GREAT LIVES
FROM
HISTORY

GREAT LIVES FROM HISTORY

American
Series

Volume 4
Mic-She

Edited by
FRANK N. MAGILL

SALEM PRESS

Pasadena, California   Englewood Cliffs, New Jersey

Library of Congress Cataloging-in-Publication Data
Great lives from history.
    Bibliography: v. 1, p.
    Includes index.
    Summary: A five-volume set of biographical
sketches of some 400 Americans, presenting their
contributions and impact on United States history
and development and including individual bibliog-
raphies.
    1. United States—Biography. [1. United States
—Biography] I. Magill, Frank Northen, 1907-   .
CT214.G74   1987   920'.073 [B] [920]   86-31561
ISBN 0-89356-529-6 (set)
ISBN 0-89356-533-4 (volume 4)

LIST OF BIOGRAPHIES IN VOLUME FOUR

LIST OF BIOGRAPHIES IN VOLUME FOUR

GREAT LIVES
FROM
HISTORY

ALBERT A. MICHELSON

Born: December 19, 1852; Strelno, Prussia
Died: May 9, 1931; Pasadena, California
Area of Achievement: Physics
Contribution: Michelson was the first American to win a Nobel Prize for
  Physics, which he received for determining the length of the standard
  meter in terms of wavelengths of light. His significant contributions to
  physics and optics include measurement of velocity of light, of the ether
  drift, of the rigidity of earth, and of the diameter of stars, as well as development of the interferometer.

Early Life

Albert Abraham Michelson was born December 19, 1852, at Strelno
(modern Strzelno), which was Polish in population and tradition but was located in German territory at that time. His mother, Rosalie Przlubska, was
the daughter of a businessman, and the effect of her early teachings made
Albert resist the lure of easy money all of his life. At the time of Albert's
birth, his father, Samuel Michelson, was the proprietor of a dry-goods shop.
Political upheavals in Europe in 1848 accelerated anti-Semitism there, and
late in 1855, the Michelsons decided to emigrate to California. They traveled
by steamer to Panama; made the laborious trip across the Isthmus by
muleback, canoe, and train; and boarded another boat to San Francisco,
where Samuel's sister and brother-in-law, Belle and Oscar Meyer, were living. The Michelsons settled in Murphys, a mining town in the heart of the
gold country, where Samuel opened a store. Young Albert took violin lessons
from a local prospector who was a fine musician. Albert's parents realized
that he was very bright and decided that he needed a better education than
was available in the mining town. They boarded him with his cousins in San
Francisco to finish the last two years of grammar school, and he matriculated
to San Francisco Boys High School. The principal, Theodore Bradley, recognized the boy's exceptional mechanical abilities and took him into his own
home. While Albert was in high school, his father moved the family to Virginia City, Nevada, and opened a business there. After graduation at sixteen,
Albert went to the famous mining town and took the competitive examination for the United States Naval Academy at Annapolis at the Storey County
Court House. He lost the appointment to the son of a man who had been injured in the Civil War. Undaunted, the young man solicited letters of recom-
mendation and made the long train trip alone across the country, determined
to petition the president for an appointment. Arriving in Washington, he
learned that President Ulysses S. Grant walked his dogs at a regular hour.
Young Michelson waited on the White House steps and approached the
president with his petition. The president advised him that the appointments-

at-large had been filled, but Michelson implored the president to consider another appointment. Impressed with the young man who would not take no for an answer, the president suggested that Albert visit Annapolis. Three days later, President Grant named him the eleventh appointee-at-large. This characteristic of attempting the impossible became a pattern in Michelson's life.

Michelson entered Annapolis in June, 1869. He made a striking figure clad in his naval uniform with his chiseled features, jet-black hair, and deep-set hazel eyes. He appeared taller than his five feet seven or eight inches because of an elegant and dignified bearing. While at the academy, he excelled in optics, acoustics, and drawing but always had time for fencing, boxing, music, and painting. His spirited independence and youthful exuberance were not evident in gunnery class, and a superior officer scolded that he might eventually be of some use to his country if he paid more attention to his gunnery than to science. No one knew at that time that this ensign would become one of America's greatest scientists.

Upon graduation, Albert served for two years at sea and then returned to the academy as an instructor in the department of physics and chemistry headed by Admiral William T. Sampson. He met the admiral's niece, Margaret Heminway, and they married in 1877 and had two sons and a daughter.

Life's Work
The speed of light had interested scientists for centuries, including Galileo Galilei, Armand-Hippolyte-Louis Fizeau, and Jean-Bernard-Léon Foucault. This was to become the all-consuming question of Michelson's life. Anxious to use demonstrations in his physics class, he gathered crude pieces of apparatus lying about the laboratory, spent ten dollars of his own money, and modified Foucault's earlier experiment. The young ensign was able to make a more accurate measurement of the speed of light than had ever before been achieved. The superintendent of the United States Navy's nautical almanac office, Simon Newcomb, appointed Michelson to a position in a government-sponsored project to determine the velocity of light. Albert quickly surpassed his peers and even his seniors, as he had an uncanny ability to devise experimentation techniques.

In 1880, Michelson secured a leave of absence from the navy and spent two years in Europe studying under Hermann von Helmholtz at the University of Berlin, Georg Hermann Quincke at Heidelberg University, and Marie Alfred Cornu at the Collège de France and the École Polytechnique in Paris. Scientists of the nineteenth century believed that light was propagated through a luminiferous ether which filled all space around the earth. The inquisitive Michelson wondered whether the existence of this luminiferous ether could be proved or disproved. This was a big idea, but big ideas appealed to him. He began studying light interference patterns and reasoned that an instrument was needed for measuring distances that would be far beyond the range of the most powerful microscope invented. In 1881, he developed this delicate instrument, which became known as the Michelson interferometer, and performed his first ether-drift experiment in Europe. He calculated a negative result on the motion of the ether relative to the earth, but scientists at that time hesitated to accept this challenge to their belief.

Michelson decided to devote his life to science, reasoning that staying in the navy would thwart this career. He resigned to become professor of physics at Case School of Applied Science in Cleveland, Ohio. He was appointed corresponding member of the British Association for the Advancement of Science in 1884, named associate fellow of the American Academy of Arts and Sciences in 1885, and received his first honorary Ph.D. from Western Reserve University the following year. In 1885, he met Professor Edward Williams Morley, a well-established chemist. Michelson must have learned much from this versatile scientist, and Morley's influence on Michelson's work has not been adequately acknowledged. They collaborated on light experiments, and Michelson worked day and night, neglecting food and rest. He reached the point of nervous exhaustion and had to take time away from the experiments. When he returned, Michelson and Morley submitted a joint paper to the *American Journal of Science* reporting negative results from the ether-drift experiment. In 1887, they conducted an experiment to see if light traveled in the same velocity in any direction and discovered no observable difference. Scientists of the nineteenth century had reasoned that since the earth moves around the sun at approximately eighteen miles per second, the speed of a light beam traveling with the earth's orbital motion should be greater than that of a beam traveling in the opposite direction. The negative result of the Michelson-Morley experiment provided the raw material which stimulated the theory of relativity. It proved that there were not different velocities of light. This discovery was catastrophic to the mechanical theory of science, which had received support since the time of Sir Isaac Newton. The two scientists worked together until 1889.

Michelson left Case Institute to teach at Clark University between 1889 and 1892. His first sojourn into astronomy began at this time when he took his equipment to Lick Observatory in California and actually measured Jupiter's satellites. In 1892, he moved to the University of Chicago and assumed the position as head of the department of physics but continued working on experiments in astronomy, spectroscopy, geophysics, and optics. He also lectured to graduate students. By the end of the nineteenth century, he was considered to be one of the twelve greatest scientists in the world, yet he was very modest: When Michelson was teaching, he gave credit to all the scientists for their contributions, but the students noticed that when he started describing current experiments and results which were clearly more significant than the preceding ones, he neglected to cite the author. The puzzled students questioned another instructor about this strange behavior. The instructor laughingly resolved the problem. The mysterious experiments had been those of Albert Abraham Michelson, and the renowned scientist had not wanted to call undue attention to his own work.

Michelson was more interested in his scientific work than in a social life, and his first marriage ended in divorce in 1897. Some sources present an austere, forbidding, overwrought picture of him at that time, but in December, 1899, he married Edna Stanton, a former student, and life with his second wife and their three daughters seemed to be happier.

Michelson continued to be very productive during this period of time and developed an echelon spectroscope with high enough resolution to indicate optical evidence of molecular motion associated with temperature. By 1905, he had completed a ruling engine which had 110,000 lines on a six-inch square of glass, which he referred to as the "she-devil." This instrument was later used by astronomers to discover the innermost secrets of the atom.

In 1907, Michelson received the Nobel Prize for Physics for establishing the length of the meter in terms of cadmium light. A few years earlier, the International Conference on Weights and Measures had made the metric system standard and deposited a platinum-iridium bar in a well-guarded vault at Severes. The Franco-Prussian War brought to the forefront the idea that the bar, which established the length of the meter, would be lost. Scientists suggested that measurement of a length of light wave would be more permanent. Michelson attempted this experiment, as he was able to measure the wavelengths of various gases with his versatile interferometer. After experimenting with sodium and mercury, he settled for the bright red line of cadmium light. He announced that 1,553,163.5 wavelengths of the red line of the metal cadmium were equal to the length of the platinum-iridium standard. The Nobel Prize was awarded to him for accomplishment in precision measurements.

Michelson was also very interested in zoology. He related the phenomenon of the iridescent colors of hummingbirds, butterflies, and beetles to interference and reflection of light. In his book *Studies in Optics* (1927), he noted that the diamond beetle had diffraction grating ruled on its wings as fine as two thousand to the inch.

Michelson remained active in naval affairs throughout his life. He commanded the Illinois Naval Militia for years. During World War I, he served as a lieutenant commander and patented five optical range-finders for naval vessels.

Ever reaching for new planes, he used his interferometer to indicate the substance of the earth's interior, and, in 1920, he was the first to measure the angular diameter of a distant star. The Royal Astronomical Society of England recognized this achievement by presenting its gold medal to him, but this was only one of numerous medals and prizes from scientific societies which he was awarded. Michelson received six honorary Ph.D.'s during his lifetime. Although he disliked publicity, he did realize the value of promotion in obtaining money for his projects, and was very gracious in his dealings with people.

In his later years, Michelson still held himself erect, maintaining the quiet demeanor of his youth. His hair was white, and he wore a close-cropped gray mustache. He enjoyed tennis, bridge, chess, and billiards. He would discuss these subjects socially, but he preferred to keep his science and art, which were so dear to his heart, in the laboratory and the studio.

Michelson always believed that his greatest experiment was still ahead of him. He considered it great fun to do the arduous work involved in setting up experiments and overseeing the technical difficulties. When he was in his seventies, he once again determined to measure the velocity of light. He worked with George Ellery Hale at Mount Wilson Observatory on five sets of light measurements between 1924 and 1927. He was dissatisfied with these tests because of the obstruction of valley haze and smoke and constructed an experiment in a vacuum tube where light could travel in empty space. He was directing this work when he became ill, but the dedicated man, then in his late seventies, carried on the work from his sickbed. He dictated the introduction of a scientific paper to astronomer Francis Pease, and when the report was published posthumously, the title was "On a Method of Measuring the Velocity of Light," the same title of his first paper when he was an ensign in the navy. He died May 9, 1931, of a cerebral hemorrhage.

Summary

Albert Abraham Michelson obtained world attention for American science at a time when European scientists were inclined to characterize Americans as lacking in scientific capabilities. It is evident that his contributions helped forward the theory of relativity, though it would be an overstatement that Albert Einstein's theory was a generalization of the Michelson-Morley experiment or that the theory of relativity could not have been arrived at without this experiment. Michelson has often been called "the man who measured the stars," but he was more than this. His major contributions include precision optical measurements of the velocity of light, of the ether drift, of the length of the standard meter, of the angular diameters of stars, and of the rigidity of the earth; developmental experimentation in the young field of spectroscopy; and invention of the harmonic analyzer, in addition to the Michelson interferometer. His efforts extended to the precision of measurement represent an extraordinary contribution to scientific knowledge.

Michelson always had the greatest respect for the navy, where he received his start. The navy did not forget him and, in 1948, honored his memory with the construction of a laboratory for basic and applied research at the United

States Naval Ordnance Test Station at China Lake in the Mojave Desert. In 1969, Michelson Hall, housing the science department, was dedicated at Annapolis in honor of its graduate of the class of 1873. The building stands over the area of the old seawall where Michelson made his earliest measurements of the speed of light. His papers, accumulated over a period of thirty years by Ted McAllister, curator of Michelson Museum at the Naval Weapons Center at China Lake, have been transferred to this facility.

Very few Americans are chosen for the Hall of Fame. Michelson was selected to receive this honor; the tribute ceremony and unveiling of the bust took place on October 21, 1973, at the Hall of Fame for Great Americans at New York University. His own words were chosen as the inscription on the bronze tablet which accompanies the sculpture: "It seems to me that scientific research should be regarded as the painter regards his art, as the poet his poems, and the composer his music." Michelson was a splendid scientist, a fine naval officer, a talented artist, and an honored educator. He will be remembered for his significant contributions to physics and optics.

Bibliography

Bennett, Jean M., D. Theodore McAllister, and Georgia M. Cabe. "Albert A. Michelson, Dean of American Optics: Life, Contributions to Science, and Influence on Modern Day Physics." *Journal of Applied Optics* 12 (October, 1973): 2253. Excellent article which not only summarizes Michelson's life but also details his scientific experiments in a readable fashion. Compiled by the curator of the Michelson Museum, who spent thirty years compiling the Michelson papers. One of the most concise sources available. Well documented. Thorough bibliography.

Holton, Gerald. *Thematic Origins of Scientific Thought*. Cambridge, Mass.: Harvard University Press, 1973. Systematically attacks any relationship between Einstein, Michelson, and the "crucial" experiment. Persuasive that the Michelson-Morley experiment had no effect on Einstein's theory of relativity.

Jaffe, Bernard. *Men of Science in America*. New York: Arno Press, 1980. Jaffe has done a considerable service for students of the history of science in this assortment of materials dealing with scientists in the United States. Sound and scholarly, the book presents Michelson's participation as a catalyst in the revolution of modern physics.

_____. *Michelson and the Speed of Light*. Garden City, N.Y.: Doubleday and Co., 1960. A well-balanced biography of Michelson. Includes descriptions of his experiments. Designed for popular reading but contains relatively few errors. Excellent bibliography. Thematic approach correlated chronologically.

Livingston, Dorothy Michelson. *The Master of Light: A Biography of Albert A. Michelson*. New York: Charles Scribner's Sons, 1973. An admirable book which falls short of being a scientific biography as it lacks the critical analysis of scientific and technical matters essential in such a work. Written by Michelson's daughter, it gives a picture of the man rather than the scientist.

Ronan, Colin A. *Science: Its History and Development Among the World Cultures*. New York: Hamlyn Publishing Group, 1982. Mentions Michelson in passing but provides a detailed account of the events, in chronological order, in the fields of science during Michelson's life. Relates to the Michelson-Morley experiment.

Swenson, Loyd S., Jr. *Genesis of Relativity: Einstein in Context*. New York: Burt Franklin and Co., 1979. Good detail of the Michelson-Morley experiment and its contribution to the theory of relativity. Readable and within reach of the average student. A valuable study.

Evelyne L. Pickett

LUDWIG MIES VAN DER ROHE

Born: March 27, 1886; Aachen, Germany
Died: August 7, 1969; Chicago, Illinois
Area of Achievement: Architecture
Contribution: One of the greatest architects and architectural educators of
the twentieth century, Mies Van Der Rohe left a legacy of famous buildings and a legacy in furniture design unmatched by any other member of
the Modern Movement.

Early Life

Born Ludwig Mies to Michael Mies, a master mason, and his wife,
Amalie, both German, Ludwig Mies Van Der Rohe was to add a version of
his mother's maiden name to his own in adulthood, believing that *mies*,
which in German means "bad" or "poor," was professionally a liability. He
was, however, known to intimates as "Mies" throughout his life.

His father owned a stone-cutting shop, and Mies Van Der Rohe got his
first experience with building materials while helping his father. He was educated in the Aachen Cathedral School, which could trace its existence back
to the time when Aachen (formerly Aix-la-Chapelle) had been the first capital of Charlemagne's Holy Roman Empire. In his childhood, much of the
medieval city was extant (much of it was lost during World War II), and he
spoke of its architecture as an important influence on him in his formative
years.

At the age of thirteen, he became a student in the local trade school,
studying there for two years, during which time he was also a part-time
apprentice to a brick mason. With a natural talent for drawing, at the age of
fifteen he joined an interior decorating firm specializing in stucco ornamentation, soon becoming their designer. In 1904, he entered a local architect's
office, and a year later, he moved to Berlin. He had, by then, some deep
knowledge of stone, but knew little about how to use wood; he took employment with Bruno Paul, who had a distinguished reputation for his use of
wood in both his architecture and his furniture design.

In 1907, Mies Van Der Rohe left Paul to work on a private commission.
His first house, designed in the popular eighteenth century German style,
possessed an air of proportion and a fineness of detail which were to be common aspects of his architecture. The next year, the prestigious Peter Behrens
firm hired him, and during his time there, two other young architects, who
were, like Mies Van Der Rohe, to have important careers, passed through
the firm: Walter Gropius and Le Corbusier. Behrens carried on the tradition
of the early nineteenth century architect Karl Friedrich Schinkel (1781-1841),
who had advocated the sensitive use of fine materials, gracious space and balance in design, and careful and fastidious concern for detail. The Behrens

group was committed to the union of engineering and architecture, accepting the facts of industrialization and mass production without presuming that beauty had to give way to utility. AEG, the German equivalent of General Electric in America, used Behrens to design their buildings, their building fixtures, and even the letterhead for their stationery. Mies Van Der Rohe was involved in the building of the Turbine factory for AEG which Behrens had designed with interesting anticipations of later architectural ideas, and Behrens put him in charge of the construction of the German Embassy in St. Petersburg, Russia.

On his own by 1913, Mies Van Der Rohe designed some intriguing domestic buildings, still, albeit, in the old tradition, but showing a sensitive and original grasp of space and proportion. He served in World War I in the German army as an engineer, supervising the building of roads and bridges. A solidly built young man with the bland good looks of the German burgher, it would have been difficult to tell by looking that he possessed the imagination, energy, and will to impose his ideas of architecture and design upon the entire Western world.

Life's Work

After the war, Mies Van Der Rohe committed himself as a designer to the architecture of what has been called the "Modern Movement," and he became a prominent member of the group of German architects and designers determined to make a new kind of building using the materials of twentieth century industrial technology: steel, glass, and reinforced concrete. The German economy was so disastrously affected by the war that little major building took place, but Mies Van Der Rohe exhibited five major projects which were to establish his reputation. These plans, the "Glass Skyscrapers" (1919-1921), the "Concrete Office Building" (1922), the "Brick Country House" (1923), and the "Concrete Country House" (1924), exemplify, in part in their titles, the new direction taken by their creator. Uninterested in politics, he accepted, nevertheless, the proposition that architecture should be a sign of a society's vitality, that it was an important expression of it own time. He was a member of several organizations supporting the new movement in the arts, and the director of several exhibitions of contemporary architecture during the 1920's.

By the mid-1920's, Mies Van Der Rohe had established his reputation as an innovator but had constructed very few buildings. During this lean period, he put his experience in the crafts to the problem of designing furniture which would be consistent with the new architecture, and it was to be this work which would result in his development of the famous tubular steel chair that was to bear his copyright.

In 1928, he was awarded a commission for the German Pavilion at the International Exposition to be held in Barcelona, Spain. Although the building was to exist only during the period of the fair, it was to be remembered by photographs and drawings as one of the most important buildings of the Modern Movement and was to become a touchstone building in modern architecture. Although he had revealed bits and pieces of his ideas in previous buildings during the 1920's, this was the first time that he was free to express his ideas without the limitations and impositions of ordinary contracts. The building itself was simply to be a showpiece unwedded to any particular function, the funds were generous, and he was allowed the use of first-class materials and first-class artisans.

The trademarks of his career were displayed with astonishing success: roof weight was to be carried not by walls but by steel columns, and the walls, as a result, were to function as aesthetic planes and screens in space, with as little enclosed area as possible, so that the whole structure had an open-aired aspect. He managed to join the austerity of modern design, the materials of twentieth century industry, to the traditional materials of the past builders, such as marble and onyx. He showed in one simple building that technology, the skeletal design, and modern materials could be used aesthetically.

In 1929-1930, his Tugendhat House in Brno, Czechoslovakia, applied the same principles to a private dwelling. Again, he freed the walls from load-bearing, refused to box in anything save service areas such as bathrooms and kitchens, used an abundance of glass walls as exteriors, and only loosely distinguished living areas by the steel columns carrying the roof and curved planes of richly polished onyx and ebony. As in the Barcelona building, the furniture was specially designed to complement, and compliment, the light, airy openness.

In 1930, Mies Van Der Rohe became the director of Germany's famous Bauhaus, the school founded by Walter Gropius to teach art and design in the modern mode, and in which the fusion of the functional and the beautiful was explored in the production of everything from cutlery to plans for entire towns. There had been continual conservative criticism of the school since its inception in 1919, and in the early 1930's, the Nazis, on coming to power, closed it down. Mies Van Der Rohe resisted for a few months, received permission to reopen, but on unacceptable terms, and gave it up in 1933. Out of favor with the Fascists, who suspected the intellectual community in general, Mies Van Der Rohe received few commissions and lived on royalties from his furniture designs.

In 1938, he left Germany and took the post of Director of Architecture at the Armour (later Illinois) Institute of Technology in Chicago. He became an American citizen in 1944.

Welcomed to Chicago by Frank Lloyd Wright, whose work he deeply admired (and who was later to complain about Mies Van Der Rohe's "flat-chested" architecture), he brought the best aspects of the Bauhaus into conjunction with American architectural education, putting emphasis, as always, upon the symbiotic relationship of modern technology and modern design. Fully committed to the steel skeleton as aesthetically valid, he led his school away from "façade" architecture. He had always been an articulate spokesman for the new ideas, and in his role of educator and practitioner he continued to express the theories of the Modern Movement with gnomic attractiveness.

He was to remain at the school until 1958, and during that period, he was to work away at the design of an entirely new campus for the institute, using his ideas of variations on the skeletal steel configuration to build a campus of artistic oneness, even for buildings which in the hands of past architects were considered too special for such treatment. By 1947, he was so firmly established as a major figure that the Museum of Modern Art in New York held an exhibition of his work (as they did again in 1986).

His career, however, has not been without resistance, even from those who admired him. His Farnsworth House, designed and built between 1945 and 1950, won the important Twenty-five-year Award from the American Institute of Architects in 1981. Its owner complained about getting an expensive one-room glass box and was sued for its payment, but she was not far from the truth in the sense that Mies Van Der Rohe had designed a simple, glass-walled box with the roof and the floor riding on cantilevered supports—in a sense, a transparent house through which the natural setting (it was a country retreat) flowed. For good or ill, it was to have an important influence on house design.

The same can be said for his work in urban, high-rise apartment design. His Lake Shore Drive apartments (1948-1951) were to be the first of the high-rise city dwellings made almost solely of glass and steel, and they were to be the prototype for the new age of urban architecture. He also provided a model for the urban housing development with his Lafayette Park project in Detroit (1955-1963), in which he mixed one-story, two-story, and high-rise apartment complexes in a garden and park setting with special attention to keeping the parking areas on the perimeters of the property.

His Seagram Building in New York City is one of the best examples of the application of his design theories to the needs of the corporate world. Facing on Park Avenue, it occupies one of the most expensive pieces of real estate in the world, yet Mies Van Der Rohe preserved half the site as open space, using it as a jeweled base for the building by the tasteful addition of greenery, pools, pink granite paving, and marble benches. The building itself is an uncompromising exercise in his use of steel and glass, but the steel is bronze-clad, the glass is topaz-gray, and the incidental furnishings are of comparable richness. It set a new standard not only in design but also in siting and in dressing a building which the business world has insisted on imitating ever since, sometimes with success (if they could get Mies Van Der Rohe to do the work), and sometimes with less happy results.

His own buildings have, in the main, been formidable variations on the Seagram theme, and examples of his work can be seen in cities all over the world. In his later years, Mies Van Der Rohe confined himself almost exclusively to corporate projects with the emphasis on high-rise offices and apartment buildings. His thrusting, concrete-cased structures lapped in steel and glass, both richly colored, decorated by equally handsome I-beam mullions, are visual confirmations of the power of the industrialized world. Since his death in 1969, that enthusiasm for his work or for the work of his followers has continued, and his influence on renewed or revived or rebuilt city and town centers is ubiquitous.

Summary

If credit for the revolution of modern architecture must be shared by Mies Van Der Rohe with Le Corbusier, Walter Gropius, and Frank Lloyd Wright, and if Gropius anticipated everyone with the matchbox style in his famous Fagus Werke in 1911, it was Mies Van Der Rohe who was eventually to dominate (indeed, almost corner) the market in urban center planning and particularly in post–World War II skyscrapers.

He became the most international of architects, who tended, in the past, to be confined in their commissions to their native land, although their influence might transcend space and time. Mies Van Der Rohe, like Gropius, straddled the Atlantic, Mies Van Der Rohe taking the Bauhaus to Chicago, Gropius taking it to Harvard. As a practitioner, however, Mies Van Der Rohe is everywhere in the Western world, and his work is standing in major and minor cities often cheek-to-jowl with that of his followers.

There is the rub: Mies Van Der Rohe, with no expense spared, using rich materials, brought together with craftsmanlike skill and fastidiousness, produced buildings of stunning aesthetic clarity and simplicity. Standing alone, they are often great works of art. Surrounded by equally tall imitations, they can lose that power simply because their creator is one of those artists who is easily emulated. The copies, less lavish materially, less lovingly constructed, often parodic in their determination to be like the original, are a principal reason for the monotony of late twentieth century city cores. The clutter of glass-and-steel monoliths, reflecting one another across narrow streets and looking alike from town to town, is the sad legacy of Mies Van Der Rohe's domination of urban architecture.

Bibliography

Blaser, Werner. *Mies Van Der Rohe.* Rev. ed. New York: Praeger Publishers, 1972. Originally published in 1965, this book is particularly interesting because it is based upon conversations with Mies Van Der Rohe and allows him to discuss the development of his ideas in relation to specific buildings.

Carter, Peter. *Mies Van Der Rohe at Work*. New York: Praeger Publishers, 1974. Divided into chapters dealing with technical aspects of Mies Van Der Rohe's work but easily understood by the lay reader. A helpful chart shows the number of projects and their progression toward the big building.

Hilbersheimer, L. *Mies Van Der Rohe*. Chicago: Paul Theobald and Co., 1956. A bit short on text but the commentary is succinct nevertheless. Includes generous photographs.

Johnson, Phillip C. *Mies Van Der Rohe*. New York: Museum of Modern Art, 1947. Published on the occasion of the 1947 Exhibition and prepared with the help of Mies Van Der Rohe himself, this volume offers a well-written, illustrated account of his career until the time of the show.

Pawley, Martin. *Mies Van Der Rohe*. London: Thames and Hudson, 1970. Pawley, quite properly, claims only to write an introduction and notes to what is really a book of pictures (some in color), but these pictures are by an excellent photographer, Yukio Futagawa. The best way to understand Mies Van Der Rohe is to see the buildings in person, but good photographs help.

Spaeth, David A. *Mies Van Der Rohe*. New York: Rizzoli International Publications, 1985. Popular critical biography, taking Mies Van Der Rohe through his entire career. Ample use of his own statements, with technical jargon kept to a minimum. Well illustrated with excellent photographs and generous use of drawings.

Speyer, A. James. *Mies Van Der Rohe*. Chicago: Art Institute of Chicago, 1968. Published at the time of the Retrospective Exhibition at the Institute, the book concentrates on specific projects, bringing photos, plans, and short, sensible commentaries together.

Charles H. Pullen

ROBERT ANDREWS MILLIKAN

Born: March 22, 1868; Morrison, Illinois
Died: December 19, 1953; Pasadena, California
Areas of Achievement: Physics, education, and administration
Contribution: As a skilled and meticulous experimenter, Millikan made major contributions to twentieth century physics; as a textbook author, university teacher, and supervisor of research, he greatly influenced the way that physics was studied in the United States; as an administrator, he was responsible for the rise to prominence of the California Institute of Technology.

Early Life

Robert Andrews Millikan was born in Morrison, Illinois, on March 22, 1868, the son of Silas Franklin Millikan, a Congregational preacher, and Mary Jane (Andrews) Millikan, a graduate of Oberlin College and former dean of a small college in Michigan. When Robert was five years old, the family, which was to include three sons and three daughters, moved westward to Iowa, where they settled permanently in Maquoketa two years later.

Robert began his education at home under his mother's tutelege, continuing in the local public schools through high school. He recalled his childhood experience as being typical for a Midwestern American boy of the late nineteenth century, with plenty of work, thrift, fun, healthy exercise, and little formal exposure to science.

He entered Oberlin College in 1886 and initially embarked on a classical course of study, later shifting to physics, in which he was largely self-taught. After receiving an M.A. from Oberlin in 1893, he enrolled as the sole graduate student in physics at Columbia University, where he came under the strong influence of Michael Pupin, a self-made scientist who had arrived in the United States virtually penniless from Eastern Europe in 1874. (Pupin's autobiography, *From Immigrant to Inventor*, published by Charles Scribner's Sons in 1923, is well worth reading as illustrative of the period.) Encouraged and financially aided by Pupin, Millikan set off for a year of study in Europe after completing his Ph.D. in 1895. A year later he was invited to come to the University of Chicago as an assistant in physics by Albert A. Michelson, America's best-known experimental physicist at the time and under whom Millikan had taken a summer course in 1894.

Early photographs show Millikan to have been a handsome young man of good stature and athletic build. As he aged, his hair turned white and he gave the appearance of a confident elder statesman of science. He was outgoing and sociable and enjoyed interacting with persons on all levels. His marriage in 1902 to Greta Blanchard produced three sons and endured until she predeceased him by a few weeks in 1953.

Life's Work

Millikan was given heavy teaching responsibilities at Chicago, the more so because Michelson did not enjoy working with students. Millikan took his duties seriously, throwing himself into classroom teaching and laboratory instruction, and writing textbooks and laboratory manuals in physics. These ventures into text writing, usually in collaboration with others, were highly successful. The books were revised many times and widely used for decades. It is interesting to note that Millikan was one of the first authors to incorporate historical material as background into physics texts. When the History of Science Society was formed in 1923, he was a founding member.

By dint of working twelve hours a day, six days a week, at the University of Chicago, Millikan also embarked on a research program, achieving notable success in two areas. Through his "oil drop" method he showed that electric charge always occurs in exact multiples of a fundamental unit quantity whose numerical value he was able to calculate. His second area of success was the photoelectric effect, an action that occurs when electrons are emitted from the surface of certain metals under illumination by light of suitable wavelength. The results obtained by Millikan in 1916 exactly confirmed the theoretical prediction made by Albert Einstein in 1905. Einstein had based his theory on a belief in "quanta," units of energy first introduced by Max Planck in 1899. It is curious to note that Millikan, despite his experimental confirmation of Einstein's equation, could not bring himself to accept the existence of quanta until several years later, since these new entities were so much at variance with the ideas of classical physics. In 1923, Millikan was awarded the Nobel Prize for Physics for these experiments. By that time he had moved to the California Institute of Technology and declined to make the journey to Stockholm for the ceremony, pleading the urgency of his research and teaching. (It should be remembered that, in those days, such a trip would have required him to be away from California for more than a month.)

In 1915, Millikan was elected to membership in the National Academy of Sciences, the prestigious body established during the Civil War to provide scientific assistance to the federal government. A year after Millikan's election, that organization moved to form the National Research Council for the purpose of mobilizing for defense the nation's scientific talent. Millikan was a member of the organizing committee of the council and subsequently was named its executive officer and director of research. Among the areas of concern were submarine detection and chemical warfare. When the United States became actively involved in World War I, Millikan moved to Washington for the duration of the war, donning an army uniform and becoming a lieutenant colonel in the Signal Corps.

After the war, Millikan was instrumental in having the National Research Council expand its function to establish and supervise a program of postdoctoral fellowships for young Americans entering scientific professions.

Funding for the program was provided by the Rockefeller Foundation. The aim of the program was twofold: The individual National Research Council Fellow could engage in research unencumbered by heavy teaching duties (as Millikan had been), and the institutions where they chose to take their fellowships would benefit from their presence. As a result of this program, American scientific competence was strengthened.

Following Millikan's return to the University of Chicago in 1919, he found himself being sought after by the Throop College of Technology in Pasadena, California, having come to their attention through contacts he had made while in Washington, D.C. Initially, Millikan served at Throop only in a visiting capacity, but by 1921 he had moved there permanently as professor of physics and chairman of the Executive Council. Although he refused the title of president, he insisted that the name of the institution be changed to the California Institute of Technology. He convinced a group of wealthy and influential Californians that "Caltech," as it became known, was a unique state asset, well worthy of the support of businessmen, philanthropists, and ordinary citizens.

Until his retirement in 1945, at the age of seventy-seven, Millikan worked tirelessly to enhance the prestige of Caltech, not only in the United States but also worldwide. One way of achieving this was to have an eminent European physicist as guest lecturer nearly every year. Among such visitors were Niels Bohr, Max Born, Albert Einstein, H. A. Lorentz, Erwin Schrödinger, and Arnold Sommerfeld. The generous funding provided by the trustees of Caltech made it possible for such visitors to lecture at other academic institutions as well, on their way to or from Pasadena, thereby benefiting the entire American physics community. Furthermore, each year a group of National Research Council Fellows found Caltech a stimulating place to be.

In addition to his administrative duties, Millikan continued an active research program, usually in collaboration with his doctoral candidates or postdoctoral fellows. A new area of study that attracted him was cosmic rays, those mysterious rays that caused electroscopes to lose their charge spontaneously. Millikan devoted great attention to this phenomenon during the 1920's and early 1930's. His research made it clear that these rays were of extraterrestrial origin, but he failed to recognize their true nature. For years, Millikan argued, often acrimoniously and in public, that the rays were electromagnetic—that is, similar to light but at invisible wavelengths. Other investigators, notably Arthur H. Compton, another American recipient of the Nobel Prize for Physics, had evidence that the rays consisted of charged particles, namely protons. Millikan was eventually proved wrong in this case.

Summary

Robert A. Millikan, a proud and dedicated man, was a leading figure in the American scientific community during the first half of the twentieth century, a period during which science in the United States rapidly rose to world-wide preeminence. Millikan traveled often to Europe, where he was well-known and respected in scientific circles as early as 1912. His success as an experimenter was widely recognized, but there were others, such as Michelson, of whom this could be said. What distinguished Millikan was his unswerving devotion to the *promotion* of science, not only in his personal laboratory but also in its institutional context and in the development of first-class educational opportunity for America's young scientific talent. He viewed science as a positive, vital element in the growth of America as a nation, a growth that had taken place dramatically in his own lifetime. He never failed to respond to critics of science who argued that science was inimical to religion or was responsible for human misery through loss of employment when resulting technology eliminated some jobs. As an advocate of the scientific component of modern society, he epitomized a man of science for the general public. He was described by *Time* magazine as "a man of twinkling blue-gray eyes and sparkling wit who knows how to make scientific complexities charming as well as awesome."

After his death in 1953, Millikan was eulogized by a colleague, L. A. DuBridge, as a contributor to knowledge, a creator of a scientific institution, and an inspiration to hundreds of students as well as a contributor to the maturing of science in America.

Bibliography

Compton, Arthur H. *The Cosmos of Arthur Holly Compton*. Edited by Marjorie Johnston with an introduction by Vannevar Bush. New York: Alfred A. Knopf, 1967. A collection of scientific and humanistic essays by a younger fellow physicist of Millikan, his adversary in the cosmic ray controversy. Contains a number of references to Millikan's work and a book review of Millikan's autobiography, listed below.

DuBridge, L. A., and Paul S. Epstein. "Robert Andrews Millikan." *National Academy of Sciences Biographical Memoirs* 33 (1959): 241-282. Written by two of Millikan's colleagues at the California Institute of Technology, this article surveys his life, work, and personality. Includes a full bibliography of Millikan's writings.

Kargon, Robert H. *The Rise of Robert Millikan: Portrait of a Life in American Science*. Ithaca, N.Y.: Cornell University Press, 1982. A carefully written, fully documented critical study of Millikan's life as illustrative of science in America during his lifetime—not a full biography. Kargon has drawn heavily on the Millikan papers deposited in the Archives of the California Institute of Technology. Contains a number of photographs not previously published.

Kevles, Daniel J. *The Physicists: The History of a Scientific Community*. New York: Alfred A. Knopf, 1978. Written by a contemporary historian of science, with documentation, this work contains significant coverage of Millikan's activities.

Millikan, Robert A. *The Autobiography of Robert A. Millikan*. New York: Prentice-Hall, 1950. Written when the author was nearly eighty years old, it present a firsthand account of how life and science had changed in America during his lifetime; narrates the details of his own career as he saw it. Includes photographs of Millikan, family members, and colleagues.

——————. *The Electron: Its Isolation and Measurements and Determination of Some of Its Properties*. Edited with an introduction by Jesse W. M. DuMond. Chicago: University of Chicago Press, 1963. A facsimile edition of Millikan's original account of his electron studies as published in 1917. The editor, a friend and colleague of Millikan, has provided a valuable biographical study of Millikan and his work.

——————. "The Electron and the Light-Quant from the Experimental Point of View," in *Physics*, 54-66. New York: Elsevier Publishing Co., 1965. Millikan's Nobel Prize address describing his own investigations and discussing their significance in relation to the work of others.

——————. *Electrons (+ and −), Protons, Photons, Neutrons and Cosmic Rays*. Chicago: University of Chicago Press, 1935. Essentially an updating of *The Electron*. In both these volumes, Millikan addressed himself to the educated layman, putting the more mathematical passages at the end as appendices.

——————. *Evolution in Science and Religion*. New Haven, Conn.: Yale University Press, 1927. Three invited lectures given at Yale University some years earlier dealing with the compatibility of science and religion, a favorite theme with Millikan.

Sopka, Katherine R. *Quantum Physics in America, 1920-1935*. Edited by I. Bernard Cohen. New York: Arno Press, 1980. Includes some discussion of Millikan's work and influence on physics in America.

Katherine R. Sopka

WILLIAM MITCHELL

Born: December 29, 1879; Nice, France
Died: February 19, 1936; New York, New York
Area of Achievement: The military
Contribution: An advocate of air power in the armed forces, Mitchell worked to create a separate air force and to develop strategic doctrines that would utilize its potential in the conduct of modern war.

Early Life

William Lendrum Mitchell was born during his parents' visit to France in 1879. His paternal grandfather, Alexander Mitchell, was born in Scotland, migrated to Wisconsin, and became a successful businessman and investor. His grandfather served in Congress, a path followed by his father, John Lendrum Mitchell, who served in both houses of Congress as representative of Wisconsin. Mitchell, one of nine children, attended private schools in Wisconsin and received his college degree from George Washington University after his military enlistment.

"Billy" Mitchell's military career began with the declaration of war against Spain in 1898. He enlisted as a private with the Wisconsin volunteers and was quickly commissioned a lieutenant in the Signal Corps. He served on the staff of General Fitzhugh Lee, and when Cuba fell to American troops, he transferred to the Philippines, where the war continued in 1899 against Philippine nationalists led by Emilio Aguinaldo. There, he served on the staff of General Arthur MacArthur, whose son, Douglas, later served on the court-martial board that convicted Mitchell of insubordination and ordered his five-year suspension from active military duty.

After the war in the Philippines ended in 1902, Mitchell returned to the United States with the army Signal Corps. He was assigned to duty in Alaska, where he commanded units charged with laying three thousand miles of telegraphic lines connecting the territory with the United States. In 1912, he was sent to the army's General Staff School as a young and promising officer. His first real encounter with the untried but intriguing flying machine was in 1908, when he served as an army representative to a demonstration flight of a Wright brothers airplane at Fort Myer. He later learned the fundamentals of piloting from Orville Wright and soloed in 1914. Always sensitive to technological changes that modified traditional doctrines of warfare, Mitchell quickly appreciated the tactical uses of manned flight.

As a young officer serving outside the United States, Mitchell gained new insights into the geopolitical implications of modern warfare. His experiences in Cuba, the Philippines, and Alaska focused Mitchell's attention on the strategic significance of the Pacific area. Before the United States entered World War I, he was sent to Spain as an observer and then to France in 1917.

After the war, he traveled in Europe, and he toured the Pacific and Far East in 1923 and 1924. He understood the significance of the growing power of Japan better than many of his military contemporaries, leading him to argue forcefully for air power as America's first line of defense, especially in the Pacific. He formed close relationships with the important early air-power spokesmen abroad and after World War I was awarded not only the Distinguished Service Cross but also France's Croix de Guerre, as well as special commendations by the British and Italian governments.

Life's Work

After 1900, the potential development of motorized air power for military purposes struggled for recognition and adequate financial support. The War Department, through the Board of Ordinance and Fortification, believed that dirigibles were of greater value than fixed-wing aircraft for military use, especially for reconnaissance. It was not until 1909 that Orville and Wilbur Wright produced a test aircraft for the army's Signal Corps. Mitchell agreed with other military strategists that air power should be used not for tactical support for ground troops or strategic bombing, but for observation, in part because technological problems prevented the production of fast, large, and reliable aircraft capable of sustained air operations. The First Aero Squadron, composed of Curtiss biplanes, was activated for service in Mexico in 1916 to support "Black Jack" Pershing's expedition into northern Mexico to pursue Pancho Villa's revolutionary force. Mechanical and maintenance problems, however, soon grounded all aircraft. Between 1916 and 1918, American intervention in World War I provided the new advocates of air power with ample opportunities to perfect superior aircraft and to develop new strategies for the deployment and use of winged aircraft.

The Air Service of the American Expeditionary Forces (AEF), under the direction of the Signal Corps, initially asked for five thousand pilots and planes to accompany the ground forces to France. The Army Air Service grew rapidly under the supervision of three ambitious young officers, operating very much on their own: Brigadier General Mitchell, Brigadier General Benjamin D. Foulois, and Colonel Reynal C. Bolling, soon joined by a senior officer, Major General Mason M. Patrick. Mitchell assumed the position of air combat commander and chief advocate of the AEF's air-power contribution to the war in France. Mitchell argued for a separate role for American pilots at the front: to observe and to protect the separate operational front assigned to the American land forces under the command of General John J. Pershing by the joint Allied command. A combined attack of air and land forces was planned for the St. Mihiel salient in September, 1918. Mitchell was given the command of six hundred aircraft—a combined force of American, French, Italian, and Portuguese air forces—and coordinated assault operations with a joint attack by American and French ground forces, successfully reducing the salient and capturing more than fifteen thousand prisoners. The victory not only established the integrity of American infantry forces but also proved the success of combined air-land operations.

With the return of peace in 1919, American advocates of air power returned to the United States prepared to lobby for public and governmental support for the establishment of a permanent and well-financed commitment to military aviation. Mitchell was the most enthusiastic advocate for a new role for air operations in modern warfare. The debate on air power after 1919 involved both the army and the navy, often focusing on the activities of Mitchell and creating a sharp split between the two services on the future of air power in the United States military. While both services acknowledged the essential usefulness of air operations, the navy rejected the proposition that air power alone could win future wars. Mitchell's advocacy of aerial warfare both antagonized and threatened the navy's efforts to build adequate public support in the postwar era. Mitchell defined four basic functions for the new air service: to destroy the enemy's air effectiveness, to destroy enemy ground targets, to demoralize enemy ground forces, and to gather information. The suggestion by Mitchell that adequate air power was the key to coastal defense irritated naval strategists. Focusing on the Pacific as an area of future military operations, Mitchell suggested that air power was the most efficient substitute for naval power; aircraft development thus warranted adequate congressional support and a separate institutional identity. In 1920, the reorganization of the army elevated the Air Service to an equal rank with other military services.

Never adept at mediating interservice arguments over the role of air power in the armed forces, Mitchell planned a dramatic demonstration. He secured a role for the Air Service in bombing tests planned by the navy in 1921 to test the vulnerability of battleships to air attack. The captured German battleship *Ostfriesland* was anchored near Chesapeake Bay, and Mitchell's pilots sent it to the bottom with heavy bombs, in disregard of the rules set by the navy for the demonstration. Mitchell's success strengthened his congressional supporters, but alienated his colleagues in the military. This incident led the army to remove Mitchell from the center of political debate over appropriations and reorganization by sending him to Europe, where he consulted with other primary architects of modern aerial warfare: General Sir Hugh Trenchard of Great Britain's Royal Air Force and General Giulio Douhet of the Italian air force, author of *Command of the Air* (1921). Mitchell agreed with Douhet that strategic bombing, when directed against enemy urban centers and their civilian populations, could effectively diminish morale and support for a war; nevertheless, Mitchell still viewed strategic air power as a substitute for naval power and the key to the coastal defense of the United States. American strategic bombing in World War II later proved Douhet's vision to have been more accurate.

Mitchell's return to the United States did nothing to further the creation of a separate air force. Tired of his constant lobbying efforts, Major General Mason M. Patrick transferred Mitchell to a field position and reduced his rank to colonel. Mitchell's outspoken accusations of negligence on the part of American military leaders prompted President Calvin Coolidge to appoint a special review board to investigate charges that the neglect of air power bordered on "treason," and Dwight W. Morrow was selected to head the special panel of inquiry. While the review board endorsed increased attention to aviation development, the army moved to silence Mitchell's criticisms of incompetence, negligence, and "almost treasonable administration" of national defense, accusations Mitchell had directed not only against the navy but also against the army itself. President Coolidge personally ordered a court-martial hearing, which to no one's surprise found Mitchell guilty and ordered his suspension from military service for five years. He resigned his commission in January, 1926, but continued to speak and write extensively in favor of separate and coequal status for the air service. His ideas of strategic air operations were later tested extensively by American operations in the European theater under American air general Henry H. Arnold, although with mixed results.

Mitchell's unrelenting and impolitic advocacy of a separate and independent air arm may have dissuaded more effective and influential supporters from aiding his cause. His critics referred to him as the "General of the Hot Air Force." He called his army critics the "longbowmen." While the Morrow board recommended changing the Army Air Service to the Army Air Corps (AAC) and increasing its strength to eighteen hundred planes, the air force remained under the command of the General Staff of the Army. In the 1920's, Congress, concerned with tax and budget reductions, generally ignored pleas to increase allocations for AAC personnel and equipment. The most pressing need of the air force was the development of a heavy bomber to accomplish the type of strategic bombing Mitchell continued to advocate.

By 1930, Mitchell was the most persuasive spokesman for Douhet's "morale" warfare. The proper targets in future wars were the "vital centers," areas of civilian population where transport, food supplies, and material support were located. He defended the destruction of such civilian centers as the key to short and decisive wars, avoiding the horrible trench warfare of World War I. While many Americans could not accept the strategic destruction of civilian populations as humane warfare, Mitchell intellectually "prepared them to accept it." The intensive bombing of centers of civilian populations such as Hamburg, Dresden, and Hiroshima in World War II was the outcome of his writings, although he never advocated "throwing the strategic bomber at the man in the street." His emotional and partisan defense of an independent air arm coequal with surface forces made him the martyr of the modern Air Force.

Summary

What Alfred Thayer Mahan did for naval strategy at the turn of the century, Mitchell did for strategic air-power development in the 1920's and 1930's. Based on his firsthand observation of the futility of land warfare in World War I, he believed that the proper development and deployment of specialized aircraft and the targeting of civilian centers could shorten future wars by destroying an enemy's industrial capabilities. He envisioned military aircraft capable of many tasks—pursuit, attack, bombardment, reconnaissance, and the delivery of airborne troops behind enemy lines, an idea he first proposed in 1919. His vision of a separate role for military aircraft was not unique; his writings and lectures were refined by exchanges with his counterparts in the emergence of the new air age, Trenchard and Douhet being only two of his well-known colleagues.

Mitchell understood that modern warfare required the destruction of the weak and the old, women and children, and that air power "put a completely new complexion on the old system of making war." He set forth his ideas by lecture and by book. He published *Winged Defense* in 1925 and *Skyways* in 1930. His refusal to work through a bureaucratic system of conservative procurement and governmental reluctance to finance innovative weapon systems in the 1920's led directly to his court-martial in 1925. As a civilian, he continued to espouse the strategic use of air power until his death in 1936. He lectured, he wrote, he testified before Congress, and he used the press to push his particular views. Indifference he found impossible to tolerate. The irony of Mitchell's career was that the real systemization of his thoughts on strategic warfare and "vital centers" came after 1926, when he joined the ranks of civilians.

Bibliography

Craven, Wesley Frank, and James Lea Cate, eds. *The Army Air Forces in World War II*. 7 vols. Chicago: University of Chicago Press, 1949-1958. Reprint. Washington, D.C.: Office of Air Force History, 1984. The standard history of the use of air power, deployment of forces, theater of operation, and air power development during World War II.

Dupuy, R. Ernest, and Trevor N. Dupuy. *The Encyclopedia of Military History*. Rev. ed. New York: Harper and Row, Publishers, 1986. The standard reference source for students of military history, containing sections on strategy, tactics, weaponry, and war and battle chronologies.

Earle, Edward Mead, ed. *Makers of Modern Strategy: Military Thought from Machiavelli to Hitler*. Princeton, N.J.: Princeton University Press, 1943. This anthology contains a well-written, if slightly dated, essay on three great architects of aerial warfare: Douhet, Mitchell, and Alexander de Seversky. Douhet's doctrine influenced American air-power theory through Mitchell's interpretation and popularization of his arguments.

Hurley, Alfred F. *Billy Mitchell: Crusader for Air Power*. New York: Franklin Watts, 1964. A biographical portrait of Mitchell that is considered the most factual and objective. It has been reprinted by Indiana University Press (1975) and should be used to balance Mitchell's often exaggerated claims for his own ideas and the superiority of air-power.

Millet, Allan R., and Peter Maslowski. *For the Common Defense: A Military History of the United States of America*. New York: Free Press, 1984. The best single history of America at war. The authors integrate naval and air force developments with the conduct of war by conventional surface forces. Mitchell's contributions are balanced by adequate attention to the navy's assessment of the role of military aircraft in the post–World War I era.

Mitchell, William. *Memoirs of World War I: "From Start to Finish of Our Greatest War."* New York: Random House, 1960. Mitchell's memoirs were first published in 1960, twenty-four years after his death.

_____. *Winged Defense: The Development and Possibilities of Modern Air Power, Economic and Military*. New York: G. P. Putnam's Sons, 1925. To understand the development of Mitchell's thought and the development of strategic air-power doctrines, there is no better place to start than this work.

Weigley, Russell F. *The American Way of War: A History of United States Military Strategy and Policy*. Bloomington, Indiana University Press, 1977. Weigley's excellent study of the evolution of American military strategy devotes a chapter to Billy Mitchell's thought, writings, and advocacy of directing air-power to the destruction of the "vital centers." He also traces the interpretation of Mitchell's doctrines as they were applied to strategic bombing in World War II, where its results often fell short of those promised by its advocates, including Alexander de Seversky.

Ronald M. Benson

JAMES MONROE

Born: April 28, 1758; Westmoreland County, Virginia
Died: July 4, 1831; New York, New York
Area of Achievement: Politics and statesmanship
Contribution: As President of the United States and author of the Monroe
  Doctrine, Monroe set forth one of the basic principles of American foreign
  policy.

Early Life

James Monroe was born April 28, 1758, in Westmoreland County, Virginia. He came from a good but not distinguished family of Scottish origin. His father was Spence Monroe, and his mother was Elizabeth Jones Monroe, sister of Judge Joseph Jones, a prominent Virginia politician. James was the eldest of four children. His formal education began at the age of eleven, at a private school operated by the Reverend Mr. Archibald Campbell, which was considered the best school in the colony. At the age of sixteen, after the death of his father, Monroe entered the College of William and Mary upon the advice of his uncle, Judge Jones, who was to have a very formative influence upon Monroe's life.

At the College of William and Mary, the Revolutionary War intruded, and Monroe, with his education unfinished, enlisted, in the spring of 1776, as a lieutenant in a Virginia regiment of the Continental Line. Slightly more than six feet tall, with a large, broad-shouldered frame, the eighteen-year-old was an impressive figure. He had a plain face, a rather large nose, a broad forehead, and wide-set, blue-gray eyes. His face was generally unexpressive, and his manners were simple and unaffected. He fought in the battles at Harlem and White Plains, and he was wounded at Trenton. During 1777 and 1778, he served as an aide, with the rank of major, on the staff of William Alexander, Lord Stirling. As an aide, Monroe mingled with the aides of other commanders and other staff officers, among them Alexander Hamilton, Charles Lee, Aaron Burr, and the Marquis de Lafayette. This interlude broadened his outlook and view of the ideals of the Revolution, which he carried with almost missionary zeal the remainder of his life. After participating in the battles of Brandywine, Germantown, and Monmouth, Monroe resigned from Stirling's staff in December, 1778, and returned to Virginia to apply for a rank in the state line. Unable to secure a position, Monroe, upon the advice of Judge Jones, cultivated the friendship of Governor Thomas Jefferson, and he formed a connection as a student of law with Jefferson that continued until 1783. This was the beginning of a long and valuable relationship, especially for Monroe. In 1782, Monroe was elected to the Virginia legislature, thus beginning a political career that lasted for more than forty years and brought him eventually to the highest office in the land.

Life's Work

In 1783, Monroe was elected to the Congress of the Articles of Confederation. He was an active and useful member, and he gained invaluable experience. He cultivated a friendship with James Madison, who was introduced to him by Jefferson. Monroe was identified with the nationalists, but his strong localist and sectional views made him cautious. He was particularly opposed to John Jay's negotiations with Don Diego de Gardoqui, the first Spanish minister to the United States, which threatened the western navigation of the Mississippi River. Monroe helped to defeat the negotiations, thereby gaining great popularity in the Western country, which lasted all of his political life.

Monroe's congressional service expired in 1786. He returned to Virginia intending to become a lawyer. By this time, he had married Elizabeth Kortright, the daughter of a New York merchant, on February 16, 1786. She was attractive but formal and reserved. Years later, she proved to be a marked contrast to her predecessor as hostess of the White House, Dolley Madison.

Monroe set up a law practice at Fredericksburg, Virginia, but he was not long out of politics. He was again elected to the Virginia legislature. He was also a delegate at the Annapolis Conference, but he was not chosen for the Federal Convention. In 1788, Monroe was elected to the Virginia convention for ratification of the Constitution. Here he joined with the opponents of the Constitution, fearing that the government would be too strong and would threaten Western development.

Monroe soon joined the new government, however, after losing a race for the House of Representatives against James Madison. He was elected to the United States Senate in 1790 and served there until May, 1794. He took an antiadministration stand, opposing virtually all of Secretary of the Treasury Alexander Hamilton's measures. It was a surprise, therefore, when he was selected as the new United States minister to France in June, 1794. Relations between the United States and France were at a low ebb. President George Washington apparently believed that Monroe, whose pro-French attitude was well-known, would improve relations as well as appease the Republican Party at home.

Moved by his sympathies and a desire to satisfy the French, Monroe addressed the French National Convention in a manner that brought a rebuke from Secretary of State Edmund Randolph. Monroe was unable to defend Jay's treaty to the French, and he was considered too pro-French in the United States. In 1796, he was recalled by the new secretary of state, Timothy Pickering. When he returned, Monroe responded to innuendoes about his conduct with a nearly five-hundred-page pamphlet entitled *A View of the Conduct of the Executive, in the Foreign Affairs of the United States* (1797), revealing his belief that he had been betrayed by the Administration.

Although attacked by Federalists, among Westerners and his friends, his reputation was enhanced.

Monroe's diplomatic career was not finished. After an interlude as governor of Virginia (1799-1802), Monroe was chosen to return to France to assist Robert R. Livingston in negotiations to purchase New Orleans. Monroe always believed that his arrival in France was the decisive factor in convincing Napoleon Bonaparte to shift his position and offer the entire Louisiana Territory to the United States. Livingston had, however, already opened the negotiations and, with Monroe's assistance, closed the deal.

In 1804, Monroe went to Spain to "perfect" the American claim that the Louisiana Purchase included West Florida. The Spanish would not budge, and Monroe returned to England in 1805. In London, Jefferson matched Monroe with William Pinkney to negotiate with the British to end the practice of impressments and other disputes which had arisen between the two countries. The Monroe-Pinkney Treaty of December, 1806, gained few concessions but apparently satisfied the two American ministers. President Jefferson and Secretary of State Madison, however, rejected the treaty, and Jefferson did not submit it to the Senate.

Monroe returned to the United States in December, 1807, in an angry mood. He allowed his friends to present him as a presidential contender against Madison. Although Monroe's ticket was swamped in Virginia, ending his effort, he still had support in Virginia, for he was elected to the Virginia legislature in 1810, and the next year, to the state's governorship.

In 1811, Monroe and Madison were reconciled. Monroe accepted the offer of secretary of state. Relations between the United States and Great Britain had so deteriorated that Monroe concluded, as had Madison, that war must result. Monroe sustained the president's policy and the declaration of war on June 18. As secretary of state, Monroe supported Madison's decision to enter negotiations with the British and helped him select an outstanding negotiating team. Thereafter, Monroe had little influence upon the negotiations that resulted in the Treaty of Ghent, which ended the War of 1812.

Monroe emerged from the war with his reputation generally unscathed, and he was a leading contender for the presidency. The congressional caucus in 1816, however, partially influenced by a prejudice against the Virginia dynasty, accorded him only an eleven-vote margin to win the nomination. The discredited Federalists offered only token opposition, and Monroe won easily. His years in the presidency (1817-1825) are often referred to as the Era of Good Feelings. The Federalist Party gradually disappeared and offered no opposition. Monroe was reelected in 1820, only one vote short of a unanimous vote. He sought to govern as a president above parties. He took two grand tours, one to the North and the other to the South, and was well received wherever he went. Monroe also appointed some Federalists to office.

The outward placidity of these years, however, was belied by ferment below the surface. The question of slavery was raised to dangerous levels in the debate over restrictions upon the admission of Missouri to statehood. Monroe did not interfere in the debate, and he readily signed the compromise measure. Other issues during his presidency revealed the dissension within his party—for example, the debate over Jackson's invasion of Florida, army reduction, and internal improvements.

Diplomatic successes included neutralizing the Great Lakes, arbitrating the fisheries question, establishing the northern boundary of the Louisiana Purchase as the forty-ninth parallel, and joint occupation of Oregon with Great Britain. Much of the success of these negotiations was a result of Monroe's able secretary of state, John Quincy Adams. After Jackson's foray into Florida, Adams got Spain to transfer Florida to the United States and to settle the border extending to the Pacific Ocean.

The Monroe Doctrine, issued in 1823, capped off these diplomatic successes. It arose out of American fears that European nations would intervene to subdue the newly independent countries in South America. Invited by the British to join in a statement warning against intervention, Monroe, at the urging of Adams, issued a unilateral statement warning Europe not to interfere in the affairs of the Western Hemisphere.

In 1824, the unity of the party was shattered by a contest between several strong rivals for the presidency. William H. Crawford, Monroe's secretary of the treasury, secured the caucus nomination from a rump group of congressmen, but other contenders, including Adams, Jackson, and Henry Clay, threw the vote into the House of Representatives. Clay threw his support to Adams, who won the presidency. In the aftermath, new coalitions were formed and eventually another two-party system emerged.

Monroe did not exert any political leadership during this period. It was not his temperament to operate in the new style of politics emerging as the Age of the Common Man. In many ways, he was obsolete when he left the presidency. His last years were spent making claims upon the government for past service. He received $29,513 in 1826, and he got an additional thirty thousand dollars in 1831, but this did not stave off advancing bankruptcy. In 1830, upon the death of his wife, he moved to New York City to live with a daughter and her husband. He died there on July 4, 1831.

Summary

Monroe, the third of the Virginia triumvirate, has generally been ranked below his two predecessors in intellectual ability, although he has been ranked higher than either for his administrative skills. Monroe was more narrowly partisan and sectional, but he tried to be a president of all the people. The question has been raised, however, as to what extent he understood the role of the president as a party leader. It is to be noted that the party disintegrated under his presidency, but that may be a result, in part, of the decline of the Federalist Party as a viable opposition.

During his last years, Monroe was much concerned about his reputation. His concern reflects the essentially political cast of his mind. His letters throughout his life concerned almost exclusively political matters. An experienced and even a sensitive politician, he was an anachronism by the end of his presidency. The last representative of the generation of the Founding Fathers, his idea of government by consensus was out of place in the new democratic politics of the era of the common man.

Monroe's legacy was his Americanism. If he was at times narrow and sectional, he was always an American. His Monroe Doctrine aptly expressed the feelings of his fellow Americans that the Western Hemisphere was where the principles of freedom would be worked out and show the way to Europe and the rest of the world. His career was long and successful, and his public service, if not brilliant, was useful to his country.

Bibliography
Ammon, Harry. *James Monroe: The Quest for National Identity*. New York: McGraw-Hill Book Co., 1971. The most comprehensive biography. This book is well researched and well written. The interpretations are favorable to Monroe.

Cresson, William P. *James Monroe*. Chapel Hill: University of North Carolina Press, 1946. Until Ammon's book, this was the standard biography. Engagingly written, it lacks rigorous analysis. The point of view of the author is also favorable to Monroe.

Dangerfield. George. *The Era of Good Feelings*. New York: Harcourt Brace and World, 1952. Brilliantly written, this work, although superficial in many places, is still the best account of Monroe's presidency.

Monroe, James. *The Autobiography of James Monroe*. Edited by Gerry Stuart Brown. Syracuse, N.Y.: Syracuse University Press, 1959. Monroe's own view of his early career (the narrative extends only to 1805). Partly written to advance his claims upon the government, and partly to leave his own record of his career, Monroe's narrative does not always achieve objectivity.

Morgan, George. *The Life of James Monroe*. Boston: Small, Maynard and Co., 1921. Reprint. New York: AMS Press, 1969. Entertainingly written, but thin on analysis and weak on some subjects. The book is also marred by the biases of the author in favor of Monroe.

Perkins, Dexter. *Hands Off: A History of the Monroe Doctrine*. Rev. ed. Boston: Little, Brown and Co., 1955. In part a summary of a three-volume study by the same author and the considered judgment of the authority on the Monroe Doctrine.

Styron, Arthur. *The Last of the Cocked Hats: James Monroe and The Vir-*

ginia Dynasty. Norman: University of Oklahoma Press, 1945. Less a biography than a collection of the author's favorable opinions of Monroe. Written in a spritely manner, but there is more style than substance.

C. Edward Skeen

DWIGHT L. MOODY

Born: February 5, 1837; Northfield, Massachusetts
Died: December 22, 1899; Northfield, Massachusetts
Area of Achievement: Religion
Contribution: In mass evangelistic campaigns, Moody preached a message of
salvation and brought spiritual revival to the United States and England.

Early Life

Dwight Lyman Moody was born February 5, 1837, in Northfield, Massachusetts, the sixth of nine children. His father, Edwin Moody, died when
Dwight was four, leaving the family with no provision for their future. With
determination, hard work, and assistance from others, Dwight's mother, Bet-
sey Holton Moody, kept the family together and reared them in a strict, loving, devout home. Because he was impatient with school and needed to
work, Moody had very little formal schooling. Always conscious of this lack,
he was for many years hesitant to speak in public and only gradually attained
the ability to preach.

At the age of seventeen, Moody left Northfield and obtained work as a
shoe salesman in the store of his uncle, Samuel Holton. Ambition, boundless
energy, natural wit, and unorthodox selling methods made him an unusually
successful salesman.

As a condition of employment, Moody had to attend Holton's church, the
Mount Vernon Orthodox Congregationalist Church. Reared as a Unitarian,
Moody had never heard the message that was preached at Mount Vernon:
that Jesus Christ had died for all men, risen from the dead, and lived to be
the Savior and friend of all who trusted Him. Moody resisted this idea for
some time, but when his Sunday-school teacher asked him privately for a
response, Moody gave himself and his life to Christ. From that date forward,
April 21, 1855, Moody had a new purpose in life.

In 1856, Moody moved to Chicago and within two years was earning more
than five thousands dollars a year. His ambition was to succeed in business
and accumulate the wealth to support his philanthropic work.

Needing an outlet for his energy and Christian zeal, Moody started a mission Sunday school in 1858. In two years, the regular attendance grew to 450
children. By 1864, the school had outgrown two buildings, and members
wanted to form a church. The Illinois Street Church was founded that year,
later becoming Moody Memorial Church.

In 1860, Moody resigned his business position to devote himself full time to
Christian work. He joined the fledgling Young Men's Christian Association
(YMCA) and, in 1865, became its president. Through the years, he was one
of the foremost fund-raisers for YMCA buildings and activities. During the
Civil War, the YMCA held evangelistic services for the soldiers, and though

still unpolished, Moody became an effective and practiced preacher. He also visited personally with the soldiers.

In 1862, Moody married Emma Revell, a beautiful and well-educated girl of nineteen. They differed sharply in personality traits. While Emma Moody was poised, retiring, and conservative, her husband loved publicity and practical jokes and was impulsive, quick-tempered, and outspoken. Though she suffered from poor health, he was robust and was always active. Practical and orderly, she handled most of her husband's correspondence and the family's finances. He depended on her good judgment and learned self-discipline from her. With all of his brusqueness, he was warm, tenderhearted, and sensitive to others. Humble and peace-loving he was quick to apologize when he had wronged another. Under his wife's influence, Moody mellowed and improved in manners and speech.

In the 1860's, the YMCA expanded its work among the poor of Chicago. The association set up a distribution system for food and clothing using Moody's mission staff as workers. Moody organized literacy and Americanization classes. Also, the YMCA sponsored evangelism of the poor and, under Moody's leadership, citywide distribution of religious tracts.

As president of the YMCA, Moody became responsible for traveling to national conventions. At the same time, he participated in Sunday-school conventions and interdenominational "Christian conventions." Since he played a prominent role in YMCA work and the Sunday-school movement, Moody was well-known as a colorful and effective speaker. At a convention Moody heard Ira Sankey sing and persuaded Sankey to leave his home and business and to join him as an associate. This partnership led Moody in a new direction.

Life's Work

After much prayer and soul-searching, Moody concluded that God was calling him to full-time evangelism. In June, 1873, Moody and Sankey sailed for England. After an inauspicious beginning, the two met with minor success in Newcastle and then preached to huge crowds in Edinburgh and Glasgow.

Throughout 1874, Moody moved slowly through Scotland and Ireland and reached England in 1875. Moody would select a local person to coordinate plans for the campaign, and he insisted on cooperation among the local churches. He encouraged people to hold prayer meetings to pray for his work.

Attendance at the revivals required a huge building and, at times, a special temporary structure was built. Meetings were publicized in circulars and through home visitation.

As the evangelists approached London, the question was whether London would accept this uneducated preacher with his simple and direct messages.

Short and heavy set, he wore a full beard on his round, ruddy face. Good-humored with a rich, full laugh, he walked quickly and spoke loudly. Despite criticism from the press, Moody's popularity seemed assured from the beginning of his London meetings. It was estimated during the four-month campaign that Moody spoke to more than two million people.

Moody returned to the United States as an international figure, receiving numerous requests for speaking engagements. After a short time at Northfield, Moody and Sankey held campaigns in Brooklyn, Philadelphia, and New York. After these campaigns, a visit to the South and a tour of the Midwest brought the two evangelists back to Chicago. In the fall of 1876, they began a revival in Chicago that lasted until mid-January, 1877. Following this revival, they held campaigns in Boston, Baltimore, St. Louis, Cleveland, and San Francisco.

Moody proved to be a sought-after speaker for the remainder of his life, and he traveled in North America and Britain with his message of revival. Recognizing a need for trained laymen to work in the churches, he established schools to instruct new converts. The Northfield School for Girls opened in 1879, followed by the Mount Hermon School for Boys in 1881. Their purpose was to provide a preparatory school education that would encourage the development of Christian character and prepare the students for Christian service. Moody did not consider himself an educator; rather, he obtained funds, facilities, and personnel for his schools.

In 1880, Moody held the first summer Bible conference at Northfield, with his friends and himself as speakers. The goal was to give laymen increased understanding of the Bible and to foster spiritual renewal. These laymen would then return to work in their churches with greater power. In 1886, the conference was expanded to include college students.

Chicago was the setting for another of Moody's ventures into education. Friends had long hoped for a permanent school there, and Miss Emma Dryer, with Moody's encouragement, had founded a small training school. Under Moody's direction, the Chicago Bible Institute officially opened on September 26, 1889. The school's purpose was to train Christian workers and equip them to serve in city missions. After Moody's death, the name was officially changed to Moody Bible Institute.

In 1894, Moody became convinced that masses of people could be reached if Christian books were available in inexpensive editions. A colportage department was begun at the Chicago Bible Institute, with students often distributing the books. In his later years, Moody developed a concern for prisoners, and books from the institute's colportage line were provided to prison libraries.

Moody had continued his revival preaching from 1878 to 1899, and he was speaking at Kansas City when his fatal illness struck. He hastened home to Northfield, and there he died on December 22, 1899.

Summary

A man of incredible energy and authority, Moody was an evangelist to the masses and brought spiritual renewal to urban centers, both in the United States and abroad. The most significant religious leader of the Gilded Age, he instituted new strategies and techniques in mass evangelism that have been used by later evangelists. These included his methods of planning, organization, and publicity. By enlisting cooperation among the churches, he proved that evangelism could be above denominationalism.

Living in the midst of a change from traditional conservatism to a liberal outlook in theology, Moody nevertheless maintained a deep belief in a literal interpretation of the Bible and its fundamental creeds. His message typified the thought of the evangelical Protestant movement. Out of the millions who heard him speak, many became converted and carried on his message.

In Moody's era, Christian elementary and secondary schools had not come into existence. The schools he established at Northfield were innovative in their approach as Christian education. The Chicago Bible Institute was the second significant Bible school started up in the United States and became the impetus for others. His use of lay people in his work—Moody himself was never ordained—and his Christian schools ushered in the age of the lay worker in the Church.

Moody's influence was felt in evangelical circles long after his death. Probably more than his theology, his personality and fierce concern for mankind have inspired others to continue his work. His compassion, humility, and earnest message of salvation remain an example for other evangelists.

Bibliography

Findlay, James F., Jr. *Dwight L. Moody: American Evangelist, 1837-1899*. Chicago: University of Chicago Press, 1969. The single best scholarly biography. Includes an analysis, though inadequate, of Moody's personality, theology, and techniques of evangelism. Examines critical shifts in the social and religious thought of the nineteenth century, placing Moody in historical perspective. A review of Moody's home life and later accomplishments is included.

Getz, Gene A. *MBI: The Story of Moody Bible Institute*. Chicago: Moody Press, 1969. Getz details the early history of the Moody Bible Institute and describes Moody's role in its beginnings and early years. A comprehensive account of the growth and expansion of the institute and its varied ministries.

Gundry, Stanley N. *Love Them In*. Chicago: Moody Press, 1976. Balanced, comprehensive evaluation of Moody's theology and how it related to his evangelistic campaigns. Within the historical context, Gundry considers Moody's doctrine in matters such as Calvinism, perfectionism, speaking in tongues, and the life of the believer. He stresses how Moody viewed the

Gospel and its message of salvation.

Hopkins, C. Howard. *History of the Y.M.C.A. in North America*. New York: Association Press, 1951. A valuable resource as it examines the interplay of influences between Moody and the YMCA. Details the work Moody did for the YMCA in organization, fund-raising, and evangelism.

McLoughlin, William G., Jr. *Modern Revivalism: Charles Grandison Finney to Billy Graham*. New York: Ronald Press, 1959. Attempting to explain the significance of revivalism in the social, intellectual, and religious life of America, McLoughlin examines the lives of major revivalists, including Moody. He analyzes their social environment and their effect on American life. Includes a description of the work of Moody's associate, Ira Sankey.

Moody, William R. *Dwight L. Moody*. Rev. ed. New York: Macmillan Publishing Co., 1930. Just before his death, Moody commissioned his son to write this official biography. Though eulogistic, it is complete and invaluable in any study of Moody's life.

Pollock, John. *Moody*. Chicago: Moody Press, 1983. A readable, inspirational biography. Although it is not a theological analysis, Moody's personality is illuminated, and the detailed story gives information not found in other biographies.

Sankey, Ira D. *My Life and the Story of the Gospel Hymns*. Chicago: Bible Institute Colportage Association, 1907. Since Ira Sankey was Moody's associate in his evangelistic campaigns, his autobiography gives insight into the way Moody conducted services. Also included are anecdotes which further aid in the understanding of Moody's personality.

Elaine Mathiasen

J. P. MORGAN

Born: April 17, 1837; Hartford, Connecticut
Died: March 31, 1913; Rome, Italy
Areas of Achievement: Banking and philanthropy
Contribution: As an extraordinarily successful investment banker and a
conspicuous philanthropist, one of the most prominent art collectors of his
day, Morgan symbolized an era of aggressive capitalism.

Early Life

John Pierpont Morgan had remarkable parents: Junius Spencer Morgan
(1813-1890) owned part of a large mercantile house in Hartford, advanced to
a larger one in Boston, and finally became partner, then successor to the very
wealthy George Peabody, an American who made his career banking in London. Junius settled there in 1854 and lived in England for the remainder of
his life. Morgan's mother, Sarah Pierpont, came from the family of a brilliant
preacher in Boston, much given to abolitionism and other reforms. Young
Morgan received his formal education in Hartford, in Boston, in Vevey, Switzerland, and at the University of Göttingen. Seriously ill as a teenager, he
had a long and successful convalescence in the Azores. At age twenty, he
began his career as a clerk in Duncan, Sherman, and Company in New York.
Two years later, while traveling in the Caribbean to study the sugar and cotton markets, he bought, without authorization, a cargo of unwanted coffee
with a draft on his employers. They complained but accepted the profit of
several thousand he earned by wholesaling the coffee in New Orleans.

In 1860, Morgan set up his own company. He had plenty of business from
his father in London and also took advantage of many opportunities to buy
and sell in the booming commercial city of New York. In 1861, he married
Amelia Sturges, after courting her for several years. She was clearly in the
advanced stages of tuberculosis, but Morgan, daring in love as well as in business, gave up all commercial activities and took his stricken bride to Algiers
and then to Nice, hoping to cure her. He failed, returning to the United
States as a widower in 1862. He formed a partnership with his cousin, Jim
Goodwin, and called the firm J. P. Morgan and Company, Bankers.

Writers hostile to Morgan claim that he selfishly pursued profit during the
Civil War years, trading in gold against the government's fluctuating greenbacks, buying a substitute for three hundred dollars under the Conscription
Act, and on one occasion buying obsolete arms from the federal government
in the East and then selling them to General John C. Frémont in the West at
an enormous profit. Morgan never apologized for his own actions, but writers friendly to him have argued that recurrent fainting spells, from which he
suffered as a young man, made him unfit for military duty, that he served the
Union cause well as an agent for Junius Morgan, who was staunchly pro-

Union and placed United States bonds in England, and, finally, that two other men arranged and carried out the affair of the arms. Morgan was involved only as their banker, extending a short-term loan. Furthermore, the weapons were improved by rifling the barrels, and the young entrepreneurs, whatever their motives, did what the disorganized Department of the Army could not manage: They delivered arms at a reasonable price to the desperately needy Western army. On one point, however, there is no dispute: Morgan spent that part of the war that followed his disastrous first marriage in making money as rapidly as he could. In September, 1864, he took in new partners and reorganized as Dabney, Morgan and Company. At twenty-seven, he was a leader in the financial life of the United States' largest city. Yet he was already launched in his career of philanthropy, helping to raise money for the wounded and widowed and working effectively to establish and enlarge the Young Men's Christian Association (YMCA). In 1865, he married Frances Tracy, one of the six daughters of attorney Charles Tracy. The Tracys were fellow communicants at St. George's Episcopal Church in the Bowery, which Morgan had joined in 1861 and attended for the remainder of his life.

Largely free, at this point, of the illnesses and spells that had marred his youth, Morgan stood well over six feet, with powerful shoulders, penetrating eyes, and the air of one born to command. In later life, he would grow portly and suffer painfully from acne rosacea, an inflammation of the skin which settled especially in his nose. He doted on his and Frances' four children, Louisa, Jack (John Pierpont Morgan, Jr.), Juliet, and Anne. In the summer of 1869, Morgan and his wife, accompanied by two relatives, rode the new transcontinental railroad to Utah and to California, where they toured extensively by stagecoach and horseback. Returning East, the Morgans occupied a comfortable new home at Six West Fortieth Street. In 1871, troubled by nervous disorders, Morgan briefly considered retiring. Instead, he accepted a new partnership with the powerful Drexels of Philadelphia. He would be a full partner and would head their New York office under the title of Drexel, Morgan, and Company.

Life's Work

To understand the later fame of Morgan, the investment banker, one must first understand how and why he became involved with the railroads of the United States. From their earliest beginnings around 1830 to the Civil War, American railroads were generally small affairs, connecting neighboring cities or connecting cities with important rivers or seaports. Most companies supposed that they could not manage more than five hundred miles of track. The two systems which thoroughly refuted this thinking, the New York Central and the Pennsylvania, were quite exceptional until Congress, offering large land grants, encouraged the building of transcontinental railroads.

Some firms can begin business with very little capital investment and grow on earnings; others, including railroads and electric power systems, are expensive to build and cannot be put into operation or earn money until everything is in place, including the employees. Thus, the quantities of federal land given to the Western railroads were not the source of huge profits that they have been claimed to be. The railroads had to be built and operating, and the land had to be well along toward settlement, before any of those lands were salable. Railroads, the most important and transforming feature of the American economy in the nineteenth century, relied entirely on borrowed capital for their construction and initial operation. Furthermore, they had to be public corporations, their stock for sale in markets throughout the world; otherwise, the enormous sums required would not be forthcoming. This feature led inevitably to the separation of management from stockholders, too numerous and too scattered to exercise a coherent will on railroad affairs. Yet stockholders all had one thing in common: They wished to protect their investments. It was therefore logical that investment bankers, whose income derived largely from marketing stocks and bonds, would wish to protect their own business positions by assuring the quality of the stocks and bonds being sold. Morgan was thus drawn into railroad affairs by a desire, born of necessity, to see that railroads were properly and efficiently managed, so that the stockholders and bondholders would be properly rewarded for their investments. Furthermore, he clearly saw what Cornelius Vanderbilt, Thomas A. Scott, and Jay Gould had seen earlier: The future of American railroading lay in building large, integrated systems, in which a single corporation controlled not only trunk lines but also feeders and operated without competition.

His first adventure was a colorful skirmish with the most notorious railroad pirates of the age, Gould and Diamond Jim Fisk, in a battle for the control of the Albany and Susquehanna. There is a legend that Morgan kept control of a crucial stockholders meeting by hurling the burly Fisk down a flight of stairs, scattering his henchman as though they were tenpins. If true, this was the only time Morgan gained control of a railroad by hand-to-hand combat. In 1879, he performed a more sedate but much more lucrative feat in marketing William Vanderbilt's 250,000 shares (eighty-seven percent of those in existence) of New York Central Stock without suffering any depreciation or exciting any move to displace the railroad's management.

The year 1880 brought another enormous challenge, converted into enormous profits, not because Drexel, Morgan, and Company charged high brokerage fees but because they were handling so much money. In this case, it was a question of marketing forty million dollars in bonds for the improvement of the Northern Pacific, a transcontinental that had suffered bankruptcy and reorganization in the Panic of 1873. Great though his resources were, Morgan could not finance such enormous sales of stocks and bonds entirely through his own and his father's partnerships. He brought in other major banking houses, in the United States and abroad, discreetly organized in syndicates. To help protect the investments so arranged, Morgan, or one of his trusted partners or friends, became director of the refinanced railroad. Morgan later helped to finance and manage dozens of railroads.

Morgan was involved in the finances of the federal government on four major occasions. With other leading bankers, he helped refinance the federal debt under President Ulysses S. Grant. In the summer of 1877, Morgan committed another of his unexpected and extraordinary moves: He loaned the army money with which to pay its troops, largely engaged in the Western Indian wars, after a distracted Congress had adjourned without renewing their appropriation. Since the army was not authorized to borrow, Morgan had paid out more than two million dollars at his own risk; Congress, however, appropriated funds to repay the banker. Much more effort was required to save the United States Treasury's gold reserve in the depression of 1893. A combination of laws, more popular than wise, had forced the Treasury to sell gold until it was on the brink of bankruptcy; the Panic of 1893 had further started a general flight of gold back to Europe. To save the situation, Morgan had to form a syndicate of American and European bankers both to loan gold to the government at acceptable rates and to check the flow of gold from the Treasury out of the country. Furthermore, Grover Cleveland, whose party was rapidly coming under the control of Populists and Bryanites, was extremely reluctant to accept help from the only people who could give it, the "monied interests of Wall Street."

Morgan's greatest triumphs and defeats came at the end of his life. In 1901, he formed a combination to buy out Andrew Carnegie and merge his steel colossus with several other companies. The resulting United States Steel Corporation, the first "billion dollar corporation," renewed charges of monopoly and chicanery. Morgan then turned to a merger of the Northern Pacific with its regional rival, the Great Northern, by means of a holding company, the Northern Securities Company. Theodore Roosevelt, the Progressive president, ordered a prosecution which the government won in 1904, and the merger fell apart. Morgan, however, ever the patriot, returned in 1907 to lead yet another syndicate of bankers to prevent a financial panic. One of the New York banks saved on that occasion had chiefly working people for its depositors; Morgan ordered his company to save them even if he lost money; in fact, he did. In the last year of his life, Morgan was summoned before the Pujo Committee, which charged him with destroying competition by controlling all the large banks, railroads, and steel companies of the United States through interlocking directorships and stock proxies. Morgan stoutly denied the charge, claiming that his methods guaranteed the proper management of business by men of high character.

At St. George's Church, Morgan led the vestry in hiring W. S. Rainsford, an Emerson-inspired Progressive who introduced a community center, a house for Deaconesses (Episcopal women doing social work, in this case), an industrial school, a summer camp, and a seaside resort for working-class women and children, all of which Morgan helped plan and most of which he financed. He also helped maintain the church near his summer home, served on the committee that planned the cathedral, and attended every national triennial convention of his church until his death.

Always something of a collector, Morgan began buying rare and old works of art on a stupendous scale after the death of his father. As a collector, Morgan displayed the decisiveness and flair that had characterized his business career. A trustee of the Metropolitan Museum from its fledgling days, he became its most active member in the last fifteen years of his life and left it priceless collections of paintings, ceramics, armor, and other objets d'art. For his collection of rare manuscripts and books, he built his own library next to the home at 219 Madison Avenue which he had built in 1881. It would later be administered as a public reference library. Collecting art went nicely with Morgan's lifelong habit of traveling abroad. He spent almost every summer in England, France, Italy, and, on several occasions, Egypt, where he often visited archaeological digs. He died during one of his periods of travel in Rome, Italy, on March 31, 1913.

Summary

J. P. Morgan's power grew because of the unusual combination of boldness and good sense, ruthlessness and responsibility, that made up his complex personality. The failure of the American people, between 1836 and 1913, to have any sort of central bank created rare opportunities for investment bankers with strong connections to foreign centers of capital. Hating waste, inefficiency, and conflict, Morgan used his growing financial power to impose order on the railroad and steel industries, inevitably reducing competition and calling into question the Adam Smith economics that most educated people took seriously. Democrats also feared the growing power of rich men who appeared responsible to no one but themselves. Morgan, thus, stirred up controversy and antagonism; yet, on his death in 1913, he left a legacy of responsibility in business and civic affairs and a priceless collection of art for the enjoyment of, literally, millions.

Bibliography

Allen, Frederick Lewis. *The Great Pierpont Morgan*. New York: Harper and Brothers, 1949. The most readable of the biographies and the only one that does justice to Morgan while stating the full case against him.
Canfield, Cass. *The Incredible Pierpont Morgan: Financier and Art Collector*. New York: Harper and Row, Publishers, 1974. Richly illustrated and with superb color plates, this is a delightful book on Morgan.

Chandler, Alfred D., Jr. *The Visible Hand: The Managerial Revolution in American Business*. Cambridge, Mass.: The Belknap Press of Harvard University Press, 1977. A comprehensive business history, placing Morgan exactly in context.

Gras, N. S. B., and Henrietta Larson. "J. P. Morgan: 1837-1913." In *The Coming of Managerial Capitalism: A Casebook on the History of American Economic Institutions*, edited by A. D. Chandler and R. S. Tedlow, 257-288. Homewood, Ill.: Richard D. Irwin, 1985. An outstanding short treatment of Morgan's business affairs and their significance.

Hoyt, Edwin P., Jr. *The House of Morgan*. New York: Dodd, Mead and Co., 1966. This is uniquely valuable in tracing the careers of four generations of Morgans.

Hughes, Jonathan. *The Vital Few: American Economic Progress and Its Protagonists*. Boston: Houghton Mifflin Co., 1966. A splendid interpretive history with a graceful chapter on Morgan.

Rainsford, W. S. *The Story of a Varied Life: An Autobiography*. Garden City, N.Y.: Doubleday, Page and Co., 1922. Rainsford was Rector of Morgan's church for twenty-two years and, for all of his spiritual condescension, the only informed witness to Morgan's strenuous service.

Satterlee, Herbert L. *J. Pierpont Morgan: An Intimate Portrait*. New York: Macmillan Publishing Co., 1939. A narrative chronicle by Morgan's son-in-law, in whose eyes the financier was a great and good man. Dull, but full of family information not available elsewhere.

Sinclair, Andrew. *Corsair: The Life of J. Pierpont Morgan*. Boston: Little, Brown and Co., 1981. A stylishly written book in the muckraking tradition, slightly marred by the repetition of the unlikely theory that Morgan resented his rich and powerful father right up to the old gentleman's death in 1890.

Tomkins, Calvin. *Merchants and Masterpieces: The Story of the Metropolitan Museum of Art*. New York: E. P. Dutton, 1970. Richly illustrated, this work places Morgan's collecting and ambitions for the museum in proper context.

Robert McColley

LEWIS HENRY MORGAN

Born: November 21, 1818; Aurora, New York
Died: December 17, 1881; Rochester, New York
Areas of Achievement: Anthropology and natural history
Contribution: Extending kinship studies, first among the Iroquois, then to
    cultures around the world, Morgan devised a theory of social and cultural
    evolution that provided both a theoretical paradigm for late nineteenth
    century anthropology and a theory of early family evolution that Karl Marx
    used in his interpretation of history.

Early Life

Lewis Henry Morgan was born November 21, 1818, in Aurora, New York,
to Harriet Steele and Jedediah Morgan. Morgan's father, a wealthy land-
holder, died when Morgan was eight, and the farm's operation was placed in
the hands of young Morgan's older brothers. After receiving an education at
the Cayuga Academy in Aurora and being graduated from Union College in
1840, Morgan decided to pursue a career in law. In Aurora, while reading for
his bar exams, Morgan joined a secret men's organization called the Grand
Order of the Iroquois. Morgan's participation and leadership in this organization proved to be the beginning of his ethnological career. In order to
model the order after the political organization of the six Indian nations of
New York, known as the Iroquois Confederacy, Morgan and other members
of the club made trips to several Iroquois reservations to study their history
and culture.

Later, Morgan took an active role in protesting the loss of Iroquois land,
specifically reservations of the Seneca—one of the six Iroquois nations—to a
land company, and he even traveled to Washington to present a petition to
the president and the Senate on behalf of the Seneca. For his support of the
Seneca Indians in this matter and his continuing interest in their culture, the
Seneca adopted Morgan as a member of the Hawk clan.

In 1844, Morgan moved to Rochester, New York, and opened a law office.
This career move did not deflect Morgan from his preoccupation with Indian
studies. Not only did he supply Indian artifacts to the Regents of the University of New York, for what would later become a collection of the New York
State Museum, but he also wrote a series of articles that appeared under the
title "Letters on the Iroquois Addressed to Albert Gallatin," published in the
American Whig Review (1847-1848). These letters he later revised and
expanded into *League of the Ho-dé-no-sau-nee, or Iroquois* (1851), now considered the first full ethnography of an American Indian group. Morgan
dedicated the book to Ely S. Parker, a Seneca Indian whom Morgan met in
an Albany bookstore and who was instrumental in helping Morgan collect
Seneca data. If Morgan never lived among the Indians, as some writers have

claimed, neither was he an armchair ethnologist. He read what books he could find on the Iroquois and then complemented this reading with extensive fieldwork. Indeed, Morgan proved to be one of the first ethnologists to rely heavily on data collected in the field for the construction of ethnological theories.

The publication of Morgan's work on Iroquois history and culture drew the attention of others in the new science of ethnology, including the Indian agent, historian, and ethnographer Henry Rowe Schoolcraft and archaeologist Ephraim George Squier. After the publication of his book on the Iroquois, Morgan hoped to put aside his study of Indians and devote himself to his career in law. His marriage to his cousin Mary Elisabeth Steele, in 1851, strengthened his desire to succeed in his law career.

Life's Work

Morgan's early law career in Rochester proved unspectacular. Unknown and without influential friends, Morgan supported himself on local collection cases and occasional criminal cases. In time, he became known more for his public lectures at the Mechanic's Institute and at the Rochester Athenaeum than as a trial lawyer. These lectures, as well as his book on the Iroquois, eventually introduced Morgan to the elite society of Rochester. Through these contacts, he invested in railroad and mining companies in the Upper Peninsula of Michigan. By the late 1850's, through wise investments, he had acquired a modest fortune that allowed him to retire from legal practice in the early 1860's. Except for brief stints in the New York assembly in 1861 and the New York senate from 1868 to 1869, Morgan devoted the remainder of his life to ethnology.

Morgan's return to anthropological studies really began in 1857. In 1856, Morgan attended the meetings of the American Association for the Advancement of Science. Impressed with the papers he heard, Morgan decided to return the following year and deliver a paper on Iroquois kinship. This paper grew out of Morgan's earlier research and his discovery that the Iroquois determined kinship differently from the way of Anglo-Americans. Morgan suspected that other Indian tribes exhibited similar kinship patterns, but he had no opportunity to test this theory until the summer of 1858, while traveling in upper Michigan. There, Morgan met some Ojibwe Indians and was excited to discover that their system of kinship was essentially the same as that of the Iroquois. It occurred to Morgan that kinship systems might be linked to a people's economy. Morgan noted that North American Indian kinship systems, which he termed classificatory, seemed to be associated with a hunting-gathering horticultural economy. Assuming that kinship systems changed slowly and then only when a people's economy changed, Morgan believed such systems to be quite old. If they were ancient and if similar systems could be found in other parts of the world, Morgan believed that this would constitute proof of the migration of American Indians from the Old World.

Because the origin of the American Indian remained an important question throughout the first half of the nineteenth century, Morgan believed that discovering an Old World connection would be a major contribution to the young science of ethnology. Seeking an answer to these questions, Morgan made four trips, between 1859 and 1862, to Indian tribes west of the Mississippi River to collect kinship information. On these trips, he interviewed missionaries, schoolteachers, merchants, government agents, Indian traders, and steamboat captains, checking and rechecking the data he received from his talks with Indians from various reservations. He also sent questionnaires to missionaries and government agents around the world to learn how other non-European cultures determined kinship. Out of these travels and research came his *Systems of Consanguinity and Affinity of the Human Family* (1871). Discovering that the method of designating kinship which he first found among the Iroquois Indians also existed in Asia, Morgan became convinced of the Old World origin of the American Indians.

Morgan's trips to the West and his examination of conditions in various Indian communities made him sharply critical of the federal government's handling of Indian affairs. His shock and frustration over educational and health facilities available to Indians poured out in a series of articles triggered by the public outcry at the death of General George A. Custer and his troops at Little Big Horn. In "Factory Systems for Indian Reservations," "The Hue and Cry against the Indians," and "The Indian Question," all published in the *Nation*, Morgan castigated the government for its treatment of Indians and blamed Custer's death on the government's long-standing mismanagement and indifference to reservation administration. Morgan claimed that Indians could not be civilized quickly and that teaching them farming might not be the best approach to changing their behavior. Change would take time, and American society would have to be patient in their expectations for the Indian.

Along with many others, Morgan sharply criticized government Indian policy. His reputation, however, rests not on these attacks but on his study of Indian kinship, which led him to theorize about the history and nature of the family. His evidence convinced him that the family had evolved through gradual stages from promiscuity to monogamy. This idea contributed to the development of Morgan's theory of human social and cultural evolution through stages of savagery, barbarism, and civilization. He developed these ideas in his next and best-known work, *Ancient Society: Or, Researches in the Lines of Human Progress from Savagery through Barbarism to Civilization* (1877). After the publication of *Ancient Society*, Morgan published little. A section on the evolution of house architecture and home life originally intended for *Ancient Society* and deleted by the publishers because of its length, was published separately as *Houses and House-Life of the American Aborigines* in 1881.

Although Morgan's primary contribution to American scholarship came through his work in anthropology, he also made contributions to natural history. Intrigued by the question of whether animals operated through instinct or reason, Morgan set out to investigate this question through an extensive study of the American beaver. Through his thorough examination of beaver behavior, Morgan concluded that beaver, in particular, and animals, in general, did indeed use reason. With the publication of *The American Beaver and His Works* (1868), Morgan became the foremost authority on the beaver. The study impressed both famed Harvard zoologist Louis Agassiz and English evolutionist Charles Darwin.

Summary

Morgan began writing at a time when American ethnology still stressed collection and classification, with little emphasis on the interpretation of these accumulating data. His evolutionary theory moved American ethnology beyond mere classification to a larger consideration of humankind and their place in space and time. By placing American Indian ethnology into the larger context of human social evolution or human history, Morgan proved a pioneer in the development of the science of anthropology.

Morgan's legacy to anthropology is considerable. His studies of kinship and theories of social evolution became the paradigm for anthropological study in the second half of the nineteenth century and influenced, in both Europe and the United States, the development of social anthropology into the twentieth century. His accomplishments were recognized by Charles Darwin, Henry Adams, Francis Parkman, and Karl Marx. Morgan's election to membership in the American Academy of Arts and Sciences, the National Academy of Science, and the American Association for the Advancement of Science, in which he served as president, indicates the esteem in which he and his ideas were held by the scientific community.

The work of Lewis Henry Morgan embodied much of the optimistic spirit that prevailed in nineteenth century America, a spirit that enthusiastically emphasized laws of progress for both the individual and society. Morgan's theory of social evolution—the evolution of society through levels of savagery and barbarism to civilization—well expressed this fundamental belief in progress.

Bibliography

Bieder, Robert E. *Science Encounters the Indian, 1820-1880: The Early Years of American Ethnology*. Norman: University of Oklahoma Press, 1986. Contains a chapter on Morgan discussing his views on Indians and considering his influence on American anthropology.

Eggan, Fred. *The American Indian: Perspectives for the Study of Culture Change*. Chicago: Aldine Publishing Co., 1966. A series of lectures given by Eggan at the University of Rochester's Morgan Lectures, which focused on Morgan's contributions to the study of American Indian social organization.

Fortes, Meyer. *Kinship and the Social Order: The Legacy of Lewis Henry Morgan*. Aldine Publishing Co., 1970. Also lectures in the University of Rochester's Morgan Lecture series. Fortes explores the larger scope of Morgan's ideas on kinship and social order in contemporary anthropology.

Morgan, Lewis Henry. *Lewis Henry Morgan: The Indian Journals, 1859-1862*. Edited by Leslie A. White. University of Michigan Press, 1959. Morgan's journals of his four trips, relating experiences among the Western Indians.

_____. *Pioneers in American Anthropology: The Bandelier-Morgan Letters, 1873-1883*. Edited by Leslie A. White. Albuquerque: University of New Mexico Press, 1940. A collection of letters between Morgan and his foremost American disciple.

Resek, Carl. *Lewis Henry Morgan: American Scholar*. Chicago: University of Chicago Press, 1960. A brief but well-written biography of Morgan.

Stern, Bernhard Joseph. *Lewis Henry Morgan: Social Evolutionist*. Chicago: University of Chicago Press, 1931. A dated but still useful biography of Morgan, written by a sociologist and social theorist.

Stocking, George W. *Race, Culture, and Evolution: Essays in the History of Anthropology*. New York: Free Press, 1968. Contains a chapter in which Morgan's anthropological theories are considered, along with those of his English contemporaries E. B. Tylor and Herbert Spencer.

Robert E. Bieder

THOMAS HUNT MORGAN

Born: September 25, 1866; Lexington, Kentucky
Died: December 4, 1945; Pasadena, California
Area of Achievement: Genetics
Contribution: Through his ability to work closely with colleagues in unselfishly pursuing a scientific problem, Morgan's *Drosophila* research pioneered modern chromosome theory and genetic research.

Early Life

Born September 25, 1866, in Lexington, Kentucky, Thomas Hunt Morgan was the son of Charlton Hunt Morgan and Ellen Key Howard. His paternal uncle was General John Hunt Morgan, commander of Morgan's Raiders, under whom his father served during the Civil War. Through his mother's family he was related to Francis Scott Key, author of "The Star-Spangled Banner."

Morgan's boyhood was spent in Kentucky and in the mountains of western Maryland. During his childhood vacations in the mountains, he spent much of his time collecting fossils, birds, and bird's eggs. He continued in his scientific interests during his college years at the University of Kentucky, from which he was graduated in 1886. In the summer after his college graduation, he worked at the Boston Society of Natural History's marine laboratory in Annisquam, Massachusetts, prior to entering graduate school at The Johns Hopkins University in Baltimore.

At The Johns Hopkins University, his major professor was William Keith Brooks, by whom he was influenced to study embryology, especially in marine organisms. Since Brooks's research was on how an organism's parts went together or how these parts developed, it was to be expected that Thomas Hunt Morgan's early work was descriptive. His 1890 doctoral dissertation on sea spiders was entitled "A Contribution to the Embryology and Phylogeny of the Pycnogonids."

Among the influential factors shaping his life was his introduction to the marine laboratory at Woods Hole, Massachusetts. He spent his first summer there in 1888, while still a graduate student. So conducive was this environment to research that Morgan spent nearly every summer there for the remainder of his life, even after he moved to California in the late 1920's. During his teaching days in the East, he would actually pack all of his experimental specimens, whether plant or animal, and ship them on the train to the marine laboratory.

Morgan's first academic teaching appointment came in 1891, when he was named associate professor of biology at Bryn Mawr. There he remained until 1904, working closely with his faculty colleagues R. G. Harrison and Jacques Loeb. Among his outstanding students were Nettie M. Stevens, who worked in regeneration and cytology, and Lilian V. Sampson, whose research was in embryology and regeneration. Morgan and Sampson were married in 1904, the same year that he accepted a position as professor of experimental zoology at Columbia University, in New York.

Life's Work

The twenty-four years spent at Columbia would be the most productive period in Morgan's life. By the time of his arrival in New York, he was addressing the research issue of genetics, which would lead him to his greatest achievements. Sex determination was one of the first topics of investigation in this area, a subject whose literature he reviewed in 1903: "Recent Theories in Regard to the Determination of Sex." Work on honeybees, phylloxera, and aphids during the next five years led him toward the chromosome interpretation of sex determination. As one of his students wrote:

> This was one of Morgan's most brilliant achievements, involving great skill and patience in the collecting and care of the animals, insight in seeing what were the critical points to study, and ability to recognize and to follow up unexpected facts. The results were of importance in serving to demonstrate the role of the chromosomes in sex determination, at a time when that importance was seriously questioned by many biologists.

Before adopting the uniquely suitable *Drosophila* as a laboratory animal for genetic research, Morgan had worked for a time with both mice and rats. By 1910, however, he published his first paper on *Drosophila*: "Hybridization in a Mutating Period in *Drosophila*." The particular strain about which he reported had been started in 1909, although Morgan had been supervising a graduate experimenting with breeding *Drosophila* in the dark even before that time.

The fruit fly was ideal for genetic work because it produced a new generation every two to three weeks, was virtually immune to disease, and, perhaps most important, had only four pairs of chromosomes, compared to the usual plus or minus twenty-four in most mammals.

By 1910, the so-called fly room at Columbia University had come into being. Into a rather small room were crowded eight desks—some were assigned permanently, others went to visiting researchers—where, for the next seventeen years, Thomas Hunt Morgan and his colleagues—undergraduates, graduates, faculty, and visitors from around the world—would work to lay the foundations of the modern chromosome theory of heredity. All this would be learned from a small fly which would breed in a milk bottle that was provided with a piece of rotting fruit.

The first of the major discoveries based on the *Drosophila* research was announced in July, 1910, in a paper in which Morgan revealed the sex-linked inheritance of white eyes. The next major step came as a second sex-linked characteristic, rudimentary wings, appeared as a mutant in one of the cultures. When white eyes and rudimentary wings were crossed, there was evidence for a new step in the development of chromosome theory:

> White and rudimentary happen to lie far apart in the X chromosome, with the result that it was not apparent in this first cross that they were linked. . . . But in 1911 cases of linkage had been recognized—most obvious in the relation between yellow body and white eyes—and Morgan then laid down the essence of the modern chromosome theory of heredity. The basis of linkage is nearness together in chromosomes, and recombination between linked genes is due to exchange of parts between homologous chromosomes. . . .

Five years later, Thomas Hunt Morgan and three of his fly-room colleagues published *The Mechanism of Mendelian Heredity* (1915). Here for the first time appeared an attempt to interpret the field of genetics in terms of chromosome theory. From this landmark publication came scientific vindication for Gregor Mendel and a foundation upon which all future chromosome research could be built.

Despite the sophistication of Morgan's research and its results, he insisted on working with the simplest of equipment. His early cultures of *Drosophila* were cultivated in an odd assortment of milk bottles. In each bottle it was customary to place a piece of paper for identification purposes; Morgan often used the envelopes torn from correspondence which he had just opened. Flies were ultimately examined with a hand lens. According to one of his students and collaborators, Morgan was always generous with his own personal funds (to the point of lending money to students), but rather miserly with budgetary allotments for which he was responsible.

Another unique characteristic of the research done in Morgan's laboratory at Columbia was the unselfish cooperation on the part of all those who worked there. As one of the participants (A. H. Sturtevant) explained:

> This group worked as a unit. . . . What mattered was to get ahead with the work. There can have been few times and places in scientific laboratories with such an atmosphere of excitement and with such a record of sustained enthusiasm. This was due in large part to Morgan's own attitude, compounded of enthusiasm combined with a strong critical sense, generosity, open-mindedness, and a remarkable sense of humor.

The slender, bearded Morgan was always ready to contribute boundless energy and an incisive mind to the solution of any problem.

However important Morgan's fly work may have been in opening new approaches to chromosome theory research, his methods of research were fundamental to the changes which would come in twentieth century biology. Morgan and his generation of biologists had studied under professors who, by training and practice, were descriptive biologists, to whom the more important focus was on structure rather than on function. Morgan's success in his *Drosophila* work through quantitative and experimental analysis would encourage others to free themselves from the shackles of descriptivism.

At Johns Hopkins, Thomas Hunt Morgan had worked with W. K. Brooks, a descriptive biologist. Fortunately, he had also encountered H. Newell Martin and W. H. Howell, who helped him appreciate physiological approaches. Even more powerful influences on his future research strategies had been brought to bear by two European trained scientists, Jacques Loeb and Hans Dreisch. From his training the Prussian-born Loeb had concluded that the methods of physics and chemistry were the only way that research could advance knowledge about life.

> Loeb concluded that behavior, like all events in nature, was deterministic. . . .
> Analysis on the physical or chemical level demanded synthesis on the biological
> level. The use of quantitative methods, analysis, and experimentation offered
> the best means, . . . of raising biology to the status of a rigorous science.

Morgan and Loeb met in 1891, when the two joined the faculty at Bryn Mawr. Loeb's stay at Bryn Mawr was brief, because he moved to the University of Chicago in January of 1892, but the two men had become fast friends and sympathetic scholars. Every summer for many years at the Woods Hole marine lab, the two men worked in collaboration, often disagreeing about conclusions but never about methodology. Once Loeb moved to the Rockefeller Institute in 1910, the two scholars could enjoy interchanges of ideas almost year-round.

Morgan's second influential European friend was Hans Driesch, whom he met when he spent some time doing research at the Naples Zoological Station in 1894-1895. These sojourns were not only academically stimulating but also personally pleasant, since Morgan's father was revered by the Italians for his service as American consul at Messina when he befriended the Italian patriot Giuseppe Garibaldi.

Driesch believed that biology, like physics and chemistry, should be made quantitative and mechanical; indeed, thought Driesch, the indispensable tools of biology were math and physics. Morgan's leanings toward the value of experimentation and quantification were encouraged by his friendship and collaboration with Driesch. They worked together at Naples, traveled in Europe, and published papers on ctenophore development in 1895.

From his inspiring experiences at the Naples Zoological Station, Morgan concluded that American biology would remain relatively stagnant until there was a comparable marine laboratory facility in the United States. A library, outstanding facilities, an immediate source of marine organisms, freedom to work, and, perhaps most significant of all, a place to exchange ideas, were the elements which made Naples such a fruitful place to work. These would be the conditions which Morgan would seek to incorporate into the Woods Hole Marine Biological Laboratory, especially after he became a trustee there in 1897.

Summary

According to the Nobel Prize presentation speech in 1933, Morgan's greatness lay in his ability "to join two important methods in hereditary research, the statistic-genetic method adopted by Mendel, and the microscopic method. . . ." Morgan was fortunate also in his choice of an object for his experiments and in the brilliance of the students and collaborators he gathered about him in the fly room. "With perfect justice we speak about the Morgan school, and it is often difficult to distinguish what is Morgan's work and what is that of his associates. But nobody has doubted that Morgan is the genuine leader." Morgan's work, concluded the Nobel committee, can be expressed in four rules: "the combination rule, the rule of the limited number of the combination groups, the crossing-over rule, and the rule of the linear arrangement of the genes in the chromosomes." Without Morgan's investigations in human hereditary research, modern human genetics would be impractical. "Morgan's discoveries are simply fundamental and decisive for the investigation and understanding of the hereditary diseases of man."

In addition to Morgan's impact on biological study through his *Drosophila* research, he was similarly influential in his role as coeditor of a series of biological monographs published by the Lippincott Company. Morgan, along with Loeb, and W. J. V. Osterhout, intended to further the progress of science in the United States along the lines of scientific investigation favored by the three editors. Although Loeb was European by birth and training, and Morgan was European-influenced, the two were trying to break away from the domination of European speculative biology. The Lippincott series was conceived by its editors as a fresh start in the direction of quantitative and mechanistic biology. During the critical decade after 1918, the three men labored to choose monographs which they believed would be instrumental in shaping a new American biology. Morgan ultimately would accept the directorship of a new Division of Biology at the California Institute of Technology in order to establish his ideas firmly within the framework of a great university. Morgan is regarded in the West as one of the fathers of modern genetics. His work helped make possible the great strides in hereditary research leading to our modern understanding.

Bibliography
Allen, Garland E. "T. H. Morgan and the Emergence of a New American

Biology." *The Quarterly Review of Biology* 44 (June, 1969): 168-187. A useful analysis of the factors instrumental in shaping Morgan's attitudes and methodology. It should be used in conjunction with the Sturtevant memoir listed below.

Mayr, Ernst. *The Growth of Biological Thought: Diversity, Evolution and Inheritance.* Cambridge, Mass.: The Belknap Press of Harvard University Press, 1982. A history of ideas in biology which is fundamental for understanding the context and impact of Morgan's scholarly contribution.

Moore, Ruth E. *The Coil of Life: The Story of the Great Discoveries in the Life Sciences.* New York: Alfred A. Knopf, 1961. A popular account ranging from Antoine-Laurent Lavoisier's experiments to developments in DNA research. Less formidable for the average reader than the volume by Mayr.

Morgan, T. H., A. H. Sturtevant, H. J. Muller, and C. B. Bridges. *The Mechanism of Mendelian Heredity.* Rev. ed. New York: Henry Holt, 1922. Under Morgan's leadership, these inhabitants of the Columbia fly room demonstrated how their *Drosophila* research illustrated chromosome theory.

Nobelstiftelsen [the Nobel Foundation]. *Physiology or Medicine, 1922-1941.* Amsterdam: Elsevier Publishing Co., 1965. The official source for remarks made by the Nobel Prize Committee about the award winners and the speech written by the recipient.

Sturtevant, A. H. *A History of Genetics.* New York: Harper and Row, Publishers, 1965. Sturtevant, T. H. Morgan Professor of Biology, Emeritus, from the California Institute of Technology, writes from the perspective of a founding father on the history of genetics from Mendel to World War II. Interesting intellectual pedigree charts included as an appendix.

_____. *Selected Papers of A. H. Sturtevant: Genetics and Evolution.* Edited by E. B. Lewis. San Francisco: W. H. Freeman and Co., 1961. An edition of thirty-three Sturtevant papers from 1913-1956, edited by an intellectual grandson of Thomas Hunt Morgan, E. B. Lewis, who worked at the California Institute of Technology as a research fellow from 1931 to 1936.

_____. "Thomas Hunt Morgan." *Biographical Memoirs, National Academy of Science* 33 (1959): 283-325. An indispensable account by one of Morgan's students who assisted in writing *The Mechanism of Mendelian Heredity* (1915). This is the source to which most general accounts refer.

James H. O'Donnell III

ROBERT MORRIS

Born: January 31, 1734; Liverpool, England
Died: May 8, 1806; Philadelphia, Pennsylvania
Areas of Achievement: Finance and politics
Contribution: Combining an intimate knowledge of the political workings of the early Revolutionary and Confederation periods with his experience as America's leading merchant, Morris saved the young United States from financial collapse and the consequent danger of losing its war for independence from Great Britain.

Early Life

Robert Morris was born January 31, 1734, in Liverpool, England. Few details are known of his early life. The name of his mother is unknown. His father, also Robert Morris, was a tobacco agent at Oxford in Maryland, on the Chesapeake. At some time, the younger Robert was brought to Maryland, and at age thirteen, he briefly attended a school in Philadelphia. Following this, he was placed with a prominent shipping family, the Willings. By 1754, armed with a substantial inheritance from his father and his own considerable talents, he was made a partner in the new firm of Willings, Morris and Company. Remarkably, in a period when business arrangements were much less formal and durable than those made in the twentieth century, the firm survived and thrived for twenty years. Morris actively directed it for a large part of that time. The company expanded over the years, concentrating on the importation of British and Colonial manufactures and the exportation of American goods and on owning ships, a general exchange and banking business. Morris, along with the firm, came to hold a leading position in the trade of Philadelphia and in America generally by the time of the first crisis with Great Britain over the question of taxation in 1765: the Stamp Act crisis.

Life's Work

Morris first became prominent in public affairs in 1765, during the resistance to the Stamp Act, as one of the signers of the nonimportation agreement. Later in the year, he served on the citizens' committee appointed to force the collector of the stamp tax in Philadelphia to desist from carrying out the duties of his office. The following year, Morris was named warden of the Port of Philadelphia. Although not immediately committed to the patriot cause when the First Continental Congress met in Philadelphia in 1774, a few months later, he was among its leading representatives. It is said that his mind was made up upon hearing the news of the Battle of Lexington. In October, 1775, he was elected to the Pennsylvania Assembly, the last to meet under the Colonial charter. From there, he was sent the following month as delegate to the Continental Congress.

Morris quickly emerged as one of the leading members of the Congress, the driving force in many of its committees between 1775 and 1778. He was a member of both the Committee of Secret Correspondence and the Secret Committee of Commerce, and Morris played a leading part in managing the purchase of goods and ships on a scale unprecedented in the American experience. It was a period of confusion, the mixing of personal and public affairs, the problems of a fluctuating currency, a long lapse between the placing of orders and their fulfillment, and a hopelessly overtaxed accounting and bookkeeping system.

Criticisms and charges were made against Morris as against several others. John Adams for one, however, was quite clear in his opinion. Writing to Horatio Gates, he said,

> You ask me what you are to think of Robert Morris? . . . I think he has a masterly Understanding, an open Temper and an honest Heart. . . . He has vast designs in the mercantile way. And no doubt possesses mercantile ends, which are always gain; but he is an excellent Member of our Body.

In March, 1778, Morris signed the Articles of Confederation on behalf of Pennsylvania. When his term in Congress expired in November of the same year, Morris was ineligible for reappointment under the terms of his state's democratic constitution. During his period out of national office, Morris concentrated on his business affairs. The Willing and Morris partnership was terminated in 1777, but between 1778 and 1781, Morris formed nine major partnerships and took part in a large number of lesser concerns. He derived great profit from the West India trade and from privateering and attempted to corner the tobacco market. By 1781, Morris was acknowledged as the leading merchant in the United States and its richest citizen.

In 1781, Morris was a big man in every sense. He stood at six feet tall, with blue eyes and graying sandy hair. He had the assurance of the self-made man. He was outgoing, warm, and generous. He was a most lavish host and his wife, Mary, a dazzling hostess. He lived a princely life, and wherever he went, he was the center of a social whirl. Primarily he was a man of action rather than reflection; he displayed zeal, great ability, an amazing grasp of detail, and tremendous executive ability.

Therefore, it was no surprise that Congress turned to Morris that same year when the country was on the verge of financial collapse and public credit was all but destroyed. His wealth and political experience as well as his personal abilities made him the obvious choice for the new post of superintendent of finance or, as he was soon known, "Financier of the Revolution." Morris assumed office at a time when depreciation of paper currency made money more expensive to print than its face value and when the armies of the republic were, as a result of apathy and mismanagement, lacking in pay, clothing, and supplies. Outside the public realm, however, the economy was sound. Morris was well aware that drastic and fundamental measures were needed. His program aimed at restoring public credit by establishing a national bank and mint to bind people to the national government through economic self-interest; to reorganize the Treasury in order to cut out extravagance and waste; to issue notes based on his private credit—known as "Morris notes"—in order to bolster that of the government; and to fund the Confederation's debts by raising revenues from the states.

In addition to these long-term objectives, Morris faced the immediate problem of the plight of the armies. It was largely because of his efforts that a successful contracting system was established to supply and provision General George Washington's forces and that transport was secured to place the army in a physical position to lay siege to the British at Yorktown. The American victory at Yorktown was significant but did not immediately promise an end to war. Through Morris' reforms, the Continental army went into winter quarters in 1782 better supplied than at any time previously, and well equipped to fight.

The efforts Morris made to restore public credit were intimately connected with political battles raging in the country. His major problem lay in raising revenue from the reluctant states. The Financier headed a powerful group in Congress which advocated an effective central government, and he developed the detailed policies and groundwork for the later successful challenge to the Articles of Confederation and their replacement by the Constitution of the United States as well as the triumph of the Federalists led by Alexander Hamilton. At this time, however—1783—Morris and his friends were unable to overcome the fears of central authority held by many in the states. Morris personally was subjected to much abuse and, after a protracted battle in Congress, the Financier resigned.

He left office in 1784 with the accounts in detailed order and a surplus of twenty-two thousand dollars, a remarkable achievement. James Madison, no ally of Morris, said,

> My charity, I own, cannot invent an excuse for the . . . malice with which the character and services of this gentleman are murdered. I am persuaded that he accepted his offices from motives which were honorable and patriotic. I have seen no proof of misfeasance. I have heard of many charges which were palpably erroneous. Every member in Congress must be sensible of the benefit which has accrued to the public from his administration; no intelligent man out of Congress can be altogether insensible of it.

Morris never completely left politics. He remained in Pennsylvania politics, heading the state's delegation to the Constitutional Convention in 1786. Throughout the remainder of his life, he was an intimate friend of Washington and was even seriously considered by Thomas Jefferson for the post of secretary of the navy in 1800. In the optimistic postwar atmosphere in the

United States, however, Morris became ever more deeply entangled in speculation in land, and his affairs became ever more precarious owing to the protracted credit squeeze brought on first by postwar depression in the American economy, then by the failure of the Bank of England in 1793, and finally by the French Revolution and its subsequent invasion of Holland and the resulting British naval blockade. Many important debts owed to Morris were tied up in these countries, and he was unable to collect. After several years of juggling his accounts, Morris' affairs collapsed, and he was jailed as a debtor in 1798. Despite the efforts of his friends, Morris' debts were so large and so complex that he was released only in 1801, when a federal law was passed allowing bankrupts to live outside prison. From that time until his death in 1806, Morris lived quietly on the charity of family and friends.

Summary

Robert Morris was a controversial figure in his time. His wealth, ostentatious life-style, and high-handed and sometimes crude mode of political behavior made him the target of much popular suspicion in a period of revolutionary ferment and anti-aristocratic and antimonarchical feelings. Added to this, Morris was a centralizer in an age when the American Colonies had for years declared against the control of a distant, centralized empire, and the states remained committed to the promotion of their own local interests. Finally, Morris was unequivocally identified with the Middle States and appointed his cronies and business associates to government positions at a time when sectional antagonism was already a factor in American life. Even today, Morris remains controversial. His political defeat in 1783, his rather ignominious decline after 1793, enmeshed in what today would be considered quite unethical business practices, and his death in poverty serve to diminish his importance in the eyes of posterity.

Nevertheless, Morris must rank as one of the more important founders of the United States. Through his actions rather than his words, he was involved at almost every critical stage in the birth of the young republic. He played a most significant part in pulling his country through a crisis which might well have spelled the end of its independence. For four years, he was the most powerful figure in government. In March, 1783, Joseph Reed wrote to General Nathanael Greene,

> Mr. Morris has been for a long time the *dominus factotum*, whose dictates none dare oppose, and from whose decisions lay no appeal; he has, in fact, exercised the power really of the three great departments, and Congress have only had to give their fiat to his mandates.

Moreover, Morris laid the foundations and the detailed policies of the group soon to be called Federalists. Through his financial policies, Morris established an economic interest in altering the Articles of Confederation to make for an effective national government by establishing national responsibility for paying Revolutionary War debts at a time when Congress had no power of direct taxation and requisitioning from the states was ineffective. Morris also went some way toward reestablishing public credit by a combination of foreign loans, domestic loans from the Bank of North America, and the issuance of "Morris notes" which circulated at or near par and were backed by his own private credit. He established order in a chaotic government and rationalized requisition and procurement systems, relying heavily and, on the whole, successfully on the issuance of secret competitive bidding for government contracts. Morris established efficiency in government at a time notorious for waste and extravagance.

The achievements of Robert Morris were both political and financial. Upon his policies was erected the sound financial and constitutional structure, completed by the Federalists under more favorable circumstances, which has been so important to the long-term stability of the United States.

Bibliography
Carp, E. Wayne. *To Starve the Army at Pleasure: Continental Army Administration and American Political Culture, 1775-1783*. Chapel Hill: University of North Carolina Press, 1984. Not as much of a cure for insomnia as its title suggests, this book ably shows the severe problems facing the Continental armies. Chapters 7 and 8 in particular show the tremendous difference made by Morris as Financier and his role in the victory at Yorktown. Carp casts doubt about the outcome of Yorktown without Morris' contributions.

Dos Passos, John. *The Men Who Made the Nation*. Garden City, N.Y.: Doubleday and Co., 1957. Dos Passos does not like Morris. He is antagonized by Morris' wealth and political power and views him generally as a threat to democracy. He questions the Financier's political and financial morality. Yet chapter 4, especially, is good for a sense of the speculative atmosphere of the 1780's and 1790's and for illustrating the fact that Morris was certainly not alone in going to ruin.

Ferguson, E. James. *The Power of the Purse: A History of American Public Finance, 1776-1790*. Chapel Hill: University of North Carolina Press, 1961. This is an enlightening book which shows the ideological aspects of financial policies and explains the economics of the time in layman's terms. The role of Morris figures very prominently.

Ferguson, E. James, and John Catanzariti, eds. *The Papers of Robert Morris, 1781-1784*. 5 vols. Pittsburgh, Penn.: University of Pittsburgh Press, 1973-1980. These are the papers of Robert Morris when he was Financier, at the height of his power and influence. They show the range of his interests at the time as well as allowing insights into his mind. The introductory essay by Ferguson is a model of clarity and perception.

Oberholtzer, E. P. *Robert Morris: Patriot and Financier*. New York: Macmillan, 1903. This was the first work to draw on the Morris papers, which had recently been acquired by the Library of Congress after their rescue from a rubbish heap in France. It is very favorable to its subject.

Sumner, William Graham. *The Financier and the Finances of the American Revolution*. 2 vols. New York: Dodd, Mead and Co., 1891. Reprint. New York: Augustus M. Kelley, 1968. Despite the lack of access to Morris' papers as financier, this is a more perceptive work than that of Oberholtzer.

Swiggett, Howard. *The Forgotten Leaders of the Revolution*. Garden City, N.Y.: Doubleday and Co., 1955. The author's declared aim to inject personal and familial information into his mainly public and political account, in the case of Robert Morris, becomes an attempt to discredit the Financier. Chapters 6 and 8 spend more time trying to prove how devoid of financial judgment and common sense Morris was than on what he actually did as a public servant.

Ver Steeg, Clarence L. *Robert Morris: Revolutionary Financier*. Philadelphia: University of Pennsylvania Press, 1954. This is recognized as the best of the more recent studies of Morris. It concentrates on Morris as Financier, though his early career is briefly but adequately covered. It is short and well written. Highly recommended.

Stephen Burwood

SAMUEL F. B. MORSE

Born: April 27, 1791; Charlestown, Massachusetts
Died: April 2, 1872; New York, New York
Areas of Achievement: Telegraphy and invention
Contribution: Persevering through the trials of experimentation and the sluggishness of public approval, Morse developed and implemented a system of electric communication which revolutionized the availability of information and forever changed the sense of world distances.

Early Life

In the shadow of Boston, a center for politics and communications, was born Samuel Finley Breese Morse, whose life and work would revolutionize those pursuits. First son of the young Calvinist minister Jedidiah Morse and his New Jersey wife Elizabeth Breese, "Finley," as the child was called, was born on April 27, 1791, in Charlestown, Massachusetts. Three years later, a brother, Sidney Edwards, was born, and the next year, Richard Cary followed.

The Morses had great expectations of their sons, who were born into a family with a strong history of education: Their mother's grandfather had been president of Princeton College, and their father, Pastor Morse, earned a degree from Yale and wrote the first geography text in America. When the boys started school, however, they showed distinctly different aptitudes for study. Their father characterized Finley as the hare, quick to lose interest and change paths; Sidney, he said, was the tortoise of the family, stubborn and steadfast; Richard, the youngest Morse to survive birth, was more like Sidney than he was like Finley. Though the younger siblings were of different temperaments, they would often later come to the aid of their older brother: easing his financial woes, caring for his children after his first wife's death, offering an editorial forum for discourses on the telegraph.

Morse's parents believed that the discipline of education would benefit their firstborn. They sent him off to Phillips Academy in Andover, Massachusetts, at the tender age of seven. His aptitude in the classroom was not legendary, though his aptitude for drawing proved somewhat greater and was encouraged by the family. By the time he studied at Yale, Morse was able to sponsor his affinity for cigars and wine with miniature portraits on ivory. Further encouragement from a meeting with the artist Washington Allston, whom Morse would later credit as his mentor, prompted him to set some goals. Young Morse yearned to go abroad to study painting with Allston and Benjamin West. With some persuasion, his parents agreed to send him to England. There, at the Royal Academy of London, he learned to work in other media: charcoal, marble, oils. West lent his work a critical eye and often turned the callow artist back to finish works he had thought completed.

Soon, England recognized his talent and diligence with a gold medal from the Adelphi Society of Arts for his sculpture of the dying Hercules.

Morse returned to the United States (via a nearly two-month voyage), convinced of the historical genre's preeminence as "the intellectual branch of art." Commissions of such works were not readily available, however, and he had to resort to portrait work for subsistence. His pursuit of commissions took him up and down the Eastern seaboard. In Concord, Massachusetts, he met his bride-to-be, Lucretia Pickering Walker. The wedding was postponed until he could save enough money to set up winter housekeeping in Charleston, South Carolina, where he had been awarded a commission for a portrait of President James Monroe.

Charleston, however, was only a temporary residence, and eventually Morse was forced by impecunity to leave his wife in New Haven, where his entire family seemed to be toiling without benefit of regular salary. He traveled continually to paint and dreamed of the means to live in the same house as his wife and children. That dream was never realized while Lucretia lived. In fact, he learned of Lucretia's death days after the event, while he was in Washington to paint the Marquis de Lafayette.

The Lafayette portrait, which hangs in New York's City Hall, is not without critical acclaim. At least one art historian deems it worthy of nomination to the Golden Age of American portrait painting. Portrait painting, especially for civic commission, offered a regular income, but the two large-scale historical works Morse hoped to exhibit for profit did not. Morse conceived of these historical pieces in a grand manner. The one, *Congress Hall*, otherwise known as *The Old House of Representatives*, shows the National Hall during a session of Congress and includes likenesses of the congressmen, achieved from individual sittings, as well as Jedidiah Morse, Benjamin Silliman, and a Pawnee chief. The other, *The Louvre*, shows a room at the museum, the Salon Carré, complete with more than forty great paintings. When he thought of these works initially (nearly ten years apart), Morse wanted to create something which would appeal to the common man, though the historical genre was to his mind the most elevated of art forms. With *Congress Hall*, Morse thought each man would at least recognize his representative and have an interest in seeing him at work. *The Louvre*, he thought, would open the treasures of the Old World to Americans, who were rarely privileged to see these masterpieces.

Morse dreamed of an additional historical commission to decorate panels at the new Capitol, but the commission went to someone else; in this case, perhaps, art's loss directly contributed to science's gain.

Life's Work

When there is a question of who was the first to invent a machine or a process, research often shows more than one person working with similar ideas, though the one has no knowledge of the others' works. Such was the case with the invention of the telegraph. In 1832, while Morse was returning from Europe aboard the packet ship *Sully*, isolated from libraries, laboratories, and scientific journals, he formulated his first hypotheses regarding the possibility of transmitting information by electric impulses.

His only formal education in matters of electricity had been lectures during his junior year at Yale when Silliman and Jeremiah Day gave demonstrations there. Morse himself experimented with electricity in the basements of Yale, apparently for reasons of native curiosity. Outside the classroom, Silliman, who was Morse's neighbor, and James Dwight Dana, an acquaintance with more than passing knowledge of electromagnetism, rounded out Morse's knowledge of electricity.

Long out of Yale by 1832, Morse had not read current scientific journals and was not aware that, at the same time, there were men experimenting in England with semaphore telegraphs—that is, those which worked with visual signals. On board the *Sully*, he was inspired in a conversation on electromagnetism with Dr. Charles T. Jackson to note that information could be sent electrically. With that grain of thought he began investigating possibilities for transforming the potential into a reality.

Morse's shipboard sketch pad shows his early ideas for a code based on dots and dashes and for devices to send and record messages. Upon his arrival at his brother's house in New York City, he began work on a prototype. With an old canvas stretcher and saw-tooth type that he had forged at his sister-in-law's hearth, he produced a rudimentary model of a machine which would make electricity useful to mankind. The forces which had confronted Morse as artist, however, now played upon Morse the inventor: The initial stroke of genius demanded systematic revisions and fresh income if it were to be developed fully. Nevertheless, Morse was too active to be incapacitated by despair over lack of remuneration for his art or invention. He was busy running the National Academy of Design (he was among its founders), running for mayor of New York, and accepting the first art professorship at New York University (NYU).

To further his telegraphic work, Morse contracted several partners. These partners agreed that any new discoveries made to the telegraph would become public under Morse's name. The original partners, Leonard Dunnell Gale, Alfred Vail, and that cantankerous man, most often cast as a villain in stories of the telegraph, F. O. J. "Fog" Smith, contributed money and ideas to development of the telegraph.

Two crucial contributions by scientists made Morse's telegraph work. A professor, Joseph Henry, had discovered a principle that, though made public in 1831, did not come to Morse's attention until after he had made preliminary investigations. Henry discovered that increasing the number of turns in a coil increased the power of the current. Morse's partner Gale, who brought

Henry's law to Morse's attention, was responsible for persuading Morse to change his primitive battery, designed for quantity, into one of intensity. This factor, with Morse's concept of an electric relay, enabled the telegraph to be effective over great distances.

Morse continued wrapping wires around and around his NYU studio, testing and demonstrating his remarkable new device. In 1837, he applied for his first telegraph patent in the form of a caveat to protect his preliminary inventions. They included a code of dots and dashes (to become, eventually, the "Morse code"), a mechanism for sending information and another for receiving, a method of laying wire, and a code dictionary. That same year, Morse began petitioning Congress to accept and implement his system on a national basis.

Congress let the initial telegraph offer pass them by as Morse set sail for Europe to secure foreign patent rights. Europe, though enthusiastic about the abilities of the electromagnetic telegraph, would not bless it with the official sanction of patent.

This European excursion, however, was not completely futile. Morse learned the newly discovered photographic process of Louis-Jacques-Mandé Daguerre and resorted to it as a means to gain additional funds for his research concerning the telegraph. His trained artistic eye and his direct knowledge of the process from study with Daguerre in France made him an ideal teacher. In time, the success of Morse's students, who literally kept him from the brink of starvation, earned for him the epithet "Father of Photography."

Physically, Morse showed the effects of years of struggle. He looked haggard, and his clothes were shabby with wear. In this condition Morse returned to Washington, D.C., wooing Congress with demonstrations. At last, Congress awarded him money to build a line between Baltimore and Washington in 1843. This line reported to the Capitol the results of the national presidential conventions held in Baltimore and broadcast the first formal message, "What hath God wrought?"

Once financial remuneration was forthcoming with the spread of lines across the country, Morse became the subject of suit and countersuit as others tried to claim rights of invention and expansion in this new and as yet unregulated field. Morse energetically fought off these attacks. His mind was active with thoughts of a transatlantic cable, a new wife, and a home in the country that he could share with his children. After the trials and disappointments of his earlier years, Morse lived to enjoy universal approbation and financial success. At the time of his death, on April 2, 1872, his invention was in use throughout the world.

Summary

Morse lived at the vanguard of a communications revolution. Trained as a painter, he combined knowledge of composition that would convey a message without words with the technology of Daguerre's picture-taking method to train the men who would record the Civil War through the eye of the camera. The photographic images, along with the news of the war transmitted instantly by telegraph, reported the immediate and shocking news of the war to the folks at home. This ability to unite and make useful abstract theories is a trademark of the American inventor.

Morse as a communicator, through his portraits and historical genre paintings, through working on the public relations of trying to fund experimentation, and in having the foresight and magnanimity to encourage Congress to establish this new machine under the auspices of postal system, was always ready to serve. Even when pressed with other responsibilities, he ran for mayor of New York City, appeared at the statue erection in Central Park, and helped found the National Academy of Design. In each case, his motivation was the desire to contribute to society rather than to promote himself.

Though Morse was a nativist, he worked to make the telegraph a force for international communication, and his success in making the world much smaller was clearly demonstrated in the memorial services held upon his death: Telegrams arrived at the nation's capital from as far as Egypt and from all over the United States as well.

Bibliography
Boorstin, Daniel J. *The Americans: The Democratic Experience*. New York: Vintage Books, 1974. Includes an examination of the spirit and character peculiar to the American innovator-entrepreneur.
Harlow, Alvin F. *Old Wires and New Waves*. New York: D. Appleton-Century Company, 1936. A comprehensive look at long-distance communication via signal, from Trojan War signal fires to the American telephone.
Larkin, Oliver W. *Art and Life in America*. New York: Holt, Rinehart and Winston, 1960. Though not as specific as the author's *Samuel Morse and American Democratic Art*, published in 1954 in Boston by Little, Brown and Co., this text seems more readily available. Explores Morse's standing among other artists of the period. Very good on the contrasts between pursuit of the arts in the New World and the Old.
Mabee, Carleton. *The American Leonardo: A Life of Samuel F. B. Morse*. New York: Alfred A. Knopf, 1944. The standard Morse biography. Mabee writes a unified account of a man whose varied interests are a delight and challenge to follow.
_____. *Memorial of Samuel Finley Breese Morse, Including Appropriate Ceremonies of Respect at the National Capitol and Elsewhere*. Washington, D.C.: Government Printing Office, 1875. One measure of a man's life is the mourning of his passing. The ceremonies described here were particularly modern, uniting electronically virtually the entire world in a

common bond of gratitude and sorrow.

Morse, Samuel F. B. *Samuel F. B. Morse: His Letters and Journals*. 2 vols. Edited by Edward Lind Morse. New York: Houghton Mifflin Co., 1914. Begins with Morse's first thoughts of telegraphic communication while aboard the packet ship *Sully*.

Vail, Alfred. *The American Electro Magnetic Telegraph*. Philadelphia: Lee and Blanchard, 1845. Reprint. *Eyewitness to Early American Telegraphy*. New York: Arno Press, 1974. Explains the workings of the telegraph, illustrated with fully labeled diagrams.

Ellen Clark

WILLIAM THOMAS GREEN MORTON

Born: August 9, 1819; Charlton, Massachusetts
Died: July 15, 1868; New York, New York
Areas of Achievement: Dentistry and anesthesiology
Contribution: Morton discovered anesthesia by ether inhalation. Rival claims
to priority resulted in the most acrimonious debate in the history of
medicine.

Early Life

William Thomas Green Morton was born to James Morton, a farmer of
Scottish descent, and his wife, Rebecca Needham, a native of Charlton. A
sternly religious upbringing, a wholesome and plain family life, and a boyhood filled with farm tasks formed Morton's character. His father insisted on
a proper education, enrolling him in several country academies from the age
of twelve. The boy wanted to become a physician, but his hopes vanished
when a business venture undertaken by his father failed.

In 1836, Morton moved to Boston, making a living as a clerk and salesman
for several firms. He hated the drudgery and crassness of business life, choosing a career in dentistry with the opening of the first American dental school,
the Baltimore College of Dental Surgery, in 1840. One year later, he apprenticed himself to Horace Wells, a young dentist from Hartford, before establishing his own practice in Farmington, Connecticut. In 1842, he met Elizabeth Whitman, daughter of a prominent Farmington family. The Whitmans
were disturbed by their daughter's interest in him, the owner of no property
and a dentist, dentists then being regarded as ignorant "tooth-pullers." Determined to marry, Morton convinced them that dentistry was a temporary
occupation; he intended to become a physician. The marriage took place in
May of 1844; the first of the Mortons' children, William James Morton,
became an important neurologist and a pioneer in the use of X rays.

Morton was a tall, dark-haired, handsome man, neat and methodical, mild
and agreeable in manner. He maintained his dignity and composure through
the long years of the bitter ether controversy, never attempting to retaliate
against his enemies despite the relentless attacks on his character.

Life's Work

Prior to his marriage, Morton had formed a partnership in Boston with
Wells in order to exploit the development of a noncorrosive dental solder for
attaching false teeth to plates. Artificial teeth were hinged monstrosities set
over the roots of old teeth, leaving the face swollen, the solder coloring and
corroding the teeth. The two young dentists devised enameled teeth which
they attached with their new solder to a hingeless plate. To fit the plate
snugly in the mouth, however, required the removal of the roots of the old

teeth. No one would accept their innovations unless they found a means to overcome the extremely painful extractions.

By the end of 1843, the partnership failed for lack of patients. Wells returned to Hartford, Morton remained in Boston, both intent on succeeding in dentistry. During their development of the solder, they sought the advice of an expert chemist, Charles T. Jackson, a European-trained physician, chemist, and geologist. In 1844, Morton became Jackson's private student, boarding in his house, first alone and then with his wife, hoping to prepare himself for entrance into Harvard Medical School.

During 1844-1845, his dental practice flourished, and his income enabled him to buy a farm in West Needham (modern Wellesley) near Boston. Morton became a specialist in prosthetic dentistry and prospered by his thoroughness and his skill in excavating and filling cavities.

During the summer of 1844, Morton discussed with Jackson the need to control pain. He had tried many pain remedies, but none was satisfactory. Jackson gave him a bottle of ether and urged him to try his "toothache drops" as a local painkiller for filling teeth. He also learned from Jackson that physicians used ether as an inhalant in treating respiratory ills, believing it to be a possible cure for tuberculosis and other lung diseases.

Morton used the ether drops, finding that he could remove tooth decay and fill cavities painlessly. He noticed that often the region near the tooth became numb and wondered whether ether had wider possibilities. Morton wanted to experiment with ether. What happens upon inhaling it? Was it dangerous? Might it be an effective painkiller for all aspects of dentistry, including the extraction of the stumps and roots of old teeth? He experimented with ether inhalation into 1846, using animals of all kinds, including his pet spaniel.

In August of 1846, Morton purchased a new supply of ether in Boston. His two apprentices submitted to ether inhalation but became excited rather than quieted. He sought Jackson's advice on September 30, careful not to tell him about his inhalation experiments but only about the problems he was having with different samples of ether. Jackson informed him that ether varied considerably in quality and that he must use only pure, highly rectified ether.

Events happened swiftly on September 30; obtaining the best-quality ether, Morton induced unconsciousness in himself for about seven minutes, recovering with no ill effects. That same day, a patient, Eben Frost, came to him with a painful toothache. Morton persuaded him to have his tooth extracted under ether.

During the next two weeks, he successfully etherized about one hundred patients, developing an inhaler in the form of a glass globe that had two necks to allow both ether and air to be inhaled. Suddenly, his horizons widened beyond dentistry. A young surgeon, Henry Jacob Bigelow, appeared at his office, having become aware of his ether experiments and wanting to observe some painless tooth extractions. Through Bigelow, Morton arranged a public demonstration at Massachusetts General Hospital on October 16, 1846. John Collins Warren, the preeminent surgeon in Boston and founder of Massachusetts General and of the *New England Journal of Medicine*, agreed to perform surgery on an etherized patient.

Warren removed a three-inch tumor from the neck of a young man, Gilbert Abbott, with Morton administering the inhalant. Before a large audience, the hitherto exceedingly painful operation proceeded smoothly, with no cry or struggle from Abbott, the first public demonstration that ether could prevent the pain of surgery. Anesthesia quickly became routine at Massachusetts General, (The Boston physician Oliver Wendell Holmes introduced the name "anesthesia" in November.) The very newness of the procedure caused concern, however, and the case records of etherized patients at the hospital never mentioned anesthesia; only after its general acceptance were the records altered to record that it had been used.

Prior to the surgical demonstration, Morton visited Richard M. Eddy, patent commissioner in Boston, to inquire whether his painless tooth extraction method could be patented. The visit reveals his determination to secure a monopoly; he planned to sell licenses for the use of ether and gain a royalty on the price of all inhalers. On October 21, Eddy informed him that the process was patentable but that Jackson should be included, since he had provided essential information. Jackson knew Eddy and convinced him that he had been essential to the discovery. While Morton did not share their opinions, he agreed to an arrangement whereby Jackson received ten percent of the profits, while turning over the responsibility of the patent to Morton. He received the patent on November 12.

Morton failed to appreciate the professional opposition to his scheme of licenses and royalties. Bigelow, in a hectic meeting, told him that he should give his discovery to the world for the relief of human suffering. Morton, however, believed that he had to control his procedure to prevent its misuse, granting licenses only to qualified people, and candidly admitted that he wanted to make a living from his discovery. He did convince Bigelow of his good intentions and expressed his willingness to surrender the patent if the government would take it over and reward him for the discovery.

Problems began immediately. Morton had just received a bill for one thousand inhalers when he learned that they were inferior to a simple bell-shaped sponge saturated with ether. The Massachusetts Medical Society protested the procedure because it was for private profit and a secret remedy. (Morton had disguised the nature of the agent by adding a red dye and calling it "Letheon.") He soon saw his hopes of controlling anesthesia and gaining a financial reward dashed. As physicians realized that the readily available ether was the active agent, there was no need to buy a patented preparation.

Morton may have been disappointed by the turn of events, but surgeons were not. Surgical anesthesia spread with unprecedented speed, far more rapidly than earlier innovations as vaccination or later ones as antisepsis. Bigelow was once again the key figure in alerting physicians to the discovery. His detailed report in the *Boston Medical and Surgical Journal* was the first in a professional journal, copies of which spread the news throughout the United States and Europe. Etherization was in use in American, English, and French hospitals by the year's end. By 1848, anesthetics were in use in dentistry, obstetrics, and therapeutics, as well as in surgery.

The ugliest aspect of the ether controversy was the dispute between Morton and Jackson. In mid-November of 1846, Jackson was claiming full credit for the discovery of anesthesia. He asserted that he had been experimenting with ether since 1841, had discovered its anesthetic properties, and had instructed Morton in how to use it in his dental practice and in how to seek a surgical demonstration. Jackson used his prestige and influence to press his case in both the popular press and professional journals and before such bodies as the American Academy of Arts and Sciences and the French Academy of Sciences.

For the remainder of his life, Morton had to face attacks on his character and ability, Jackson using Morton's faulty education and the fact that he was a mere dentist to make him out to be an unscrupulous profit-seeker and fraud. His life became exceedingly troubled. He lost his dental practice, and creditors demanded payments on loans; he was ruined financially. Supporters petitioned Congress to give adequate compensation for his discovery of anesthesia. In the 1850's, Congress introduced two bills appropriating $100,000, but active supporters of Jackson, Wells (who successfully used nitrous oxide for tooth extractions), and several other claimants prevented any appropriation. A direct appeal by Morton to President Franklin Pierce led to a promise of a reward, but the presidential promise proved worthless. With the coming of the Civil War, the cause was lost. During that war, Morton served with distinction as an anesthetist in field hospitals.

In 1868, Morton went to New York in an agitated state over a pro-Jackson article in the *Atlantic Monthly*, determined to defend himself with a reply. While there, he suffered a fatal stroke. Following his interment, Boston citizens donated a monument bearing a moving tribute to him as the inventor of anesthetic inhalation. In 1873, Jackson visited the site; still obsessed with Morton, he began to scream and flail wildly. He had to be restrained, and he remained confined to a mental institution until his death in 1880.

Summary

Anesthesia is America's greatest contribution to nineteenth century medicine. Until 1846, all surgical operations were done without anesthesia: The patient was strapped or held down, struggling in agony over the cutting, speed being the prime requisite of a surgeon. Anesthesia freed the patient of pain, while giving the surgeon the gift of time.

The ether controversy reflected the medical profession's disarray in the 1840's: full of disputes over causes and cures with no central authority to confer legitimacy to an innovation. In addition, Morton violated four norms of the medical profession. He patented his "Letheon," patented pain cures being synonymous with quackery. He indulged in promotional advertising. He was a dentist, dentists being regarded with mistrust as mere empirics. Last, he engaged in a bitter, unprofessional quarrel over priority which tarnished both the image of anesthesia among physicians as well as whatever reputation the disputants possessed.

Despite the violation of these taboos, Morton's discovery spread with remarkable speed, because the benefits of ether were so evident. It did prevent pain. Leading surgeons saw ether as primarily benevolent and humane; it relieved human suffering, hence its rapid, general acceptance.

Bibliography

Davis, Audrey B. "The Development of Anesthesia." *American Scientist* 70 (September, October, 1982): 522-528. A superb essay by a historian of science, relating the development of anesthesia to the context of nineteenth century surgery and dentistry.

Fülöp-Miller, René. *Triumph over Pain*. Translated by Eden Paul and Cedar Paul. New York: Literary Guild of America, 1938. A comprehensive study of the search for pain relief, focusing on the American discovery of anesthesia. Not a scholarly work, but absorbing reading.

Ludovici, L. J. *The Discovery of Anesthesia*. New York: Thomas Y. Crowell, 1962. A fine biography of Morton. More concerned with the personalities of the characters and why they behaved as they did than other works.

MacQuitty, Betty. *Victory over Pain: Morton's Discovery of Anaesthesia*. New York: Taplinger Publishing Co., 1971. A clear, dramatic story of Morton and his career set against life in pre–Civil War America. Well written, with an emphasis on Morton's struggle to secure recognition.

Pernick, Martin S. *A Calculus of Suffering: Pain, Professionalism, and Anesthesia in Nineteenth-Century America*. New York: Columbia University Press, 1985. A brilliant book. Pernick goes beyond a history of surgical anesthesia to consider how the medical profession confronted the discovery and the implications of anesthesia for society. Social history at its finest.

Woodward, Grace Steele. *The Man Who Conquered Pain: A Biography of William Thomas Green Morton*. Boston: Beacon Press, 1962. The most vivid, elegantly written biography of Morton. Woodward's study was based on hitherto unavailable letters and other unpublished material of the Morton family. Very good at describing the medical atmosphere of early nineteenth century Boston.

Albert B. Costa

JOHN R. MOTT

Born: May 25, 1865; Livingston Manor, New York
Died: January 31, 1955; Orlando, Florida
Area of Achievement: Religion
Contribution: The central figure in at least four worldwide Christian movements, Mott combined missionary zeal and personal piety with administrative efficiency. Cowinner of the Nobel Peace Prize in 1946, he is widely regarded as the father of the ecumenical movement, the most significant religious movement of the twentieth century.

Early Life

John Mott was born May 25, 1865, in the farming community of Livingston Manor, New York, the third of four children and the only son of John Stitt Mott and Elmira Dodge Mott. When he was only four months old, his father, a farmer, moved the family to Postville, Iowa, where he entered the lumber business and soon became the leading lumber and hardware dealer in town. While working in his father's lumberyard, Mott learned to keep meticulously accurate and detailed records, which he continued to do throughout his life. John Mott expressed his individuality early when, at age eleven, on his own initiative he added the initial "R" (for "Raleigh") to his name.

Mott acquired from his mother much of his personal piety, together with an almost insatiable desire for knowledge. Elmira was an earnest Methodist and subscribed regularly to such magazines as *Harper's Weekly*, *The Youth's Companion*, *The Christian Advocate*, and *The Guide to Holiness*, all of which were eagerly devoured by young Mott. The family also had a relatively large library, and his mother told him much about European history and public affairs, both absorbing interests of his in later years. At the age of thirteen, Mott came under the influence of an Iowa Quaker evangelist, J. W. Dean. Shortly thereafter, a young circuit-riding Methodist pastor, the Reverend Horace E. Warner, not only instilled in him the desire and purpose to obtain a college education but also convinced his parents to make it possible for him to do so.

In the fall of 1881, Mott, at age sixteen, enrolled in Upper Iowa University, a small Methodist preparatory college at nearby Fayette. His primary interests in his years there were English literature, history, and philosophy, with special emphasis on politics, constitutional law, and logic. He joined the Philomathean Society, a debating club, and won prizes in historical and political oration and debate. Mott's debates and orations, in preparation for a political career, were to prove highly useful to him in later years, as did his nearly complete mastery of *Robert's Rules of Order* (1876).

During his years at Upper Iowa, Mott was not particularly religious, although he did become a charter member of the local Young Men's Christian Association (YMCA). His decision to transfer to Cornell University in Ithaca, New York, seems to have been motivated primarily by a need for wider horizons in his preparation for a career in politics and law, but also by a desire to attend a large secular institution in hopes of escaping religious influences. Such was not to be. On Friday evening, January 15, 1886, Mott attended a lecture by J. E. K. Studd, famous English cricketer from Cambridge (later to be knighted and become Lord Mayor of London), and heard Studd utter three sentences which changed his life. As Mott took his seat, having arrived late, Studd announced his text: "Seekest thou great things for thyself? Seek them not. Seek ye first the kingdom of God." Mott later wrote, "These words went straight to the springs of my motive life. I have forgotten all else that the speaker said, but on these few words hinged my life-investment decision. I went back to my room not to study but to fight." Following an interview with Studd the next day, Mott wrote his parents of his decision "to devote my whole life and talents to the service of Jesus."

Mott immediately began a period of intensive Bible study and prayer, along with holding religious services in the local jail. He was elected vice president of the Cornell YMCA, whose membership rapidly grew from forty to 150. In the summer of 1886, he was selected to represent Cornell at the first international and ecumenical Christian Student Conference, a gathering of 251 young men from eighty-nine colleges and universities in the United States and Canada, at Mount Hermon, Massachusetts, under the leadership of the evangelist Dwight L. Moody. Mott returned to Cornell from Mount Hermon determined to complete his education and to devote his life to missionary work. He was elected president of the Cornell YMCA and its membership rapidly grew to 290. He also was instrumental in raising the money for a building for the Cornell YMCA. In 1888, he was graduated with degrees in philosophy, history, and political science, along with membership in Phi Beta Kappa.

Life's Work

Rejecting several opportunities for further study and travel, Mott agreed to a trial period of one year as student secretary of the International Committee of the YMCA. This involved extensive traveling to college campuses and coordination of campus Christian activities. Mott was to remain in this position not one year but for the next twenty-seven years until 1915, at which time he became the committee's general secretary until 1931. Only four months into his new job, however, Mott also accepted the additional responsibility of chairman of the newly organized Student Volunteer Movement for Foreign Missions, the missionary branch of the YMCA, the YWCA, the American Inter-Seminary Missionary Alliance, and the Canadian Intercollegiate Missionary Alliance. This post Mott would hold until 1920, and he continued to solicit funds for it most of his life. Its slogan, The

Evangelization of the World in This Generation, was the title of one of his most important books (1900). Mott had an almost uncanny ability to seek out other capable leaders and to inspire them by his own contagious enthusiasm and zeal. In addition to Mott's extensive travels, he sent out others to work with student Christian groups on various campuses. By 1925, his efforts had resulted in the recruitment of more than ten thousand American and Canadian student volunteers for various mission boards.

In November of 1891, Mott married Leila Ada White, an English teacher and graduate of Wooster College, at her family home in Wooster, Ohio. Leila accompanied him in much of his travel and was a devoted wife and partner for nearly sixty-one years, until her death in 1952. The Motts had four children: John Livingstone, Irene, Frederick Dodge, and Eleanor, all of whom grew up in Montclair, New Jersey, while their father commuted to offices in New York City when not traveling elsewhere. Mott is described by his biographers as six feet tall, with handsome features and an impressive bearing. His reddish-brown hair, gray in later years, topped a large, finely molded head. Photographs indicate his most impressive facial feature to have been his thick, shaggy eyebrows. His entire physique suggested strength: square shoulders and square head, firm mouth, and dark brown, piercing eyes. Small wonder that at least one student is said to have emerged from a conference with Mott and commented, "It was like being in to see God!"

Mott defined his life's work as one of weaving together Christian movements—particularly among students—all over the world. In 1893, he organized the Foreign Missions Conference of North America in an effort to unite missionary work on that continent. He was repeatedly elected to its executive committee and was made an honorary life member in 1942. Mott also was one of the leaders in founding the World's Student Christian Federation in Badstena, Sweden, in 1895, and he became its first general secretary. In this role, he organized student movements in China, Japan, India, New Zealand, and Australia, as well as in Europe and the Near East. International meetings were held in such unlikely places as Tokyo, Constantinople, Jerusalem, Peking, and Madras. By 1925, the WSCF claimed the membership of more than 300,000 young men and women in more than three thousand colleges and universities in twenty-seven different nations. Mott served as chairman of its executive committee from its inception until 1920, then as general chairman until 1928.

A high point in Mott's career came in June of 1910, when he was elected chairman of the World Missionary Conference, attended by more than twelve hundred delegates, in Edinburgh, Scotland, which Mott himself called "the most notable gathering in the interest of the worldwide expansion of Christianity ever held, not only in missionary annals, but in all Christian annals." Mott was also made chairman of a "continuation committee" to carry on the work of the Edinburgh conference until the next one. He toured the Far East in this role and organized regional missionary councils in various nations, including India, Japan, Korea, and China. Mott spent his days organizing these councils and his evenings addressing huge throngs of students. Although he spoke through interpreters, his impassioned words were interrupted time and again by applause. Mott deserves much of the credit for the leading role assumed by the "younger churches" in later missionary conferences throughout the world. Against strong opposition, he recruited Roman Catholic and Eastern Orthodox Christians into ecumenical groups. The "continuation committee" was succeeded by the International Missionary Council in 1921, with Mott as its chairman. In 1942, when he retired from that position, he was named its "honorary chairman."

Mott's travels on behalf of various Christian causes were prodigious. Following extensive trips throughout the United States and Canada, he made his first visit to Europe in 1891. For the next sixty years, he crossed the Atlantic both ways almost annually, occasionally twice or three times, and the Pacific at least fourteen times, in all logging well over two million miles and visiting eighty-three countries. One indication that these travels were far from pleasure junkets is that Mott was often afflicted by motion sickness—not only on sea travels, but on trains as well. When he accepted the Nobel Peace Prize in 1946 (after his first intercontinental flight), this "world citizen" received congratulatory messages from seven chiefs of state and numerous other world leaders. He died January 31, 1955, a few months before his ninetieth birthday, and was buried in the Washington Cathedral. Among his last recorded words were these: "While life lasts I am an evangelist."

Summary

For many years, Mott was the central figure in at least four major world Christian movements: president of the World's Alliance of YMCAs, general secretary and later chairman of the World's Student Christian Federation, chairman of the International Missionary Council, and the first honorary president of the World Council of Churches. As an American Methodist layman, he was awarded an honorary doctor of divinity degree by the (Russian) Orthodox Theological Institute of St. Sergius, in 1940. He declined many prestigious opportunities during his career, including President Woodrow Wilson's offer to become United States Ambassador to China and offers of the presidencies of Princeton University, Oberlin College, and Yale Divinity School. At President Wilson's request, he served on the Mexican Commission in 1916 and the Special Diplomatic Mission to Russia (the "Root Mission") in 1917, utilizing the latter as an opportunity to bring the Russian Orthodox Church into the ecumenical network. Mott was awarded the Distinguished Service Medal for his fund-raising work and other service during World War I, at the conclusion of which he also made significant contributions to the peace conferences at Versailles. In addition to the Nobel

Peace Prize, which he shared with the pacifist Emily Greene Balch in 1946, he was the recipient of seven honorary degrees, the Imperial Order of Meija from Japan, the Order of the Saviour from Greece, the Order of the Holy Sepulchre from Jerusalem, the Prince Carl Medal from Sweden, the Order of the White Rose from Finland, the Second Order of the Crown from Siam, the Order of Polonia Restituta from Poland, the Order of the Italian Crown, and he was made a chevalier, and later an officer, of the French Legion of Honor. He raised more than $300 million for his various Christian causes, most of it for World War I relief work.

Although a brilliant organizer and fund-raiser, Mott was also a man of deep spiritual strength. "Organize as though there were no such thing as prayer," he said, "and pray as though there were no such thing as organization." President Wilson once called him "the world's most useful man."

Mott was typical of much of early twentieth century American religious thought. An evangelical liberal, he eagerly embraced the "social gospel" and applied it to missions and other burning issues of his day. Mott was probably influenced as well by the "social Darwinism" of the period; there was unbounded optimism in the popular slogan The Evangelization of the World in This Generation. This slogan did not originate with Mott, although he made it his own. Yet it is also clear that he knew the difference between the "evangelization" of the world and its "conversion." He simply wanted the Christian Gospel to be preached to the entire world and sincerely believed it could be done in a single generation. Perhaps in part because of his lack of a seminary education, Mott was not deterred by theological niceties in urging ecumenical cooperation. He made the words of Jesus, "that they all may be one," into an ecumenical rallying cry.

In his speech responding to the 1946 Nobel Peace Prize, Mott characterized his career: "My life might be summed up as an earnest and undiscourageable effort to weave together all nations, all races, and all religious communions in friendliness, in fellowship, and in cooperation." In its 1965 tribute to him, on the one hundredth anniversary of his birth, the General Board of the National Council of Churches called Mott "the greatest missionary statesman since the Apostle Paul." If anyone ever deserved the title of father of one of the most important religious movements of the twentieth century, the ecumenical movement, it was John R. Mott.

Bibliography

Fisher, Galen M. *John R. Mott: Architect of Cooperation and Unity*. New York: Association Press, 1952. Written shortly before his death, this volume is very positive throughout in its analysis of Mott's many contributions. The book contains many quotations from distinguished churchmen in praise of Mott's work. The concluding chapter compares Mott's service with that of Saint Paul.

Hopkins, Charles Howard. *John R. Mott, 1865-1955: A Biography*. Grand Rapids, Mich.: William B. Eerdmans Publishing Co., 1979. The definitive biography of Mott, by an emeritus professor of history at Rider College, Philadelphia, this is a detailed, straightforward, and well-documented account of Mott's career and influence. The result of fifteen years of research, this volume tends to emphasize Mott's social concern and the details of his travels, perhaps to the neglect of his Evangelicalism and churchmanship.

Mackie, Robert C. *Layman Extraordinary: John R. Mott, 1865-1955*. New York: Association Press, 1965. A brief monograph of nearly unbridled praise and enthusiasm on behalf of Mott and his accomplishments.

Mathews, Basil. *John R. Mott: World Citizen*. New York: Harper and Brothers, Publishers, 1934. This book was authorized by Mott to describe the principles and experiences of his life as examples for young people. An excellent portrayal of his personality and character written some twenty years before his death, this volume portrays Mott as one who applied the principles of business to the work of Christian Missions.

Mott, John R. *Addresses and Papers*. 6 vols. New York: Association Press, 1946-1947. Mott wrote at least sixteen books himself, as well as many shorter works, which are included in these volumes. His personal papers and his comprehensive archives of the World's Student Christian Federation are in the Mott Collection of the Yale Divinity School Library, New Haven, Connecticut.

Rouse, Ruth. *John R. Mott: An Appreciation*. Geneva: World's Student Christian Federation Press, 1930. A well-balanced portrayal of Mott in mid-career by an admirer and historian of the ecumenical movement.

_____. *The World's Student Christian Federation: A History of the First Thirty Years*. London: S.C.M. Press, 1948. Mott wrote the foreword to this volume, which traces the WSCF from its origins prior to Vadstena, Sweden, in 1895, to High Leigh, England, in 1924, with appropriate attention to Mott's contributions.

C. Fitzhugh Spragins

JOHN MUIR

Born: April 21, 1838; Dunbar, Scotland
Died: December 24, 1914; Los Angeles, California
Areas of Achievement: Exploration and conservation
Contribution: Combining his skills as a scientist, explorer, and writer, Muir
    played a significant role in the conservation movement and in the develop-
    ment of the United States National Park system.

Early Life

John Muir was born April 21, 1838, in Dunbar, Scotland. His mother, Ann
Gilrye Muir, would give birth to three sons and five daughters, John being
the eldest son and the third child. She married Daniel Muir, who as a child
grew up under the harshest poverty imaginable. He eventually gained stature
as a middle-class grain merchant and became a Presbyterian of severe Fun-
damentalist religious beliefs. He worshiped a God of wrath who found evil in
almost every childish activity. Typically, John and his playmates would leave
the yard, and his tyrannical father would fly into a rage and punish the innocent lad. When his father did not have the total devotion of his entire family, he would punish them with the greatest severity.

In 1849, at age eleven, John and his family immigrated to the United States
in search of greater economic opportunity. The Muirs moved to Portage,
Wisconsin, an area that had a fine reputation for wheat growing, where they
purchased farmland. John marveled at the beauty of the countryside. He
kept busy with farm chores and read at night when he was thought to be
asleep. He also developed an early love of machinery and began the practice
of waking at one in the morning to go to his cellar workshop to build things
out of scraps of wood and iron. His father considered his inventions a waste
of time, but John built a sawmill, weather instruments, waterwheels, and
clocks. In 1860, at age twenty-two, he displayed his inventions at the state
fair in Madison. His gadgets were well received, but his dour father only lectured him on the sin of vanity.

At this juncture in his life, John decided to leave home to make his own
way. First, he moved to nearby Madison and attended the University of
Wisconsin. He followed no particular course of study; he took classes that
interested him. He seemed more concerned with learning than with earning
a degree. Muir excelled in the sciences and also enjoyed the outdoor laboratory of nature. A tall, disheveled, bearded man with penetrating, glacial-blue
eyes, Muir eventually grew tired of the regimentation of college. He liked
books, but he loved experience more. Some men from the university were
leaving to fight in the Civil War. Muir was twenty-five years old and in his junior year of school, but he decided to leave also.

From Madison, he journeyed into Canada to take odd jobs and to study the botany of the area. Later, he turned up in Indianapolis, Indiana, working in a carriage shop. With his inventive mind, he proved a success in the factory environment until one day he suffered an eye injury while working on a machine. The puncture wound effected both eyes, and soon he lost his eyesight. After a month of convalescence in a darkened room, his vision slowly returned. With a new lease on life and his eyesight fully restored, Muir decided to abandon the factory world and enjoy nature.

Life's Work
In September of 1867, Muir began a walking tour that would take him from Louisville, Kentucky, to the Gulf Coast of Florida. He found the wild life and plants of the South fascinating. His travels took him through Kentucky, Tennessee, Georgia, and Florida, until he reached the Gulf at Cedar Key. He had no particular route planned, other than to head south. He was not disappointed in what he found on his four-month trek and decided to continue his journey. He had often read the exciting travel accounts of Alexander von Humboldt, who had explored widely in South America. That was Muir's dream also, but it was interrupted by a three-month bout with malaria. When he was almost recovered, he set off for Cuba, but, upon reaching that tropical island and after waiting for a southbound ship for a month, he settled on a new destination.

Muir believed that California offered the best climate for his malarial disorder and also afforded an environment of substantial botanical interest. He made the long journey to the West and settled in beautiful Yosemite Valley, which was snuggled in the Sierra Nevada. At times, he worked as a sheepherder and at a lumber mill, but he spent most of the time exploring the beautiful countryside, taking notes of his findings, and looking for one more glorious site of the wondrous Sierra. In 1869, Muir and a friend built a one-room cabin of pine logs near Yosemite Falls, and this became his home. He had famous visitors such as Asa Gray, the Harvard botanist, the novelist Therese Yelverton, and the renowned Transcendentalist, Ralph Waldo Emerson. With all, he shared the exhilarating scenes of the high country.

After four years in Yosemite Valley, Muir moved to San Francisco and dreamed of other trips. He traveled up the coast to Oregon and Washington and climbed Mount Shasta and Mount Rainier. He also made six excursions to Alaska, where he climbed mountains and studied glaciers. His favorite area was Glacier Bay in southern Alaska, but he loved any place where he could find a mountain to climb. During his stay in Alaska, he also studied the customs of the Tlingit Indians.

Muir also found time for romance. A friend introduced him to Louisa Strentzel, daughter of horticulturalist Dr. John Strentzel and owner of a large fruit ranch east of San Francisco, near the town of Martinez. Louisa and John were married on April 14, 1880. At the same time, he became the overseer of the Strentzel ranch and introduced changes that brought production to peak efficiency. Muir grafted one hundred varieties of pears and grapes onto the best strains. His effective management of the ranch provided him with economic security. For the next ten years, he neglected his writing and mountain climbing, but he and his wife grew reasonably prosperous and reared their two daughters, Wanda and Helen.

Nine years after his marriage, Muir took an important trip back to Yosemite. With him was Robert Underwood Johnson, an old friend and editor of the influential *The Century*. The two were dumbfounded by the changes that had taken place in the Sierra during such a short time. Sheep and lumberjacks had created great devastation in the valley and high country. Forest land was bare and grass root structures were severely damaged by the sharp hoofs of the sheep. Johnson was moved to action. He promised to lobby influential congressmen, and he encouraged Muir to convince the American public of their conservationist cause and the need to take action before it was too late. Muir accepted the challenge and, in two well-argued articles published in *The Century*, he convinced many readers of the desperate need to preserve some of the natural wonders of the California highlands.

In 1890, the federal government rewarded the efforts of Muir, Johnson, and other conservationists by creating Yosemite National Park. Other victories followed when Congress created Rainier, the Grand Canyon, the Petrified Forest, and parts of the Sierra as national preserves. The following year, Muir worked for the passage of legislation that eventually allowed President Benjamin Harrison to set aside thirteen million acres of forest land and President Grover Cleveland, twenty-one million acres more. Muir continued the conservationist cause by helping to create the Sierra Club in 1892. He became the club's first president, and the members vowed to preserve the natural features of the California mountains.

With the total support of his wife, Muir decided to abandon the ranch work and concentrate on furthering his writing career. In 1894, he published *The Mountains of California* and followed it with *Our National Parks* (1901), *Stickeen* (1909), *My First Summer in the Sierra* (1911), *The Yosemite* (1912), and *The Story of My Boyhood and Youth* (1913). In these works, he richly illustrated the growth of a conservationist mind and presented forceful arguments for preservation and ecological protection.

In his last years, Muir traveled to Europe, South America, and Africa, always learning and experiencing what he could. Seventy-six years of life and accomplishment came to an end in December of 1914, when Muir died in Los Angeles on Christmas Eve.

Summary

For John Muir, it had been a full life. Forced to make a decision at an early age between machines and inventions on the one hand and nature and conservation on the other, he chose the path of mountains, flowers, and preservation. In nature, he found his cathedral, and there he preached the gospel of conservation, preservation, and ecology. He walked the wilderness paths with Ralph Waldo Emerson and Theodore Roosevelt; in the end, he convinced many of his contemporaries of the rightness of his ideas.

He lived at a time when the United States was becoming a great industrial leader in the world. Still, he was able to point to the wisdom of preserving many natural wonders of the American West. While an earlier generation had plundered the East, his efforts and those of others helped to save significant portions of the West, to create large national parks and forest preserves, and to protect the ecological systems so necessary for the survival of nature.

Bibliography
Badè, William Frederic. *The Life and Letters of John Muir.* 2 vols. New York: Houghton Mifflin Co., 1924. The best collection of Muir's letters.
Cohen, Michael. *The Pathless Way: John Muir and the American Wilderness.* Madison: University of Wisconsin Press, 1984. Although there is much biographical information in this book, it is mostly an intellectual history of Muir and his ideas as he expressed them in his writings.
Fox, Stephen R. *John Muir and His Legacy: The American Conservation Movement.* Boston: Little, Brown and Co., 1981. This is a biography of Muir, a chronological history of the conservation movement from 1890 to 1975, and an analysis of what conservation means in historical terms.
Melham, Tom. *John Muir's Wild America.* Washington, D.C.: National Geographic Society, 1976. A good place to begin the study of Muir. Beautiful illustrations and sound background history.
Nash, Roderick. *Wilderness and the American Mind.* New Haven, Conn.: Yale University Press, 1967. This work traces the idea of wilderness from an early view as a moral and physical wasteland to its present acceptance as a place to preserve. John Muir emerges as one of many significant figures in this intellectual transformation.
Smith, Herbert F. *John Muir.* New York: Twayne Publishers, 1964. Approaches Muir through his writings as literary works and places him in the context of Transcendentalist literature.
Turner, Frederick. *Rediscovering America: John Muir in His Time and Ours.* New York: Viking Press, 1985. A good, sound coverage of Muir's life in the context of his times and the development of the United States.
Wolfe, Linnie Marsh. *Son of the Wilderness: The Life of John Muir.* New York: Alfred A. Knopf, 1945. A well-written biography based on solid research that shows the many-faceted dimensions of Muir's personality.

John W. Bailey

HERMANN JOSEPH MULLER

Born: December 21, 1890; New York, New York
Died: April 5, 1967; Bloomington, Indiana
Area of Achievement: Genetics
Contribution: The first scientist to induce mutations with X rays and the founder of the field of radiation genetics, Muller became a crusader for radiation protection.

Early Life

Hermann Joseph Muller was a third-generation American born to H. J. Muller, Sr., and Frances Lyons. His paternal grandparents emigrated from Koblenz, Germany, after the unsuccessful revolution of 1848. Muller's father was a partner in a family-owned brass artworks shop in New York City. Muller was reared a Unitarian, his father being a freethinker with Socialist sympathies who had abandoned the family's Catholic ancestry. Muller's mother was of partly Jewish and Congregationalist English ancestry. When Muller was ten, his father died of a stroke and his mother supported the family on a meager income from the shop. Muller was a gifted student, receiving scholarship support to study at Columbia College, obtaining his bachelor's degree in 1910. Muller's love for science settled in the new field of genetics, which he explored in course work with Edmund Beecher Wilson and later with Thomas Hunt Morgan. Joining Muller in this enthusiasm for genetics were two students who entered Columbia two years after he did, Calvin Blackman Bridges and Alfred Henry Sturtevant. These five men were the major contributors to the development of classical genetics, the theory of the gene, and the field of cytogenetics.

Muller was a diminutive five feet, two inches tall, but this boyish height was counterbalanced by his pattern baldness and muscular physique. Although Muller had to support himself and his mother with many outside jobs, he maintained contact with "the fly lab," as the group called itself. After receiving a master's degree in physiology in 1912, Muller succeeded in having Morgan serve as his dissertation supervisor. Until 1910, Morgan had not made a major discovery with fruit flies. Between 1910 and 1915, when Muller completed the work for his Ph.D., the fly lab had introduced the concepts of sex-linked inheritance and crossing over, the mapping of genes, and the relation of genes to character formation. Some of the work involved individual discovery, but much of it was a cooperative effort in what was one of the first research teams, a model that is now characteristic of modern science.

Muller's role in the fly lab was that of a zealot. He believed that all biological phenomena ultimately stemmed from the activity of genes, and he tried to interpret all heredity through this model. Morgan and Muller differed both in personality and in scientific style, Morgan favoring experimental data that forced a theory to emerge and Muller favoring the reasoning that generated experiments and tossed out weak hypotheses. Muller, as a theoretician, provided abundant models and insights into the new discoveries, but Morgan rewarded credit and authorship to the careful execution of experiments. Muller felt resentful that Sturtevant and Bridges were financially supported through Morgan's efforts while he had to support himself with time-consuming jobs that were unrelated to his research. This incompatibility of temperament eventually led to Muller's estrangement from the fly lab and a lifelong reputation as a difficult man, preoccupied with issues of priority.

Life's Work

Muller's major theoretical contributions to genetics were in gene theory. He pointed out that genes were the only molecules that had the property of copying their errors and that, thus, the copying property must be a fundamental feature of life. He clarified the concept of mutation, which then included numerous different abnormal processes, by restricting it to a change within the individual gene or what is now called a gene mutation. He extended the primacy of the gene to evolution and asserted that the gene was the basis of life, life having originated with the first replicating molecule capable of copying its variations. These ideas, developed between 1920 and 1926, were frequently resisted as fanciful or naïvely speculative by many of his contemporaries, but they gradually gained acceptance after the molecular revolution of the 1950's when the chemical structure of genes proposed by James Dewey Watson and Francis Harry Compton Crick provided a material basis for these views.

Muller was also a gifted experimenter, and he designed complex genetic stocks that enabled geneticists to repeat the work of others and to use them as tools for genetic studies, theoretical and applied. In 1916, after receiving his Ph.D., Muller was recruited by Julian Sorell Huxley to join the faculty at the newly founded Rice Institute. He returned to Columbia in 1920, while Morgan was on leave, and then secured a position at the University of Texas, where he worked from 1920 to 1932. During these years, Muller pursued the study of the gene and mutation. He demonstrated that mutation frequency was measurable and that temperature affected the frequency. He proved that gene mutation was not restricted to the process of sperm or egg formation but could occur throughout the life cycle. He studied environmental effects by comparing the behavioral and physical traits of a pair of identical twins reared apart, concluding that it would take an army of experts to tease apart the genetic and environmental components in human behavior.

In 1926, Muller made the most important experimental contribution of his career. He reasoned, after a thorough review of the literature on biological effects of radiation, that X rays might damage individual genes. With his carefully designed stocks, he proved that ionizing radiation produced mutations. He demonstrated this fact quantitatively for a class of mutations that kills half the sons of the mothers who carry the induced mutation on a sex chromosome. This work he reported in 1927 to the International Congress of Genetics in Berlin. The work was rapidly confirmed by many geneticists, and Muller found himself an international celebrity and the leading authority on radiation genetics. In the years that followed, Muller and his students showed that gene mutation frequency rises proportionally to the dose received; that there is no apparent threshold dose, the low or attenuated doses spread out over a month having the same amount of mutations induced as the identical dose when administered over a short interval of time. Muller also demonstrated that ionizing radiation induced breakage of chromosomes, and this breakage resulted in many changes such as rearrangements of the sequences of genes, losses of chromosomes, and fatal early abortion of the embryos receiving such damaged sperm or eggs. By 1945, Muller and his students applied these findings to interpret the mechanism of radiation sickness among the victims of the first atomic bombings in Hiroshima and Nagasaki.

Muller's political views shifted from Socialist to Communist. He supported the Bolsheviks and visited the Soviet Union in 1922 to set up research programs in fruit fly genetics. He attracted postdoctoral students from the Soviet Union to his Texas laboratory. In 1932, he helped edit and distribute an underground newspaper, *The Spark*, and the FBI kept him under surveillance. He criticized the American eugenics movement as racist, sexist, and misguided in a paper he delivered at the third and last International Congress of Eugenics. That same year, he left Texas for Berlin on a Guggenheim fellowship, but the Nazis came to power before the year was over and Muller accepted an invitation to set up a laboratory in the Soviet Union. Between 1933 and 1937, at Leningrad and then in larger quarters in Moscow, Muller had a flourishing research school that studied problems of gene size, shape, boundaries, and number. This work was interrupted in 1936 by the arrest and execution of two of Muller's students and by the growing antigenetic movement of Trofim Denisovitch Lysenko, who secretly had the Communist Party's support to replace genetics with a curious theory of environmental modification or training of heredity. Muller and Lysenko clashed in public debate, and by 1937 Muller realized that the cause was lost and he escaped by volunteering to fight in the Spanish Civil War. After the siege of Madrid, Muller was helped by Huxley, who recommended him for a job in Edinburgh.

Once again, Muller established a productive laboratory with graduate students from many Commonwealth nations, only to find his work interrupted by the onset of World War II. In 1940, Muller returned to the United States as an interim professor at Amherst, but he relinquished the job when the war ended in 1945. Because of his erratic past, many universities were not interested in hiring him, but Indiana University took that chance, and the following year, 1946, Muller was awarded the Nobel Prize for Medicine. Muller continued to speak out on the importance of genetics to the future of mankind until his death, on April 5, 1967.

Summary

Muller was unusual in speaking out on issues related to genetics; this frequently embroiled him in controversy. He was a staunch critic of those who attacked the teaching of evolution in public schools. He advocated the teaching of biology free of religious or supernatural interpretation. He denounced Lysenko as a gangster at a time when more liberal scientists looked upon the genetics controversy in the Soviet Union as a clash between two worldviews. He criticized the medical profession for not protecting its own practitioners and for taking too paternalistic an attitude when using radiation excessively on patients. He fought hard for radiation protection at a time when the United States Atomic Energy Commission tried to hide the occurrence and the effects of fallout from weapons testing. He was often mistrusted and misinterpreted because of his past. He believed in a strong national defense, including weapons testing, during the years of the Cold War and only came to support the international move to ban atmospheric testing when the quantity of fallout began to reach dangerous levels. Although he denounced the cruder eugenics of his generation, he championed differential breeding and favored the breeding of more intelligent, more cooperative, and healthier people as a response to the increasing load of mutations that he identified as a concern in the industrial nations. He was an idealist who believed in education and the use of knowledge to transform mankind outwardly and inwardly. At the same time, he rejected coercion as a basis for bringing about change. As a critic and a crusader, he was an exemplar of a vital American tradition.

Bibliography

Carlson, Elof Axel. *Genes, Radiation, and Society: The Life and Work of H. J. Muller*. Ithaca, N.Y.: Cornell University Press, 1981. This is the first full account of Muller's life and his scientific accomplishments. It is based on more than thirty thousand letters, his 375 published articles, and numerous interviews with his students, colleagues, and critics. Carlson was Muller's student, and his view of his subject is essentially sympathetic.

Ludmerer, Kenneth M. *Genetics and American Society*. Baltimore: Johns Hopkins University Press, 1972. This study deals largely with the eugenics movement and the failure of many of the United States' leading geneticists to criticize many of the false claims made by advocates of compulsory sterilization laws and restrictive immigration. Muller's views are downplayed in the otherwise informative and scholarly work.

Medvedev, Zhores. *The Rise and Fall of T. D. Lysenko*. New York: Columbia University Press, 1969. The criminality and self-deception that characterized the Lysenkoist movement are revealed in this account by a dissident critic of political and scientific repression in the Soviet Union. Medvedev did not know Muller; he was a youth when the controversy broke out.

Morgan, T. H., A. H. Sturtevant, H. J. Muller, and C. B. Bridges. *The Mechanism of Mendelian Heredity*. New York: Henry Holt and Co., 1915. This summation of the fly lab's contributions to classical genetics established the now-prevailing theory of inheritance, replacing contending views in Europe and the United States. It led to an American dominance in genetics throughout the rest of the twentieth century.

Muller, H. J. *Out of the Night: A Biologist's View of the Future*. New York: Vanguard Press, 1935. This was Muller's only venture into popular writing. He was still communistic in spirit, and the book's eugenic utopia reveals a Socialist bias. The book presents a proposal for sperm banks and eugenic breeding which was superseded by his articles after 1957, when he recognized the importance of what he termed "germinal choice," the freedom to choose the genetic worth that one wishes for one's children.

_____."The Problem of Genic Modification." In *Proceedings of the Fifth International Congress of Genetics: Berlin, 1927*. Berlin: International Congress of Genetics, 1928. Muller's original paper on the artificial induction of mutations is one of the classics of science. In it, Muller spells out his research program for the next twenty years of his life.

Elof Axel Carlson

EDWARD R. MURROW

Born: April 25, 1908; Greensboro, North Carolina
Died: April 27, 1965; Pawling, New York
Area of Achievement: Broadcast journalism
Contribution: The pioneer of news broadcasting, Murrow set the standard for objective reporting while warning against the potential for manipulation by electronic journalism.

Early Life

Egbert Roscoe Murrow was born April 25, 1908, in Greensboro, North Carolina. Called "Egg" by family and friends, he changed his name to the more acceptable "Edward" as a young man. When he was still a child, his family moved to the Pacific Northwest, where Murrow spent summers working in the logging camps. In high school, he was a superachiever on several levels: a successful athlete, valedictorian of his class, student body officer, and, prophetically, star of the debate team. Following his graduation, the rangy, six-foot, two-inch young man returned to the logging camps. In 1926, after one year of this hard labor, he had saved sufficiently to enroll at Washington State University.

His popularity continued in college, enhanced by his dark, handsome looks—a physical appearance which would prove useful in his final career choice. In college, he majored in speech, honing his communication skills; he also added acting to his list of credits and began to cultivate the taste for elegant, expensive clothes for which he would later be known.

As the president of the student government, Murrow was a delegate to the annual convention of NSFA, the National Student Federation of America, of which he was elected president. Immediately following his graduation with a B.A. in speech, he moved to New York City to undertake his new, unpaid responsibilities. His tenure with NSFA afforded him travel throughout Europe, where he began to establish a network of friends and acquaintances that would eventually encompass the most influential people of the time. During these early Depression years, he also traveled frequently within the United States; these experiences were to affect his developing social and political conscience. Murrow resigned from NFSA in his second year as president (1931) to take a salaried position with the Institute of International Education.

In this position, he was assistant to Stephen Pierce Duggan, director of the institute, a reformer who believed in the betterment of mankind and in the principle of noblesse oblige. Duggan and the Eastern Establishment, to whom he introduced his young protégé, further contributed to Murrow's political development as well as adding to his list of valuable contacts.

In 1934, Murrow married Janet Brewster. He was earning five thousand dollars a year, a comfortable sum by Depression standards, when he accepted a position at Columbia Broadcasting System (CBS) Radio. Eventually, he was made European director for CBS in London. This posting marked the beginning of the CBS wartime news team and Murrow's own beginning as the major influence in broadcast journalism.

Life's Work

For an energetic, talented, and idealistic young reporter, there could have been no better vantage point from which to view the ensuing struggle than prewar London. By 1939, Murrow had established a crew which included Eric Sevareid, Bill Henry, William Shirer, and Cecil Brown, among others. Murrow charged them to report the human side of the news, not only the facts but also how the average person reacted to the facts. He also urged them to speak naturally, to be honest, and to be neutral. One of his greatest achievements was the training of this impressive group of reporters, who could communicate over the air a sense of the drama unfolding around them. For the first time, broadcast journalism eclipsed print in popularity. Without endless rewrites, copy editors, layouts, and printings, it was demonstrated that the electronic medium could accurately report the news and do so faster.

As radio's most recognizable personality, Murrow himself did not realize the extent of his influence or his huge listenership until a 1941 trip to the United States. At a banquet in his honor, the poet Archibald MacLeish, commenting on Murrow's reports on the attack of London, acknowledged his achievement:

> You burned the city of London at our doors and we knew that the dead were our dead . . . were mankind's dead . . . without rhetoric, without dramatics, without more emotion than need be . . . you have destroyed . . . the superstition that what is done beyond 3,000 miles is not done at all.

Never content to sit back and be the London bureau chief, Murrow needed to face danger, to be present to absorb the flavor of the events he reported. He stood on a rooftop and watched the bombing of London. He flew twenty-five bombing missions, refusing even the president of CBS's plea that he cease such a dangerous practice. He was in Vienna when the city was occupied by the Nazis and saw at firsthand the atrocities of which they were capable. He walked among the half-dead inmates of the concentration camp at Buchenwald soon after it had been liberated. His harrowing broadcast describing this experience was reprinted in the media and replayed over and over on the air.

Many years previously, Murrow had begun smoking. As early as 1942, this pleasure had become an addiction; he was smoking up to three packs of unfiltered cigarettes a day. He was already exhibiting a "weak chest" and other pulmonary problems. His restless nature, probing mind, need for experience, and inability to relax all led him to periodic exhaustion, requiring hospitalization.

On November 6, 1945, Janet Murrow, at age thirty-five, gave birth to a son, Charles Casey Murrow. With the war over, it was time for the family to return to New York. Murrow took the position of vice president and director of public affairs for CBS.

This was a difficult period of adjustment. Postwar New York was brash and wealthy, in stark contrast to war-torn London; Murrow missed his old friends and colleagues and the excitement of covering the war. After eighteen months in the position, Murrow resigned to return to broadcasting the news. He settled into a comfortable life, doing what he knew and loved best at a salary of $125,000 a year, an amount necessary for a man who enjoyed fine clothes, a good address, fast cars, and the best restaurants.

Augmenting this income were royalties from the *Hear It Now* recordings. This record was the brainchild of Fred Friendly, a colleague whose partnership would span the remainder of Murrow's broadcast career. Released in 1948, the record brought together the actual recorded speeches of such personalities as Winston Churchill, Franklin D. Roosevelt, Adolf Hitler, Huey Long, Will Rogers, and Edward VIII, with Murrow narrating. A quarter of a million copies were sold in the first year.

See It Now, the documentary program that established Murrow's reputation as a television journalist, debuted on November 18, 1951, the result of another partnership with Fred Friendly. A precursor to the present-day documentary, the program was improvised and rife with technical problems: blackouts, loss of picture, and so on. The show explored contemporary issues: from what it was like underground with coal miners in West Virginia to the experience of riding a school bus following desegregation in the South. A particularly moving segment was on Korea at Christmas. Rather than focus on military strategies, Murrow interviewed average soldiers and their reactions to the war. Before being canceled, this show won three Peabodys, four Emmys, and various other awards from *Look, Saturday Review*, the New York Newspaper Guild, and others.

Along with *See It Now*, Murrow's other venture into television was *Person to Person*, a program which took cameras into the homes of the rich and famous while Murrow interviewed them by remote from the studio. *Person to Person* was an enormous commercial success, widening his audience to include millions of viewers who would never have watched *See It Now*. Through *Person to Person*, Murrow became as familiar as the celebrities he interviewed, vastly increasing his credibility. The show also served to document an era, featuring interviews of such diverse subjects as Marilyn Monroe, Fred Astaire, Fidel Castro, and John F. Kennedy and his new wife, Jacqueline.

In early 1953, Murrow was targeted by the House Committee on Un-American Activities. He had been too consistently critical of Joseph McCarthy; he was prominent and, through his activities in the 1930's, he was vulnerable. Murrow fought back with a segment of *See It Now* entitled "A Report on Senator Joseph R. McCarthy." His strategy was to catch McCarthy in his own contradictions by splicing together his various speeches with Murrow's voice-over narration. Murrow ended with a speech spoken directly to the camera, not read as was his normal practice:

> He [McCarthy] didn't create this situation of fear, he merely exploited it; and rather successfully. Cassius was right. "The fault, Dear Brutus, is not in our stars, but in ourselves."

By the following morning, CBS had received one thousand telegrams applauding the telecast. Murrow, returning from lunch the next day, was mobbed on Fifth Avenue. *Variety* labeled him "practically a hero." McCarthy's power was beginning to wane.

In 1961, exhausted from his years in broadcasting and disillusioned with CBS, Murrow accepted the directorship of the United States Information Agency in the Kennedy Administration. His tenure ended after three years, after surgery for cancer of the lung. Awarded the Presidential Medal of Freedom in 1964, Murrow died at his farm in New York on April 27, 1965, at the age of fifty-seven.

Summary

Edward R. Murrow spent his life following the dictates of his conscience: struggling with the top executives at CBS, with Kennedy, with McCarthy, and even with his adoring public. With a profound commitment to fair reporting, Murrow set the standard for broadcast journalism.

He became a dedicated anti-Fascist in the early 1930's, working with the Emergency Committee to bring out of Europe ninety-one scholars whose lives and works were endangered. These activities would figure prominently in smear tactics made against him by the House Committee on Un-American Activities. Although his head-on collision with McCarthy was considered by many to be television's "finest hour," Murrow himself agonized over its production. His objectivity and his dedication to balanced presentation were lacking. He called it a "half hour editorial."

In a career-long relationship, flawed at times with serious bitterness, CBS found the perfect vehicle in Murrow. Not only had nature bequeathed him a mellifluous baritone voice and dark good looks, but he was also a trained and skillful debater. His speaking ability, his passionate social conscience, and his dedication to providing the truth infused his broadcasting with a rare vitality. Yet Murrow was taxed by television in a way that his audiences would never guess: He was incredibly camera shy. He had been nervous on the radio, but television added the dimension of the camera. His hands trembled, the heat of the lights made him perspire and squirm; under the table, his nervous leg jumped.

Murrow's most enduring battle was with broadcasting itself, to see that it upheld its integrity. Repeatedly—to colleagues, in speeches, and in articles—he warned of the potential of broadcasting to manipulate the news and the public. At the same time, he believed that broadcasting had the potential to be "a real aid in keeping the light of Western Civilization burning." In his lifetime, he saw that light burn dangerously low.

Bibliography
Friendly, Fred W. *Due to Circumstances Beyond Our Control*. New York: Random House, 1967. In this occupational memoir of his sixteen years at CBS, Friendly presents a critical, disturbing picture of commercial television. He also discusses *See It Now* from a production point of view.
Kendrick, Alexander. *Prime Time: The Life of Edward R. Murrow*. Boston: Little, Brown and Co., 1969. Kendrick was one of the so-called Murrow Boys, trained in his tradition. This training gives him an insider's view in this profusely illustrated and anecdote-rich biography. Often insightful, he captures Murrow's involvement and his conscience but stops short of any criticism. Good for an overview of the sins of commercial television.
Murrow, Edward R. *In Search of Light: The Broadcasts of Edward R. Murrow, 1938-1961*. Edited by Edward Bliss, Jr. New York: Alfred A. Knopf, 1967. These selections were made from five thousand broadcasts, which spanned Hitler's seizure of Austria to Kennedy's inaugural address. Bliss, a longtime CBS staffer, has chosen broadcasts which add dimension to history or show Murrow's perspective on the development of his style.
_____. *This Is London*. New York: Simon and Schuster, 1941. Texts of his London radio broadcasts from August, 1939, to December, 1940, when he was chief of the European bureau for CBS. The broadcasts read well because Murrow was not only a good speaker but also a sensitive writer with a good grasp of the language. An excellent source for a historical perspective.
Paley, William S. *As It Happened: A Memoir*. New York: Doubleday and Co., 1979. This autobiography by the founder and president of CBS describes the heyday of radio and television programming, including controversies with Murrow, Daniel Schorr, and the CIA. Often pretentious, he presents a one-sided view without attempting to be analytical. Important for the corporate view of broadcasting.
Sperba, A. M. *Murrow: His Life and Times*. New York: Freudlich Books, 1968. Exhaustive biography. Almost obsessive in its documentation of each detail of Murrow's life. In this well-balanced, critical presentation, Sperba

penetrates the reasons for Murrow's actions and the sources of his beliefs while communicating Murrow's passion for proper news reportage. The definitive biography.

Terrill Brooks

THOMAS NAST

Born: September 27, 1840; Landau, Germany
Died: December 7, 1902; Guayaquil, Ecuador
Areas of Achievement: Art and politics
Contribution: As one of the greatest American cartoonists, Nast created lasting works of art that expressed his personal and political convictions while reflecting the hopes and dreams of a generation.

Early Life

Thomas Nast was born September 27, 1840, in army barracks in Landau, Germany. His father, also called Thomas, was a musician in the Ninth Regiment Bavarian Band. The elder Nast and his wife, Apollonia Apres, had three children before Thomas was born. Two boys died at a very early age, so that Nast's only playmate was an older sister. In 1846, the Nast family decided to move to the United States, because of the father's political affiliations and the threat of revolution in Germany. While the elder Nast served in the French and American navies, his family moved to New York. He joined them four years later.

Young Thomas Nast had by this time developed considerable artistic talent. His crayon drawings thrilled fellow students and teachers, but Nast did not enjoy school. Finally, his parents allowed him to take art classes instead, first with Theodore Kaufmann and later, Alfred Fredericks. Nast's formal education soon ended, when he showed some of his work to Frank Leslie, publisher of *Frank Leslie's Illustrated Newspaper*. Leslie was impressed with the boldness, if not talent, of this short, round-faced, pudgy, fifteen-year-old German with dark hair and olive skin. After Nast's successful completion of a difficult assignment, Leslie hired him at four dollars a week.

Nast worked diligently for *Leslie's Illustrated Newspaper* over the next four years, receiving much technical training from Sol Eytinge, a coworker and good friend. Nast's drawings during this early period frequently reflected his humorous personality in their subject matter and his study of the English illustrators, John Leech, Sir John Gilbert, and Sir John Tenniel, in methodology. Perhaps most significant for the future, however, was Nast's first battle with corruption. Frank Leslie discovered that while dairy owners sold "swill milk" from diseased cows, New York city officials were looking the other way. With Nast's vivid depictions of the squalid conditions in these dairies, *Leslie's Illustrated Newspaper* brought the issue to the forefront of the news and created a public outcry, which quickly defeated the promoters of the contaminated milk. In this first campaign against corruption, Nast learned that his art could have tremendous political power—a lesson he would not forget.

When Nast left *Leslie's Illustrated Newspaper* in 1859, to work for the *New*

York Illustrated News, he covered events such as the funeral of John Brown and the John Heenan–Tom Sayers fight in England. Then, hearing of Giuseppe Garibaldi's invasion of Italy, Nast left England to join the great liberator. While witnessing and recording only a few skirmishes, Nast found upon his return home in February, 1861, that his reputation had grown considerably. Later that year, on the day before his twenty-first birthday, a dignified looking Nast with a recently grown mustache (which became his trademark) married the refined and lovely Sarah Edwards. She would become not only the mother of his five children but also the author of many of the captions for his artwork. Their Niagara Falls honeymoon was a pleasant escape from the realities of a country torn by the Civil War.

Life's Work

At the outbreak of the Civil War, Nast determined to do what he could for the sacred Union. A more devoted patriot could not be found, especially one with his battlefield experience. Consequently, *Harper's Weekly*, a pictorial newspaper begun in 1857, hired Nast to illustrate the events of the war. This association with *Harper's Weekly* would provide Nast the perfect forum for the expression of his ideas and the development of his art.

Nast soon began to create imaginative works which aroused the patriotism and commitment of his Northern audience, pictures which made the Confederate soldier the embodiment of evil and the Union soldier the defender of justice. Nast's fervent support of the Union was recognized by President Abraham Lincoln, who called Nast his best recruiting sergeant.

After the Civil War, Nast used his art to support the Republican Party, which to him represented freedom and equality for the slaves and punishment of the treasonous South. Thus, when President Andrew Johnson adopted a lenient Reconstruction policy for the South, Nast retaliated with his first use of caricature, the comic distortion of identifiable men. In 1868, Nast used this art form in the campaign to elect Ulysses S. Grant, the hero of the war, to the presidency. With his satiric caricatures of the Democratic presidential candidate from New York, Governor Horatio Seymour, Nast not only helped Grant but also established a national reputation for himself.

The following year marked the beginning of Nast's most widely acclaimed political battle. In his crusade against the corrupt Tweed Ring of New York city, Nast's work matured in technique, composition, and power. Nast's enemies were the Tammany Hall Democrats who controlled the New York state legislature, the immigrants, the courts, the police, and, to some extent, organized crime. Nast made the four Tweed Ring leaders—city boss William Marcy Tweed, Peter Barr Sweeny, Richard Connolly, and A. Oakey Hall—famous with his caricatures. A cartoon entitled "Shadows of Forthcoming Events" (June 4, 1870) revealed the areas of corruption—schools, elections, street cleaners, the fire department, the board of health, saloons—and the men who were responsible for these conditions.

For two years, Nast bombarded the enemy with artistic accusations. His most viciously direct cartoon indicating ring members was "Who Stole the People's Money?" (April 19, 1871), in which corrupt officials stood in a circle, pointing to one another and proclaiming, "Twas Him." Ring members became so frightened over this cartoon that Tweed tried to stop Nast's attacks by threats and then bribery. Nast, true to his principles, vowed not only to continue his fight but also to put the Ring leaders behind bars. With increased public awareness and an honest tabulation of the ballots, the Tweed Ring was defeated in the 1871 election. Although Nast did not win a single-handed victory over the Tweed Ring, one of his caricatures of Tweed did help officials in Spain identify and capture the American fugitive, who died in jail in 1878.

During the early 1870's, Nast continued to support the Republican Party and its candidates, especially Grant, his hero. Nast even created the symbol for the Republican Party, the Republican elephant, and popularized the Democratic donkey in his cartoons. For his assistance in the 1876 campaign of Rutherford B. Hayes, the Republican Party offered Nast ten thousand dollars, but he refused to accept money for expressing his convictions.

Nast became disillusioned with the Republican Party, however, when President Hayes restored home rule to the South in the Compromise of 1877. By 1884, Nast's political dilemma had reached its climax. He could not back James G. Blaine, Republican presidential candidate, since Blaine sponsored Chinese exclusion, a policy contrary to Nast's belief in equality. Nast therefore abandoned the Republicans for the Democratic candidate, Grover Cleveland, whose fiscal policy and personal and political philosophies were more acceptable. Yet, even though Cleveland won the election, Nast's political influence would never be the same. In 1886, the forty-six-year-old Nast ended his fruitful career with *Harper's Weekly*.

Though Nast continued free-lance work and even tried to establish his own paper with the motto Principles, not Men, he soon realized that only one area of his work remained popular—his Christmas sketches. For more than twenty-five years, the Christmas issue of *Harper's Weekly* had contained Nast's drawings of Santa Claus, the jolly, fat, fur-clad, white-bearded legend whom Americans still recall at the holiday season. Nast's inspiration for the character came from his childhood memories of Pelze-Nicol—the local name for the German Saint Nicholas who awarded good children with toys and bad ones with switches. Appropriately, Nast's last publication was a Christmas drawing for *Leslie's Weekly* in 1901.

Summary

Thomas Nast more completely represents life in late nineteenth century United States than most prominent men of his day, for he not only lived it, but he also captured its essence in his artistic creations. His career began at a time when intense nationalism was of primary importance to his country; his Uncle Sam became the symbol of patriotic feeling. After the Civil War, an era of political Reconstruction caused heated debates among American politicians. Nast became a pictorial contributor to these debates as a Radical Republican. Wherever he saw a threat to American democracy, he pounced on it—whether it took the form of the Ku Klux Klan in the South or the Tweed Ring in New York.

Nast's caricatures and cartoon symbols were given life by the intensity of his principles. The popularity of his Tammany tiger, empty dinner pail, and rag baby of inflation reveals more about society in this period than any political speech or statistical study. For twenty-five years, Nast was a molder of public opinion, intuitively sensing the public mood and responding with drawings which stirred the public mind to thought or action.

Yet by the 1890's, things had changed. The public had grown tired of moral and political crusades. Nast's popularity decreased rapidly, his finances dwindled, and, in 1902, he was forced to accept a gift from his beloved country— a consulship in Ecuador, where he died from yellow fever.

Nast's death indicated the end of an era, but he left a powerful legacy of images: the Republican elephant, the Democratic donkey, Uncle Sam, and the jovial figure who spreads happiness to all mankind, Santa Claus. Moreover, he left the story of a dedicated American whose pursuit of a perfect society with liberty and justice for all could never end.

Bibliography
Harper's Weekly, 1859-1886. The original publications of Nast's drawings are an essential source of information in tracing his development and analyzing his contribution.

Keller, Morton. *The Art and Politics of Thomas Nast*. New York: Oxford University Press, 1968. Shows how Nast's work reflected the post–Civil War belief that society can be reformed. Weak regarding Nast's artistic techniques.

Levy, Alan. "Thomas Nast's Triumphant Return to Germany." *Art News* 78 (March, 1979): 118-119, 122-123, 125. Details the discovery of Nast's work in his native land. Noting the great success of the 1977 Nast Festival in Landau, Levy suggests that Nastomania has gripped Germany.

Murrell, William. *A History of American Graphic Humor*. New York: Macmillan, 1933-1938. An early work showing the evolution of cartoons from Nast's day to Walt Disney's. Chapter 3 is devoted to Nast. Helpful in placing Nast's work in the appropriate context.

Nast, Thomas. *Thomas Nast's Christmas Drawings*. Introduction by Thomas Nast St. Hill. New York: Dover Publications, 1978. A reprint of the work published by Harper and Brothers in 1890, which compiled Nast's Christmas drawings of almost thirty years. Three illustrations and the introduction by Nast's grandson have been added.

Paine, Albert Bigelow. *Th. Nast: His Period and His Pictures*. New York: Macmillan, 1904. Nast selected Paine to write this comprehensive biography. Provides sympathetic insight into Nast's personal life while presenting the history of an era. Used by all subsequent biographers.

Provenzo, Eugene F., Jr. "Thomas Nast and the Church/State Controversy in Education (1870-1876)." *Educational Studies* 12 (Winter, 1981-1982): 359-379. An informative article discussing Nast's fight against funding for parochial schools, especially Catholic ones.

Vinson, J. Chal. *Thomas Nast: Political Cartoonist*. Athens: University of Georgia Press, 1967. A scholarly work that condenses the Paine biography, concentrating on those aspects of Nast's career that made him a powerful influence on the politics of his day.

Alice Taylor

JOHN VON NEUMANN

Born: December 28, 1903; Budapest, Hungary
Died: February 8, 1957; Washington, D.C.
Areas of Achievement: Mathematics, mathematical physics, and computer science
Contribution: A brilliant mathematician who laid the mathematical foundations of modern physics and computer science, von Neumann affirmed the importance of autonomous scientific research during the anti-Communist McCarthy era.

Early Life

The eldest of three boys, John von Neumann was born in Budapest on December 28, 1903. In the United States, he came to be known universally as Johnny, perhaps because he was already known by the Hungarian Jancsi. Von Neumann belonged to the group of Hungarian mathematicians and physicists including Eugene Wigner, Edward Teller, Leo Szilard, and Dennis Gabor, who have substantially contributed to twentieth century science. In addition to knowing one another, some of them even attended the same high school, Budapest Lutheran.

Von Neumann's father, Max von Neumann, was a successful banker who had been elevated to the nobility. The Hungarian honorific "Margittai" was later Germanized to "von." The family was Jewish and bilingual in Hungarian and German. When John entered the gymnasium at age ten, he came into contact with László Rátz, a teacher who perceived his mathematical talents and arranged with his father for special tutoring. Von Neumann worked concurrently on a degree in chemical engineering, awarded by the Eidgenössische Technische Hochschule of Zurich in 1926, and a doctorate in mathematics, which was awarded by the University of Budapest, also in 1926.

Although von Neumann then held positions at the University of Berlin and at the University of Hamburg, he also visited Göttingen, where there was an amazing group of physicists and mathematicians, including David Hilbert, Werner Heisenberg, Max Born, and Erwin Schrödinger. The visitors included Albert Einstein, Wolfgang Pauli, Linus Pauling, J. Robert Oppenheimer, and Norbert Wiener.

After coming to the United States as a visiting professor at Princeton University in 1930, he accepted a permanent position in 1931. In 1933, he was invited to join the permanent faculty of the Institute for Advanced Study, also located at Princeton University, and became the youngest faculty member at the institute. He married Marietta Kövesi in 1930; she was Catholic, and he at least nominally became a Catholic during his first marriage. His daughter, Marina, was born in Princeton in 1935. The marriage ended in divorce in 1937. In 1938, he visited Hungary and married Klára Dán, who joined him in Princeton.

Von Neumann was one of the rare men of extraordinary scientific genius who was as engaging personally as he was brilliant mentally. Colleagues relate anecdotes concerning his foibles, but all with a touch of nostalgia because his charm as well as his intelligence endeared him to those who knew him best. Von Neumann was of medium size, slender as a young man, plump as he grew older. His colleagues teased him about dressing like a banker— perhaps because he was the son of a banker; he habitually wore three-piece suits with a neatly buttoned coat and a handkerchief in his pocket. Cheerful and gregarious, he was a great raconteur. Not at all athletic, he had to watch his appetite for rich gravies, sauces, and desserts. He drove erratically, regularly acquiring speeding tickets and wearing out approximately a car a year. According to his friends, he was not mechanical enough to change a tire on his car, but his wife attributed to him a great skill at releasing zippers.

Because of his powers of concentration, he could appear absentminded. He would sometimes start out on a trip and then have to call home to find out with whom he had an appointment and where it was to be. He loved off-color limericks and repeated them at parties. Especially fond of children, he enjoyed their toys so much that friends would give him toys as gifts on special occasions. Von Neumann's associates described him as sociable, witty, and party-loving.

History intrigued von Neumann. He had systematically read and learned most of the names and facts in the twenty-one volumes of the *Cambridge Ancient History* (1923-1939). During World War II, his colleagues were amazed at how frequently his forecasts were borne out by later events. Once asked by his colleague Herman Goldstine to recite Charles Dickens' *A Tale of Two Cities* (1859), von Neumann continued for so long that it was clear that he was prepared to recite from memory the entire book, even though he had read it twenty years before. While he had a photographic memory of books he had read decades earlier, he was quite capable of forgetting what his luncheon menu had been. When his wife once asked him to get her a glass of water, he came back and asked her where the glasses were—even though they had lived in the same house for seventeen years.

Life's Work

Von Neumann's first group of mathematical papers involved presenting an axiomatic treatment of set theory. Related to this concern with set theory was the problem of the freedom of contradiction of mathematics. Bertrand Russell and Alfred North Whitehead, in *Principia Mathematica* (1910-1913), contended that all mathematics derives from logic and is without contradiction. In 1927, following David Hilbert, who wanted to separate number from experiential logic, where seven is related to seven objects, von Neumann argued that all analysis could be proved to be without contradiction. Three years later, the German mathematician Kurt Gödel upset these theories by showing that "in any sufficiently powerful logical system, statements can be formulated which are neither provable nor unprovable within that system unless the system is logically inconsistent." Von Neumann was entirely comfortable with theoretical issues of this kind.

In a series of important papers, culminating in his book entitled *The Mathematical Foundations of Quantum Mechanics* (1944), von Neumann showed that two different theories, Erwin Schrödinger's wave mechanics and Werner Heisenberg's matrix mechanics, are equivalent. His work on the mathematical foundations of quantum theory had brought him into the small, closely knit circle of theoretical physicists, and so he shared from the beginning an awareness of the technological possibilities of the energy which could be generated by nuclear fission.

The first self-sustaining nuclear chain reaction was produced by a group of physicists headed by Enrico Fermi in Chicago on December 2, 1942. It was not until spring of 1943 that physicists and mathematicians were summoned to Los Alamos, New Mexico, where the Manhattan Project, charged with developing an atom bomb, had established a research laboratory. Von Neumann was already engaged in scientific defense work, particularly in connection with the motions of compressible gases, but he did not arrive at Los Alamos until the fall of 1943. His contributions to the work at Los Alamos were substantial. He assisted in the development of a method of implosion and a means of calculating the characteristics of nuclear explosions.

Prior to and during the Manhattan Project, von Neumann became interested in problems of turbulence, general dynamics of continua, and meteorological calculation. Because these problems took too long to calculate even with the assistance of desk calculators, he became convinced that progress in developing electronic computing machines was essential.

The issue of who deserves the credit and patents for inventing the computer is complex and hotly debated. According to his colleague Stanislaw Ulam, von Neumann's contribution to the development of the computer was that he formulated the methods of translating mathematical procedures into a language of instructions for a computing machine. He developed the idea of a universal set of circuits in the machine, "a flow diagram," and a "code," or fixed set of connections which could solve a great variety of problems. Prior to that, each problem required a special and different set of wiring in order to perform operations in a given sequence. When von Neumann was awarded the Fermi Prize of the Atomic Energy Commission, he was especially cited for his work on using electronic computing machines.

After World War II, von Neumann was increasingly called upon to act as an adviser to the government. From the perspective of the peace movement of the 1960's and 1970's, the arms race between the United States and the Soviet Union seemed irresponsible and inhumane. In the 1940's and 1950's, the very vivid memories of World War II contributed to the intense anti-Soviet atmosphere of the Cold War. After the Soviet Union tested its own atom bomb, von Neumann supported work on the hydrogen bomb in order to maintain American ascendancy in the arms race. Unlike the physicist Edward Teller and Lewis Strauss, one of the commissioners of the Atomic Energy Commission, von Neumann insisted upon limiting his role to that of a technical expert; he resisted pressures to join scientists who publicly supported banning nuclear tests; he also engaged in political lobbying in support of development of the hydrogen bomb.

In 1954, when J. Robert Oppenheimer, formerly the director of the Manhattan Project, was attacked as a security risk and hearings concerning his loyalty were conducted, von Neumann expressed complete confidence in Oppenheimer's integrity and loyalty. He acknowledged that their views concerning the importance of developing the hydrogen bomb differed, but he unequivocally opposed the political harassment of scientists. In October, 1954, the president offered von Neumann a position on the United States Atomic Energy Commission. According to his friend Stanislaw Ulam, von Neumann was flattered and proud that he, even though foreign-born, would be entrusted with such responsibility, but he was concerned about the Oppenheimer affair. Convinced that work on the commission was of great national importance, he accepted the post. In a written statement prepared for the hearing before the Special Senate Committee on Atomic Energy, which took place on January 31, 1946, von Neumann stated that "science has outgrown the age of independence from society." Observing that the combination of politics and physics could render the earth uninhabitable, he commented that regulation is necessary in both spheres. Restricting himself as a scientist to the scientific, he supported health and safety measures and protection by government police power, but unequivocally asserted the importance of freedom of information: "There must, however, be no restriction in principle on research in any part of science, and none in nuclear physics in particular, and absolutely no secrecy or possibility of classification of the results of fundamental research."

A proponent of armament during the Cold War, von Neumann incorrectly predicted a massive war between the United States and the Soviet Union immediately after World War II; still, he accurately foresaw that the Soviet Union would take control of Eastern European countries, including his native Hungary, and crush all opposition to Communism.

In the summer of 1955, von Neumann slipped in a corridor and injured his left shoulder. Diagnosis of the injury revealed that he had bone cancer. During this illness, he surprised his Jewish colleagues by consulting a Catholic priest, but it is likely that he had received instruction in Catholicism at the time of his first marriage. Until the last, he continued to function as a member of the Atomic Energy Commission; he also worked on a number of projects, including the texts for the honorary Silliman lectures to be given at Yale. The painful nature of his illness prevented him from concentrating with his accustomed intensity. He was forced to leave the lectures entitled *The Computer and the Brain* unfinished, but they were published posthumously in 1958.

Summary

When von Neumann answered a questionnaire in 1954 distributed by the National Academy of Science, which asked him to name his three most important contributions to mathematics, he identified his work on the rigorous formulation of quantum theory as one of those three. His papers on this topic represent one-third of his total work. As his most important contributions, von Neumann selected his work on the mathematical foundations of quantum theory and ergodic theorems and his theory of operators. In making this selection, von Neumann may have been motivated by a keen desire to maintain the importance of mathematics on a conceptual level in solving the problems of the physical sciences. Von Neumann's interest in the development of the electronic computing machine was prompted in part by the need for swift answers to problems in mathematical physics and engineering. Later, he pioneered in the use of computing machines to assist in weather prediction. In addition to working on the mathematics of weather prediction, he believed that control over climate might one day be possible.

Von Neumann was essentially the creator of game theory, a new branch of mathematics. He later coauthored a treatise with Oskar Morgenstern, *Theory of Games and Economic Behavior* (1944), which attempts to schematize mathematically the economic exchange of goods and to solve problems concerning monopoly, oligopoly, and free competition.

In his theory of automata, an area of study in which von Neumann was a pioneer, he effectively demonstrated that in principle it is possible to build machines which can reproduce themselves. His posthumously published lectures, *The Computer and the Brain* (1958), return to these problems and draw upon ideas and terminology from mathematics, electrical engineering, and neurology to outline a theory of representation of logical propositions by electrical networks or nervous systems.

Bibliography

Goldstine, Herman. *The Computer from Pascal to von Neumann*. Princeton, N.J.: Princeton University Press, 1972. A history of the computer, written by a very close and loyal friend of von Neumann.

Heims, Steve J. *John von Neumann and Norbert Wiener: From Mathematics to the Technologies of Life and Death*. Boston: MIT Press, 1980. A biased attack on von Neumann which uses his life as a means of editorializing in favor of a ban on nuclear tests.

Nagy, Dénes, and Ferenc Nagy. "Neumann János." In *Magyarok a természettudomány és technika történetében*, edited by Ferenc Nagy and Dénes Nagy, 215-218, 407-415, 423-449. Budapest: Omikk, 1986. Accurate and useful biographical treatment.

Neumann, John von. *Collected Works*. Edited by A. H. Taub. 6 vols. Elmsford, N.Y.: Pergamon Press, 1961-1963. Standard edition of the works of von Neumann.

Shurkin, Joel. "John von Neumann." In *Engines of the Mind: A History of the Computer*. New York: W. W. Norton and Co., 1984. A survey of the difficulty in ascertaining who deserves credit for the development of the computer, inaccurate concerning von Neumann's life. Opposes Goldstine's view.

Stern, Nancy. "John von Neumann's Influence on Electronic Digital Computing: 1944-1946." *Annals of the History of Computers* 2 (1980): 349-361. Discussion of von Neumann's contribution to the development of the computer.

Ulam, Stanislaw. "John von Neumann." *Bulletin of the American Mathematical Society* 64, no. 3, pt. 2 (1958): 1-49. Biography and highly mathematical assessment of von Neumann's career.

Wigner, Eugene. *Symmetries and Reflections*. Cambridge, Mass.: MIT Press, 1970. Autobiography of Wigner, a friend and colleague of von Neumann.

Jeanie R. Brink

SIMON NEWCOMB

Born: March 12, 1835; Wallace, Canada
Died: July 11, 1909; Washington, D.C.
Area of Achievement: Science
Contribution: Combining intellectual prowess and organizational ability, Newcomb, the best-known American scientist at the turn of the century, revolutionized dynamical astronomy.

Early Life

Although primarily of New England stock, Simon Newcomb was born in Wallace, Nova Scotia, Canada, on March 12, 1835, the elder son of John Burton Newcomb, an itinerant country schoolteacher, and Emily Prince, the daughter of a New Brunswick magistrate. He spent his youth traveling with his father from village to village in Nova Scotia and Prince Edward Island. On reflection, he believed that he had had relatively little formal education, although he had attended his father's schools on occasion. (Newcomb later claimed that scientific geniuses were born, not created through formal education; he may have had his own experience in mind.)

At sixteen, Newcomb was apprenticed to a Dr. Foshay for five years of training in medical botany. After only two years, Newcomb ran away to the United States, having concluded that Foshay was an uneducated quack. Newcomb found employment as a country schoolteacher and tutor in Maryland. A frequent visitor to Washington, D.C., he became acquainted with Joseph Henry, secretary of the Smithsonian Institution, and J. E. Hilgard of the United States Coast Survey. He impressed them with his intellectual prowess; less evident at this point were his abrasiveness and sense of self-importance. Through their recommendations, he gained an audience with the Nautical Almanac Office in Cambridge, Massachusetts. In early 1857, he was appointed astronomical computer with the almanac on a trial basis, entering what he would later call in his autobiography the "world of sweetness and light."

Life's Work

During the next four years, Newcomb increased his sophistication as a mathematical astronomer. Taking advantage of his location and the relatively undemanding responsibilities of a computer, he studied mathematics at Harvard University with Benjamin Peirce, gaining a B.S. degree in 1858. Thereafter, he continued his efforts at self-education. He gained a reputation for industry and the ability to grasp material quickly. A sign of his maturing as a scientist was his election to membership in the American Association for the Advancement of Science in 1859.

Two years later, Newcomb left Cambridge to assume a professorship in mathematics in the United States Navy and an assignment at the Naval Observatory. His initial duty was to take observations with a transit instrument and then to reduce his observations and those of the other astronomers using the instrument. He soon discovered that the Naval Observatory lacked a uniform system of reducing data, making Newcomb's task of combining the data more difficult. This confusing situation revealed to Newcomb the importance of organization to the efficient completion of a scientific endeavor.

During the next sixteen years, Newcomb investigated a number of research problems regarding the sun, moon, and planets, concentrating on the orbit theory. In 1866, he published his theory of Neptune's motion; his tables of the motion of Uranus appeared in 1874, and his treatise on the moon in 1878.

This was also a period of personal and professional change. In 1863, Newcomb married Mary Caroline Hassler. His growing family (he would eventually have three daughters) and the realization that he preferred theoretical mathematical research to observation led him to contemplate a career change. He alternately attempted to become superintendent of the Naval Observatory and to obtain an appointment as a theorist in the Nautical Almanac Office. The navy blocked the former efforts because it wanted a naval officer to run the observatory. His superior at the observatory, having no desire to lose him, offered a compromise: In 1869, Newcomb was relieved of his responsibilities for routine observations so that he could concentrate on the tables of lunar motion. In 1870, he was sent to Europe by the United States government to observe a solar eclipse and to collect additional data from European observations on lunar motion. Newcomb's consultations with some of Europe's leading astronomers confirmed both the significance of the problems he was investigating and the quality of his own work. In September, 1877, he was appointed superintendent of the Nautical Almanac Office, which had, by this time, moved to Washington, D.C.

His major research program for the Nautical Almanac Office was the development of new theories and tables for planetary motion. At first, he funded the program by restructuring the *American Ephemeris and Nautical Almanac*, the primary product of the Nautical Almanac Office, so that it required less calculation, thus freeing up staff. Later, he persuaded Congress to support the research directly. Newcomb divided the program into three separate parts: the four inner planets, Jupiter and Saturn (which were given to George W. Hill), and Uranus and Neptune (which was only an updating of Newcomb's earlier work). It was not until 1895 that the program was essentially completed.

Photographs of the mature astronomer show a large head and a graying beard, usually in need of a trim. Contemporaries describe him as a dominating presence at a scientific meeting. They had many opportunities to see him. He belonged to numerous organizations, astronomical societies, and academies, including the National Academy of Sciences and the American Astronomical Society; he was elected the first president of the latter.

Newcomb authored hundreds of items, among them some widely read popular astronomical works, a text on spherical astronomy, mathematics texts (in the 1880's and 1890's, he taught mathematics at The Johns Hopkins University, becoming a professor in 1884), and papers on psychic research (he was a skeptic) and economics. He even wrote three novels.

In 1897, at the age of sixty-two, he was automatically retired by the navy with the rank of captain, although he continued to work for the Nautical Almanac on a consulting basis. He was promoted to the rank of rear admiral (retired) in 1906. He died on July 11, 1909, in Washington, D.C., and was buried with military honors in Arlington National Cemetery.

Summary

Simon Newcomb began his scientific career at an opportune time. The American scientific community was sufficiently mature and large so that there were jobs available for bright young men, but not so mature or large as to exclude mathematical astronomers who lacked formal educational credentials. For a man of Newcomb's background, the 1850's were the ideal time to start a career.

Newcomb was lucky also because his chosen field of endeavor was reaching the peak of its importance. The predicted discovery of Neptune in 1846 had demonstrated the great power of celestial mechanics. Astronomers were concerned with predicting and determining the position of stars, planets, and the moon. Newcomb was involved in the central astronomical research problem. By the end of the century, however, it was the "new" astronomy, astrophysics, which was the important field. The essential question had become the composition of the stars and planets. Newcomb's work became relatively peripheral.

There was yet a third way in which Newcomb's timing was perfect. With the death of Joseph Henry in 1878, the American scientific community lost its leader. There was no obvious successor. A void had developed which Newcomb consciously attempted to fill over the years, with great success— the product of his visibility as a scientist, his extensive popular writings, and his international reputation.

According to the traditional American success story, the individual who is poor and self-educated gains success through hard work and dedication. Normally, however, the success is in the fields of business or politics. Simon Newcomb proved that it could happen in science.

Bibliography

Clerke, Agnes M. *A Popular History of Astronomy During the Nineteenth Century*. 2d ed. New York: Macmillan, 1887. Still the best overview of the astronomical research of the period. This edition provides a sense of Newcomb's position in international astronomy just prior to the completion of his major research program at the Nautical Almanac.

Dupree, A. Hunter. *Science in the Federal Government: A History of Policies and Activities to 1940*. Cambridge, Mass.: Harvard University Press, 1957. The best survey of scientific activity in the federal government. It places Newcomb's career and the history of the institutions he worked for in a larger context.

Newcomb, Simon. *The Reminiscences of an Astronomer*. Boston: Houghton Mifflin Co., 1903. Still the basic source of information on Newcomb's early life.

Norberg, Arthur L. "Simon Newcomb's Early Astronomical Career." *Isis* 69 (1978): 209-225. A scholarly analysis of Newcomb's life and work through 1870.

_____. "Simon Newcomb's Role in the Astronomical Revolution of the Early Nineteen Hundreds." In *Sky with Ocean Joined: Proceedings of the Sesquicentennial Symposia of the U.S. Naval Observatory*. Edited by Steven J. Dick and LeRoy E. Doggett, 74-88. Washington, D.C.: United States Naval Observatory, 1983. Focuses on Newcomb's research program on planetary tables.

Weber, Gustavus A. *The Naval Observatory: Its History, Activities and Organization*. Baltimore: Johns Hopkins University Press, 1926. Although badly dated, this is the only general history of this institution which covers the entire period of Newcomb's life. It provides unique insight into the bureaucratic structure within which Newcomb functioned.

Marc Rothenberg

REINHOLD NIEBUHR

Born: June 21, 1892; Wright City, Missouri
Died: June 1, 1971; Stockbridge, Massachusetts
Areas of Achievement: Theology and social and political ethics
Contribution: The leading American formulator of Neoorthodox theology, Niebuhr used the political and social arenas to place the Christian faith in the center of the cultural and political world of his day.

Early Life

Reinhold Niebuhr was born June 21, 1892, in Wright City, Missouri, the fourth child of Lydia and Gustav Niebuhr. Lydia was the daughter of an Evangelical Synod missionary, and Gustav was a young minister for the denomination. Reinhold later said that his father was the first formative religious influence on his life, combining a vital personal piety with a complete freedom in his theological training. This combination reflected the stance of the German-originated Evangelical Synod with its "liberal" de-emphasis of doctrine and its stress on heartfelt religion. Although he never exerted pressure, Gustav began early to talk to his son about the ministry, and by the time he was ten Reinhold had made the decision to be a preacher.

In 1902, the Niebuhr family moved to Lincoln, Illinois, where Gustav became pastor of St. John's Church. It was there that Reinhold experienced an incident which he was later to recount as a great influence on his thinking about the nature and destiny of humankind. During a recession, a local grocer for whom Reinhold worked, Adam Denger, had extended considerable credit to a number of unemployed miners. Embarrassed by his generosity and unable to pay him back, many of them moved away without even saying good-bye. Despite Denger's belief that God would protect him if he did what was right, he went bankrupt, and his young assistant, Reinhold, grew up to preach against sentimentality and reliance on special providence.

Niebuhr attended Elmhurst College in Elmhurst, Illinois, and Eden Theological Seminary in St. Louis, Missouri, both Evangelical Synod schools, but he found himself uninterested in any specific academic discipline. While Niebuhr was at Eden in April, 1913, his father, Gustav, suffered an attack of diabetes and died. Niebuhr went on to Yale Divinity School and received his M.A. in 1915, but rather than continue his graduate studies, he chose to accept a parish of the Evangelical Synod.

Life's Work

The board of the Evangelical Synod chose for Niebuhr a newly organized parish in Detroit, Michigan, the location of the Ford Motor Company. That institution came to have a powerful impact on the thinking and actions of Niebuhr taking on symbolic proportions and illustrating the tyranny of power.

Niebuhr experienced the problems common to all young ministers, many of which are told in his delightful *Leaves from the Notebook of a Tamed Cynic* (1929), a kind of diary of his years as parish minister. This book marked the beginning of a transition in Niebuhr's thought which eventually led to a rejection of all the liberal theological ideals with which he had ventured forth in 1915.

He said that the theological convictions he later came to hold began to dawn on him in Detroit

> because the simple little moral homilies which were preached in that as in other cities, by myself and others, seemed completely irrelevant to the brutal facts of life in a great industrial center. Whether irrelevant or not they were certainly futile. They did not change human actions or attitudes in any problem of collective behavior by a hair's breadth.

The problems of collective behavior to which he refers were the extreme working conditions and financial insecurity of the mass of industrial workers, especially employees of the Ford Motor Company, contrasted with the complacency and satisfaction of the middle and upper classes. People from all these groups were found among the membership of Niebuhr's church. He began to agonize about the validity and practicability of the optimistic liberal ideals which he was preaching each week.

Niebuhr's sermons began to contain more and more references to social and political issues, and he became more involved in social activity, speaking on behalf of the industrial workers in Detroit and other cities and lobbying for the formation of labor unions. Although he was not directly involved in World War I, the tragedy of that event led him to join and ultimately to become the head of the pacifist Fellowship of Reconciliation. He was also instrumental in organizing the Fellowship of Socialist Christians in the late 1920's.

In 1928, Henry Sloane Coffin, then president of Union Theological Seminary, offered Niebuhr a teaching post at Union. Although he considered himself inadequately prepared for teaching, particularly theology, he accepted Coffin's offer to teach "just what you think," with his subject area labeled "Applied Christianity." The thin, eagle-eyed, balding minister soon became one of the most sought-after professors on the Union campus as he brought his experiences with world political and religious figures to the campus. He continued to preach, traveling every weekend to colleges and universities around the country, and he continued to take part in an ever-increasing number of religious and secular organizations, besides his full-time teaching.

In 1931, Niebuhr married Ursula Keppel-Compton, daughter of a doctor and niece of an Anglican bishop, who was a student at Union. Ursula shared her husband's political interests and became a great help and collaborator with him in his work. He later acknowledged that his wife was the more diligent student of biblical literature (she taught courses in biblical literature at Barnard College) and that she was responsible for many of his viewpoints.

Niebuhr's theology compelled him to become involved in an extraordinary range of activities. He was a pioneer in the movement for racial justice, strongly supporting the Tenant Farmers' Union and the Conference of Southern Churchmen. He was involved in the work of a cooperative farm in Mississippi, an effort to enable the sharecroppers in the South to improve their conditions. He participated in the World Conference on Church, Community, and State in Oxford in 1937. Later, he worked on the United States Federal Council of Churches. After World War II, he was a key member of the World Council of Churches Commission on a Just and Durable Peace. He made hundreds of transatlantic trips, and his influence became strong in other countries, especially in Britain, where he had many ties.

Just before a worship service during the summer of 1934, Niebuhr casually jotted down a short prayer and used it in the worship. The prayer was, "O God, give us serenity to accept what cannot be changed, courage to change what should be changed, and wisdom to distinguish the one from the other." After the service Niebuhr gave the notes to Chandler Robins, dean of the Cathedral of St. John the Divine, and the "serenity prayer" gradually made its way into the religious folklore of America.

Because of his strenuous schedule in connection with war activities, Niebuhr was near nervous collapse at the end of each school year from 1938 to 1940. Contrary to his doctor's orders, he kept up the pace. His Neoorthodox theology, which he called Christian Realism, led him to conclude that because of humankind's freedom to sin, true sacrificial love could never triumph in history. Nevertheless, it was his belief that this sacrificial love was ultimately right and true, and that this love might be approximated in history to divert or stop the abuse of power.

In February, 1952, Niebuhr suffered several small strokes. He was hospitalized for several weeks, being partially paralyzed on his left side. At last his rigorous schedule was curtailed; he was unable to do any work at all. He spent much of the rest of his nineteen years as an invalid or semi-invalid. Niebuhr continued his writing and made what appearances he could. He officially retired from teaching in 1960, becoming Professor Emeritus at Union and Research Associate at Columbia University's Institute for War and Peace Studies. He died June 1, 1971, one of the most influential thinkers of the twentieth century.

Summary

From the naïve liberalism of 1915 Niebuhr moved toward what he called Christian Realism. The events in which he had become involved forced him to recognize not only the effects of power in society, like that of Ford Motor Company over its thousands of helpless workers, but they also made him painfully aware of the corruption that had been imposed on the Christian norm. When confronted with the brutal realities of the industrialized city of Detroit, he came to realize the inadequacy of liberal thought with its naïve belief in the ultimate goodness of humankind to deal with evil in society. He began first to express his opposition to liberal viewpoints in terms of Marxist politics, but came to the conclusion that Marxism had essentially all the same illusions, again maintaining the ultimate goodness of human beings once capitalism was destroyed. Gradually he articulated his search for an alternative to liberal and orthodox theologies and ethical views. In *Beyond Tragedy* (1937), he focused on the symbol of the Cross of Christ as pivotal in understanding the human situation. While on the surface it appeared that evil had triumphed over the sacrificial love of Jesus, from the eschatological, or "beyond history," vantage point available to Christians, the Cross transcends tragedy.

Perhaps Niebuhr's clearest statement of Christian Realism is found in *The Nature and Destiny of Man* (1949). There he explains the paradox of selfless love, a divine attribute, coming into human society. While the inherent evil of human society prevents the triumph of love in this world, in historical existence, it will triumph in the end. Niebuhr's emphasis is not on a future vindication, although that is essential for his thought. Rather, he focuses on the acting out of sacrificial love by humans. While that love can never be fully embodied in any human motive or action, it was the ultimate standard. Niebuhr saw the possibility of divine love having an impact on history only in a life which ends tragically, the ultimate example being that of Jesus Christ. He threw himself into the exercise of divine love, trying to rectify social and political evils, and in many ways he ended his own life tragically in that pursuit. Theologically there was no preexisting group that fully agreed with him; his ideas were too orthodox for the liberals and too liberal for the orthodox.

Bibliography
Bingham, June. *Courage to Change: An Introduction to the Life and Thought of Reinhold Niebuhr*. New York: Charles Scribner's Sons, 1961. A biographical study of Niebuhr's life as well as a thorough examination of his theology. Bingham, a close friend of Niebuhr, tends to be less than critical, and the lack of footnotes reduces the utility of the volume as a reference work. Nevertheless, an excellent introduction to Niebuhr's life and thought, containing much material not found elsewhere.
Fackre, Grabriel J. *The Promise of Reinhold Niebuhr*. Philadelphia: J. B. Lippincott Co., 1970. A brief (less than one hundred pages) overview of Niebuhr's life and thought, synthesizing many of his views and concepts into a manageable and coherent whole. May serve as a starting point, but

too abbreviated to function as a comprehensive account of Niebuhr's life and thought.

Fox, Richard Wightman. *Reinhold Niebuhr: A Biography*. New York: Pantheon Books, 1985. An extremely well-written biography, reading at times like a good novel yet thorough and critical. Makes extensive use of unpublished materials; meticulously documented throughout. By far the best historical treatment of Niebuhr, though not as strong on theology.

Hofmann, Hans. *The Theology of Reinhold Niebuhr*. New York: Charles Scribner's Sons, 1956. Hofmann traces the development of Niebuhr's theology first by examining his major writings in chronological order, then by structuring his thought into a logical system. Uses lengthy quotations from Niebuhr's works. Marred by failure to relate Niebuhr's thought to his life experiences; still very useful for a clear and comprehensive understanding of his ideas.

Kegley, Charles W., and Robert W. Bretall, eds. *Reinhold Niebuhr: His Religious, Social and Political Thought*. New York: Macmillan Publishing Co., 1956, 1984. A collection of essays which critically interpret all phases of Niebuhr's work. Also contains an important intellectual autobiography by Niebuhr himself. Particularly significant for American studies is Arthur Schlesinger, Jr.'s "Reinhold Niebuhr's Role in American Political Thought and Life." Indispensable volume for Niebuhr studies.

Patterson, Bob E. *Reinhold Niebuhr*. Waco, Tex.: Word Books, 1977. Part of Word's "Makers of the Modern Theological Mind" series, this concise and well-written biography gives a positive interpretation of Niebuhr's thought from a moderate Evangelical viewpoint.

Robertson, D. B. *Reinhold Niebuhr's Works: A Bibliography*. Boston: G. K. Hall and Co., 1979. Rev. ed. Washington, D.C.: University Press of America, 1983. The most complete listing available of Niebuhr's published works, including both books and articles. Also contains a full listing of books about Niebuhr, as well as a large number of articles and dissertations.

Stone, Ronald H. *Reinhold Niebuhr: Prophet to Politicians*. Nashville: Abingdon Press, 1972. Carefully traces and analyzes the stages of Niebuhr's political ethics. Well organized and documented, although tedious at points. Perhaps the best treatment of the development of Niebuhr's theology of Christian Realism as it both shaped and was shaped by his political thought and activities.

Douglas A. Foster

CHESTER W. NIMITZ

Born: February 24, 1885; Fredericksburg, Texas
Died: February 20, 1966; near San Francisco, California
Area of Achievement: The military
Contribution: Nimitz commanded American forces in the Pacific during World War II and played a crucial role in winning the important and difficult Battle of Midway. After the war, he became Chief of Naval Operations.

Early Life

Chester William Nimitz was born on February 24, 1885, in the German immigrant community of Fredericksburg, Texas, the son of Chester B. Nimitz and Anna Henke Nimitz. Although his father had died before he was born and the family was never well-off financially, he enjoyed a happy childhood with his cherished and hardworking mother and his not-so-hardworking but happy-go-lucky stepfather (who was also his uncle), William Nimitz. Perhaps the most important male influence on the boy, however, was that of his grandfather, Charles Henry Nimitz, who filled his mind with tales of nautical adventure. Despite such talk of the sea, Nimitz's ambition as a teenager was to become a soldier, so impressed was he by officers from the Army post at Fort Sam Houston. There were no vacancies at West Point, however, so he attended the United States Naval Academy instead, and was graduated on January 30, 1905, seventh in a class of 114.

Blond and handsome, kindly and humorous, above all capable of laughing at himself when the need arose, young Nimitz was prime material for a happy marriage; yet nuptials did not occur until April 9, 1913, when he wed Catherine B. Freeman of Wollaston, Massachusetts. They had four children: Catherine (born 1914), Chester (born 1915), Anna (born 1919), and Mary (born 1931).

Life's Work

Nimitz's early interests were in engineering and submarines. During World War I, he served on an oiler and also with the submarines, ending the war as a lieutenant commander. In the postwar period, he had the usual kinds of assignments that rising officers enjoyed: attendance at the Naval War College, teaching in ROTC, service with battleships, and command of a cruiser. He never became an aviator, a fact that might have caused problems for a lesser man during World War II, when he was called upon to command an aircraft carrier–oriented fleet. Nimitz became an admiral in 1938 and in 1939 took charge of the Bureau of Navigation, the office that controlled personnel assignments.

This latter post gave him access to President Franklin D. Roosevelt, who, along with almost everyone else, took a liking to the new admiral. In early 1941, Roosevelt offered Nimitz command of the Pacific Fleet, but he declined because of lack of seniority—a lucky move: Had he accepted the offer, he, instead of Admiral Husband E. Kimmel, might have had to take the blame for the disaster at Pearl Harbor later that same year.

After the invasion at Pearl Harbor, Kimmel was dismissed and Nimitz was named to replace him as Commander in Chief Pacific (CINCPAC), as of December 31, 1941. From his desk in Pearl Harbor, Nimitz would lead all the American forces, Army as well as Navy and Marines, in the North, Central, and South Pacific areas; he also was in direct command of all naval units in those areas by virtue of wearing a different hat. Thus, in a sense, he was his own boss, being both theater commander and theater naval chieftain. This arrangement worked well, but did not eliminate all command problems in the war against Japan.

One of Nimitz's difficulties was with General Douglas MacArthur, commander of the Southwest Pacific Area (SWPA). MacArthur wanted his theater to be the scene of the principal thrust against Japan, even if that meant reducing Nimitz's activity to nothing. Probably MacArthur would have been happiest if Nimitz and his theater had been put under SWPA command. The Navy Department would never have allowed either the lesser or the greater of MacArthur's ambitions to come true, but Nimitz had to operate throughout the war with the knowledge that the Army in general, and MacArthur in particular, wanted a greater share of material and command.

Nimitz also had to contend with his own boss, Admiral Ernest J. King, Chief of Naval Operations and Commander in Chief of all American warships around the world. King was a ferocious man, just as harsh as Nimitz was kindly, and he worried about CINCPAC's aggressiveness. King thought that Nimitz might not be willing to dismiss those who fell short of perfection; he also wondered at first about Nimitz's willingness to take enormous risks in fighting the Japanese. Perhaps the real problem was that King could not resist the temptation to become personally involved in running the Pacific war. Another thing that bothered King about Nimitz was the latter's reluctance to do battle against MacArthur. King was responsible for upholding the Navy's prerogatives in the face of demands from his equals in the highest councils of war—the British, the Army, and the Army Air Forces; therefore, he could not afford to be affable, or so he seems to have reckoned. Nimitz, on the other hand, outranked all the generals and admirals in his own theater and was not in a position to thwart MacArthur's plans directly; he, therefore, could approach the war in a more genial frame of mind. For all that, King and Nimitz made a good team, each compensating for the other's rare moments of bad judgment.

Since Nimitz was tied for the most part to his desk, the battles in his theater were conducted either by commanders at sea or on the invaded islands:

Admirals Frank Jack Fletcher, William F. Halsey, and Raymond A. Spruance, and Marine Generals A. Archer Vandegrift and Holland M. Smith, among others. Nevertheless, as Commander in Chief, Nimitz bore the ultimate responsibility for their campaigns, except insofar as King himself sometimes determined the overall strategy—and except for the times when Halsey's services were lent to MacArthur.

Undoubtedly, the most important battle in which Nimitz's role was most personal and crucial was that fought near the island of Midway. The Pacific Fleet was much inferior to that of Japan, and so it was vital for the Americans, if they were to hold Midway, to know what the Japanese intended to do. Fortunately, Nimitz could tap the resources of a brilliant cryptologist, Lieutenant Commander Joseph J. Rochefort, Jr., who had recently broken the Japanese naval code and thereby was able to predict the enemy's plan. It was Nimitz himself, however, who had to decide whether to believe Rochefort's evidence, and it was also Nimitz who next had to convince a headstrong King that Rochefort was right. Even after that, there were plans to be made and risks to be taken. It was Nimitz who decided not to use the United States' elderly battleships in the coming fight because they would only get in the way; a nonaviator, he nevertheless put his faith in his aircraft carriers. It was Nimitz who decided on the deployment of those carriers, although Fletcher and Spruance were in command afloat. The result of all these plans and decisions, along with the skill and luck of those on the scene, was an overwhelming American victory, one of the great turning points of the war.

Nimitz was farther removed from the controls during the battles on and around Guadalcanal in August and November, 1942. These were King's pet projects, and conducted on the scene by the South Pacific commanders, who reported to Nimitz. Though close victories, they served to confirm the verdict of Midway: From then on, it was not a question of whether the United States would win the war against Japan but of how soon and at what cost. If Nimitz took too long or spent too much American blood, the public might demand that MacArthur be given the lion's share of men, material, and tasks. Nimitz was responsible more than any other single person for the fact that his forces moved ahead as rapidly as they did and, for the most part, with no more bloodshed than necessary. His campaigns in the Gilberts, the Marshalls, the Marianas, Iwo Jima, and Okinawa were all successful. During the reconquest of the Philippines, however, Nimitz was in general an onlooker: Halsey still reported to him but was operating according to MacArthur's plan. Thus, there was no unity of command during the Battle of Leyte Gulf (October 23-26, 1944); the only common commander of all American forces at Leyte was President Roosevelt himself. Nimitz did intervene once in order to correct an unfortunate move by Halsey.

World War II ended with Nimitz and MacArthur accepting Japan's surrender, both of them now wearing the five stars of the new American ranks, respectively Fleet Admiral and General of the Army; this was an honor shared by only five other officers as of V-J Day.

On December 15, 1945, Nimitz succeeded King as Chief of Naval Operations. It was a time of demobilization, but the biggest issue facing the new chief was that of unification of the services. Although CINCPAC's joint command had worked well, and although command disunity had bedeviled the Leyte Gulf campaign, Nimitz nevertheless agreed with most Navy men in objecting to unification on the national level. Sailors feared that the new Air Force might try to take over the Navy's aerial component, while the Army, having lost its airplanes, might attempt to seize control of the Marine Corps as compensation. Yet when Congress "unified" the services in 1947, the Navy Department retained its airplanes and the Marines. Nimitz deserves some of the credit for his department's victory: He had made himself welcome at the White House of President Harry S Truman, a man who, unlike Roosevelt, had originally favored the Army.

Although five-star officers do not retire in the usual sense, Nimitz nevertheless went off active duty in December, 1947. In 1949, however, Truman offered to reappoint him as Chief of Naval Operations in the wake of the so-called Admirals' Revolt against the Defense Department, an incident touched off by Navy–Air Force rivalry. What Truman wanted was a conciliator, but Nimitz declined the offer. Instead, he spent his retirement as regent of the University of California, as United Nations plebiscite administrator for Kashmir (1949-1950), and as roving ambassador for the United Nations (1950-1952). In the late 1950's, he helped E. B. Potter edit an important textbook of naval history, *Sea Power: A Naval History* (1960).

By 1965, Nimitz was suffering from osteoarthritis and pneumonia; the latter had bothered him off and on for many years despite his generally robust condition. Strokes and heart failure followed, and he died in San Francisco on February 20, 1966.

Summary

Despite King's occasional misgivings, Nimitz's career proves that nice guys do not necessarily finish last. He fully deserved his elevation to five-star rank for his all-important role in the Battle of Midway and his more distant but still vital part in subsequent American Pacific victories. His postwar services also justified the honor. Although he disliked controversy, and therefore did not subsequently write his memoirs or even allow a biography in his lifetime, he nevertheless was able to carry out the duties of a great commander without inordinate displays of ego or temper. Whether such a pleasant man could have held off the War Department and the British in Washington during World War II is another question, but perhaps the American Joint Chiefs of Staff and the Anglo-American Combined Chiefs of Staff would have benefitted from his reasonable and amiable presence. He was too quiet a man to make good "copy" for the press, as was the case with some other famous World War II commanders, but he achieved as much greatness or more.

Bibliography

Buell, Thomas B. *Master of Sea Power: A Biography of Fleet Admiral Ernest J. King*. Boston: Little, Brown and Co., 1980. This book does not rank with Potter's biography of Nimitz (see below), but it is quite worthwhile and helps the reader to see Nimitz from the point of view of Washington and London.

Dull, Paul S. *The Imperial Japanese Navy, 1941-1945*. Annapolis, Md · Naval Institute Press, 1970. This is a highly successful attempt to see the war in the Pacific from the Japanese Navy's viewpoint.

James, Dorris Clayton. *The Years of MacArthur: Volume II, 1941-1945*. Boston: Houghton Mifflin Co., 1975. A gigantic, brilliant biography. James accomplishes the nearly impossible: He provides a balanced, fair treatment of one of America's most controversial leaders.

Morison, Samuel E. *The Two-Ocean War: A Short History of the United States Navy in the Second World War*. Boston: Little, Brown and Co., 1963. Admiral Morison, himself a professional historian, oversaw the production of the Navy's multivolume official history of World War II; this is a one-volume distillation of that effort.

Potter, E. B. *Nimitz*. Annapolis, Md.: Naval Institute Press, 1976. This is a long but well-written, authoritative, and masterful biography by an eminent naval historian. It is by far the most important source for any sketch of Nimitz's life.

Potter, E. B., and Chester W. Nimitz, eds. *Sea Power: A Naval History*. Englewood Cliffs, N.J.: Prentice-Hall, 1960. A useful textbook covering all the history of naval warfare.

Prange, Gordon W., Donald M. Goldstein, and Katherine V. Dillon. *Miracle at Midway*. New York: McGraw-Hill Book Co., 1982. One of Prange's posthumous books, perhaps a bit flawed because it was put together after his death; nevertheless, it provides interesting and dramatically told insights concerning Nimitz's most famous battle.

Spector, Ronald H. *Eagle Against the Sun*. New York: Free Press, 1985. A well-balanced, well-written, and up-to-date account of the Pacific war by a highly respected, rising young historian.

Karl G. Larew

RICHARD M. NIXON

Born: January 9, 1913; Yorba Linda, California

Areas of Achievement: Government and diplomacy

Contribution: A realist in foreign policy, Nixon renewed American relations with the People's Republic of China, achieved détente with the Soviet Union, and ended the United States' involvement in Vietnam. Ironically, because of his "Watergate coverup," he aroused public and congressional opposition to the "imperial presidency."

Early Life

Richard Milhous Nixon was born in Yorba Linda, in Southern California, on January 9, 1913, the son of Francis A. Nixon and Hannah Milhous Nixon. "Frank" Nixon was a small businessman, and Richard as a boy worked in the family store, driving into Los Angeles early each morning to buy fruits and vegetables and then going on to school. He attended public schools, was graduated from Whittier College in 1934, and from Duke University's law school in 1937. As a young man Nixon was above average in height, strong, but slender, weighing a little more than 150 pounds. His most prominent physical characteristics were and would remain a prominent, "ski-slide," nose, a dark beard despite frequent shaving, and a rather stiff manner. Despite a good record in law school, he found no job in New York City or even with the Federal Bureau of Investigation, which may have made him wary of the "Eastern Establishment." He practiced law in California from 1937 to 1942, in 1940 marrying Thelma Catherine "Pat" Ryan. They had two daughters, Patricia and Julie. Soon after the United States entered World War II, Nixon, a Quaker, became a lawyer with the Office of Price Administration but in the summer of 1942 joined the United States Navy and served as a transportation officer in the South Pacific. He was released from active duty as a lieutenant commander.

Life's Work

In 1946 Nixon ran as a Republican for United States representative from the Twelfth District of California, winning after a harsh campaign. Reelected in 1948, in 1950 he sought a senate seat from California, defeating the popular Helen Gahagan Douglas after another controversial campaign. In both house and senate, Nixon's record was one of moderate conservatism but also one of strident anticommunism, which fitted America's mood in the early Cold War. He helped secure the conviction of Alger Hiss for perjury in a case which made Nixon famous. He won the Republican nomination for vice president in 1952 largely because his youth, his "hard line" position, and his being from the West balanced the presidential candidate, General Dwight D.

Eisenhower. Nixon found himself to be vice president in charge of the Republican Party because of Eisenhower's wish to remain above partisan politics. He relished his trips abroad for Eisenhower, to Asia, Latin America, and the Soviet Union. He was again a controversial campaigner in 1956 because of his harsh attacks on opponents. Admired by party regulars because of his faithful partisan services, Nixon easily secured the Republican nomination for president in 1960. Nixon lost to Senator John F. Kennedy, probably because of televised debates in which Nixon showed his exhaustion from campaigning while Kennedy gained an image of vigor and competence. The margin of defeat was extremely narrow in the popular vote—119,000 out of 68,838,000 cast—but 303 to 219 electoral votes.

Nixon then practiced law in California, seeking the governorship in 1962 but losing to Edmund G. Brown. He again became controversial by bitterly attacking the press after the election, in effect accusing its people of deliberately defeating him. Moving to New York, he joined a Wall Street law firm, becoming a partner in 1964. With the overwhelming defeat that year of Senator Barry Goldwater, Nixon again became a major contender for the presidential nomination. He continued to travel widely abroad, meeting important leaders, and maintained his political contacts, campaigning for many Republican candidates in 1966. In 1968 he again won the presidential nomination and defeated Vice President Hubert Humphrey by 510,000 popular votes out of 63,160,000 cast for the two men, and by 301 to 191 electoral votes, probably because of public disillusionment with the Democrats' handling of the Vietnam War and their catastrophically divided presidential convention.

As president, Nixon was most interested in foreign policy, commenting that a competent cabinet could look after the country. Reflecting his moderate conservatism, his administration did nothing about civil rights except to oppose some laws already enacted, sought to win Southern segregationists into the Republican Party, stressed "law and order" issues, tried to shift some emphasis to state and local government through revenue sharing, sought reform of the welfare system, and took some steps toward environmental protection. Strangely, it did not cut down "big government" much or reduce tax burdens. Vice President Spiro T. Agnew and Attorney General John Mitchell became especially controversial because of Agnew's attacks on the "media" and Mitchell's recommending one questionable nominee for the Supreme Court and then one unsuitable one. The Senate rejected both. The administration was also hurt by its changing responses to "stagflation," a new term for a slowing economy with continued inflation, a situation created by the Vietnam War and then by a sudden oil price rise because Arab states were angry at the American aided Israeli victory in the Yom Kippur War of 1973. Nixon's task was made no easier by his facing a Congress controlled by Democrats.

Nixon revealed his foreign policy position by appointing as his chief adviser Dr. Henry A. Kissinger of Harvard University. Kissinger, a student of *Realpolitik*, fitted Nixon's own wish for realism. Nixon had shed his earlier bitter anticommunism and also recognized the fact that because of the Vietnam War Americans would no longer support endless intervention abroad. Seeking to end United States involvement in Vietnam without South Vietnam's collapsing, he bombed and invaded Cambodia, helped a South Vietnamese invasion of Laos, and tried "Vietnamization," a massive buildup of South Vietnam's armed forces accompanied by the withdrawal of many thousands of United States troops. He later intensified United States bombing of North Vietnam and ordered the mining of its major harbors, all this to apply sufficient pressure for a peace settlement. His reelection in 1972 left North Vietnam only Nixon to deal with, and in January, 1973, the United States and North Vietnam signed an agreement which ended the United States' involvement in Vietnam but which was so loosely worded that the war never really ended and South Vietnam fell in 1975.

With the Soviet Union Nixon concluded agreements for grain sales and, most important, arms limitation. A 1972 agreement, called the "strategic arms limitation treaty" (SALT I), limited antiballistic missiles and, in effect, granted to two superpowers equality in nuclear weapons. By warning the Soviet government and ordering a middle-level alert of United States armed forces, Nixon may also have kept the Soviet Union from intervening in the Middle East during the Yom Kippur War. Nixon's major foreign policy triumph was his 1972 trip to Beijing, China, and meetings with Mao Tse-tung and Chou En-lai. While Nixon and Kissinger could not solve all the problems between the two countries, the renewal of contact led ultimately to the renewal of Chinese-American diplomatic relations, which had ended in 1949. Nixon also paved the way for a renewal of American trade with China, which aided China in its modernization. Chinese-American relations may also have restrained some Soviet actions. The only exceptions to a record of sound diplomacy were Nixon's aiding the overthrow and murder of Chilean President Salvador Allende in 1973 and his support for Pakistan despite its murderous behavior toward its own people in East Pakistan as the latter broke away to become Bangladesh.

Nixon was overwhelmingly reelected in 1972, defeating Senator George McGovern by 520 to 17 electoral votes and by 47,170,000 to 29,170,000 popular votes. Public opinion polls revealed massive approval of Nixon's foreign policy, especially detente and relations with China, but fairly strong disapproval of his handing of domestic matters. Unfortunately, high officials in the Nixon campaign sponsored or allowed a burglary of the national Democratic headquarters in the Watergate building. This was probably a symptom of the Administration's atmosphere, one of near siege, of feeling surrounded by enemies and of sharing Nixon's demand for overwhelming reelection as a vindication of himself. There was also a rejection by "Middle America" of everything that McGovern allegedly stood for: left-wing liberalism and the "counterculture" of the 1960's. When others tried to cover up their roles in "Watergate," Nixon himself became involved in the "cover-up." Tape recordings made of conversations in the president's office, intended to be the basis of a historical record, proved Nixon's role in attempted deception. About to be impeached by the House of Representatives, Nixon resigned the presidency on August 9, 1974; he was the first president in the United States' history to do so. Earlier, Vice President Agnew, himself under indictment, had resigned, and under the new Twenty-fifth Amendment, Nixon had appointed Representative Gerald R. Ford, who thus became president after Nixon.

In retirement, first at San Clemente, California, and later at Saddle River, New Jersey, Nixon was quiet for a time and then began to travel again, to Europe and twice to China. With the help of able assistants, he produced four books in addition to his memoirs: *The Real War* (1980), *Leaders* (1982), *Real Peace* (1984), and *No More Vietnams* (1985). He also took part in a number of televised interviews, entertained members of the press, and with other former presidents represented the United States at the funeral of assassinated Egyptian President Anwar el-Sadat in 1981. He was in general silent on President Gerald Ford, critical of President Jimmy Carter, and supportive of President Ronald Reagan. His books reveal a mixture of a wish for lasting world peace and a hard-line approach toward the Soviet Union.

Summary

In some ways, Nixon represented millions of post–World War II Americans: Well educated, he was a professional man and also a veteran who wanted to succeed in life and also build a better world for his family. He was highly ambitious, driven by the example of his father, who never really succeeded, but also controlled by his mother's example of piety and manipulativeness. He thus created the public image of a patriotic young man of ambition but decency. As such, he was repeatedly elected to public office but was sometimes defeated and was always suspect to millions of voters. Behind the public image remained the real man who revealed himself occasionally: remote, lonely, under tremendous stress in his drive to succeed, and angry at those who opposed him. When, during the Watergate crisis, this inner person was revealed, there was public shock and his defenders melted away. He had built up presidential power and prestige, and there arose opposition to what was named the "imperial presidency." His legacy, aside from foreign policy successes, was one of increased public distrust of government.

Bibliography
Brodie, Fawn M. *Richard Nixon: The Shaping of His Character*. New York: W. W. Norton and Co., 1981. The best attempt at a "psychobiography,"

based on exhaustive interviews with relatives, classmates, and others; connects Nixon's character with his behavior in office.

Evans, Rowland, Jr., and Robert D. Novak. *Nixon in the White House: The Frustration of Power*. New York: Random House, 1971. A critical but penetrating analysis of the Nixon Administration's early successes and errors, on a case-by-case basis, ranging from appointments to legislative strategy.

Kissinger, Henry A. *White House Years*. Boston: Little, Brown and Co., 1979.

_____. *Years of Upheaval*. Boston: Little, Brown and Co., 1982. These two volumes form a highly personal account of Nixon's foreign policy by his chief adviser and secretary of state. Egocentric, reluctant to admit errors or even his ignorance of parts of the globe, Kissinger subtly places himself ahead of the president.

Nixon, Richard M. *Leaders*. New York: Warner Books, 1982. A superb example of Nixon's later writings, highly egocentric and revealing Nixon's wish to be seen as a pragmatist with ideals, who knew and dealt with so many great men. Especially revealing is Nixon's treatment of Winston Churchill and Charles de Gaulle.

_____. *RN: The Memoirs of Richard Nixon*. New York: Grosset and Dunlap, 1978. Revealing even when they try to conceal, as in refusing to admit guilt for Watergate or the cover-up, these offer Nixon's version of what he wants as his public image. Emphasizes his parents' positive qualities, his own struggles, but above all the presidency, Nixon overstating his administration's achievements.

_____. *Six Crises*. Garden City, N.Y.: Doubleday and Co., 1962. Memoirs of Nixon in the Congress and the vice presidency, including the Checkers speech, trips abroad, and defeat for the governorship of California.

Safire, William. *Before the Fall*. Garden City, N.Y.: Doubleday and Co., 1975. An "insider's account" which covers such conversations as Nixon's comments on trips to China and Russia, and internal struggles within the Administration.

White, Theodore H. *Breach of Faith: The Fall of Richard Nixon*. New York: Atheneum Publishers, 1975. The best account of Watergate, the cover-up, and Nixon's resignation, based on interviews as well as the presidential tape recordings, and revealing of who in the Administration was how deeply involved.

Wills, Garry. *Nixon Agonistes: The Crisis of the Self-Made Man*. Boston: Houghton Mifflin Co., 1970. Nixon as the self-made man who built flaws in himself, the classical liberal believing in competition, a representative of America itself, placed in the setting of the disorderly decades of the 1950's and 1960's.

Robert W. Sellen

SANDRA DAY O'CONNOR

Born: March 26, 1930; El Paso, Texas

Area of Achievement: Law
Contribution: The first woman to serve as a Supreme Court justice, O'Connor is also known for her keen mind, conservatism, and strict constructionist views.

Early Life
Sandra Day O'Connor was born on March 26, 1930, in El Paso, Texas, to Harry A. and Ada Mae Wilkey Day. The family owned a 155,000-acre ranch in southeastern Arizona, which her grandfather Henry Clay Day established in the 1880's, when Arizona was still a territory. As a youngster, Sandra rode horses, helped with the cattle, and did many things boys did. Because of the ranch's isolation, her parents sent her to El Paso when she was five; there, she lived with her grandmother and attended Radford School, a private school for girls. Because of her love for the ranch, she returned at thirteen to attend school. The nearest school was twenty-two miles away, and commuting meant leaving before daylight and returning in the dark, so the next year she was back at Radford. After a year, she switched to Austin High School and was graduated at age sixteen.

Sandra laid the foundation for her later success at Stanford University. There she majored in economics, earned a B.A. degree with honors in 1950, and went to law school. She earned the LL.B. degree in two years, ranked third out of the 102 students in her class, and was an editor of the *Stanford Law Review*. One of her fellow editors and the top-ranking student in the class was future Supreme Court justice William H. Rehnquist. Another student in the class below hers was John Jay O'Connor. The two married soon after Sandra's graduation in 1952.

During the early years of her marriage, O'Connor accommodated her career to the demands of family life. During her husband's last year of law school, she tried to get a job with a law firm in California but was unsuccessful because of the reluctance of many firms to hire a female attorney. She found government more accepting of women and worked for the first year of her marriage as a deputy attorney for San Mateo County. When John O'Connor was graduated, he worked for three years in Frankfurt, West Germany, in the Judge Advocate General's Corps of the United States Army. His wife joined him in Frankfurt as a civilian quartermaster corps attorney, specializing in contracts. The O'Connors then returned to the Maricopa County/Phoenix area, because its size and growth rate offered opportunities to newcomers, and Sandra had the first of their three children in 1957. The children, all born within six years, were all sons. Scott and Jay attended Stanford and Brian went to Colorado College. For several years, O'Connor worked part-time with a partner in their own law office, and she became active in civic affairs. She served on the Maricopa County Board of Adjustments and Appeals, was on the Governor's Committee on Marriage and Family, worked for the Arizona State Hospital as an administrator, and volunteered for the Salvation Army and a school for minorities. Other volunteer activities with professional implications included acting as a court referee in juvenile cases and making recommendations to the judge, establishing a legal referral service for the county bar, and writing and grading bar exams for the state bar. She also became active in the Republican Party, serving as district chair. By 1965, when she decided to resume her career full-time, O'Connor had an established family, excellent legal credentials, and a variety of experiences in public service. Bright, gracious, and attractive, she was also a hard worker.

Life's Work

Initially, O'Connor's career centered on state government. From 1965 to 1969, she was Arizona's assistant attorney general. She also chaired the Maricopa County Juvenile Detention Home's board of visitors (1966-1968) and served on the Arizona State Personnel Commission (1967-1969). In 1969, Governor Jack Williams appointed her to a vacant seat in the Arizona Senate. As a Republican, she won election to that seat in 1970 and again, easily, in 1972.

In the Arizona senate, O'Connor was known for her careful work, her attention to factual accuracy, and her ability to handle her staff well and get things done. When she became majority leader in 1972, she was the first woman in that post in the United States. Her voting record ranged from moderate to conservative. She favored limiting government spending, restoring the death penalty, and some selected feminist issues. Specifically, she voted for the Equal Rights Amendment and supported revisions in women's protective legislation (such as the maximum hours women were allowed to work), and favored enhanced property rights for women who owned property jointly with their husbands.

She also seemed, on balance, to favor women's right to abortion. For example, she voted, in 1970, to repeal Arizona's laws that essentially made abortion illegal. Later, she opposed a resolution seeking a constitutional ban on abortion, and she opposed an attempt to limit access to abortion. On the other hand, she voted to restrict state funds for poor women's abortions and also supported the right of hospital employees to refuse to perform abortions. This voting record was considered the best indication of her social and political views when the Senate voted to confirm her Supreme Court nomination in 1981.

Meanwhile, in 1974, O'Connor decided on another career change and ran successfully for election as a judge on the Maricopa County Superior Court. On the bench, she acquired a reputation for being both tough and fair. She did not shirk from imposing the death penalty. She also favored open hearings and indicated concern for prison conditions.

O'Connor remained politically active. She was an alternate delegate to the 1972 Republican National Convention and cochaired Richard M. Nixon's reelection committee in Arizona. In 1976, she backed Ronald Reagan in his losing attempt to wrest the nomination from President Gerald Ford.

Her judicial career continued to prosper. In 1979, she won appointment to Arizona's Court of Appeals. Initially, she was regarded as competent but undistinguished. The following summer, however, she attended a judicial conference in England with Chief Justice Warren Burger. She also gained national attention in legal circles when in January, 1981, she participated in a program on federalism and the state courts, in which she expressed her judicial philosophy. She then turned her remarks into an article in the Summer, 1981, issue of *William and Mary Law Review*. She thought that if state courts had already given a matter full and fair treatment, then federal judges should refuse to intervene or hear appeals: In other words, federal and state judges were equally competent.

O'Connor was the right woman at the right moment. To offset criticism of his opposition to the Equal Rights Amendment in 1980, Reagan promised to appoint the first woman to the Supreme Court. Justice Potter Stewart gave him the opportunity when he retired in June, 1981. Reagan chose O'Connor, probably because of her conservative credentials, her strict constructionist views of the Constitution, and her ability to elicit widespread support. The nomination was hailed by senators as ideologically diverse as Barry Goldwater and Edward Kennedy. Feminists anticipated a justice who would support legalized abortion and other issues of the women's movement. The American Bar Association was not overwhelmingly impressed but did say that she met the qualifications. The Senate approved her nomination with ninety-one votes, in time for O'Connor to join the other justices in deciding which cases they would hear during the 1981-1982 term.

During O'Connor's first year on the Court, she made it clear that she was a conservative. She joined conservatives Burger and Rehnquist on sixty-two out of eight-four opinions and opposed those two conservative allies only five times. Her votes paralleled those of fellow Arizonan Rehnquist even more closely. Out of 137 cases, she voted 123 times with Rehnquist. She watched out for and defended states' rights and acted to curb excessive appeals. On five-to-four split decisions, she was with the majority in voiding the death sentence for a sixteen-year-old killer, supporting a procedure making the challenge of public money to parochial schools more difficult, upholding a state law which said that aliens could not work as parole officers, narrowing the double-jeopardy concept to make retrials easier, and supporting affirmative action hiring under Title IX. She was rarely accused of creatively reading into a law what was not explicitly there.

Her private life fit in with her new position. Husband John moved his law practice to Washington, and the couple became popular with Washington society. An athletic person, she regularly played tennis. As the first woman on the Court, she has received many requests to speak but has not spent much time on the lecture circuit or deliberately sought media attention.

During her second year on the Supreme Court, feminist enthusiasm for O'Connor cooled. She did split with her conservative allies in eliminating pension plans that failed to offer women equity with men, but she disappointed feminists when she refused to allow her pension-plan decision to become retroactive. She also disappointed prochoice advocates when she supported the minority opinion to uphold a series of local laws curbing women's access to abortion. Given the fact that abortion is legal in the United States as a result of a Supreme Court decision, not federal legislation, her abortion views caused major concern.

O'Connor is still very much a part of the conservative faction, but some observers think that they detect a growing self-confidence and independence. Two of her decisions reflect a concern for minority rights. First, she joined the majority in limiting peremptory challenges to exclude minority jurors when the defendant is the same minority. Second, she argued that if a crime is interracial (black defendant, white victim), then prospective jurors could be questioned on racial bias if the death penalty is involved. Although showing some signs of moving toward the center, O'Connor has most often voted with Rehnquist and Burger.

Summary

As the first woman on the Supreme Court, Sandra Day O'Connor has acted much as any conservative male justice might have done. It is difficult to attribute any aspect of her judicial record to her being female. Yet, if she had not been a woman, she probably would not have been appointed to the Court. Her judicial experience simply was not that extensive or outstanding, yet she was undeniably competent, and her appeal was bolstered by political connections and a personal friendship with Justice Rehnquist. Timing was also a factor. The women's movement was prominent enough to make an issue out of the fact that no woman had ever before served on the Court, and Reagan needed a feminist issue in 1980. If her decisions have not always been to the liking of feminists, she has in other ways been an excellent role model for women in general.

Bibliography
Kerr, Virginia. "Supreme Court Justice O'Connor: The Woman Whose Word Is Law." *Ms.* 11 (December, 1982): 52, 80, 82-84. An in-depth analy-

sis of O'Connor's decisions during her first year on the Supreme Court from a feminist perspective. The author finds O'Connor ambivalent on feminist issues—favoring some and opposing others—but expresses the hope that O'Connor will turn out to be a feminist.

Lacayo, Richard. "Establishing Her Independence." *Time* 127 (May, 1986): 85. O'Connor's relatively low public profile has not generated much media attention. Authors keep trying to find some signs of independence to make a story. This is a 1986 attempt. Also reviews some of her key 1985-1986 decisions.

Lewis, Neil A. "Justice O'Connor's First Six Months." *The New Republic* 186 (March, 1982): 17. Contains some incisive observations on the confirmation hearing and early court decisions.

Press, Aric, and Diane Camper. "The Court's New Tough Guy." *Newsweek* 99 (June, 1982): 69-70. Gives a brief summary of O'Connor's first year on the Court.

"Sizing Up Ms. Justice." *Newsweek* 102 (July, 1983): 57. A brief article that outlines certain O'Connor decisions which disillusioned feminists.

Weil, Denie S. "Personal Priorities." *Working Woman* 11 (January, 1986): 89-91, 114-115. The thrust of this article is how O'Connor successfully combined family and career responsibilities.

Woods, Harold, and Geraldine Woods. *Equal Justice: A Biography of Sandra Day O'Connor*. Minneapolis: Dillon Press, 1985. A brief, laudatory biography aimed at the adolescent reader.

Judith Ann Trolander

JAMES EDWARD OGLETHORPE

Born: December 22, 1696; London, England
Died: June 30, 1785; Cranham Hall, Essex, England
Area of Achievement: Colonization
Contribution: With his social vision, promotional genius, military ability, and personal guidance, Oglethorpe established the colony of Georgia and frustrated the Spanish effort to push the British out of southeastern North America.

Early Life

James Edward Oglethorpe was born in London, the seventh and last child of Sir Theophilus and Lady Eleanor Wall Oglethorpe, two Jacobites who surrounded young Oglethorpe with intrigue and endowed him with the family's strong moral courage, conviction, loyalty to the crown, and military and parliamentary tradition. Oglethorpe received the education of an English gentleman, first at Eton and then at Corpus Christi College, Oxford, where Jacobite sentiment was strong. Oglethorpe then held a commission in the British army but resigned to join Prince Eugene of Savoy in fighting the Turks. He gained a reputation for military prowess at the Battle of Belgrade (1717). After a brief Jacobite flirtation at Saint Germain, France, where his widowed mother and sisters attended the pretender James III (also known in history as James the Old Pretender), Oglethorpe returned to the family estate of Westbrook at Godalming in Surrey. The move ended his Jacobite interest.

In 1722, Oglethorpe was elected to Parliament, succeeding his father and two elder brothers as representative for Haslemere, a seat he would hold for thirty-two years. In Parliament, Oglethorpe shook off suspicions about his Jacobitism. He won respect for integrity and hard work, and, more important, for his ambitions and interests, he cultivated several powerful friends. In Parliament, Oglethorpe opposed royal extravagance and the machinations of Robert Walpole and advocated naval preparedness, mercantile and colonial expansion, relief for the oppressed, and, later, the Industrial Revolution. Oglethorpe's humanitarianism, probably a product of his family's high-mindedness, first appeared in *The Sailor's Advocate* (1728), an anonymously published pamphlet attacking the Royal Navy's practice of impressment. The pamphlet went through eight editions. Throughout his life, Oglethorpe also professed antislavery beliefs. It was Oglethorpe's interest in penal conditions, however, that led him to his life's work.

Life's Work

In 1729, Oglethorpe was named chairman of a committee to inquire into the state of England's jails. In three reports issued in 1730, the committee cataloged the abuses of debtors' prisons. The reports electrified the public, in part because of their lurid detail and in part because such exposés were rare in an indifferent age. Oglethorpe's investigation convinced him that the nation and the debtors would be better served by settling the debtors in British colonies. There they could render service to the Crown by colonizing and defending new territory and producing crops and other goods needed in the mother country, while remaking their own lives. Such an argument was hardly new to England in the eighteenth century, for since the Elizabethan age colonizers had promised similar benefits. What gave Oglethorpe's appeal energy was the renewed public interest generated by his reports on penal conditions and his friendship with such influential men at court and in Parliament as John Lord Viscount Perceval (later the first Earl of Egmont) and Dr. Thomas Bray (founder of several religious and philanthropic societies), who shared his interest in reform and in America.

Oglethorpe, Egmont, and eighteen other associates received a charter in June, 1732, creating the "Trustees for establishing the colony of Georgia in America." The proprietary grant was for a period of twenty-one years, after which the colony would revert to the Crown. The associates benefited from the British government's interest in placing a buffer colony on Carolina's southern frontier to protect against French, Spanish, and Indian attacks and also from its desire to increase imperial trade and navigation. Relief for domestic unemployment was a third consideration, but it lagged behind the former two. Indeed, the interest of defense and the production of exotic crops and naval stores for the mother country so outweighed the humanitarian objective that few debtors were actually recruited for the colony.

Oglethorpe quickly proved himself an energetic promoter for a project that would evoke the most vigorous and extravagant promotional literature in the British North American experience. In 1732, at his own expense, he published *A New and Accurate Account of the Provinces of South Carolina and Georgia*, stressing the commercial and agricultural advantages of the colony. Georgia's strategic position, combined with Oglethorpe's and the Trustees' appeals, helped secure regular financial support from Parliament. When his mother died in 1732, leaving Oglethorpe free of domestic responsibilities, he decided to accompany the first group of settlers to the colony—a move that fundamentally influenced the colony's development.

In November, 1732, Oglethorpe and 116 emigrants set sail for Georgia on the *Anne*. Arriving in America in January, 1733, after a successful voyage, Oglethorpe directed the settlers to the Savannah River. There he chose the site for the principal city. Oglethorpe conciliated the local Indians, securing from them both a grant for the land and an agreement whereby they would cut their ties to the French and Spanish. He laid out Savannah's distinctive pattern of squares and grids, which dominates the city even today, and then parceled out the land according to the Trustees' system of entailed grants

designed to hold the settler to the soil. The cumbersome land system—
which prohibited the holder from selling his property or bequeathing it to
any but a male heir—would cause much trouble soon enough, but Oglethorpe imposed military discipline on the first settlers. He made a treaty with
the Lower Creeks and fortified the southern reaches of the colony.

In 1734, Oglethorpe set out for England to answer charges that he was
overspending and being uncommunicative. Accompanied by several Indians,
Oglethorpe received an ecstatic public welcome. The press revived interest in
the colony. Strengthened by the public showing, Oglethorpe gained additional support from the Trustees, including new restrictions on the colony
that prohibited the sale of rum and black slavery and regulated the Indian
trade through a licensing system. Meanwhile, Oglethorpe's policy of religious
toleration encouraged other emigrants to join the experiment—a policy that,
in 1734, led a group of Salzburger Lutherans to seek asylum in Georgia.
Other German groups followed, including subsequent contingents of
Salzburgers and Swiss Moravians, and Scotch Highlander Presbyterians came
as well. The British government was cool toward Oglethorpe's efforts to
attract non-British emigrants, but Oglethorpe persisted. The colony needed
people.

It also needed Oglethorpe's attention. Rumors of insurrection drew Oglethorpe back to Georgia in 1735. He brought John and Charles Wesley and a
new batch of settlers with him. The Wesleys soon fell into disputes with
Oglethorpe and the settlers and returned to England. Oglethorpe did better
with George Whitefield, who came later and established an orphanage that
Oglethorpe supported. Oglethorpe found the Georgia government in disarray. Lines of authority were blurred and the Trustees retained essential
power in their hands, but Oglethorpe's unwillingness to delegate authority
hardly helped matters. Oglethorpe further fanned the colony's troubles by
his own intransigence. Vain and unbending, he insisted on enforcing the new
restrictions he brought from London and honoring the Trustees' unpopular
land policy. Traders from South Carolina resented the licensing system for
the Indian trade, farmers chafed at restrictions on establishing a plantation-
style agriculture, and the Spanish complained about Oglethorpe's southward
movement, which included a new settlement at Frederica in 1736 and a fort
on Cumberland Island soon after. In London, malcontents from Georgia told
tales of incompetence and venality in Oglethorpe's administration. Oglethorpe responded by going to London, where he pacified the Trustees and
answered all charges. He returned to Georgia in 1738 with a regiment of soldiers that he had raised at his own expense.

Military matters thereafter preoccupied Oglethorpe in Georgia. With war
between Spain and England imminent, Oglethorpe repaired relations with
the Indians. He persuaded the Chickasaw and Lower Creeks not to join
Britain's enemies should war occur and even settled differences between the

Creeks and Choctaw. He also put down a mutiny among his own men, personally grabbing the ringleaders as they shot at him. When Parliament declared war on Spain in 1739, a war, known as the War of Jenkins' Ear, that eventually became part of the larger War of Austrian Succession, Oglethorpe moved rapidly. He led a futile attack on St. Augustine in 1740, which failed partly from Oglethorpe's indecision. Although personally brave, Oglethorpe had little experience commanding a military expedition. His inability to distinguish between the trivial and the significant—a trait that afflicted his civil administration as well—further embarrassed his campaign. Oglethorpe redeemed his military reputation in 1742 when, in a series of skirmishes known collectively as the Battle of Bloody Marsh, he and his men rebuffed a superior Spanish force invading St. Simon's Island. The Spanish withdrew their army from Georgia, never again to threaten seriously the British presence in North America. In 1743, Oglethorpe made another unsuccessful feint against St. Augustine, but by then Georgia was safe and Oglethorpe's American career was ending.

Civil discontent in the colony had distracted Oglethorpe while he fought to save the empire. Colonists ignored the Trustees' regulations, malcontents launched new campaigns against Oglethorpe and the Trustees in England, and the Moravians left for Pennsylvania rather than bear arms in Georgia's defense. Questions of finance especially nagged Oglethorpe. His own expenses became entangled with those of the colony, for he had borrowed against his English property to pay for Georgia's defense—money for which he would be only partially reimbursed. To add to Oglethorpe's problems, the colony storekeeper had kept poor accounts and made unwarranted expenditures. In 1740, the Trustees limited Oglethorpe's civil responsibilities so that he could concentrate on military matters.

In 1743, Oglethorpe went to England to respond to criticism and to answer charges brought by a subordinate to a court-martial. He was exonerated, but his colonizing days were over. He never returned to America. Georgia was going its own way already. Indicative of Oglethorpe's declining influence in Georgia's future was the Trustees' decision in 1750 to remove the restrictions on rum and slavery and to accept Georgia's development along the lines of South Carolina as a slave-based plantation society.

Oglethorpe married Elizabeth Wright, heiress of Cranham Hall, Essex, in 1744. The match gave him a fortune and the country estate where he lived for the rest of his life. He fought against the Jacobites in 1745, but rumors of his family's Jacobite associations trailed after him and led to charges of misconduct in not pursuing the retreating Jacobites vigorously enough at Lancashire. Oglethorpe was acquitted, but his military career was over. Using an assumed name, however, he did fight on the Continent against the French during the Seven Years' War, and did earn the friendship of William Pitt for his endeavors and promotions to general in 1765. In Parliament, Oglethorpe became something of a liberal Whig free-lance, distrusting the Hanoverian ministers, supporting civil rights for religious dissenters in the Colonies, attacking arbitrary power, and associating with the antislavery movement in England. After he lost his seat in 1754, Oglethorpe retired from public life. Oglethorpe devoted attention to his estate and to literary and artistic circles, where he became friends with Samuel Johnson, James Boswell, David Garrick, Sir Joshua Reynolds, Hannah More, and Edmund Burke, among others. He died in 1785.

Summary

From his earliest colonizing promotionals, Oglethorpe had recognized the place of Georgia in the larger British North American schema. Indeed, imperial considerations of defense and commerce, more than humanitarianism, made Georgia possible. Oglethorpe's negotiations with powerful Indian tribes marked the growing recognition among British administrators and settlers that European rivalries in southeastern North America dictated accommodations with the Native American population which held the balance of power. However clumsy, Oglethorpe's military moves underscored the fact that in the eighteenth century England would have to fight for territory on North America. Parliament's willingness to underwrite Georgia bespoke the growing strategic importance of the North American colonies in Great Britain's imperial design. In the age of imperial rivalries, visionaries needed also to be soldiers. Oglethorpe's repulsion of the Spanish at Bloody Marsh in 1742 effectively ended Spanish incursions in the southern mainland colonies and secured Great Britain's southern frontier.

Oglethorpe was the last of the great proprietary colonizers in British North America. Like William Penn, he was a visionary imbued with a strong sense of mission. Oglethorpe's promotion of Georgia captured anew the prospect of America's destiny, and like Penn, it included recruitment of non-British settlers to promise a New World elysium out of religious and cultural diversity. Unlike Penn, Oglethorpe did not temper his social vision sufficiently with practicality. Although a gentle and even generous man, Oglethorpe bridled at criticism and was egotistic and self-righteous. He never fully adapted to the democratizing tendencies of colonial life, preferring to impose rules on his charges rather than take them into his confidence. Where Penn acceded to local demands for greater self-governance, Oglethorpe insisted on compliance with all regulations. A country whig in temperament and politics in England, Oglethorpe unwittingly played the autocrat in America. His life in Georgia demonstrated how much the British colonial establishment in the late seventeenth through the early eighteenth centuries rested on the energy and enthusiasm of powerful individuals. It also served to show the limits of Old World authority in the New. Oglethorpe had founded Georgia, protected it, and given it purpose, but he could not control the social, economic, and political impulses of diverse peoples in a setting that demanded popular participation and promised individual wealth. To have done so would have defeated the idea of America that inspired Oglethorpe to believe in the Georgia experiment, and the people to risk it.

Removed from the hurly-burly of Georgia, Oglethorpe seems to have understood that fact himself. He championed America's sons of liberty during the American Revolution, and before his death in 1785 he called on John Adams, the United States minister to England, acknowledging America's promise as England's, indeed Europe's, own redemption. By his continued hope for America, the old soldier did not die.

Bibliography
Boorstin, Daniel J. *The Americans: The Colonial Experience*. New York: Random House, 1958. Boorstin's influential treatment of Oglethorpe and Colonial Georgia criticizes the Trustees for their inability to adapt to the American environment. Boorstin finds in the failure of Oglethorpe's and the Trustees' vision of Georgia the clue to the success of other forms of community in America. By comparing the Georgia experiment with those of Massachusetts and Pennsylvania, Boorstin places Oglethorpe's thought and actions in the context of American utopianism.
Church, Leslie Frederic. *Oglethorpe: A Study of Philanthropy in England and Georgia*. London: Epworth Press, 1932. This older study remains valuable for its detail on Oglethorpe's philanthropic interests, his ties to religious figures and interest, especially the Wesleys, and his social and political connections in England.
Coleman, Kenneth. *Colonial Georgia: A History*. New York: Charles Scribner's Sons, 1976. A valuable synthesis of Georgia history, Coleman's account offers an excellent brief introduction to Oglethorpe's ideas and actions and how a multiethnic, multireligious colony developed from his policies. Coleman is especially good at relating the politics of Colonial Georgia and Oglethorpe's and the Trustees' ineffective governance.
Ettinger, Amos Aschbach. *James Edward Oglethorpe: Imperial Idealist*. Oxford: The Clarendon Press, 1936. Ettinger's lively and sympathetic account is the fullest and best biography of Oglethorpe. Ettinger approached Oglethorpe in the tradition of George Macauley Trevelyan, who believed the eighteenth century was the age of the individual. As such, Ettinger found Oglethorpe's personality and interest formed from his family traditions of loyalty to the crown, military service, and parliamentary responsibility. Although the bulk of Ettinger's biography focuses on Oglethorpe's American experience, the book also details Oglethorpe's Jacobite connections, parliamentary career, and literary friendships. Still, Ettinger's narrative views Oglethorpe's post-Georgia years as an anticlimax for the "imperial idealist."

Lane, Mills, ed. *General Oglethorpe's Georgia*. Savannah: Beehive Press, 1975. Lane collects and publishes a very good sampling of Oglethorpe's letters relating to the Georgia years and provides a useful introduction to Oglethorpe and Georgia, including accounts of Colonial discontent.

Spalding, Phinizy. *Oglethorpe in America*. Chicago: University of Chicago Press, 1977. Spalding reassesses Oglethorpe's life in the light of the many new materials available since Ettinger completed his research. In a balanced account of Oglethorpe, Spalding weighs Oglethorpe's ideas against his actions. He argues that Oglethorpe was not blind to American realities and that his ideas regarding a yeoman society were not necessarily doomed by the American environment.

Ver Steeg, Clarence L. *Origins of a Southern Mosaic: Studies of Early Carolina and Georgia*. Athens: University of Georgia Press, 1975. In his important and provocative examination of the origins of Georgia, Ver Steeg discards most previous interpretations and argues that, although strategic considerations loomed largest in shaping policies toward Georgia, each Trustee had his own motives regarding the colony's settlement and development. In the absence of any grand design, Oglethorpe had to contend with the contradictions among both Trustees and settlers about Georgia's purpose.

Randall M. Miller

GEORGIA O'KEEFFE

Born: November 15, 1887; Sun Prairie, Wisconsin
Died: March 6, 1986; Santa Fe, New Mexico
Area of Achievement: Art
Contribution: O'Keeffe's distinctive way of seeing, enlarged and often from unusual perspectives though never distorted, made her, by the time of her death, the foremost American exponent of representational expressionist painting.

Early Life

Georgia Totto O'Keeffe was born in Sun Prairie, Wisconsin, the second child of Francis and Ida O'Keeffe. She was of Irish, Hungarian, and Dutch descent and was christened with the surname of her patrician Hungarian grandfather, George Totto. One of her early childhood recollections, recalled many years later in an interview, was of her older brother Francis, Jr., then two years old and playing on a brightly colored quilt. Francis received all the attention, while Georgia would be thrust back on the blanket unceremoniously whenever she crawled off. O'Keeffe remembered that she craved attention and wanted to be thought pretty, though attention and praise were rare in a family with six children.

O'Keeffe's mother found farm life and its isolation oppressive, while her father was haunted by fears of the tuberculosis which had claimed his brother's life and seemed to recur in his family. The result was that he sold the family's large and prosperous farm and moved his family to Williamsburg, Virginia, in 1901. As a result, O'Keeffe acquired a sense of maturity and independence very early in her life, boarding at the Sacred Heart Academy, a Roman Catholic convent school on the outskirts of Madison, Wisconsin, even after her family had moved east. Though O'Keeffe had been reared an Episcopalian, Sacred Heart Academy offered her a chance to pursue studies in drawing and painting. O'Keeffe had shown promise even from her Saturday lessons with Sarah Mann, an amateur painter in Sun Prairie, and O'Keeffe's mother hoped to nurture her daughter's talent.

O'Keeffe joined her family in Williamsburg in the spring of 1903, and she attended Chatham Episcopal Institute that fall. Chatham, located about two hundred miles from Williamsburg, also offered an art program, and O'Keeffe excelled in it. She studied for two years there under the tutelage of Elizabeth May Willis, the school's principal and art instructor. In September, 1905, O'Keeffe journeyed west again, this time to attend the prestigious Art Institute of Chicago. Her art studies at the institute were as successful as those in her other schools, but several events combined to prevent O'Keeffe's return the following fall. Most immediate of these was a severe case of typhoid fever. Though it had abated by fall, O'Keeffe's father had, at the same time, faced a series of business reverses which would eventually translate into severely strained family finances.

By 1907, O'Keeffe was ready to attend school again, this time at New York City's Art Students League. In this year, while taking classes with the conservative painter William Merritt Chase (whose style most closely resembled that of John Singer Sargent), O'Keeffe first saw the then controversial drawings of Auguste Rodin on display at a gallery called "291" (from the number of its Fifth Avenue address), which was run by Alfred Stieglitz. Ironically, though O'Keeffe did not even approach the intimidating Stieglitz at this first meeting, the artist-photographer would, ten years later, give her her first solo show and become her husband in December, 1924.

The success O'Keeffe would enjoy almost without interruption after 1917 was preceded by a series of one-year teaching positions. O'Keeffe held these in Amarillo, Texas, in 1912-1913, as drawing supervisor in its elementary schools; at Columbia College, South Carolina, in 1915-1916; and at West Texas Normal College in 1916-1917, and she taught summers at the University of Virginia, all on the strength of her talent and outstanding recommendations. Despite her studies at the Art Institute of Chicago, at the Art Students League of New York, at the University of Virginia, and at Teachers College, Columbia University, in New York, she was never able to remain at one institution long enough to take an academic degree. Nevertheless, O'Keeffe's years in Texas would give her a love of desert landscapes which would figure significantly in her career as it developed.

Life's Work

O'Keeffe's career began in earnest on April 3, 1917, with the opening of her first solo show. It was sponsored by Stieglitz and featured striking charcoal sketches, which O'Keeffe had made in 1916 and shipped to her friend Anita Pollitzer, a fellow student from her Art Students League days. Though she did not ask Pollitzer to show them to Stieglitz, O'Keeffe hoped that her friend would do so, and this is precisely what happened. Stieglitz was fascinated by them and thus began not only their correspondence but also one of the most famous collaborations, personal as well as professional, in art history.

It is difficult to describe adequately the coups as well as the controversy of O'Keeffe's first shows. They were coups because O'Keeffe's work displayed bold originality, unlike the work of any American artist of that time. That the artist was a woman astounded the art world, for women artists were then commonly relegated to teaching. Even Stieglitz, who always associated with the avant-garde, had previously given space at 291 to only one other female artist. O'Keeffe's shows were controversial because her work was seen as inordinately sensual, and many critics, filled with the Freudian enthusiasms of the day, were anxious to append elaborate psychological programs to her works. Some protested that O'Keeffe was boldly displaying her sexuality on canvas; others, more ready to accept innovation, recognized that they were present at the birth of a remarkable new talent. While O'Keeffe spurned and was often embarrassed by these analyses, Stieglitz, always the entrepreneur, reveled in them. Controversy sells paintings, and that O'Keeffe suddenly found herself championed by the women's movement, then in its infancy, helped to keep her work before the public.

To some extent, Stieglitz's famous photographic series of O'Keeffe, in which many of the pictures were decidely erotic, helped continue often far-fetched interpretations of her work. Even so, the hundreds of photographs which Stieglitz took of O'Keeffe constitute a portfolio unlike any other in photographic history. It is a masterpiece in itself, and it would have made O'Keeffe famous had she not painted a single work.

There were, however, natural strains in the marriage of O'Keeffe and Stieglitz. He was twenty-three years her senior, and his brilliant career as a pioneer in photography and champion of American art had peaked precisely at the time of his marriage to O'Keeffe. Her career, on the other hand, was on the ascendant, and her ambition was limitless. While Stieglitz loved the heady atmosphere of the New York art world and summers at his family's home in Lake George, New York, in the company of members of his family, O'Keeffe, who had always been a private person, came to find both places confining and invasive. She also realized that Stieglitz was, because of his age as well as his nature, becoming increasingly dependent upon her. Significantly, it had been Stieglitz who suggested that the couple marry in late 1924, this despite their having lived together since 1917. While returning to New York from the simple ceremony in New Jersey, their car went off the road in a minor traffic accident. No one was hurt, but when asked how she felt, O'Keeffe replied that she felt as though she had just undergone an amputation. It was never clear whether she was referring to the accident or to the marriage ceremony.

Thus began, given the time, one of the most unconventional marriages ever documented in the American art world. By 1929, the pattern that O'Keeffe would follow until Stieglitz's death in 1946 was firmly set. From her years spent in Texas, she had always loved the American Southwest; there, she spent summers without Stieglitz (who remained in New York), first in Taos, New Mexico, the artists' colony favored by D. H. Lawrence, and soon afterward at nearby Ghost Ranch. By the mid-1940's, she would purchase two homes there and move between the one at Ghost Ranch and the other, fourteen miles away, at Abiquiu, as her inspiration dictated. In the fall, she would return to Stieglitz in New York, the trunk of her car filled with the striking pictures of bones, flowers, and desert landscapes. A selection from these would then appear in a late fall show held at An American Place, Stieglitz's intimate gallery and the successor to 291. O'Keeffe allowed Stieglitz absolute control of these annual exhibitions, and it was he who, from the earliest stage of her career, set the high prices for which O'Keeffe's works always sold. Just as important, he controlled the number of paintings which would be sold in any one year, thus keeping the market value high. Stieglitz retained absolute rights as O'Keeffe's agent and exhibitor and provided the business acumen that O'Keeffe lacked. He thus continued to bolster O'Keeffe's career and kept her name before the public, selling her works even during the Depression years, which were so devastating for many artists. Their marriage survived, not merely as a business arrangement but because both recognized the perfect balance of their opposite personalities.

The Depression and war years treated O'Keeffe's career kindly. Stieglitz came to recognize the important works that came from O'Keeffe's New Mexico summers and encouraged her annual trips even though he missed her companionship deeply. Accompanying her to her remote homes was impossible, since there were no medical facilities and living conditions were unbelievably primitive. O'Keeffe, nevertheless, thrived in this atmosphere, and Stieglitz understood her need for it. The art world and general public recognized it and O'Keeffe's talent, and, in 1942, Daniel Catton Rich proposed to O'Keeffe a major retrospective of her works at the Art Institute of Chicago, where he served as curator of painting. This retrospective was an irresistible temptation for O'Keeffe, since she had studied at the institute in 1905 and an exhibition there meant national recognition. It was also a blow to Stieglitz, however, who had always retained exclusive exhibition rights to O'Keeffe's works. Even so, Stieglitz recognized the importance of the show, and it was held with great success in January, 1943. When New York's Museum of Modern Art proposed a similar show in 1946, it was plain that O'Keeffe had a firm place in the international art world. Honorary doctorates, first from the College of William and Mary in 1938, then from the University of Wisconsin at Madison in 1942, pleased her immensely, especially because of her scattered formal training. She had built a solid career without an academic degree and at the time had never even visited, much less studied, in Europe.

Stieglitz died of a sudden brain hemorrhage on July 13, 1946, when O'Keeffe was in New Mexico. For the next three years, O'Keeffe directed the distribution of his personal collection of art and private papers. The largest portion of his personal collection was given to the Metropolitan Museum of Art to keep it in New York, the city Stieglitz had always loved, but the Institute of Fine Arts in Chicago also received a bequest, and the Beinecke Rare Book and Manuscript Library at Yale University took possession of Stieglitz's enormous correspondence and papers. Slowly, O'Keeffe began to build a new life for herself, exclusively in the New Mexico hills in which she had always thrived.

Increased interest in abstract expressionism as well as O'Keeffe's advanced age and lack of annual New York shows meant less exposure for her new works during the 1950's. It was in these years that she began to travel extensively, visiting Europe for the first time in 1953, and in later years, Japan and India. She incorporated the layered technique of Japanese silk paintings into her own works, using it to portray the ridged foothills behind her home at Ghost Ranch. She did continue to produce new works and to show them, however, at the Worcester Art Museum in Massachusetts in 1959, at several shows in the Southwest in the mid-1960's, and at the Whitney Museum in New York in 1970.

By 1971, O'Keeffe was eighty-four, and her eyesight suddenly diminished. It was about this time that a young sculptor named Juan Hamilton came to her to ask for work. Hamilton soon became O'Keeffe's full-time assistant and protége. Their relationship was symbiotic; each encouraged the other, and O'Keeffe completed a major series of oils, called *A Day with Juan*, which stemmed from their trip to Washington, D.C. O'Keeffe continued to paint until weeks before her death, and she died quietly after a long, full life.

Stieglitz had said that O'Keeffe possessed the timeless beauty of an earth goddess, and *Newsweek* magazine considered that she had the ageless beauty few women enjoy. It is undeniable that she remained strikingly handsome to the end of her life. Her dark features highlighted her classic bone structure, and the severity of her clothes (almost always well tailored, expensive, and black and white) added to her dramatic appearance. She wore no makeup, except in her early youth, and always kept her hair short, at first from necessity, since her battle with typhoid had caused her to lose her hair, and it was slow to grow back. By her twenties, however, she realized how well the style suited her, and she wore her hair combed straight and tightly fastened at the back. When photographed, she often had a small, enigmatic smile, the corner of her mouth curved just slightly upward. She often said that she wore only black and white because she was so sensitive to color. The shockingly brilliant colors of her earlier paintings as well as the subtle gradations of color in her later works certainly prove this to be true.

Summary

It would be difficult to name a painter more thoroughly American than O'Keeffe or, for that matter, a better example of the completely self-reliant and successful woman most modern American women strive to be; nevertheless, O'Keeffe never considered her style to be a specifically American one, nor (in her later life at least) did she publicly support projects of the woman's movement. She wanted to be known, not as the best American painter or the best woman painter, but simply as an artist who had made the best possible use of the gifts she possessed.

O'Keeffe had always worked against prevailing currents of personal behavior and artistic style. She was a member of the Women's National Party before women were allowed to vote, yet she refused to see contemporary feminist Gloria Steinem and to lend her name to modern women's causes. She lived openly with Stieglitz for almost seven years when many found such a way of life scandalous; yet, in her later years, she regretted not having had children, and some have seen her relationship to Hamilton as akin to that of mother and son. In her art, she championed expressionism, while most American painters worked in the tradition of naturalism; even so, she disliked abstract expressionism and never favored cubism, even in the 1930's, when so many imitated the style of Pablo Picasso. In short, O'Keeffe remained what she had to be to retain her genius: a thoroughgoing original.

Bibliography

Goodrich, Lloyd, and Doris Bry. *Georgia O'Keeffe*. New York: Praeger Publishers, 1970. Goodrich was director of the Whitney Museum and was responsible for organizing O'Keeffe's exhibition there in 1959. Bry helped settle the Stieglitz estate, acted as O'Keeffe's agent, and, in the late 1970's, was involved in litigation concerning ownership of O'Keeffe works. Their book contains observations on the evolution of O'Keeffe's style and general biographical information.

Hoffman, Katherine. *An Enduring Spirit: The Art of Georgia O'Keeffe*. Metuchen, N.J.: Scarecrow Press, 1984. Primarily a discussion of paintings which reflect recurring themes in O'Keeffe's works. The introductory chapters discuss the artistic milieu in which O'Keeffe painted. Reproductions of works discussed appear in black and white.

Lisle, Laurie. *Portrait of an Artist: A Biography of Georgia O'Keeffe*. New York: Seaview Books, 1980. Contains good material on O'Keeffe's early life, teaching career, and relationship with Stieglitz. It concludes with reflections on O'Keeffe at age ninety-two, her life at Ghost Ranch, and her relationship with Juan Hamilton.

"Obituary: Georgia O'Keeffe Dead at Ninety-eight: Shaper of Modern Art in U.S." *The New York Times*, March 7, 1986: 1. Provides an interesting survey of O'Keeffe's career, her marriage to Stieglitz, and a discussion of several of her most important paintings.

O'Keeffe, Georgia. *Georgia O'Keeffe*. New York: Viking Press, 1976. A magnificent studio book with full-color reproductions of the most famous O'Keeffe paintings. The book measures a full two feet across when opened and was prepared from paintings selected by the artist herself.

_____ . *Some Memories of Drawings*. New York: Atlantic Editions, 1974. O'Keeffe's own reflections on her methods, style, and the circumstances which inspired some of her works.

Pack, Arthur N. *We Called It Ghost Ranch*. Abiquiu, N.M.: Ghost Ranch Conference Center, 1966. Written by the man who founded the New Mexico resort hotel at which O'Keeffe first stayed and who built one of the New Mexico houses she subsequently bought and in which she lived for the remainder of her life. Ghost Ranch property is now used as a conference center by the Presbyterian church.

Stieglitz, Alfred. *Georgia O'Keeffe: A Portrait*. New York: Metropolitan Museum of Art, 1978. The controversial and eloquent photographic tribute of Stieglitz to his wife, successful as much because of O'Keeffe's mysterious beauty as Stieglitz's own skill as photographer.

Robert J. Forman

FREDERICK LAW OLMSTED

Born: April 26, 1822; Hartford, Connecticut
Died: August 28, 1903; Waverly, Massachusetts
Areas of Achievement: Social criticism and landscape architecture
Contribution: Olmsted traveled extensively in the antebellum South and wrote some of America's best critical descriptions of slavery on the eve of the Civil War. He designed Central Park in New York City and other urban parks across the country. Olmsted is considered the father of the profession of landscape architecture in the United States.

Early Life

Frederick Law Olmsted was born on April 26, 1822, in Hartford, Connecticut, the son of a prosperous dry-goods merchant. His family's material wealth and deep roots in the community gave Olmsted both the economic freedom and the personal confidence to pursue a leisurely course toward his major life works. On the other hand, he was physically frail and suffered from an eye problem that hampered his efforts at formal education. Olmsted was attracted to strenuous outdoor physical activity as compensation for his physical weakness and developed a keen appreciation of nature and the outdoors. During his early years, Olmsted acquired a taste for travel, and by the time he was in his mid-teens he had made several lengthy trips through various regions of the northeastern United States and Canada.

Olmsted matriculated at Yale, where he studied engineering, but his eye problem prevented regular study, and after practical training in surveying he worked briefly and unhappily for a dry-goods firm in New York City. This was followed by an extremely unpleasant year's experience as a sailor on a voyage to China. Returning to Yale, he studied agricultural science and engineering and then undertook practical training as a farmer on 130 Staten Island acres purchased by his father. As he became absorbed with scientific agriculture, Olmsted began to publish articles on rural subjects and drifted toward a career as a writer.

Life's Work

In the 1850's, Olmsted embarked upon his first noteworthy career as he traveled extensively and published accounts of his journeys. His first book, *Walks and Talks of an American Farmer in England* (1852), was well received and demonstrated his aptitude for keen social observation. It is also significant that Olmsted was quite favorably taken with the landscape and rural life of the country, reflecting his continuing interest in the scenic. With sectional tension between North and South escalating, he was commissioned by *The New York Times* to travel through Dixie and report on the region's social and economic conditions.

Olmsted was chosen because of his connections among rationalist intellectual circles, his moderate antislavery views, and his established literary reputation. Although the publisher of *The New York Times* was himself a moderate Free-Soiler, Olmsted was not chosen primarily because of his views on slavery but because of his reputation as a perceptive observer who could produce an objective report on the "peculiar institution."

Accordingly, in December of 1852, Olmsted began a fourteen-month tour that took him through much of the South and as far as Texas and across the Rio Grande. He sent back lengthy letters over the signature "Yeoman," which were published on the first page of the newspaper, beginning in February, 1853. These were followed by several volumes under various titles, which were finally distilled into his classic two-volume work, *The Cotton Kingdom* (1861). Olmsted's works were immediately hailed by contemporaries as the most important sources of objective information about the life and customs of the slaveholding states and became significant references as Europeans discussed the relative merits of the Northern and Southern causes in the American Civil War. Olmsted's works remain essential sources for modern historians, who regard them as classic contemporary portrayals and analyses of the plantation slavery system of the antebellum South. If Olmsted had done nothing else, his descriptions of slavery would have established his lasting reputation, but, remarkably, even as he was producing these works, he was embarking upon a second career for which he would become even better known.

In 1857, because of his continuing interest in landscape, Olmsted accepted the position of superintendent of the preparatory work on Central Park in New York City. Soon after, with his partner Calvert Vaux, Olmsted won the competition to provide a new design for the park. He signed his plans with the title "Landscape Architect" under his name, supposedly becoming the first to use this title formally. In 1858, he became the park's chief architect and began to implement his and Vaux's plan to make the park both materially and artistically successful. His work was interrupted by service during the Civil War as general secretary of the United States Sanitary Commission, the forerunner of the American Red Cross, but by this time his philosophy of landscape design was well established.

Olmsted started from the premise that it is essential for man to maintain a balance between civilization and nature in his life and that for the citydweller, particularly, it is imperative that places should be provided as a retreat from the pressures of overcrowded, overly civilized urban existence. While he had an appreciation for nature in the raw, "wilderness," Olmsted's real preference was for the pastoral, a natural environment which was ordered, designed, structured, but which provided the illusion of nature's own handiwork. Thus, the construction of Central Park would involve the movement of tons of dirt, the creation of lakes, sunken roads, bridges, and other features to manufacture the illusion of nature for the city dweller. Ironically, considering the fact that much of his later career was spent in the service of the wealthy and influential, Olmsted's interest in urban parks was shaped in part by a strong democratic impulse to provide facilities where all classes could find refuge and recreation.

In 1863, Olmsted left Washington to become superintendent of John C. Frémont's Mariposa mining estates in California, and while there he became a leading figure in the movement to set aside the Yosemite and Mariposa "big tree" reservations which culminated in the establishment of Yosemite Park. Yosemite eventually became part of the national park system. Olmsted was a consistent promoter of preserving scenic regions and often manufactured "wilderness" areas as part of his design scheme for urban parks.

After the Civil War was concluded, Olmsted returned to New York City and carried Central Park nearly to completion. When the project was begun, the site was an area containing pig farms and squatters' shacks which had no distinguishing physical features; twenty years and the labor of more than thirty-eight hundred workers were required to construct the hills, lakes, and paths which became so important to New Yorkers. Central Park established Olmsted's reputation and became the prototype for urban parks across the United States.

Olmsted's services were now much in demand, and he moved on to design additional parks for New York City and other cities across the nation, the Capitol grounds in Washington, D.C., a preservation plan for the Niagara Falls area, and numerous college campuses. Some consider his design for the system of lagoons, wooded islands, and plantings in Chicago's Jackson Park for the Columbian Exposition in 1893 his crowning achievement. He also became a fervent advocate of suburban living, balancing the features and values of both city and country in new planned communities on the borders of older urban centers. Olmsted and Vaux designed suburbs for several cities, the most famous being Chicago's Riverside, which opened in 1869.

Emotionally exhausted by the constant political maneuvering and compromise required for work in the public sector, in his later years Olmsted retreated to the service of precisely those wealthy plutocrats whose stranglehold on scenic outdoor areas his urban parks had helped to break. His clients included Andrew Carnegie, Leland Stanford, and George Vanderbilt, for whom he helped design the famous Biltmore estate in North Carolina. Olmsted suffered a mental collapse in 1893 and disappeared from public view until his death in 1903.

Summary

Frederick Law Olmsted was one of those amazingly talented individuals who was able to achieve striking success in several areas. He was a gifted social observer and writer who left some of America's best contemporary descriptions and analyses of the life and economy of the antebellum South. Shaped by an aesthetic appreciation for wilderness and the pastoral and by a strong democratic impulse, Olmsted became a passionate advocate of the need for balance between urban and natural experiences if one were to maintain a healthy existence. He thus became the first great proponent and designer of large urban parks which would be open to all people and allow city dwellers to maintain that necessary balance in their lives. His Central Park in New York City was the progenitor of the urban parks movement in the United States, and Olmsted fathered the profession of landscape architecture.

Bibliography

Fein, Albert. *Frederick Law Olmsted and the American Environmental Tradition*. New York: George Braziller, 1972. Evaluates Olmsted's significance in the broad development of environmentalism.

Huth, Hans. *Nature and the American: Three Centuries of Changing Attitudes*. Berkeley: University of California Press, 1957. Discusses Olmsted's work as a landscape architect, as well as his efforts in the campaigns to preserve Yosemite and the area around Niagara Falls.

Newton, Norman T. *Design on the Land: The Development of Landscape Architecture*. Cambridge, Mass.: The Belknap Press for Harvard University Press, 1971. Includes an assessment of Olmsted's role in the development of the profession.

Olmsted, Frederick Law. *The Slave States Before the Civil War*. Edited by Harvey Wish. New York: G. P. Putnam's Sons, 1959. Wish has written an excellent introduction discussing Olmsted's life and publications.

Roper, Laura Wood. *FLO: A Biography of Frederick Law Olmsted*. Baltimore: Johns Hopkins University Press, 1973. The definitive biography, combining social history with a nuanced portrait of its subject. Makes generous use of Olmsted's letters. Massively documented, though lacking a bibliography.

Runte, Alfred. *National Parks: The American Experience*. Lincoln: University of Nebraska Press, 1979. While the focus is upon cultural and economic influences in the creation and shaping of the American national park system, this work also discusses the contributions of Olmsted to park design, wilderness appreciation, and the Yosemite and Niagara Falls campaigns.

Tobey, George B. *A History of Landscape Architecture: The Relationship of People to Environment*. New York: American Elsevier, 1973. Includes considerable material dealing with Olmsted.

James E. Fickle

EUGENE O'NEILL

Born: October 16, 1888; New York, New York
Died: November 27, 1953; Boston, Massachusetts
Area of Achievement: Drama
Contribution: O'Neill is commonly considered a great American playwright, honored as a writer who experimented ambitiously in a variety of dramatic modes.

Early Life

Eugene Gladstone O'Neill was born in a Broadway hotel at a corner of Times Square on October 16, 1888. His father, James O'Neill (1846-1920), came to the United States from Ireland when he was ten and established himself as a talented Shakespearean actor, expected to inherit the mantle of Edwin Booth. In 1883, the elder O'Neill opened as the protagonist Edmond Dantès in a dramatization of *The Count of Monte-Cristo* (1844-1845), by Alexandre Dumas, *père*. The play proved a spectacular success, and James O'Neill toured with it for the next fifteen years, earning up to forty thousand dollars annually to assuage his incessant fear of poverty. Later, the father came to believe that he had sacrificed his opportunity for greatness upon the altar of materialism. His son took this regret as a cautionary lesson and resolved never to compromise his artistic integrity for money.

Eugene's mother, Ellen Quinlan O'Neill (1857-1922), was a devout Catholic, educated in a convent in South Bend, Indiana, where she won a medal for her piano-playing but seriously considered becoming a nun. She fell in love with the dashing James O'Neill when his company toured South Bend. She accompanied her husband on his road trips for many years, all the while resenting their nomadic itinerary of frequent one-night stands, hotel rooms, and irregular meals. Eugene, once established as a playwright, developed an emphatic fondness for settled routine and a detestation of trains and hotels.

Ellen O'Neill found an escape from her aversion to theatrical traveling by becoming an increasingly addicted morphine user. She withdrew from many of her child-rearing responsibilities, leaving Eugene to be mothered, during his first seven years, by a Cornish nursemaid, Sarah Sandy, who exposed her charge to sensational horror stories. The elder O'Neill sent his son to Catholic preparatory schools in New York and Connecticut. In 1906, Eugene entered Princeton University, drank heavily, and studied very little; after a brick-throwing episode, he was failed in all of his courses and never returned to the university. For the next two years, he spent most of his time touring Manhattan in the company of his alcoholic older brother, James, Jr. (1878-1923).

On October 2, 1909, Eugene secretly married the non-Catholic Kathleen Jenkins, the beautiful daughter of a once-wealthy New York family. Two weeks later, the bridegroom left her to prospect for gold in Honduras. There he found not shining metal but a severe case of malaria; he was to use his knowledge of the tropical jungle in *The Emperor Jones* (1920). Even though Kathleen gave birth to a son, Eugene, Jr., on May 5, 1910, O'Neill refused to live with them upon his return, ignoring his firstborn until after the child's eleventh birthday. On July 10, 1912, Kathleen Jenkins was awarded an interlocutory divorce decree.

The year 1912 proved to be the crucial year of Eugene O'Neill's life: The nuclear O'Neill family—father, mother, two sons—spent the summer together in O'Neill's parents' New London, Connecticut, home, with Eugene writing for the local paper. In December, 1912, he was diagnosed as tubercular; Ellen O'Neill refused to accept the physician's findings, withdrawing into morphine-induced fantasies. Miserly James O'Neill first placed Eugene in Connecticut's Fairfield County State Sanatorium, a bleakly depressing charity institution, many of whose patients died. After staying there from December 9 to 11, Eugene had himself discharged. On Christmas Eve, James entered his son in a private institution, Gaylord Farm, which proved distinctly more therapeutic: Eugene was discharged as an arrested case on the third of June, 1913; *The Straw* (1921), one of his most deeply felt early plays, is a heavily autobiographical depiction of his stay there.

Life's Work

During his sanatorium stay, O'Neill crystallized his career goal: he would be a playwright. His most pervasive influence was the intense, self-tortured, somber Swedish writer, August Strindberg. In his acceptance speech for the Nobel Prize for Literature, awarded to him in 1936, O'Neill singled out Strindberg as "that greatest genius of all modern dramatists. . . . It was reading his plays . . . that, above all else, first gave me the vision of what modern drama could be, and first inspired me with the urge to write for the theater myself."

After his discharge from the institution, O'Neill boarded for a year with a private family and used this time to write thirteen plays, of which he included six one-act plays in a volume, *Thirst* (1914), subsidized by his father; he later disowned this collection, preventing its republication during his lifetime. From September, 1914, to May, 1915, he was a student in Professor George Pierce Baker's playwriting class at Harvard, remembered by classmates as handsome, thin, shy, and restless.

In 1916, O'Neill fell in love with the high-spirited journalist Louise Bryant, already the mistress and soon to be the wife of the celebrated war correspondent John Reed (1887-1920). The two men liked each other, and the trio formed a turbulent triangle which persisted close to the day of O'Neill's second marriage to Agnes Boulton on April 12, 1918. Indeed, Agnes reminded O'Neill of Louise: Both women were slender, pretty, and sophisticated; Agnes, however, was quiet and softly feminine, in contrast to Louise's strident manner. The marriage to Agnes Boulton lasted eleven years; its first two years are vividly described in her account, *Part of a Long Story* (1958). The union resulted in two children. Shane O'Neill (1919-1975) was never able to settle on a career and became a hopeless heroin addict. Oona O'Neill (born 1925) married Charles Chaplin (1889-1977). O'Neill's firstborn son, Eugene O'Neill, Jr., tall and handsome with a resonant voice, began a brilliant career as a classicist at Yale but turned increasingly alcoholic, resigned his academic post, and, in his fortieth year, committed suicide. O'Neill held himself apart from his children throughout his life, although he did make sporadic, intense, but always short-lived attempts to reach them intimately.

O'Neill's first important play, *The Emperor Jones*, dramatizes, in eight scenes, Brutus Jones's fall from "emperor" of a West Indian island to a primitive savage who is slaughtered by his rebellious people. Jones is a former Pullman porter who escapes imprisonment for murder, finds his way to the island, and there establishes himself as a despot by exploiting the natives' fears and superstitions. While the play's first and last scenes are realistic, the intervening six are expressionistic, consisting of Jones's monologues and the visions of his fearful mind as he struggles through a tropical jungle. O'Neill manages to merge supernatural beliefs with psychological effects in a powerful union that shows his dramatic affinity with two noted German expressionists, Georg Kaiser (1878-1945) and Ernst Toller (1893-1939).

Desire Under the Elms (1924) is usually considered O'Neill's finest play of the 1920's, his first in the classic Greek mode. It is a modern treatment of the Phaedra-Hippolytus-Theseus myth, set on a New England farm in 1850. The father, seventy-five-year-old Ephraim Cabot (Theseus), returns to his farm with a passionate new wife, thirty-five-year-old Abbie (Phaedra), who falls in love with her twenty-five-year-old stepson, Eben (Hippolytus). Like Phaedra, Abbie confronts the young man in a superb scene; unlike Phaedra, Abbie wins him. They become lovers and have a child, which Abbie kills in infancy to demonstrate her primary love for Eben. He insists on sharing her guilt; they go to jail together, remorseful over their infanticide but not over their adultery. O'Neill dramatizes in this play not only sexual but also materialistic desire: Desire for the farm causes Abbie to marry old Ephraim; resentment of his father's usurpation of the farm from his abused, dead mother causes Eben to exact vengeance upon the father he hates. The play's multiple setting effectively counterpoints the older and younger generations, external nature and domestic temperament.

Determined to compress within his career virtually all stages of drama, O'Neill challenged Aeschylus with his longest work, *Mourning Becomes Electra* (1931), a thirteen-act trilogy. The action is a modern adaptation of the *Oresteia* (458 B.C.), with O'Neill following *Agamemnon* faithfully with his *The Homecoming*, and *Libation Bearers* fairly closely with *The Hunted*, but departing freely from *Eumenides* in *The Haunted*. The Trojan War becomes the American Civil War, with the Mannon family (House of Atreus) awaiting the return from the fighting of Ezra Mannon (Agamemnon). The daughter, Lavinia (Electra), has discovered that her mother, Christine (Clytemnestra), has been having an affair with Adam Brant (Aegisthus). In *The Haunted*, the playwright abandons Aeschylus in favor of Freud by having Orin (Orestes), racked by remorse for his mother's suicide, not murder (as in Aeschylus), but transfer his incestuous feelings for his mother to his sister, who has come to resemble his mother. Lavinia rejects him, Orin commits suicide, and Lavinia realizes that she has always loved her father and hated her mother. She closes the drama by rejecting marriage to a loyal suitor, instead immuring herself, with the Mannon dead, alone in the Mannon house. This work had the most laudatory initial reception of any O'Neill play, but a number of critics have since tempered the original enthusiasm, deploring the drama's implausibly implacable determinism, the overly clinical, self-analytic speeches of its leading characters, and the absence of even the slightest elements of humor or warmth.

From 1934 to 1946, O'Neill did not have a play produced. He spent these years largely in a Chinese-style mansion, Tao House, built to his specifications in Contra Costa County, California. He devoted most of his work to an ambitious cycle of eleven related plays dealing with the rise and fall of an American family from 1775 to 1932, to be called *A Tale of Possessors Self-Dispossessed*, which would offer his adverse judgment on America's increasing enslavement to possession and greed. "We are the clearest example," he declared, "of 'For what shall it profit a man if he gain the whole world and lose his own soul?'" The only play of this cycle surviving in completed form is *A Touch of the Poet*, set in a Massachusetts tavern in 1828 and treating the marriage of Sara Melody, of Irish descent, and Simon Harford, of Yankee stock. O'Neill wrote various drafts of the cycle's other plays but, fearing that they might eventually be performed in unfinished form, he and his third wife, Carlotta, burned the manuscripts during the winter of 1952-1953. A third draft of *More Stately Mansions* escaped the flames and was produced in 1967.

O'Neill had met Carlotta Monterey when she played the society girl in his *The Hairy Ape* (1922). She was a sultry brunette, usually cast as the sexually magnetic adventuress eventually to be overcome by the virtuous wife. She and O'Neill began their romance in 1928 and married in 1929, three weeks after Agnes Boulton had been granted a Reno divorce. Carlotta loved O'Neill deeply but possessively, routinized his life, limited his contacts with friends, and helped estrange him from his children, whom he disinherited in his will, making her his literary executor. In his middle and later years, O'Neill both impressed and often intimidated people with his "black Irish" appearance: dark, brooding eyes; spare, rangy, five-foot, eleven-inch frame; quiet, deep voice; and mysterious, reserved, often morose temperament.

From 1944 to his death in 1953, an uncontrollable hand tremor, similar to that caused by Parkinson's disease, forced him to stop writing; he tried to dictate but found that method unworkable. His final years were marked not only by physical pain but also by increasing trouble with his children and dissension with his wife. He died of bronchial pneumonia, just past the age of sixty-five.

Most critics regard two plays written at the end of the 1930's as O'Neill's greatest, comparable to the finest dramatic achievements of the twentieth century. The first, *The Iceman Cometh* (1946), is one of his bleakest dramas, set in a squalid barroom in 1912 and portraying more than a dozen drunken wrecks who alternately feed upon and poison one another's illusions. The sum of their pipe dreams represents the total content of man's capacity for deception and repudiates any affirmation. The play's theme—that human beings cannot live without illusions, no matter how ill-founded—parallels that of Henrik Ibsen's *The Wild Duck* (1884). Opposing the alcoholic customers of Harry Hope's saloon in this work is a hardware salesman, Hickey, who kicks away their crutches of self-deception out of professed confidence that the truth shall set them free. Yet Hickey turns out to have murdered his long-betrayed wife, not only out of love—as he at first insists—but also out of a lifetime of hatred and self-loathing. Hickey, the derelicts discover, has been a false messiah; they gladly relapse into their drunken delusions. O'Neill has here written a despairing masterpiece about the impossibility of salvation in a man-centered world.

O'Neill's other, perhaps even more magnificent, achievement is the confessional family play he prepared himself for many years to write, *Long Day's Journey Into Night* (1956). This is O'Neill's most personal play: The O'Neills are called the Tyrones. His father and elder brother retain their own first names, James. Ellen O'Neill becomes Mary Tyrone, while Eugene names himself Edmund—the name of the O'Neill brother who died in infancy. Did O'Neill, as he claims in his preface, "face [his] dead at last . . . with deep pity and understanding and forgiveness for all the four haunted Tyrones"? A qualified yes is in order, for the author represses the painful data of his first marriage, first son, and first divorce, instead portraying himself as a sensitive, irresponsible, twenty-three-year-old would-be poet without commitments.

The play lives up to its title: It consumes the time from 8:30 A.M. to midnight on a day in August, 1912, in New London—The O'Neill/Tyrone summer residence. It has the unified formality of French classical drama, with the Tyrone quartet bound together by links of resentment, grief, guilt, and recrimination, yet also by tenderness, compassion, and love. Two events charge the action: Mary Tyrone's final relapse into morphine addiction and the diagnosis of Edmund as tubercular. In the day's course, she moves away from the other three but especially from her younger son; he moves toward her, in vain agony. Who is to blame for their maladies? All, replies O'Neill—and no one. As Mary says,

> None of us can help the things life has done to us. They're done before you realize it, and once they're done they make you do other things until at last everything comes between you and what you'd like to be, and you've lost your true self forever.

Summary

In power, insight, scale, and ambition, Eugene O'Neill is unsurpassed among American dramatists. He began as a realist-naturalist in a native tradition that includes Edwin Arlington Robinson and Robert Frost in poetry, and Frank Norris, Stephen Crane, and Theodore Dreiser in fiction. His middle period is marked by intermittently effective plays, influenced by many European modes, particularly expressionism, and by the ideas of Friedrich Wilhelm Nietzsche, Sigmund Freud, and Carl Gustav Jung. His last work is both his best and his most characteristically American: It demonstrates a fierce determination to dig beneath the illusions and lies of everyday behavior, to assert a profoundly tragic sense of man's shortcomings, and to reconcile himself to the melancholy state of a flawed and often unjust universe. Like tragedians from Aeschylus to Samuel Beckett, O'Neill has a desolate view of life. His talent in dramatizing that view was often flawed by self-conscious portentousness. In at least two plays, however—*The Iceman Cometh* and *Long Day's Journey Into Night*—O'Neill climbed dramatic heights unscaled by any other American and rivaled by only a handful of world-renowned modern playwrights: Henrik Ibsen, August Strindberg, Anton Chekhov, George Bernard Shaw, Bertolt Brecht, and Samuel Beckett.

Bibliography

Alexander, Doris. *The Tempering of Eugene O'Neill*. New York: Harcourt, Brace and World, 1962. This biography treats O'Neill's life and career up to *Anna Christie* (1921). Alexander devotes several chapters to O'Neill's parents and brother, follows him to Greenwich Village and Provincetown, then to his marriage to Agnes Boulton and his first dramatic successes. The book stresses O'Neill's maturation as an artist.

Bogard, Travis. *Contour in Time: The Plays of Eugene O'Neill*. New York: Oxford University Press, 1972. A study of O'Neill's works that unites theatrical knowledge with finely honed critical insights. Professor Bogard also provides illuminating accounts of both the American and European theaters in the first half of the twentieth century.

Boulton, Agnes. *Part of a Long Story*. Garden City, N.Y.: Doubleday and Co., 1958. Boulton begins with her first meeting of the twenty-nine-year-old playwright in 1917 and stops with the birth of their son Shane in October, 1919. A promised second volume was never written. She relates not only the first years of O'Neill's second marriage but also his version of his first marriage and suicide attempt.

Bowen, Croswell. Assisted by Shane O'Neill. *The Curse of the Misbegotten.* New York: McGraw-Hill Book Co., 1959. Bowen is a journalist and biographer who is here considerably assisted by O'Neill's younger son. The "curse" is the inability of the O'Neills to tell one another their love and concern, thus dooming themselves to emotionally impoverished lives. Much valuable material about Eugene O'Neill's life.

Gassner, John, ed. *O'Neill: A Collection of Critical Essays.* Englewood Cliffs, N.J.: Prentice-Hall, 1964. Gassner, an eminent authority on drama, has collected fifteen essays on O'Neill's achievement. Included are adverse views from distinguished critics such as Eric Bentley, as well as laudatory articles by Stark Young, John Henry Raleigh, Travis Bogard, and others. A discriminating selection.

Gelb, Arthur, and Barbara Gelb. *O'Neill.* New York: Harper and Row, Publishers, 1962. This volume of more than one thousand pages treats O'Neill's life and works in monumental detail. The writing is often pedestrian, but the information is usually fascinating enough to maintain the reader's interest.

Sheaffer, Louis. *O'Neill: Son and Artist.* Boston: Little, Brown and Co., 1973.

_____ . *O'Neill: Son and Playwright.* Boston: Little, Brown and Co., 1968. These two volumes comprise close to thirteen hundred pages and will be the definitive O'Neill study for many years. Shaeffer, a former journalist, devoted sixteen years to this titanic labor; they were worth it. He emphasizes a wealth of biographical lore, obtained not only from documents but also from personal interviews. Indispensable.

Gerhard Brand

J. ROBERT OPPENHEIMER

Born: April 22, 1904; New York, New York
Died: February 18, 1967; Princeton, New Jersey
Area of Achievement: Physics
Contribution: As director of the Los Alamos Laboratories, Oppenheimer was in charge of the team of scientists who developed the nation's first nuclear weapons.

Early Life

J. Robert Oppenheimer was born April 22, 1904, in New York City, the firstborn son of wealthy Jewish parents. Oppenheimer and his younger brother Frank were educated at the New York Society for Ethical Culture, where Oppenheimer became interested in science and literature. An aloof, serious young boy, he did poorly in sports but loved sailing and horseback riding.

In 1922, Oppenheimer entered Harvard, where he majored in chemistry and was introduced to physics. After graduating, Oppenheimer went to England in 1925, to study physics at Cambridge. Oppenheimer had planned to study experimental physics but proved inept at laboratory work. Theoretical physics fascinated him, but the creative, sustained, and solitary mental effort necessary for effective work drove him to the point of mental collapse. After a summer's vacation, however, Oppenheimer recovered his stability. Realizing that he was not cut out for lab work, he left Cambridge to study at the University of Göttingen, Germany, then a center for theoretical physics.

Oppenheimer made a reputation at Göttingen, writing papers dealing with aspects of the then new theory of quantum physics. In 1927, Oppenheimer was awarded a doctorate from Göttingen. After a year's further study with leading European physicists, he returned to the United States in 1929.

Life's Work

Oppenheimer hoped to build an American center for the study of physics. In 1929, he was appointed assistant professor of physics at the University of California, Berkeley, where Ernest Lawrence was building a reputation as one of the nation's leading experimental physicists. Together, Oppenheimer and Lawrence made Berkeley the best-known graduate school for physics in the nation during the 1930's.

At Berkeley, Oppenheimer became a famous, charismatic teacher. Tall, thin, with striking blue eyes, he stood before the blackboard with chalk in one hand and an ever-present cigarette in the other. He was best known for his ability to communicate abstruse theoretical material clearly. Although some found Oppenheimer an arrogant intellectual snob, to favored students he was "Oppie," a charming mentor who introduced them to art, Eastern literature, gourmet foods, and fine wines as well as physics.

Independently wealthy, Oppenheimer had lived a sheltered life and paid little attention to economic or world events. In the 1930's, as the Great Depression worsened and Adolf Hitler came to power in Germany, Oppenheimer began to take more interest in politics. Also in the 1930's, he became involved with various local reform groups, many of which were affiliated with the Communist Party. Communism was popular among many intellectuals because it seemed to offer hope for social justice at home and resistance to Fascism overseas. Many of Oppenheimer's friends were leftists. His brother, Frank, became a Communist Party member.

In November, 1940, Oppenheimer married Kathryn Puening. She had been married three times before, once to a dedicated Communist who had been killed during the Spanish Civil War; she was also a Party member.

In 1942, the United States, at war with the Axis, began a crash program to produce an atomic weapon. Oppenheimer was chosen to head the Los Alamos Laboratories, near Santa Fe, New Mexico, where the proposed weapon would be assembled and tested. At Los Alamos, Oppenheimer coordinated the work of more than three thousand scientists, technicians, and military personnel. His performance as director of the Los Alamos scientific staff, which included past and future Nobel Prize winners, was superb. His skills as a communicator helped him coordinate the project that produced the first nuclear weapon.

On July 16, 1945, the first atom bomb was tested. Oppenheimer said later that, as the first mushroom cloud rose above the New Mexico desert, he recalled a line from the Hindu scriptures, "I am become death, the shatterer of worlds." In August, 1945, American bombers dropped atomic weapons on Hiroshima and Nagasaki, and World War II was brought to an end by the Japanese surrender.

After the war, Oppenheimer returned to academic life, first teaching at Berkeley and then moving to Princeton, New Jersey, where he was appointed director of the Institute for Advanced Study. His service at Los Alamos had made him one of the nation's most famous scientists, and he was in demand as a government consultant on atomic energy. From 1947 to 1952, he was chairman of the General Advisory Committee of the Atomic Energy Commission.

In the postwar years, Oppenheimer often spoke publicly about his fear that nuclear energy would lead to world destruction unless controlled and shared. He and other influential scientists hoped that the new discoveries in physics would become an international resource, controlled and used for the good of the world as a whole. Yet as the Cold War between the United States and the Soviet Union worsened, such hopes faded.

In 1950, the Soviet Union exploded a hydrogen bomb. Shortly thereafter, Americans were shocked to learn that a member of the British delegation to

Los Alamos during World War II, Klaus Fuchs, had admitted to passing information about the project to the Soviets. After these revelations, government security became much tighter, and demagogues seized on public concern to whip up hysteria about possible Soviet sympathizers in the State Department, in the public entertainment industry, and among the nation's scientists.

Oppenheimer's left-wing connections had been well-known when he was chosen to head the Los Alamos project. He had been under Federal Bureau of Investigation surveillance for years and had continued to work on highly secret projects. In December, 1953, at the height of the Cold War hysteria, Oppenheimer's security clearance was suspended.

In the spring of 1954, the Personnel Security Board of the Atomic Energy Commission conducted hearings on the Oppenheimer case. His old associations were rehashed. He was also accused of injuring American security by being less than enthusiastic about the development of the hydrogen bomb. Despite a parade of character witnesses which included many prominent scientists, the board voted in June, 1954, to revoke Oppenheimer's security clearance. Oppenheimer returned to Princeton, where he continued to serve as director of the Institute for Advanced Studies until his retirement in 1966.

In 1963, he was given the Enrico Fermi Award by the United States government. This award was given to those who had made contributions to "development, use, or control of atomic energy." The presentation to Oppenheimer has been seen as a gesture of rehabilitation by the government. Yet his security clearance was not restored. Oppenheimer died February 18, 1967, of cancer, at his home in Princeton.

Summary

Oppenheimer is famous for two things: He directed the project which produced the first atom bomb, and he was stripped of his security clearance during a period of national paranoia. Those who denied him access to the nation's technological secrets did not allege that he was a Soviet spy or that he had at any point violated the trust placed in him. Rather, he was accused of having had Communist friends, relatives, and students, of having failed to be sufficiently security-conscious, and of failing to support the development of the hydrogen bomb.

The Oppenheimer case remained a *cause célèbre* for many years. The inherent drama of Oppenheimer's rise and fall made the case a fitting subject for a play, a television documentary, and, in the 1980's, a British Broadcasting Corporation television miniseries.

Oppenheimer's most lasting contribution was scientific. His ability to communicate, to direct, to teach in the true sense—drawing from each member of his team and incorporating all insights into a working whole—made the achievement at Los Alamos possible.

Oppenheimer himself was aware of the irony of that achievement. A man dedicated to the pursuit of knowledge, he could yet be appalled at the cost of the pursuit. In 1946, in a farewell address to the staff at Los Alamos, he said, "If atomic bombs are to be added to the arsenals of a warring world, or to the arsenals of nations preparing for war, then the time will come when mankind will curse the names of Los Alamos and Hiroshima." He went on to express the hope that the world would unite "before this common peril, in law, in humanity."

Bibliography
Curtis, Charles P. *The Oppenheimer Case: The Trial of a Security System.* New York: Simon and Schuster, 1955. A journalistic and declamatory account of Oppenheimer's 1954 hearing.
Davis, Nuel Pharr. *Lawrence and Oppenheimer.* New York: Simon and Schuster, 1968. A highly readable popular biography of Berkeley's two leading physicists; also gives a good picture of the scientific community at mid-century. Good bibliography.
The Day After Trinity: J. Robert Oppenheimer and the Atomic Bomb. Produced by Jon Else and KTEH-TV; written by Janet Peoples, David Peoples, and Jon Else. Santa Monica, Calif.: Pyramid Films, 1981. Videorecording. This excellent documentary film focuses on Los Alamos and the World War II years.
Goodchild, Peter. *J. Robert Oppenheimer: Shatterer of Worlds.* Boston: Houghton Mifflin Co., 1981. Published in conjunction with the BBC series on Oppenheimer, this is an objective, often critical analysis of Oppenheimer's personality and of United States security. Copiously illustrated.
Kunetka, James W. *Oppenheimer: The Years of Risk.* Englewood Cliffs, N.J.: Prentice-Hall, 1982. A concise, well-balanced biography dealing with Oppenheimer's public service from 1942 to 1954. Describes the postwar controversies over security and the development of the hydrogen bomb in some detail.
Oppenheimer, J. Robert. *Robert Oppenheimer: Letters and Recollections.* Edited by Alice Kimball Smith and Charles Weiner. Cambridge: Harvard University Press, 1980. Letters from Oppenheimer to friends and colleagues interspersed with biographical information.
Szasz, Ferenc Morton. *The Day the Sun Rose Twice: The Story of the Trinity Site Nuclear Explosion.* Albuquerque: University of New Mexico Press, 1984. A short history of the successful first test of the atom bomb, using Manhattan Project papers. Not about Oppenheimer per se, but deals with his role at the test.

Jeanette Keith

JESSE OWENS

Born: September 12, 1913; Oakville, Alabama
Died: March 31, 1980; Tucson, Arizona
Area of Achievement: Sports
Contribution: The winner of four gold medals at the Berlin Olympics in 1936,
Owens served as an inspirational model of success for American blacks,
and later became a symbol and eloquent spokesman for America as a land
of opportunity for all.

Early Life

James Cleveland Owens was born on September 12, 1913, in Oakville,
Alabama, a remote little farm community on the northern edge of the state.
His father, Henry Cleveland Owens, and his mother, née Mary Emma Fitzgerald, were sharecroppers, descendants of slaves. James Cleveland, the last
of nine children who survived infancy, was called J. C. When he was eight or
nine years old, the family moved to Cleveland, Ohio, for better work and
educational opportunities. On his first day of school, he introduced himself
as "J. C.," but his teacher misunderstood him to say "Jesse." The young
Owens bashfully accepted the mistake, thus taking on the name by which he
would become famous.

At Fairmount Junior High School his exceptional athletic ability caught the
eye of a physical education teacher, Charles Riley. A white man, Riley became Owens' coach, his moral monitor, and his surrogate father, teaching
him citizenship as well as athletic techniques. Riley worked long hours with
his pupil and continued to do so through high school. While on his high
school track team, Jesse set several interscholastic records. In 1932, he failed
to win a place on the United States Olympic squad, but by the time he had
finished high school, in 1933, he had won much acclaim as a track athlete of
extraordinary promise.

Owens wished to attend the University of Michigan. No track scholarships
were available in that day, however, and Jesse's parents could not afford tuition. He therefore matriculated at Ohio State University, athletic boosters
having arranged for him to work at part-time jobs to pay his expenses. He
waited on tables in the dining hall, operated an elevator in the State House,
and served as a page boy for the Ohio legislature.

Poorly prepared for college work and distracted by athletics, he was never
a good student. After his first term he was constantly on academic probation;
once he had to sit out the indoor track season because of bad grades. All the
while he excelled in sports, setting numerous Big Ten and national track
records. His finest day was May 25, 1935, at the Big Ten championships in
Ann Arbor. Within a single hour he set new world records in the 220-yard
sprint, the 220-yard hurdles, and the long jump, and tied the world record in

the 100-yard dash. Well over a year before the Berlin Games of 1936, Owens emerged as a young man destined for Olympic fame.

His physique, style, and personality made him a sportswriter's dream. He carried about 165 pounds on a compact frame of five feet, ten inches. A model of graceful form, he ran so smoothly that each performance seemed effortless. Whether on or off the track, he frequently flashed a warm, spontaneous smile. Never did he refuse an interview or autograph. In the face of racial insults and discrimination, he kept a mild, pleasant demeanor. Like most blacks of his generation, Owens survived by turning the other cheek, by presenting himself as a modest individual who did not openly retaliate against the bigotry of his day.

At the Olympic trials in the summer of 1936, he finished first in all three of the events he had entered. Several weeks later, he took the Berlin Olympics by storm. First, he won the 100-meter dash in 10.3 seconds, equaling the world record. Next he took the gold medal in the long jump with a new Olympic distance of 8.06 meters. Then he won the gold in the 200-meter race with a new Olympic mark of 20.7 seconds. Toward the end of the week, he was unexpectedly placed on the American team for the 400-meter relays. He ran the opening leg in yet another gold-medal, record-making effort.

By the end of that fabulous week in Berlin, an attractive yarn attached itself to the name of Jesse Owens. Supposedly, he was "snubbed" by Adolf Hitler, who reportedly refused to congratulate him publicly after his victories. Actually, the story was concocted by American sportswriters, who were all too willing to read the worst of motives into Hitler's behavior and to assume innocent excellence from America's newest hero. Although it had no basis in fact, the story of "Hitler's snub" was repeated so often that people took it as truth. It remains one of the great anecdotes of American popular culture.

Life's Work

For several years after the Berlin Olympics, life did not go smoothly for Owens. American officials had planned a barnstorming tour for the track team immediately after the Berlin Games. At first, Owens cooperated, running exhibitions in Germany, Czechoslovakia, and England. Having received numerous offers from the United States to capitalize on his Olympic fame, he balked when the team departed from London for a series of exhibitions in Scandinavia. The Amateur Athletic Union suspended him from any further amateur competition.

Accompanied by his Ohio State coach, Larry Snyder, Owens returned to the United States only to find that all the "offers" were phony publicity stunts by unscrupulous entrepreneurs. They never seriously intended to give a young black man—not even an Olympic hero—a steady job at decent pay. Instead, Owens found a lucrative assignment in the presidential campaign of

Alf Landon, who paid him to stump for black votes. That turned out to be a futile effort but no more futile than a subsequent string of unsatisfactory jobs. For a time, Owens directed a band for Bill "Bojangles" Robinson on the black nightclub circuit. Tiring of that, he organized traveling basketball and softball teams, raced against horses at baseball games and county fairs, served for a summer as a playground director in Cleveland, and briefly worked as a clothes salesman. He suffered his biggest failure in a dry-cleaning venture that went bankrupt within six months.

Now married with three young daughters, Owens at twenty-seven years of age returned to Ohio State to finish his baccalaureate degree. Unfortunately, he could not bring his grade average up sufficiently to earn his degree. At the outbreak of World War II, he took a government appointment as director of a physical fitness program for blacks. Two years later, he took a job with Ford Motor Company in Detroit, in charge of Ford's black labor force. Dismissed from that position at the end of the war, by 1946 Owens no doubt winced when he looked back on the ten years since his Olympic victories. During that decade he had held ten jobs or so, all confined to the segregated black community.

Finally, in the 1950's, Owens broke out of that ghetto existence. When, after the onset of the Cold War, America needed a successful black to display to the world as an exemplar of the cherished American ideal of equal opportunity, Jesse Owens fit the bill. Having moved to Chicago in 1949, he worked with the Southside Boys Club and gave addresses to both black and white audiences in the greater Chicago area. Soon, he was in great demand throughout the United States as a spokesman for American patriotism and the American Dream. In 1951, he returned to Berlin with that message. In 1955, he toured India, Malaya, and the Philippines under the sponsorship of the United States Department of State, and the following year, he attended the Melbourne, Australia, Olympic Games as a personal representative of President Dwight D. Eisenhower. Never again would Owens be shunted aside as a black man in a white man's world. For the last two decades of his life, he gave more than one hundred speeches a year in praise of athletics, religion, and the flag.

Becoming politically more conservative as he got older, Owens refused to join the Civil Rights movement. His moderate position put him out of touch with the younger, angrier generation of blacks. He was rejected as an "Uncle Tom" in the 1960's. After Tommie Smith and John Carlos gave their world-famous black-fist salutes at the Olympic Games held in Mexico City in 1968, Owens demanded apologies, but to no avail.

He received numerous honors during his final years. In 1974, the National Collegiate Athletic Association presented him its highest recognition, the Theodore Roosevelt Award for distinguished achievement. Two years later, President Gerald R. Ford bestowed on him the Medal of Freedom Award for his "inspirational" life, and in 1979, Democratic president Jimmy Carter honored him with the Living Legends Award for his "dedicated but modest" example of greatness. Less than a year later, on March 31, 1980, Jesse Owens died of lung cancer. Ironically, America's greatest track and field athlete fell victim to a twenty-year habit of cigarette smoking.

Summary

When Jesse Owens achieved stardom in the Berlin Olympics of 1936, rigid racial segregation pervaded baseball, football, and basketball in the United States. Owens and Joe Louis stood virtually alone as black athletes who had excelled against whites. Black Americans viewed them as examples of success, inspirational models of black ability, symbols of racial pride and dignity.

Although he was America's first Olympic superstar, Owens did not become a widely acclaimed hero until after World War II. As Americans transposed their hatred of Hitler and the Nazis to Stalin and the Communists, Owens' rags-to-riches story confirmed American values as superior to Communist claims to a better way of life. "In America, anybody can become somebody," Owens often said, and American politicians, the media, and the public at large loved him for it. Especially to people in the nonaligned Third World, he was an effective spokesman for American democracy.

Four years after Owens' death, the 1984 Los Angeles Olympics demonstrated his perennial popularity. At Los Angeles, Carl Lewis won gold medals in the same four events that Owens had dominated half a century earlier, with much better statistical results. Yet Owens' fame remained undiminished. Each time Lewis won a race, he was compared to Owens. Old film clips from the Berlin Games were aired repeatedly on television, showing the graceful Owens in action. Numerous interviews with family and friends kept his memory alive. Arguably, Jesse Owens was the posthumous star of the Los Angeles Olympics.

His life illustrates the principle that an athlete becomes a national hero only when his achievements, personality, and image coincide with momentous events to fulfill a cultural need beyond the athletic arena. So long as people struggle against the odds of racial prejudice and economic deprivation, the story of Jesse Owens will be told. He overcame the odds.

Bibliography

Baker, William J. *Jesse Owens: An American Life*. New York: Free Press, 1986. The only complete, critical biography available. Based on archival research, the black press, interviews with family and friends, and FBI files on Owens, all fully documented. A candid appraisal of Owens' limitations and vices as well as his achievements and virtues, set against the background of American society.

_____. *Sports in the Western World*. Totowa, N.J.: Rowman and

Littlefield, 1982. Places Owens in the larger context of sport history, briefly focusing on his Olympic victories in the face of Hitler's ambitions in 1936. A survey, undocumented, but with a good critical bibliography of sport history.

Edwards, Harry. *The Revolt of the Black Athlete.* New York: Free Press, 1970. A firsthand account of the movement for black athletes' rights in the 1960's by the leader of the revolt that culminated in Mexico City. Depicts Owens as a lamentable representative of an older generation's acquiescence to racial abuse. A fiery, argumentative treatise.

Mandell, Richard D. *The Nazi Olympics.* New York: Macmillan Publishing Co., 1971. The best treatment of the Berlin Games of 1936. Strong on Nazi ideology and technical efficiency behind the Games, also on daily events and profiles of athletes. Well documented from German as well as English sources, a gem of cultural history.

Owens, Jesse, with Paul Neimark. *Blackthink: My Life as Black Man and White Man.* New York: William Morrow and Co., 1970. A tirade against black power advocates, especially against black athletes who openly protested American racism. Mostly autobiographical, with Owens illustrating his own acquaintance with bigotry, concluding that patience and moral character rather than angry rebellion would produce social change. Evoked hostile response from black readers, prompting Owens to collaborate once again with Paul Neimark to produce *I Have Changed* (New York: William Morrow and Co., 1972), another collection of stories from his life to explain his present point of view.

_____. *Jesse: A Spiritual Autobiography.* Plainfield, N.J.: Logos International, 1978. An indulgent use of anecdotes in the service of homilies. As always, Owens' recollections cannot be taken at face value. Some are outright fabrications; most are romantically embellished.

_____. *The Jesse Owens Story.* New York: G. P. Putnam's Sons, 1970. A lightweight, ghost-written autobiography directed towards a teenage readership. More inspirational than factually accurate; anecdotal, not analytical. Undocumented and untrustworthy, the Jesse Owens story as Owens himself wanted it told.

Quercetani, Roberto L. *A World History of Track and Field Athletics, 1864-1964.* London: Oxford University Press, 1964. Useful reference for Owens' achievements in comparison with other athletes before and since his day. Covers his intercollegiate as well as his Olympic victories.

William J. Baker

THOMAS PAINE

Born: January 29, 1737; Thetford, England
Died: June 8, 1809; New York, New York
Areas of Achievement: Politics, literature, and science
Contribution: Paine was a participant in both the American and French revo-
lutions, and, through his writings, he attempted to foment revolution in
England as well. He was interested in the new scientific ideas of his age,
spent considerable energy on the design of an iron-arch bridge, and tried
to resolve the age-old conflicts between science and religion by espousing
Deism.

Early Life

Thomas Paine was born January 29, 1737, in Thetford, England. His
father, Joseph Pain (the son later added a final "e" to his name), was a
Quaker staymaker. Working as a craftsman, he provided whalebone corsets
for local women. Paine's mother, Frances Cocke, the daughter of a local
attorney, was an Anglican, older than her husband and of difficult disposition. As a daughter died in infancy, the Pains were able to concentrate all of
their efforts on their son. He was taught by a local schoolmaster from the age
seven to thirteen and then apprenticed to his father to learn the trade of a
staymaker. This was clearly not entirely to his liking, as he managed at one
point to run away and spend some time at sea. Upon his return, he practiced
his craft in various places in England. In 1759, Paine married Mary Lambert,
but his wife died a year later. Dissatisfied with his occupation, he tried others, including a brief stint at schoolteaching and perhaps also preaching. Still
seeking his niche in the world, Paine returned home for a time to study for
the competitive examination to become an excise collector. He passed the
exam and obtained positions collecting customs revenues from 1764 to 1765
and from 1768 to 1774. He was twice dismissed from his posts for what
higher authorities saw as laxity in the performance of his duties. The second
dismissal came after Paine participated in efforts to obtain higher wages for
excisemen, during the course of which he wrote a pamphlet, *The Case of the
Officers of the Excise* (1772). The time he spent on these endeavors, as well
as his arguments, contributed to the loss of his position. Paine was married to
Elizabeth Ollive in 1767, and, while continuing as an exciseman, he also
helped her widowed mother and siblings run the family store. By 1774, the
business was in bankruptcy, Paine and his wife had separated, and he was
without a government position, with little prospect of regaining one. It was at
this point in his life that Paine, so far a failure at everything he had tried to
do, obtained a letter of introduction from Benjamin Franklin and moved to
America.

Life's Work

Paine arrived in the Colonies at an auspicious moment. A dispute over "taxation without representation," simmering between England and her colonists since the passage of the Stamp Act in 1765, had led to the Boston Tea Party and then to the passage of the so-called Intolerable Acts. Paine obtained a position as editor for the new *Pennsylvania Magazine*, published in Philadelphia. Meanwhile, American feelings had boiled over, and the Revolutionary War had begun. As an author, Paine had finally found where his true talents lay. In January of 1776, he wrote *Common Sense*, a pamphlet attacking the king, advocating independence, and outlining the form of government that should be adopted. The work was a tremendous success, a consequence of its timely arguments as well as its clear, forceful language. Reprinted in numerous editions, passed from hand to hand, it reached an audience of unprecedented size. At age thirty-nine, Paine had at last achieved a measure of success. He went on to become the leading propagandist of the American Revolution.

During the war, Paine served as secretary to a commission on Indian affairs and as secretary to the Committee for Foreign Affairs of the Second Continental Congress. He resigned, under pressure, from the second position during a bitter political debate over the actions of Silas Deane. He later served as a clerk for the Pennsylvania Assembly and participated in a diplomatic venture to France, seeking additional help for the fledgling nation. He is best known, however, for his continued efforts to promote the American cause. By 1783, he had written a total of sixteen *Crisis* papers as well as other pamphlets. In the *Crisis* papers, with ringing language meant to stir the soul and bolster the war effort, he appealed to patriotic Americans to rally to the cause.

As the war came to a conclusion, Paine turned his efforts to providing some measure of financial security for himself. He appealed to the national Congress and a number of state legislatures for compensation for his previous literary efforts on behalf of the American cause. He was ultimately granted a small pension by Congress, land by the New York legislature, and money by the Pennsylvania government. The Virginia legislature refused to come to his aid after he wrote a pamphlet, *The Public Good* (1780), arguing that all the states should cede their Western land claims to the national government. In this work and others, Paine's talents were utilized by those who wanted to bolster the powers of the central government. In 1786, he wrote a pamphlet, *Dissertations on Government; the Affairs of the Bank; and Paper Money*, in which he defended the Bank of America, chartered by Congress and the state of Pennsylvania as an instrument to raise money for the government and to aid commerce. In the course of this work, he condemned paper money, maintaining that anything but gold or silver was a dangerous fraud. Always interested in science and new technology, he also busied himself with designing an iron-arch bridge that would be able to span greater distances than was possible with existing methods. Unable to obtain sufficient money or interest for his project in the United States, he left for France in 1787 and from there made several trips to England, primarily to raise support for a workable model.

Paine arrived in France just as the French Revolution began to unfold, although this drama did not at first engage his attention. With the publication of Edmund Burke's *Reflections on the Revolution in France* (1790), Paine again took up his pen for a radical cause, producing, in two parts, *The Rights of Man* (1791, 1792). Whereas the conservative Burke emphasized the value of traditions and claimed that all change should come about gradually, Paine argued for government based on consent, defended revolution as a corrective remedy for unjust government, suggested ways to bring revolution to England, and proposed an early form of social welfare. The second part of *The Rights of Man* led to his being tried and convicted in absentia in England for seditious libel. Paine barely escaped arrest by the English authorities and took passage to France, where he became intimately involved in the course of the French Revolution.

When Paine returned to France in 1792, it was as an elected delegate to the French Assembly. There he was caught up, and ultimately overcome, by the tide of the revolution. Paine associated with the political representatives of the middle and upper classes, with literary figures, and with those who spoke English, never having mastered French sufficiently to converse without a translator. Despite his attacks on monarchy in his previous writings, the depths of French radicalism, the swiftness of change, and the quick trial and execution of the king all went beyond what he could support. Associated with the Girondist faction of French politics and an object of increasing antiforeign sentiment, Paine was arrested after the Jacobins achieved power; he subsequently spent ten agonizing months in jail while prisoners around him were carted off to the guillotine. Once the virulence of the revolution ran its course, Paine seemed less of a threat to those in power. As a result, a new American minister to France, James Monroe, was able to appeal for his release from prison, arguing that Paine was an American, rather than English, citizen.

While in prison, Paine began the last work for which he achieved fame, or, in this case, infamy: *The Age of Reason* (1794). The first part of this book was an attack on religion and a defense of Deism, while the second part was specifically aimed at Christianity and included numerous pointed refutations of biblical passages. It was a work that sparked in rebuttal many pamphlets in England and the United States and was also the source of much of the hostility directed against Paine in later years.

Paine's spell in prison had undermined his health and warped his judgment, although he had never been astute in practical politics. Remaining in

France, even though after 1795 he was no longer a member of the French Assembly, he wrote a pamphlet attacking George Washington and meddled in American foreign policy. In 1802, after an absence of fifteen years, he returned to the United States, taking up residence in, among other places, Washington, D.C., and New York City. He wrote letters and a few pamphlets, but he was anathema to the Federalists and a political liability to the Republicans. He died on June 8, 1809, in New York City, and his body was taken to the farm in New Rochelle, which the New York government had given him years before, and buried. Some time after his death, his bones were clandestinely dug up by an Englishman who took them off to England hoping to exhibit them; they ultimately disappeared.

Summary

Thomas Paine said that his country was the world, and his life illustrates the truth of this statement. His numerous pamphlets and books zeroed in on the main issues of his time, while the clarity and strength of his language have given his works an enduring appeal. He wrote in support of freedom from arbitrary government and against what he saw as outdated religious superstitions. In addition, he was an active participant in two major revolutions, as well as a friend and acquaintance of major figures in three countries. He was also the center of some controversy, at times difficult to tolerate, exhibiting a disinclination to bathe, a lack of care about his apparel, a propensity to drink, and a tendency to impose on the hospitality of friends for months, and even years, at a time. He was a complex and interesting individual who sparked debate in England, America, and elsewhere among his contemporaries—debate which has continued among historians since his death.

Paine's interest for Americans, though, stems primarily from his authorship of *Common Sense* and the *Crisis* papers. He has frequently been described as the right man in the right place at the right time. The first pamphlet sold 120,000 copies in three months and went through twenty-five editions in 1776 alone. It met the needs of the moment and substantially helped push Americans toward independence. In it, Paine attacked monarchy as being "ridiculous" and George III for being the "Royal Brute of Great Britain." He thought it absurd for England, an island, to continue to rule America, a continent. Paine maintained not only that it was "time to part" but also that it was America's obligation to prepare a refuge for Liberty, "an asylum for mankind." After independence was declared, Paine, in the first of his numerous *Crisis* papers, noted that in "times that try men's souls," the "summer soldier" or the "sunshine patriot" might "shrink from the service of his country," but the true patriot will stand firm, conquer tyranny, and obtain the precious prize of freedom.

These stirring words, more than anything else he did or wrote in his long and controversial life, assured Paine's place in history. Simply put, he was the most important propagandist of the American Revolution. As such, his later sojourns in England, France, and ultimately back in the United States constitute merely an interesting postscript to his real contribution to American history.

Bibliography
Aldridge, Alfred Owen. *Man of Reason: The Life of Thomas Paine*. Philadelphia: J. B. Lippincott Co., 1959. This scholarly work, based on research in England and France, attempts to give a fair assessment of a complex man. Although the book at times is laudatory, Aldridge basically sees Paine's life as a tragedy.
Clark, Harry Hayden. "Toward a Reinterpretation of Thomas Paine." *American Literature* 5 (May, 1933): 133-145. Argues that Paine was less influenced by Quakerism than previous writers thought and also was less radical. Clark examines the growth of Paine's mind, pointing to the influence of science and Deism and noting the extent to which Paine defended *laissez-faire* economics.
Conway, Moncure Daniel. *The Life of Thomas Paine*. 2 vols. New York: G. P. Putnam's Sons, 1892. The best nineteenth century biography, written by the first scholar to do extensive research on Paine, this is still a useful work. Conway also published a collection of Paine's writings.
Dorfman, Joseph. "The Economic Philosophy of Thomas Paine." *Political Science Quarterly* 53 (September, 1938): 372-386. Examines the economic ideas expressed in Paine's major pamphlets and his other ideas that had economic implications, downplaying their radicalism.
Edwards, Samuel. *Rebel! A Biography of Tom Paine*. New York: Praeger, 1974. This is a popular biography that covers all of Paine's life. It defends the achievements of Paine's early years, emphasizing his radicalism, but is more critical of the older Paine, noting his eccentric behavior. Edwards accepts as fact some scandalous stories about Paine.
Foner, Eric. *Tom Paine and Revolutionary America*. New York: Oxford University Press, 1976. This scholarly biography of Paine concentrates on his American years and on his radicalism. Foner analyzes Paine's political and economic thought and emphasizes the degree to which he was consistent throughout his life.
Hawke, David Freeman. *Paine*. New York: Harper and Row, Publishers, 1974. The most complete biography of Paine. Hawke downplays Paine's radicalism, noting that he frequently was only reflecting the ideas of his times, and emphasizes the degree to which he wrote pamphlets for pay. This is a scholarly work that portrays Paine with all of his warts.
Jordan, Wintrop D. "Familial Politics: Thomas Paine and the Killing of the King, 1776." *Journal of American History* 60 (1973): 294-308. This article

discusses the appeal of *Common Sense* and its significance in preparing the way for a republic by attacking the idea of monarchy in general and the "brute" George III in particular.

Paine, Thomas. *The Complete Writings of Thomas Paine*. Edited by Philip S. Foner. New York: Citadel Press, 1945. An accessible and well-prepared edition of Paine's works; Foner also edited a paperback edition of Paine's major pieces.

Penniman, Howard. "Thomas Paine—Democrat." *American Political Science Review* 37 (April, 1943): 244-262. Concerning the economic and political ideas in Paine's writings after 1791, this article emphasizes the degree to which Paine was a radical and a democrat.

Robbins, Caroline. "The Lifelong Education of Thomas Paine (1737-1809): Some Reflections upon His Acquaintance Among Books." *American Philosophical Society Proceedings* 127 (October, 1983): 135-142. Robbins argues that Paine, no scholar, read books primarily for information and also learned from friends and associates.

Williamson, Audrey. *Thomas Paine: His Life, Work, and Times*. London: George Allen and Unwin, 1973. This defensive work was written by an Englishman and emphasizes Paine's years in England. Offers some new information on Paine's early years but on the whole is a rambling account.

Maxine N. Lurie

THEODORE PARKER

Born: April 24, 1810; Lexington, Massachusetts
Died: May 10, 1860; Florence, Italy
Areas of Achievement: Religion and reform
Contribution: A scholar with a strong social conscience, Parker was an influential Transcendentalist who helped shape American Unitarianism and was a leader in the abolitionist cause during the 1850's.

Early Life

Theodore Parker was born April 24, 1810, in Lexington, Massachusetts, into a family with a history of patriotic activity, including service at Lexington and Bunker Hill. Parker grew up on stories about this heritage and often referred to it when he was crusading for the liberty of black Americans. His parents John and Hannah (Segur Stearns) Parker inspired many aspects of his life. The youngest of eleven children, Parker was a bit spoiled by his mother, who often read the Bible to him and who encouraged the development of his strong conscience. Books were readily available in Parker's home as his father frequently purchased them and had access to a lending library. At school, although he could not attend full-time, Parker quickly showed his scholarly potential but was terrified by the theology of divine retribution found in the primers of that day; it was an interpretation he later rejected totally. The loss of his mother when Parker was thirteen years old left him with more and more work to do at home, and his formal secondary education ended three years later. Parker spent the next seven years teaching school and trying to accumulate enough money in order to attend the Harvard Divinity School.

In 1832, with the help of an uncle, Parker was able to open his own school at Watertown, Massachusetts. The school was quickly successful, so that, while he was still aiding his elderly father, Parker's financial situation improved. At his boardinghouse, he met Lydia Cabot, his future wife. She was the sort of woman he preferred: loving, cooperative, and supportive. Although he was often to work with strong-minded, intellectual women, Parker was never comfortable with them. Parker became friends with the Reverend Convers Francis, who provided books and scholarly guidance. Francis introduced the young Parker to the antislavery movement and to the idealistic philosophy of scholars such as Immanuel Kant and G. W. F. Hegel, which strongly influenced his thought. He also began to explore modern biblical criticism. In 1834, Francis found a scholarship for him, and Parker sadly left Watertown for the Harvard Divinity School. Over the next two years he earned a degree and a reputation for frugal living, hard study, light-heartedness, and theological radicalism.

Life's Work

It took Parker a year to get a pulpit after he was graduated. Perhaps he was tainted with Transcendentalism or, as Unitarian ministers often were, perceived as too intellectual. Perhaps his awkward bearing, prematurely balding head, square frame, and large hands hardened by farm work resulted in a poor impression. Whatever the cause, Parker used the time to fill temporarily empty pulpits, to marry Lydia, and to begin his translation of and commentary on W. M. L. De Wette's *Beiträge zur Einleitung in das Alte Testament* (1806; *A Critical and Historical Introduction to the Canonical Scriptures of the Old Testament*, 1843). It was on this book that his scholarly reputation was grounded. Parker was among the first Americans to study and apply the higher biblical criticism that was being developed by German scholars.

In May, 1837, Parker accepted a call from a church in West Roxbury, Massachusetts. Over the next decade, Parker worked on developing his philosophical and theological ideas. He was already in the Transcendentalist school with Ralph Waldo Emerson and Henry David Thoreau, for he was convinced that sensory data confirmed only limited phenomena. The great moral truths, he believed, being self-evidently true, transcended such confirmation. These were known to the human conscience and depended on no outside authority. In May, 1841, he preached a sermon entitled "The Transient and Permanent in Christianity," arguing that all the supernatural trappings of the religion and even Jesus himself might be proven false or nonexistent without weakening the essential truth of Christianity. Each person must find the Kingdom of Heaven within himself, he argued.

Unitarianism, which was still largely a branch of Congregationalism, supposedly rejected creeds, but these ideas which Parker elaborated in subsequent years outraged many. After his 1841 sermon, Parker could find few ministers who were willing to exchange pulpits with him, and the friends who did, including those who did not agree with him, faced congregational protests and even withdrawals. Undaunted, Parker criticized his colleagues freely, and eventually he was asked to resign from the Boston Association of Congregational ministers, a demand which he refused.

Convinced of God's enduring love—eternal damnation was, he believed, impossible, for it would make eternal life a curse—he renounced the religion of guilt and retribution that had tormented his childhood. A good man, a kind man, a just man, a loving man was a Christian regardless of whether he believed the traditional theology of that sect. Reason was a God-given tool, but in religion, as in Transcendentalist philosophy, intuition carried man to greater truths. With this emphasis on the individual's discovery of truth within himself, it should have been impossible for Parker to argue that anyone's beliefs were wrong. Yet he often did.

While becoming controversial among Boston's ministers, Parker was also becoming known as a Transcendentalist philosopher. His articles and reviews appeared in many journals and were a staple of the Transcendentalist organ *The Dial*, which first appeared in 1840. In this same period, Parker's friend George Ripley founded the Utopian community Brook Farm. Like Ralph Waldo Emerson, Parker chose not to join. Many who did also joined his West Roxbury congregation, and Parker often visited the farm. This exposure to intellectuals stimulated Parker's thought, which appeared as seven lectures which constituted the book *A Discourse on Matters Pertaining to Religion*, published in 1842. Writing—he had finished the two volumes on De Wette and another volume of collected articles—lecturing, preaching, parish duties, and disputes took their toll, and in September, 1843, he and Lydia left for a year in Europe. He spent this vacation visiting scholars and philosophers whom he admired.

Upon his return from Europe, Parker, more convinced than ever that Transcendentalism was the only viable form of religion, intended to prove his point. The demands of his congregation and calls for lectures which had to be written quickly always prevented him from doing the scholarly work he wanted. The old controversies were quickly renewed when, in December, 1844, he suggested the possibility that God might send man greater Christs in the future. His piety and respect for Jesus were undeniable, yet he was willing neither to limit God's love and power nor to assume that the revelation of one age was adequate for another.

Yet more and more, he was heard with respect, and early the next year a Boston group created a church for him. Although sad to leave friends in West Roxbury, Parker was eager to be part of the intellectual ferment of the city, and the new Twenty-eighth Congregational Society, under his leadership, became the largest parish in Boston and possibly in the United States. Parker made many new friends, including such luminaries as William Lloyd Garrison, Charles Sumner, Julia Ward Howe, and Horace Mann, and became mentor of a few young Unitarian ministers such as Starr King.

In Boston, the childless Parker family was enlarged by the adoption of a young, distant cousin of Lydia. Parker also worked on his beloved library, which was becoming one of the largest private collections in New England, though increasingly in the 1850's lecture fees which had bought books were diverted to support the needs of fugitive slaves. From 1847 to 1850, Parker wrote for and helped edit *The Massachusetts Quarterly Review*, a new Transcendentalist journal. Although never the intellectual force that its founders intended it to be, the *Review* did give Transcendentalists, including Parker, an outlet for their ideas.

In the 1840's, Parker moved into the general social reform movement of the mid-nineteenth century. The cozy, self-satisfied, formulistic rut that even Unitarians had fallen into was not for him. He spoke of the virtues (though against the state imposition) of temperance, the importance of equality for women, the evils and unchristian nature of the Mexican War, and the need for penal reform as well as many other reforms.

Increasingly, however, justice for blacks came to dominate not only his reform impulse but virtually all of his efforts. In 1845, Parker joined Emerson and Charles Sumner in refusing to speak at the New Bedford Lyceum because blacks had been refused membership. He was driven by the memory of his forebears' fight to win liberty from Great Britain to make liberty a reality for all. While he did not know the peculiar institution at first hand, he recognized its transcendent evil quality just as he recognized the transcendent virtues of Christianity. He amassed a powerful statistical argument that slavery was not economical, but his true power as an abolitionist came from his fervor in invoking the higher law of morality in opposing slavery. Did the Bible accept slavery? he asked, and if the answer was affirmative, he insisted, then the Bible was wrong. On the issue of slavery, as on theological issues, the intuitive truth was not to be denied. Parker would do as he believed Jesus had done: reject statute in favor of what he knew to be right.

Galvanized to greater effort by the Fugitive Slave Law of 1850, Parker became a leader of the Boston Vigilance Committee organized to prevent return of escaped slaves to the South. He called for resistance in the same spirit that the Stamp Act had once been resisted. Men who came for William and Ellen Craft, runaway slaves who were parishioners of Parker, were driven from Boston by abuse and threats. When he married the Crafts, Parker, with an eye for the dramatic gesture, presented to William a Bible for the care of their souls and a sword for the care of his wife's freedom. It would be a sin to hate those who would reenslave them, he told the Crafts, but not to kill in order to preserve their freedom if no other means were available.

Parker's radicalism grew. When Thomas Sims was being taken back to Georgia in 1852, Parker eloquently denounced the "kidnaping" in public and urged the Vigilance Committee to attack the ship on which Sims was confined. The passage of the Kansas-Nebraska Act in 1854 only made matters worse, and Parker, in May of that year, helped organize an abortive raid on the courthouse where the recently arrested fugitive Anthony Burns was held. After Burns was taken away, Parker was indicted along with several others who had supported the raid. Parker was delighted with the idea of presenting his own defense and prepared quite a speech for that purpose. When the indictment was quashed on technical grounds, he had to be satisfied with publishing the defense.

Although he refused to attend a secessionist convention called by radical abolitionists, Parker was increasingly convinced that only war could eliminate slavery, and war was more acceptable to him than slavery. Although saddened by the violence of John Brown's antislavery victories in Kansas, he supported Brown and was a member of the secret Boston Committee of Six that provided moral and financial support for further efforts. He was out of the country at the time of the catastrophic raid on Harper's Ferry but wished he were home to defend the right.

As the 1850's passed, Parker's once-robust health declined, while his activities increased. In addition to his duties as minister of a congregation formally numbering some seven thousand, he continued writing and antislavery activism. He was delivering approximately one hundred lectures each year all over the East and North. In 1856-1857, he was slowed by pleurisy and other respiratory problems to a mere seventy lectures, but after a vacation in the spring of 1858 and an operation for fistula, he seemed on the road to recovery. He was back to work too soon, and although he managed to preach for New Year's Day of 1859, the next Sunday the congregation gathered only to receive a note that because of a serious lung hemorrhage Parker would not be able to come. Parker was suffering from the greatest killer of the nineteenth century: tuberculosis. His congregation sent him overseas in the hope that better climates would help, but as was so often the case before antibiotics, the disease could not be stopped. He died May 10, 1860, in Florence, Italy.

Summary

Theodore Parker's life reflected much of the American spirit of reform and practicality. As a Transcendentalist, he was part of the first truly American school of philosophy, and his essays have been favorably compared to the work of Emerson. Parker never reached the poetic heights of Emerson, but he was better at clearly and systematically laying out the framework of his thought. He also injected a theme of empirical testing into the intuitive scheme of Transcendentalism. Parker was too good a scholar to accept the miraculous blithely. The less likely an event, the more proof he wanted before he would accept it.

Parker was also an important force in the development of liberal religion. His thought was critical and concrete rather than abstract and metaphysical. He rejected creeds and regarded atheism as impossible, except as the denial of the existence of higher law. Divorcing the essentials of Christianity from all authority but the individual's reason and conscience was clearly a step toward modernity and today's Unitarian-Universalist position that a sincere desire to find spiritual truth is the only requisite for membership.

Parker's reform efforts were also part of the reform tradition that has reappeared periodically throughout American history. His belief that the church should be a driving force in political reform might seem to defy the Jeffersonian tradition of separation of church and state, but Parker did not favor imposition of morality by legislation. The church was to lead by its example and show the society how much better it might be. Parker's reform spirit also had American democratic and egalitarian qualities. Even Abraham Lincoln seems to have learned from him, for Parker used a number of variations of the famous phrase about government of, by, and for the people. At least one example of this was communicated to Lincoln by his law partner, William Herndon, a friend of Parker. As he worked himself to death in the cause of abolitionism, Parker showed many of the finest characteristics of American reformers.

Bibliography
Albrecht, Robert C. *Theodore Parker*. Boston: Twayne Publishers, 1971. A short but reasonably handled biography.
Chadwick, John W. *Theodore Parker: Preacher and Reformer*. Boston: Houghton Mifflin Co., 1900. Written by a Unitarian minister who knew and was inspired by Parker, this biography is rather uncritical but is important for its discussion of Parker's role in the development of Unitarianism.
Collins, Robert E. *Theodore Parker: American Transcendentalist: A Critical Essay and a Collection of His Writings*. Metuchen, N.J.: Scarecrow Press, 1973. After a long interpretive essay by Collins, selections from Parker's writings are included for comparison with works by Emerson on similar subjects. Collins' conclusion that Parker was a more important Transcendentalist than Emerson is an overstatement.
Commager, Henry Steele. *Theodore Parker*. Boston: Little, Brown and Co., 1936. Commager sometimes lets interpretive passages obscure the basic chronological structure of his book. He does a superb job, however, of setting Parker's life and work in context.
Fellman, Michael. "Theodore Parker and the Abolitionist Role in the 1850's." *Journal of American History* 61 (December, 1974): 666-684. An unusual interpretation portraying Parker as a thoroughgoing racist. Although the author has found some damning quotes, they come from rather scattered sources, and he ignores Parker's eloquent denunciations of black inequality. Parker did harbor some typical nineteenth century misconceptions about race, but this article overstates his views.
Parker, Theodore. *The Slave Power*. Edited by James K. Hosmer. Boston: American Unitarian Association, 1916. Reprint. New York: Arno Press, 1969. This is a collection of Parker's abolitionist writings and is the most convenient source in which to find the text of his most powerful antislavery orations.
Wilber, Earl M. *A History of Unitarianism*. Boston: Beacon Press, 1977. A standard work on the subject, the section on American Unitarianism is very useful.

Fred R. van Hartesveldt

FRANCIS PARKMAN

Born: September 16, 1823; Boston, Massachusetts
Died: November 8, 1893; Boston, Massachusetts
Area of Achievement: Historical scholarship
Contribution: Parkman was the greatest of the nineteenth century American patrician historians. He combined extensive research with an unparalleled literary artistry that continues to excite the imagination of readers. For many years, Parkman's seven-part series *France and England in North America* (1865-1892) was regarded as the definitive history of the three-sided struggle among the Indians, French, and English for dominion over the continent.

Early Life
Francis Parkman was born in Boston on September 16, 1823, the son of Francis and Caroline (Hall) Parkman. His paternal grandfather had been one of the city's wealthiest merchants; his father was pastor of the Old North Church and a pillar of Boston's Federalist-Unitarian establishment. On his mother's side, he traced his ancestry to the Puritan John Cotton. Because of his fragile health, Parkman was sent at the age of eight to live on his maternal grandfather's farm and attended school in nearby Medford. He returned to Boston at age thirteen, finished his preparatory work at the Chauncey Place School, and entered Harvard in 1840. He had acquired from his roamings on a stretch of untamed woodland at the edge of his grandfather's farm a romantic attachment to nature in the wild. His reading of the novels of James Fenimore Cooper sparked his interest in Indians, "the American forest," and the "Old French War." He was temperamentally a compulsively intense personality, driven by "passion" and "tenacious eagerness." During his sophomore year at Harvard, he appears to have decided upon what became his life's work: to write the dual story of the conquest of the Indians by the French and English and their struggle in turn for mastery. "The theme," he later recalled, "fascinated me, and I was haunted by wilderness images day and night."

At Harvard, Parkman was active in student extracurricular affairs, serving as president of the Hasty Pudding Club. He received sufficiently respectable grades in his course work for selection to Phi Beta Kappa. He spent his summer vacations tramping and canoeing in the forests of northern New England and the adjacent parts of Canada. Parkman hoped—in vain, as events turned out—that a strenuous regimen of outdoor living would strengthen his sickness-prone physique. He simultaneously took the opportunity to begin collecting material for his planned history project, filling his notebook with measurements of forts, descriptions of battle sites, reminiscences of survivors, and names and addresses of people in possession of old letters. In the autumn of 1843, he suffered a nervous illness and temporarily left Harvard for a tour of Europe to recuperate. He returned in time to be graduated with his class in August, 1844. At his father's behest, he went on to law school at Harvard. Although profiting from his exposure to the rules for the testing and use of evidence, he could not muster much enthusiasm for the law as such. His interests were primarily literary. His first appearance in print came in 1845, when he published in the *Knickerbocker Magazine* five sketches based upon his vacation trips. Although he was awarded his LL.B. in January, 1846, he never applied for admission to the bar.

After receiving his law degree, Parkman set out on what proved to be the formative experience of his life—a trip to the Western plains, partly in the hope of improving his health, partly to observe at first hand Indian life. Camping for several weeks with a band of Sioux Indians, he immersed himself in their habits, customs, and ways of thinking. During those weeks he contracted a mysterious ailment that left him a broken man physically on his return to Boston in October, 1846. His eyesight was so impaired that he could barely read, and he suffered from a nervous condition that made him unable to concentrate for longer than brief spurts. He still managed to dictate to a cousin who had accompanied him an account of their adventures that was serialized as "The Oregon Trail" in the *Knickerbocker Magazine* over a two-year span beginning in February, 1847. The account came out in book form in 1849 under the title *The California and Oregon Trail* (the shorter title was resumed with the 1872 edition). Parkman's experience with the Sioux shattered any illusions he may have gained from reading novels about the noble savage. "For the most part," he underlined, "a civilized white man can discover very few points of sympathy between his own nature and that of an Indian. With every disposition to do justice to their good qualities, he must be conscious that an impassable gulf lies between him and his red brethren. Nay, so alien to himself do they appear, that, after breathing the air of the prairie for a few months or weeks, he begins to look upon them as a troublesome and dangerous species of wild beast."

Life's Work

In 1848, Parkman began work on what became *History of the Conspiracy of Pontiac and the Indian War After the Conquest of Canada* (1851). He had a frame built of parallel wires to guide his hand while writing with his eyes closed in a dark room. For the most part, however, he relied upon others reading the source materials to him and transcribing his words. At first, his progress was painfully slow—the readings limited to a half-hour per sitting and his output averaging six lines a day. Gradually, however, he pushed himself to work for longer periods and successfully completed the two volumes within two and a half years. The work dealt with the Indian uprising in 1763-1765 against English occupation of the Western territories after the French surrender. His purpose, he explained, was "to portray the American forest and the American Indian at the period when both received their final doom." He divided his story into two distinct phases. During the first, the Indians triumphantly pushed the English back; in the second, the English turned the tide in a successful counterattack. Parkman's portrayal of Pontiac as the central figure on the Indian side was effective drama but inaccurate history. Later scholars have found that Pontiac was simply one Indian chief among many. The work's larger importance lies in how Parkman, in his introductory background chapters, sketched in outline the theme that he would develop more fully in his seven-part *France and England in North America*: the collision of rival cultures culminating in the English triumph on the Plains of Abraham in September, 1759.

History of the Conspiracy of Pontiac and the Indian War After the Conquest of Canada appeared in 1851. The first installment of *France and England in North America*, titled *Pioneers of France in the New World*, did not come out until 1865. The delay was partly a result of the amount of research involved. The major difficulty, however, was health problems and family tragedies that would have broken the spirit of a weaker personality. On May 13, 1850, Parkman married Catherine Scollay Bigelow, the daughter of a Boston doctor. The couple had one son and two daughters. In 1853, however, he suffered a relapse in his nervous condition that forced him to give up his historical work temporarily. A man who always needed an interest, Parkman, during his enforced withdrawal from scholarship, wrote his only novel, *Vassall Morton* (1856). Its hero, reflecting Parkman's own image of himself, is a high-spirited, outdoors-loving young man of high social position who succeeds in overcoming melodramatic trials and tribulations. Unfortunately, Parkman himself was unable to cope with his own personal crises at that time. The death of his son in 1857, followed by that of his wife within a year, precipitated a severe breakdown in 1858. Although these health problems kept him out of the fighting, the Civil War had a major influence on his approach to the rivalry between the French and the English in the seventeenth and eighteenth centuries as a struggle, akin to the one under way in his own time, between "Liberty and Absolutism."

Pioneers of France in the New World focuses upon the founding of Quebec in the early seventeenth century under the leadership of Samuel de Champlain. The next volume in the series, *The Jesuits in North America in the Seventeenth Century* (1867), had as its major protagonists the Jesuit missionaries, such as Jean de Brébeuf, Charles Garnier, and Isaac Jogues, who tried to convert the Canadian Indians to Roman Catholicism. The third volume, which appeared in 1869 as *The Discovery of the Great West*, traces the explorations of Robert La Salle in the area of the Great Lakes and then down the Mississippi River and across what is now Texas and Arkansas in the 1670's and 1680's. Parkman's next two titles, *The Old Régime in Canada*

(1874) and *Count Frontenac and New France Under Louis XIV* (1877), chronicle the political, social, and military history of New France during the last half of the seventeenth century. Their major theme is the corruption that came to pervade, and undermine, French colonial society despite the valiant, but unsuccessful, bid by Louis de Buade Frontenac to reverse the decay. Fearful lest he die before reaching the climax of his story, Parkman jumped ahead in the two volumes of *Montcalm and Wolfe* (1884) to deal with the final phase of the French-English struggle starting in the early 1750's and culminating in the surrender of Canada in 1763. In 1892, he filled in the gap with the two-volume *A Half-Century of Conflict*, in which he dealt with the fifty years of intermittent conflict from Frontenac's death in 1698 to the beginning of the French and Indian War in the 1750's.

The work rested upon painstaking research in primary sources. Parkman even boasted that the "statements of secondary writers have been accepted only when found to conform to the evidence of contemporaries, whose writings have been sifted and collated with the greatest care." His relied primarily upon the massive compilations of documents that had been published during the "documania" that had swept the United States in the aftermath of the War of 1812. At the same time, Parkman spent freely from the money he inherited from his father to purchase documents and have copies made of archival materials in this country and abroad. When formerly inaccessible La Salle documents became available, he rewrote *The Discovery of the Great West* to incorporate the new information. The revised version appeared in 1879 with the new title *La Salle and the Discovery of the Great West*.

Parkman never succumbed to the illusion of late nineteenth century scientific history that the facts spoke for themselves. "Faithfulness to the truth of history," he emphasized,

> involves far more than a research, however patient and scrupulous, into special facts. Such facts may be detailed with the most minute exactness, and yet the narrative, taken as a whole, may be unmeaning or untrue. The narrator must seek to imbue himself with the life and spirit of the time. He must study events in their bearings near and remote; in the character, habits, and manners of those who took part in them. He must himself be, as it were, a sharer or a spectator of the action he describes.

In pursuit of that goal, Parkman personally visited the sites about which he wrote. One of his major strengths was his feeling for the physical setting in which his story unfolded. His early writings occasionally suffered from labored prose and excessive detail. As time went on, however, his descriptions became terser, his imagery sharper. Parkman saw heroic leaders as the primary shapers of history. His own special forte was the delineation of personality. His technique was to build up a composite portrait by drawing upon his protagonist's own words and the accounts by contemporaries before assaying the individual himself. His appraisal of Frontenac strikingly illustrates his mastery of character portrayal.

> What perhaps may be least forgiven him is the barbarity of the warfare that he waged, and the cruelties that he permitted. He had seen too many towns sacked to be much subject to the scruples of modern humanitarianism; yet he was no whit more ruthless than his times and his surroundings, and some of his contemporaries find fault with him for not allowing more Indian captives to be tortured. Many surpassed him in cruelty, none equalled him in capacity and vigor. When civilized enemies were once within his power, he treated them, according to their degree, with a chivalrous courtesy, or a gentle kindness. If he was a hot and pertinacious foe, he was also a fast friend; and he excited love and hatred in about equal measure. His attitude towards public enemies was always proud and peremptory, yet his courage was guided by so clear a sagacity that he never was forced to recede from the position he had taken.

Notwithstanding such attempts at evenhandedness when dealing with individuals, Parkman shared the prejudices of his time and class. He was a vocal opponent of woman's suffrage; his comments on what he called "the mazes of feminine psychology" were almost uniformly unflattering. No democrat, he made no secret of his contempt for society's lower orders. He dismissed the hardworking German farmers of Pennsylvania as "a swarm of . . . peasants . . . who for the most part were dull and ignorant boors." He was no more enamored of the poorer whites of Colonial Virginia, considering them "of low origin," "vicious," and "as untaught as the warmest friend of popular ignorance could wish." He saw universal manhood suffrage as "the source of all the dangers which threaten the United States"; he pictured the immigrants of his own time as "barbarians . . . masses of imported ignorance and hereditary ineptitude." He was a social Darwinist before the publication of *On the Origin of Species* (1859). When describing in *The Oregon Trail* the "cannibal warfare" he witnessed among fishes in a pond, he ridiculed the dreams by softhearted philanthropists of a peaceful millennium. From minnows to men, he philosophized, life was incessant conflict, and he had no doubt that the outcome of the struggle for North America among the Indians, French, and English accorded with the "law of the survival of the fittest."

A thoroughgoing ethnocentrism marred Parkman's outlook. He pictured the Indians as barbarous savages: treacherous, deceitful, "a murder-loving race" filled with "insensate fury" and animated by "homicidal frenzy." "The Indians," he wrote in a typical descriptive passage, "howled like wolves, yelled like enraged cougars." Their white opponents "were much like the hunters of wolves, catamounts, and other dangerous beasts, except that the chase of this fierce and wily human game demanded far more hardihood and skill." As he put the matter bluntly in an 1886 public letter which dealt with contemporary white-Indian relations, "a few hordes of savages cannot be permitted to hold in perpetual barbarism the land which might sustain a hundred millions of civilized men." Despite his admiration for some individual Frenchmen, they were an inferior breed compared to the Anglo-Saxon. "The Germanic race, and especially the Anglo-Saxon branch of it," he wrote in his conclusion to *The Old Régime in Canada*, "is peculiarly masculine, and, therefore, peculiarly fitted for self-government. It submits its action habitually to the guidance of reason.... The French Celt is cast in a different mould.... he is impatient of delay, is impelled always to extremes, and does not readily sacrifice a present inclination to an ultimate good." That the English won and the French lost was no accident. "The cause lies chiefly in the vast advantage drawn by England from the historical training of her people in habits of reflection, forecast, industry, and self-reliance,—a training which enabled them to adopt and maintain an invigorating system of self-rule, totally inapplicable to their rivals."

Despite the almost constant pain he suffered, Parkman did not surrender to invalidism. He had a wide circle of friends and carried on an extensive correspondence. He had an excellent sense of humor, and his writings are dotted with sharp quips. He never lost his love for the outdoors and continued his camping trips as much as his health permitted. He took up flower-growing as a hobby during the 1850's, when incapacitated from pursuing his scholarly work, and grew so fascinated that the study of horticulture became a passion second only to history. His major achievement in this line was his development of a hybrid crimson lily named *Lilium Parkmanni* in his honor. His specialty, however, was roses, and his *The Book of Roses* (1866) was regarded for many years as the best guide to their cultivation. He served as a member of the Harvard Overseers (1868-1871 and 1874-1876) and as a fellow of the corporation (1875-1888), he was one of the founders of the Archeological Institute of America in 1879, and he played a leading role in the establishment of the American School of Classical Studies in Athens, Greece. Shortly after finishing *A Half-Century of Conflict*, he suffered an attack of pleurisy that proved almost fatal. He died November 8, 1893, of peritonitis at his home at Jamaica Pond in Boston.

Summary

Commentators have differed about Parkman's place in American historiography. There are those who put him with the literary historians of the romantic school such as John L. Motley, William H. Prescott, and George Bancroft. Others see him as a forerunner of the late nineteenth century scientific historians. In a sense, both views are correct: Parkman had a foot in both camps. He attracted an immense readership during his lifetime. His friend Henry Adams summed up the predominant contemporary appraisal when he rated Parkman "in the front rank of living English historians." At the same time, Parkman enjoyed a higher reputation among professional academic historians than any other of his fellow amateurs except possibly Adams himself. Those who dealt with the same period not simply followed Parkman's chronological framework but also relied heavily upon his work for information. One scholar went so far as to state that "Parkman never makes a mistake, certainly never a glaring one." Even Vernon L. Parrington in his *Main Currents in American Thought* (1927-1930) acknowledged that the "Brahmin mind has contributed to American letters no more brilliant work." As late as 1953, the account in the standard *Literary History of the United States* (1948) concluded that "Parkman's whole method may be accurately summarized as an attempt to bring back the past just as it was."

More recently, Parkman's reputation has suffered an eclipse. Judged by modern standards, he had major shortcomings as a historian. The French-English rivalry in the New World was only a minor aspect of the worldwide struggle under way between those powers, but Parkman largely failed to explore the dynamics of that broader conflict. Even as regards its North American phase, Parkman's episodic, narrative approach focusing upon heroic personalities runs counter to the prevailing tendency to emphasize the role of larger social, economic, and cultural forces. The heaviest attack has come from ethnographers over Parkman's treatment of the Indians; he has even been accused of deliberately distorting evidence to put the Indians in the worst possible light. Such criticisms miss the point. As Frederick Jackson Turner rightly observed, Parkman was "the greatest painter of historical pictures that this country—perhaps it is not too much to say, that any country—has produced." The chorus of praise greeting the 1983 republication of *France and England in North America* in the Library of America series attests Parkman's "extraordinary power" as a literary artist. Notwithstanding its limitations, Parkman's history constitutes what a reviewer of the new edition aptly called "our great national epic."

Bibliography
Doughty, Howard. *Francis Parkman.* New York: Macmillan Publishing Co., 1962. Although biographical in format, this work is primarily an appraisal of Parkman's writings, focusing upon their literary and artistic qualities from the point of view of a layman rather than a professional historian.
Gale, Robert L. *Francis Parkman.* New York: Twayne Publishers, 1973. A rather pedestrian biographical survey followed by volume-by-volume summaries of the major works.
Jennings, Francis. "Francis Parkman: A Brahmin Among Untouchables." *William and Mary Quarterly* 42 (July, 1985): 305-328. An important attempt to debunk Parkman's reputation for accuracy and impartiality by exposing his racism and his distortion of the evidence in order to place the Indians in the worst possible light.

Pease, Otis A. *Parkman's History: The Historian as Literary Artist.* New Haven, Conn.: Yale University Press, 1953. A brief but perceptive analysis of "the preconceptions and interests" shaping Parkman's historical approach.

Van Tassel, David D. *Recording America's Past: An Interpretation of the Development of Historical Studies in America, 1607-1884.* Chicago: University of Chicago Press, 1960. Places Parkman in the context of the development of historical scholarship in the United States.

Vitzthum, Richard C. *The American Compromise: Theme and Method in the Histories of Bancroft, Parkman, and Adams.* Norman: University of Oklahoma Press, 1974. Primarily an exercise in "literary criticism" based upon detailed textual explication.

Wade, Mason. *Francis Parkman: Heroic Historian.* New York: Viking Press, 1942. The fullest and most detailed biography, based upon thorough research of Parkman's correspondence, journals, and notes. The work is marred only by the author's tendency toward hagiography.

John Braeman

ROSA PARKS

Born: February 4, 1913; Tuskegee, Alabama

Area of Achievement: Civil rights
Contribution: By refusing to give up her bus seat to a white man, Parks provided Montgomery's black leaders with the incident that sparked a successful bus boycott and resulted in the further expansion of the Civil Rights movement and the rise to leadership of Dr. Martin Luther King, Jr.

Early Life
On February 4, 1913, Rosa Louise McCauley was born in Tuskegee, Alabama. Her father, James, was a carpenter, and her mother, Leona, had been a teacher. Some years later her father left, and the family, including her younger brother Sylvester, moved in with grandparents on a farm near Montgomery. Rosa attended the Montgomery Industrial School for Girls and Alabama State College. In 1932 she married Raymond Parks, a barber; they were both active members of the National Association for the Advancement of Colored People (NAACP), and Rosa was a youth adviser in the organization. She worked variously as a clerk, an insurance saleswoman, and then a tailor's assistant (seamstress) at the Fair Department Store in Montgomery, for seventy-five cents an hour.

In 1955, Rosa Parks was a slim, neat, rather plain woman, with rimless glasses and hair drawn straight back from her forehead down across her ears to the back of her neck. Like most of Montgomery's fifty thousand blacks, she had had problems with the city's segregated bus system; in 1943 she had been put off a bus because, after paying her fare at the front, she had walked down the aisle to the back instead of getting off and reboarding the bus by the back door. The first four rows of seats in a bus were always reserved for whites; the next two or three could be used by blacks only if no whites sat in that area. During 1955, three black women had been arrested for not giving up their seats to whites, but no action had been taken by the factionally fragmented black community. The black Women's Political Council had been unsuccessful in its attempt to organize a boycott protesting the March, 1955, arrest of fifteen-year-old Claudette Colvin, who had been taken off a bus in handcuffs.

Life's Work
On Thursday, December 1, 1955, Rosa Parks left an ordinary day's work and took a seat on her bus for the quarter-hour ride home. As the bus filled, she and three other blacks in the fifth row were told by the driver to stand so that a white man might sit. The others moved but Rosa Parks refused, because she was tired. The driver called the police, who arrested her.

Parks called Edgar Daniel Nixon, a leader in the Brotherhood of Sleeping Car Porters and president of the Montgomery chapter of the NAACP. Nixon was refused information when he called the police station and had to have a colleague, liberal white lawyer Clifford Durr, find out the charges. Two and a half hours later, Nixon paid the fifty dollars' bail and took Parks home. He believed that the arrest presented a good opportunity for a boycott, and he and Durr urged this on the Parkses and Mrs. McCauley.

Nixon was soon in touch with Ralph D. Abernathy, pastor of the First Baptist Church, the Reverend H. H. Hubbard, president of the Baptist Ministerial Alliance, and the young Dr. Martin Luther King, Jr., new minister of the Dexter Avenue Baptist Church. Forty black leaders met the next day and planned a one-day boycott, to take place the following Monday, to support a set of limited demands to be made on the bus company.

The Montgomery *Advertiser*, which had reported the arrest of a "Negro woman" in a small article on page nine in its December 2 issue, on December 4 (a Sunday) ran a front-page story about the planned boycott. Leaflets had been distributed in black areas of Montgomery, telling of the proposed Monday evening meeting at the Holt Street Baptist Church. By agreement with Nixon, who had shown him a leaflet, the *Advertiser*'s city editor, Joe Azbell, reported that the paper had learned of the meeting from a white woman whose illiterate black maid had asked her to read the leaflet for her.

At dawn on Monday, December 5, the early buses were empty. At nine-thirty that morning, in a five-minute hearing, Parks was convicted of violating the city code and fined ten dollars plus four dollars in court costs. Her attorney, Fred D. Gray, appealed the case to the Montgomery Circuit Court, challenging the constitutionality of the city code; he and Nixon signed the hundred-dollar appeal bond.

Another front-page article in the December 5 Montgomery *Advertiser* reported the planned "top secret mass meeting of Negroes" at the Holt Street Baptist Church at seven o'clock Monday evening. Five thousand jammed the church and overflowed onto the sidewalk as Parks was introduced and black leaders addressed the crowd. This meeting marked the emergence of Dr. Martin Luther King, Jr., as a civil rights leader and inaugurated the Montgomery bus boycott, a major phase in the Civil Rights movement, which culminated in the December 21, 1956, decision by the United States Supreme Court declaring segregation on city buses unconstitutional.

As the bus boycott swung into high gear, Parks was fired from her job and became again a helper, doing volunteer work and making speeches to aid the boycott. The pressures, however, proved too great: Raymond Parks became ill, and in 1957 they moved to Detroit. Raymond worked as a barber again, and Rosa sewed at home until she got a dressmaker's job. Later she became receptionist-secretary and then staff assistant to United States Representative John Conyers, a Democrat. She served as deaconess of St. Matthews

A.M.E. Church and was active in the Women's Public Affairs Committee and the Southern Christian Leadership Conference, which sponsored an annual Rosa Parks Freedom Award. Shaw College in Detroit awarded her an honorary degree, and the A.M.E. Church's Women's Missionary Society honored her in 1971. In January of 1980, the Martin Luther King, Jr., Center for Social Change in Atlanta awarded her the Martin Luther King, Jr., Nonviolent Peace Prize. In November of 1980, *Ebony* magazine's readers voted her a five-thousand-dollar prize as the woman who had done the most to advance the cause of black America (Jesse Jackson won the prize as her male counterpart). In 1985, at seventy-two, Parks was still a part-time worker for Conyers, active in the community and speaking out against apartheid.

Summary

Hailed as the mother of the modern Civil Rights movement, Rosa Parks was less its mother than its opportunity, in a black community theretofore too divided for effective concerted action. An ordinary woman, committed to a cause but not a leader, she was the catalyst, the spark, which, skillfully applied at the right point in time, ignited the Civil Rights movement. She became a constant symbol for the movement, in which she played only a minor role. Her life serves as a reminder that great social movements are dependent not only on issues and charismatic leaders but also—and ultimately—on the mass of ordinary people, the "bus riders" who, after Rosa Parks decided she was too tired to give up her seat, decided they were not too tired to walk to and from their jobs for a year, until the boycott was successful. As *Time* magazine reported on January 16, 1956, a black minister asked an old woman, during the boycott, whether she was tired, to which she replied, "My soul has been tired for a long time. Now my feet are tired, and my soul is resting."

Bibliography

"Alabama." *Time* 67 (January 16, 1956): 20. National coverage of the boycott, generally favorable to the boycotters.

Bennett, Lerone, Jr. "Great Moments in Black History: The Day the Black Revolution Began." *Ebony* 32 (September, 1977): 54-64. Effectively written article by a noted black historian; provides good historical context.

Greenfield, Eloise. "Rosa Parks." *Ms.* 3 (August, 1974): 71-74. One of the magazine's articles in its series "Stories for Free Children," this account, albeit geared to a young audience, is well written and informative, especially on the general circumstances surrounding segregation.

Low, W. Augustus, and Virgil A. Clift, eds. *Encyclopedia of Black America*. New York: McGraw-Hill Book Co., 1981. The entry on Parks's action places it in its historical context.

Montgomery *Advertiser*. December 2-8, 1955. Articles by city editor Joe

Azbell cover the beginnings of the bus boycott effectively and generally without bias.

Nash, Tony. "Essence Woman." *Essence* 16 (May, 1985): 34. Brief but informative article about Parks's life to 1985.

Ploski, Harry A., and James Williams, eds. *The Negro Almanac: A Reference Work on the Afro-American.* 4th ed. New York: John Wiley and Sons, 1983. This informative piece characterizes Parks as a civil rights activist.

Stevenson, Janet. "Rosa Parks Wouldn't Budge." *American Heritage* 23 (February, 1972): 56-64, 85. Detailed coverage of the events at the beginning of the bus boycott, with a summary of the conduct and results of the yearlong campaign.

"Thirty-fifth Anniversary Services Awards." *Ebony* 36 (November, 1980): 142-143. Sketches of both Parks and Jackson, winners of the magazine's Thirty-fifth Anniversary Service Awards; clear indication of how widely Parks is regarded as a significant factor in the Civil Rights movement.

Marsha Kass Marks

VERNON L. PARRINGTON

Born: August 3, 1871; Aurora, Illinois
Died: June 16, 1929; Winchcombe, England
Area of Achievement: American history and literature
Contribution: Parrington's three-volume *Main Currents in American Thought* (1927-1930) was a landmark work that not only helped shape how the generation coming to maturity in the 1930's viewed the United States' past but also did much to stimulate interest in American intellectual history as a field of study.

Early Life

Vernon Louis Parrington was born August 3, 1871, in Aurora, Illinois, the son of John William and Louise (McClellan) Parrington. A graduate of Waterville (modern Colby) College in his native Maine, Parrington's father had moved to Illinois and, after a stint as a school principal, began the practice of law. He served as an officer in the Union Army during the Civil War, and then, after moving to Kansas in 1877, he farmed and was elected judge of the local probate court. Vernon attended the preparatory department of the College of Emporia and then its collegiate division before transferring to Harvard as a junior. Given his upbringing on the Western plains, he had an unhappy two years at Harvard—an experience that did much to shape his hostility to the upper-class Eastern establishment. After he was graduated from Harvard in 1893, Vernon returned to the College of Emporia as an instructor in English and French and there received an M.A. in 1895. In 1897, he began work at the University of Oklahoma as an instructor in English and modern languages. The following year, he was promoted to professor of English. In 1908, however, Parrington lost his job when the newly elected Democratic governor fired the president and fourteen faculty members—including Parrington—who were deemed insufficiently politically sound or religiously orthodox by Southern Methodist standards.

Parrington managed to find a position as assistant professor of English at the University of Washington in Seattle. In 1912, he was promoted to full professor. He was a highly popular teacher whose courses on American literature and thought drew impressive enrollments. He appears to have begun work in 1913 on what would become *Main Currents in American Thought: An Interpretation of American Literature from the Beginnings to 1920* (1927-1930). A related article, "The Puritan Divines, 1620-1720," appeared in the first volume of *The Cambridge History of American Literature* (1917). He edited and wrote the introduction to *The Connecticut Wits*, published in 1926. Apart from *Main Currents in American Thought*, Parrington's other publications did not amount to much: an occasional review, a few encyclopedia articles, a brief appreciation of the novelist Sinclair Lewis, and an essay,

"The Development of Realism," in *The Reinterpretation of American Literature* (1928). Parrington married Julia Rochester Williams on July 31, 1901; the couple had two daughters and a son.

Life's Work

As a student at the College of Emporia, Parrington had accepted without question his father's allegiance to the Republican Party, the school's Presbyterian religious orthodoxy, and belief in the inevitability of progress. At Harvard, exposure to Darwinian ideas eroded his religious faith. During his first years of teaching, his interests were primarily literary and aesthetic. Parrington dabbled at writing poetry, and he was strongly impressed by English Utopian Socialist William Morris' attacks upon the shoddiness and commercialism of the machine age and extolling of the work of the Middle Ages, which Morris romanticized as the time when craftsmanship reigned supreme. By the late 1890's, however, under the impact of the agrarian revolt that swept over Kansas, the major focus of Parrington's interest had shifted to reform politics. "I become," he confessed in 1918, "more radical with each year, and more impatient with the smug Tory culture. . . ." His Populist sympathies shaped his approach in *Main Currents in American Thought*. "The point of view from which I have endeavored to evaluate the materials," he admitted, "is liberal rather than conservative, Jeffersonian rather than Federalistic. . . ."

The first volume, dealing with the period from settlement to 1800, was turned down by the first two publishers to whom Parrington submitted the manuscript, because of doubts about its sales potential. He was so discouraged that he abandoned work on the projected second volume. The literary critic and historian Van Wyck Brooks, however, who had read and liked the manuscript, interested Alfred Harcourt of Harcourt, Brace and Company. Harcourt agreed to publish the work if Parrington would finish the second volume carrying the story to 1860. The two volumes appeared in 1927, with the first bearing the subtitle "The Colonial Mind: 1620-1800" and the second "The Romantic Revolution in America: 1800-1860." The work was an immediate success; Charles A. Beard spoke for most of the reviewers when he hailed Parrington for writing "a truly significant book . . . that promises to be epoch-making, sending exhilarating gusts through the deadly miasma of academic criticism." *Main Currents in American Thought* was awarded the Pulitzer Prize for history in 1928. When liberal or left-wing intellectuals were polled in the late 1930's about the authors who had most influenced their thinking, Parrington's name was prominent among those listed. As late as 1952, when a sample of American historians were asked to name their "most preferred" American histories published between 1920 and 1935, *Main Currents in American Thought* received more votes than any other.

Main Currents in American Thought had the subtitle "An Interpretation of

American Literature," and the larger part of the text was devoted to literary figures. Yet Parrington had scant interest in literature as literature. "With aesthetic judgments," he confessed in the foreword to volume 2, "I have not been greatly concerned. I have not wished to evaluate reputations or weigh literary merits. . . ." When dealing with the work of literary figures, he focused primarily upon their political and social views. Writers who had been uninvolved with such issues were summarily dismissed. Thus, he devoted less than three pages to Edgar Allan Poe and still less to Henry James. He brushed aside criticism upon this point with the reply that he was not writing the history of American literature but was rather concerned "with the total pattern of American thought." As an intellectual historian, however, Parrington had major blind spots. As a later critic pointed out, "he showed slight interest or competence in metaphysics and theology; he scarcely touched scientific thought and development, or the rise of the social sciences; he ignored legal thought, intellectual institutions, and the nonliterary arts."

Parrington had been much influenced by the emphasis placed by the French historian Hippolyte Taine in his book *History of English Literature* (1863-1864) upon the role of the social environment in shaping literary expression. "Ideas are not godlings that spring perfect-winged from the head of Jove," he wrote in an unpublished essay of 1917. Rather, "they are weapons hammered out on the anvil of human needs." Accordingly, the historian's task was "to understand how ideas are conditioned by social forces." The most important social force was economics—the "subsoil" upon which literature and ideas rested. Unfortunately, Parrington was not consistent in applying this economic determinism. On the one hand, he dismissed ideas that he disliked as rationalizations of selfish interests. On the other, he extolled those with whom he sympathized for their "creativity" and "originality." Increase Mather, for example, was a supporter of the established order because he was "a beneficiary of things as they were, certain to lose in prestige and power with any relaxing of the theocracy"; Roger Williams, however, was "a social innovator on principle, . . . and his actions were creatively determined by principles the bases of which he examined with critical insight."

In sum, *Main Currents in American Thought* amounted to a catalog of Parrington's biases. He pictured American history as a struggle between two sets of forces: the aristocracy versus the democratic majority; the defenders of selfish privilege against the champions of the rights of man and social justice; the capitalists versus the farmers and laborers. The work was organized around a series of biographical-critical sketches of individuals representing those conflicting forces: John Cotton versus Roger Williams; Alexander Hamilton versus Thomas Jefferson; Henry Clay versus Andrew Jackson; Daniel Webster versus Ralph Waldo Emerson. The metaphor of a ship's voyage was utilized to provide a unifying theme. The ideas with which Parrington sympathized were the progressive currents carrying the vessel forward;

those to which he was hostile were "reefs," "barriers," a "dragging anchor." Similar value judgments were freely applied to individuals. The target of his animus would be described as "the victim of a decadent ideal," "studiously conventional," or so closed-minded as to be "shut up within his own skull-pan"; the object of his favor would be pictured as an "unshackled thinker," "an adventurous pioneer," or a man of "fine idealism."

Parrington directed his sharpest barbs against the Puritans—perhaps a reflection of the slights of which he believed himself the object while at Harvard. Typical was his portrayal of Cotton Mather: "What a crooked and diseased mind lay back of those eyes that were forever spying out occasions to magnify self! He grovels in proud self-abasement. He distorts the most obvious reality. . . . His egoism blots out clarity and even the divine mercy." More broadly, he juxtaposed Puritanism to the liberating force of the Enlightenment. Puritanism represented "an absolutist theology that conceived of human nature as inherently evil, that postulated a divine sovereignty absolute and arbitrary, and projected caste divisions into eternity." By contrast, the Enlightenment

> asserted that the present evils of society are the consequence of vicious institutions rather than of depraved human nature; and that as free men and equals it is the right and duty of citizens to re-create social and political institutions to the end that they shall further social justice, encouraging the good in men rather than perverting them to evil.

In his treatment of the Founding Fathers, Parrington took the view put forward by his friend and University of Washington colleague J. Allen Smith in his book *The Spirit of American Government* (1907) that the framers of the Constitution had as their major purpose to clip the wings of a threatening democracy. He portrayed Hamilton as "a high Tory." "Accepting self-interest as the mainspring of human ambition," he elaborated, "Hamilton accepted equally the principle of class domination." Parrington did feel an almost grudging admiration for John Adams: "A stubborn intellectual independence and a vigorous assertiveness were his distinguishing characteristics. . . . He was no believer in unchecked government by wealth. His honest realism taught him the sophistry of Hamilton's assumption that gentlemen of property are equally gentlemen of principle, and that wealth voluntarily abdicates selfish interest. He feared the aggressions of the rich as much as the turbulence of the poor." Parrington's special hero was Thomas Jefferson:

> To all who profess faith in the democratic ideal Jefferson is a perennial inspiration. A free soul, he loved freedom enough to deny it to none; an idealist, he believed that the welfare of the whole, and not the prosperity of any group, is the single end of government.

Parrington pictured the conflict between Henry Clay and Andrew Jackson as a continuation of the struggle over the Constitution and the Hamilton-Jefferson battle of the 1790's. At a philosophical level, Parrington portrayed the issue as a clash between the egalitarian and humanitarian idealism of the Rousseauian tradition in French Romantic thought and the cold, calculating rationalism of English liberalism, represented by Adams Smith, with its exaltation of the beneficent workings of the pursuit of self-interest. He lamented the growing ascendancy of the belief in what he sarcastically termed "the natural right of every free citizen to satisfy his acquisitive instinct by exploiting the natural resources in the measure of his shrewdness." Even in the West, where once the democratic frontiersman had held sway, egalitarianism gave way to get-rich-quick "speculative psychology" under the impact of "abundant wild lands, rapid increase in population, and an elastic credit, operating on a vast scale." Even Abraham Lincoln was found to have had his "instinctive democracy" compromised by the new Whiggish "philosophy of progress [that] had displaced the older agrarianism."

Parrington died on June 16, 1929, while on vacation in England, before completing a third volume that would have continued the history to the 1920's. Parrington's publisher issued the unfinished and in parts fragmentary manuscript in 1930 under the subtitle "The Beginnings of Critical Realism in America." The volume exuded a mix of pessimism and hope. The pessimism grew out of the reign of plunder carried on by business in the years since the Civil War—what Parrington, in one of his most striking metaphors, called "The Great Barbecue." Nevertheless, he was optimistic that the revolt underway among American intellectuals during the 1920's against middle-class philistinism might yet manage "to unhorse the machine that now rides men and to leaven the sodden mass that is industrial America." He simultaneously reaffirmed his faith that "Jeffersonian democracy still offers hope." He was, however, ambivalent about what substantive policies were required. In correspondence, he expressed a vague sympathy with Marxism, but *Main Currents in American Thought* resounded with hostility to "the coercive state." Parrington even eulogized the Southern spokesmen for states' rights as "the best liberals of the time." He thus remained trapped in what he saw as the irresolvable dilemma facing the would-be reformer: "We must have a political state powerful enough to deal with corporate wealth, but how are we going to keep that state with its augmenting power from being captured by the forces we want it to control?"

Summary

The popularity of *Main Currents in American Thought* owed much to the fit of Parrington's prejudices with those of American intellectuals and would-be intellectuals of the time. In the 1920's, the Puritans were the favorite target of the self-consciously enlightened as the source of all the shortcomings found in American life: sexual repression, Prohibition, religious Fundamentalism, the Ku Klux Klan, and the middle-class philistinism that Sinclair Lewis satirized in *Babbitt* (1922). Here, then, Parrington was simply reinforcing existing stereotypes. His animus against business would similarly fit the mood of the Depression years. Parrington is typically linked with Frederick Jackson Turner and Charles A. Beard as one of the founders of so-called Progressive history, but he had neither their intellectual power nor their long-term influence. Later scholarship has left most of his interpretations in shambles; even his style, with its melodramatic rhetoric, appears contrived and overdone to the modern reader. The most generous appraisal of his lasting contribution is that he directed the attention of scholars to American intellectual history as a legitimate and important field of study.

Bibliography
Colwell, Stephen. "The Populist Image of Vernon Louis Parrington." *Mississippi Valley Historical Review* 49 (1962): 52-66. According to Hofstadter, "corrects certain notions about Parrington's Populist activities in the 1890's, but only at the cost of minimizing the impact of Populism on his thinking."
Gabriel, Ralph H. "Vernon Louis Parrington." In *Pastmasters: Some Essays on American Historians*, edited by Marcus Cunliffe and Robin W. Winks, 142-166, 438-440. New York: Harper and Row, Publishers, 1969. A rambling and disjointed sympathetic appraisal.
Harrison, Joseph B. *Vernon Louis Parrington: American Scholar*. Seattle: University of Washington Book Store, 1929. A brief appreciation that is gushingly admiring of Parrington as a "humanist and liberal."
Hofstadter, Richard. *The Progressive Historians: Turner, Beard, Parrington*. New York: Alfred A. Knopf, 1968. Contains the fullest available account of Parrington's life. Hofstadter makes a valiant effort to treat Parrington as a major thinker but is sufficiently astute an analyst to recognize that he was not.
Skotheim, Robert A. *American Intellectual Histories and Historians*. Princeton, N.J.: Princeton University Press, 1966. Includes an examination of Parrington's place in the development of American intellectual history that is devastating on the shortcomings of *Main Currents in American Thought*.

John Braeman

GEORGE S. PATTON

Born: November 11, 1885; San Gabriel, California
Died: December 21, 1945; Heidelberg, Germany
Area of Achievement: The military
Contribution: Though never a theoretician, Patton was a masterful tactician who demonstrated the advantages of mobility and aggressive offensive action as essential elements of modern warfare.

Early Life

George Smith Patton, Jr., was born on November 11, 1885, in San Gabriel, California. His father, George Smith Patton, was descended from a well-established Virginia family rooted in the culture of genteel Southern aristocracy and steeped in the military tradition one commonly associates with that class. His mother, Ruth Wilson, was the daughter of B. D. Wilson, a California businessman who made a sizable fortune in the winery business. Owing to the affluence of his family, Patton's childhood was happy and largely care-free. He did suffer from dyslexia, and as a result his parents decided to enroll him in a private school just prior to his twelfth birthday. His classmates represented some of the wealthiest families in Southern California, but it was with the tradition of his paternal forebears that Patton's affinities lay.

The year 1902 proved to be critically important in Patton's early life. He had decided to pursue a career in the military and thus sought appointment to the United States Military Academy at West Point, New York. He also met Beatrice Banning Ayer, the daughter of Frederick Ayer, a wealthy industrialist from Massachusetts. She would later become his wife—and her marriage to him would on more than one occasion prove beneficial to Patton's career. There were no senatorial or congressional vacancies available at West Point in 1902, so Patton enrolled for one year at Virginia Military Institute, his father's alma mater. During that year, Patton's father worked untiringly to ensure his son's appointment to West Point, and his efforts were rewarded the following year.

At nineteen, Patton was tall—slightly over six feet—very athletic, and quite handsome. An arm injury prevented his playing varsity football, but he took up the broadsword, excelled in the high hurdles, and became a skilled horseman. In fact, three years after graduating from West Point, he competed in the Modern Pentathlon event in the 1912 Stockholm Summer Olympics and finished fifth. Patton had two physical traits, however, which were of great concern to him—a high-pitched, almost squeaky voice, and a very fair and placid facial expression. To correct the latter he practiced in front of a mirror to develop what he called "my war face." There was little that could be done about his voice, but his frequent use of profanity may well have been designed to compensate for what he considered to be a flaw.

Life's Work

Patton was graduated from West Point in June, 1909. He married Beatrice in May of the following year, and in March, 1911, their first daughter, Beatrice, was born. Following his initial assignment at Fort Sheridan, near Chicago, Patton utilized family influence to secure a tour of duty at Fort Myer in Washington, D.C. Knowing that advancement in the peacetime army would be painfully slow, Patton actively sought to make contact with the "right people." His personal wealth and family connections certainly facilitated his efforts—a fact well illustrated in 1915, when he secured an assignment to a cavalry regiment at Fort Bliss, Texas, while the rest of his outfit went to the Philippines. It proved to be a particularly fortuitous assignment for Patton, who met and served as aide to General John J. Pershing when the latter was ordered into Mexico in 1916. Patton, who served with distinction in Mexico, regarded Pershing as a model soldier and continued to serve as his aide when the latter was chosen to head the American Expeditionary Force to France in 1917.

Once in France, Patton relinquished his staff position for a combat command. He was particularly interested in the tank, which promised to be the cavalry arm of the modern army. His dream of leading a tank unit in combat became a reality during the St. Mihiel campaign. During one engagement he was wounded, but he continued to direct his tanks to their targets by runners. When the newspapers ran the story of the "Hero of the Tanks" who directed his men while lying wounded in a shellhole, Patton became an instant hero. His actions won for him the Distinguished Service Cross and the Distinguished Service Medal. Later, he would admit to his father that he had always feared that he was a coward but had now begun to doubt it.

The peacetime army was a difficult place for Patton. He tried desperately to gain appointment as commandant to West Point and even sent a personal letter to Pershing in which he poignantly argued that he could transmit his ideal of "blood and gutts [*sic*]" to the cadets under his command. The argument failed, but the sobriquet remained for all time.

Denied West Point, Patton pursued the course one might expect of an ambitious young officer on the rise. In 1923, he attended the Command and General Staff College at Fort Leavenworth, Kansas, and in 1931, he entered the Army War College. During the intervening years, he served tours of duty in Hawaii and in Washington, D.C. His commanding officer in Hawaii described him as "invaluable in war. . . but a disturbing element in time of peace," a prescient evaluation, indeed. Patton lost his father in 1927 and his mother the following year. He consoled himself with the knowledge that he had not been a failure in their eyes and had achieved more, perhaps, than they had dreamed for him. Now he was free to fulfill his own destiny.

In 1938, Patton was ordered back to Fort Myer to replace General Jonathan Wainwright. He was fifty-three years old at the time, and although the war clouds were gathering in Europe and Asia, it seemed likely that age alone might preclude his being considered for a possible combat command. Following the outbreak of war in Europe, however, two decisions by Army Chief of Staff George Marshall changed all that. The German blitzkrieg convinced Marshall that the United States Army needed an armored force. He ordered the creation of two armored divisions and chose Patton to command the Second Armored Division—destined to win fame as "Hell on Wheels." Patton, obviously elated, wrote to his friend and army colleague, Terry Allen, "Now all we need is a juicy war."

Patton got his war and saw his first action in North Africa when, as part of Operation "Torch," his forces landed on the beaches of Morocco. Following the debacle at Kasserine Pass in Tunisia, he was ordered to assume command of the United States Second Corps. He chose Omar N. Bradley as his deputy and initiated a program of rigid training and discipline designed to redeem the valor of American arms. His subsequent victory over the Germans at Al-Guettar was therefore a source of great satisfaction to him. As initially planned, Patton gave up the Second Corps to Bradley to assume command of the Seventh Army which was to participate in the invasion of Sicily.

The Sicilian campaign was one of triumph and tragedy for Patton. Convinced that American forces had been assigned a subordinate role in the operation, he nevertheless managed to turn adversity into advantage by taking the historic town of Palermo and then beating General Bernard Law Montgomery and the vaunted British Eighth Army to Messina. Unfortunately, his shining victories were soon tarnished by the revelation of the famous slapping incident—actually two of them—wherein he struck two enlisted men who had been hospitalized for "battle fatigue." Patton's violent temper and his susceptibility to radical shifts in mood were well-known. Some of his biographers have suggested that he may have suffered from what is known as subdural hematoma, the result of head injuries sustained in falls from and kicks by some of his horses. Whatever the cause, the results were devastating.

Bradley was chosen to command American ground forces preparing for the Normandy invasion, and it was not until the summer of 1944 that Patton was given command of the newly activated Third Army. Determined to redeem himself, Patton's accomplishments as commander of the Third Army were truly remarkable. His forces liberated almost all of France north of the Loire River and were responsible for relieving the besieged 101st Airborne Division at Bastogne during the Ardennes Offensive. Patton considered the latter to be the Third Army's most brilliant operation and "the most outstanding achievement of this war."

As the war began to wind down, Patton expressed his fear of the "horrors of peace." His intemperate remarks expressing hatred of the Russians and contempt for the Jews were most embarrassing to the American High Command. Consequently, when the press subsequently reported that he had compared the Nazi Party to the Democratic and Republican parties, Dwight Eisenhower, Supreme Allied Commander in Europe, had little choice but to relieve him of command. On December 9, 1945, the day before he was to leave to return to the United States, the car in which he was riding slammed into a truck. Patton suffered severe lacerations, a broken nose, and two fractured vertebrae. At best it was feared that he would be a semi-invalid, but that was not to be. He died on December 21, 1945, and was buried in Hamm, Luxembourg.

Summary

The name of George Patton is and perhaps always will be synonymous with war—particularly World War II. No doubt Patton would have relished that association. He regarded war as the greatest of human endeavors and the battlefield as a place of honor. Patton idolized the great military leaders of the past—Hannibal, Caesar, and Napoleon—and spent much of his life preparing himself to be a worthy follower of the tradition they represented. Like them he would one day lead great numbers of men into battle. It was his destiny.

Patton achieved his destiny, though he did so late in life. World War II was his stage, and though he occupied it for only a brief period of time and never in more than a supporting role, he created a legend. He played to an appreciative audience as a tenacious, innovative, and daring battlefield commander. Had he lived, years of peace might have dimmed the luster of his star. Death intervened to prevent that, and before the applause faded, George Patton was born into immortality.

His death prompted a flood of praise, most of which paid tribute to his skills as a great fighting general. Perhaps the accolade he would have appreciated most, however, came from a former adversary, Field Marshal Gerd von Rundstedt, who, in a postwar interview with American military personnel, said simply, "Patton was your best."

Bibliography

Ayer, Fred, Jr. *Before the Colors Fade: Portrait of a Soldier, George S. Patton, Jr.* Boston: Houghton Mifflin Co., 1964. An attempt to analyze Patton the man rather than the legendary battlefield general. This work, authored by Patton's nephew, is highly impressionistic and rather superficially researched.

Blumenson, Martin. *Patton: The Man Behind the Legend, 1885-1945*. New York: William Morrow and Co., 1985. Blumenson's skills as a writer and military historian are evident in this biography. The author reminds his readers that the Patton legend was molded from human clay.

_____, ed. *The Patton Papers: 1885-1940*. 2 vols. Boston: Houghton

Mifflin Co., 1972. Blumenson's judicious selection from the voluminous Patton Papers allows the reader to see Patton as he saw himself and to know his fears, failures, strengths, and weaknesses.

Essame, Herbert. *Patton: A Study in Command*. New York: Charles Scribner's Sons, 1974. This very favorable biography of Patton focuses on his talents as a battlefield commander. Based exclusively on published sources, this synthetic work adds little that is new to the general's life story.

Farago, Ladislas. *The Last Days of Patton*. New York: McGraw-Hill Book Co., 1981. Focusing on the events surrounding Patton's tragic death in December, 1945, Farago attempts a more detailed investigation of the incident than was conducted at the time.

_____. *Patton: Ordeal and Triumph*. New York: I. Obolensky, 1963. Considered by many to be the definitive biography of George Patton, this impressive work was the basis for the critically acclaimed film *Patton*, released in 1970.

Patton, George S. *War as I Knew It*. New York: Houghton Mifflin Co., 1947. This work is best when viewed as a critique of the role of the battlefield general and the problems associated with high command. As military history it suffers from too much detail.

Kirk Ford, Jr.

LINUS PAULING

Born: February 28, 1901; Portland, Oregon

Areas of Achievement: Chemistry, biology, medicine, and world peace

Contribution: Pauling is the only person to have won two unshared Nobel Prizes, and these prizes, in chemistry and in peace, symbolize his contributions. In the 1930's and 1940's his scientific discoveries helped to make the United States an important center for structural chemistry and molecular biology. In the 1950's and 1960's his activities in the peace movement helped to mobilize the American public against the atmospheric testing of nuclear weapons.

Early Life

Linus Carl Pauling was born in Portland, Oregon, on February 28, 1901, the son of Herman William Pauling and Lucy Isabelle (Darling). His mother was a daughter of Oregon pioneers who could trace their ancestry in America to the seventeenth century. His father's family was German and had come to the United States after the revolutionary upheavals of 1848 in Europe. During childhood, Pauling and his two younger sisters led a peripatetic existence as their father, a traveling drug salesman, tried to find a position that suited him. The family eventually settled in Condon, Oregon, where, in a two-room schoolhouse, Linus' education began. Life in Condon proved to be financially unrewarding, however, and in 1909, the Paulings moved back to Portland. Shortly after settling in a new drugstore, Herman died suddenly of a perforated gastric ulcer. He was only thirty-two years old.

Herman's death created severe difficulties for the family. Linus became a shy adolescent who spent most of his time reading. His intellectual energies also found an outlet in schoolwork, and he moved at an accelerated pace through Portland's individualized grammar-school system and through Washington High School. The most important event of this period occurred when Lloyd Jeffress, a friend, showed him how sulfuric acid could turn white sugar into a steaming mass of black carbon. So excited was Linus by what he saw that he decided then and there to become a chemist.

Pauling was able to pursue a career as a chemical engineer at Oregon Agricultural College by working at various jobs during the school year and in the summer. Because of the need to support his mother, he was forced to interrupt his education for a year and teach quantitative analysis. This hiatus gave him time to read science journals, and he came across papers on the chemical bond by Irving Langmuir and Gilbert Newton Lewis. These papers provoked his lifelong interest in chemical bonding and structure. In his senior year, he met Ava Helen Miller, a freshman in the general chemistry class he was teaching. At first she was not attracted to this curly-haired, blue-eyed young man who was "so full of himself," and Pauling, though attracted to her, was reluctant to show it because of his position as a teacher. After the course was over, and by the time of Pauling's graduation from college in 1922, they were very much in love.

Pauling's graduate career took place at the California Institute of Technology (CIT) in Pasadena, where three professors, Arthur A. Noyes, Roscoe G. Dickinson, and Richard C. Tolman, helped to shape his career. Noyes acted as Pauling's father figure, and behind the scenes he made sure that his protégé remained a chemist (Pauling was being tempted by theoretical physics). Dickinson trained Pauling in X-ray diffraction, a technique for discovering the three-dimensional structures of crystals. Tolman was Pauling's mentor in theoretical physics. After a successful year at CIT, Pauling returned to Oregon to marry Ava Miller. She returned with him to Pasadena, where they began a close relationship that continued until her death fifty-seven years later.

After receiving his Ph.D. from CIT in 1925, Pauling spent a brief period as a National Research Fellow in Pasadena. He was then awarded a Guggenheim Fellowship to study quantum mechanics in Europe. He spent most of his year and a half abroad at Arnold Sommerfeld's Institute for Theoretical Physics in Munich, but he also spent a month at Niels Bohr's institute in Copenhagen and a few months in Zurich. Upon his return to California in 1927, Pauling began a career as teacher and researcher at CIT that would last for thirty-six years.

Life's Work

Structure has been the central theme of Pauling's scientific work. Most of his early research was on the determination of the structures of molecules, first by directing X-rays at crystals, later by directing electron beams at gas molecules. As these X-rays and electron techniques provided Pauling with experimental tools for discovering molecular structures, so quantum mechanics gave him a theoretical tool. For example, he used quantum mechanics to explain why the carbon atom forms equivalent bonds. In 1939, he wrote about many of his structural discoveries in *The Nature of the Chemical Bond and the Structure of Molecules and Crystals* (1939), one of the most influential scientific books of the twentieth century.

Pauling's interest in biological molecules began in the 1930's with his studies of the hemoglobin molecule, whose striking red color and property of combining with oxygen appealed to him. Interest in hemoglobin led naturally to an interest in proteins, and with Alfred Mirsky he published a paper on the general theory of protein structure in which they suggested that proteins had coiled configurations that were stabilized by weak intermolecular forces and hydrogen bonds.

On one of Pauling's visits to the Rockefeller Institute to visit Mirsky, he met Karl Landsteiner, the discoverer of blood types, who introduced him to another field—antibodies. Pauling's first paper on antibody structure appeared in 1940. During World War II, his work shifted toward practical problems, for example, the discovery of an artificial substitute for blood serum. This was only part of the extensive work that he did for the government. He also invented an oxygen detector, a device that depended on oxygen's special magnetic properties and that found wide use in airplanes and submarines. He also spent much time studying explosives and rocket propellants. At the end of the war, he became interested in sickle-cell anemia, which, he speculated, might be a molecular disease caused by an abnormal hemoglobin molecule. Working with Harvey Itano, Pauling showed in 1949 that this indeed was the case.

While a guest professor at Oxford University in 1948, Pauling returned to a problem that had occupied him in the late 1930's—to find precisely how the chain of amino acids in proteins is coiled. By folding a piece of paper on which he had drawn such a chain, he discovered the alpha helix, a configuration of turns held together by hydrogen bonds, with each turn having a nonintegral number of amino-acid groups. Pauling and Robert B. Corey published a description of the helical structure of proteins in 1950, and this structure was soon verified experimentally.

During the early 1950's, Pauling became interested in deoxyribonucleic acid (DNA), and in February, 1953, he and Corey published a structure for DNA that contained three twisted, ropelike strands. Shortly thereafter, James Watson and Francis Crick published the double-helix structure, which turned out to be correct. Watson and Crick profited from X-ray photographs of DNA taken by Rosalind Franklin, a research tool denied Pauling because of the refusal of the United States State Department to grant him a passport for foreign travel. He was finally given a passport when he received the 1954 Nobel Prize for Chemistry for his research into the nature of the chemical bond.

With the heightened publicity given him by the Nobel Prize, Pauling began to devote more of his attention to humanitarian issues connected with science. For example, he became increasingly involved in the debate over nuclear fallout and in the movement against nuclear-bomb testing. In 1958, he and his wife presented a petition signed by more than eleven thousand scientists from around the world to Dag Hammarskjöld, secretary-general of the United Nations. Pauling defended his petition before a congressional subcommittee in 1960, and he risked going to jail by refusing to turn over his correspondence with those who helped to circulate the petition. For all these efforts, he was awarded the Nobel Peace Prize for 1962 on October 10, 1963, the day that the partial nuclear test-ban treaty went into effect.

Through the mid-1960's, Pauling was a staff member at the Center for the Study of Democratic Institutions (CSDI). He had left CIT primarily because of the negative reaction of many members of the CIT community to his peace efforts, and in Santa Barbara he hoped to be able to work effectively in both areas, science and peace. While at CSDI, he participated in discussions on peace and politics, and he proposed a new model of the atomic nucleus in which protons and neutrons were arranged in clusters.

Pauling left Santa Barbara in 1967 to become research professor of chemistry at the University of California at San Diego, where he published a paper on orthomolecular psychiatry that explained how mental health could be achieved by manipulating the concentrations of substances normally present in the body. During this time, Pauling's interest became centered on a particular molecule—ascorbic acid (vitamin C). He examined the published evidence about vitamin C and came to the conclusion that ascorbic acid, provided that it is taken in large enough quantities, helps the body fight off colds and other diseases. The eventual outcome of Pauling's work was the book *Vitamin C and the Common Cold*, published in 1970, while he was a professor at Stanford University. This interest in vitamin C in particular and orthomolecular medicine in general led to his founding in 1973 the institute that now bears his name: the Linus Pauling Institute of Science and Medicine. During his tenure at the institute, Pauling was involved in a controversy about the relative benefits and dangers of the ingestion of large amounts of vitamins. In the early 1970's, he became interested in using vitamin C for the treatment of cancer, largely through his contact with the Scottish physician Dr. Ewan Cameron. Their collaboration resulted in a book, *Cancer and Vitamin C* (1979), in which they marshaled evidence for the effectiveness of vitamin C against cancer. In the 1980's Pauling obtained financial support to have his ideas about vitamin C and cancer tested experimentally in his own laboratory as well as in the laboratories of the Mayo Clinic. Positive results were obtained in animal studies at the Linus Pauling Institute, but negative results were obtained with human cancer patients in two Mayo Clinic studies, and so the controversy remained unresolved.

Summary

Throughout his life Pauling has seen himself as a Westerner, with a strong belief in those values that Frederick Jackson Turner called the "traits of the frontier": self-sufficiency, strength combined with inquisitiveness, a masterful grasp of material things, restless nervous energy, and love of nature and hard work. One can see these traits in Pauling's scientific work, as his curiosity drove him from one area to another. He liked to work on the frontiers of knowledge, not in crowded fields, and many of his greatest discoveries have occurred in the area between disciplines—between chemistry and physics, chemistry and biology, chemistry and medicine.

A master showman, Pauling cleverly fought for the recognition of his ideas. He was passionate in defending his scientific views, even when most of his colleagues did not accept them, as in his ideas about vitamin C. Despite his involvement in many scientific controversies, scientists have recognized the overwhelming importance of his contributions. On the occasion of Pauling's eighty-fifth birthday, Crick called him "the greatest chemist in the world." When Pauling was born, chemistry was a discipline dominated by Europeans, mainly Germans. Pauling's work symbolized and helped to make real the dominance of chemistry by Americans.

Pauling's influence on America was not restricted to chemistry. J. D. Bernal stated that if one person could be given credit for the foundation of molecular biology, that person would be Linus Pauling. Another field—molecular medicine—was created by Pauling's discovery of the first molecular disease, sickle-cell anemia. Besides helping revolutionize and found several scientific disciplines, Pauling had a major influence on American society through his many speeches and writings on peace. He helped to change the climate of American public opinion on nuclear weapons, which made the 1963 test-ban treaty possible. In fact, he was prouder of his efforts on behalf of peace than he was of his scientific accomplishments. Yet he did not see these contributions as separate: They were both part of his single-minded quest for truth.

Bibliography
Judson, Horace Freeland. *The Eighth Day of Creation: Makers of the Revolution in Biology*. New York: Simon and Schuster, 1979. The story of molecular biology told mainly in the words of the people who created it. Judson interviewed Pauling, and the book contains a good account of Pauling's work in molecular biology.
Olby, Robert. *The Path to the Double Helix*. Seattle: University of Washington Press, 1974. In terms of scientific accuracy and objectivity, Olby's is probably the best historical account of the discovery of the double helix. The book has a good discussion of Pauling's research on the alpha helix and DNA.
Pauling, Linus. "Fifty Years of Progress in Structural Chemistry and Molecular Biology." *Daedalus* 99 (Fall, 1970): 988-1014. This article is also available in a book, *The Twentieth-Century Sciences: Studies in the Biography of Ideas*, edited by Gerald Holton (New York: W. W. Norton, 1972). The article contains the most extensive autobiographical reminiscences that Pauling has ever written. The emphasis is on his scientific work, and the account is intended for the general reader.
_____. *The Nature of the Chemical Bond and the Structure of Molecules and Crystals: An Introduction to Modern Structural Chemistry*. 3d ed. Ithaca, N.Y.: Cornell University Press, 1960. Pauling's magnum opus, and the best summary of his work in structural chemistry. The book is intended for students of chemistry, and it has become a classic.

_____. *No More War!* New York: Dodd, Mead and Co., 1983. The best extended treatment of Pauling's thinking about war, nuclear weapons, and peace. This edition contains an addendum to each chapter in which Pauling reflects on the changes, for better or worse, that have occurred in the quarter century since the first edition.

Pauling, Linus, and Roger Hayward. *The Architecture of Molecules*. San Francisco: W. H. Freeman and Co., 1964. This book gives an excellent introduction to Pauling's structural imagination. Roger Hayward was a distinguished scientific illustrator, and the book has fifty-seven full-color illustrations of molecular structures accompanied by Pauling's clear and incisive discussions.

Rich, Alexander, and Norman Davidson, eds. *Structural Chemistry and Molecular Biology: A Volume Dedicated to Linus Pauling by His Students, Colleagues, and Friends*. San Francisco: W. H. Freeman and Co., 1968. A festschrift for Pauling on his sixty-fifth birthday. J. H. Sturdivant's discussion of Pauling's scientific work is particularly good.

White, Florence Meiman. *Linus Pauling: Scientist and Crusader*. New York: Walker and Co., 1980. This short biography is intended for young people ten years of age and older, but because it was written with the cooperation of Linus and Ava Helen Pauling, it contains some interesting anecdotes about and insights into the human side of its subject.

Robert J. Paradowski

CHARLES WILLSON PEALE

Born: April 15, 1741; Queen Anne County, Maryland
Died: February 22, 1827; Philadelphia, Pennsylvania
Areas of Achievement: Painting, curatorship, and natural history
Contribution: Peale combined a sense of patriotism in his portraits of revolutionary and early national leaders with a faith in democracy by establishing the first public museum of art and science in America.

Early Life
Charles Willson Peale was born April 15, 1741, in Queen Anne County, Maryland. His mother was Margaret Triggs of Annapolis, Maryland; his father, Charles Peale, Jr., a convicted forger, had been banished to the Colonies in 1735. Peale had five children, of which Charles Willson was the eldest. In 1750, when Charles was only nine years old, his father died, leaving his widow with five small children. She took the family back to Annapolis and worked as a seamstress there.

Young Charles received whatever education was available, and in 1754, when he was thirteen, his mother apprenticed him to a saddle maker. During the next seven years he learned that craft. At age twenty, the young man completed his apprenticeship and borrowed the money he needed to begin his own business. In February, 1762, he married Rachel Brewer, the first of his three wives. Although successful as a saddle maker, Peale gradually diversified, adding clock making, watch repair, harness making, carriage repair, and sign painting to his skills.

By age twenty-one, Peale, a slender, light-complexioned man with brown hair and eyes, seemed well started on a career. Yet he longed for something more: He wanted to become a painter. Soon he began painting, using himself, his wife, and friends as subjects. When a neighbor offered him a fee of ten pounds to paint his and his wife's portraits, Charles decided that he needed instruction. He traveled to Philadelphia, bought an art book and what supplies he could afford, and returned home. In 1763, he visited the painter John Hesselius, who lived at a nearby plantation. Peale offered Hesselius an expensive saddle in return for some instruction and for a chance to watch him paint.

The next year his carriage-making partner absconded with most of the funds from their business. Deeply in debt, Peale sold most of his leather goods and supplies but failed to pay all of his bills. Then he joined the country party in the hotly contested election. His group won, but his creditors belonged to the losing side and they sued for the repayment of his debts. With the sheriff bearing warrants searching for him, Peale sailed to New England, beyond the reach of his creditors. He later recalled this incident as the turning point in his life: Having lost his business, he turned his attention to art as a full-time occupation. Peale returned to Maryland in 1766 after friends arranged a settlement of his affairs that would keep him out of debtor's prison. Shortly after his return, Peale's association with the local merchants and planters led them to gather funds to send him to England for formal training as a painter.

Life's Work

With his neighbors paying his way, Peale sailed for England in December, 1766. In London, early the next year, he began working in the studio of Benjamin West. There Peale tried many types of artistic endeavors, including oil portraits, miniatures, busts in plaster of Paris, and mezzotints. While in London he showed a painting and several miniatures at the exhibit of the Society of Artists of Great Britain. In early 1769, he became homesick for Maryland and his wife and child, so he returned home.

Back in the Colonies, Peale turned his energies to painting full-length portraits of the Maryland gentry. In 1772, he visited Mount Vernon, where he did a portrait of George Washington in his Virginia militia uniform, the only painting of Washington done before the American Revolution. Despite Peale's success at doing portraits for the scattered planters, he hoped to move to Philadelphia so that the family could live together. Before that happened, however, the strains between England and the Colonies broke into open revolt.

In 1776, the Peales moved to Philadelphia because Charles thought that an urban center offered more opportunity. A man of strong patriotic feelings, he enlisted in the city militia and was soon elected a first lieutenant. Peale's unit participated in the battles of Trenton and Princeton, and by June, 1777, he received an appointment as a captain of infantry. Early the next year, the British occupied Philadelphia and Peale was out of the army, serving instead on several civil and military committees as well as being an elected representative to the Pennsylvania legislature. In late 1780, his bid for reelection to the legislature failed, and he retired from local politics.

Throughout the disruptions caused by the war and his political activities, Peale continued to paint. In fact, the executive council of Pennsylvania commissioned him to do a portrait of Washington in the middle of the war. He bought a home in Philadelphia during 1780 and during the next several years added a studio and an exhibition room. He continued to paint portraits and miniatures of leading military and political figures throughout the revolutionary era. At the same time, Peale strove to gain some economic security for his family. He opened a portrait gallery to show his work in 1782 and several years later offered the public an exhibition of "moving pictures."

In 1786, Peale opened the Philadelphia Museum. At the time, there were no museums in America, and the few museums that existed in Europe were open only for the privileged classes. Peale saw his museum as a logical part of the American Revolution. In addition to making the government open to the citizens, he would make art and science available too. Also, by charging a modest fee he hoped for a satisfactory family income. His museum was the first such venture in the United States, and it put Peale at the head of a group of American scientists, artists, and intellectuals then living in or around Philadelphia.

In 1790, Rachel Brewer Peale, Peale's first wife, died, and a year later he married Elizabeth DePeyster. As the museum collections grew, Peale moved his operations twice. In 1802, the Pennsylvania government allowed him to relocate in the vacant state house (Independence Hall). Between moves, Peale found time to buy some mastodon bones, and in 1801 he organized an expedition to Newburgh, New York, to excavate the rest of the beast's remains. While digging, the searchers unearthed a second mastodon, and from these bones Peale and his associates assembled one complete skeleton for display. By this time the museum contained hundreds of birds, mammals, and insects, in addition to Peale's paintings. To display them he introduced the practice of using their natural habitat as background, a distinct change from the then current practice of using single-color or neutral backgrounds.

Peale retained his broad range of interests throughout his adult life. He developed a type of fireplace, experimented with plows and types of seeds, and introduced the physiognotrace for making profiles, then so popular. At the same time he continued to paint, and he met or corresponded with the most prominent artists, scientists, and intellectuals of the day. In 1804, Elizabeth DePeyster Peale, Peale's second wife, died, and the next year he married Hannah Moore, his last wife. He remained active in artistic and scientific activities in Philadelphia, helping to found the Pennsylvania Academy of the Fine Arts that same year. In 1810, he retired, deeding the museum to his son, Rubens Peale.

Although he claimed to be retired, Peale's curiosity and drive continued. He corresponded frequently with Thomas Jefferson, wrote essays, gave public addresses, and continued his active interest in American scientific and artistic activities. In the winter of 1818-1819, he traveled to Washington, D.C., where he painted portraits of President James Monroe and also of John Quincy Adams and Henry Clay. Back in Philadelphia he also did portraits of the officers and scientists of Stephen H. Long's 1819 Scientific Expedition being sent west to explore the Missouri Valley. In 1822, Peale reassumed management of the museum and remained active in Philadelphia until his death in 1827.

Summary

Peale's paintings give later Americans a view of late Colonial American society unmatched anywhere else. By no means a brilliant artist, he was nevertheless a keen observer and a highly competent craftsman. His early portraits show the elegance of plantation society along the Chesapeake Bay. He participated in both military and political aspects of the American Revolution, and through long acquaintance with many leading figures in early American history he had repeated chances to depict them. For example, Peale painted many portraits of George Washington, who is known to have sat for him at least seven different times. Local and regional leaders, too, sat for his work as he painted individuals from presidents and statesmen to his neighbors and family during the first half century of national independence.

Peale was also an inventor, natural scientist, and museum curator. His Philadelphia Museum began as a sort of hall of fame for early national heroes but soon evolved into the nation's first repository for scientific and natural specimens. Here Peale's contributions were varied. Offering such displays to the public was new and daring. Yet his skills in preserving and displaying specimens were impressive, too. He used habitat settings for the displays, varied the museum holdings, and used the lighting and surroundings to depict his material in a natural manner. Peale depicted his own view of his contributions to American society in a self-portrait painted when he was eighty-one years old. There he appears smiling and urging the public to enter while he lifts a curtain showing the museum display room. To him, the ultimate result of American democracy was making not simply politics, but also art, science, and knowledge available to each citizen.

Bibliography

Briggs, Berta N. *Charles Willson Peale, Artist and Patriot.* New York: McGraw-Hill Book Co., 1952. A popular account of Peale's life. Although the author included no sources, the work is based on solid scholarship.

Miller, Lillian B., ed. *The Selected Papers of Charles Willson Peale and His Family.* Vol. 1, *Charles Willson Peale: Artist in Revolutionary America, 1735-1791.* New Haven, Conn.: Yale University Press, 1983. A detailed, scholarly collection of Peale family papers, including letters, diaries, and legal notices. Of more interest to scholars than the general reader, it offers an intimate glance into life in Colonial America.

Richardson, Edgar P., Brooke Hindle, and Lillian B. Miller. *Charles Willson Peale and His World.* New York: Harry N. Abrams, 1982. This book grew out of an exhibit of Peale's art at the Metropolitan Museum of Art in New York City. Each contributor provides a thoughtful essay focusing on a particular aspect of Peale's career or character.

Sellers, Charles Coleman. *Charles Willson Peale.* 2 vols. Philadelphia: American Philosophical Society, 1947. A biography which includes generous excerpts from Peale's diary, letters, and autobiography. This is the first of Seller's several books on Peale. It is chiefly narrative and makes only a modest effort at analysis.

_____. *Charles Willson Peale.* New York: Charles Scribner's Sons,

1969. This lavishly illustrated full-length biography is based on Sellers' 1947 two-volume study, but includes new material and corrections of minor errors in the earlier version. The narrative is clear and interesting, and the conclusions are well presented.

_____. *Mr. Peale's Museum: Charles Willson Peale and the First Popular Museum of Natural Science and Art.* New York: W. W. Norton and Co., 1980. The author focuses on Peale and his family to discuss their role in early museum operations, and the growth of American art and natural science. Places Peale within the broad context of American intellectual and artistic development during the first half century of independence.

_____. *Portraits and Miniatures of Charles Willson Peale.* Philadelphia: American Philosophical Society, 1952. Meant for the serious student of early American portrait art, this volume includes an assessment of Peale's skills and techniques. It provides an alphabetical listing and discussion of 1,046 of his works and reproductions of 471 of his paintings.

Roger L. Nichols

ROBERT EDWIN PEARY

Born: May 6, 1856; Cresson, Pennsylvania
Died: February 20, 1920; Washington, D.C.
Area of Achievement: Arctic exploration
Contribution: After several unsuccessful attempts, Peary became the first
man to reach the geographic North Pole, on April 6, 1909.

Early Life

Robert Edwin Peary was born on May 6, 1856, in Cresson, Pennsylvania, a
backwoods farm community. His New England forebears were Frenchmen
(Peary is an American modification of the Gallic Pierre) who had made bar-
rel staves for their livelihood. His father died when he was three and his
mother, Mary Peary, was forced to rear her only child on meager resources.

His mother was extremely possessive and forced her son to dress in girlish
clothes. Robert was nicknamed "Bertie," and he was regarded as a sissy by
his peers. He would spend the remainder of his life attempting to compensate for his tortured early years.

Peary studied civil engineering at Bowdoin College in Brunswick, Maine,
and resolved to outdo his rivals. He became active in sports, drama, and
debate. Symbolically, he dressed up as Sir Lancelot at his college fraternity
masquerade party. For graduation exercises, he composed an epic poem in
which he imagined himself to be Sir Roland.

Life's Work

Peary received a degree in civil engineering in 1877 from Bowdoin College. After his graduation, he served as a draftsman for the United States
Coast and Geodetic Survey. While in that position, he applied for and
received a commission in the Civil Engineer Corps of the United States Navy
in 1881.

In 1886, Peary borrowed five hundred dollars from his mother, took a summer leave of absence from the navy, gathered a crew, and embarked on what
would be the first of eight expeditions to the Arctic. Peary, along with a Danish skiing companion, made a one-hundred-mile journey over the inland ice
from the southwest coast of Greenland. The purpose of his first expedition
was to acquire some fame by discovering what existed on north Greenland's
ice cap: Was Greenland an island continent, or did it, as some geographers
believed, thrust its ice cap right up to the North Pole? This expedition accomplished little. Yet Peary quickly learned what he needed to do in the future,
and when his leave of absence expired, he returned to duty in Nicaragua with
an obsession to return to the Arctic and to continue his quest for fame.

His second expedition was delayed until 1891. In 1888, he returned to his
navy job on the Nicaraguan canal route for what would be a two-year tour.

That same year, Peary married Josephine Diebitsch, the daughter of a professor at the Smithsonian Institution. She was a tall, spirited woman whose appearance closely resembled his mother's. Peary's mother moved in with the newlyweds. This uncomfortable arrangement lasted a year. Josephine soon realized that her husband was really married to his Arctic adventures; to solve her dilemma, she accompanied him on his second expedition. By this point, Peary had become skillful in getting what he needed to continue his explorations. He pulled strings and used his gifted oratorical skills and enormous self-confidence to obtain ten thousand dollars from financial backers and an eighteen-month leave of absence from the navy.

The stern, blue-eyed Peary sported a reddish-blond mustache; despite his serious nature, his overall appearance resembled that of the walruslike Ben Turpin, the silent-screen comedian. His face was already wrinkled from his time in Nicaragua and from exposure to Arctic blizzards and sun. His six-foot, sturdy physique, with broad shoulders and narrow hips, his finely tuned body which had already passed its thirty-fifth birthday, was ready for the mental and physical challenges ahead.

For his second trip to the Arctic, which began in 1891, his strategy was to take with him a party of six "campaigners," including Dr. Frederick Cook, and a seventh person, his wife, Josephine. Josephine attracted much attention from the newspapers: She would be the first white woman to winter at such a high altitude in Greenland. Once in position, Peary planned to conduct a "white march" over the great ice of northeast Greenland and to claim for the United States a highway to the North.

On June 6, 1891, the *Kite* sailed from Brooklyn, destined for the northwest coast of Greenland. Cook, nicknamed the Sigmund Freud of the Arctic, proved to be a helpful passenger; his obsession to reach the North Pole went back to his own deprived childhood, during which he won prizes in geography and worked in his free time to help support his poverty-stricken family. To pay for medical school, he had worked nights as a door-to-door milkman.

The *Kite* was in the process of ramming its way through the ice of Baffin Bay when Peary broke his lower right leg by striking it against the iron tiller. Cook quickly set the leg in splints, and Josephine relieved Peary's pain with morphine and whiskey. Peary would later praise Cook as a helpful and tireless worker who was patient and cool under pressure.

On July 30, 1891, the party landed on the foot of the cliffs in Inglefield Gulf, immediately north of Thule, the United States Greenland military base. With his right leg strapped to a plank, Peary continued to demonstrate leadership as he carried a tent ashore and supervised the construction of a prefabricated, two-room cabin named Red Cliff House. As the party settled in for the long polar night, the Etah Eskimos flocked from hundreds of miles away to see the first white woman to come to their country.

Peary soon began to recover from his broken leg. Josephine recorded in her journal that, within three months, he had discarded his crutches and had begun running foot races with Cook to build up his leg. The Eskimos watched as the white man took snow baths in subzero temperatures. To demonstrate his endurance to the Eskimos, he wore a hooded parka and caribou socks and slept in the open all night without a sleeping bag.

Peary realized that, to endure in the Arctic, he would have to adopt the survival techniques of the Eskimos. He learned from the Eskimos that expeditions required dog teams, sleighs, fatty meat for nourishment, and light fur garments. Yet he treated the Eskimos, who would continually come to his aid, as subhumans. He refused to learn their language, in contrast to Cook and Matthew Henson, and he rejected the hospitality of their igloos.

During May of 1892, Peary set out eastward, on his white march across the ice cap of north Greenland. Initially, the Eskimos and Cook accompanied him. Cook had gone ahead as a forward scout. When the two men rendezvoused, Peary ordered Cook to return to look after Josephine. The Eskimos feared that the evil spirit Tormarsuk presided in the interior, and they departed with Cook.

Peary and Eivind Astrup, a Norwegian ski champion, proceeded forward. In sixty-five days, the two men completed the unbelievable distance of six hundred miles over unknown terrain. On July 4, he named an easterly inlet Independence Bay, planted two American flags, and held a small celebration with the Norwegian skier. After they had rested, they turned around to retrace the six hundred miles back.

The trip would bring Peary fame; yet he had made costly cartographic errors that would eventually cause the death of a Danish scientist who attempted to confirm Peary's "discoveries." From Navy Cliff, Peary had believed that he had seen the Arctic Ocean, but he had actually been one hundred miles from the coast. Independence Bay had not been a bay but rather a deep fjord, and his conclusion that Peary Channel marked the northern boundary of the Greenland mainland was erroneous. In 1915, the United States government withdrew Peary's maps of Greenland, and Peary's reckless, unscientific behavior became legend.

When he returned, Peary raised twenty thousand dollars on the lecture circuit. Cook resigned from Peary's organization when Peary refused to allow him to publish ethnological findings on the Eskimos. No one in the group was allowed to publish anything, except in a book bearing Peary's name as author.

Peary's next expedition included Josephine, who was pregnant, a nurse, an artist, eight burros, and a flock of carrier pigeons. On September 12, 1893, Josephine gave birth to the first white child to be born at that altitude. The Peary's nine-pound daughter was named Marie Ahnighito Peary; her middle name came from the Eskimo woman who had chewed bird skins to make diapers for the blue-eyed child, nicknamed the Snow Baby.

The birth of the child was the only happy event of this expedition, as discontent broke out among the crew. Peary's drive and relentless nature began to cause problems. Astrup had a nervous breakdown and committed suicide on a glacier. Most of the remainder of the crew could no longer tolerate Peary, and they took the next supply ship back to the United States, as did Josephine, her child, and her nurse.

On future expeditions, Eskimos would lose their lives for Peary; Peary himself lost eight of his toes to frostbite. Now a near cripple, he simply stuffed his boots with tin-can lids to protect his stumps. Nothing short of death itself would stop Peary's single-minded quest.

Peary's first serious attempt to reach the North Pole began during the four-year expedition starting in 1898. Matthew Henson, a black who had mastered the skills of Arctic exploration, was the only member from the original crew. The 1898-1902 mission failed to get to the North Pole, but Peary was able in 1902 to travel to eighty-four degrees, seventeen minutes north. On his seventh mission, in 1905-1906, Peary reached eighty-seven degrees, six minutes north, only 174 nautical miles from the North Pole, before having to retreat.

In 1908, Peary, though crippled, aging, and weatherbeaten, knew that he had the physical and mental resources for one final attempt to reach the North Pole. It would be his eighth and final trip. Several millionaires in the Peary Arctic Club pledged $350,000 for the final outing and *The New York Times* paid four thousand dollars in advance for the exclusive story. The National Geographic Society of Washington and the American Museum of Natural History in New York bestowed their prestige on him. The United States Navy once again released him with pay after President Theodore Roosevelt personally intervened.

In 1905, at a cost of $100,000, Peary had built, according to his own design, a schooner-rigged steamship named the *Roosevelt*. He took six men with him, the most loyal being Matthew Henson, who had nursed Peary and had saved his life on numerous occasions. A remarkable man, he had mastered everything for the mission, including the language of the Eskimos, who worshiped him as the Maktok Kabloonna (black white man). Both Peary and Cook, who was involved in a rival expedition, believed that the best companion for such an outing was a nonwhite, since whites, ultimately, could not seem to get along.

The flag-decorated *Roosevelt* got under way from New York Harbor on the steamy afternoon of July 6, 1908. At Oyster Bay, Long Island, President Roosevelt came aboard and shook hands with every member of the crew. At Sydney, Nova Scotia, Peary's wife Josephine, fourteen-year-old Marie, and five-year-old Robert, Jr., once again bade farewell to Peary. At Anoatok, on the northwest coast of Greenland, the Eskimos reported to Peary that Cook had already passed westward on his march to the Big Nail.

Peary ordered Captain Bob Bartlett to begin ramming the *Roosevelt* through the ice packs and to head toward Cape Sheridan, the proposed wintering berth, which was 350 miles away. On September 5, the *Roosevelt* had reached her goal of eighty-two degrees, thirty minutes latitude—a record north for a ship under her own steam.

Cape Sheridan became home base. Ninety miles northwest lay Cape Columbia, which Peary decided would be the ideal jumping-off spot. Four hundred and thirteen miles of Arctic Ocean ice separated Cape Columbia from Peary's goal, the North Pole, the Big Nail, ninety degrees north latitude.

Peary was ready for the final chance to realize the greatest dream of his life. On the appointed Sunday morning, twenty-four men, 133 dogs, and nineteen sleighs departed. The expedition was broken up into five detachments: Each one would break trail, build igloos, and deposit supplies in rotation. Peary would follow the group from the rear as each exhausted team rotated back toward land.

On April 1, Bartlett took a navigational fix and determined a reading of eighty-seven degrees, forty-seven minutes north latitude. He took no longitudinal reading, which made his determination dubious, but Peary was convinced that he was 133 nautical miles on a direct beeline to the North Pole. Peary then surprised and disappointed Bartlett and ordered him home. The only qualified nautically trained witness who might verify the North Pole sighting finally departed.

Peary continued on with Henson, four Eskimos, five sleighs, and forty dogs. On April 6, 1909, at ten in the morning, after a labor of twenty years, Peary became the only white man to reach the North Pole. Once there, Peary draped himself in the American flag. Henson later recalled in his memoirs that his fifty-three-year-old commander was a dead-weight cripple, a mere shadow of the civil engineer in Nicaragua. One of the Eskimos remarked, "There is nothing here. Just ice!"

Summary

En route from his last mission to the Arctic, Peary learned that Cook had claimed to reach the Pole on April 21, 1908, nearly a year before Peary. Later, Cook was so hounded by the press and others that he took to wearing disguises and left the country for a year. When he returned, he spoke in his defense on the lecture circuit. Ultimately, his claims were disregarded, but the controversy was kept alive by the press because the dispute made a good story. Peary's claims were not scientifically documented. The National Geographic Society did a hasty, perfunctory examination of Peary's trunk of instruments in the middle of the night in a railway baggage station and agreed that Peary had discovered the North Pole.

In the 1930's, Dr. Gordon Hayes, an English geographer, scrupulously and fairly examined Cook's and Peary's claims. He concluded that neither one had got within one hundred miles of the North Pole. Nevertheless, Peary is credited with reaching the North Pole, attaining the fame he so desperately desired. After much lobbying and a congressional hearing, Peary was promoted to rear admiral. Peary served for a year as chairman of the National Committee on Coast Defense by Air during World War I. He retired and received a pension of sixty-five hundred dollars a year. He had achieved his goal, and the United States and the world recognized him for the twenty years of supreme sacrifices he had made.

Shortly after his return from the Arctic, Peary began suffering from anemia. On February 20, 1920, he died from that affliction at the age of sixty-four. He was buried with full honors at Arlington National Cemetery in Washington, D.C. His casket was draped with the remnants of the American flag with which he had covered himself as he stood atop the world on the North Pole. The National Geographic Society constructed a huge globe of white granite, representing the Earth and inscribed with Peary's motto, "I shall find a way or make one," and a legend proclaiming him Discoverer of the North Pole.

Bibliography
Cook, Frederick A. *My Attainment of the Pole*. New York: Polar, 1911. Cook's own descriptions of his expedition. Some claim that it was a hoax and others state that he only got to within a hundred miles of the North Pole.

Diebitsch-Peary, Josephine. *My Arctic Journal: A Year Among Ice-Fields and Eskimos*. New York: Contemporary Publishing Company, 1893. Peary's wife gives her account. Includes "The Great White Journey."

Henson, Matthew A. *A Black Explorer at the North Pole: An Autobiographical Report by the Negro Who Conquered the Top of the World with Admiral Robert E. Peary*. Foreword by Robert E. Peary. Introduction by Booker T. Washington. New York: Walker and Co., 1969. Henson's account. Henson began his life in poverty, attained fame, and ended his life as a parking attendant and a seventeen-dollar-a-week messenger in Brooklyn. He lived to be eighty-eight, and in his last years he suffered extreme poverty.

Hunt, William R. *To Stand at the Pole: The Dr. Cook-Admiral Peary North Pole Controversy*. New York: Stein and Day, 1982. Contains detailed account of the controversy over which man (Cook or Peary) got to the North Pole first. The mystery is not answered. Contains an excellent bibliography.

Peary, Robert E. *The North Pole*. New York: Stokes, 1910. Peary wrote three books—the others are *Nearest the Pole* (Doubleday, 1907) and *Northward over the "Great Ice"* (Stokes, 1898). *The North Pole* is Peary's own account of reaching the Pole. Exciting as an account but criticized by others.

Rasky, Frank. *Explorers of the North: The North Pole or Bust.* New York: McGraw-Hill Book Co., 1977. Chapters 10 and 11 are devoted to Peary. A human account of the explorer, warts and all. Short, readable, extremely detailed report of the important events. Good starting point.

Rawlins, Dennis. *Peary at the North Pole: Fact or Fiction?* New York: Luce, 1973. Argues that Peary never made it to the North Pole.

John Harty

CHARLES SANDERS PEIRCE

Born: September 10, 1839; Cambridge, Massachusetts
Died: April 19, 1914; Milford, Pennsylvania
Area of Achievement: Philosophy
Contribution: Largely unrecognized by contemporaries, except for his contribution to pragmatism, Peirce developed a system of philosophy that
attempted to reconcile the nineteenth century's faith in empirical science
with its love of the metaphysical absolute. His difficult and often confusing
ideas anticipated problems central to twentieth century philosophy.

Early Life

Charles Sanders Peirce, born on September 10, 1839, in Cambridge, Massachusetts, was the son of Benjamin Peirce, one of America's foremost
mathematicians. During his childhood, Charles's mother, Sarah Hunt (Mills)
Peirce, took second place to his dynamic father, who personally supervised
the boy's education and provided a role model that inspired but also proved
impossible to emulate. Convinced of his son's genius, Benjamin Peirce
encouraged his precocious development. Charles began the study of chemistry at the age of eight, started an intense scrutiny of logic at twelve, and
faced rigorous training in mathematics throughout his childhood. In the latter case, he was seldom given general principles or theorems. Instead, he was
expected to work them out on his own.

At sixteen, Peirce entered Harvard, where his father was professor of
mathematics. Contrary to expectations, Peirce proved a less than brilliant
student, and he was graduated, in 1859, seventy-first out of a class of ninety-
one. Probably too young and certainly too much the nonconformist to fit into
the rigid educational system of nineteenth century Harvard, Peirce's inauspicious beginning in institutional academics was prophetic. Though he would
continue his education, receiving an M.A. from Harvard in 1862 and a Sc.B.
in chemistry the following year, his future did not lead to a distinguished
career in academics or, indeed, in any conventional pursuit. His lot in life, in
spite of so much promise, was frustration and apparent failure.

Peirce's difficulty in adjusting to the world of ordinary men was related to
his unusual and often trying personality. Always his father's favorite, Peirce
became convinced of his own genius and impatient with those who failed to
recognize the obvious. Shielded and overindulged as a child, Peirce never
developed the social skills required for practical affairs nor the self-discipline
necessary to make his own grandiose vision a reality. Such problems were
exaggerated by his passion for perfection and his abstract turn of mind.
Peirce found real happiness only in the rarefied world of his own philosophical speculation.

As a youth, Peirce both attracted and repelled. Always prone to the dramatic gesture and, when he was inclined, a brilliant conversationalist, he could be an entertaining companion, but he could also use his rapier wit as a weapon. Of medium height, dark, swarthy, and fastidious in matters of dress, the handsome young Peirce reveled in his reputation as a lady's man and spent much energy in seeking the "good life." He actually paid an expert to train his palate so that he could become a connoisseur of fine wines. In 1862, Peirce married Harriet Melusina Fay, three years his senior and infinitely more mature and self-possessed. A feminist and intellectual in her own right, "Zina" worshiped her captive "genius" and labored for years to keep him out of serious trouble while restraining his extravagance. Yet she could also be jealous and possessive, and, though Peirce would experience some stability under Zina's influence, the marriage was doomed.

Life's Work

Upon his graduation from Harvard, Peirce went to work for the United States Coast and Geodetic Survey, a position acquired through his father's influence. Benjamin Peirce served as a consulting geometer for the organization and became its superintendent in 1867. Charles Peirce remained with the survey in various capacities until 1891, when he was asked to resign. This bureaucratic career, while terminated in less-than-desirable circumstances, was not without accomplishments. His deep commitment to the experimental method helped put the survey on a firm scientific basis, and Peirce himself became internationally known for his work on gravity research. He also continued an association with Harvard, once again through his father's influence, holding temporary lectureships in logic in 1865-1866 and 1869-1870 and from 1872 to 1875 serving as assistant at the Harvard Observatory. His observatory work on the measurement of light provided data for the only book he published during his lifetime *Photometric Researches* (1878). Peirce hoped for a permanent appointment at Harvard, but his lack of a Ph.D., his erratic life-style, and a typically personal quarrel with Harvard president Charles W. Eliot made the dream impossible.

More important than his actual work, the atmosphere and personal contacts at Harvard helped mold his philosophical outlook. Never idle, Peirce spent his spare time studying the work of Immanuel Kant, the ideas of the medieval scholastics, and various theories in logic and mathematics. The most useful forum for his developing ideas was the so-called Metaphysical Club. In the meetings of this unusual group, which included William James, Oliver Wendell Holmes, Jr., Francis E. Abbot, and Chauncey Wright, among others, Peirce had the opportunity to test his theories before a critical audience. It was there that he used the term "pragmatism" to describe the relationship between a conception and its effects which allows one to understand the actual meaning of the original conception by knowing its effects. While Peirce intended his idea as a theory of meaning, William James, more than twenty years later, would popularize the term and expand it far beyond the original intention. In fact, objecting to his friend's interpretation, Peirce, in 1905, coined the term "pragmaticism" to distinguish his thought from James's version.

In his Harvard years, Peirce began to write articles for *The Journal of Speculative Philosophy* and other scholarly publications, as well as more popular magazines such as *Popular Science Monthly*. Such articles, along with numerous book reviews, provided his major public outlet for the remainder of his life. Ignored by much of the philosophical community, these writings contained important contributions to logic, mathematics, and metaphysics.

Peirce finally got his chance to teach when he was hired as a part-time lecturer at The Johns Hopkins University in 1879. Apparently an effective teacher, he produced some of his best work in logic and scientific methodology at Johns Hopkins. Yet his erratic behavior, coupled with his divorce from his first wife and remarriage to a twenty-six-year-old French woman, the mysterious Mme Juliette Pourtalai, made it difficult for the authorities to accept him, no matter how brilliant, as part of the faculty. In 1884, Peirce was dismissed from his position because of unsuitable activities of a moral nature, probably connected with his divorce and remarriage.

Peirce's second marriage began a phase of his life which would be philosophically productive but personally frustrating, ending in self-imposed exile. In 1887, his academic career hopelessly in shambles and his labors for the survey drawing to a conclusion, Peirce moved to Milford, Pennsylvania, a resort area on the Delaware river. With a small inheritance, he was able to purchase land and begin construction of an elaborately planned home he called "Arisbe." Though Peirce was able to live in his retreat for the remainder of his life, the mansion was never really completed. Typically, Peirce had overextended himself. When he lost his government salary in 1891 and suffered severe losses in the depression of 1893, he began a long slide into poverty. His closest and always tolerant friend, William James, tried to help as much as possible, arranging for a series of lectures in Boston in 1898 and finally convincing Harvard to allow the notorious philosopher to give a series of lectures at the university in 1903. No effort, however, even by America's most famous philosopher, would make Peirce acceptable to established society in the nineteenth century. Finally, James began collecting donations for a Peirce fund from interested and unnamed friends. From 1907 until his death in 1914, Peirce was largely supported by this fund, which amounted to about thirteen hundred dollars a year. Peirce, who had often been jealous of James and attacked his version of pragmatism with undisguised contempt, paid his friend a typical compliment by adopting Santiago (St. James) as part of his name in 1909.

Even in his last years, which were marred by illness, Peirce was productive. He continued to work in isolation, leaving behind a massive collection of papers. Ironically, Harvard, the institution which had so often rejected him, recognized his worth and purchased the manuscripts from his widow. Between 1931 and 1935, the six volumes of the *Collected Papers of Charles Sanders Peirce*, edited by Charles Hartshorne and Paul Weiss, were published by Harvard. This collection began what amounted to a revolution in American academic philosophy, making the ideas of Peirce a touchstone for twentieth century philosophical inquiry.

Unfortunately, the exact nature of Peirce's contribution to understanding is by no means clear. Numerous scholars have spent careers examining his writings, never reaching a consensus. The confusion is rooted in the nature of Peirce's work itself. Not satisfied with a contribution in a single area of inquiry, Peirce envisioned a vast architectonic system ending in a complete explanation of all human knowledge. In short, Peirce strove to be a modern Aristotle. While admirable, this goal ran up against a central dilemma in human thought, providing a source of tension within Peirce's system as well as within the world in which he lived.

Science, in the last years of the nineteenth century, revealed a limited vision of reality, of what could be known. The world, according to this view, consisted of matter and could be fully explained through the scientific method. Many thinkers, unable to accept this so-called positivistic version of reality, countered with an explanation based on the mind itself as the source of everything. Best represented in the idealism of Georg Wilhelm Friedrich Hegel, this view had spawned many variations. Peirce could not fully accept either position. Positivism seemed to deny the possibility of metaphysics or, perhaps better, a universe with meaning which could be understood by men. Idealism seemed hopelessly subjective, denying the possibility of actually knowing the physical universe.

Peirce set out to reconcile the irreconcilable by carefully examining immediate experience. Characteristically, this examination would be grounded on clear and precise thinking such as his famous "pragmatic maxim." He also rejected nominalism and accepted the position of the medieval scholastic Duns Scotus on the reality of Universals. Peirce insisted that cognition itself is reality, and everything that is real is knowable. The structure of experience is revealed in what he called "phaneroscopy." This term is typical of Peirce's obsession with the invention of new words to explain concepts, which is one of the reasons his ideas are so difficult. Phaneroscopy is roughly analogous to the modern concept of phenomenology. From his phenomenological basis, Peirce deduced three categories or qualities of experience which he termed Firstness, Secondness, and Thirdness. This division of experience allowed him to move from an essentially psychological analysis to logic itself through what he called the "semiotic," or the doctrine of signs. By signs, Peirce essentially meant those things in the mind which stand for the real things of the world. A word, for example, would be a sign but only one kind of sign. Peirce's analysis of signs and their relationships was a vast and complicated explanation of how human beings think and provides the logical basis for his whole system.

A complete discussion of this difficult and obscure argument is not possible in this context, but most modern philosophers would agree that it constitutes Peirce's most important contribution to philosophy, particularly logic. Its obscurity, however, has led to many different interpretations. Phenomenologists, for example, find considerable comfort in his explanation of experience, while the logical positivists, who seldom agree with phenomenologists, also see their ideas reflected in Peirce's theory of signs. In fact, most philosophical systems in the twentieth century find some part of Peirce's ideas important in either a positive or a negative way.

Peirce's logic, however, was only the foundation of a broad system that included a complete theory of knowledge as well as cosmological speculations. This system, while not as widely accepted as his semiotic, includes a number of important concepts. For example, Peirce develops what he calls "tychism," or the doctrine of chance, which explains irregularities within nature. This idea should be balanced with "synechism," which is the doctrine that continuity is a basic feature of the world. Here again, Peirce reconciles the irreconcilable, and the result provides a reasonable picture of the actual condition of scientific inquiry. Synechism represents scientific law, which Peirce calls habit, without which one could not understand the operation of the natural world. Tychism, however, explains how change is possible and prevents a deterministic version of reality, which is the logical result of scientific law. Science then, while based on research which, if pursued to infinity, will result in "truth," must in the practical world be based on probability. Even in logic itself, one cannot be sure that all statements are correct. While not denying absolute truth, this concept, which Peirce called "fallibilism," provides a healthy corrective to those who are convinced that they have found the ultimate answer to reality.

Summary

Few can profess to understand all of Peirce's philosophy, and his work will probably never appeal to the average person unschooled in the mysteries of philosophical discourse. Yet his attack on the central dilemma of modern thought, created by scientific advance and its inevitable clash with human values, is the necessary starting point for many twentieth century philosophers and, through their work, has a profound influence on the way the world is viewed. It may be true that Peirce ultimately failed in his attempt to reconcile the "hard" world of science with cherished human values represented by the "soft" world of idealism, but, unlike his tragic personal life, his philosophy was certainly a glorious failure. Moreover, Peirce remained a true optimist who believed in the inevitability of human progress through reason. His system of thought, while far from perfect, did provide a view of reality that would make such progress possible. His first rule of reason demanded that the road to new knowledge always be left open. The greatest sin against reasoning, he believed, consisted in adopting a set of beliefs which would erect a barrier in the path of the search for truth.

Bibliography
Almeder, Robert F. *The Philosophy of Charles S. Peirce: A Critical Introduction*. Totowa, N.J.: Rowman and Littlefield, 1980. An analysis of Peirce's philosophy, stressing his epistemological realism, which contains a perceptive and detailed discussion of his theory of knowledge.
Conkin, Paul K. *Puritans and Pragmatists: Eight Eminent American Thinkers*. Bloomington: Indiana University Press, 1968. One of the finest overviews of American intellectual history. Places Peirce within the context of the development of American thought between Jonathan Edwards and George Santayana.
Goudge, Thomas A. *The Thought of C. S. Peirce*. Toronto: University of Toronto Press, 1950. One of the most perceptive studies of Peirce's thought. Sees Peirce's philosophy as resting on a conflict within his personality which produced tendencies toward both naturalism and Transcendentalism.
Moore, Edward C. *American Pragmatism: Peirce, James, and Dewey*. New York: Columbia University Press, 1961. An analysis of American pragmatism based on its three primary figures. Provides an excellent comparison of their different positions.
Potter, Vincent G. *Charles S. Peirce: On Norms and Ideals*. Amherst: University of Massachusetts Press, 1967. An analysis of Peirce's attempt to establish aesthetics, ethics, and logic as the three normative sciences. The author places particular emphasis on the role of "habit" in the universe.
Reilly, Francis E. *Charles Peirce's Theory of Scientific Method*. New York: Fordham University Press, 1970. A discussion of Peirce's ideas concerning the method and the philosophy of science.
Skagestad, Peter. *The Road of Inquiry: Charles Peirce's Realism*. New York: Columbia University Press, 1981. Focuses on Peirce's theory of scientific method but also contains an introduction with considerable biographical information.
Thayer, H. S. *Meaning and Action: A Critical History of Pragmatism*. Indianapolis: Hackett Publishing Co., 1961. A comprehensive analysis of pragmatism, covering philosophers both in the United States and Europe.

David Warren Bowen

WILLIAM PENN

Born: October 14, 1644; London, England
Died: July 30, 1718; Ruscombe, England
Areas of Achievement: Religion, politics, and colonization
Contribution: A leading Quaker, Penn contributed to the early development of the sect through his traveling ministry, his numerous religious tracts, intervention with English authorities for toleration, and establishment of Pennsylvania as a refuge for dissenters.

Early Life

William Penn was born October 14, 1644, on Tower Hill in London, England. His mother was the widow Margaret Vanderschuren, the daughter of John Jasper, a Rotterdam merchant. His father, Sir William Penn, was an admiral in the British navy who first achieved prominence under Oliver Cromwell and, after the Restoration of the monarchy in 1660, went on to further success under the Stuarts. Despite some ups and downs in his career, the elder Penn accumulated estates in Ireland, rewards for his services, providing sufficient income so that the younger Penn was reared as a gentleman and exposed to the upper echelons of English society.

Penn received his early education at the Chigwell School, followed by a stint at home with a tutor who prepared him for entrance into college. In 1660, he was enrolled at Christ Church, Oxford University, where he remained until March, 1662, when he was expelled for infraction of the rules enforcing religious conformity. He then went on a grand tour of the Continent and spent a year or two at Saumur, France, studying languages and theology at a Huguenot school. After returning to England, he spent a year as a law student at Lincoln's Inn. His legal studies were somewhat sporadic and were never completed, a pattern that was typical for gentlemen of the day. They did, however, influence his subsequent writings and his ability to argue his own cause as well as those of others.

In Ireland, first as a child and later while acting as an agent for his father, Penn was exposed to Quakerism. It was in 1666, while managing the family estates, that he was converted by Thomas Loe, a Quaker preacher. Much to the horror of his father, young Penn took to preaching at Quaker meetings, quickly achieving prominence among the members of the still relatively new nonconforming sect. Parental disapproval continued until a reputedly dramatic reconciliation at the admiral's deathbed.

Life's Work

It was as a Quaker that Penn found his true calling. In 1668, he was in London preaching at meetings, and he produced his first religious tract, *Truth Exalted*. From that time onward, he spent a good portion of his life traveling, preaching, and writing religious tracts. He made several extended trips to the Continent, speaking at Quaker meetings as well as trying to convert others to the faith. By the end of his life, he had written some 150 works, most of them on religion. Some were descriptions of Quaker doctrines, such as *No Cross, No Crown* (1669); others were defenses of Quaker principles and actions—for example, *Quakerism: A New Nick-Name for Old Christianity* (1672).

There was no toleration in England in the 1660's for those who dissented form the Anglican Church. As a result, Penn, like numerous other Quakers, was arrested for attending Quaker meetings, for preaching, and for publishing a religious tract without a license. Indeed, several of his works were written while he was in prison. As a result of his experiences, as well as of observation of his coreligionists and friends, Penn became an advocate of religious toleration. He wrote several tracts, including *England's Present Interest Discovered* (1675), which pleaded with the government to recognize liberty of conscience for all, not only for Quakers. Penn used his position and friendship with the Stuart kings, Charles II and James II, to aid others.

Support for civil rights also came out of Penn's advocacy of religious toleration. His arrest for preaching at a Friend's meeting in 1670, a violation of England's stringent religious laws, led to two trials which ultimately contributed to the independence of juries. In the first case, Penn and his fellow Quaker William Mead were found not guilty of unlawful assembly by a jury which refused to alter its verdict after being ordered to do so or else "go without food or drink." Members of the jury were then fined; they appealed their case and ultimately were vindicated in their right to establish a verdict free from coercion.

Politically, Penn was caught, both in his beliefs and friendships, between the liberal dissenting Whig politicians and the conservative followers of the Stuart court. In 1678, he gave his support to Algernon Sidney's bid for a seat in Parliament, while maintaining his friendship with the Duke of York. Penn's attempt to keep his balance in the volatile English political scene of that period failed with the Glorious Revolution, when England exchanged the Catholic Duke of York, James II, for Mary, his Protestant daughter, and her husband, William of Orange. Accused of treason and at one point placed under arrest, Penn fled and for several years after 1691 went into hiding. It was not until after the turn of the century, under the rule of Queen Anne, that he again safely participated in the English political scene. Penn's position between the two major camps of the period is also evident in his writings and in the constitutional provisions he made for his colony, Pennsylvania, since they exhibit both liberal and conservative features.

For Americans, Penn is best known for his colonization efforts. His interest in the New World stemmed from his association with the great Quaker leader and preacher George Fox, who traveled through the Colonies. Penn's first involvement was in West Jersey, where he acted as an arbitrator in a complex dispute between two Quakers with claims to that colony. He ultimately became one of the proprietors of West Jersey, as well as, after 1682, of East Jersey. Yet because Quaker claims to the government of the Jerseys were under question, he sought a colony of his own, and it was on Pennsylvania that he expended most of his efforts. In 1681, he obtained a charter from Charles II for extensive territories in America, ostensibly as payment owed to his father; the grant gave him rights to the government as well as the land of the colony.

In establishing Pennsylvania, Penn wanted both to create a refuge for Quakers where they would be free to worship without fear of imprisonment and a government with laws based upon their principles. At the same time, as proprietor of the colony, he hoped that the venture would be profitable. He started by preparing a constitution and laws for the colony, consulting numerous friends for their suggestions and comments. The resulting first Frame of Government proved too complex for the colony and was followed by other modified versions. Penn also worked to obtain both settlers and investors for his project and advertised it in pamphlets such as *A Brief Account of the Province of Pennsylvania* (1681) and *A Further Account of the Province of Pennsylvania and Its Improvements* (1685), which were published in several languages and distributed in both England and on the Continent. Expecting to be the resident proprietor and governor of the new colony, Penn made plans to move there. He journeyed to America twice, first in 1682 and again fifteen years later, in 1699, each time remaining for about two years. Both times he scurried back to England to protect his proprietorship, the first time from a controversy with Lord Baltimore, the proprietor of neighboring Maryland, over boundaries, and the second, to respond to a challenge from English authorities to all proprietary governments.

In the long run, Penn's colony was a success for everyone but him. His anticipated profits never materialized—a serious disappointment because, with advancing age, he was increasingly in financial difficulty. The Quaker settlers also proved to be a disappointment in their failure to get along with one another as well as with Penn. Indeed, they proved to be an exceedingly contentious lot, and the boundary controversy with Maryland was not solved in Penn's lifetime. After 1703, Penn negotiated with English authorities to sell his province back to the Crown, a deal which fell through because he suffered an incapacitating stroke in 1712. Pennsylvania, however, grew rapidly, and Philadelphia, the capital city that he had carefully planned, was an impressive success.

Penn is remembered for more than simply his religious writings and the establishment of Pennsylvania. In 1693, he wrote *An Essay Towards the Present and Future Peace of Europe*, which offered proposals for the establishment of peace between nations. In 1697, he proposed a plan of union for the Colonies, suggesting the creation of a congress of representatives from each colony which would meet once a year.

Penn was also a warm, affectionate, and concerned family man. In 1668, he married Gulielma Maria Springett; they had eight children, only three of whom survived childhood. In 1696, two years after his first wife's death, he married Hannah Callowhill, fathering another five children. Unfortunately, his children, like his colony, were a source of disappointment. His oldest son, and favorite, Springett, died at the age of twenty-one. His second son, William Penn, Jr., renounced Quakerism and was something of a rake. The surviving children of his second marriage were, at the time of his death, still young; it was to them that he left his colony of Pennsylvania.

Also contributing to Penn's woes in his later years was a festering problem with his financial agent, Philip Ford. Both were at fault, Ford for making inappropriate charges and Penn for a laxity in supervising his personal affairs. The result was that Ford's wife and children (after his death) pushed for payment—including Pennsylvania—for what they claimed were debts; they had Penn arrested and put in prison. When the dust settled, the Ford claims were taken care of and Pennsylvania had been mortgaged to a group of Penn's Quaker friends.

Summary

Although Penn was never more than a brief resident in the Colonies, his contributions to American history were substantial. He played a prominent role in the proprietorships of both East and West Jersey and was the founder of Pennsylvania. Penn was one of a handful of influential Quaker preachers and authors, and although his ideas were not original, he powerfully expressed and defended the sect's beliefs in numerous pamphlets, as well as in the laws and Frames of Government of Pennsylvania. As a colonizer, his efforts ensured a Quaker presence in America and the sect's role in the political and religious life of the middle colonies.

Penn's advocacy of religious toleration, of protection of the right to trial by jury, and of constitutional government carried across the Atlantic; as a result, provisions for all three were made in the colonies with which his name was associated. Penn thought that settlers would be attracted to America not only for its land but also for the freedoms it could offer, maintaining that Englishmen would only leave home if they could get more, rather than less, of both. He worked to make this happen. Thus, Penn used his connections among Whig and court groups on the English political scene to protect his fellow Quakers, his colony, and his proprietorship.

As the founder of Pennsylvania, he was the most successful of English proprietors and yet personally was a financial failure. He was a gentleman and a Quaker who could be contentious, particularly in religious debates, stubborn in maintaining his position against all opposition, and anything but humble in his life-style. In many ways, he was an uncommon and contradictory individual.

Penn's place in American history rests on his success in helping establish one colony and in founding another. The name Pennsylvania, standing for "Penn's woods," continues as a reminder of his significance. Sometimes overlooked, but also important, are his contributions to the fundamental political traditions which Americans have come to take for granted.

Bibliography
Beatty, Edward C. O. *William Penn as Social Philosopher*. New York: Columbia University Press, 1939. Reprint. New York: Octagon Books, 1975. Beatty examines Penn's philosophical and social ideas, viewing him as a political theorist, statesman, pacifist, humanitarian, and family man.
Bronner, Edwin B. *William Penn's Holy Experiment: The Founding of Pennsylvania, 1681-1701*. New York: Columbia University Press, 1962. Concerned with Penn's vision in establishing Pennsylvania and how it worked out. Contrasts plans and reality.
Dunn, Mary Maples. "The Personality of William Penn." *American Philosophical Society Proceedings* 127 (October, 1983): 316-321. Dunn portrays Penn as a restless rebel, a poor judge of people, and always the aristocrat.
_____. *William Penn: Politics and Conscience*. Princeton, N.J.: Princeton University Press, 1967. Argues that Penn was a creative thinker who, along with others of his age, wrestled with the question of what was constitutional government. The key to Penn's political ideas was liberty of conscience; a key to his behavior was the desire to protect his title to Pennsylvania.
Dunn, Richard S. "William Penn and the Selling of Pennsylvania, 1681-1685." *American Philosophical Society Proceedings* 127 (October, 1983): 322-329. Discusses Penn as a salesman and businessman.
Endy, Melvin B., Jr. *William Penn and Early Quakerism*. Princeton, N.J.: Princeton University Press, 1973. Concentrates on Penn's religious thought and its relationship to his political and social life. Also evaluates his significance for early Quakerism.
Illick, Joseph E. *William Penn the Politician: His Relations with the English Government*. Ithaca, N.Y.: Cornell University Press, 1965. Illick is primarily concerned with Penn as a practical politician who threaded his way through the perilous waters of English politics. Penn, as proprietor, is viewed as more successful, despite some ups and downs, in his dealings with the English government than with his own colonists.
Lurie, Maxine N. "William Penn: How Does He Rate as a Proprietor?" *Pennsylvania Magazine of History and Biography*, October, 1981: 393-417. Compares and contrasts Penn as proprietor with those who established other proprietary colonies.

Morgan, Edmund S. "The World and William Penn." *American Philosophical Society Proceedings* 127 (October, 1983): 291-315. A good, brief discussion of Penn's life which tries to put his experiences in the context of the English society. Emphasis is on Penn as a Protestant, a gentleman, and an Englishman.

Nash, Gary B. *Quakers and Politics: Pennsylvania, 1681-1726*. Princeton, N.J.: Princeton University Press, 1968. Concentrates on Penn's conflicts with the settlers in Pennsylvania, as well as their problems with one another. Nash emphasizes the religious and economic background of the disagreements. Good source for information on the dynamics of early Pennsylvania politics as well as on Penn.

Peare, Catherine Owens. *William Penn: A Biography*. Philadelphia: J. P. Lippincott Co., 1956. The standard modern work on Penn. A readable account with a sometimes excessively flowery style. There are numerous other, older, biographies, but this one is the best.

Penn, William. *The Papers of William Penn*. Edited by Mary Maples Dunn, Richard S. Dunn, et al. Philadelphia: University of Pennsylvania Press, 1981- . This is the result of a project to collect and make available the widely scattered papers of Penn. Volumes are well annotated and a pleasure to use. In addition to the printed volumes, there is also a more complete microfilm series.

Maxine N. Lurie

FRANCES PERKINS

Born: April 10, 1880; Boston, Massachusetts
Died: May 14, 1965; New York, New York
Areas of Achievement: Social reform and politics
Contribution: A firm believer in social justice, Perkins dedicated her life to others as a social worker, as an advocate of industrial workers, and as secretary of labor. The first woman cabinet member in United States history, she helped shape much New Deal legislation; in the process, she furthered the interests of laborers, the elderly, and women.

Early Life

Fannie Coralie Perkins (she changed her name to Frances around 1902 to change her fortune) was born April 10, 1880, in Boston, Massachusetts. She was one of two daughters of Fred W. Perkins and Susie E. Bean Perkins. Both of her parents were originally from Maine; for generations, their ancestors had been farmers, businessmen, and seamen.

Two years after Perkins was born, her family moved to Worcester, Massachusetts, where her father started a retail and wholesale stationery business. Although never wealthy, the Perkins family enjoyed a comfortable existence which included summers spent at the family farm in Newcastle, Maine. In the mid-1890's, Perkins, described by her contemporaries as a rather plump and plain brunette, enrolled in Worcester Classical High School, a college preparatory institution. Shy but articulate and argumentative, she was graduated in 1898 and then attended Mount Holyoke College in South Hadley, Massachusetts. While at Mount Holyoke, Perkins majored in chemistry and physics. Yet a course in American history, taught by Anna May Soule, which required students to go into the factories of Holyoke, Massachusetts, and to survey the working conditions which they found there, had the greatest impact on her. This experience, combined with a reading of Jacob Riis's study, *How the Other Half Lives* (1890), provided Perkins with an awareness of urban problems. During her senior year of college, Perkins joined the National Consumers' League, which was dedicated to abolishing child labor and the sweatshop system. She also heard a speech delivered by social worker Florence Kelley and for the first time entertained the possibility of devoting her life to the welfare of others.

Perkins was graduated from Mount Holyoke in 1902; lacking experience to enter the field of social welfare, she taught briefly at schools in New England and did volunteer work. From 1904 to 1907, she taught at Ferry Hall in Lake Forest, Illinois. Her free time was spent working in settlement houses in Chicago, especially at Jane Addams' Hull House. This experience confirmed Perkins' desire to enter the field of social service. She returned to the East Coast in 1907; receiving her master's degree from Columbia University in

1910, she became executive secretary of the New York City Consumers' League. In that capacity, she worked tirelessly to achieve state passage of a fifty-four-hour bill for women and children. From that experience, she also learned the political maneuvering necessary to achieve legislative success.

In the aftermath of the Triangle Shirtwaist fire, which caused the deaths of 146 female factory workers, Perkins became executive secretary of the Committee on Safety of the City of New York. Assuming the position in May, 1912, she acted as the committee's representative before the New York Factory Investigating Commission. Carefully attired in simple, dark dresses and small tricorn hats which became her trademark, she worked closely with other commissioners such as Alfred E. Smith and Robert Wagner. In the years ahead, both men would further her political career. Together, this group lobbied for the enactment of state legislation regulating industrial and labor conditions. Such action served as a confirmation of Perkins' belief that social legislation, rather than trade unionism, should be the focus of efforts to improve the lives of workers.

Life's Work

On September 26, 1913, Perkins married Paul Caldwell Wilson, an economist for the Bureau of Municipal Research in New York. In a break with tradition, Perkins chose to retain her maiden name. In 1916, the couple welcomed the arrival of a daughter, Susanna Winslow Wilson. After the birth of her child, Perkins kept busy through volunteer work. In 1918, however, her husband lost most of his money through unwise investments; Perkins was forced to seek paid employment to support her family. Her husband's deepening depression was a constant source of worry; from 1930 until his death, Paul Wilson spent more and more time living in institutions.

In 1918, Perkins' friend Smith was elected governor of New York; he soon appointed her an industrial commissioner, one of the leaders of the New York State Labor Department. Over the next decade, as she worked for Smith, Perkins became active in the fields of factory inspection, workmen's compensation, and labor-management mediation. She also continued to lobby for the enactment of labor legislation. Gradually, she became a partisan of Democratic politics and worked tirelessly on campaigns to reelect Smith.

In 1926, Smith appointed Perkins chief industrial commissioner of the state of New York; she was reappointed to that position by his successor, Franklin D. Roosevelt. The Roosevelt years (1929-1933) in the New York statehouse witnessed the advent of the Great Depression. During that era, Perkins insisted on the gathering of reliable job statistics; she lobbied for protective legislation for women, emergency relief, and state unemployment insurance. Her ideas served as a model of vigorous state response to economic crisis.

In 1933, Roosevelt, the newly elected President of the United States, named Perkins to be secretary of labor. He did this over the objections of labor leaders, who opposed the appointment not only because Perkins was a woman but also because she was not a trade unionist. At first reluctant to accept this responsibility, which would necessitate frequent separations from her family, Perkins eventually assented, thereby becoming the first woman cabinet member in United States history. During her years in Washington (1933-1945), she maintained an unswerving loyalty to Roosevelt; she also helped draft and support much New Deal legislation, including the Federal Emergency Relief Act, the National Recovery Act, the Civilian Conservation Corps, the Social Security Act, and the Fair Labor Standards Act. At the same time, she helped rebuild the Department of Labor, purging it of unsavory elements. She strengthened the women's and children's bureaus and created a Bureau of Labor Statistics. Furthermore, Perkins helped mediate in labor-management disputes.

Despite Perkins' apparent success as secretary of labor, there were many who disliked her for her sex and for her liberal sympathies. In the late 1930's, she became the victim of a vicious campaign which alleged that she possessed Communist sympathies because she had refused the deportation of Harry Bridges, a radical labor leader. The House Committee on Un-American Activities launched a campaign to impeach Perkins, but the House Judiciary Committee endorsed her actions and the charges were dropped. Although vindicated, Perkins found that her political credibility was badly damaged.

During World War II, Perkins continued to run the Department of Labor; her major goal was to uphold those gains made by workers during the 1930's. At that time, she took a moderate course on women's issues, opposing the registration of female workers for national labor service, the creation of child-care centers at government expense, and the passage of the proposed Equal Rights Amendment.

Upon the death of Roosevelt, Perkins served briefly in the Truman Administration, resigning her post as secretary of labor on July 1, 1945. Yet she was not ready to retire. From 1946 to 1953, she served on the United States Civil Service Commission. To raise money to meet expenses, she also spoke frequently on her years in the Roosevelt Administration. In 1946, she wrote *The Roosevelt I Knew*, a memoir which she readily admitted was biased in FDR's favor.

With her husband's death in 1952, Perkins gained a new freedom of action which allowed her to lecture at universities across the United States. In 1957, she began a long-term relationship with Cornell, which culminated in her yearly appointment as a visiting professor at the School of Industrial and Labor Relations. Although her eyesight was failing, she participated fully in the life of the university. This relationship lasted until her death in New York City, from a series of strokes, in May, 1965. Ever generous with her talents, Perkins had given of her knowledge and abilities until the end of her life.

Summary

Frances Perkins' graduating class at Mount Holyoke chose as its motto the biblical injunction, "Be ye steadfast." This motto, which frequently was quoted at reunions and in class mailings, summed up what many students believed they had gained from their college education. It implied that Mount Holyoke women should have a social conscience and work strenuously to improve the world around them. Perkins, more than any of her classmates, exhibited the meshing of words with action. A pioneer when few women received higher education, Perkins readily acknowledged that it was her duty to help those less fortunate than herself. A deep religious faith sustained her in this commitment.

Perkins was typical of other college-educated women who chose to enter the field of social work. Many, intrigued by the experiences of Jane Addams and Florence Kelley, eagerly entered settlement houses. What was unusual was Perkins' degree of commitment to her work. Beginning at Hull House and then expanding her interests to the problems of the laboring masses in New York State, she rapidly became an expert in a field normally thought inappropriate for women. Sustaining her in her work were men who recognized her expertise and talents. At a time when many men wary of placing women in offices of public trust, both Smith and Roosevelt gave Perkins an opportunity to develop her abilities to the fullest.

In 1933, when she became the first woman cabinet member, Perkins had the opportunity to give her ideas national exposure. Placed in a position in which resentment developed against her, Perkins nevertheless helped to shape much revolutionary New Deal legislation. As a result of her efforts, emergency relief was provided to the unemployed, young men were given constructive labor to perform, and regulations were created mandating minimum wages, maximum hours, and decent working conditions. Through the Social Security Administration, old-age insurance was created and provisions were made to assist the unemployed and the handicapped. All these reforms quickly became accepted aspects of American life.

Although not a radical feminist, Perkins also furthered the position of women in American society. Afraid to champion the Equal Rights Amendment because it would have outlawed protective legislation, Perkins helped women through her insistence that neither they nor their children be exploited on the job. Furthermore, she served as an important example to women desiring a life of government service. During the New Deal, she encouraged many to become a part of the Roosevelt Administration.

Surely Perkins' own marital situation was an unusual one. Despite her husband's long-term illness, she remained intensely loyal to him and, even while in Washington, visited him weekly in New York. To a great extent, her devotion to her work was mandated by the necessity to support her family and to pay large medical bills. It should be remembered, however, that Perkins deeply believed in her work. Refusing to accept defeat, she lobbied long and hard for the government regulations which would assist Americans coming from the lower rungs of the economic ladder. The result was a life extraordinarily rich in experience and in concern for others.

Bibliography

Bernstein, Irving. *Turbulent Years: A History of the American Worker, 1933-1941*. Boston: Houghton Mifflin Co., 1970. A detailed history of labor problems during the New Deal. Emphasis is placed on organized labor; also explained is Perkins' role in mediating worker disputes.

Chambers, Clarke A. *Seedtime of Reform: American Social Service and Social Action, 1918-1933*. Ann Arbor: University of Michigan Press, 1967. A study detailing the social movement of which Perkins was a part. Chambers contends that it was individuals such as Perkins who kept Progressive social welfare ideas alive during the 1920's and 1930's so that they could see fruition in the New Deal.

Lash, Joseph P. *Eleanor and Franklin*. New York: W. W. Norton and Co., 1971. Mainly a study of the personal professional relationship of the Roosevelts; the study casts an interesting light on Perkins' activities as perceived by her associates.

Martin, George. *Madam Secretary: Frances Perkins*. Boston: Houghton Mifflin Co., 1976. Undoubtedly the finest and most complete biography of Perkins. Exhaustively documented, the book provides a balanced yet affectionate view of the private and public activities of America's first woman cabinet member.

Mohr, Lillian Holmen. *Frances Perkins: "That Woman in FDR's Cabinet!"* Croton-on-Hudson, N.Y.: North River Press, 1979. Concentrates on Perkins' public activities in the 1920's, 1930's, and 1940's. Carefully researched and clearly written, it nevertheless fails to evoke the drama of Perkins' life and work.

Perkins, Frances. *The Roosevelt I Knew*. New York: Viking Press, 1946. One of the best biographies of Roosevelt, written by a member of his inner circle. Unabashedly favorable to FDR, the volume provides autobiographical data on Perkins' experiences working with Roosevelt in Albany and Washington.

Ware, Susan. *Beyond Suffrage: Women in the New Deal*. Cambridge, Mass.: Harvard University Press, 1981. Putting Perkins' career in its proper perspective, this volume is essential for examining the development of the women's "network" which moved into posts in the federal government and the Democratic Party in the 1930's.

_____. *Holding Their Own: American Women in the 1930's*. Boston: Twayne Publishers, 1982. A survey of the variety of activities in which women engaged in the United States in the 1930's. Ware contends that the work of Perkins as secretary of labor symbolized the progress made by many women during the Depression decade.

Marian E. Strobel

MATTHEW C. PERRY

Born: April 10, 1794; Newport, Rhode Island
Died: March 4, 1858; New York City
Areas of Achievement: The naval service and diplomacy
Contribution: In a naval career spanning almost half a century, Perry, besides
   commanding ships and fleets with distinction in peace and in war, proposed and accomplished reforms in naval architecture, ordnance, and
   organization, and through skillful negotiation introduced Japan into the
   modern community of nations.

Early Life

Matthew Calbraith Perry was born April 10, 1794, in Newport, Rhode Island. His father, Christopher Raymond Perry, was the descendant of original
Quaker settlers of Rhode Island but served in privateers and Continental
warships in the Revolution. The senior Perry met his Irish wife, Sarah Wallace Alexander, when he was a paroled prisoner in Ireland in 1781. Their eldest son, Oliver Hazard Perry (1785-1819), was the hero of the Battle of
Lake Erie in 1813 and Matthew Perry's greatest hero.

In 1809, Matthew Perry was assigned as a midshipman to the schooner *Re-
venge*. A year later he transferred to the frigate *President*, in which he served
in 1811 in the engagement with HMS *Little Belt* and in the War of 1812, when
he was wounded slightly in the inconclusive fight with HMS *Belvidera*.

On December 24, 1814, he married Jane Slidell (1797-1879), daughter of a
New York merchant, who bore him ten children. Their three sons and one of
their sons-in-law were all navy or marine officers.

In 1815, Perry was assigned to the brig *Chippewa*, which was part of the
Mediterranean Squadron, and at the end of this cruise he applied for furlough and commanded one, and perhaps more, of his father-in-law's merchant ships.

Life's Work

In 1819, Perry returned to naval service as first lieutenant in the corvette
Cyane, which escorted the first settlers sent to Liberia by the American
Colonization Society and patrolled the coast of West Africa to suppress the
slave trade. Two years later, he was commanding the schooner *Shark* in African waters and the West Indies, where the navy was attempting to suppress
piracy. Perry was of great assistance to the Liberian settlers in their efforts to
establish their republic and was primarily responsible for the selection of the
site of Monrovia.

From 1824 to 1827, Perry served as first lieutenant and later as acting commander in the battleship *North Carolina* in the Mediterranean Squadron. At
this time the two responsibilities of the squadron, commanded by Com-

modore John Rodgers, were the protection of American shipping during the Greek war of independence and the implementation of a naval treaty with Turkey. Rodgers achieved both goals.

After service in the Charlestown naval yard, Perry was given command of the sloop-of-war *Concord* and in 1830 was responsible for conveying Minister John Randolph to St. Petersburg. This voyage was followed by two more years in the Mediterranean.

By this time Perry had developed all the skills which distinguished the rest of his naval career: total mastery of seamanship, a commanding presence, a great sense of duty and personal rectitude, negotiating skills of a high order, and a capacity for sympathy with people of diverse cultures. Much of this no doubt derived from his devout Episcopalianism, but it also was a product of high intelligence, which was reflected in a broad range of scholarly interests, particularly in history, ethnology, languages, and science.

When Perry was serving in the Mediterranean in this cruise, President Andrew Jackson was seeking agreements by which the European powers would agree to pay for spoliation of American commerce during the Napoleonic wars. In 1832, Perry commanded a squadron sent to Naples to support the efforts of American negotiators to collect payments from the Kingdom of the Two Sicilies. This show of strength apparently tipped the scales to produce the agreement of October, 1832.

The three greatest achievements of Perry's career were his efforts to modernize the navy, his service in the Mexican War, and his command of the expedition which first established formal relations with Japan.

From 1833, when he accepted command of the New York recruiting station, until 1843, when he ended his tenure as commander of the Brooklyn naval yard, Perry campaigned for naval reform. In an 1837 article, he outlined in detail the inadequacies of the United States Navy, which was eighth in the world, trailing even Turkey and Egypt and far behind Great Britain and France in naval architecture and ordnance. Perry is correctly considered the "father of the steam navy." He campaigned for construction of steam warships, and he initiated the action which led to the creation of the navy's Engineering Corps. He argued for the adoption of shell guns, invented the collapsible smokestack, advocated iron hulls for river gunboats, and recommended the creation of an independent Lighthouse Board. In addition, he was deeply involved in efforts to cure the old navy's problem of manpower procurement. In the early nineteenth century, crews were usually made up by robbing the merchant service and by recruiting foreigners and social misfits. Perry agitated for the creation of an apprentice system and for a school ship for their training. The attempted mutiny on the *Somers* in 1842 discredited this system, but that failure led to implementation of another of Perry's proposals: the creation of the Naval Academy.

In 1843, Perry was assigned to the command of the African Squadron, and in this capacity he negotiated a treaty with the local chiefs on the Ivory Coast, in which the chiefs agreed not to molest missionaries or plunder trading ships. He also was influential in settling differences between the immigrants and the native population of Liberia.

In the Mexican War, Perry first served as vice commodore of naval forces on the Mexican coast, subordinate to Commodore David Conner. He captured Frontera in October, 1846, and sailed fifty miles up the Rio Grijalva to attack Villahermosa and to capture nine enemy warships there. In November, he participated in the capture of Tampico, and the following month occupied Ciudad de Carmen. In March, 1847, he succeeded Conner as commodore and landed naval guns and gun-crews to support the troops Conner had landed to besiege Vera Cruz.

By the time Vera Cruz surrendered on March 29, 1847, Perry was commanding the largest American fleet up to that time—twenty-three vessels. In April he attacked Tuxpan, destroying the forts and carrying off the guns captured by the Mexicans when an American brig ran aground.

His second attack on Villahermosa in June, 1847, was his greatest achievement in the war. He again advanced up the Grijalva to the underwater obstacles laid down by the enemy, then landed eleven hundred men and led them personally on their three-mile march through Mexican defenses to capture Villahermosa.

The Japan expedition originated in Perry's memorandum to the secretary of the navy in the winter of 1851, in which he suggested that friendly relations could be achieved with Japan by a show of naval strength. He did not want command of the expedition, but he accepted it in January, 1852. His selection of ships and officers was careful, and his logistical planning was so effective that the colliers for refueling his steamers were in their assigned positions throughout the voyage. Before he could depart, however, he was ordered to investigate charges of British interference with American fishermen on the Canadian coast. His report on his findings led to the reciprocity treaty of 1854.

Perry's squadron arrived at Okinawa, then an independent kingdom, in May, 1853, and he established relations which enabled him to negotiate a treaty in the following year. After a side trip to the Bonin Islands, where, on Chichi Jima, he bought fifty acres as a possible coaling station, the squadron reached Tokyo Bay on July 8, 1853.

Perry's behavior with the Japanese was remarkable for its combination of austere reserve, firmness, and cordiality. The Japanese sent minor officials to order the American ships away, but Perry dealt with them only through his subordinates, insisting on dealing with officials who could speak for the emperor. When Japanese guard boats attempted to ring his ships, he ordered them off under threat of opening fire. Finally, when it did not appear that the Japanese would accept President Fillmore's letter under any conditions,

Perry informed them that if they would not accept it within a sufficient time he would land at Edo (Tokyo) in force and deliver it himself.

On July 14, Perry was invited to land with an armed retinue at Kurihama, near the mouth of Tokyo Bay, and, amid great formality on both sides, two Japanese officials accepted Fillmore's letter.

After wintering in Hong Kong, Perry returned to Japan in February, 1854, for further negotiations and landed in March. By the treaty of March 31, the Japanese granted two fueling ports, at Hakodate on Tsugaru Strait on southern Hokkaido and at Shimoda on the Izu Peninsula on Honshū. While the treaty did not make arrangements for trade, it did give Americans free access to the areas around the ports and arranged for shipwrecked American sailors to be sent to those ports for repatriation. Perry examined the port of Shimoda and, after sailing to Hakodate to insure that it was acceptable, he returned to Shimoda in June and reached further agreements with the Japanese on currency exchange, pilotage, and port dues. After sailing to Okinawa to negotiate the Treaty of Naha in July, 1854, he led his forces back to Hong Kong and with the treaty returned to the United States by commercial steamers.

In his last years, Perry enjoyed enormous public respect for his achievements in Japan. He devoted his time to service on the Naval Efficiency Board, which was engaged in weeding out overage naval officers, and concentrated much of his attention on the preparation of the official narrative of the Japan expedition and on writing several articles which revealed a great sense of the importance of the Pacific in future American naval and political strategy. He was convinced that Russia would be America's future Pacific rival and that it was crucially important to acquire coaling stations and naval bases in the western Pacific. Meanwhile, as a result of his achievements, the European powers were able to obtain treaties with Japan, and a trade agreement between the United States and Japan was achieved in 1858. Perry died in New York City on March 4, 1858.

Summary

Perry distinguished himself in his long naval career both as a commander and as a diplomat. Possessing not only the great skills in combat leadership that made him the most distinguished American naval officer of the Mexican War but also a remarkable combination of tact, firmness, patience, and empathy that enabled him to achieve great results as a negotiator, he succeeded both in founding the modern United States Navy and in using naval power to establish mutually productive relations with Japan. Perry's success in the latter case led him to the conclusion that the Pacific was to become his country's future arena of power and influence, and he made proposals for establishing naval bases in the Pacific which, if they had not disappeared in the domestic crisis in which the United States found itself in the 1850's, might well have prevented the rupture of Japanese-American relations in the 1930's. Perry recognized international political realities in the Pacific at a time when virtually every other American was concerned with the task of conquering and developing the continent and securing domestic harmony. When the United States finally accepted international responsibility, it was obliged to fight a terrible war with the country with which Perry had established amicable relations and to maintain the presence in the Pacific which he had favored in the first place.

Bibliography

Barrows, Edward M. *The Great Commodore*. Indianapolis: Bobbs-Merrill Co., 1935. The best biography until it was superseded by that of Morison. Somewhat dated on the subject of the Japan expedition.

Griffis, William Elliott. *Matthew Calbraith Perry: A Typical American Naval Officer*. Boston: Copples and Hurd, 1887. A friendly account, flawed by a misleading title and by occasional errors of fact. Provides most of the essential information on Perry's life.

Hawks, Francis L. *Narrative of the Expedition of an American Squadron to the China Seas and Japan*. Edited by Sidney Wallach. New York: Coward-McCann, 1952. A convenient modern abridgement of the journals and reports of the Japan expedition. (The original was published in three volumes in 1856.)

Knox, Dudley. *A History of the United States Navy*. New York: G. P. Putnam's Sons, 1936. A standard work which devotes a chapter to the Japan expedition and provides a good survey of the naval background of Perry's career.

Kuhn, Ferdinand. "Yankee Sailor Who Opened Japan." *National Geographic Magazine* 104 (July, 1953): 85-102. A general account of Perry's achievements in Japan, well illustrated with contemporary prints, many of them by Japanese artists.

Morison, Samuel Eliot. *"Old Bruin": Commodore Matthew Calbraith Perry, 1794-1858*. Boston: Little, Brown and Co., 1967. The definitive biography, by the most distinguished American naval historian. Full account of Perry's personal and professional life, with thorough treatment of social and political background, including the *Somers* affair and the achievements of Perry's father and brother.

Paullin, Charles Oscar. "The First American Treaty with Japan: 1851-1854." In *Diplomatic Negotiations of American Naval Officers, 1778-1883*, 244-281. Baltimore: Johns Hopkins University Press, 1912. Paullin was the outstanding student of this subject, and this chapter is a sound, basic account of Perry's accomplishments in Japan.

Pineau, Roger, ed. *The Japan Expedition, 1852-1854: The Personal Journal of Commodore Matthew C. Perry*. Washington, D.C.: Smithsonian Institution Press, 1968. A fine edition of Perry's journal, hitherto unpublished, with splendid color plates of watercolors and prints made during the voyage.

Walworth, Arthur. *Black Ships Off Japan*. New York: Alfred A. Knopf, 1946. A popular account of the Japan expedition, essentially accurate though its interpretation of Perry's character and behavior should be checked against that of Morison.

Robert L. Berner

OLIVER HAZARD PERRY

Born: August 20, 1785; South Kingston, Rhode Island
Died: August 23, 1819; near Port of Spain, Trinidad
Area of Achievement: The naval service
Contribution: Perry's skillful seamanship and tactical tenacity in the War of
   1812 provided an example of leadership and courage to the officers and
   crews of the young republic's fledgling navy.

Early Life

Born to a family of Rhode Island seamen, Perry's father, Christopher Raymond Perry, broke with the clan's tradition of Quaker pacifism to fight in the American Revolution. Four of Christopher's sons served in the United States Navy, one of whom was Matthew C. Perry, the famed naval commander and diplomat who opened Japan to Western commerce and thought. Reared in Newport, Rhode Island, and educated by his mother, Sarah Wallace Perry, Oliver signed on as a midshipman on his father's vessel, USS *General Greene*, at the age of fourteen. Four years later, he was a lieutenant on the twenty-eight-gun frigate USS *Adams*. Between 1803 and 1806, during the Tripolitan War, he served aboard the *Constellation*, captained the twelve-gun frigate *Nautilus*, and eventually transferred to the forty-four-gun frigate *Constitution* in Commodore John Rodgers' squadron. During the next six years, he directed the construction of various gunboats and commanded a schooner in American waters. In 1811, he married Elizabeth Champlin Mason of Newport. They eventually had five children, two of whom became military officers.

Life's Work

The outbreak of war found Perry commanding a gunboat flotilla at Newport, but in early 1813 he reported to Presque Isle (modern Erie), Pennsylvania, where he immediately began constructing vessels and organizing a crew in the midst of a wilderness. Captain Perry found himself engaged in a naval arms race with Captain Robert H. Barclay of the Royal Navy, who was patrolling Lake Erie and building his own vessels at a rapid pace. Perry's flotilla was under the overall command of Commodore Isaac Chauncey, stationed at Sackett's Harbor, New York, on the southeastern shore of Lake Ontario.

While the ship construction proceeded at Presque Isle, Perry joined Chauncey and General Henry Dearborn and superintended the naval gunfire and amphibious landing support of the attack on Fort George at the mouth of the Niagara River, May 27, 1813. Perry's conduct in this operation was a model of interservice cooperation. The success of the Fort George attack allowed Perry to move to Lake Erie five small vessels and fifty sailors.

At Presque Isle, Perry spent the spring and summer building, equipping, officering, and manning his small fleet of ten vessels, the largest of which were the USS *Lawrence* and the USS *Niagara*, each of 480 tons burden. To take his flotilla onto the lake, Perry had to cross the bar outside the harbor, a feat he could not accomplish in the presence of an enemy force since the shallow waters required that the guns and equipment of the vessels be removed before the ships could pass over. For inexplicable reasons, Captain Barclay relaxed his vigilance and allowed his foe the opportunity in early August to enter the lake unmolested. The battle for Lake Erie may well have been won at the Presque Isle bar, since crossing it allowed the Americans to achieve superior naval power on the lake.

Hoisting his flag on the *Lawrence* and with Lieutenant Jesse Duncan Elliott commanding the *Niagara*, Commodore Perry set out to fight Barclay's force and to cooperate with General William Henry Harrison's army, then encamped at Fort Meigs (west of modern Toledo, Ohio). Harrison could not advance toward Detroit unless Perry secured his lines of supply along the western shore of Lake Erie. After conferring with General Harrison, Perry located Barclay's fleet at Fort Malden, near the mouth of the Detroit River, but confrontation was delayed because of contrary winds and illness among Perry's crew. The Americans retired to Put-in-Bay in the Bass Islands, near modern Sandusky, where Perry received crew reinforcements from Harrison and awaited Barclay's decision to leave the protection of Fort Malden. Though outgunned, Barclay had to risk an engagement because Perry's dominance of the lake denied the British supplies for their troops in the Detroit vicinity.

The encounter, on September 10, 1813, should have been easily won by the Americans because Perry's two twenty-gun vessels gave a decided weight of metal advantage over the single twenty-gun HMS *Detroit* commanded by Barclay. Moreover, the initial wind advantage enjoyed by the British was lost because of a change in direction that allowed the Americans the power of initiative. Perry intended the *Lawrence* to engage the *Detroit* and the *Niagara* to attack HMS *Queen Charlotte*, the second largest of the British vessels. Not only did Elliott not engage the *Queen Charlotte*, but he also allowed that vessel to support the *Detroit* against the *Lawrence*. The result was that despite the heavy damage his flagship inflicted upon the *Detroit*, Perry found his vessel a wreck, her guns disabled, and most of her crew casualties. He transferred his flag to the undamaged *Niagara*, which he then took into action and quickly destroyed and captured the British vessels. His succinct message to General Harrison—"We have met the enemy and they are ours; two ships, two brigs, one schooner, and one sloop"—constitutes a model laconic after-action report. Elliott's conduct in this battle remains controversial and left a legacy of dispute with Perry that lasted long after the latter's death.

Perry's victory dramatically changed the military situation in the Middle

West. Harrison quickly retook Detroit and pursued the British-Canadian-Indian forces eastward. Perry's vessels supported him, and when the two armies met at the Battle of the Thames on October 5, the naval captain acted as an aide to the general and assisted in the forming of the battle line.

Perry relinquished his command and made a triumphant tour to Newport. President James Madison promoted him to the permanent rank of captain, and Congress added five thousand dollars to the seventy-five hundred dollars in prize money that was his due and requested that the president give him a gold medal. In July, 1814, Perry took command of the newly commissioned USS *Java* at Baltimore but was unable to take the vessel to sea because of the British blockade and the ship's still uncompleted state. While in this capacity, he commanded a battery of seamen who harassed the British fleet as it withdrew down the Potomac after the raid on Washington.

On the return of peace with Britain in 1815, Perry took a squadron into the Mediterranean to assist Commodore Stephen Decatur in redressing American grievances against Algiers and Tripoli, whose cruisers had captured numerous American vessels and seamen since 1812. During this cruise, he engaged in a number of diplomatic efforts. He also became involved in a dispute with Marine Captain John Heath, which grew so embittered that, in a fit of passion, Perry struck the *Java*'s marine detachment commander. The incident resulted in a court-martial and a mild reprimand. Still unsatisfied, Heath would eventually engage Perry in a duel that ended with both unhurt and Perry not firing his weapon.

In 1819, Perry undertook a diplomatic mission to Venezuela. He conducted the delicate venture successfully but died of yellow fever contracted during the trip. Perry was buried on Trinidad. In a token of respect for his military prowess and post-battle humanitarianism, his funeral procession received full British honors. Seven years later, his body was returned to Newport for reburial and was marked with a granite obelisk erected by the state of Rhode Island.

Summary

The key to Oliver Hazard Perry's reputation is victory on Lake Erie. There, he demonstrated the elements of professionalism, presence, and determination that elicited the admiration of his officers and men. As he had done earlier at Fort George, in his support of General Harrison's ground force Perry exhibited a degree of interservice cooperation uncharacteristic of many subsequent army-navy efforts. One of the few heroes in a war that was very divisive, his achievement of capturing a Royal Navy fleet was unprecedented in American history. Yet Perry was more than a distinguished warrior and seaman. His diplomatic efforts in North Africa and South America were typical naval endeavors of his day, and they set the tone for his younger brother's famous expedition to Japan. In the final analysis, his career, like that of John Paul Jones, Stephen Decatur, Thomas Macdonough, and James Lawrence, provided an example of valor, dedication, leadership, and patriotism that influenced American sailors for years to follow.

Bibliography

Dutton, Charles J. *Oliver Hazard Perry*. New York: Longmans, Green and Co., 1935. The standard but undistinguished biographical study.

Forester, Cecil S. *The Age of Fighting Sail: The Story of the Naval War of 1812*. Garden City, N.Y.: Doubleday and Co., 1956. A popular history by the author of the Horatio Hornblower stories, this is a good introduction to the problems confronted by Perry and his contemporaries.

Hitsman, J. Mackay. *The Incredible War of 1812: A Military History*. Toronto: University of Toronto Press, 1965. Written from a Canadian perspective, this is a solid history with a strong focus on the war on the Great Lakes.

MacKenzie, Alexander Slidell. *The Life of Commodore Oliver Hazard Perry*. 2 vols. New York: Harper and Brothers, 1840. A highly laudatory account by a naval officer who served under Perry, this study is notable for the numerous personal recollections that MacKenzie collected and for its defensive tone in the Perry-Elliott and Perry-Heath controversies.

Mahan, Alfred Thayer. *Sea Power in Its Relations to the War of 1812*. 2 vols. Boston: Little, Brown and Co., 1905. Volume 2 contains this distinguished naval historian's account of the Battle of Lake Erie; Mahan stoutly defends Perry's conduct.

Morison, Samuel Eliot. *"Old Bruin": Commodore Matthew Calbraith Perry, 1794-1858: The American Naval Officer Who Helped Found Liberia*. Boston: Little, Brown and Co., 1967. This account by a famous naval historian of the career of Perry's younger brother provides both family background and an analysis of the United States Navy in the early nineteenth century.

David Curtis Skaggs

JOHN J. PERSHING

Born: January 13, 1860; Laclede, Missouri
Died: July 15, 1948; Washington, D.C.
Area of Achievement: The military
Contribution: A career soldier, Pershing was ready when called upon to lead the American Expeditionary Force to Europe in World War I, helping to preserve democracy in the first global conflict.

Early Life

The oldest of John and Elizabeth Pershing's nine children, John Joseph Pershing was born in Laclede, Missouri, in the year preceding the outbreak of the Civil War. Tensions ran high in this Midwestern state, and Pershing's father suffered for his staunch support of the Union, which he served as a sutler. Pershing early aspired to a career in law, and initially his goal appeared attainable. A brief period of postwar prosperity, however, soon gave way to virtual bankruptcy for the family, and when Pershing's father gave up storekeeping to work as a traveling salesman, John took to farming and odd jobs. One of them, as janitor for the nearby black school in Prairie Mound, led to a permanent position as a teacher there. In 1882, he attended the Normal School in Kirksville, obtaining a bachelor's degree in elementary didactics. That same year, he took the test for appointment to the United States Military Academy and received a nomination. To meet the age limitation for entrants, he changed his birth month from January to September.

After a month in a Highland Falls, New York, preparatory school, Pershing enrolled with 129 other young men at West Point. Somewhat older than his classmates, he commanded their respect, holding his five-foot, ten-inch frame ramrod-straight and casting a stern glance at the world from steel-gray eyes; the mustache and silvered hair would come later. Pershing proved an adequate student and a first-rate leader, whom schoolmates elected class president each year. In each of his four years, he held the top position for cadets, culminating in his selection as first captain of the Corps of Cadets in his final year. In 1886, he was graduated and commissioned a second lieutenant of cavalry.

Life's Work

A career as a soldier did not hold great promise in the late nineteenth century. Pershing spent his first years with the Sixth Cavalry, fighting in the last of the Indian Wars. Later, he commanded a troop in the Tenth Cavalry, an all-black unit with whom Pershing gained unusually good rapport. His service on the frontier was broken by a tour at the University of Nebraska, where he transformed a slovenly cadet corps into one of the country's finest detachments of college trainees. During his off-duty time, he earned a law degree and gave serious thought to resigning. In 1898, he returned to his alma mater as a tactical officer, instructing West Point cadets in the fundamentals of soldiering. In that year, troubles with Spain over Cuba erupted into a war, and Pershing sought duty with the force being organized to invade the Caribbean island.

Unable to go to Cuba as a cavalryman, Pershing obtained a temporary assignment as a quartermaster. In that position, he gained important insight into the follies of the army's system for providing supplies to its line units. That lesson was stored away for future use in Europe during the first global conflict of the twentieth century.

Pershing was promoted to captain in 1901, fifteen years after he was commissioned. Because promotions were based on seniority, he expected little further advancement. The early years of the new century saw him in the Philippines, leading American soldiers in a pacification effort against nationals who resisted the United States government's efforts to bring Western-style democracy to the islands. Pershing earned a reputation as a successful negotiator with Philippine leaders, and his remarkable march around Lake Lanao was noted not only in the Philippines but also in Washington, D.C.

A tour on the newly formed general staff gave Pershing the opportunity to meet the woman he would eventually wed: Frances Warren, daughter of Wyoming senator Francis E. Warren, a Republican and member of the Senate's military committee. Pershing and Frances were married in January, 1905, and left almost immediately for Japan, where Pershing was to serve as a military observer during the Russo-Japanese War.

Then, in 1906, Pershing's efforts on behalf of his country were generously rewarded. In an unusual move, President Theodore Roosevelt nominated the captain for promotion to brigadier general, allowing him to jump over almost a thousand officers senior to him and bypass the field grade ranks (major, lieutenant colonel, and colonel). The new general spent much of the next decade in the Philippines, returning to the United States for assignment at the Presidio, San Francisco, in 1914. Almost immediately, Pershing left for El Paso, Texas, to organize a force that would invade Mexico to capture the bandit Pancho Villa.

While Pershing was in Texas, his family, which now included three girls and a boy, remained in California. On August 26, 1915, tragedy struck the Pershings. Coals ignited wax on the ground floor of their wood-frame quarters, and Frances and the three girls perished in the ensuing fire; only Pershing's son, Warren, was saved. With stoic courage, Pershing made his way to California, accompanied the bodies to Wyoming for burial, then returned to his troops on the Mexican border.

The Punitive Expedition which Pershing commanded from 1915 to 1917 was ostensibly organized in retaliation for raids conducted by Villa within the United States city of Columbus, New Mexico. Pershing's force of twenty

thousand men traversed the Mexican desert for months, while political negotiations continued between President Woodrow Wilson and the various factions trying to seize permanent control of the government in Mexico. The
force withdrew in 1917, when the war in Europe forced Wilson to shift his
attention to that region of the world.

In May, 1917, Pershing was notified that he had been selected to organize
an American force for duty with the Allied forces in Europe. Hastily assembling a small staff, he traveled to England and then to France, where he
spent a year shaping a force that would ultimately consist of more than one
million Americans. Handpicked subordinates wrestled with problems of
obtaining supplies, coordinating troop movements, quartering the divisions
and separate units, feeding and clothing the newly arrived recruits, and training men to survive as individuals and fight as units. Pershing's time was occupied in constant inspections and in wrangling with Allied commanders,
especially marshals Philippe Petain of France and Douglas Haig of England,
both of whom wanted to detail small American units for duty with French
and British units already employed on line against the Germans. Convinced
that Americans should fight in American units, commanded by American
officers, Pershing held out against their constant requests. Only reluctantly
did he finally commit some battalions of the First Infantry Division for duty
with the French. His strategy paid off in the late summer of 1918, when the
American First Army achieved smashing victories against the Germans along
the Saint-Mihiel salient and then in the Meuse-Argonne area of France.

The entrance of American forces into the war helped deal the final death
blow to Germany's hopes for conquest. In November, 1918, the Germans
agreed to the terms of surrender, and Pershing was faced with the problems
of dismantling the huge military machine he had worked so hard to assemble.
For the better part of the next two years, he was engaged in returning troops
to America and drafting detailed reports of the actions of his army during the
war. In 1920, Congress passed a law designating Pershing general of the
armies, allowing him to keep the four-star rank that had been bestowed upon
him temporarily while he was in command of the American Expeditionary
Force (AEF). There was some talk of Pershing running for president, and he
allowed his name to appear on the ballot in the Nebraska primary as a favorite son candidate; a poor showing convinced him, however, to abandon that
campaign.

In July, 1921, President Warren G. Harding and Secretary of War John
Weeks named Pershing chief of staff of the army. In that position, the hero of
World War I fought a three-year battle against the Congress and a large con-
tingent of American people who wanted to return the American military to
its prewar position: small and poorly funded. Pershing argued (in vain) for
larger permanent forces and an active program to train men for future service through the National Guard and Army Reserve. Despite his pleas, the

size of the army shrunk, its budget dwindled, and its capability to mobilize evaporated. In September, 1924, Pershing retired.

The following years were far from quiet ones, though, since duty with various government commissions kept the general busy. In 1924, he served with the delegation trying to resolve the Tacna-Arica boundary dispute between Peru and Chile. He later served with the American Battle Monuments commission and continued to provide sage advice to his successors in the office of the chief of staff. In 1936, Pershing became seriously ill, but he recovered and once again offered his services to the country when America became embroiled in World War II. President Franklin D. Roosevelt sought his advice, and in fact Pershing helped convince the president to keep General George C. Marshall in Washington, D.C., rather than let him assume field command in Europe. Marshall, a protégé of Pershing who had been a key staff officer in the AEF, often consulted his mentor during World War II.

Pershing received special honors when the Congress ordered a medal struck in his honor in 1946. He died on July 15, 1948. In accordance with his wishes, he was buried at Arlington National Cemetery, under a simple headstone, among the soldiers whom he had led in "the Great War."

Summary

Pershing's lifelong career of service to his country has secured for him a place among American military heroes. The epitome of the American soldier-leader, he was purposely self-effacing when placed in political circles, remaining true to the principle of military subordination to civilian control with great conviction. His efforts as a stern disciplinarian, a brilliant organizer of large forces, and a staunch believer in the capabilities of the American soldier were a vital element in the Allied success in World War I. In addition, his consistent support for the citizen-soldier helped set the model for future generations of planners and shaped the future of American military organization for the remainder of the century. Finally, his sagacious tutelage of subordinates such as George C. Marshall and George S. Patton provided America the military leadership it needed to rise to the challenge posed by Adolf Hitler and his confederates in World War II.

Bibliography

American Military History. Washington, D.C.: Office of the Chief of Military History, 1969. Official history of American military involvement at home and abroad; includes accounts of the Indian Wars, the Punitive Expedition in Mexico, and World War I, providing excellent background and highlighting Pershing's contributions when in command.

Editors of *Army Times*. *The Yanks Are Coming: The Story of General John J. Pershing*. New York: G. P. Putnam's Sons, 1960. Short biography, with many photographs. Good summary of Pershing's major accomplishments.

Goldhurst, Richard. *Pipe, Clay and Drill: John J. Pershing: The Classic American Soldier*. New York: Reader's Digest Press, 1977. A solid biography that places Pershing's actions within the larger context of American political enterprises. Detailed chapters on the Punitive Expedition.

Liddell-Hart, Basil Henry. *Reputations Ten Years After*. Boston: Little, Brown and Co., 1930. Hart's chapter on Pershing provides an antidote to hagiographic portraits that were popular immediately after the war and points out Pershing's difficulties in dealing with high-ranking officials of Allied forces.

O'Connor, Richard. *Black Jack Pershing*. Garden City, N Y : Doubleday and Co., 1961. An objective biography, highly readable and informative, of modest length.

Smythe, Donald. *Guerrilla Warrior: The Early Life of John J. Pershing*. New York: Charles Scribner's Sons, 1973. A detailed, scholarly account of the early years of Pershing's life through his participation in the Punitive Expedition.

_____. *Pershing: General of the Armies*. Bloomington: Indiana University Press, 1986. With this volume, Smythe concludes his definitive biography of Pershing. Focuses on Pershing's role as commander in chief of the American Expeditionary Force in World War I and his tenure as chief of staff of the army.

Vandiver, Frank. *Black Jack: The Life and Times of John J. Pershing*. 2 vols. College Station: Texas A and M University Press, 1977. A comprehensive biography, based largely on records in the Library of Congress, National Archives, and other collections. Places Pershing's actions in the context of America's coming of age as a world power.

Weigley, Russell A. *A History of the United States Army*. New York: Macmillan Publishing Co., 1967. A scholarly yet highly readable account of the growth of the American military establishment; chapter on World War I provides excellent summary of Pershing's actions and an assessment of his accomplishments as commander of the American Expeditionary Force.

Laurence W. Mazzeno

WENDELL PHILLIPS

Born: November 29, 1811; Boston, Massachusetts
Died: February 2, 1884; Boston, Massachusetts
Area of Achievement: Social reform
Contribution: Phillips was one of the foremost orators and writers in the American antislavery movement and other social movements from 1837 until 1884.

Early Life

Born in Boston on November 29, 1811, Wendell Phillips traced his American ancestry to the Reverend Mr. George Phillips, who came to Massachusetts with John Winthrop in 1630 on the *Arbella*. His father, John Phillips, was a prominent Boston politician, who served as a judge, as the presiding officer of the state senate, and as the first mayor of Boston under that city's corporate charter, as well as on the Harvard Board of Overseers. One of his relatives was the founder of Phillips Andover Academy, while another founded Phillips Exeter Academy. Wendell's mother, Sarah Walley, was the devoutly Calvinist daughter of a middle-class Boston merchant. Although Sarah came from a less distinguished family than her husband, she could trace her American ancestry to the early seventeenth century.

As a child, Phillips received the typical education of a Boston patrician. He attended Boston Latin School, where he won distinctions for his oratory, was graduated from Harvard College in 1831, and then studied at Harvard's new law school under Justice Joseph Story until 1834.

As a young lawyer, Phillips could look forward to what appeared to be a certain and successful future. Phillips was already financially secure from his inheritance. Politically, Phillips was fully in the tradition of conservative New England Federalists. He wrote in his Harvard class book of 1831, "I love the Puritans, honor Cromwell, idolize Chatham and Hurrah for Webster." He was connected by social class, and often by blood, to the most powerful and important families in Massachusetts. He was already noted as an unusually talented speaker and writer. In addition, he was healthy, physically fit, tall, handsome, and aristocratic in his bearing. Later in life, when proper Bostonians shunned him for his abolitionist activities, Phillips condescendingly retorted that his detractors were "men of no family."

By 1835, Phillips was on his way to building a successful and profitable law practice. Phillips was not particularly enthusiastic about law practice, but he probably would not have needed to continue in the field for very long. Like his father, Phillips could have looked forward to a successful career in politics, which would have been enhanced by his remarkable speaking ability, brilliant mind, and superb debating skills. In October, 1837, Phillips solidified his position in Boston society when he married Ann Terry Greene, the orphaned daughter of a wealthy and prominent Boston merchant. In that year, however, Phillips abandoned his law practice and society life for a full-time career as an abolitionist agitator, social reformer, and professional orator.

Life's Work

In 1837, Phillips' life changed dramatically. In March, he gave a short speech supporting abolition at the Massachusetts Anti-Slavery Society. By the end of 1837, Phillips was a professional abolitionist speaker. This shift—from a socially prominent lawyer to a leading speaker for a despised group of radical reformers—was the result of his heritage, his marriage, and the events of the mid-1830's.

As an educated patrician, Phillips firmly believed in noblesse oblige. It was not inconsistent for him to champion the rights of an oppressed minority. Indeed, moderate opposition to slavery was part of his Federalist political background and his Puritan social and cultural heritage. Phillips was, in fact, a profoundly religious man whose Puritan background no doubt led him to a movement such as abolition, which sought to root out the United States' most sinful institution—slavery.

Phillips' relationship with Ann Terry Greene was critical to his development as an abolitionist. When he met Greene, she was already a committed abolitionist, active in the Boston Female Anti-Slavery Society. While courting Ann in 1836, Wendell met William Lloyd Garrison and the other abolitionists whom he soon would join. Although an invalid most of her life, Ann was actively involved in Wendell's career, giving him both intellectual and emotional support. Phillips claimed not only that Ann made him into an abolitionist but also that she was always ahead of him in analyzing the social issues of the movement. Throughout their marriage, Ann encouraged Phillips to remain uncompromising in his opposition to slavery, in his support of the freemen, and in support of the rights of women. Their only major political disagreement was over the rights of the Irish. Ann retained the anti-Irish bias of most Bostonians of her class; Wendell saw the Irish as an exploited class, much like blacks, and thus in need of an eloquent champion to further their search for social justice. When he met Ann in 1836, Phillips was not yet an abolitionist. Two events, one in 1835 and the other in 1837, coalesced with his relationship with Ann and his background to bring Phillips into the anti-slavery movement.

In 1835, a mob dragged the abolitionist editor William Lloyd Garrison through the streets of Boston with a rope around his body. Phillips witnessed the event with shock and outrage. At the time, Phillips was not sympathetic to abolition. Yet he considered himself to be fully a son of the American Revolution. As such, he believed in free speech for all, even radicals such as Garrison. The threatened lynching of Garrison violated Phillips' sense of order and constitutional rights. The young patrician lawyer now had a new view of the abolitionists—as protectors of civil liberties, because they were the victims of intolerance.

Phillips was even more profoundly affected by the death of Elijah Lovejoy, an abolitionist printer in Alton, Illinois. In 1837, Lovejoy was thrice attacked by mobs which threw his press into the Mississippi River. When a fourth press arrived in Alton, Lovejoy vowed to defend it. In the process, he was killed. At a meeting called to denounce this event, James T. Austin, Massachusetts' antiabolitionist attorney general, took the floor and gave an eloquent speech attacking Lovejoy. Austin compared Lovejoy's killers to the revolutionaries who organized the Boston Tea Party and declared that Lovejoy was "presumptuous and imprudent" for challenging the sentiments of the day. Phillips, still relatively unknown in Boston and not yet a committed abolitionist, immediately took the floor to answer Austin. His response electrified the crowd in Boston's Faneuil Hall; the printed version had a similar effect on those who read it. Pointing to the portraits of revolutionary leaders on the wall of Faneuil Hall, Phillips declared,

> Sir, when I heard the gentleman [Austin] lay down principles which place the murderers of Alton side by side with Otis and Hancock, with Quincy and Adams, I thought those pictured lips would have broken into voice to rebuke the recreant American, the slanderer of the dead. . . . Sir, for the sentiment he has uttered, on soil consecrated by the prayers of Puritans and the blood of patriots, the earth should have yawned and swallowed him up.

Phillips then went on to defend the rights of free speech and of the press and to attack those who would deny it to abolitionists.

This speech was the beginning of Phillips' career as the greatest abolitionist speaker of the day. Indeed, in an age of great orators, Phillips may have been the best. Besides speaking on abolition, Phillips often gave lectures on artistic and cultural topics and on other political issues. He was in constant demand and made a good living from his speaking tours. Phillips gave one nonpolitical lecture, entitled "The Lost Arts," more than two thousand times in his career and earned more than $150,000 from it.

As an antislavery agitator, Phillips was noted for his "eloquence of abuse." Northern politicians who supported slavery risked the wrath of his wit. Edward Everett was "a whining spaniel," Senator Robert Winthrop "a bastard who has stolen the name Winthrop," and Daniel Webster "a great mass of dough." Abraham Lincoln, who had once represented a slaveowner in a fugitive slave case was "the slave hound from Illinois." When lecturing, Phillips could be abusively eloquent without even using words. During one speech, he mentioned the name of a United States attorney who was notorious for his support of the Fugitive Slave Law. Phillips then stopped his speech, asked for a glass of water, rinsed his mouth, spat the water out, and continued.

Besides his marvelous rhetoric, Phillips made important intellectual contributions to the antislavery movement. Phillips accepted Garrison's analysis that the Constitution was "a covenant with death and an agreement in Hell" that favored slavery. Since Phillips could not conscientiously support the Constitution, he ceased to practice law shortly after joining the abolitionist movement. Yet he applied his legal training and knowledge to his speeches, articles, and pamphlets. His analysis of the Constitutional Convention, *The Constitution a Pro-Slavery Compact: Or, Selections from the Madison Papers* (1844), was particularly important to the Garrisonian analysis of the American government.

More important than his antislavery theory was the role he developed as a professional agitator. Phillips was harsh, extreme, and unfair in his speeches and his pamphlets. His rhetoric, however, was purposeful. He sought to enrage the people of the North by dwelling on the horrors of slavery. In a speech on slavery, he would assert that "The South is one great brothel, where half a million women are flogged into prostitution." His goal was to force his audiences to contemplate the evil of slavery. Phillips succeeded far better than any of his contemporaries.

In 1860, Phillips opposed Lincoln, as he had almost all other politicians, because the latter was not sufficiently antislavery. During the Civil War, however, Phillips' agitation was sympathetic to Lincoln and the cause of the Union. He intuitively understood that the war would destroy slavery, and he supported the Emancipation Proclamation, even though it did not extend to all slaves in the nation.

Unlike many abolitionists, Phillips did not discontinue his work with the end of the war and the adoption of the Thirteenth Amendment. In 1865, he severed his relationship with his longtime associate Garrison because the latter wanted to dissolve his American Anti-Slavery Society. Phillips thought that the job of the abolitionists remained unfulfilled. Emancipation alone was insufficient; Phillips was farsighted enough to realize that freedom required granting full political and social equality to former slaves. Thus, Phillips remained a tireless supporter of equal rights for the freedmen throughout the 1870's.

With the Constitution no longer proslavery, Phillips felt free to participate in politics. In 1870, he ran for governor of Massachusetts on the Labor Reform ticket and received twenty thousand votes. By this time, Phillips divided his energies between caring for his invalid wife, agitating for the rights of the freedmen, and opposing the exploitation of workers in the emerging industrial economy. He agitated for an eight-hour day and a reorganization of the nation's economy to protect the poor and the working classes from the robber barons of the Gilded Age. By the time of his death in 1884, Phillips was a full-fledged labor radical, as indicated by his last major publication, *The Labor Question* (1884).

Summary

In 1881, Phillips was invited back to his alma mater to give the Phi Beta Kappa address. In his speech, entitled "The Scholar in a Republic," Phillips argued that the role of an educated man in a free society is "to help those less favored in life." This had been the life of Phillips. In an age of great orators, he was among the best. Born to lead the elite, he led instead a movement which sought freedom for those at the bottom of society. He provided hard logic, brilliant rhetoric, and a measure of upper-class cachet for the antislavery movement. Phillips flourished on the fringes of American politics, consciously creating an "office" for himself as an agitator. Phillips never made policy. Yet, by helping to create an antislavery constituency, Phillips was able to influence politics and politicians throughout his career. In the process of opposing slavery, Phillips helped legitimize the professional agitator in American politics and society.

Bibliography

Bartlett, Irving H. *Wendell and Ann Phillips: The Community of Reform, 1840-1880*. New York: W. W. Norton and Co., 1979. A brief biography of Phillips and his wife, based on a large collection of Phillips family letters discovered in the 1970's. Includes many letters written to and from Ann and Wendell Phillips. Focuses on the private life, as well as the public life, of the Phillipses.

_____. *Wendell Phillips: Boston Brahmin*. Boston: Little, Brown and Co., 1961. A sympathetic modern biography of Phillips. Covers his entire career, focusing almost entirely on his public life.

Filler, Louis, ed. *Wendell Phillips on Civil Rights and Freedom*. New York: Hill and Wang, 1965. A short collection of some of Phillips' greatest speeches. This volume begins with his brilliant defense of Elijah Lovejoy's right to publish an antislavery newspaper.

Hofstadter, Richard. "Wendell Phillips: The Patrician as Agitator." In *The American Political Tradition*. New York: Alfred A. Knopf, 1949. A superb essay on Phillips and his role as an agitator. One of the first modern reappraisals of Phillips.

Korngold, Ralph. *Two Friends of Man: The Story of William Lloyd Garrison and Wendell Phillips*. Boston: Little, Brown and Co., 1950. Study of the two leaders of the radical or Garrisonian wing of the abolitionist movement.

Stewart, James B. *Holy Warriors*. New York: Hill and Wang, 1976. A superb short history of the antislavery movement which places Phillips in the context of other abolitionists. An excellent introduction to history of abolition.

Wiecek, William M. *The Sources of Antislavery Constitutionalism in America: 1760-1848*. Ithaca, N.Y.: Cornell University Press, 1977. Study of abolitionist constitutional thought, which places the ideas and theories of Phillips in context with other antislavery thinkers.

Paul Finkelman

FRANKLIN PIERCE

Born: November 23, 1804; Hillsborough, New Hampshire
Died: October 8, 1869; Concord, New Hampshire
Area of Achievement: Politics
Contribution: After service in his state's legislature and in both houses of
  Congress, Pierce became the nation's fourteenth president, serving during
  the turbulent years between 1853 and 1857.

Early Life
  Franklin Pierce was born on November 23, 1804, in Hillsborough, New
Hampshire. His father, Benjamin, was an American Revolutionary War veteran and two-term state governor (1827-1828, 1829-1830). His mother, Anna
Kendrick, was Benjamin's second wife. Frank, as family and friends called
him, was the sixth of their eight children.
  Frank attended local schools before enrolling in Bowdoin College. Overcoming homesickness and early academic nonchalance, he was graduated
fifth in the class of 1824. Classmates there included John P. Hale, the 1852
Free-Soil Party's presidential candidate; Calvin Stowe, the husband of Harriet Beecher Stowe; and writers Henry Wadsworth Longfellow and Nathaniel
Hawthorne. Pierce became close friends with Hawthorne, and the novelist
later penned his campaign biography. Pierce taught school during semester
breaks, but his major interest during his college years seemed to be the college battalion, in which he served as an officer.
  After graduation, Pierce studied in several law offices including that of
later United States Senator and Supreme Court Justice Levi Woodbury of
Portsmouth. He was admitted to the bar in 1827 and immediately assisted in
his father's successful bid for the governorship. When his father was
reelected in 1829, he simultaneously gained a seat in the state legislature.

Life's Work
  His political rise was steady. When first elected to the legislature, Pierce
was named chairman of the Committee on Education. Later he served as
chairman of the Committee on Towns and Parishes. In 1831, Governor Samuel Dinsmoor named him his military aide with the rank of colonel, and that
same year and the next he served as Speaker of the House. In March, 1833,
though he was not yet thirty years old, he was elected to the United States
House of Representatives. By this time, his political course was already set.
He had enjoyed rapid success because of his support for his father and the
Democratic Party. From then on, he gave total loyalty to the party and to its
experienced politicians.
  Pierce served in the House from 1833 to 1837 before advancing to the Senate for one term (1837-1842). His service was undistinguished. He deferred

to his elders (when he entered the Senate, he was its youngest member). He made no memorable speech and sponsored no key legislation. He served on several committees, eventually gaining the chairmanship of the Senate Pension Committee. He consistently accepted the Southern view on slavery, and was strongly antiabolitionist, a staunch defender of the Democratic Party, and a strong opponent of the Whig program. For example, he supported the Southern position on the Gag Rule and defended Andrew Jackson's opposition to internal improvements.

It was during these years that Pierce made the political contacts and created the impression that would result in his later nomination and election to the presidency. He came to be known as an accommodating person, fun loving, and always anxious to please. He seemed perfectly content to follow party policy and he gave proper respect to his elders. He was a New Englander whom Southerners trusted. He formed a close friendship with Jefferson Davis during these years.

In 1834, Pierce married Jane Means Appleton, the daughter of a former Bowdoin College president and Congregational minister. Throughout their married life, she suffered from a variety of physical illnesses, anxiety, and depression; in addition, she held strict Calvinistic views on life. In contrast to her sociable husband, she felt very uncomfortable in social settings and consequently stayed away from Washington as much as she could. Like many congressmen of that age, Pierce lived in a boardinghouse with several colleagues, and he joined them in drinking to try to compensate for the boredom of his existence. Pierce was no alcoholic, but he was incapable of holding any liquor. The smallest amount inebriated him. This problem, combined with his wife's unhappiness, which was exacerbated by the death of a newborn child, convinced Pierce in 1842 that he should go back to New Hampshire. There he promised his wife that he would never drink again or return to Washington.

In New Hampshire, Pierce became a successful lawyer. He did not spend much time analyzing legal principles because he was easily able to ingratiate himself with juries and win his cases that way. He was of medium height and military bearing, dark, handsome, and an excellent dresser. People who met him at social and political gatherings liked him immediately.

During these years, Pierce also played an active role in New Hampshire's Democratic politics. He was a driving force in most of the party's campaigns, achieving good success, though he lost out to college classmate Hale in a party dispute over Texas annexation. President James K. Polk offered him the attorney generalship, and his party wanted to return him to the Senate. He declined both offers.

When the Mexican War broke out, Pierce's long-held interest in military matters and his desire for more excitement than his Concord law practice provided caused him to volunteer as a private. Before he donned his uniform, he had gained the rank of brigadier general. He made many friends among the enlisted men, and General Winfield Scott named him one of the three commissioners who attempted to negotiate an unsuccessful truce. His combat record was much less sparkling. During his first combat in the Mexico City campaign, his horse stumbled, banging Pierce against the saddle horn and then falling on his leg. He fainted. Though still in pain when he was revived, he continued, only to twist his knee and faint again when he encountered the enemy. Later, he became bedridden with a severe case of diarrhea. He was happy when the conclusion of the war enabled him to return home.

Pierce resumed his legal and political pursuits. He supported the Compromise of 1850 and became president of the state constitutional convention. He helped rid the state party of an antislavery gubernatorial candidate and thereby improved his reputation in the South. When his former law tutor, Levi Woodbury, the state's choice for the 1852 Democratic presidential nomination, died in September, 1851, Pierce became New Hampshire's new favorite son. Remembering his promise to his wife, however, he said he would consider the nomination only in case the convention deadlocked. That was precisely what happened. None of the Democratic front-runners, James Buchanan, Lewis Cass, Stephen A. Douglas, and William L. Marcy, was able to obtain the necessary two-thirds of the convention ballots. On the thirty-fifth stalemated ballot, Pierce's name was introduced. He was a Northerner with Southern principles and a person everyone seemed to like. These characteristics carried the day. On the forty-ninth ballot, he gained the nomination. When his wife learned the news, she fainted from shock.

The 1852 presidential campaign between Pierce, Whig candidate Winfield Scott, and Free-Soiler Hale was issueless. Pierce made no formal speeches; according to the custom of the time, he allowed his supporters to campaign for him. Hawthorne quickly wrote a laudatory biography, and others worked to overcome the accusation that Pierce was a drunkard, a coward, and an anti-Catholic. (The latter accusation came from an anti-Catholic provision remaining in the revised New Hampshire constitution.) In a Boston speech the previous year, he had called for the enforcement of the Fugitive Slave Law yet voiced his belief that it was inhuman, so he had to work hard to repair damage in the South from that remark. He never denied the statement but insisted he had been misrepresented, and this seemed to satisfy his critics. He won the general election 254 to 42 in electoral votes, although he had a popular margin of only forty-four thousand.

At first, Pierce made good progress in organizing his administration. Then tragedy struck. He, his wife, and their eleven-year-old son, Benjamin, were riding the train from Boston to Concord when, without warning, their car toppled off the embankment. Benjamin was killed. Neither Pierce nor his wife was ever able to recover from the shock. They vainly sought to find meaning in the freak accident. Pierce wondered if his son's death was God's punishment for his sins. Jane Pierce concluded that God had taken the boy so her husband could give his undivided attention to the presidency.

Pierce thus entered office in a state of turmoil. The feeling of insecurity that caused him to want to please others and follow his party's line now received further reinforcement from the guilt and self-doubts resulting from his son's death.

His wife's reaction only added to his burdens. Quite by accident, she learned from a friend that her husband, far from not wanting to return to Washington as he had insisted, had actually worked hard to get the nomination. She had lost her son; now she learned that her husband had deceived her. She locked the bedroom door, seldom even appearing for public functions. Eventually she spent most of her time writing little notes to her dead son apologizing for her lack of affection during his life.

Pierce became president determined to adhere to old-line Democratic policy with a strong dose of expansionist ideas. Unfortunately, everything he tried seemed to fail. He attempted to broaden the base of support for his administration by giving patronage to all segments of the party, but loyal supporters, especially Southerners, became angry. He made decisions on what he considered to be principle but lost political support in the process. Most significantly, he did not seem to understand that slavery, especially its expansion into the territories, was a powder keg. He had always considered public opinion to be the stuff of demagogues, so he believed he could ignore the strong negative feelings about slavery which were gaining ground in the North.

Pierce seemed incapable of providing effective direction to his administration. His cabinet, the only one in history to remain intact for an entire term, was weak, but its members had to exert their authority since he did not. Jefferson Davis, the secretary of war, emerged as the most powerful of the group.

The tragedy of Franklin Pierce was that he was president during a time of major crisis and conflict. Pierce's presidency was dominated by controversy and even violence: the Kansas-Nebraska Act, Bleeding Kansas, Bloody Sumner, the Ostend Manifesto, the Gadsden Purchase, the destruction of the Whig Party and the birth of the Republican Party. The nation cried out for leadership, for some kind of direction, but Pierce was unable to provide it. Events seemed to provide their own impetus, and he seemed incapable of directing them. His pro-Southern and antiabolitionist attitudes, his desire to please, and his uncertainty about his own capabilities did not allow him to act effectively.

The Kansas-Nebraska Act demonstrated the problem quite clearly. Pierce believed that this law providing for popular sovereignty would effectively solve the controversy over slavery in the territories. He never understood why it resulted in violence instead. Increasingly, slavery was becoming a moral issue, but he continued to treat it as merely another solvable disagreement. He and the nation paid the price.

Despite the ever more obvious failure of his presidency, Pierce hoped for renomination, authoring his 1855 annual address as a campaign document. He excoriated the new Republican Party. He reminded Americans about the need for compromise and recognition of the concept of states' rights. He claimed that despite the South's longtime willingness to compromise, as, for example, in the Missouri Compromise, the North now refused to respond in kind. The Kansas-Nebraska Act was good legislation, Pierce argued, and it could solve the problem of slavery in the territories if it were allowed to; Republicans and other antislavery fanatics had to recognize that the South had rights too. No one could arbitrarily limit slavery. Pierce believed that such fanaticism would result only in national disruption, and did anyone really want to destroy the interests of twenty-five million Americans for the benefit of a few Africans?

Pierce's battle cry brought down a torrent of criticism. When the Democratic National Convention met in 1856, it chose James Buchanan as its candidate, snubbing Pierce and making him the only president who wanted to run for reelection not to receive his party's renomination for a second term. He was bitterly disappointed and went on a three-year tour of Europe. When the Civil War erupted, Pierce first supported the Union effort, but he quickly reverted to his pro-Southern position. In a July 4, 1863, Concord speech, he blasted Lincoln's policy on civil rights and emancipation and proclaimed the attempt to preserve the Union by force as futile. While he spoke, word filtered through the crowd of the Union victory at Gettysburg. Once again events had passed Pierce by. He lived another six years, but he played no further public role. He died on October 8, 1869, in Concord, New Hampshire.

Summary

Franklin Pierce's life was filled with contradiction. He was an outgoing man who married a recluse. He was a Northerner, but he held Southern attitudes on the major issue of the day, slavery. He gained the presidency because he seemed to be what the nation wanted: an amiable man whom neither Northerners nor Southerners found offensive. Yet it was this appealing inoffensiveness, actually a lack of firm purposefulness, which doomed his presidency from the start. The nation's problems needed determination and skill of the highest order; in Franklin Pierce, the nation gained an irresolute man, overcome with personal problems, who did not understand the crisis around him and was carried along by events instead of directing them.

Bibliography

Freehling, William W. "Franklin Pierce." In *The Presidents: A Reference History*, edited by Henry F. Graff. New York: Charles Scribner's Sons, 1984.

A highly critical evaluation of Pierce. The New Hampshire politician is portrayed as a weak, vacillating individual whose mediocrity was the major reason why he was electable in 1852 and why he failed during his term.

Kane, Joseph N. *Facts About the Presidents: A Compilation of Biographical and Historical Data.* 3d ed. New York: H. W. Wilson Co., 1974. A compilation of basic factual information on all the American presidents. Unusual or unique aspects about each president's administration are included.

Nevins, Allen. *Ordeal of the Union: A House Dividing, 1852-1857.* Vol. 2. New York: Charles Scribner's Sons, 1947. An excellent discussion of the Pierce years with insightful commentary on how his personality affected his policy. Nevins believes that Pierce's basic weaknesses doomed his presidency because they prevented him from taking the strong positions on national issues that the times required.

Nichols, Roy F. "The Causes of the Civil War." In *Interpreting American History: Conversations with Historians*, vol. 1, edited by John A. Garraty, 286-287. New York: Macmillan Publishing Co., 1970. A brief discussion of the White House relationship of Mr. and Mrs. Pierce. Nichols points out that Jane Pierce never recovered from the death of her son and became a virtual recluse in the White House.

_____. *Franklin Pierce: Young Hickory of the Granite Hills.* Philadelphia: University of Pennsylvania Press, 1931. This is the standard biography of the fourteenth president, detailed yet appealingly written. It emphasizes that, rather than outstanding ability, Pierce's physical attractiveness, his Mexican War military reputation, his ability to convince people with his oratory, his party regularity, and his pro-South policy gained him the 1852 Democratic nomination and eventually the presidency.

Taylor, Lloyd C., Jr. "Jane Means Appleton Pierce." In *Notable American Women, 1607-1950*, vol. 3, edited by Edward T. James. Cambridge, Mass.: The Belknap Press of Harvard University Press, 1971. A brief sketch of Pierce's wife which discusses how religious rigidity fostered a repressed personality which gave way under the strain of public life and the death of a young child.

John F. Marszalek

POCAHONTAS

Born: c. 1596; Werowocomoco on the Pamunkey River, Virginia
Died: March, 1617; Gravesend, Kent, England
Area of Achievement: Race relations
Contribution: Through friendship with the English settlers and her marriage
   to John Rolfe, at a crucial time Pocahontas contributed to peaceful relations between Indians and white settlers, thereby helping to ensure the
   success of the Jamestown colony. Her story has become legend, one of the
   many which constitute an idealization of the founding of America.

Early Life

Pocahontas, known to her own people as Matoaka and, in her adult life,
christened Rebecca, was born around 1596. She was the favorite daughter of
Powhatan, overlord of the various Algonquian-speaking tribes in tidewater
Virginia. Powhatan made his capital village at Werowocomoco on the
Pamunkey River, though for a brief period after 1609 he resided at Powhatan
town at the Falls of the James River (the site of modern Richmond). The
Powhatan Confederacy numbered about nine thousand at the time of their
discovery by the English.

"Matoaka" (also "Matoax" and other variations) can be termed Pocahontas' secret name, as—according to the custom of the northeast woodland Indians—it was known only to her family and clan. To these people, she was
thus "Little Snow Feather." Her public name, Pocahontas, which fitted her
personality, was translated by the English as "Bright Stream Between Two
Hills," but actually in her native language it was an adjective meaning play-
ful, sportive, frolicsome, mischievous, or frisky. As a child, Pocahontas was
tall, tomboyish, and athletic. William Strachey wrote in 1612,

> Pocahontas, a well featured but wanton young girle Powhatans daughter,
> sometymes resorting to our Fort of the age then of 11. or 12. yeares [would]
> gett the boyes forth with her into the market place and make them wheele, fall-
> ing on their hands turning their heeles upwards, whome she would follow and
> wheele so her self naked as she was all the fort over. . . .

On exploring expeditions up the James and Chickahominy Rivers, John
Smith, who for a while was president of the colony, became acquainted with
Pocahontas. It seems that Pocahontas was infatuated with the dashing young
captain. In the course of their friendship, they taught each other words from
their own languages. The story of Pocahontas' famous rescue of Smith has
historians divided as to its basis in fact. Smith did not mention the incident
until the publication of his *The Generall Historie of Virginia, New-England
and the Summer Isles* (1624). The event, which was said to have happened in
December, 1605, was not included in Smith's *A True Relation of Such Occur-*

rences and Accidents of Noate as Hath Hapned in Virginia Since the First Planting of That Collony (1608), but possibly it was deleted by the publisher. According to Smith's later account, which appeared after Pocahontas' death, he and other Englishmen had been captured by the Indians fifteen miles south of the Falls of the James, paraded through several Indian villages, and brought to Werowocomoco, where Smith was condemned to have his head beaten in. A moment before the intended execution, Pocahontas took Smith's "head in her arms and laid her owne upon his to save him from death." Apparently, upon being spared, Smith was made an adopted son of Powhatan.

Pocahontas' friendship with the English colonists grew, and several times she sent warnings to Jamestown of impending hostility. She probably made her first journey to Jamestown in the spring of 1610, when she accompanied her father, who was returning a visit made by the new governor, Lord De La Warre. She, her brother, and a party of braves went to Jamestown in 1611, delivering parched corn, which the Indians had agreed to furnish. She dined at the governor's house and attended church.

Indian relations, however, began to worsen, as the acting governor, Sir Thomas Dale, sought to extend the colony further into the interior, including the construction of Henrico town on the upper James. In 1613, while visiting the Potomac Indians, Pocahontas was kidnaped by Captain Samuel Argall and held hostage. Dale assigned her to live just outside Henrico town on the one-hundred-acre farm of the Reverend Alexander Whitaker. Pocahontas would be released if the Indians returned their English captives and also tools and weapons that had been stolen from the English. Powhatan, however, would not agree to the demands. At her new abode, Pocahontas quickly adapted to English dress and ways. Not permitted to engage in her own Indian worship, she agreeably received instruction by the Reverend Whitaker in the English catechism and memorized the Apostles' Creed, the Lord's Prayer, and the Ten Commandments. In the spring of 1614, upon confession of faith, she was baptized and became a member of the Church of England. Pocahontas now had a new English name, Rebecca. She attracted the attention of John Rolfe of Varina, a plantation across the river from Henrico town. His love for Pocahontas was returned, and as an ultimate result of their relationship, she would become a romanticized figure in history.

Life's Work

The attachment between the cultivated and college-educated Englishman and the Indian princess seems to have been strong and genuine. Rolfe had arrived in Virginia in 1610 with his son and English wife, who had soon died. He was the first Englishman to raise tobacco successfully; it was tobacco that would put the colony on its feet economically. Rolfe, enamored of Pocahontas when he met her at Jamestown, sought permission to marry her. Marriage between a white person and an Indian was prohibited, however, by both the Church of England and the Virginia Company. In a long letter to Dale in early 1614, Rolfe stated that his intentions were

> for the good of the Plantacon, the honor of or Countrye, for the glorye of God, for myne owne salvacon, and for the Cnvertinge to the true knowledge of God and Iesus Christ an vnbeleivinge Creature, namely Pohahuntas To whome my hart and best thoughts are and have byn a longe tyme soe intangled & inthralled in soe intricate a Laborinth. . . .

Dale finally approved the marriage, and so did Powhatan, although the Indian chief did not attend the wedding, sending instead Pocahontas' uncle and two brothers. Thus, on April 5, 1614, Rolfe and Pocahontas were married at the Jamestown church, with the Reverend Richard Bucke officiating. King James I, however, strongly denounced the wedding.

Two years later, Rolfe, Pocahontas, and their one-year-old son, Thomas, accompanied Dale to England aboard the *Treasurer*, a ship ironically still captained by Samuel Argall, Pocahontas' abductor. The ship arrived at Plymouth on June 16, 1616. For nine months, Pocahontas enthralled London society. She was received by the Bishop of London at Lambeth Palace and by King James and Queen Anne at the Court of St. James. Various entertainments were staged for her benefit, including a masque devised by Ben Johnson. The Rolfes lodged at the Bell Savage Tavern.

In March, 1617, the Rolfes prepared to return to America. Pocahontas was suffering from a pulmonary ailment (perhaps a form of tuberculosis or pneumonia), induced by the damp and polluted air of London. The family boarded ship at London, and downriver, with Pocahontas critically ill, the vessel docked at Gravesend. Pocahontas died in the third week of March 1617. Her last words were: "Tis enough that the child liveth." She was buried in the chancel of St. George's Church in Gravesend. John Rolfe returned to Virginia and was killed in the Great Massacre of March, 1622, by the very Indians among whom he had married. Young Thomas Rolfe stayed in England, residing with several families and finally moving in with John Rolfe's younger brother, Henry, in London. Thomas Rolfe returned to America at age twenty in 1635. He married Jane Poythress, and from the union there would be a vast progeny, of whom many over the successive generations were to be famous, including Senator John Randolph of Roanoke. The old St. George Church at Gravesend, England, was destroyed, and the remains of Pocahontas were lost. At the site of the church, however, a new one has been erected, and today, it is the nondenominational Anglo-American Chapel of Unity, with a plaque and windows which honor Pocahontas. In a garden at the church (the old tombstones having been removed), there is also a bronze statue of Pocahontas (a replica of a statue by William Ordway Partridge at Jamestown), which was presented by the people of Virginia. An oil portrait of Pocahontas, executed while she was in London, was the source for a number of engravings that circulated in that city. The artist is unknown but may have been Simon van de Passe, who did the engravings. The portrait that hangs at the National Portrait Gallery in Washington, D.C., is thought to be the original.

Summary

Pocahontas deserves credit for having helped bring about a period of peace during the most difficult years in the founding of the Jamestown colony. Her presence in England stimulated financial backing for the Virginia Company and contributed to the success of a lottery held on behalf of the company's venture in Virginia. Shortly after Pocahontas died, Powhatan did also, and soon thereafter the delicate peace in the colony collapsed, a fact dramatically signified by the Indian rampage of 1622 that nearly eradicated the colony. Attitudes toward the Powhatan Indians would change, with the natives now a race to be conquered.

In a sense, the story of Pocahontas celebrates the spirit of the free individual. She, of her own volition, defied her tradition-bound society and accepted one which was regarded as more civilized. Furthermore, she risked her life in aiding the Englishmen. Her marriage to Rolfe can be interpreted to represent the individual's pursuit of happiness amid the imposition of values by institutions such as church and state.

The Pocahontas story has been romanticized into myth in the development of a self-conscious American culture. It also calls attention to the idealistic principle that all men are capable of living in harmony. The image of Pocahontas unites three worlds: the Indian wilderness, English Virginia, and post-Elizabethan London. The Pocahontas legend bolstered the European ideal of the noble savage, while among the English it underscored an ambivalent conception of the Indian, especially of their women. Frances Mossiker, in her biography *Pocahontas*, has caught the essence of the Indian princess as symbol and legend:

> The *tableau vivant* at the altar-stone—the death-defying embrace, white man and red woman aswoon with love and terror—seems fixed, frozen in time, indelibly imprinted on the mind's eye, reminding us that at least once in our history, there existed the possibility of interracial accommodation. For that one fleeting moment—with the bloodthirsty blades arrested in midair—came a flicker of hope that on this continent, at least, there would be no cause to mourn man's inhumanity to man.

Bibliography

Barbour, Philip L. *The Three Worlds of Captain John Smith*. Boston: Houghton Mifflin Co., 1964. The classic and definitive biography of John Smith. The story of Pocahontas can be seen in the context of Smith's other adventures and encounters.

Hamor, Ralph. *A True Discourse of the Present State of Virginia*. London: John Beale, 1615. Reprint. Richmond: Virginia State Library, 1957. Introduction by A. L. Rowse. Complements Smith's history in reference to Pocahontas and the Powhatan Indians. Records Pocahontas' visits to Jamestown.

Mossiker, Frances. *Pocahontas: The Life and the Legend*. New York: Alfred A. Knopf, 1976. Intended for the general reader, this work, nevertheless, is based on solid research. It emphasizes the social aspects of both the Indians and the whites and the building of a legend of Pocahontas.

Phillips, Leon. *First Lady of America: A Romanticized Biography of Pocahontas*. Richmond: Westover Publishing Co., 1973. Foreword by Clifford Dowdy. Aimed at younger readers, this is an imaginative work. It fleshes out the Pocahontas story with descriptive material which is suggested by the sources but which is not always supported by the evidence. Yet this is a delightful, humanized version.

Smith, John. *The Complete Works of Captain John Smith*. 3 vols. Edited by Philip L. Barbour. Chapel Hill: University of North Carolina Press, 1986. Contains all the known writings of Captain John Smith. A biographical directory identifies the many persons—both Indian and white—of Pocahontas' world. Ample annotation clarifies word usage and place names.

Tyler, Lyon G., ed. *Narratives of Early Virginia: 1606-1625*. New York: Barnes and Noble Books, 1952. Although devoted mainly to John Smith's writings, this collection has John Rolfe's letter to Sir Thomas Dale, asking permission to marry Pocahontas; it also includes tracts written by several participants in the Jamestown venture.

Vaughan, Alden T. *American Genesis: Captain John Smith and the Founding of Virginia*. Boston: Little, Brown and Co., 1975. A scholarly reevaluation of the early Jamestown experience, with an interpretative quality. This study makes use of recent scholarship.

Woodward, Grace S. *Pocahontas*. Norman: University of Oklahoma Press, 1969. Scholarly and well-written account, stressing Indian-white relations and the early years of Jamestown. The extensive bibliography is most useful.

Harry M. Ward

EDGAR ALLAN POE

Born: January 19, 1809; Boston, Massachusetts
Died: October 7, 1849; Baltimore, Maryland
Area of Achievement: Literature
Contribution: In addition to his achievements as one of the pioneering figures in American literature, Poe was influential in making magazine publishing an important force in the literary world of the nineteenth century.

Early Life

Edgar Allan Poe was born January 19, 1809, in Boston, Massachusetts. His mother, Elizabeth Arnold Poe, was a talented actress from an English theatrical family. Because Poe's father, David Poe, Jr., a traveling actor of Irish descent, was neither talented nor responsible, the family suffered financially. After apparently separating from David Poe, Elizabeth died in Richmond, Virginia, in 1811. The young Edgar, though not legally adopted, was taken in by a wealthy Scottish tobacco exporter, John Allan, from whom Poe took his middle name.

For most of his early life, Poe lived in Richmond with the Allans, with the exception of a five-year period between 1815 and 1820 which he spent in England, where he attended Manor House School, near London. Back in America, he attended an academy until 1826, when he entered the University of Virginia. He withdrew less than a year later, however, because of various debts, many of them from gambling; Poe did not have the money to pay, and his foster-father refused to help. After quarreling with Allan about these debts, Poe left for Boston in the spring of 1827; shortly thereafter, perhaps because he was short of money, he enrolled in the United States Army under the name "Edgar A. Perry."

In the summer of 1827, Poe's first book, *Tamerlane and Other Poems*, published under the anonym "A Bostonian," appeared, but it was little noticed by the reading public or by the critics. In January, 1829, he was promoted to the rank of sergeant major and was honorably discharged at his own request three months later. In December, 1829, Poe's second book, *Al Aaraaf, Tamerlane, and Minor Poems*, was published, and it was well received by the critics. Shortly thereafter, Poe entered West Point Military Academy, possibly as a way to get into his foster-father's good graces.

After less than a year in school, Poe was discharged from West Point by court-martial for neglecting his military duties. Most biographers agree that Poe deliberately provoked his discharge because he had tired of West Point. Others suggest that he could not stay because John Allan refused to pay Poe's bills any longer, although he would not permit Poe to resign. After West Point, Poe went to New York, where, with the help of some money raised by his West Point friends, he published *Poems by Edgar A. Poe, Sec-*

ond Edition. After moving to Baltimore, where he lived at the home of his aunt, Mrs. Clemm, Poe entered five short stories in a contest sponsored by the *Philadelphia Saturday Courier*. Although he did not win the prize, the newspaper published all five of his pieces. In June, 1833, he entered another contest sponsored by the *Baltimore Saturday Visiter* and this time won the prize of fifty dollars for his story "Ms. Found in a Bottle." From this point until his death in 1849, Poe was very much involved in the world of American magazine publishing.

Life's Work

During the next two years, Poe continued writing stories and trying to get them published. Even with the help of a new and influential friend, John Pendleton Kennedy, a lawyer and writer, he was mostly unsuccessful. Poe's financial situation became even more desperate when, in 1834, John Allan died and left Poe out of his will. Kennedy finally persuaded the *Southern Literary Messenger* to publish several of Poe's stories and to offer Poe the job of editor, a position which he kept from 1835 to 1837. During this time, Poe published stories and poems in the *Messenger*, but it was with his extensive publication of criticism that he began to make his mark in American letters.

Although much of Poe's early criticism is routine review work, he began in his reviews to consider the basic nature of poetry and short fiction and to develop theoretical analyses of these two genres, drawing upon the criticism of A. W. Schlegel, in Germany, and Samuel Taylor Coleridge, in England. Poe's most important contribution to criticism is his discussion of the distinctive generic characteristics of short fiction, in a famous review of Nathaniel Hawthorne's *Twice-Told Tales* (1837). Poe makes such a convincing case for the organic unity of short fiction, argues so strongly for its dependence on a unified effect, and so clearly shows how the form is more closely allied to the poem than to the novel that his ideas have influenced literary critics ever since.

In 1836, Poe married his thirteen-year-old cousin, Virginia Clemm, a decision which, because of her age and relationship to Poe, has made him the subject of much adverse criticism and psychological speculation. In 1837, after disagreements with the owner of the *Messenger*, Poe moved to New York to look for editorial work. There he completed the writing of *The Narrative of Arthur Gordon Pym* (1838), his only long fiction, a novella-length metaphysical adventure. Unable to find work in New York, Poe moved to Philadelphia and published his first important short story, a Platonic romance titled "Ligeia." In 1839, he joined the editorial staff of *Burton's Gentlemen's Magazine*, where he published two of his greatest stories, "The Fall of the House of Usher" and "William Wilson."

In 1840, Poe left *Burton's* and tried, unsuccessfully, to establish his own literary magazine. He did, however, publish a collection of his stories, *Tales of the Grotesque and Arabesque* (1840), as well as become an editor of *Graham's Magazine*, where he published his first tale of ratiocination, "The Murders in the Rue Morgue." In this landmark story, he created the famous detective Auguste Dupin, the forerunner of Sherlock Holmes and thus of countless other private detectives in literature and film. A biographical sketch published at that time described Poe as short, slender, and well-proportioned, with a fair complexion, gray eyes, black hair, and an extremely broad forehead.

In 1842, Poe left *Graham's* to try once again to establish his own literary magazine, but not before publishing two important pieces of criticism: a long review of the poet Henry Wadsworth Longfellow, in which he established his definition of poetry as being the "Rhythmical Creation of Beauty," and his review of Hawthorne, in which he defined the short tale as the creation of a unified effect. Between 1842 and 1844, after Poe moved to New York to join the editorial staff of the *New York Mirror*, he published many of his most important stories, including "The Masque of the Red Death," "The Pit and the Pendulum," "The Black Cat," and two more ratiocinative stories, "The Mystery of Marie Roget" and "The Gold Bug." It was with the publication of his most famous poem, "The Raven," in 1845, however, that he finally achieved popular success.

Poe left the *New York Mirror* to join a new weekly periodical, the *Broadway Journal*, in February of 1845, where he continued the literary war against Longfellow begun in a review written for the *Mirror*. The series of accusations, attacks, and counterattacks that ensued damaged Poe's reputation as a critic at the very point in his career when he had established his critical genius. Poe's collection of stories, *Tales*, was published in July, 1845, to good reviews. Soon after, Poe became the sole editor and then proprietor of the *Broadway Journal*. In November, he published his collection, *The Raven and Other Poems*.

The year 1846 marked the beginning of Poe's decline. In January, the *Broadway Journal* ceased publication, and soon after, Poe was involved in both a personal scandal with two female literary admirers and a bitter battle with the literary establishment. Moreover, Poe's wife was quite ill, a fact which necessitated Poe's moving his family some thirteen miles outside the city to a rural cottage at Fordham. When Virginia died on January 30, 1847, Poe collapsed. Although he never fully recovered from this series of assaults on his already nervous condition, in the following year he published what he considered to be the capstone of his career, *Eureka: A Prose Poem*, which he presented as an examination of the origin of all things.

In the summer of 1849, Poe left for Richmond, Virginia, in the hope, once more, of starting a literary magazine. On September 24, he delivered a lecture, "The Poetic Principle," at Richmond, in what was to be his last public appearance. From that time until he was found semiconscious on the streets of Baltimore, Maryland, little is known of his activities. He never recovered, and he died on Sunday morning, October 7, in Washington College Hospital.

Summary

Edgar Allan Poe is important in the history of American literature and American culture in two significant ways. First, he developed short fiction as a genre that was to have a major impact on American literature and publishing throughout the nineteenth century. His stories and criticism have been models and guides for writers in this characteristically American genre up to the present time. No one interested in the short-story form can afford to ignore his ideas or his fiction. Poe was influential in making American literature more philosophical and metaphysical than it had been before.

Second, and perhaps most important, Poe helped to make periodical publishing more important in American literary culture. American writers in the mid-nineteenth century were often discouraged by the easy accessibility of British novels. Lack of copyright laws made the works of the great English writers readily available at low cost. Thus, American writers could not compete in this genre. Periodical publishing, and the short story as the favored genre of this medium, was the United States' way of fighting back. Poe was an important figure in this battle to make the United States a literary force in world culture.

The problem with Poe, however, is that he is too often thought of as the author of some vivid yet insignificant horror stories. Moreover, Poe's personality is often erroneously maligned: He has been called a drunk, a drug-addict, a hack, a sex pervert, and an exploiter. As a result of these errors, myths, and oversimplifications, it is often difficult for readers to take his works seriously. The truth is, however, that Edgar Allan Poe, both in his criticism and in his dark, metaphysically mysterious stories, helped create a literature that made America a cultural force not to be ignored.

Bibliography

Allen, Hervey. *Israfel: The Life and Times of Edgar Allan Poe.* 2 vols. New York: George H. Doran Co., 1926. Reprint. New York: Farrar and Rinehart, 1956. A romantic narrative of Poe's life, valuable for the information drawn from letters between Poe and John Allan.

Buranelli, Vincent. *Edgar Allan Poe.* 2d ed. Boston: Twayne Publishers, 1977. A somewhat sketchy study of Poe's fiction, poetry, and criticism, but still a good introduction to his work.

Carlson, Eric W., ed. *The Recognition of Edgar Allan Poe: Selected Criticism Since 1829.* Ann Arbor: University of Michigan Press, 1966. A valuable collection of some of the most influential critical remarks about Poe by artists, writers, and critics.

Hoffman, Daniel. *PoePoePoePoePoePoePoe.* Garden City, N.Y.: Doubleday and Co., 1972. An idiosyncratic and highly personal account of one critic's fascination with Poe that echoes the fascination of countless readers. Often Freudian and sometimes farfetched, the book provides stimulating reading and suggestive criticism.

Jacobs, Robert D. *Poe: Journalist and Critic*. Baton Rouge: Louisiana State University Press, 1969. An extensive study of Poe's career as editor, reviewer, and critic. Shows how Poe's critical ideas derived from and influenced periodical publishing in the mid-nineteenth century.

Moss, Sidney P. *Poe's Literary Battles: The Critic in the Context of His Literary Milieu*. Durham, N.C.: Duke University Press, 1963. A well-researched study of Poe's controversial battles with Longfellow and the many literary cliques of nineteenth century American publishing.

Quinn, Arthur Hobson. *Edgar Allan Poe: A Critical Biography*. New York: D. Appleton-Century Co., 1941. Reprint. New York: Cooper Square Publishers, 1969. Although this book is somewhat outdated in its critical analysis of Poe's works, it is the best and most complete biography, informed by Quinn's knowledge of Poe's literary milieu and his extensive research into Poe's correspondence.

Quinn, Patrick F. *The French Face of Edgar Poe*. Carbondale: Southern Illinois University Press, 1957. Ironically, Poe's fiction, poetry, and criticism had more influence on French literature in the nineteenth century than on American literature. Quinn's book explains why.

Charles E. May

JAMES K. POLK

Born: November 2, 1795; Mecklenburg County, North Carolina
Died: June 15, 1849; Nashville, Tennessee
Areas of Achievement: Politics and government
Contribution: A staunch nationalist, Polk used the authority of the presidency to bring about the expansion of the nation nearly to its continental limits. He added power as well as stature to the office.

Early Life

James Knox Polk was born in Mecklenburg County, North Carolina, on November 2, 1795. His parents, Samuel and Jane Knox Polk, were members of large Scotch-Irish families whose forebears began migrating to America late in the previous century. When James was eleven, Samuel moved the family westward to the Duck River Valley in middle Tennessee, where he became both a prosperous farmer and a prominent resident. The family was staunchly Jeffersonian in its politics, while Jane Polk was a rigid Presbyterian.

Young James was small in stature—of average height or less according to various accounts—and was never robust. At seventeen, he had a gallstone removed (without anesthesia), and thereafter his health improved somewhat. It became obvious early, however, that he would never be strong enough to farm, and contrary to his father's wish that he become a merchant, Polk decided on a law career with politics as his goal. For this goal, some education was necessary. He had been a studious youth but until the age of eighteen had had little formal schooling. Thereafter, he applied himself totally and entered the sophomore class at the University of North Carolina at the age of twenty. Two and a half years later, he was graduated with honors. Characteristically, he had worked diligently, but the drain on his physical reserves was so great that he was too ill to travel home for several months.

Upon his return to Columbia, Tennessee, Polk read law in the offices of one of the state's most prominent public figures, Felix Grundy. Through Grundy's sponsorship, Polk began his political career as clerk of the state senate in 1819 and was admitted to the bar the following year. Prospering as a lawyer, he was elected to the Tennessee legislature in 1823 and aligned himself with the supporters of the state's most famous citizen, Andrew Jackson. Soon he became friendly with Jackson, a presidential candidate in 1824, aided Old Hickory's election to the United States Senate, and thereafter was always associated with his fellow Tennessean.

On New Year's Day, 1824, Polk married Sarah Childress, a member of a prominent middle Tennessee family. Described as not particularly pretty, she was vivacious, friendly, and devoted, and the marriage, although childless, was apparently happy. By this time Polk's health had improved, but he remained slender, with an upright posture and a grim face below a broad forehead. According to contemporaries, he was always impeccably dressed, as befitted a promising young lawyer and sometime militia colonel on the governor's staff. Now nearly thirty, he was considered one of the state's rising Jacksonians.

Life's Work

Impressed with his legislative record and legal as well as martial success, in 1825 the Jackson faction supported Polk's bid for a seat in the House of Representatives against four opponents. His victory by a decisive plurality after a spirited campaign solidified his position among the followers of General Jackson. For the next four years, during the administration of President John Quincy Adams, Polk was in the forefront of the Jacksonians, who were determined to overturn the alleged "corrupt bargain" that had denied Jackson the presidency in 1824 and elect their man in 1828.

During the debates on the Adams program, considered too nationalistic by most congressmen, Polk seized numerous opportunities to express his opposition and to stand with the embryonic Democratic Party. He aided in reviving the "corrupt bargain" charge and spoke for economy, majority rule, and limited government. He embraced the party position against the protective tariff, internal improvements, and banks. Only on the question of slavery did he equivocate, as he would always do. Slavery was an evil, he believed, yet doing away with it was fraught with peril. It was best that all concerned recognize its existence and live with it as peacefully as possible.

The issues before Congress during the Adams term commanded less attention than the Jacksonians' primary goal—the election of Jackson. In this effort, Polk played an increasingly important part as his abilities and devotion to the cause became more evident. In the bitter campaign of 1828, he constantly defended Jackson and carried on an extensive correspondence with him at his home in the Hermitage. Victory for Jackson followed and, despite interparty infighting for the position of successor to the new president, the future of the Jacksonian party looked promising.

In the next decade, Polk's rise in the party hierarchy was steady. He served as chairman of the House Ways and Means Committee in Jackson's first term and played a leading role in the president's victory in the Bank War. He enjoyed a growing reputation for speeches and reports showing much preparation, logic, and clarity. In 1835, he was elected Speaker of the House, and was reelected two years later. His four years in the chair, where he was the first to function as a party leader and to attempt to guide through a program, proved to be trying. The Whig Party was gaining strength while the slavery issue was intruding in the House, resulting in the passage of the infamous "gag rule." In the middle of his second term as Speaker, Polk decided to become a candidate for governor of Tennessee rather than risk probable defeat for reelection. By now the recognized leader of the party forces in his home state, he won by a narrow margin in 1839.

Once again, Polk was the first incumbent to use an office for political purposes as a party leader. Yet since the governor had little real power and Whig opposition continued strong, Governor Polk was able to accomplish little in his single two-year term. When the victorious Whig presidential candidate, William Henry Harrison, easily carried Tennessee in 1840, Polk's chances for another gubernatorial term appeared to be slim. He was defeated for reelection in 1841 and failed again two years later. For the only time in his career, he was out of office.

On the national level, Polk's position in the party remained secure. In 1840, he was a leading candidate for the vice presidential nomination on the ticket with President Martin Van Buren but withdrew when the convention decided against making a nomination. Polk then began to work toward the nomination four years later, when it was expected that the former president would again contend for the top place. In the meantime, he repaired political fences and kept in touch with Van Buren and other party leaders.

Polk's comeback leading to his nomination as the Democratic standard-bearer in 1844 is one of the best-known episodes in American political history. Expansionism, justified as "Manifest Destiny," was in the air as Texas clamored for admission to the Union while American eyes were on California and Oregon. It was expected that the presidential race would be between former president Van Buren and Whig Henry Clay. When both announced their opposition to the annexation of Texas, however, Van Buren's chances for the nomination faded. In the party convention in May, he withdrew when his cause looked hopeless, and on the ninth ballot delegates turned to Polk, who had declared for annexation weeks earlier. Although his nomination, recalled as the first "dark horse" selection, was a surprise to most voters, it was the result of much hard work and a correct recognition of the mood of the electorate.

In the ensuing campaign, Whig candidate Clay and his supporters obscured the issues by asking, "Who is James K. Polk?" Democrats responded by linking "Young Hickory" to the aged former president, vacillating on controversial matters such as the tariff and stressing annexation as a national, not sectional, question. After an exciting campaign, Polk won a narrow victory brought about in part because a number of potential Clay voters cast ballots for an antislavery candidate. In his inaugural address, President Polk announced a brief but positive program. He called for settling the Oregon question (Congress had voted to annex Texas by joint resolution a few days earlier) by its "reoccupation" and for the acquisition of California. The tariff was to be reduced to a revenue level, and the Independent Treasury, killed by the Whigs, would be reestablished. Unique among American chief executives, Polk carried out his entire program.

The new president assumed his duties, determined to be in control. He appointed able cabinet members, many of whom were friends, and he consulted them and Congress frequently, although he made his own decisions. Seldom away from his desk, he was constantly besieged by office seekers who placed an added drain on his limited strength and energy. Not surprisingly, his appointments were largely "deserving" Democrats.

Foreign affairs immediately commanded Polk's attention. Oregon, occupied jointly with England since 1818, was rapidly filling up with Americans who anticipated eventual absorption by the United States. It was "clear and unquestionable," the president declared in his inaugural, that Oregon belonged to the United States. Yet he revealed to the British minister his willingness to compromise at the forty-ninth parallel. A negative response evoked from Polk a hint of war and a request in his first annual message for congressional sanction for termination of joint occupation. For the first time, there was a presidential reference to the Monroe Doctrine as justification for action, and war talk, including demands for "Fifty-four Forty or Fight," was heard. Neither nation wanted war, so the British countered with Polk's original suggestion, it was accepted, and a treaty was completed, setting the boundary at the forty-ninth parallel, where it has remained.

In the meantime, the Mexicans had not accepted the loss of Texas, and they now maintained that the southern boundary was the Neuces River, not the Rio Grande, as the Texans claimed. Polk agreed with the Texans and also feared that the British might interfere there, as well as in California and New Mexico. As tensions increased, he sent to Mexico City an offer of some thirty million dollars for the entire area. When the offer was refused, he ordered General Zachary Taylor to move his troops into the disputed section. A predictable clash took place, but before word reached Washington, Polk had decided to ask for war. Congress responded with a declaration on May 13, 1846. Although American forces were victorious from the beginning, the Mexican War, called "Mr. Polk's War," was among the most unpopular in the nation's history. Opposition to it was voiced in Congress, in the press, and among the people. Even though the two leading generals professed to be members of the party, Whigs led the protests, which tended to increase Polk's strongly partisan attitudes.

To a greater extent than any previous chief executive, Polk took his role as commander in chief seriously. His military experience was meager, yet he planned grand strategy, was personally involved in military appointments and promotions, and took the lead in peacemaking. His emissary (although technically recalled) completed with a defeated Mexico a satisfactory treaty which ceded California and New Mexico to the United States and recognized the annexation of Texas in return for some fifteen million dollars. Polk decided to accept the offer. The Senate narrowly approved the treaty on February 2, 1848, and the continental limits of the nation had almost been reached. Near the end of his term, Polk looked longingly at other areas, such as Cuba, but nothing further was done.

In Congress, the remainder of Polk's limited program was approved. The Independent Treasury was reestablished and remained in existence into the next century. In addition, the tariff was reduced considerably. Although these successes seemed to indicate party harmony, the Democrats actually were engaged in much interparty wrangling, adding to the president's many problems.

Of more lasting effect was the revival of antislavery agitation as a result of the possible addition of territory. In the midst of the war, as an appropriations measure was debated in Congress, Representative David Wilmot of Pennsylvania proposed an amendment banning slavery in any territory acquired from Mexico. This so-called Wilmot Proviso was never approved, yet it rekindled sectional animosities which finally led to secession some fifteen years later. Polk, a slaveholder who seldom thought of slavery in moral terms—he believed that the solution was the extension of the Missouri Compromise Line to the Pacific—was not directly involved in the ensuing agitation during the remainder of his term, yet the legacy of sectional bitterness continued to be linked to his administration.

In his acceptance letter in 1844, Polk declared that he would not be a candidate for a second time, the first nominee ever to do so. As his term drew to a close, he refused to reconsider. His health remained poor, and the split within his party was unsettling. Nor did his outlook improve with the election of one of the Mexican War generals, Zachary Taylor, as his successor.

Following Taylor's inauguration, the Polks slowly made their way home, often delayed by the poor health of the former president and well-meaning attempts by supporters to entertain them. Polk never fully recovered (his main complaint was chronic diarrhea) and he died June 15, 1849, slightly more than fourteen weeks after leaving office. His considerable estate, including a Mississippi plantation, was left to his widow, who lived until 1891, witnessing the tragic sectional split and devastating war brought about in part by the events associated with her husband's presidency.

Summary

The youngest presidential candidate elected up to that time and often called the strongest chief executive between Andrew Jackson and Abraham Lincoln, James K. Polk raised the presidency in public esteem. Although humorless, partisan, and totally without charisma, he was devoted to the office and impressed all those around him with his dedication and diligence. Nothing was allowed to interfere with the carrying out of his duties (except that no business was conducted on Sundays unless in an emergency). Unlike most occupants of the office, he seldom was away from the Capitol, absent a total of only six weeks in four years.

Under his leadership, a relatively brief, successful war was fought with Mexico, the annexation of Texas was completed, the most troublesome dispute with England was resolved, and the nation expanded almost to its continental limits. These accomplishments came about despite Polk's frail constitution and sharp political differences with the Whig Party and among his fellow Democrats. Unfortunately, his successes only added to the increasing sectional tensions which would soon tear the nation apart and cause a long, costly conflict.

Bibliography

Bassett, John Spencer, ed. *The Southern Plantation Overseer as Revealed in His Letters*. Westport, Conn.: Negro Universities Press, 1925. Most of these letters, from the Polk papers, were written by overseers on Polk's plantations in Tennessee (sold in 1834) and Mississippi (sold by Mrs. Polk in 1860). The correspondence indicates that the Polks, who were apparently benevolent owners, derived much of their income from the labor of slaves.

Cutler, Wayne, et al., eds. *Correspondence of James K. Polk*. 6 vols. to date. Nashville, Tenn.: Vanderbilt University Press, 1969-1983. A well-edited, complete publication of all extant Polk papers. Also includes many letters to Polk. An indispensable source for the history of the period.

Johannsen, Robert W. *To the Halls of the Montezumas: The Mexican War in the American Imagination*. New York: Oxford University Press, 1985. An interesting study of how the American people viewed the Mexican War and its effects on their lives. Reaches the usual conclusion that the war, although immediately successful, presaged great trouble.

McCormac, Eugene Irving. *James K. Polk: A Political Biography*. Berkeley: University of California Press, 1922. Reprint. New York: Russell and Russell, 1965. First published in 1922 and somewhat dated, it was for many years the standard political biography of Polk. Still useful for an account of the political maneuvering in the Jackson years.

Quaife, Milo Milton, ed. *The Diary of James K. Polk*. 4 vols. Chicago: A. C. McClurg and Co., 1910. Reprint. *Polk: The Diary of a President, 1845-1849*. Edited by Allan Nevins. New York: Longmans, Green and Co., 1929. Only five hundred copies of the original diary were printed. Written between August 26, 1845, and June 2, 1849, it is highly personal and apparently was not written with an eye on future historians. As a result of the 1929 publication, in which selections of the earlier publication appeared, Polk's presidency was reassessed and his reputation considerably enhanced.

Schroeder, John H. *Mr. Polk's War: American Opposition and Dissent, 1846-1848*. Madison: University of Wisconsin Press, 1973. A provocative study of public opinion during the Mexican War. Conclusion is that Polk not only decided on the war before learning of the firing on American troops but also welcomed the conflict as a way to fulfill his expansionist plans.

Sellers, Charles Grier, Jr. *James K. Polk: Jacksonian, 1795-1843*. Princeton, N.J.: Princeton University Press, 1957.

_____ . *James K. Polk: Continentalist, 1843-1846*. Princeton, N.J.: Princeton University Press, 1966. These volumes constitute the best treatment of Polk and his times up to the introduction of the Wilmot Proviso, a portent of things to come. Well-balanced and thoroughly researched, the study established Polk's claim to be considered one of the "near great" presidents.

Weems, John Edward. *To Conquer a Peace: The War Between the United States and Mexico*. Garden City, N.Y.: Doubleday and Co., 1974. A popular treatment of the war. Largely undocumented but interesting and basically sound. Weems believes that Polk hoped to avoid war by making a show of force.

C. L. Grant

JACKSON POLLOCK

Born: January 28, 1912; Cody, Wyoming
Died: August 11, 1956; East Hampton, Long Island, New York
Area of Achievement: Art
Contribution: A central figure in the New York School of Abstract Expressionists during the late 1940's and early 1950's, Pollock, through his "drip" painting, produced some of the most distinctive and unique work in the history of American art.

Early Life

Paul Jackson Pollock was born January 28, 1912, on the Watkins Ranch at Cody, Wyoming. Both his mother, née Stella May McClure, and his father, LeRoy Pollock, were of Scotch-Irish ancestry and had been born and reared in Tingley, Iowa. The elder Pollock worked at various jobs during his lifetime (ranch hand, dishwasher, truck farmer, plasterer, and surveyor) but listed his occupation as "stone mason and cement work" on Jackson's birth certificate. By the time Jackson had reached ten years of age, his family (he had four older brothers) had moved six times and had lived in San Diego, Chico, Janesville, Orland, Riverside (all in California), and Phoenix, Arizona.

Pollock entered Manual Arts High School in Los Angeles in 1928 and came under the influence of an art teacher named Frederick John de St. Vrain Schwankovsky, who encouraged his growing interest in art and sparked his attachment to Eastern mysticism. Although he already knew by this time that he wanted to be "an artist of some kind," he had personal difficulties in high school (he was temporarily expelled in early 1929) and eventually left without being graduated in 1930. He then followed his older brothers, Charles and Frank, to New York City in the fall of 1930, where he joined the Art Students League and took classes from Thomas Hart Benton, John Sloan, and Robert Laurent. Benton was strongly impressed with Pollock's talent, especially his use of color; became his mentor; and continually urged the young man to pursue a career in art. Although they rarely saw each other after 1937, this close relationship between teacher and student would persist, via letters and the telephone, until Pollock's death in 1956.

During this early New York period, Pollock appeared to be the typical all-American young man: well built (although slightly thin), with a mop of auburn hair, rough-hewn good features, and a vague pugnacious air about him. Only later would the creeping effects of alcoholism and hard living be reflected in his appearance: Photographs from the 1940's and 1950's show a paunchy and balding man, his face increasingly lined and depressed. The seeds of these personal and physical problems had already been planted in the 1930's; Pollock was arrested in July, 1937, for public intoxication and disturbing the peace, and he entered treatment for alcoholism, once in 1937, again in 1938, and again in 1939.

The first public exhibition of Pollock's work came in February, 1935, when he showed a work entitled *Threshers* at the Eighth Exhibition of Watercolors, Pastels, and Drawings by American and French Artists, held at the Brooklyn Museum. He also joined the Federal Art Project of the Works Project Administration (WPA) in 1935, earning approximately ninety-five dollars per month in exchange for submitting one painting every eight weeks. He would remain with the Federal Arts Project until early 1943 and produced more than fifty paintings during this time. Only two of them are known to exist today.

In April, 1941, Pollock was classified IV-F and declared unfit for military service by his local draft board. He also met Lenore (Lee) Krasner that year at an exhibit at the McMillen gallery. He had been introduced to her briefly in 1935, but this time the relationship flowered. They became constant companions and finally married on October 25, 1945, at Marble Collegiate Church in New York City.

Pollock's career also began to flower during the early 1940's. He attracted the attention of Peggy Guggenheim, an art collector, patron, and owner of a newly established museum-gallery in New York called Art of this Century. After inviting him to submit a collage for a show in her gallery in 1943, she issued him a one-year contract which guaranteed him $150 a month plus a negotiated bonus if she sold more than twenty-seven hundred dollars' worth of his paintings during that year. She also gave him a one-man show at her gallery in November, 1943, and commissioned him to paint a mural for the entrance hall of her town house. Guggenheim's patronage allowed Pollock to give up the custodial job he had obtained after the end of the Federal Arts Project and devote himself full-time to painting. Pollock's reputation and creativity soared from this point onward.

Life's Work

With the financial security provided by his connection with Peggy Guggenheim, Pollock entered the most creative period of his career. Show followed show as he exhibited his work at such prestigious galleries and museums as the New York Museum of Modern Art (1944-1945), the Cincinnati Art Museum (1944), the David Porter Gallery in Washington, D.C. (1945), The Arts Club of Chicago (1945), the San Francisco Museum of Art (1946), and the Whitney Museum of American Art in New York (1946). He sold his first painting to a museum during this period. In 1944, the Museum of Modern Art, acting on the advice of Alfred Barr, purchased Pollock's *The She-Wolf* for its permanent collection. He also received increasingly favorable notices in the art press, which praised his sense of color and surface, his fluent design, and his "exuberance, independence, and native sensibility."

Pollock's work underwent a clear creative evolution during this period. His work during the 1930's revealed the strong influence of Benton and David Alfaro Siqueiros, both advocates of the social realism school of art that attracted so many young painters during the difficult years of the Depression. Although often heavily stylized in their portrayal of reality, the social realists insisted that art carry a clear social or political message and thus serve a "useful" purpose. Paintings such as *Going West* (1934-1935) and *The Covered Wagon* (1934) demonstrate the impact of social realism on Pollock's early work. Yet as he entered the 1940's, Pollock became more and more interested in the work of such painters as Pablo Picasso, Joan Miró, Piet Mondrian, Henri Matisse, Wassily Kandinsky, and Hans Hofmann, and his work became increasingly abstract and, according to many critics, surrealistic. Yet his paintings from this period, such as *The She-Wolf*, *Guardians of the Secret* (1943), *The Troubled Queen* (1945), and *Red* (1946), show the gradual development of a style that, while reflecting the influence of other abstract painters, was also uniquely his own.

As Pollock evolved into a mature and unique artist, his personal life continued along its rather rocky course. In the fall of 1945, he and Lee left New York City and purchased (with a loan from Peggy Guggenehim) a farmhouse, barn, and five acres of land on Fireplace Road in East Hampton, Long Island. He would live and work there for the remainder of his life. Two years later, in 1946, Guggenheim closed her gallery and planned to return permanently to Europe. Before leaving, she arranged for the art dealer Betty Parsons to take over Pollock's contract and market his work. Pollock renewed this contract in 1949, but, when it expired in January, 1952, he signed an exclusive agreement with the Sidney Janis Gallery in New York City. He would remain with Janis until his death. Pollock also continued to suffer from alcoholism throughout these years and entered treatment with an East Hampton doctor in 1948, to arrest his chronic drinking. Thanks to this doctor's efforts, Pollock did manage to stay sober until 1950 but then reverted to his old behavior. From this point onward, he would visit a series of doctors and psychiatrists in an effort to cure his problem, but permanent success eluded him.

Beginning in 1946 or 1947, Pollock began experimenting with what would become his most important contribution to modern art, his "drip" or "action" painting. Action painting was a style pioneered by Hans Hofmann, who insisted that a finished painting is only the record of the intense personal feelings that an artist experienced while creating it. Moreover, the painting should also reflect the spontaneous, uncontrolled, and prerational actions that the artist made during the creative process. In this sense, the action of painting became more real and important than the painting itself. Pollock carried this idea to new extremes. He would roll out a large canvas on the floor of his East Hampton studio and drip and splatter paint on its surface as he worked in an energetic frenzy around its border. Pollock argued that the finished product was not accidental, that his actions were guided by internal psychic forces that were unleashed while he worked, and thus the painting represented a manifestation of his inner being on canvas. Examples of work produced during his drip period include *Lucifer* (1947), *Number 5* (1948), *Birds of Paradise* (1949), *Lavender Mist* (1950), *Autumn Rhythmn* (1950), and *Number 8* (1950), and all demonstrate a spontaneous freshness of statement and an exciting combination of dynamic composition and color. Many sophisticated art critics recognized the creative genius at work in these paintings and hailed Pollock as the most important American artist of the era. Critics for the popular press, however, generally dismissed him as a fraud and claimed that any three-year-old child could produce a Pollock "dribble" painting. The general public tended to agree with this assessment, and Pollock's work became the target for numerous jokes, cartoons, and ridicule. As a result, he continued to have difficulty selling his paintings and had to rely on the generosity of his patrons and an occasional grant to make ends meet.

Beginning in 1953, Pollock began to explore other styles of painting, as represented by his *Easter and the Totem* (1953) and *Sleeping Effort* (1953), but he still frequently returned to his drip technique in such works as *White Light* (1954) and *Scent* (1955). Yet this later work was produced during the all-too-brief creative spurts that punctuated an otherwise protracted period of artistic inactivity. In 1954, for example, Pollock produced only a handful of paintings and, in 1955, he hardly painted anything at all because, as he told a friend, he wondered whether he could say anything with his art anymore. He even contemplated a trip to Europe to renew his creativity but never went beyond obtaining a passport. Although his standing among knowledgeable art critics continued to escalate, his well of inspiration had dried up because of the severity of his alcoholism. His personal behavior had also become increasingly belligerent, as demonstrated by the fights he often provoked at the various taverns he frequented.

The year 1956 initially seemed to hold out some promise for Pollock. In May of that year, the New York Museum of Modern Art notified him that it was planning a one-man show of his work to honor him at midcareer. His wife was sufficiently satisfied that he had his drinking under control that she left for a vacation in Europe in July. A month later, on August 11, Pollock, with two female friends, lost control of his car on Fireplace Road and crashed into a clump of trees. One of the passengers survived but Pollock and the other passenger were killed instantly. He was buried at Green River Cemetary in Springs, Long Island, on August 15, 1956.

Summary

As with many artists before him, and undoubtedly many after, appreciation for what Jackson Pollock had accomplished during his short career grew after his death. By defying all traditional conventions and taking tremendous artistic and aesthetic risks, especially with his drip paintings, Pollock shattered old barriers and expanded the horizon of modern art into realms that few even dreamed existed. He also freed American art from its dependence on European innovation and at least temporarily pushed it to the forefront of the art world's avant-garde. In the process, he paved the way for the recognition of American artists within the international art community and helped create a market for their work. Many younger American artists, such as Robert Rauschenberg, Claes Oldenburg, Roy Lichtenstein, and Andy Warhol, benefited from his fearless desire to do what no one else had ever done, to push art beyond all previous limits, no matter what the cost.

That cost proved to be extraordinarily high. Public rejection and ridicule, alcoholism, eventual creative burnout, and a tragic death proved to be the price Pollock paid for his artistic courage. In many ways, he epitomized the rootless and innovative artists who were attracted to New York City at the end of World War II, young artists who celebrated absolute freedom and art as an intense personal commitment in their work but who ultimately fell victim to a society that neither understood nor appreciated them during their lifetimes. Jackson Pollock and his colleagues tried to stimulate the aesthetic imagination of the America of Disneyland, backyard barbecues, and television game shows. They lost in the short term, but their long-range influence would prove to be both liberating and exciting.

Bibliography
Friedman, B. H. *Jackson Pollock: Energy Made Visible*. New York: McGraw-Hill Book Co., 1972. Highly opinionated account of Pollock's life and work by a friend who met the artist late in the latter's career. Despite a rather confusing and overly dramatic style, the author provides some interesting insight into Pollock's personal demons.
Hunter, Sam. *Jackson Pollock*. New York: Museum of Modern Art, 1956. Originally intended to be a catalog to accompany Pollock's one-man show at the Museum of Modern Art in 1956, this book was expanded after the artist's death to be a retrospective of his entire career.
Motherwell, Robert, and Ad Reinhardt, eds. *Modern Artists in America: First Series*. New York: Wittenburg Schultz, 1951. Includes an excellent analysis of what Pollock was trying to say in his drip paintings. Motherwell always held Pollock in high regard.
O'Connor, Francis V. *Jackson Pollock*. New York: Museum of Modern Art, 1967. This book was published to supplement a major retrospective exhibit of Pollock's art in 1967. It includes a detailed chronology of Pollock's life and career, numerous excerpts from his correspondence, and black-and-white reproductions of most of his important work.
O'Hara, Frank. *Jackson Pollock*. New York: George Braziller, 1959. An appreciation of Pollock's career by a noted poet who also worked as a staff

member at the Museum of Modern Art. This book provides a concise and intelligent survey of Pollock's place in American art. An excellent starting point.

Potter, Jeffrey. *To a Violent Grave: An Oral Biography of Jackson Pollock*. New York: G. P. Putnam's Sons, 1985. These reminiscences, gathered from many sources by a friend of Pollock, document his problems with alcoholism, his troubled personal life, and his self-obsession. The book is valuable as a supplement to other studies, but it sheds little light on Pollock's art.

Robertson, Bryan. *Jackson Pollock*. New York: Harry N. Abrams, 1960. A massive collection of black-and-white and color reproductions of Pollock's paintings and drawings. Little biographical information on Pollock is included in this volume.

Rubin, William S. "Jackson Pollock and the Modern Tradition." *Artforum* 5 (February-May, 1967): 14-22, 28-37, 18-31, 28-33. A highly esoteric examination of Pollock's art that attempts to clarify the influences upon which he drew and his impact on the development of modern art in the United States.

Christopher E. Guthrie

PONTIAC

Born: c. 1720; on the Maumee River, Ohio
Died: April 20, 1769; Cahokia, Illinois
Areas of Achievement: Native American leadership and diplomacy
Contribution: Pontiac was one of a series of great Indian leaders, including the Mohawk Joseph Brant, the Miami Little Turtle, the Shawnee Tecumseh, the Sac Black Hawk, and the Oglala Sioux Crazy Horse, who sought to maintain independence for the Indians in North America.

Early Life

Little is known of Pontiac's early life; there is next to no documentation of it, and many reports are conflicting. He belonged to the Ottawa nation by birth but was not full-blooded; one of his parents was either Chippewa or Miami. This was not unusual, as the Ottawas, Miamis, and Chippewa were friendly neighbors, and intermarriage was common. Probably Pontiac was born in the Ottawa village that in 1718 was still on the north side of the Detroit River but by 1732 was located on the other side of the river at the site of modern Walkerville, Ontario.

No accounts of his childhood or early manhood have been preserved. Probably his youth was passed in typical Ottawa fashion. One of the first ceremonies in which he took part was that in which he received his name. An Ottawa tradition of the nineteenth century referred to him as "Obwandiyag" (the prefix "O" being a pronoun in Ottawa), and it is said that the name was pronounced *Bwon-diac*. "Bon" or "bwon" means "stopping"; thus, "obwon" means "his stopping," "stopping it," or "stopping him." No meaning, however, has been discovered for "diyag" or "diac." Pontiac was married; he had at least three sons.

The Ottawa political and social organization was loose and rather fluid. The Ottawas had no single chief; instead, each village had its chiefs, both civil and military. The village would break up as winter approached, and family hunting parties might go in any direction. They would regroup in the spring, either near a French fort, where they would trade their winter's catch of furs, or in their village, where they planted crops. The Ottawa nation, like many other Indian nations, was actually a confederation. There were at least four groups that made up the Ottawas: the Kiskakons, Sinagoes, Sables, and Nassauaketons.

It is impossible to describe the Ottawas of the 1740's, when Pontiac came to maturity, without also describing the influence of European culture upon them. By 1720, the Indians were already largely dependent upon French trade, which would become a large part of their culture. They relied on goods imported from France, such as steel knives and axes (formerly the Indians had used stone), brass kettles (they had fashioned kettles from clay), steel needles (in place of bone), and fabrics. There were also novelties: guns, liquor, horses, and several new communicable diseases. Relations among Indian nations had been altered drastically by the presence of the Europeans and their forts or trading posts for more than a century; as far back as 1645, the Iroquois had attempted to replace the Hurons as principal middlemen in the lucrative fur trade, launching a series of devastating attacks that displaced almost every Indian nation east of the Mississippi and north of the Ohio River. The Iroquois annihilated several entire nations and pushed the Ottawas to the Mississippi Valley, where they encountered the hostile Sioux; the Ottawas were forced to retreat to the south shore of Lake Superior and eventually to the Straits of Mackinac. It is hard to conceive of the Ottawas in Pontiac's time in isolation from the French and other Europeans; the French had a string of forts in the Great Lakes dependent on Montreal and others to the south on the Maumee, Wabash, Allegheny, and Mississippi rivers. Pontiac lived near the post at Detroit called Fort Pontchartrain.

Pontiac's life was indelibly marked by the outbreak of war between England and France in 1744, when he was approximately twenty-four years old. In the United States, this is known as King George's War, while in Europe it is called the War of the Austrian Succession (1744-1748). In origin it was a European quarrel, but once England and France were on opposite sides, fighting broke out between their colonies in North America for supremacy on the continent. At the beginning of the war, the Great Lakes were so deep within French territory that the war barely touched the Indians living in that region; the English, however, had already made contact with the French-dominated Indians at Sandusky Bay and on the Wabash River. There was sporadic fighting between the French and English throughout the next decade, Pontiac consistently siding with the French. This warfare culminated in the French and Indian War (1755-1760) and the defeat of the French general the Marquis de Montcalm by James Wolfe on the Plains of Abraham outside Quebec. The British gained nominal control of the eastern half of the North American continent.

Life's Work

The war usually known as Pontiac's War closely followed the French and Indian War. Its causes lay in the replacement of the French by the British. In 1760-1761, each of the French forts on the Great Lakes was taken over by a British commander. Most important, a totally new policy toward the Indians was put in force. This was the real cause of Pontiac's War, although Francis Parkman and other American historians following him have focused on different causes. Far from being a European war, it was largely American, beginning only when the European powers made formal peace with one another. The war continued for five years, until 1766; although it is identified with Pontiac and bears his name, this is misleading. Pontiac was able to express the aspirations of many Indians from a broad variety of nations.

Although Pontiac is known above all as a warrior, his major accomplishment was as a diplomat. Given the multiplicity of Indian leaders, Indian diplomacy was extremely complex. Its fluidity and constantly changing nature has made it one of the most difficult domains for the historian or reader to grasp. In addition to the intricate, shifting quality of Native American confederations and agreements, there was the constant interference of the white men. If they found a village hostile to their advance, they often attempted to entice a few villagers to friendship and decorated them with medals, declaring them to be chiefs in the eyes of the "great white father" across the Atlantic; the proud, newly decorated puppets would return to their town and attempt to supplant the other chiefs or divide the town. This king-making was a standard feature of British diplomacy and, after 1779, of United States diplomacy. The great feat of Pontiac was that, despite the complicated fabric of relationships within and among Native American groups, he was able to forge a strong alliance among disparate nations. By European standards, this alliance was perhaps weak, beset by constant defections, quarrels, and changes of allegiance, but by the standards of the peoples who were within the alliance—realistic standards—it was a remarkable performance. Pontiac had many exceptional qualities: He was eloquent and persuasive, resourceful, loyal, stubborn, and intelligent.

The prime grievance of the Indians of the Great Lakes and further south was the new British policy concerning the Native Americans. This appeared in a particularly stark light because of the suddenness of the change from French to British rule. For generations, the Indians had lived with the French, growing dependent on their material culture and accustomed to their habits. It would not be mistaken to see an analogy between the Indian revolt against the British in 1761-1766 and the later Colonial American revolt against the British in 1776.

French policy and practice was to mix with the Indians far more intimately than the British Americans were willing to mix with them. The French colonists put a high value on peaceful relations with the Indians; French officials gave the Indians presents during both peace and war, three or four times a year, and also provided the Indians with a constant supply of ammunition. This became a key issue during Pontiac's War, because the ammunition enabled the Indians to kill enough game to support their families. Not only did the French colonists live among the Indians, they frequently intermarried with them. Many Indian leaders were half-breeds.

Perhaps the most important difference between French and British rule related to the concept of land and title of the two European countries. The French colonists considered themselves tenants in the New World, maintaining themselves in peaceful occupancy by making frequent presents. The British government, however, did not regard the Indians as members of "the family of nations"; in consequence, the Native Americans, in the eyes of the British, had no rights at the bar of international justice. The Indian "tribes" were not sovereign nations and their people had no more rights than the wild animals that wandered over the land.

In 1760, British policy toward the Indians was devised by General Jeffrey Amherst, and it is difficult to imagine a policy more likely to provoke war. (It it surprising that a respected American college continues to bear his name.) Amherst ordered his officers and agents at the newly acquired forts to stop giving presents to the Indians and to deny them ammunition. For Amherst, the Indians were conquered subjects. Even his own Indian agent, William Johnson, was afraid to admit openly to the Indians the nature of Amherst's new policy. Amherst refused to employ Indians in the British armies, and shortly afterward, when the war began, his rage and inhumanity increased with each new victory of Indians allied with Pontiac. He took no prisoners, ordering any Indian falling into British hands to be immediately put to death, "their extirpation being the only security for our future safety."

It was Amherst who first used smallpox as a weapon against the Indians, spreading epidemics among them by means of "gifts" of infected blankets. As a result, entire Shawnee and Delaware villages were liquidated. Amherst frequently referred to the Native Americans as "vermin." Pontiac's successes filled him with rage, and he offered a reward for Pontiac's head; later, he doubled it. Such was the nature of the war between Pontiac and his major adversary. It was during the decade of the 1760's that the belief started to take hold among the Indians of the Great Lakes region that the British wanted to annihilate them. Pontiac's message to the other Native American nations was built upon the rejection of the British trade practices, British law, and the concept of private property—in stark contrast to the Indian notion of shared property—and, above all, British policy toward the Indians.

There were other elements in Pontiac's appeal to the different Indian nations that he skillfully played upon in speeches and appeals for help. A Delaware prophet became prominent in the Ohio Valley around 1760; sometimes called "The Impostor," he was a visionary who exhorted the Indians to purify themselves and live in their original state before the white men came to their country. By following his instructions, they would be able to drive the white people out of their country in a few years—there would be a generalized war followed by victory for the Indians and a state of bliss resembling the Christian heaven. Pontiac shared many features of this vision and translated it for other Indian nations in more practical terms. His relations to the Delaware prophet could be roughly described as resembling that of Paul to Jesus. Further, important initiatives to revolt had already been made by the Senecas, the Iroquois tribe farthest to the west, who were accustomed to freedom of action in the area that is now western Pennsylvania; they soon became Pontiac's most powerful allies. A final element in Pontiac's message was the continuing alliance with the recently defeated French. He had warm feelings for the French traders, *habitants*, and officials who remained on what was now legally British territory. Although the French, in contrast, had an ambiguous attitude toward Pontiac, and officials tried to discourage his grandiose plans, they secretly sympathized with him—he was attempting what they had recently tried to do and failed—and many *habitants* and traders openly aided him.

The results of Pontiac's diplomacy were electrifying. British forts in the Great Lakes area and farther south fell one after the other. Pontiac laid siege to Detroit; Fort Sandusky fell, as did Presqu'Île, Le Boeuf, Venango, Miamis, St. Joseph, Ouitenons, and La Baye. Indians also laid siege to Fort Pitt (formerly Duquesne), but Detroit and Fort Pitt held out. Many British-American settlers were killed. Although none of Pontiac's larger objectives was realized, there were greater losses of soldiers on the British side than on that of the Indians; at least 450 British regulars and provincials lost their lives in the war, while the British Major Gladwin estimated that the Indians lost one hundred warriors. It is impossible to calculate the number of civilians slaughtered on the frontiers, but a British official, George Croghan, estimated that not less than two thousand British subjects lost their lives. On the other hand, a vast number of Indians died in the epidemics created by General Amherst.

The forts at Detroit and Pittsburgh were reinforced, and, slowly but surely, the British demonstrated their superior force of arms. Recognizing the reality of the situation, Pontiac finally capitulated. He never liked the British, but he advocated peace in 1766, even though many other Indians continued to fight. Pontiac was virtually exiled by his own Ottawa village because his attempt to find a durable peace was not popular. Pontiac was assassinated in 1769, struck from behind by a Peoria Indian in Cahokia, Illinois, near the modern city of St. Louis.

Summary

Pontiac's War marks a watershed in the fortunes of the Native Americans. Pontiac fought to restore the relative independence enjoyed by the Western Indians under the French; he tried to force the British to change their policy, and he failed. His aims were largely ethical and conservative; he wanted the tribes to be sovereign nations, but he did not seek isolation. In essence, Pontiac fought for many of the values of the Enlightenment. Some Indian methods of warfare may strike modern readers as barbaric—the torture and dismemberment, boiling, eating of the hearts of prisoners, and so on—but these must be carefully weighed against the methods employed by the other side. The Indian war practices may seem picturesque, but their reasons are transparent: They were intended to increase the motivation of warriors. Furthermore, the Indian practices seem quaint in comparison with the bacteriological warfare waged by General Amherst and his wholesale destruction of civilian populations, which ominously foreshadow twentieth century practices during World War II of the German SS and the Soviet NKVD.

In Pontiac's War it was, above all, Indian independence that was defeated. Ironically, the British Indian policy was inherited by the British-American colonists when they declared their own independence in 1776. One of the first acts of the United States was to nullify the old treaty boundary with the Indians, and the new Americans inflicted a wound not only on the Native Americans but also on themselves, denying some of the most basic principles of their own freshly written Declaration of Independence.

Bibliography

Blackbird, Andrew J. *History of the Ottawa and Chippewa Indians of Michigan.* Ypsilanti, Mich.: The Ypsilantian Job Printing House, 1887. An Indian account of the history of the two nations and the traditions that had been passed down to the 1880's.

Eckert, Allan W. *The Conquerors: A Narrative.* Boston: Little, Brown and Co., 1970. Despite the author's claim of writing fact rather than fiction, this reconstruction of the prerevolutionary period is really fiction. It is highly readable, based on a broad reading of sources and documents.

Franklin, Benjamin. *Narrative of the Late Massacres in Lancaster County.* Philadelphia: Anthony Armbruster, 1764. A very one-sided account, by an engaging writer, of one aspect of Pontiac's war.

Kinietz, W. Vernon. *The Indians of the Western Great Lakes, 1615-1760.* Ann Arbor: University of Michigan Press, 1940. An excellent source book with observations of Indian life of the period, many translated into English for the first time.

Parkman, Francis. *History of the Conspiracy of Pontiac and the Indian War After the Conquest of Canada.* Boston: Little, Brown and Co., 1857. The best-known account of Pontiac's war, written in a fine literary style and utilizing abundant sources. Parkman believed Pontiac was the initiator and strategist of the whole war. Subsequent information, however, opens this "conspiracy" theory to doubt; Pontiac's diplomatic achievement, and difficulties encountered, were greater than Parkman claims.

Peckham, Howard H. *Pontiac and the Indian Uprising.* Chicago: University of Chicago Press, 1947. An erudite, modern biography.

Slotkin, Richard. *Regeneration Through Violence: The Mythology of the American Frontier, 1600-1860.* Middletown, Conn.: Wesleyan University Press, 1973. A sharply critical look at myths of the frontier meant for popular consumption and the harsh realities.

John Carpenter

JOHN WESLEY POWELL

Born: March 24, 1834; Mount Morris, New York
Died: September 23, 1902; Haven, Maine
Areas of Achievement: Exploration and science
Contribution: In 1869, Powell led the first party of exploration to descend the gorges of the Green and Colorado rivers by boat, stimulating interest in the geology and scenic wonders of the Grand Canyon. He also helped to establish the concepts of large-scale damming and irrigation projects as the keys to settlement and agricultural survival in the arid lands of the American West beyond the one hundredth meridian.

Early Life

John Wesley Powell was born on March 24, 1834, at Mount Morris, New York, the son of a circuit-riding Methodist minister who supplemented his income by farming and tailoring. The family moved to Ohio in 1841. The abolitionist views of the Powell family were not well received in Ohio, and John Wesley had such a difficult time at school that he was eventually placed under the direction of a private schoolmaster. This proved a significant experience, for the young Powell accompanied his tutor on biological field trips and developed a strong interest in both biological and physical science. The family eventually moved on to Illinois, where John Wesley grew to maturity. He spent several years combining a career as a teacher in Wisconsin and Illinois with sporadic attendance at several colleges, including Wheaton, Oberlin, and Illinois College. During this period he undertook extensive natural history excursions and ambitious journeys by boat down the Illinois, Des Moines, Ohio, and Mississippi rivers from St. Paul all the way to New Orleans.

When the Civil War came, Powell immediately enlisted as a private in an Illinois volunteer infantry company. He rose quickly through the ranks and became a student of military engineering and fortifications. He met and became a friend of General Ulysses S. Grant and eventually commander of his own battery in an Illinois artillery unit. He led his battery into the fierce struggle at the Hornet's Nest in the Battle of Shiloh, where he was hit by a Minié ball, requiring the amputation of his right arm. Despite his injury he continued in service, seeing action and carrying out important duties in a number of major campaigns and rising to the rank of brevet lieutenant colonel.

After the war, Powell returned to Illinois and became professor of natural history at Illinois Wesleyan College, later moving to Illinois Normal University at Bloomington. By this time he had become accustomed to taking his students into the field as part of their training, but he was increasingly obsessed with the desire to reach further afield. He was particularly drawn by the glamour and mystery of the trans-Mississippi West and began to assemble the ingredients that would allow him to make his first major expedition into that area.

Powell was instrumental in the establishment of a state natural history museum in Bloomington, and as its first curator he secured funding from several governmental and private sources to undertake a collecting expedition into the West. His friendship with General Grant enabled him to arrange for low-cost rations from army posts and for military protection for part of his trip. In 1867, the expedition, including students, amateur naturalists, teachers, and family members, set out from Council Bluffs on the first of Powell's major expeditions. The summer was spent examining the country and collecting specimens in the Colorado Rockies, and Powell remained after most of his party returned east and journeyed along the Grand River in Colorado.

The following summer, Powell returned to the Rockies with an expedition of twenty-five people, sponsorship from various Illinois state institutions, and encouragement from officials of the Smithsonian Institution, who were intrigued by his plans to explore among the rivers and high peaks of Colorado. After time collecting specimens in the Middle Park region, in late August Powell and six of his party made the first ascent of Long's Peak. They then moved into the White River basin, intending to follow it down to the Green River and on to a winter reconnaissance of the Colorado River. By now Powell had become thoroughly captivated by Western adventuring and scientific exploration and was obsessed by the unknown mysteries and legends of the Colorado. He had actively promoted his ideas and successfully publicized his activities and plans and had something of a reputation as an explorer and scientist, as well as good connections in the political and scientific communities. Although this five-foot-six, bearded veteran with only one arm hardly looked the part of the great explorer, Major John Wesley Powell was on the threshold of one of the great Western adventures.

Life's Work

The gorges of the Green and Colorado rivers were among the few remaining unexplored areas on the North American continent. The legends which had been constructed out of the tales of Indians, mountain men, and other sources told of a region of enormous waterfalls, vicious whirlpools and rapids, and enormous rock cliffs which offered no escape or refuge from the punishment of the river. Essentially Powell and his men would plunge into a river descent of nearly nine hundred miles with no real idea of what terrors and adventures lay before them. Back east, Powell made the best preparations he could. A Chicagoan built four small wooden boats, one sixteen feet long of pine, the other three twenty-one feet, of oak, with water-tight compartments. Powell secured some financial support from a variety of public and private sources, although most of the meager financing came out of his own pocket. He assembled a varied group of nine companions, and on May 24, 1869, after several weeks of training, they set off down the Green River toward the Colorado.

They were on the river for ninety-two days. Their small vessels plunged through turbulent rapids, foaming cataracts, and towering canyon walls that at least matched most of the myths and legends. Two boats were lost, one expeditioner deserted early, three others were killed by Indians as they gave up on the river journey and attempted to climb out of the Grand Canyon. A confidence man surfaced who claimed that he was the only survivor of a wreck beneath a falls that had claimed the lives of the other members of the expedition, and newspapers across the country reported that Powell's party had been defeated by the river. By the time they in fact surfaced at a Mormon settlement below the canyon, Powell and his men had explored the Colorado River and the Grand Canyon and had discovered the last unknown river and mountain range in the American West. Powell's prodigious expedition marked him immediately as an American hero and one of the great explorers in the nation's history. It also meant that he could attract support and financing for further activities.

Powell returned to the Colorado two years later and retraced his original steps, now with the sponsorship of the Smithsonian Institution and the Department of the Interior. This expedition was a more determinedly scientific endeavor, operating as a survey group, the United States Geological and Geographical Survey of the Rocky Mountains, and they undertook a careful study, survey, and mapping of the canyon country. Powell became fascinated with the question not only of how the region—its canyons, plateaus, and mountains—looked but also of how they had been formed. He undertook additional Western expeditions and employed men who explored the high plateaus of Utah, the Colorado Plateau, Zion and Bryce canyons, and the Henry and Uinta mountains. The work of Powell and his associates introduced the idea of vast processes of uplift and erosion as responsible for the topography of the canyon and plateau country. They helped to popularize the geological concept of "base level of erosion." Powell's findings and ideas were published as *Explorations of the Colorado River of the West and Its Tributaries* (1875; revised and enlarged in 1895 under the title *Canyons of the Colorado*).

Powell's interest in the topography and geology of the Western regions led him naturally to a concern about the management of its lands. In 1878 he published *A Report on the Lands of the Arid Region of the United States*, which has been described as among the most important works ever produced by an American. Powell rejected both the concept of the inexhaustibility of natural resources and the idea that the West was the "Great American Desert" and not capable of supporting substantial settlement. Powell's familiarity with the West had convinced him that its lands and climate west of the one hundredth meridian were simply not suitable for development under policies that had been shaped by the conditions in the Eastern regions. The arid lands of the West required a different strategy, and the key was water management.

Powell argued that the arid regions would not support the traditional family farm on the eastern model and that the lands of the West should be categorized and utilized according to their most efficient uses for grazing, lumbering, mining, farming, and other purposes. Water should be considered a precious resource to be allocated by the community for the benefit of society in general rather than a privileged few. Government should undertake large-scale damming and irrigation projects so that the arid regions could be "reclaimed" and become productive. Powell's ideas represented a significant departure from the conventional wisdom regarding land use and the West, and his prestige as an explorer and scientist, coupled with his office as director of the United States Geological Survey from 1881 to 1894, put him in a position to be enormously influential in shaping the establishment in 1902 of the United States Bureau of Reclamation, which helped to make water management one of the major components of the early conservation movement.

During his Western expeditions, Powell had become fascinated by the cultures of the Indian tribes of the region, and it is characteristic of the man that he became a student of anthropology and headed the Bureau of Ethnology of the Smithsonian Institution during the same period that he led the Geological Survey. In 1880 he published his *Introduction to the Study of Indian Languages*.

Major Powell's retirement in 1894 was brought about partially because of physical ailments and partially because of his frustration in trying to get his ideas implemented. Ironically, his death in 1902 coincided with the passage of the Reclamation Act, which institutionalized many of his theories concerning land and water management.

Summary

Powell's career was significant on several fronts. As an explorer, his journey down the Colorado River through the Grand Canyon in 1869 ranks as one of the epic American adventures. His scientific background and interests prepared him for important accomplishments in mapping, surveying, and studying the geology of the plateau and canyon country, and for long service as director of the United States Geological Survey. During the same period, he headed the Bureau of Ethnology of the Smithsonian Institution. Powell became most interested in the problems of proper management and utilization of the lands in the arid West and was convinced that intelligent water management was the key to its development. He is one of the fathers of the concept of "reclamation" of arid lands through the construction of dams and irrigation projects.

Bibliography

Bartlett, Richard A. *Great Surveys of the American West.* Norman: University of Oklahoma Press, 1962. A comprehensive treatment that includes the work of Powell.

Darrah, William C. *Powell of the Colorado.* Princeton, N.J.: Princeton University Press, 1951. A useful scholarly biography. Well researched, drawing on some unpublished sources, but rather colorless. Includes illustrations.

Exploring the American West, 1803-1879 (National Park Handbook no. 116). Washington, D.C.: Government Printing Office, 1982. This 128-page booklet is profusely illustrated and contains several photographs of Powell and his survey. The text is by William H. Goetzmann.

Fradkin, Philip L. *A River, No More: The Colorado River and the West.* New York: Alfred A. Knopf, 1981. Focusing upon the Colorado River and its tributaries, Fradkin discusses the federal land and water policies that shaped much of the West. Powell's role in the evolution of these developments is considered.

Goetzmann, William H. *Exploration and Empire: The Explorer and the Scientist in the Winning of the American West.* New York: Alfred A. Knopf, 1966. This Pulitzer Prize–winning book is the standard general treatment of the role of exploration in the American West. Contains a chapter dealing with Powell's life and career.

Savage, Henry, Jr. *Discovering America, 1700-1875.* New York: Harper and Row, Publishers, 1979. A very readable survey which is particularly good on the nineteenth century explorations.

Schwartz, Seymour I., and Ralph E. Ehrenberg. *The Mapping of America.* New York: Harry N. Abrams, 1980. An enormously detailed and lavishly illustrated history.

Stegner, Wallace. *Beyond the Hundredth Meridian: John Wesley Powell and the Second Opening of the West.* Boston: Houghton Mifflin Co., 1954. The standard biography. Stegner brings a novelist's gifts to his compelling narrative. Illustrations juxtapose early artists' renderings of the Grand Canyon with some of the first photographs of the region.

Wild, Peter. *Pioneer Conservationists of Western America.* Missoula, Mont.: Mountain Publishing Co., 1979. A brief, breezy, superficial account which contains a chapter on Powell's explorations and theories.

James E. Fickle

POWHATAN

Born: c. 1550; Powhata, near Richmond, Virginia
Died: April, 1618; Powhata, Virginia
Area of Achievement: Native American leadership
Contribution: Though better known in North American history as the father of the Indian princess Pocahontas, Powhatan made significant contributions to the English settlement in North America. Through his prudent leadership and goodwill, Powhatan provided the basis for a peaceful co-existence between the Indians and the English which ultimately enabled Jamestown, the first English colony in America, to thrive and expand.

Early Life

Powhatan was born around the year 1550, but his exact birth date is still in question. It has been documented that Powhatan was of foreign extraction, that his father had come from the West Indies because he had been driven from there by the Spaniards. His given name was Wahunsenacawh, but he came to be called Powhatan after the name of one of the tribes that was later to come under his rule. It is known that Powhatan had at least two brothers: Opechancanough, who later became chief of one of Powhatan's most important tribes, the Pamunkeys, and who was the most formidable enemy of the English after Powhatan's death, and Opitchepan, who succeeded Powhatan.

Unfortunately, virtually nothing has been recorded about Powhatan's early childhood. When he was a young man, he inherited six tribes, thus becoming a chief, or sachem. By force or threat of force, he expanded his reign to include thirty tribes. Powhatan's geographical jurisdiction encompassed most of tidewater Virginia. It began on the south side of the James River, extended northward to the Potomac, and stretched to include two tribes of the lower Eastern Shore of the Chesapeake Bay. In addition to the tribe from which he took his name, he controlled the Pamunkey, the Chickahominy, and the Potomac tribes. He and his people belonged to the Algonquian-speaking family which occupied the coastal areas from upper Carolina to New England and beyond. It has been estimated that Powhatan had a population of between eight thousand and nine thousand under his rule.

Powhatan's portrait, as documented by those with whom he had frequent contact, certainly mirrors his status. Early written records state that he was tall, stately, and well proportioned. Although he was perceived as having a sour look, his overall countenance was described as majestic and grave. Powhatan possessed fabulous robes of costly skins and feather capes. His love for ornamentation was evident from the fact that he was always bejeweled with long chains of pearls and beads. Powhatan has been described as wily and crafty. The English described him as possessing a subtle intelligence, and they had great respect for him.

Powhatan's principal residence was set deep in a thicket of woods in the village of Werowocomoco, on the York River not far from Jamestown. It was approximately fifty to sixty yards in length and was guarded by four decorative sentries: a dragon, a bear, a leopard, and a giant man. In typical kingly fashion, he enjoyed sitting on a throne of mats approximately one foot high. He was flanked on either side by his current favorite women. His chief men sat along each side of the house and behind them sat many women. All were adorned with jewelry, ornaments, and paint.

Powhatan's status as sachem brought with it many privileges, one of which was having many wives and, as a result, many children. He selected his favorite women to bear him children and, after they did so, they were free to leave and marry again. One of these women bore him the most loved and most famous of his daughters, Pocahontas. It was through her that Powhatan became personally involved with the first English colony in America in 1607 and ultimately decided its destiny.

Life's Work

Powhatan's main goal as sachem of such a large number of tribes was to create unity and foster harmony among them. It was under his firm guidance that the largest Algonquian group had been consolidated. Once this was accomplished, their strength and prosperity was evident.

Powhatan's people enjoyed political, economic, and artistic stability and prosperity under his domain. Although Powhatan's tactics may be deemed despotic, his political system offered protection for its people against their numerous and varied foes. The economy was a relatively sophisticated one. Three crops of Indian corn were cultivated each year. Tobacco was also grown. Their foodstuffs were richly supplemented by hunting and fishing, which were carried out in an organized, communal fashion and manifested the tribes' common goals and sense of unity. Together, the Indians hunted wild turkey, beaver, and deer, which not only reinforced their food supply but also provided them with important items for clothing and tools. For fishing, they deftly employed equipment such as the weir, net, fishhook, spear, and arrow. Their canoes were fashioned from a single log and had the capacity to carry approximately forty men. Their implements showed a high level of sophistication and were quite comparable in form and function to those of their English counterparts, except that they were not made of metal. There was also a high degree of sophistication in arts and crafts, especially pottery and basketry. They fashioned their own pipes, in which they smoked the tobacco they grew. They also created musical instruments from reeds, with which they participated in various ceremonial rites.

With the arrival of the English, Powhatan's main goal was to continue the peace, prosperity, and strength of his people. This was based on the naïve assumption that it would be possible for the two groups to coexist peacefully and that neither would prosper by the extinction of the other. Hence, Powhatan's wisdom, wiles, and capacity for negotiation were put to the test. In spite of the many trials and tribulations he suffered during this period, Powhatan never wavered from this goal. He was firmly committed to his people and instinctively sought to guard against any disruptive temptations presented by the English. He continued to rule with the same common sense with which he built his empire and to espouse a humane philosophy and sense of statecraft.

Powhatan, however, initially sensed danger from the English. They were on his land, destroying it to build homes, hunting his animals, cultivating his soil, chopping his trees, and eating his fish. Furthermore, they possessed weaponry that was far more sophisticated than that of the Indians. When Powhatan first met the English Captain John Smith, his keen instincts and political acumen told him that he was being deceived. Thus, he decided that Smith should be put to death. At the last minute, however, Pocahontas intervened, and the Englishman's life was spared.

The first tactic that Powhatan used in dealing with Smith and the English was that of trading. He sent a generous quantity of badly needed food to the starving colonists and, in return, demanded cannons, muskets, and a millstone for grinding corn. Although Powhatan's tribes were more numerous and more cohesive than the colonists, he wished to fortify them with sophisticated English weaponry for protection against any surprise attacks. Smith returned to Jamestown a free man, laden with food supplies, only to break his bargain with Powhatan by sending him bells, beads, and mirrors instead of the items he requested. Powhatan felt deceived and so refused the next request for food. His response was met with a threat from Smith's pistol and the raised muskets of his men. Powhatan became openly angry but knew that bows and arrows were no match for guns. The Indians became resentful and stole tools and weapons, and occasional outbreaks of fighting ensued. The English knew, however, that the success of their colony depended on Powhatan's goodwill, generosity, and humanitarianism, and they tried to appease him and win him over with pardons and gifts.

Powhatan, however, had already been twice deceived, was always on the alert, and adopted a wait-and-see stance. He recognized, resisted, and outwitted all attempts to subjugate him or his people. For example, when Powhatan was asked to participate in a coronation ceremony which would make him a subject of the English king, he became defiant. He did not see the wisdom or the logic of one king serving another king. He did, however, accept all the gifts that were presented to him. These included a huge bed, a red silk cape, and a copper crown. The English, for their part, continued to try to use the Indians while biding their time to build up strength with supplies from England. They never invited Powhatan to visit their colony and, even when they were in desperate need of food, they requested a lesser amount than was actually needed. Powhatan was one step ahead of them, though, and not only decided to charge them more for the corn but also demanded that they build him an English-style house modeled after the largest standing structure of the time. The English had no choice. When Powhatan realized that Captain Smith was never going to trade his weapons, he made a deal with Captain Christopher Newport, who was not on friendly terms with Smith. They traded twenty wild turkeys for twenty swords. The result was twice as favorable for Powhatan. It created further demoralization and internal strife among the members of the Jamestown community, while at the same time it strengthened and fortified the unity of Powhatan's people. Powhatan's humanitarian side, however, prevailed on most occasions. For example, when a fire destroyed the Jamestown warehouse which contained the colonists' food, Powhatan sent not only food but also his daughter Pocahontas to serve as ambassador. When Pocahontas was kidnaped by an English captain and one of the ransom demands was the return of all captured prisoners and pilfered guns, Powhatan again reacted in a shrewd manner. Although Pocahontas was known to be his favorite daughter and he had often said that she was as dear to him as his own life, he knew that the English had always been her friends and would never harm her. He blessed her impending marriage to John Rolfe, promised friendship, sent two of his sons to attend the wedding bearing many gifts, and returned the prisoners—but never the guns.

This act began an era of peace between the Indians and the English known as the Peace of Pocahontas, which lasted until the time of Powhatan's death in 1618. The sachem had achieved his goal without compromising his personal dignity or jeopardizing the strength and peace of his tribes.

Summary

Powhatan's rule provided his numerous tribes with peace, protection, and prosperity. These vast numbers of people succeeded in forming a binding alliance and uniting against common foes.

Internally, they were prudent and resourceful. They knew their land well and cultivated it with care. Their agricultural system assured them of bountiful harvests, and excess food supplies were always in abundance for emergency use. It was Powhatan himself, in fact, who presented Captain Smith with baskets of corn kernels and even provided him with planting instructions. This act of generosity and goodwill not only prevented famine in the Jamestown colony during its first winter season but also once again attested Powhatan's good faith and humanitarian nature.

There are many theories as to why Powhatan allowed the Jamestown colony to survive. Given the large numbers of people under his rule, it is quite obvious that, had he so wished, he could have easily destroyed the colony in spite of its superior weaponry. He had no apparent reason to do so, however, and perhaps he thought that fair play and a cautious approach in his relations with the English could be mutually advantageous.

The English colony never posed a real threat to Powhatan from their initial landing in the spring of 1607. It was composed of a group of quarrelsome, power-hungry men who were incapable of unifying their small group. Their rate of growth was virtually nonexistent; Powhatan had no forewarning of future events. There were only 350 people in the colony at the time of Powhatan's death. Since its founding, the colonists there had suffered such grave misfortunes that it was only with Powhatan's help that they had survived; he, in turn, reasoned that the English could help him. Their sophisticated weaponry not only would facilitate daily chores such as hunting but also would provide his people with better protection against their foes and further reinforce his own authority. This interdependence would have the potential to lead to an alliance if such a situation presented itself.

The deceit and double-crossing exchanged between the two sides was probably the normal politicking of two very astute leaders. Powhatan's tactic was to outwit the English, punish them at every opportunity, and deny them the opportunity to retaliate. It should be noted, however, that although Powhatan was often a victim of English deceit, he never allowed these discrepancies to interfere with the formation of a long-lasting peace treaty. It is highly doubtful that he allowed sentimental considerations to interfere with his political decisions. Although there is no denying that Powhatan loved Pocahontas, he also knew that her ability to deal with the English could prove fruitful to him; thus, he sent her to negotiate the return of the Indian prisoners in the Jamestown camp. He knew that Smith would yield to Pocahontas what he would yield to no one else. By appointing her as his ambassador, he was able to plant the seeds of friendship between the Old World and the New World.

Bibliography

Andrews, Matthew Page. *The Soul of a Nation*. New York: Charles Scribner's Sons, 1943. Concentrates on the founding of Virginia and the projection of New England. Emphasizes the need for a fresh appraisal of American beginnings. Powhatan and his relationships with Captain Smith and Captain Newport are discussed.

Chatterton, E. K. *Captain John Smith*. New York: Harper and Brothers, 1929. Focuses on the early life of Smith, the formation of his character, his spirit of adventure, and his place in history. Details his meetings and dealings with Powhatan and Pocahontas and provides insight into his respect and sympathy for Powhatan.

Craven, Wesley Frank. *White, Red, and Black: The Seventeenth Century Virginian*. Charlottesville: University Press of Virginia, 1971. Chronicles the history of the white, Indian, and African black in the early history of Virginia. Emphasizes Powhatan's organizational skills and strong leadership in contrast to the disorganization, lack of leadership, and internal strife of Jamestown.

Fishwick, Marshall W. *Jamestown: First English Colony*. New York: Harper and Row, Publishers, 1965. The best book on the daily life and customs of the Indians. Discusses all aspects of Powhatan and his tribes and their dealings with the English.

Fritz, Jean. *The Double Life of Pocahontas*. New York: G. P. Putnam's Sons, 1983. A fresh look at Pocahontas, her relationship with her father, and the dilemma of her entrapment between two cultures. She was purely happy in her Indian village and thoroughly fascinated by the English. Describes the tragedy that befell the Indians after Powhatan's death.

Gerson, Noel B. *The Glorious Scoundrel: A Biography of Captain John Smith*. New York: Dodd, Mead and Co., 1978. Discusses John Smith's life and ambitions, his role of leadership in the colony, and his diplomatic dealings with Powhatan. It was through his sensitivity that Powhatan was able to be appeased and won over.

Willison, George F. *Behold Virginia: The Fifth Crown*. New York: Harcourt, Brace and Co., 1951. Provides an overview of the early history of Virginia. Powhatan is discussed in terms of his humanitarianism: accepting and aiding the settlers during their times of need. Many of the English plots to subvert him are exposed.

Anne Laura Mattrella

WILLIAM HICKLING PRESCOTT

Born: May 4, 1796; Salem, Massachusetts
Died: January 28, 1859; Boston, Massachusetts
Area of Achievement: History
Contribution: Prescott proved that historical writing could achieve the permanence of literature; he introduced into American historiography all the methods of modern scholarship, and he remains the most distinguished historian of sixteenth century Spain and Spanish America in the English language.

Early Life

William Hickling Prescott was born in Salem, Massachusetts, on May 4, 1796. His father, William Prescott, a lawyer and judge who prospered in investments in industry, real estate, and the India trade, was the son of Colonel William Prescott, the hero of the Battle of Bunker Hill; Prescott's mother, Catherine Greene Hickling, was the daughter of another wealthy New England family. Prescott attended private schools in Salem and another in Boston when the family moved there in 1808. At Harvard, he suffered an injury to his left eye during a boyish fracas in the dining hall, which led to a lifetime of trouble with his eyesight. This event is the basis of the myth that he achieved literary fame in spite of blindness. Actually, he was never totally blind, but his eyesight and his general health were poor throughout his life.

When he was graduated from Harvard in 1814, Prescott's study of the law in preparation for joining his father's firm was cut short by impaired vision and rheumatic pains, and his parents sent him abroad for his health, first to the Azores, where his maternal grandfather was the American consul. He returned to Boston in 1817, after two years in England, France, and Italy, convinced that he would never be able to practice law. During the winter of 1817-1818, he was confined to a darkened room, where his sister read to him while he wrestled with the question of what career to pursue.

Prescott's first published work, an article on Lord Byron, appeared in the *North American Review* in 1821. By this time, he was determined to be a man of letters, a career made possible by the readers and secretaries whom he could afford to employ. In 1820, he married Susan Amory, the daughter of a wealthy Boston merchant, and he embarked on the systematic study of European literature. During the next nine years, he continued to publish essays on a variety of literary subjects while studying Italian and Spanish literature.

Life's Work

Prescott's study of the literature of Spain led to his determination to write a history of the reign of the fifteenth century monarchs Ferdinand and Isabella. Doubly isolated from documentary sources by his poor eyesight and his distance from Spanish libraries but blessed with sufficient wealth, Prescott employed full-time secretaries to read to him and to take dictation, and his many contacts in European libraries made possible a form of research that was remarkably complete, considering his difficulties. His friends in Europe found and made copies of often obscure documentary sources, and his remarkable memory gave him the ability to keep a large amount of historical information in mind as he organized his subject. *History of the Reign of Ferdinand and Isabella the Catholic* (1838), the result of eight years of writing, was, for a historical work, a remarkable success, both in the United States and in England. Though later historians have charged that Prescott ignored the ordinary people of Spain in concentrating on the life of the Spanish court, it must be remembered that it was politics, diplomacy, and war, not "common life," that furnished subjects for historians in Prescott's time. This first work reveals high standards of objectivity, it is thoroughly documented, and Spanish historians have always considered it a basic contribution to fifteenth century historiography. All this is even more remarkable for being the achievement of a self-trained historian.

Prescott's success with his first book encouraged him to embark on the writing of the two works for which he is most famous, his accounts of the destruction of the Aztec and Inca empires by the conquistadors of Hernán Cortés and Francisco Pizarro. *History of the Conquest of Mexico* (1843) produced for Prescott a remarkable number of honors, including memberships in various historical societies in the United States and in Europe, honorary degrees, and, most significant, a membership in the Royal Academy of History in Madrid. This work, which has been issued in two hundred editions and has been his most translated book, is considered by most students of Prescott to be his masterpiece, admired particularly for its graceful style and overall design. It is a supreme example of the work of the first great generation of American historians—Prescott, Francis Parkman, and John Lothrop Motley—who, being unburdened by any philosophy of history, subordinated deep analyses of social background and lengthy explanations of the causes of events to simple narrative history written for both the edification and entertainment of the reader.

History of the Conquest of Peru (1847) was written in two years. The speed of its composition is an indication of the success of Prescott's mastery of the subject of sixteenth century Spain, his methods of research, and particularly the remarkable network of friends he had established in Spanish libraries. This work has not enjoyed the scholarly respect which *History of the Conquest of Mexico* has achieved, but this is less because of failing powers in its author than of the subject itself: Prescott found much less to admire in Pizarro than he had found in Cortés.

In 1850, he traveled in Europe, where he was a great social success and where, among other honors, he received a doctorate from Oxford University. The first two volumes of his fourth work, *History of the Reign of Philip the Second, King of Spain*, were published in 1855, and the final, third volume appeared in December, 1858, only a month before his death on January 28, 1859. This is the least of his four major works, probably because of the bad health that plagued him while he was writing it but also because he found so little to admire in his subject.

Prescott's four historical works are his primary claim to fame as a historian and man of letters. He also published "The Life of Charles V After His Abdication" (1856) as a supplement to William Robertson's *The History of the Reign of the Emperor Charles the Fifth* (1769), and what he called "some of my periodical trumpery" appeared as *Biographical and Critical Miscellanies* in 1845.

In spite of his physical ailments, Prescott's private life was serene. He was the father of four children, he enjoyed a wide circle of personal and professional friends, and he maintained a comfortable rhythm of the seasons as he worked in his library in Boston in the winter and spent his summers at Nahant or at the ancestral Prescott farm.

Prescott was in many ways a typical Boston Brahmin, a Unitarian in religion, a Federalist in politics and later a Whig, and a man with strong social concerns for his community and a belief that wealth confers obligations on the wealthy. Early in life, he was influential in the establishment in Massachusetts of an institution for the care of the blind, and he supported the Boston Atheneum all of his life. He earned the respect of many Mexican and Spanish friends by opposing the Mexican War and the Pierce Administration's designs on Cuba, and like most New England intellectuals, he opposed the Fugitive Slave Law and voted for John C. Frémont in 1856. He was a complex man who, in spite of his physical impairment, enjoyed social activity and gracious living, and he was a frequent help to other writers and researchers, but his ambition as a historian and man of letters triumphed over the double burden of ill health and social position while his wealth made possible research which no other American of his time could have achieved.

Summary

William Hickling Prescott combined thorough research and literary gifts to produce historical works which must be considered contributions both to historical knowledge and to American literature. Though he concentrated on the colorful aspects of his subjects and ignored the more prosaic and mundane life of common people, he produced remarkable examples of narrative and helped to raise historical writing in the United States from the often parochial concerns of his predecessors while avoiding the dullness which characterizes much of the admittedly fuller social and economic histories of later generations of historians. The fact that his work is eminently readable has obscured his importance as the first American historian to employ modern methods of historical research, an achievement that is even more remarkable when one takes account of the fact that he was completely self-trained and that he was burdened with ill health all of his life. Furthermore, at a time when American literary and historical interests, in the aftermath of revolution and nation-building, were inevitably turned inward, he made American readers conscious of cultures beyond their borders while helping to give American literature an international reputation.

Bibliography
Charvat, William, and Michael Kraus, eds. *William Hickling Prescott: Representative Selections*. New York: American Book Co., 1943. This selection of passages from Prescott's writing is supplemented by a brief account of his life and discussions of his literary style and the philosophical and political premises of his work.

Darnell, Donald G. *William Hickling Prescott*. Boston: Twayne Publishers, 1975. Primarily concerned with Prescott as a man of letters, Darnell provides a brief account of his life, a balanced assessment of his achievement as a historian, and lengthy examinations of each of his four major works.

Gardiner, C. Harvey. *The Literary Memoranda*. Edited by William Hickling Prescott. 2 vols. Norman: University of Oklahoma Press, 1961. A collection of Prescott's private papers, which provide essential insight into his methods as a writer and researcher.

—————. *William Hickling Prescott: A Biography*. Austin: University of Texas Press, 1969. The definitive biography by the most distinguished Prescott scholar, based on a thorough knowledge of primary sources and not likely to be superseded. A balanced assessment of Prescott's achievement as a historian and man of letters and a full treatment of his complex personality and private life.

Levin, David. *History as Romantic Art: Bancroft, Prescott, Motley, and Parkman*. Stanford, Calif.: Stanford University Press, 1959. A study of the first generation of American historians, their romanticism, and its effects on their writing, which Levin often considers unfortunate. His assessments of Prescott should be checked against Gardiner's.

Ogden, Rollo. *William Hickling Prescott*. Boston: Houghton Mifflin Co., 1904. Apparently intended to supplement George Ticknor's biography, it devotes more attention to Prescott as a person and takes greater account of his private papers. The best biography before Gardiner's.

Peck, Harry Thurston. *William Hickling Prescott*. New York: Macmillan Publishing Co., 1905. A brief biography which makes no use of primary sources but includes a useful discussion of Prescott's literary style.

Ticknor, George. *Life of William Hickling Prescott*. Philadelphia: J. B. Lippincott Co., 1863. Ticknor, himself the author of a major history of

Spanish literature, knew Prescott intimately, but his biography provides no insight into his subject's personality and very little of his social and intellectual background. Includes useful appendices on the history of the Prescott family.

Williams, Stanley T. *The Spanish Background of American Literature*. 2 vols. New Haven, Conn.: Yale University Press, 1955. Includes a chapter on Prescott and provides insights into the sources of nineteenth century American interest in Spain and Spanish America.

Robert L. Berner

ELVIS PRESLEY

Born: January 8, 1935; Tupelo, Mississippi
Died: August 16, 1977; Memphis, Tennessee
Area of Achievement: Music
Contribution: Fusing the legacies of black and white American music, Presley helped create the cultural phenomenon of rock and roll and became its most famous and influential performer.

Early Life

Elvis Aron Presley was the son of Gladys and Vernon Presley; his twin brother, Jesse Garon Presley, died at birth and was buried in an unmarked grave in a local cemetery. There were no other children in the Presley family, and Elvis grew up especially close to his mother. His father held a variety of jobs, none very successfully, and served time in the state penitentiary for check forgery. While not actually poverty-stricken, the Presley family was poor.

In 1948, they moved to Memphis, Tennessee. Presley had already demonstrated a talent for singing, particularly in church, and in Memphis he won first place at his high school's annual variety show. He had already assimilated much of the rich musical tradition of the South: the blues and spirituals; gospel and country music, some of it reaching back to the English folk tradition; and contemporary American song, including jazz and the first stirrings of what he would help transform into rock and roll. With no formal training, Presley combined these varied influences through his inborn gifts.

After high school, Presley became a truck driver for the Crown Electric Company in Memphis. In 1953, he paid to record a single at a local studio; Sam Phillips, the owner of Sun Records, heard this single and recognized the immense talent Elvis possessed. In July, 1954, Presley recorded his first commercial tapes with Phillips in the Sun Records in Memphis.

As he began his career, Presley was of average height, and his dark hair was worn rather long for the period, with sideburns. He had full lips, which would later become famous for his "sneer," a slight lifting as he talked or sang. His eyes were dark, penetrating, and heavy-lidded. As he grew older, he would have increasing problems with his weight. When he performed, he moved freely, even wildly, about the stage; his pronounced hip movements while singing earned for him the nickname "Elvis the Pelvis." His most remarkable characteristics were his fine singing voice and his intense, charismatic presence.

Life's Work

For Sun, Presley recorded a song called "That's All Right Mama," which was released in July, 1954. Played on the local radio stations, it became an immediate hit. Other records followed, equally successful, and Presley rapidly became a regional sensation. In 1955, Phillips sold his contract with Presley to Radio Corporation of America (RCA), and Colonel Tom Parker became Elvis' manager; Parker would retain almost complete control of all financial matters until long after Presley's death.

Presley's fame spread rapidly as more and more radio stations aired his records, and his recognition spread beyond the South. He appeared on major television shows, including the Dorsey brothers' *Stage Show*, the *Milton Berle Show*, and the *Steve Allen Show*. His real explosion into national prominence came with his three appearances on the popular *Ed Sullivan Show*, between September 8, 1956, and January 6, 1957. In the last of these, Presley was shown only from the waist up, to avoid complaints over his wild gyrations. Older viewers were astonished, younger ones delighted, and almost everyone recognized that a new era in popular music had been inaugurated by this skinny Southern boy.

The years between 1955 and 1958 were the most creative and important of Presley's career. It was during this time that he recorded music the likes of which had never been heard before, and which transformed American popular songs. Violence, tragedy, and lost love mingled with unlimited promise and undefeated optimism in these songs, as Presley's remarkable performances drew upon the musical heritage he had known and then transcended it. His immensely popular recordings included "Mystery Train," "Heartbreak Hotel," "Blue Suede Shoes," "Shake, Rattle and Roll," "Teddy Bear," and what became the song most closely associated with him, "Hound Dog." The pulsing, infectious rhythm of these songs, a combination of all the songs and singers Presley had known growing up in the South, swept across the country with unprecedented popularity.

Such popularity was soon translated into films. Presley signed a contract with Hal Wallis of Paramount Studios, and, in 1956, he began filming *Love Me Tender*, the first of his thirty-three films. His early films were his best, especially *Jailhouse Rock* (1957), a gritty film which used prison as a metaphor for the fate of the popular artist, and *King Creole* (1958), in which Presley was given the opportunity to display his real, if limited, dramatic abilities. His later films were repetitious in plot and mechanical in production; they were always set in some exotic location—Hawaii, Arabia, Las Vegas—and used a breezy, romantic story line on which to hang a half dozen forgettable songs. These songs were written specifically for the films and were far removed from the energetic recordings of Presley's first years as an artist.

In 1957, Presley received his induction notice from the Memphis draft board, and in March, 1958, he entered the United States Army. While stationed at Fort Hood, Texas, for his basic training, Presley received emergency leave to visit his mother in a Memphis hospital. Gladys Presley died on

August 14, 1958, at the age of forty-six. The cause of death was a heart attack, complicated by hepatitis. His mother's death was a severe blow to Presley. The huge mansion he had built for her in Memphis, Graceland, would be his home for the remainder of his life.

Stationed in Germany, Presley met Priscilla Beaulieu, the teenage daughter of a career army officer. They began dating, and after his duty in the service, Presley convinced the Beaulieus to permit Priscilla to move into Graceland. His grandmother served as chaperone while Priscilla completed high school. Presley and Priscilla were married on May 1, 1967, in Las Vegas, Nevada. Nine months later, on February 1, 1968, their daughter and only child, Lisa Marie Presley, was born.

Presley was discharged from the army in March, 1960. There was some concern that his absence from the musical scene would have erased or diluted his popularity, but his reception by two thousand fans at Fort Dix, New Jersey, was an indication that such fears were groundless. He was soon in the studio recording new tracks for an album, and he appeared in a television special entitled *Frank Sinatra's Welcome Home Party for Elvis Presley*. It was soon apparent that Presley's time in the army had not weakened his hold on the popular imagination.

Changes were made, however, under the direction of Presley's manager, Parker. In March, 1961, Presley gave a memorial concert; it would be his last for eight years. Instead of live appearances, he concentrated on films, making an average of two a year. His records consisted mostly of songs written for the films—the title track and a variety of forgettable tunes. On occasion, he recorded some gospel albums, such as the powerful *How Great Thou Art* (1967), which demonstrated his mastery of that musical genre. The RCA record label also released collections of his best-selling hits.

During the 1960's, however, Presley displayed none of the galvanic, revolutionary musical energy that had captured the attention of millions at the start of his career. That energy still had its effect, however, as an entire generation of performers, American and British, followed in his path. Groups such as the Beatles and the Rolling Stones, and individual artists such as Bob Dylan, expanded in their own ways the musical frontier which Presley had first marked out. Ironically, the originator of this movement was conspicuous by his absence.

In 1968, Presley returned to public performances. He first recorded a television program called, simply enough, *Elvis*. The success of the program led to live appearances in resort hotels in Las Vegas and a series of concert tours across the United States. The act Presley presented in these concerts was totally different from that of his early days: He now had a large, carefully rehearsed orchestra, sizable numbers of background singers, and increasingly elaborate costumes. His popularity, always high, increased; his records began to appear at the top of the music charts for the first time since the early

1960's. In 1973, his television special *Elvis: Aloha from Hawaii via Satellite* was broadcast to forty countries throughout the world.

During the 1970's, Presley toured heavily, as well as performing regularly in Las Vegas. In part because of his schedule, in part for personal reasons, the Presley marriage deteriorated, and on August 18, 1972, Presley filed for divorce on the grounds of irreconcilable differences. The divorce was granted on October 9, 1973.

Over the years, Presley had come to rely increasingly on a wide variety of drugs: stimulants for the concerts, depressants for sleep, painkillers for comfort. His behavior became occasionally erratic and irrational, and at times, even violent. He took to carrying pistols and other weapons, insulting or attacking longtime friends, and afterward presenting them with automobiles or other expensive gifts. Some attributed these actions to regret over the failure of his marriage or to a long-standing depression at the death of his mother; other observers blamed the peculiar life-style imposed upon such a hugely popular entertainer, or the influence of drugs.

Despite these problems, and perhaps to avoid them, Presley continued to tour. In the summer of 1977, he planned another national circuit, to begin with a concert on August 17. On the afternoon of August 16, Presley was discovered unconscious in a bathroom of Graceland. Efforts by paramedics at the mansion failed to revive him, as did further attempts by doctors at Baptist Memorial Hospital. Although his death was apparently drug-related, the official statement gave the cause as heart disease.

His body was viewed by thousands as he lay in state in his mansion, and thousands more formed the miles-long procession to the cemetery. His body was later moved to Graceland, where he was buried beside his mother. Elvis Presley was forty-two years old when he died.

Summary

The career of Elvis Presley and his impact on modern culture transcend the outlines of biography and defy analysis. Rising from poverty and obscurity, Presley became a major force in shaping contemporary popular music; indeed, for some, he was the essential inspiration and source of rock and roll. While this claim may be extreme, there is little doubt that Presley was the focus that brought together the various traditions which united to produce America's most energetic and perhaps most typical music.

With his background in Southern gospel, black soul and blues, and traditional country music, Presley was able to forge something new yet totally familiar. His music was instantly recognized as the work of genius, even if the work was denounced as obscene or attacked as primitive. In its truest sense, it was primitive, because it went to the very roots of American culture.

President Jimmy Carter attempted to express this feeling in his tribute to Presley when he said that his music and his personality, fusing the styles of white country and black rhythm and blues, permanently changed the face of American popular culture. His following was immense and he was a symbol to people the world over of the vitality, rebelliousness, and good humor of his country.

Perhaps the truest summary came from rock and roll critic Greil Marcus, who wrote of the relationship between the performer and the United States: "At his best Elvis not only embodies but personalizes so much of what is good about this place."

Presley's impact is even more remarkable when it is noted that his period of truly creative work fell within the relatively short period of the late 1950's. During these years, he recorded his most memorable and influential songs, the songs for which he will always be remembered. The path to both Woodstock and Abbey Road begins at Sun Records in Memphis. This period ended with his induction into the army; following his return to civilian life, Presley spent most of the 1960's making films and recording sound tracks; he remained popular but distant from his public. It was not until 1968 that he staged a triumphant comeback and resumed live performances. Clearly, however, he had either lost or muted his energy and his unpredictable, even dangerous, appeal. Just as clearly, it made little difference, for his image had become reality to his fans.

Presley was undoubtedly the most famous entertainer in the world, known to millions only as Elvis. Others knew him as The King, perhaps of rock and roll, perhaps of entertainment, and perhaps, in some mysterious way, king of the complex experience of America itself, which he summed up so well in his performances and his presence.

Bibliography
Cotton, Lee. *All Shook Up: Elvis Day-by-Day, 1954-1977*. Ann Arbor, Mich.: Pierian Press, 1985. An exhaustive chronology of Presley's activities during his career. Proof that Presley was undoubtedly the most closely observed of contemporary performers.
Dundy, Elaine. *Elvis and Gladys*. New York: Macmillan, 1985. The influence of Gladys Presley on her son, and his relationship to her, has been an issue which has always fascinated both fans and more neutral observers. This book gives a generally balanced account.
Goldman, Albert. *Elvis*. New York: McGraw-Hill Book Co., 1981. A long, unfriendly look at Presley—the man, the performer, and the music. Although Goldman seems to have done extensive research, his dislike for his subject is apparent on every page.
Hopkins, Jerry. *Elvis: A Biography*. New York: Simon and Schuster, 1971. A well-researched, solid life of Presley, good especially for his early life and his career from the years with Sun Records to his semiseclusion in the

1960's. Contains much useful information.

_____ . *Elvis: The Final Years*. New York: St. Martin's Press, 1980. Takes up where Hopkins' earlier book left off, and completes the life. The work is carefully documented and free of sensationalism.

Marcus, Greil. *Mystery Train*. Rev. ed. New York: E. P. Dutton, 1982. In general, this is one of the best books yet written about rock and roll, and the section on Presley is a sharp, penetrating analysis of both the individual performer and his place in modern American music.

Miller, Jim, ed. *The Rolling Stone Illustrated History of Rock and Roll*. Rev. ed. New York: Random House, 1980. The article on Presley by Peter Guralnick is a well-balanced and informative survey of the performer's career and influence and provides an excellent, short biography.

Michael Witkoski

JOSEPH PULITZER

Born: April 10, 1847; Mako, Hungary
Died: October 29, 1911; Charleston, South Carolina
Area of Achievement: Journalism
Contribution: Combining a strong social conscience with a superb grasp of journalistic techniques, Pulitzer created with his *New York World* the prototype of the modern newspaper.

Early Life

Joseph Pulitzer was born April 10, 1847, in Mako, Hungary. His mother, née Louise Berger, was Austro-German and Catholic; his father, Philip Pulitzer, was Magyar-Jewish, a grain dealer affluent enough to retire by 1853, whereupon the family moved to Budapest. Pulitzer and his younger brother and sister (another brother died early) were educated by private tutors; he became fluent in German and French as well as his native Hungarian.

By the age of seventeen, Pulitzer was ready to make his own way. Brilliant, independent, and intensely ambitious, he first sought fame in the military. Having been rejected for enlistment by several European armies—his eyesight was very poor—he was approached by Union army recruiting agents, who were considerably less selective. Thus it was that Pulitzer came to the United States and, in September, 1864, enlisted in the Lincoln Cavalry. His military career was short, undistinguished, and unhappy; discharged in July, 1865, with very little money and no immediate prospects, he settled in St. Louis, Missouri, where there was a large German community.

Photographs of the beardless, bespectacled young Pulitzer show a profile seemingly tailor-made for the caricaturist: a prominent, beaky nose and an up-pointed, witchlike chin. At six feet two and a half inches, he was a tall man for his time, slender and ungainly. When he arrived in St. Louis, he spoke only the most rudimentary English. Nevertheless, his exceptional abilities and his capacity for hard work were soon noticed, and, after a series of subsistence jobs, he was hired as a reporter for the *Westliche Post*, an influential German-language paper with a strong reform bent. This association provided Pulitzer's entrée into politics, and he was elected to the Missouri state legislature in 1869. His financial acumen soon became evident as well, and by his mid-twenties he was able to enjoy a long vacation in Europe.

By the time of his marriage, in June, 1878 (his bride, the beautiful Kate Davis, was a distant cousin of the former president of the Confederacy) Pulitzer had achieved the kind of success that most immigrants could only dream of, but the direction which his life would take was not yet clear. Maintaining a desultory law practice, he continued to take an active interest in politics, but, impatient, imperious, he was ill suited to the demands of office. Later in 1878, however, he made what proved to be a decisive choice of vocation.

Life's Work

It was in December of 1878 that Pulitzer, acting through an intermediary, purchased at auction in St. Louis the bankrupt *Evening Dispatch*. The paper's sixteen-year history had been marked by failure, but it did possess a Western Associated Press franchise—a consideration which prompted the publisher of a recently established rival paper, the *Post*, to propose a merger exactly as Pulitzer had planned. For the first issue of the *Post and Dispatch* (soon to become simply the *Post-Dispatch*), Pulitzer wrote an editorial that ringingly asserted the paper's independence from special interests and its dedication to reform:

> The POST and DISPATCH will serve no party but the people; will be no organ of "Republicanisn," but the organ of truth; will follow no caucases [*sic*] but its own convictions; will not support the "Administration," but criticise it; will oppose all frauds and shams wherever and whatever they are; will advocate principles and ideas rather than prejudices and partisanship.

Although Pulitzer's great achievements are associated with New York, he laid the foundation for those achievements in St. Louis in the years from 1878 to 1883 with the *Post-Dispatch*. As publisher and editor, he was involved in every phasc of the paper's operation. He was an editor of genius, as his memos to his staff attest: Even today, his notes could serve as a course in newspaper journalism. Always a shrewd judge of talent, he hired the gifted editor of the *Baltimore Gazette*, John A. Cockerill, to serve as managing editor of the *Post-Dispatch*; Cockerill later followed him to New York. Indeed, Pulitzer's ability to find good employees and treat them well played an integral part in his success: The average salary of the reporters for the *Post-Dispatch* was the highest of any paper in the country, and at a time when vacations were a luxury, every employee of the *Post-Dispatch* enjoyed a paid two-week vacation each summer. Pulitzer was, then, an inspiring leader and a relatively enlightened employer, but working for him was difficult: He had a pronounced dictatorial streak, which became much stronger as he grew older, and he could be ruthless in his judgments.

Having developed in St. Louis the brand of journalism that was to make him the most influential newspaperman of his time, Pulitzer was ready to move to New York—where, ironically, his brother Albert was prospering with the *Morning Journal*, which he had founded in 1882. (The arrival of another Pulitzer was not welcomed by Albert; never close, the brothers were permanently estranged thereafter.) The opportunity came in 1883, when Pulitzer bought the failing *New York World* from financier Jay Gould for $346,000; the deal was closed not long after Pulitzer's thirty-sixth birthday. Although a young man, he was in poor health: His eyesight was failing, and he suffered from a nervous disorder. (In a later age, he would probably have been diagnosed as manic depressive.) Moreover, the continuing profitability of the *Post-Dispatch* notwithstanding, in purchasing the *New York World* he had incurred an enormous debt. Such were the unpromising circumstances in which Pulitzer entered the arena of New York journalism, yet within a short time his *New York World* reigned supreme: The paper that sold fifteen thousand copies daily in 1883 sold almost fifteen million daily in 1898.

Great as was his success, Pulitzer was never fully able to savor it. In 1890, still in his early forties, he was compelled by blindness and the worsening condition of his nerves to give up firsthand supervision of the *New York World*, although he kept in close touch with his editors, firing off innumerable memos. His mood swings and other manifestations of his illness made him a difficult companion for his wife and their children (four daughters, one of whom died in infancy and another of whom, her father's favorite, died at seventeen, and three sons, one of whom, Joseph Pulitzer, Jr., became a noted newspaperman in his own right, despite a conspicuous lack of paternal confidence in his abilities). Pulitzer spent much of the time in later years traveling; near the end of his life, his preferred residence was his magnificently appointed yacht *Liberty*, where, as was his custom, newspapers, magazines, and books were read to him in great abundance and where distractions and annoyances were minimized. It was on the *Liberty* that he died, on October 29, 1911. Among the provisions in his will was the establishment of the Pulitzer Prizes, annual awards in journalism and arts and letters; also included was a one-million-dollar bequest to the soon-to-be-opened Columbia School of Journalism, which he had endowed in 1903.

Summary

In countless ways, Pulitzer caught the democratic, egalitarian spirit of America, an achievement reflected in the enormous influence of his journalistic style. The *New York World* was a pioneer in increased sports coverage, especially of boxing and baseball. People from every walk of life—tradesmen and judges, firemen and Brooklyn belles—were featured in line-drawn portraits (photojournalism did not begin until the Spanish-American War), often accompanied by brief biographical sketches. That American institution, the Sunday funnies, can also be traced to the *New York World*, where, in 1894, the first colored comic strip appeared.

Pulitzer was able to accomplish so much because, to an extraordinary degree, his own character mirrored all the contradictions that distinguished late nineteenth century America. Genuinely idealistic, Pulitzer crusaded against widespread corruption and injustice, bringing to public attention, for example, the inhuman conditions in which many immigrants were forced to live and work. Certainly this sense of conscience was one key to the *New York World*'s success. At the same time, however, Pulitzer was a master of sensationalism. Others before him had used lurid stories of crime, sex, and disaster to attract readers, but Pulitzer took this material and, with bold headlines, illustrations (diagrams of murder scenes were particularly popular), and first-rate reporting, made it both appealing and acceptable to a wide range of readers. Indeed, Pulitzer rarely challenged the essentially conservative values of his readers (values which he largely shared), whether the subject was women's rights or the plight of the unemployed.

Pulitzer's legacy is most visible in the prizes that bear his name, synonymous with excellence in journalism. Less obvious but more pervasive is his impact on the way in which Americans get the news, not only in the morning paper but also on television, where sensationalism with a social conscience has enjoyed great success.

Bibliography

Barrett, James Wyman. *Joseph Pulitzer and His "World."* New York: The Vanguard Press, 1941. An anecdotal biography by the last city editor of the *New York World*. Although the focus is on Pulitzer, the last three chapters follow the fate of the *New York World* after his death to the paper's last issue in 1931. Valuable for its insider's view but rambling and undocumented.

Juergens, George. *Joseph Pulitzer and the "New York World."* Princeton, N.J.: Princeton University Press, 1966. The best single book on Pulitzer's "new journalism." Concentrates on the crucial years from 1883 to 1885, though later developments are also noted. Juergens' approach is thematic rather than chronological; he provides a clear, objective, well-documented analysis of Pulitzer's journalistic techniques and their revolutionary impact.

King, Homer W. *Pulitzer's Prize Editor: A Biography of John A. Cockerill, 1845-1896*. Durham, N.C.: Duke University Press, 1965. A colorful account of Cockerill's career before, during, and after his tenure with Pulitzer. Perhaps exaggerates Cockerill's contributions to Pulitzer's success but offers a needed corrective to other accounts.

Rammelkamp, Julian S. *Pulitzer's "Post-Dispatch," 1878-1883*. Princeton, N.J.: Princeton University Press, 1967. Stresses the significance of Pulitzer's St. Louis years, scanted in most studies. A valuable, well-documented study, as much social history (particularly concerned with the growth of the middle-class reform movement) as journalistic history.

Seitz, Don C. *Joseph Pulitzer: His Life and Letters*. New York: Simon and Schuster, 1924. Badly dated, this intimate portrait by Pulitzer's longtime business manager nevertheless remains indispensable; all subsequent biographers have drawn on it.

Swanberg, W. A. *Pulitzer*. New York: Charles Scribner's Sons, 1967. Popular biography, marred by some irritating mannerisms, but the only full-scale life of Pulitzer since Barrett's book of 1941. Generally balanced and well-researched, drawing extensively on the Pulitzer papers at Columbia University and the Library of Congress.

Wittke, Carl. *The German-Language Press in America*. Lexington: The

University Press of Kentucky, 1957. Mentions Pulitzer only in passing but provides a detailed account of the milieu in which he made his beginning as a journalist and in which his political views were formed.

John Wilson

ISIDOR ISAAC RABI

Born: July 29, 1898; Rymanow, Austria-Hungary

Areas of Achievement: Physics and statesmanship
Contribution: Rabi developed the magnetic resonance method to measure with unprecedented accuracy the properties of atomic nuclei. After World War II, he used the international nature of science to bring peoples of the world together, himself becoming a world figure in the process.

Early Life

Isidor Isaac Rabi was born July 29, 1898, in the town of Rymanow, in Galicia, the northeasternmost province of the old Austro-Hungarian Empire. After World War I, the town of Rymanow became a part of Poland. His father, David Rabi, left Galicia soon after Rabi's birth and came to the United States. Within a matter of months, David sent for his wife, Sheindel, and his infant son.

The Rabi family settled in the Lower East Side of New York City, a Jewish ghetto. While the Rabis had little money, there was a richness to their life that came from their devotion to the traditions and practices of Orthodox Judaism. The turning point in Rabi's life came when he was only nine years old. After his family moved to Brownsville, a community in the New York borough of Brooklyn, Rabi discovered the public library, where he came upon a little book on astronomy. In the pages of this book, Rabi read about the Copernican solar system with the planets orbiting around the sun. Suddenly, he understood the seasons of the year and the phases of the moon. With equal suddenness, Rabi recognized a natural explanation for events that previously had been explained only in terms of divine causes. The focus of Rabi's life then began to change from Orthodox Judaism to science.

Rabi entered Cornell University in 1916, and three years later, he was graduated with a major in chemistry. Chemistry did not inspire him, however, and Rabi spent the three years after graduation living at home, doing little besides reading in the New York Public Library. In 1922, he returned to Cornell as a graduate student of chemistry and soon discovered that the part of chemistry he liked was called physics. He transferred to the physics department at Columbia University in 1923 and obtained his doctorate in 1926. The day after he submitted his doctoral dissertation, he married Helen Newmark.

As a graduate student, Rabi knew that the most exciting physics research was occurring in Europe, where quantum mechanics was being created. In 1927, Rabi obtained a fellowship, went to Europe, and studied with Niels Bohr, Werner Heisenberg, Wolfgang Pauli, and Otto Stern. While he was in Zurich with Pauli, he received an offer from Columbia University to join the physics faculty. He returned from Europe in 1929 and began his career as a lecturer, the lowest academic rank. Thirty-nine years later, Rabi, a university professor, retired from Columbia, the first Columbia professor to hold that prestigious rank.

Life's Work

Throughout the decade of the 1930's, Rabi was consumed by physics. In 1931, he turned the molecular beam method from the study of atoms (as he had learned it during 1928 in Stern's Hamburg laboratory) to the study of atomic nuclei. In the molecular beam method, a stream of atoms or molecules move through a highly evacuated chamber. Within this chamber, the beam passes between the poles of a magnet designed so that magnetic forces are exerted on individual atoms or molecules. With Rabi's method, the responses of atoms or molecules to these subtle magnetic forces revealed basic, and unknown, properties of the nucleus. Like a virtuoso, Rabi brought modification after modification to Stern's basic method and brought the uncertainties in the data coming from his laboratory from ten percent down to five percent and ultimately to less than one percent.

The climax of Rabi's molecular beam work was the molecular beam magnetic resonance method. In this method, atoms or molecules passed, in succession, between the poles of three magnets. The second of these magnets produced an oscillating magnetic field. For certain frequencies of this oscillating field, atoms or molecules were ejected from the beam by the third magnet and thus were not registered by the detector. As the frequencies could be measured with great accuracy, this enabled properties of the nucleus to be determined with corresponding accuracy. The new precision led to unanticipated discoveries such as the quadrupole moment of the heavy hydrogen nucleus. For this work, Rabi was awarded the Nobel Prize for Physics in 1944.

World War II brought Rabi's molecular beam research to a sudden halt. Long before the United States entered the conflict, physicists had an insider's view of events in Europe. Jewish physicists were being displaced from their academic positions in Europe, and many of them came to England and the United States. Added to the concern of American physicists was the discovery of nuclear fission by the Austrian physicists Lise Meitner and Otto Frisch. With this discovery, it became apparent that a new energy, nuclear energy, was potentially available: The question was, what were German scientists doing about it?

During the summer of 1940, a magnetron—a powerful source of microwave radiation recently invented in England—was secretly brought to America by a delegation of British physicists. They wanted to enlist the aid of American physicists in the development of microwave radar. In rapid succession, the magnetron was demonstrated, the Massachusetts Institute of Technology (MIT) Radiation Laboratory was established, and Rabi left Columbia University for the Radiation Laboratory in Cambridge.

Rabi became the head of the research division and later the associate director of the laboratory. He took it upon himself to anticipate the course of the war and to anticipate the type of radar that would be needed by the military services. By the time the United States entered the war in December of 1941, a variety of radar systems had been developed, and as the conflict proceeded, radar systems from the MIT Radiation Laboratory were being used by the Allied forces in every theater of the war.

In 1943, another wartime laboratory was established in Los Alamos, New Mexico. The director of the Los Alamos laboratory, the laboratory founded to develop the atomic bomb, was J. Robert Oppenheimer. Rabi and Oppenheimer had first met in Europe in 1929, and their friendship was based on deep mutual respect. Oppenheimer wanted Rabi as his associate director, but to Rabi, the radar project was more important to the war effort, and he retained his position at the Radiation Laboratory. Rabi, however, became one of two senior advisers to Oppenheimer (the other one was Niels Bohr) and in this capacity made important contributions to the development of the atomic bomb.

When the war ended in 1945, the world was faced with a powerful new energy, and it was a matter of great importance to establish policies to control this new power. During December of 1945, Rabi and Oppenheimer spent a long day talking in Rabi's living room. During that day, a set of ideas was formulated that in the spring of 1946 became the Acheson-Lillienthal Report. This incredible document proposed to place atomic energy in the hands of an international agency and thereby to dissociate the energy of the atom from any nation's interests. In June, 1946, these ideas were presented to the United Nations by the United States' delegate, Bernard Baruch. To Rabi's great disappointment, the Russian delegate, Andrei Gromyko, rejected this proposal. Three years later, the Russians detonated their first atomic bomb, and the arms race was under way.

The Russian achievement prompted a few influential Americans to propose a crash program to develop the hydrogen bomb. Rabi was then a member of the General Advisory Committee of the Atomic Energy Committee. This committee, chaired by Oppenheimer, was called into session to consider the question of a fusion-bomb program. The committee unanimously opposed the development of such a weapon, and Rabi and Enrico Fermi wrote a minority opinion in which they expressed their moral revulsion to a weapon that cannot be confined to any military target. Once again, Rabi was on the losing side: The United States detonated a fusion bomb in 1952; nine months later, the Russians followed suit.

Throughout the postwar years, the culture of science was for Rabi a means for bringing peoples of the world together. In 1950, as a United States delegate to the fifth General Assembly of the United Nations Educational, Scientific, and Cultural Organization (UNESCO) held in Florence, Italy, Rabi proposed that European nations unite in the formation of a scientific laboratory. Two years later, the decision was made to establish the Center for European Nuclear Research (CERN) in Geneva, Switzerland. Today CERN is one of the foremost physics laboratories in the world, and Rabi is regarded as its father.

In 1954, Rabi proposed an international conference on the peaceful uses of atomic energy. This proposal, which was inspired by a speech given by President Dwight D. Eisenhower before the United Nations, was, at Eisenhower's direction, presented to the United Nations by Secretary of State John Foster Dulles. Dag Hammarskjöld, secretary-general of the United Nations, was an enthusiastic supporter of the idea. Rabi and Hammarskjöld together promoted the idea, and in 1955, the first International Conference on the Peaceful Uses of Atomic Energy was held in Geneva. This conference was, according to Hammarskjöld, the beginning of détente.

During the mid-1950's, Rabi was the chairman of the Science Advisory Committee (SAC) of the Office of Defense Mobilization. Rabi was concerned because SAC did not have direct access to the president and, as a result, the scientific implications of various policies were not adequately understood by the president. The Russian launch of *Sputnik* in 1957 prompted Eisenhower to seek the advice of SAC. Rabi proposed six specific actions, all of which Eisenhower accepted immediately. Rabi suggested that SAC needed direct access to the president (thus, SAC became PSAC, President's Science Advisory Committee) and that the president needed a science adviser. James Killian became the first assistant to the president for science and technology. Rabi remained a member of PSAC until the committee was dissolved by the Nixon Administration.

On the evening of October 21, 1986, at the Weizmann National Dinner, Rabi, as guest of honor, shared the head table with the president of Israel and many other dignitaries. In his response to the honor bestowed upon him that evening, Rabi proposed that Israel build a laboratory to be shared, as the European nations share CERN, with nations of the Middle East. At the age of eighty-eight, Rabi was still using science to bridge national, religious, and ideological differences.

Summary

When Rabi returned from his studies in Europe in 1929, he was determined, as were others, to bring American physics out from the shadows of European physics. This determination paid dividends: By the end of the 1930's, American physics was preeminent. Rabi's influence in American physics is pervasive; his research contributions are cited by contemporary physicists. His influence, however, transcends physics. He saw clearly the significance of science in the modern world and used the international character of science in the pursuit of peace.

Bibliography
Bernstein, Jeremy. *Experiencing Science: Profiles in Discovery*. New York: E. P. Dutton, 1978. The first significant overview of Rabi's work. Originally appeared in *The New Yorker*.
Kevles, Daniel J. *The Physicists: The History of a Scientific Community in Modern America*. New York: Vintage Books, 1979. This book, inspired by Rabi, is an intriguing account of the development of American physics.
Killian, James R., Jr. *Sputnik, Scientists, and Eisenhower: A Memoir of the First Special Assistant to the President for Science and Technology*. Cambridge, Mass.: MIT Press, 1977. Killian describes the formation of the President's Science Advisory Committee (PSAC)—a committee proposed by Rabi—and its activities during his tenure as Eisenhower's science adviser.
Rabi, Isidor Isaac. *Science: The Center of Culture*. New York: World Publishing Co., 1970. Rabi's insight and wisdom are revealed in this collection of his articles and speeches.
Rigden, John S. "The Birth of the Magnetic-Resonance Method." In *Observation, Experiment, and Hypothesis in Modern Physical Science*, edited by Peter Achinstein and Owen Hannaway, 205-237. Cambridge, Mass.: MIT Press, 1985. This article traces the development of Rabi's powerful magnetic-resonance method.
_____. *Rabi: Scientist and Citizen*. New York: Basic Books, 1987. The definitive biography of Rabi traces his life and work.

John S. Rigden

A. PHILIP RANDOLPH

Born: April 15, 1889; Crescent City, Florida
Died: May 16, 1979; New York, New York
Areas of Achievement: Trade unionism and civil rights
Contribution: Having a passionate desire for economic justice and an unwavering advocacy for social and political equality among all persons, A. Philip Randolph improved significantly the status of Afro-American labor and greatly advanced the civil rights of minority people throughout the United States.

Early Life

Asa Philip Randolph was born April 15, 1889, in Crescent City, Florida. His mother, Elizabeth, was from Baldwin, Florida, and the youngest of four daughters born to James and Mary Robinson. A devoted member of the African Methodist Episcopal (AME) church, Elizabeth was an intelligent and proud woman who deeply resented bigotry and segregation. James Robinson, independent and resourceful, supported his family by running a small lumber business which supplied pine logs, crossties, pulpwood, and other materials for the railroads and papermills in northern Florida. Philip's father, James William Randolph, was born in 1864, a descendant of slaves who worked for the Virginia planter, John Randolph. James acquired a rudimentary education from Northern missionaries who came South after the Civil War. He became an accomplished tailor and AME minister, serving several poor congregations in Jefferson County, Florida. Outraged by the failure of Reconstruction to secure full racial equality for black people, the itinerant preacher militantly fought to defend his community's newly acquired political rights. James was also strongly influenced by Henry McNeal Turner, the AME bishop and Georgia legislator who sought better wages and living conditions for black workers. Elizabeth and James were married in 1885. They were to have two sons, James William, Jr. (1887), and later A. Philip. In 1891, the Randolphs moved to Jacksonville, Florida, where the family lived frugally in a modest home enriched with purpose, respect, and love.

Several influences shaped Philip's formative years. He greatly admired his brother, a brilliant student, whom Philip readily acknowledged he "loved very much." As youngsters, they often played roles championing the rights of blacks. They remained close friends until William's death in 1928. Philip also revered his father and often accompanied him on house visits to his congregation. The boy basked in the prestige and respect shown his father throughout the community. His father's moving speeches and effective sermons taught young Philip the value of having a social consciousness. Contributing to the family income, Philip worked at a number of jobs including store clerk, newsboy, errand runner, boxcar loader, and railroad section hand. He attended Cookman Institute High School in Jacksonville (later Bethune-Cookman College), where he took the classical course. A diligent student, he developed his elocution skills and did much reading both in and outside class. After graduation he decided to leave the South and go North; his move was an individual example of the great migration undertaken by thousands of other Afro-Americans at the turn of the century to improve themselves economically.

Life's Work

In 1911, Randolph arrived in New York City and found residence in the Harlem section of upper Manhattan. During the day he worked odd jobs as a porter, waiter, elevator operator, and switchboard operator. In the evenings he enrolled in courses at the City College of New York; there he became interested in literature, especially the works of William Shakespeare, and honed his oratorical talent. He gave readings of the classics to church groups, to literary clubs, and at public forums. He took courses in history, political science, and economics. College life introduced him to socialism, the cause of the Industrial Workers of the World, the ideas of William D. ("Big Bill") Haywood, Eugene V. Debs, and Elizabeth Gurley Flynn. While growing up in Jacksonville, he had read the works of Booker T. Washington and W. E. B. Du Bois, but now he discovered Marxism and other radical approaches to ameliorating the difficulties facing the laboring classes.

Tall and handsome, he was a meticulous, clean-cut dresser who paid careful attention to his grooming. As he matured into a confident yet disciplined young man, his baritone voice and sharp intellect presented a figure of considerable dignity whose presence commanded one's undivided attention. He married Lucille Campbell Green in 1915, an attractive, socially exuberant manager of a Madam C. J. Walker beauty salon. Although six years his senior, she shared his interest in socialism, the classics, the welfare of Afro-Americans, and concern for the working poor. They remained together until her death in 1963.

The seminal event that launched Randolph's career as a labor and political activist occurred when he took a job as a waiter on the Fall River Line which transported people from New York to Boston. Appalled at the cramped, squalid quarters of the employees, the long hours, and the low pay, he attempted to organize his fellow workers, whereupon he was fired by the steamboat company. Undaunted, he joined the Brotherhood of Labor Organization and helped to establish the Independent Political Council (1912).

In 1915, Randolph met Chandler Owen, a brilliant young intellectual who studied social sciences at Columbia University. They held similar political views and became great friends. It was a time of radical protest against brutal, intolerable working conditions in mills, mines, factories, and railroads across the nation. They joined the Socialist Party and believed that the only way to end black racial oppression in America was to attack the capitalistic economic system, which exploited both white and black workers by pitting them against one another, driving wages and living conditions down. Appeals to religious sentiment or humanistic ideals of fair play and equity were viewed as vacuous and pusillanimous. The majority of blacks were politically disfranchised. A successful strategy, they reasoned, must appeal to the economic self-interests of the parties involved. The solution was to forge black-white labor unity, have the laboring masses take control of the economic system from the capitalist classes, and establish a more equitable social system. Pragmatic and militant, their plan of action was to educate and organize Afro-American workers. Randolph spoke from street-corner soapboxes, rallied opponents in social clubs, and debated opponents in public forums.

With Owen, Randolph published a monthly periodical, *Messenger*, subtitled "The Only Radical Negro Magazine in America." In editorials they treated many issues: the need for solidarity among black and white workers, impotent black leadership, the Socialist critique of capitalism, and creative use of boycotts by blacks to achieve their goals. For example, one 1919 editorial succinctly put it, in part:

> Black and white workers should combine for no other reason than that for which individual workers should combine, viz., to increase their bargaining power, which will enable them to get their demands.
>
> Second, the history of the labor movement in America proves that the employing class recognize no race lines. They will exploit a white man as readily as a black man. They will exploit women as readily as men. They will even go to the extent of coining the labor, blood and suffering of children into dollars. The introduction of women and children into the factories proves that capitalists are only concerned with profits and that they will exploit any race or class in order to make profits, whether they be black or white men, black or white women or black or white children.

As a pacifist, Randolph opposed the United States' participation in World War I and was jailed for a short period of time because of his antiwar position. Randolph and Owen charged that W. E. B. Du Bois had failed as a theorist and offered no sound solutions to Afro-American problems. They counseled blacks to eschew the National Association for the Advancement of Colored People (NAACP) because it was "controlled and dominated by a group who was neither Negro nor working people." The editors claimed that capitalism was the real culprit responsible for the lynchings of more than three thousand Afro-Americans that occurred between 1890 and 1920; they advocated the use of armed resistance to end this barbaric extralegal practice. Despite having fundamental political differences with Marcus Garvey, Randolph worked for a while with him and his Universal Negro Improvement Association (UNIA). Although Randolph staunchly opposed Com-

munism, he believed that the Russian Revolution was "the greatest achievement of the twentieth century." Responding to Red-baiters who made no
distinction between his support for socialism and disapproval of Communism, he remarked:

> If approval of the right to vote, based upon service instead of race and color is
> Bolshevism, count us as Bolshevists. If our approval of the abolition of pogroms
> is Bolshevism, stamp us again with that epithet. If the demand for political and
> social equity is Bolshevism, label us once more. . . .

For several years during and after the Great War, Randolph worked to organize several trade unions, with little success. In 1925, he took up the causes
of the porters and maids on the Pullman railroad cars who had failed in their
attempts to organize. The problems confronting these largely black workers
were shocking. They labored between three hundred and four hundred hours
a month barely earning seventy-five dollars monthly in good years. These
workers had to pay for their dining-car meals, uniforms, lodging, and other
expenses while supporting families and homes. To gain better wages and
shorter hours, Randolph and less than a dozen men formed The Brotherhood of Sleeping Car Porters union, with *Messenger* as its official organization. By 1928, a majority of the maids and porters had joined the union.
Randolph was labeled a dangerous agitator, Red, atheist, and radical—an
outsider who never had worked as a Pullman porter. The American Federation of Labor (AFL) refused to support the union, and the Railroad Labor
Board would not protect it. The Interstate Commerce Commission declined
to investigate labor complaints. The Brotherhood lost its first attempt to win
concessions from the Pullman Company. While a solid core remained loyal,
membership in the union declined thereafter. During the Great Depression,
when the New Dealers sought to protect the rights of labor to bargain
collectively with their employers, porters once again began joining The
Brotherhood and by 1935 voted to have the union represent them. By 1937,
the union secured an important contract with the Pullman Company, reducing hours to 240 a month, better working conditions and much higher pay. In
less than twenty years, the union grew to become the most successful black
labor organization in the nation, and Randolph was invited in 1957 to
become a vice president of the newly merged AFL-CIO.

Randolph showed as much interest in politics as he had in labor organizing. While serving as president of the Joint Committee on National Recovery
(JCNR) in 1935, he called for a united front of all black organizations (civic,
labor, political) to abolish Jim Crow laws, attain civil rights, oppose Fascism,
and improve the economic status of Afro-Americans. "True liberation," he
maintained,

can be acquired and maintained only when the Negro people possess power; and power is the product and flower of organization—organization of the masses, the masses in the mills and mines, on the farms, in the factories, in churches, in fraternal organizations, in homes, colleges, women's clubs, student groups, trade unions, tenant's leagues, in cooperative guilds, political organizations and civil rights associations.

With the coming of World War II, Afro-Americans were still being denied fair employment opportunities, and those working were not receiving the same pay as their white counterparts for doing the same work. Randolph made a bold yet brilliant move by threatening a massive nonviolent march on Washington to protest job discrimination. As enthusiasm for the protest grew, fear of hampering the nation's war economy led President Franklin D. Roosevelt to issue Executive Order 8802, forbidding racial discrimination in employment by companies having defense contracts. A Fair Employment Practices Commission (FEPC) was established to monitor the order and investigate violations.

During the late 1940's, Randolph called for the complete desegregation of the United States armed forces. An ardent spokesman for the Committee Against Jim Crow in Military Service and Training, he warned the government that he would lead a civil disobedience campaign to refuse registration and resist conscription into a Jim Crow army. Randolph's popular support no doubt influenced President Harry S Truman to begin desegregation of the military. In 1950, Randolph, along with others, established the Leadership Conference on Civil Rights (composed of more than 157 national organizations representing blacks, Hispanics, Asians, labor, major religious denominations, women, the handicapped, and the aged) to guide President Truman's efforts to achieve racial equality. The Negro American Labor Council was founded in 1960 because Randolph, as its president (from 1960 to 1966), believed that the AFL-CIO was doing "little more than paying lip service to desegregation in unions." He was the prime mover behind the historic March on Washington for Civil Rights in 1963 involving a quarter of a million people.

Randolph retired from active political and labor work in 1968 to join for a brief period the A. Philip Randolph Institute, a labor research and information center directed by Bayard Rustin.

Summary

In numerous ways, A. Philip Randolph sought to secure economic opportunities, political power, and social justice for Afro-Americans in particular and for all exploited and oppressed people in general. If the common people, the workers, unified and organized themselves, he believed that they would have the power in a democracy. In the early years, he had insisted that all ethnic groups and genders must fight together for their common rights.

Although he continued to call for interracial solidarity throughout his life, he seemed to have lost faith that most white Americans would ever overcome their bigotry and racism. By the late 1930's, he put less emphasis on his earlier belief in a united labor party and urged the formation of a "tightly organized Negro non-partisan bloc."

With this concept, he galvanized the Afro-American community for the threatened 1941 March on Washington. His masterful tactic was the most significant achievement initiated by any Afro-American to achieve racial equality since Emancipation. Extraordinary indeed, the federal government acceded to black demands. Although President Roosevelt's Executive Order 8802 was grossly undermined and the FEPC lacked strong enforcement power, for the first time in the nation's history, Afro-Americans by themselves had successfully compelled an administration to take action to improve their socioeconomic condition. It was a momentous event that marked a turning point in black-white relations. If for no other reason, this feat alone guaranteed Randolph an indelible place in the pages of United States history.

A. Philip Randolph was the consummate black political organizer of his age. He labored unrelentingly to get individuals and groups to put aside their divisive, parochial, and often petty concerns and close ranks in the formation of a mass movement for the common good. The foremost architect of the modern Civil Rights movement, he urged boycotts in the South against Jim Crow trains, buses, schools, and businesses. "Nonviolent Good Will Direct Action" is what he labeled his movement to gain social equality decades before Martin Luther King, Jr., and others emerged on the 1960's political scene. If not the man himself, then his influence and ideas were at home at the forefront of virtually every civil rights campaign from the 1930's through the 1960's, including desegregation of public accommodations and schools, ending of restrictive covenants, the Montgomery bus boycott, and the 1957 March on Washington. Randolph is to be credited for his role in passage of the 1957, 1960, and 1964 civil rights acts and the voting rights bill of 1965 as well. As one award stated: "No individual did more to help the poor, the dispossessed and the working class in the United States and around the world than A. Philip Randolph."

Bibliography

Anderson, Jervis. *A. Philip Randolph: A Biographical Portrait*. New York: Harcourt Brace Jovanovich, 1973. This work is the most complete treatment of the life and work of Randolph. Although a sympathetic account, a wide variety of sources, particularly useful interviews with Randolph and others, were used. A strength of this biography is the author's conscientious effort to provide the historical background at each phase of Randolph's long and illustrious career.

Foner, Philip S., and Ronald L. Lewis, eds. *The Black Worker: A Documen-*

tary History from Colonial Times to the Present. Vol. 6, *The Era of Post-War Prosperity and the Great Depression, 1920-1936*, and Vol. 7, *The Black Worker from the Founding of the CIO to the AFL-CIO Merger, 1936-1955*. Philadelphia: Temple University Press, 1983. These works contain an invaluable collection of primary documents on a wide range of labor issues, not only those involving Randolph. The documents give an indispensable account of the difficulties and aspirations of black trade unionism.

Garfinkel, Herbert. *When Negroes March: The March on Washington Movement in the Organizational Politics for FEPC*. New York: Atheneum Publishers, 1959, 1969. This is the first major treatment of the proposed March on Washington in 1941, initiated by Randolph. It is a well-reasoned, thoroughly documented examination of the central event in Randolph's career and should be read by all scholars of the period.

Harris, William H. *Keeping the Faith: A. Philip Randolph, Milton P. Webster, and The Brotherhood of Sleeping Car Porters, 1925-37*. Urbana: University of Illinois Press, 1977. Harris' study of the origins of The Brotherhood of Sleeping Car Porters is the best scholarly account of the creation and development of the union. The author's thorough research and thoughtful analysis of the problems, mistakes, and successes of this organization tell much about black trade unionism in particular and national opposition to it in general.

Marable, Manning. "A. Philip Randolph: A Political Assessment." In *From the Grassroots: Essays Toward Afro-American Liberation*. Boston: South End Press, 1980. Marable's essay is a critical analysis of Randolph, suggesting that the leader became increasingly cautious and conservative as he won modest victories for labor and achieved limited civil rights reforms. A provocative essay, it deserves a careful reading.

Meier, August, Elliott Rudwick, and Francis L. Broderick, eds. *Black Protest Thought in the Twentieth Century*. 2d ed. Indianapolis: Bobbs-Merrill Co., 1971. Several primary documents spanning Randolph's career in labor and politics from 1919 to 1963 are made available in this collection. The volume is also useful for ideas and insights into other significant figures.

Rustin, Bayard. *Down the Line: The Collected Writings of Bayard Rustin*. Chicago: Quadrangle Books, 1971. This collection of essays has several partisan articles on various aspects of Randolph's philosophy and activities. Most of the selections on Randolph deal with his later years and offer an interesting, if not polemical, interpretation of the labor leader by his longtime colleague and friend.

Lamont H. Yeakey

WALTER RAUSCHENBUSCH

Born: October 4, 1861; Rochester, New York
Died: July 25, 1918; Rochester, New York
Areas of Achievement: Religion and social reform
Contribution: Moving away from individualism, Rauschenbusch formulated a social gospel which influenced the Church and society to accept responsibility for social and economic injustice and to institute social reform.

Early Life

Walter Rauschenbusch was born on October 4, 1861, in Rochester, New York, of German immigrant parents. His father, August Rauschenbusch, came from a Lutheran background but became an Orthodox Baptist minister. In 1865, Rauschenbusch traveled with his mother and two sisters to Germany, where his father joined them in 1868. He attended public school there, but when the family returned to New York in 1869, he attended a private school and the Free Academy, both in Rochester.

From 1870 to 1879, Rauschenbusch enjoyed summer farm work in Pennsylvania. The farmer who employed him was kind and the work pleasant. At a farm in New York, however, he experienced at first hand unfair labor practices. The farmer kept him at hard work for long hours, feeding and paying him very little. This influenced his later thoughts on economic injustice.

Healthy and bright, Rauschenbusch was a mischievous boy but eager to work and learn. His mother encouraged in him a sense of humor, courtesy, an appreciation of beauty, and a love of nature. Rauschenbusch was taught to attend Sunday school and church and to read the Bible and pray, but the family religion did not include an interest in social issues. At the age of seventeen, he underwent a spiritual awakening and had a personal experience with God.

After his conversion and baptism, he concluded work at the Free Academy. From 1879 to 1883, he studied and traveled in Europe. He completed courses at the Evangelical Gymnasium of Gütersloh and the University of Berlin. Although urged to enter other work, he continued to move toward the ministry.

When he returned home, he studied at the University of Rochester and Rochester Theological Seminary from 1883 until 1886. During this time, another spiritual experience inspired him to resolve to live entirely by the spirit and teachings of Jesus Christ.

During the summer of 1884, Rauschenbusch pastored a German Baptist Church in Louisville, Kentucky. He found a small, neglected congregation with internal disharmony and a poor reputation with outsiders. Shy and sensitive but upright and determined, he began to raise the spiritual standards of the congregation. When he left at summer's end, he had settled disputes, united members, and nearly doubled the congregation.

When he completed his seminary studies, Rauschenbusch was six feet tall with a mustache, sideburns, and hazel eyes that sparkled with humor. His close friends were of exceptional character and ability. He applied for the mission field with the American Baptist Foreign Mission Society but was turned down, apparently because of his liberal views concerning the Old Testament.

Life's Work

When the Second German Baptist Church in New York City asked Rauschenbusch to be their pastor, he accepted and began work on June 1, 1886. The church, located in a tough West Side neighborhood known as Hell's Kitchen, was filled with discouragement and need.

At the start, he planned to preach and pastor, bringing individuals to salvation and then nurturing their faith. He soon realized, however, that Christians were unsafe in the city because of oppressive social conditions. In his church families, he saw the effects of poverty, unemployment, and malnutrition. Disease and crime were widespread in the overcrowded slum tenements. As he developed a plan of social action, he became convinced that capitalism was causing the injustice. He began to see Christian socialism as a cure for economic injustice.

Also, he recognized that one's acceptance of Christ gave one inner strength but did not change the unfair political and economic system that was ruining families. His gospel needed to expand to provide for the redemption of society. In his search for a principle to encompass the salvation of individuals and society, he studied the writings of economists, political activists, socialists, and other social reformers. He also read Jesus' teachings and the Old Testament Book of Amos.

Long hours in study and church work weakened his health, and he became ill with Russian influenza in 1888. Unwilling to neglect his parishioners, he returned to work too soon and a relapse left him deaf. Although his deafness caused him suffering and loneliness, he did not allow it to ruin his friendships or his work. In three years, the church membership increased from 143 to 213 and a new building was erected.

While developing his ideas of social reform, Rauschenbusch began to write for newspapers and journals. In 1889, he helped found *For the Right*, a monthly paper for working people that discussed their questions in terms of Christian socialism.

When the last issue was published in March, 1891, Rauschenbusch sailed for Europe. While exploring social and economic conditions in Europe, he hoped to discover new ways to serve the poor. He investigated the Salvation Army but concluded that it was treating symptoms of poverty, while he wanted to eliminate the cause.

While in Germany, Rauschenbusch formulated his idea of the Kingdom of God, the organization of society in obedience to God's will. The individual is converted and receives the power and responsibility to participate in the redemption of society. Worldwide missions would extend the Kingdom to every institution and group, and society would move progressively toward unity. God's will—justice and righteousness—would be done on earth as in Heaven. He returned home in 1891 and formed the Brotherhood of the Kingdom, whose members were committed to obeying the ethics of Jesus and spreading the spirit of Christ throughout the political, industrial, social, and scientific life of society.

At a conference of German Baptists, Rauschenbusch met Pauline Rother, a Milwaukee schoolteacher, and married her on April 12, 1893. It was a happy marriage, and Pauline became an active partner in his ministry at the New York church. Intelligent and well educated, she shared his views on Christianity and social reform. Her ability to communicate with her husband enabled her to help him in conversations and meetings. The couple had five children, and Rauschenbusch was devoted to his family.

As Rauschenbusch continued his difficult but successful work with the church in New York, he was becoming well-known as an activist and as a speaker on social reform. He also participated in the Baptist Congress, a liberal forum for Baptist leaders.

In 1897, Rauschenbusch left the pastorate to teach in the German Department of Rochester Theological Seminary. He taught German Americans to pastor the German Baptist churches, but under him many students became too liberal for the churches. Five years later, he became a professor of church history and continued teaching there until his death in 1918.

In 1907, Rauschenbusch gave *Christianity and the Social Crisis* (1907) to a publisher and sailed for Europe. When he returned, he was famous, in great demand for sermons and lectures. His book explored the biblical history of social ethics, described the need for reform, and urged Christians to promote social justice.

Personal prayer was the source of Rauschenbusch's vitality, and that part of his spiritual life is revealed in his book, *For God and the People: Prayers of the Social Awakening* (1910). It includes a collection of prayers written for various situations and an essay on the Lord's Prayer. *Christianizing the Social Order* (1912) gives a detailed and systematic explanation of his views on social problems and their relationship to Christianity. *A Theology for the Social Gospel* (1917) was written to provide a theological and intellectual basis for the social gospel. Not a substitute for the individual gospel, the social gospel expands it to include the good news of redemption for society.

The world was at war when Rauschenbusch finished his last book, and he knew that there could be no immediate regeneration of society. Seriously ill and saddened by the war, he died on July 25, 1918.

Summary

Working across denominational lines, Walter Rauschenbusch influenced and changed the thinking of American Protestantism. He moved Christianity away from individualism and into the area of social consciousness. Churches could no longer ignore the poverty and injustice around them but were made aware of their responsibility to change oppressive social and economic conditions. His theory of social ministry became the basis for the social creeds adopted by major Protestant denominations.

Rauschenbusch and his writings were instrumental in the formation of the Federal Council of the Churches of Christ in America. The organization has given leadership to the Christian movement and worked for unity, social justice, and international goodwill. The Federal Council was the forerunner of the National Council of Churches.

The direction of the work of the Young Men's Christian Association and the Young Women's Christian Association was also influenced by Rauschenbusch's teachings. He provided religious justification for their outreach to humanity and encouraged the provision of a Christian social environment.

By speaking and writing of the oppressive conditions in the cities and fighting for reform, Rauschenbusch made the public aware of the needs of the poor. The labor movement, public park movement, and Christian socialism were all influenced by his teachings. After his first book was published, he was accepted as the chief spokesman for the American Social Gospel movement. His views on social change have become a part of American Christianity and social service.

Bibliography

Handy, Robert T., ed. *The Social Gospel in America*. New York: Oxford University Press, 1966. Biographical sketches and selected writings of three prominent leaders of the Social Gospel movement: Washington Gladden, Richard T. Ely, and Walter Rauschenbusch. Depicts the growth and development of the social gospel.

Hopkins, Charles Howard. *The Rise of the Social Gospel in American Protestantism: 1865-1915*. New Haven, Conn.: Yale University Press, 1940. The relationship between Christianity and society's moral and ethical problems is explored in this comprehensive chronicle of the Social Gospel movement. Describes how the industrial revolution, social injustice, and an interest in reform led to the theology of the social gospel.

Macfarland, Charles S. *Christian Unity in the Making*. New York: The Federal Council of the Churches of Christ in America, 1948. Traces the development of the Federal Council of the Churches of Christ in America from the first attempts to unify the denominations to the establishment of the organization in 1908 and includes its history through 1930. Details the work and purpose of the council and its progress in working with various denominations and interdenominational groups.

Mowry, George E. *The Era of Theodore Roosevelt: 1900-1912*. New York: Harper and Brothers, 1958. Only briefly covering the Social Gospel movement, Mowry gives insight into the social, political, and economic problems of the early 1900's and why reform was needed. Explores conservatism, liberalism, Progressivism, and socialism.

Rauschenbusch, Walter. *Christianity and the Social Crisis*. New York: Macmillan, 1907. First of a series of major works which contributed to a social awakening and the humanization of theology in America. Examines the social ethics of the Old Testament and Jesus' teachings. Describes the need for reform and offers suggestions for change.

_____. *Christianizing the Social Order*. New York: Macmillan, 1912. Most complete and systematic explanation of Rauschenbusch's position. Specifically discusses social problems and changes needed in religion and the economic system to resolve them.

_____. *A Rauschenbusch Reader*. Edited by Benson Y. Landis. New York: Harper and Brothers, 1957. Compilation of selected Rauschenbusch writings, abridged but including main points. Preceding each chapter, Landis remarks on then-prevailing issues and describes the chapter selection.

Sharpe, Dores Robinson. *Walter Rauschenbusch*. New York: Macmillan, 1942. Comprehensive biography by his secretary and longtime friend. Sharpe portrays Rauschenbusch as a scholar, a loving husband and father, a pastor who cared deeply for his struggling parishioners, and a creative thinker who penned the theology of a social gospel. Summarizes and comments on Rauschenbusch's most important writings.

White, Ronald C., and C. Howard Hopkins. *The Social Gospel*. Philadelphia: Temple University Press, 1976. Restatement of the social gospel and expansion of its definition and history, including criticisms, personalities, and lasting effects. Examines the influence of the Social Gospel movement on issues such as human rights, social injustice, ecumenism, and social action.

Elaine Mathiasen

RONALD REAGAN

Born: February 6, 1911; Tampico, Illinois

Area of Achievement: Acting and politics

Contribution: After a succession of failed presidencies over two decades, Reagan stemmed the general feeling of instability that had begun to surround the office. Almost by sheer personality and by effortlessly exuding an enormous self-confidence, Reagan reversed many of the negative images of the presidency.

Early Life

Ronald Wilson Reagan was born February 6, 1911, in Tampico, Illinois. He was the younger of two sons; his brother John Neil Reagan was born on September 3, 1909. His father, John Edward Reagan, was born July 13, 1883, in Fulton, Illinois; his father's parents were born in County Cork, Ireland. His mother, Nelle Clyde Wilson Reagan, of English-Scottish ancestry, was born July 24, 1885, in Fulton, Illinois. When Reagan was ten years old, his family settled in Dixon, Illinois, after living in several other rural Illinois towns. Reagan's father was a shoe salesman who was troubled by alcoholism and had difficulty holding a job. His mother loved the theater, and it was in Dixon, while attending high school, that Reagan first participated in acting. In 1928, he was graduated from high school, where he played basketball and football and was on the track team; he was also president of the student body. For seven summers during his high school and college years, he worked as a lifeguard at Lowell Park near Dixon.

Reagan won a scholarship which paid half of his living expenses, tuition, and fees at Eureka College, where he majored in sociology and economics. At Eureka, he participated in student politics, athletics, and theater, playing the lead in several college productions and winning honorable mention in a drama competition sponsored by Northwestern University. He won varsity letters in football, swimming, and track, and, as in high school, was elected president of the student body. After receiving a B.A. degree on June 7, 1932, he was hired as a sports announcer for station WOC in Davenport, Iowa. WOC was a five-thousand-watt station which shared its wavelength with WHO in Des Moines; both stations became part of the NBC network within a year after Reagan's initial employment. By 1937, his coverage of major league baseball, Big Ten Conference football, and other sports events had earned for him a national reputation as a sportscaster. While covering the Chicago Cubs' training camp at Catalina Island, he was introduced to a Los Angeles motion picture agent who succeeded in getting him a screen test at the Warner Bros. studio. In 1937, he signed a two-hundred-dollar-per-week, seven-year contract with Warner Bros.

Life's Work

Reagan's first film, the 1937 production *Love Is on the Air*, was well received, with Reagan cast as a radio commentator. He played in more than twenty B pictures before his performance as George Gipp, the famous Notre Dame football star, in *Knute Rockne, All American* (1940) established his reputation as a serious actor. In 1940-1941, he was chosen one of the "Stars of Tomorrow" in an exhibitor's poll. Reagan's most memorable film role was probably that of Drake McHugh, the victim of a sadistic surgeon, in *King's Row* in 1942. This was an excellent film directed by Sam Wood, and Reagan's performance was generally described as excellent by reviewers. In all, Reagan, generally regarded as a competent but not outstanding actor, made fifty-five feature-length films, mostly for Warner Bros., between 1937 and 1964. Reagan left Warner Bros. in the 1950's and free-lanced among several studios for a few years; his career was to be rescued by television.

On April 14, 1942, Reagan had entered the United States Army as a second lieutenant of cavalry in reserve; poor eyesight disqualified him for combat duty. Until his discharge as a captain on December 9, 1945, he made training films for the army in California. It was after his three-year stint in the army that Reagan began to give serious attention to the politics of the film industry. He took fewer roles as an actor after he was elected as president of the Screen Actors Guild (SAG) in 1947. SAG was one of the major labor unions in the industry; Reagan was elected to six one-year terms as president, in which capacity he successfully negotiated several significant labor contracts. In October, 1947, he appeared before the House Committee on Un-American Activities (HUAC, as it became popularly known) as a friendly witness in its investigation of Communist influence in the film industry. He came to view HUAC and its chairman, Congressman J. Parnell Thomas, and their questionable tactics, however, with enough wariness that he did not name names of suspected Communists.

Reagan started his political life as a liberal Democrat who ardently supported Franklin D. Roosevelt. In the 1940's, however, his political outlook became much more conservative. His movement to the right of center politically came during his experience from 1954 to 1962 when he was employed by the General Electric Company, as host, program supervisor, and occasional actor on the weekly television show *General Electric Theater*. Between television appearances, Reagan traveled throughout the country for General Electric's personnel relations division. He spoke at the company's 135 plants and addressed thousands of its workers. In these speeches he often repeated the themes of the American need for free enterprise while warning against the evils of big government. In 1962, Reagan became the host of the weekly television program *Death Valley Days*; he remained with that show until he entered the race for governor of California in 1965.

Reagan switched to the Republican Party in 1962, although he had campaigned as a Democrat for Dwight Eisenhower in 1952 and 1956, and again for Richard Nixon in 1960. He had supported Harry S Truman in 1948. In October, 1964, Reagan's prerecorded speech on behalf of Barry Goldwater, "A Time for Choosing," was well received by viewers and resulted in a huge surge in campaign contributions. Reagan's friendly, low-key delivery suggested a reassuring, plain patriotism that became a hallmark of his appeal to voters in the future.

In November, 1966, Reagan defeated incumbent Democratic Governor Edward G. "Pat" Brown by more than a million votes. Reagan stumped the state with his basic speech, essentially unchanged from his days with General Electric. He called on voters to bring "common sense" back to government. He was reelected four years later when he defeated Democratic State Assembly Speaker Jesse Unruh by more than a half-million votes.

As governor, Reagan mastered the art of compromise with state legislators and was more restrained and pragmatic than his conservative rhetoric suggested. He took a hard line toward dissident students in the state's educational system, particularly at the University of California in Berkeley. He also reduced expenditures in a number of areas, including social services and education, in order to fulfill his campaign promise to reduce the size of government. These cuts, along with a prosperous state economy, resulted in substantial surpluses in the state government's revenues. In 1973, he was able to begin generous programs of income tax rebates and credits as well as significant property tax relief. A major tax law was passed during his tenure as governor which corrected a regressive state revenue system. A major achievement of Reagan's second term was the passage of the California Welfare Reform Act of 1971. This law reduced the numbers of people on the welfare rolls while increasing payments to those in need, notably those recipients of Aid for Families with Dependent Children. His successes as a governor led many political observers to regard him as a leading contender for the GOP presidential nomination in 1968.

Reagan's first run for the presidency, however, was too tentative to stop Richard M. Nixon in 1968, and he accordingly requested that the convention make Nixon's nomination unanimous. He next campaigned for the presidency against Gerald R. Ford, beginning with the New Hampshire primary in February, 1976. Reagan narrowly lost the nomination to Ford at the Republican Convention in Kansas City, Missouri; the delegate vote was 1,187 for Ford to Reagan's 1,070. Nevertheless, Reagan had laid the groundwork for 1980 by his strong showing, especially with voters in the South, and in July of that year he arrived unopposed at the Republican National Convention. In his acceptance speech, Reagan pledged to support a conservative platform which called for voluntary prayer in public schools, tuition credits for private school tuition, and strong opposition to school busing, abortion, and the Equal Rights Amendment. Reagan overcame questions about his age with a vigorous campaign against incumbent Jimmy Carter, and his disarming and engaging performance in televised debates helped him to defeat Carter at the polls on November 4, 1980. His margin in the popular vote was substantial, and he received 489 votes to Carter's 49 in the electoral college.

Ronald Wilson Reagan was inaugurated as the fortieth president of the United States at 11:57 A.M. on Tuesday, January 20, 1981, with Chief Justice Warren Burger administering the oath of office. For the first time, the ceremony was held at the West Front of the Capitol, in a symbolic allusion to Reagan's Western roots. The president gave a twenty-minute address calling for "an era of national renewal." Minutes afterward, he fulfilled a campaign promise by placing a freeze on government hiring. As the president concluded his address, at 12:33 P.M., the Iranian government released the American hostages whom they had held for 444 days. The news added to the festive spirit of the occasion.

Reagan is six feet, one inch tall and weighs 185 pounds, with light-brown hair and blue eyes. He has worn contact lenses for many years, is a nonsmoker, and drinks only on occasion. He retreats often to his ranch, Rancho del Cielo, near Santa Barbara, California. He enjoys horseback riding, chopping wood, and watching television and privately screened motion pictures.

Reagan was married for the first time on January 24, 1940, to actress Jane Wyman, whom he had met while they were both appearing in films for Warner Bros. From that marriage, which ended on July 19, 1949, they had a daughter, Maureen Elizabeth, and an adopted son, Michael Edward. On March 4, 1952, Reagan married actress Nancy Davis, the daughter of Dr. Loyal Davis, a prominent Chicago neurosurgeon. They had two children, Patrician Ann and Ronald Prescott. Reagan was the first president to have been divorced.

Reagan was shot in the chest as he left the Washington Hilton Hotel at about 2:30 P.M. on March 30, 1981, after addressing a group of union officials. His assailant, John Hinckley, Jr., was overpowered and arrested at the scene of the crime. The president was rushed to nearby George Washington University hospital, where he later was operated on to remove a bullet from his left lung. On April 11, 1981, after a remarkably quick recovery, he returned to the White House.

During his first term, Reagan concentrated on a strategy of cutting taxes for economic growth stimulation, holding back increases in government spending, and an expensive buildup of American defenses throughout the world. By 1984, inflation was under control, interest rates moved down, though not low enough, employment was up significantly, and generally the economy was upbeat. Difficult problems remained, however, such as the huge size of the federal deficit, a somewhat myopic view of government's role in domestic matters, and a Supreme Court which was perhaps too conservative in such a complex, modern world. Solutions for the plight of minorities and the American farmer remained to be found. Nevertheless, the Reagan presidency set standards against which present and future programs will be judged.

Summary

Ronald Reagan has fashioned two careers in his long years in the public eye. He has held only two public offices, first as governor of the largest state in the union, then as President of the United States; he began his second career at the top. His years in the governor's mansion in Sacramento co-incided with an era of national protest, foreign war, and social change; his years in the White House have been marked by economic recession and recovery, problems of unemployment, complicated foreign affairs, and ex-panding American military buildup.

Yet Ronald Reagan was well-known to the public before he undertook a career in public service in the 1960's. His first career was in film and televi-sion, and most voting-age Americans initially encountered him in the dark-ened film theater or at home on television. It was during the Hollywood years that Reagan's vision of American was formed. He learned more in the film world than simply acting: He acquired an easy way with an audience, and also experienced the competition and studio politics that led him into the larger arenas of the New Deal, SAG, and HUAC—all of which constituted the apprenticeship for his second career.

Reagan's optimistic attitude appealed to voters, and his conservatism pro-duced a number of programs that have changed American government in fundamental ways. By June, 1986, public approval of President Reagan's per-formance was higher than ever before, according to a Gallup Poll. The poll also found that Reagan was more popular than any previous President in the second year of his second term since World War II. A crest of public support in 1981, when fifty-eight percent of Americans approved of his performance, had tapered off in 1982 and 1983 to forty-four percent, rising again in 1984 to fifty-six percent approval and sixty-one percent in 1985. Despite the Iranian arms crisis which marred the later half of his second term, few presidents in the twentieth century have demonstrated such staying power in the polls, including Dwight Eisenhower and Franklin D. Roosevelt. Indeed, perhaps Reagan's greatest achievement is to have restored the office of President of the United States to a position of power and prestige.

Bibliography
Adler, Bill. *Ronnie and Nancy: A Very Special Love Story*. New York: Crown Publishers, 1985. The most interesting part of this book follows Reagan's career from Hollywood actor and political activist to television personality and General Electric spokesman and on to governor of California and

president. There are fascinating glimpses into the inside workings of
campaigning and, to a lesser extent, life in the White House. There is also
a frank discussion of the most successful public marriage in recent American history.

Cannon, Lou. *Reagan*. New York: G. P. Putnam's Sons, 1982. This substantial and highly critical biography is the work of a veteran reporter and
White House correspondent for *The Washington Post*. Although dated—
writing his conclusion midway through his subject's first term, Cannon
confidently assesses him as a one-term president—it provides a perspective on Reagan to be considered with other, more positive viewpoints.
Illustrated and well documented, with an extensive bibliography.

Evans, Rowland, and Robert Novak. *The Reagan Revolution*. New York:
E. P. Dutton, 1981. An informed analysis of the Reagan administration,
which the authors portray as "revolutionary"; they favorably compare
Reagan's first one hundred days in office to that celebrated span in Franklin D. Roosevelt's first term. In seeking the presidency, the authors suggest, Reagan hoped to restore the United States to world leadership, to
halt the pervasive growth of government, and to revive free enterprise.

Gelb, Leslie H. "The Mind of the President." *The New York Times Magazine*
October 6, 1985, scc. 6: 20-24, 28-32, 103, 112-113. The author concludes
that Reagan is unique in the history of American presidents because he
alone possesses the mind of both an ideologue and a politician. Reagan
"has all the moral force and power that swell from absolute conviction."
His success stems from the fact that he is a "natural horsetrader" who has
mastered the art of political compromise in order to achieve his own political ends.

Greenstein, Fred. I., ed. *The Reagan Presidency: An Early Assessment*. Baltimore: Johns Hopkins University Press, 1983. A collection of scholarly essays that came out of a November, 1982, conference at Princeton University on the first two years of the Reagan presidency. The authors attempt
to judge Reagan's performance in four major policy areas—fiscal, foreign,
defense, and domestic. They examine Reagan's ideological objectives and
the ways in which they have been translated into public policy.

Hannaford, Peter. *The Reagans: A Political Portrait*. New York: Coward,
McCann and Geoghegan, 1983. Written by a former aide, this book provides many details about Reagan's political life, including a thorough treatment of his days as Governor of California. The author reveals the intense
struggle between Reagan's 1980 campaign manager John Sears and the
others in the candidate's inner circle of advisers. An interesting portrait
written from the standpoint of an "insider."

Reagan, Ronald, with Richard G. Hubler. *Where's the Rest of Me?* New
York: Dell Publishing Co., 1981. Reagan originally wrote this autobiography in 1965 long before he dreamed of becoming President of the United

States. It is a frank, witty, and moving account of his life. The title comes from his most famous line from his best movie, *King's Row*, in 1942. The book reveals much of the charm, optimism, and common sense that made him such a phenomonally successful politician.

Thomas, Tony. *The Films of Ronald Reagan*. Secaucas, N.J.: The Citadel Press, 1980. The only book-length study of Reagan's film career. Reagan took his acting seriously, in spite of what his political opponents may say. He was an able actor usually assigned to poor roles. Workmanlike in his professional duties, he was seldom criticized for being less than convincing within his acting range. The author concludes that Reagan's career was a respectable one.

Weintraub, Bernard. "The Reagan Legacy." *The New York Times Magazine*, June 22, 1986, sec. 6: 12-21. This article examines Reagan's firm belief that his impact on America will prove to be just as far-reaching as Franklin Roosevelt's. The author concludes that Reagan has reestablished the primacy of the presidency as an institution after nearly two decades of White House disarray. Weintraub quotes Senator Edward M. Kennedy, who, despite his frequent criticism of Reagan's economic, social, and civil-rights policies, acknowledges that "he has contributed a spirit of good will and grace to the Presidency and American life generally and turned the presidency into a vigorous and forceful instrument of national policy."

Arthur F. McClure

RED CLOUD
Makhpíya-Lúta

Born: 1822; Blue Creek, near North Platte, Nebraska
Died: December 10, 1909; Pine Ridge, South Dakota
Areas of Achievement: The military and political leadership
Contribution: Red Cloud led the Dakota Sioux Indians through a difficult
period, effectively resisting the onrush of American westward advance and
later helping the Sioux make the transition to reservation life under American rule.

Early Life

In 1822, Red Cloud was born into the Oglala subtribe of the Teton branch
of Dakotas (more popularly known as Sioux) on the high plains of what is
now Nebraska. His father, a headman in the Brulé subtribe, was named
Lone Man, and his mother was Walks-as-She-Thinks, a member of the
Saone subtribe. There is disagreement over the origins of the name Red
Cloud. Some sources contend that it was a family name used by his father
and grandfather, while others claim that it was coined as a description of the
way his scarlet-blanketed warriors covered the hills like a red cloud.

Very little is known about Red Cloud's early life. His father died when he
was young, and he was reared in the camp of Chief Old Smoke, a maternal
uncle. He undoubtedly spent his boyhood learning skills that were important
to Sioux men at the time, including hunting, riding, and shooting. Plains Culture Indians sometimes conducted raids against enemies, and Red Cloud
joined his first war party and took his first scalp at age sixteen. Thereafter,
he was always quick to participate in expeditions against Pawnee, Crows, or
Ute. Other Oglala frequently retold Red Cloud's colorful exploits in battle.
During a raid against the Crows, he killed the warrior guarding the ponies
and then ran off with fifty horses. This was a highly respected deed among
Plains Indians, whose horses were central to their way of life. On an expedition against the Pawnees, Red Cloud killed four of the enemy—an unusually
high number in a type of warfare in which casualties were normally low.

In the early 1840's, most Oglala bands camped around Fort Laramie on the
North Platte River, where they could obtain a variety of goods from white
traders. Red Cloud was part of a band known as the Bad Faces, or Smoke
People, under the leadership of his uncle, Old Smoke. Another band in the
area, the Koya, was led by Bull Bear, the most dominant headman among
the Oglala and commonly recognized as their chief. The two groups frequently quarreled. One day in the fall of 1841, after young men of both sides
had been drinking, a member of the Bad Faces stole a Koya woman. Bull
Bear led a force to the Bad Face camp and shot the father of the young man
who had taken the woman. The Bad Faces retaliated, and when a shot to the

leg downed Bull Bear, Red Cloud rushed in and killed him. This event led to a split among the Oglala that lasted for many years. It also elevated Red Cloud's standing among the Bad Faces, and shortly after the incident he organized and led a war party of his own against the Pawnee.

Soon after recovering from wounds suffered in that raid, Red Cloud married a young Dakota woman named Pretty Owl. Sources disagree as to whether he thereafter remained monogamous or took multiple wives, a common practice among prominent Sioux. Nor is there agreement on how many children he fathered, although five is the number most accepted by scholars. Over the next two decades, Red Cloud's reputation and status continued to grow. By the mid-1860's, he was a ruggedly handsome man of medium stature with penetrating eyes and a confident and commanding presence. He was also a band headman and a leading warrior with an increasing following among the Bad Faces. Sioux social and political structure was very decentralized; no one person had authority over the whole group. Instead, certain leaders were recognized as chiefs on the basis of ability and achievement. An important member of his band, at this time Red Cloud was not yet a chief.

Life's Work
In the several decades before the Civil War, traders began operating in Sioux territory, followed by wagon trains, telegraph construction, and more. The Sioux welcomed most of the traders and at least tolerated most of the wagon trains, even though whites disrupted hunting by killing indiscriminately and chasing many animals away from traditional hunting grounds. By the closing years of the Civil War, American traffic across the northern plains increased even further. The discovery of gold in the mountains of Montana in late 1862 enticed more whites to cross Sioux land, leading to friction and occasional clashes. The final straw came when the government sent soldiers in to build forts and protect passage along a popular route known as the Bozeman Trail that linked Montana with the Oregon Trail.

In 1865, many Sioux, including Red Cloud, took up arms in resistance. Several Dakota leaders signed a treaty in the spring of 1866 that would open the Bozeman Trail, but Red Cloud and his many followers held out, insisting on a removal of soldiers. The government tried to ignore Red Cloud for a time, but the Sioux almost completely closed down travel and obstructed efforts to construct the forts. This was the high point in Red Cloud's career as a military strategist. He led his men to a number of victories, most notably the annihilation of Captain William J. Fetterman and eighty-two soldiers in an incident known to whites as the Fetterman Massacre and to Indians as the Battle of a Hundred Slain. In November of 1868, when, after negotiations, the army withdrew the troops and abandoned the forts, Red Cloud finally ended the war.

This victory increased Red Cloud's standing among his people, although he still was not the Sioux's exclusive leader. The United States government, however, assumed that he was the head chief and dealt with him as such. In the late 1860's, there was talk of creating a reservation for the Dakota, and Red Cloud surprised everyone by announcing that he would go to Washington, D.C., and talk about the idea. Some have argued that he was motivated by a desire to gain the status among the Sioux that he already enjoyed in the view of federal officials. On the other hand, he may have realized that since many white Westerners opposed a reservation and preferred the extermination of Indians, a reservation, combined with the withdrawal of troops from all Sioux lands, an important objective to Red Cloud, might be the best compromise he could achieve. He and twenty other Sioux leaders were escorted to the nation's capital in 1870 with great ceremony. Red Cloud did not win everything he wanted, but he clearly emerged as the most famous Native American of his time. He was applauded by many Easterners who sympathized with Indians and saw Red Cloud as a symbol of justifiable response to white advance.

In 1871, Red Cloud settled on the newly created reservation, at the agency named after him. Then, only a few years later, gold was discovered in the Black Hills portion of the reserve, and the government pressured the Sioux to sell the area. When negotiations broke down, events quickly escalated into the Sioux War of 1876-1877. With one eye on the government, Red Cloud publicly opposed the armed action undertaken by some Dakota to stop the flood of prospectors onto their lands, but privately he seemed to sanction such moves. Red Cloud frequently became embroiled in political battles with federal agents on the reservation. He tried to win whatever provisions and concessions he could to ease his people's suffering, and he resisted government efforts to break down traditional cultural and political life. When many Sioux became involved in the controversial Ghost Dance in 1889-1890, Red Cloud avoided early commitment to or open encouragement of participation. Many dancers, however, believed that they indeed had his support. Red Cloud's frequent compromise position and his seeming cooperation with government agents sometimes made him suspect among some of his people, and, as a consequence, his influence steadily eroded. He died on the reservation on December 10, 1909.

Summary

Red Cloud emerged as a military and political leader at a dramatic and tragic time in the history of the Dakota Sioux Indians. Onetime powerful nomadic buffalo hunters, they were going through far-reaching changes. American westward advance constricted their land base, destroyed the buffalo upon which their economy depended, and ultimately brought about their impoverishment. Moreover, government attempts to destroy traditional Sioux ways of life on the reservation, while never completely successful, resulted in cultural shock.

For a time, Red Cloud resisted militarily as effectively as any Native American leader ever had. Then, when American domination became clear, he attempted delicately to balance the two worlds of Indian and white, hoping to win the best results possible for his people under the circumstances. This was a very difficult task, and he did not satisfy everyone. He was attacked from both sides—by whites for not doing more to encourage his followers to assimilate into the white world, and by some Sioux for being too willing to give in to government authorities.

Red Cloud stood as a symbol to many Indians (and some whites) of strong defense of homelands and culture, while to other whites he epitomized the worst in Indian treachery and savagery. For both sides, the name Red Cloud conveyed immense power and meaning. In the 1960's and 1970's, with the rise of the Red Power movement and a rejuvenation of Indian culture, he again became a symbol—this time to a generation of young Indian (and sometimes white) political activists who found inspiration in what they saw as his defiance in the face of unjust authority.

Bibliography
Cook, James H. *Fifty Years on the Old Frontier*. New Haven, Conn.: Yale University Press, 1923. Neither scholarly nor complete in its coverage of Red Cloud, it does contain some interesting, colorful, and firsthand descriptions of the Sioux leader and some of his exploits by a prominent frontiersman and close friend.
DeMallie, Raymond J., ed. *The Sixth Grandfather: Black Elk's Teachings Given to John G. Neihardt*. Lincoln: University of Nebraska Press, 1984. Does not focus on Red Cloud's life specifically but provides some direct accounts of various events in his life, especially surrounding the 1875-1876 Black Hills controversy, as told by Black Elk and other Sioux participants to poet John Neihardt.
Hyde, George E. *Red Cloud's Folk: A History of the Oglala Sioux Indians*. Norman: University of Oklahoma Press, 1937. Less complete and authoritative than the more recent book by James C. Olson, but generally well written and reliable. Focuses on the earliest period of which historians have any knowledge of Dakota history to about the end of the Sioux War of 1876-1877.
_____. *A Sioux Chronicle*. Norman: University of Oklahoma Press, 1956. A continuation of *Red Cloud's Folk* that carries the story of the Oglala to the tragedy at Wounded Knee in 1890. Contains less information about Red Cloud, since his role was diminishing by the end of the 1800's. It does offer useful material on Red Cloud's part in Sioux history after the creation of the reservation in the 1870's.
Olson, James C. *Red Cloud and the Sioux Problem*. Lincoln: University of

Nebraska Press, 1965. The best and most complete account of Red Cloud. Except for some background information on the Dakota Sioux and Red Cloud's early life, it begins with the period immediately after the Civil War and ends with the death of Red Cloud in 1909.

Robinson, Doane. *A History of the Dakota or Sioux Indians*. Aberdeen, S.D.: News Printing Co., 1904. Reprint. Minneapolis, Minn.: Ross and Haines, 1958. First printed by the South Dakota State Historical Society in 1904, this book bears the mark of scholarship in an earlier era in its attitude toward Indians. It is so factually solid and complete that it still stands as an important source for information on Red Cloud.

Utley, Robert M. *The Last Days of the Sioux Nation*. New Haven, Conn.: Yale University Press, 1963. An excellent history of the events surrounding the famous Massacre of Wounded Knee, including material about Red Cloud's participation in that event that reveals something about his role in Sioux society in 1890.

Larry W. Burt

WALTER REED

Born: September 13, 1851; Belroi, Virginia
Died: November 22, 1902; Washington, D.C.
Area of Achievement: Medicine
Contribution: Reed served as the head of the commission that designed and conducted the experiments which revealed beyond a doubt that yellow fever was transmitted by the bite of an infected mosquito, thus making control of this terrible disease possible.

Early Life

Walter Reed was born September 13, 1851, in the small town of Belroi, Virginia, near Gloucester. He was the youngest of five children. His mother, Pharaba White, was the first wife of his father, Lemuel Sutton Reed, a Methodist minister. From the very first, it seemed as if Reed were destined to live a gypsylike existence. As an adult, he would reside in a nearly endless series of army camps; as a child, his family moved frequently as his father was sent to parish after parish in the regions of southeastern Virginia and eastern North Carolina. In 1865, however, the Reeds achieved some stability with a move to Charlottesville, Virginia, and Walter was able to attend school with some regularity. In 1866, he entered the University of Virginia, receiving the M.D. degree in 1869.

Feeling the need for more clinical experience, Reed next enrolled in the medical school of Bellevue Hospital in New York City, where, at the age of nineteen, he completed study for his second M.D. degree. A year's internship followed in New York's Infant's Hospital, after which he became a physician in two other hospitals in the New York area while also serving as a sanitary inspector for the Brooklyn Board of Health.

Life's Work

Unhappy with the insecurity of life as a public physician, yet having no good prospects for private practice, Reed decided upon a career in the military and, in 1875, passed the examinations which earned for him a commission as first lieutenant in the Army Medical Corps. He married Emilie Lawrence in 1876, and shortly afterward was transferred to Fort Lowell in Arizona. His wife soon joined him, and their son Lawrence was born in 1877. A daughter, Blossom, followed in 1883. The Reed children lived much the same restless life as their father had as a youngster as they followed him in almost annual moves from army post to army post in Arizona, Nebraska, Minnesota, and Alabama.

These wanderings in the West were interrupted briefly in 1889, when Reed was appointed surgeon for army recruits in Baltimore. While stationed there, he sought and was given permission to work in The Johns Hopkins Hospital where he took courses in bacteriology and pathology. It was not, however, until 1893, when Reed returned to the East to stay, that his career finally began to flourish. In that year, he was promoted to the rank of major, assigned the position of professor of bacteriology and clinical microscopy at the recently established Army Medical School in Washington, D.C., and given the position of curator of the Army Medical Museum as well.

In 1896, Reed received his first real opportunity to demonstrate his ability as a medical investigator when he tracked down the cause of near-epidemic malaria among troops in the Washington barracks and in nearby Fort Myer, Virginia. In addition, in 1898, he chaired a committee that investigated the spread of typhoid fever in army camps. All this was excellent preparation for the task that Reed was about to undertake, and the task for which he is famous—that of resolving the riddle of yellow fever's transmission. The disease had been the scourge of the Caribbean Islands and the regions bordering on the Gulf of Mexico, as well as other port cities in North America and Brazil, for more than two centuries and had claimed hundreds of thousands of lives. Its abrupt but mysterious appearances and disappearances had long been the subject of controversy among physicians. Many believed the disease to be contagious, while many others were convinced that it was caused by local climatic conditions which created poisoned air (miasmata). By the end of the nineteenth century, much of the medical world had accepted the contagionists' view, believing that the disease was spread by fomites (items such as clothing or bedding used by a yellow fever victim).

Yet for at least a century, a few physicians had been skeptical of both explanations. Dr. John Crawford of Baltimore is sometimes credited with advancing a mosquito theory toward the end of the eighteenth century, as are Josiah Nott of Mobile, Alabama, and the French naturalist Louis Daniel Beauperthuy at about midpoint in the nineteenth century. The real credit for a mosquito theory, however, belongs to the Cuban physician Carlos Juan Finlay, who, in 1881, not only suggested that mosquitos were responsible for the transmission of yellow fever but also narrowed the focus to the *Aëdes aegypti* (then called *Stegomyia fasciata*) mosquito. Finlay's difficulty was that he could not prove his theory.

In 1896, an Italian physician, Giuseppe Sanarelli, claimed to have isolated the causative agent of yellow fever and Reed, along with army physician James Carroll, was assigned the task of investigating that claim. They soon demonstrated it to be groundless, but this was only the beginning of Reed's work on yellow fever. He volunteered for duty during the war with Spain over the question of Cuban independence, but only got to Cuba after the war was over, arriving in Havana in 1899, to investigate a typhoid outbreak, and again in 1900, as the head of a commission sent to investigate the reasons for an outbreak of yellow fever among American troops still stationed on the island. Carroll, Aristides Agramonte, and Jesse Lazear made up the remainder of the commission.

At first, they made little progress with yellow fever, for their efforts were directed toward showing that the bacillus which Sanarelli believed to cause yellow fever was actually part of the group of hog cholera bacillus. It was only after Reed had investigated an outbreak of a disease originally thought to be malaria among soldiers in Pinar del Rio, that the commission settled down to its task. The disease in question turned out to be yellow fever, and the circumstances surrounding the death of one of the soldiers who had been a prisoner and locked in a cell particularly intrigued Reed because none of his cellmates had got yellow fever, not even the one who had taken his bunk and bedding. This fact seemed to discredit the fomite theory, and Reed wrote later that at this point he began to suspect that some insect was capable of transmitting the disease.

It was also at this point that several important findings began to converge. In 1894, Sir Patrick Manson had suggested that mosquitoes might be responsible for the transmission of malaria and in 1897, Sir Ronald Ross had proved it. On the other hand, malaria was a very different disease from yellow fever. One of the reasons why Finlay had been unable to prove that the *Aëdes aegypti* mosquito was responsible for spreading yellow fever was that he (and everyone else) was unaware of the long period (generally nine to sixteen days) of incubation the yellow fever virus requires in the stomach of a mosquito before that mosquito is capable of passing the disease along to a human host. In May of 1900, Henry Rose Carter of the United States Marine Hospital Service published his observations on outbreaks of the disease in Mississippi which for the first time revealed the lengthy incubation period.

Then, in the summer of 1900, the members of the commission met with Finlay, who placed the records of his experiments at their disposal. They had decided to test Finlay's theory using human subjects for the experiments.

Reed returned to Washington, but was back in Cuba in September, upon learning that Lazear, who had permitted himself to be bitten by an infected mosquito, was dead from yellow fever and that Carroll was seriously ill with the disease. It seemed that Finlay had indeed been correct, and Reed at this juncture designed and conducted the experiments that produced twenty-two more cases in soldier volunteers, proving once and for all that the female *Aëdes aegypti* mosquito was responsible for epidemic yellow fever. Armed with this knowledge, Major W. C. Gorgas was able to free Havana of the disease quickly and then eradicate it in Panama (making construction of the canal possible), while others wiped out yellow fever in urban centers elsewhere in the hemisphere. More than three decades would elapse before another form of the disease called jungle yellow fever would be discovered in some of the monkey populations of that area and in those of Africa. With this discovery came the realization that the disease could not be completely eradicated, but only controlled.

Unfortunately, Reed did not live long enough to see the whole of this triumph of man over yellow fever. After completing his experiments in Cuba, he returned, in 1901, to Washington, a hero and the recipient of many honors. He resumed his teaching duties but died in late 1902 of complications that developed following surgery on his ruptured appendix.

Summary

In no small part because of a sensationalist American press, Reed (as Cuban physicians and historians in particular have pointed out) has probably received too much credit for the solution of the age-old mystery of yellow fever's transmission. Yet Reed himself was always modest about his role in the matter and quick to pass along that credit to Finlay, and to his associates Carroll, Lazear, and Agramonte.

In truth, however, Reed was entitled to a lion's share of the credit. Finlay had not been able to prove the truth of his mosquito hypothesis, and Reed's colleagues were narrow specialists; Carroll was a bacteriologist, Lazear, a mosquito specialist, and Agramonte, a pathologist. Thus, it was Reed who successfully drew the work of these and others together and organized the experiments that made the final definitive breakthrough.

While his early career gives no hint of this kind of ability, his activities in investigating malaria and typhoid outbreaks during the years immediately prior to his yellow fever work surely prepared him well for that work. In all these undertakings, Reed revealed a fine scientific mind, and his success in the tropical medicine field, heretofore dominated by Europeans, brought much prestige to American science and American scientific education. Thus it is fitting that the small monument over his resting place in Arlington National Cemetery bears the inscription, "He gave to man control over that dreadful scourge Yellow Fever."

Bibliography
Bean, William B. *Walter Reed: A Biography*. Charlottesville: University Press of Virginia, 1982. Despite its lack of documentation, it is clear that this study, by the leading authority on Reed, has been extensively researched, and as a full-length biography it has the virtue of providing a balanced account of Reed's life rather than concentrating excessively on his yellow fever work alone. Thus, it provides an excellent description of medicine and the military between the Civil War and the war with Spain.
_____. "Walter Reed: He Gave Man Control of That Dreadful Scourge—Yellow Fever." *Archives of Internal Medicine* 89 (1952): 171-187. A succinct depiction of Reed's accomplishments.
Carmichael, Emmett B. "Walter Reed: Army Surgeon-Bacteriologist-Epidemiologist." *Alabama Journal of Medical Science* 8 (1971): 446-457. A brief biography of Reed that focuses on his work on yellow fever and the honors that he received for that work.

Carter, Henry Rose. *Yellow Fever: An Epidemiological and Historical Study of Its Place of Origin.* Edited by Laura Armistead Carter and Wade Hampton Frost. Baltimore: Williams and Wilkins, 1931. The author, himself one of the major actors in the drama of the conquest of yellow fever, provides the most thorough examination of the history of the disease as well as an account of its ultimate surrender to science.

Chappell, Gordon S. "Surgeon at Fort Sidney: Captain Walter Reed's Experiences, 1883-1884." *Nebraska History* 54 (1973): 419-443. Focuses on Reed's year of service as the chief medical officer at Fort Sidney, a Nebraska military post. An interesting glimpse of a slice of Reed's early career.

Gilmore, Hugh R. "Malaria at Washington Barracks and Fort Myer." *Bulletin of the History of Medicine* 29 (1955): 346-351. This is a brief description of the careful epidemiological investigation of a malaria outbreak among soldiers in the Washington, D.C., area carried out by Reed in 1896.

Kelly, Howard A. *Walter Reed and Yellow Fever.* 3d rev. ed. Baltimore: Norman, Remington Co., 1923. The first scholarly and satisfactory biography of Reed despite its uncritical nature. It traces his life from birth to death, but, as the title indicates, it places most of the emphasis on the work done by Reed and his associates on yellow fever.

Truby, Albert E. *Memoir of Walter Reed: The Yellow Fever Episode.* New York: Paul B. Hoeber, 1943. This work, as the title indicates, is not biographical in nature but rather concentrates on the methods and techniques employed by Reed and his colleagues to demonstrate that the mosquito was indeed the carrier of yellow fever. In the process, the study also provides a fine background sketch of the Army Medical Corps and the conditions in Cuba with which Reed met upon his arrival.

Wood, Laura N. *Walter Reed: Doctor in Uniform.* New York: Julian Messner, 1943. A biography for young people which, although fanciful at times, particularly in the words put in the mouths of the leading characters, is nevertheless well researched and well indexed.

Kenneth F. Kiple

FREDERIC REMINGTON

Born: October 4, 1861; Canton, New York
Died: December 26, 1909; Ridgefield, Connecticut
Areas of Achievement: Art and writing
Contribution: In his drawings and bronzes, Remington recorded the Old
  West before it vanished, thus preserving it for later generations.

Early Life

Born October 4, 1861, in Canton, New York, Frederic Sackrider Remington was the only child of Clara Bascomb Sackrider and Seth Pierrepont Remington, a newspaper editor and publisher. Remington's early childhood was marked by the four-year absence of his father, who was a lieutenant colonel in the Civil War. Upon his father's return, Remington eagerly listened to his tales of the cavalry and the West; perhaps Remington's lifelong fascination with the horse can be traced to this period. At any rate, Remington grew up sketching horses, cowboys, Indians, and soldiers. His artistic ability pleased his father, whom he idolized, but did not satisfy his practical mother, who envisioned for him a career in business. School never received much of his attention; instead, his childhood revolved around fishing, swimming and other outdoor activities.

In 1878, after two years at a military academy in Massachusetts, Remington entered Yale and its newly established School of Art and Architecture. In the college weekly, *Courant*, he published his first drawing, *College Riff-Raff* (1879), a cartoon of a bruised football player. Despite his interest in art, he was soon bored by the study of classical painting and sculpture, but he discovered a new diversion, football. Tall, robust, and burly, he was a natural football player and became a forward on the varsity team. In 1880, Remington's father died, leaving him a modest inheritance. Finding himself financially independent, at least momentarily, he left Yale against his mother's wishes, after having completed less than two years. In Canton, he tried several jobs, but none was to his liking. In the summer of 1880, upon meeting Eva Adele Caten of Gloversville, New York, he fell deeply in love and asked her father for her hand, but he was refused on the grounds that his future was not promising. Remington, dejected, left to find his fortune in the West. Working as a cowboy and a scout did not make him rich, but as a result of the trip he sold a sketch, *Cow-boys of Arizona: Roused by a Scout* (1882), to *Harper's Weekly*, his first appearance in a major magazine, a milestone even if the sketch was redrawn by a staff artist.

In 1883, Remington bought a sheep ranch in Kansas. Yet the difficult and lonely work induced him to sell it in 1884. With the last of his inheritance, he invested in a saloon. Although the business was successful, his unscrupulous partners tricked him out of his share. After selling a few drawings to a Kansas City art dealer, he began seriously to consider an art career. In retrospect, he said of his interest in drawing, "I knew the wild riders and the vacant land were about to vanish forever. . . . Without knowing exactly how to do it, I began to record some facts around me and the more I looked the more the panorama unfolded." Thus, he began the task of chronicling the West before it disappeared.

Returning to New York, Remington again approached Eva's father, who relented, perhaps because Eva would have no other. After being married on October 1, 1884, he and his bride set out for Kansas City to establish their home. A steady income was not to be found, however, so after less than a year Eva returned to New York, and Remington resumed his travels through the West. At one time, he prospected for gold, at another, he rode with an army unit in search of Apaches, but always he sketched.

Realizing that New York City, with its many publishers, was the place for an aspiring illustrator, he returned in 1885 and, with Eva, set up a household in Brooklyn. The early days were difficult as he doggedly tried to sell his drawings, but the turning point came in 1886, when *Harper's Weekly* published on its cover his drawing *The Apache War: Indian Scouts on Geronimo's Trail* (1886). Soon Remington's work began to appear regularly in major magazines.

Life's Work

In the years following 1886, Remington became recognized as the foremost illustrator of his day. Over his lifetime, his drawings, numbering more than twenty-seven hundred, were published in forty-one different periodicals. His illustrations, with their Western themes, struck a responsive chord in the American public, whose curiosity had been aroused by the tales of gold and Indians, circulating out of the Wild West.

After 1886, Remington went West every summer to sketch and to collect Indian artifacts and cowboy paraphernalia. At other times, he traveled on assignment for magazines. In 1888, he covered the army campaign against the Apache. In 1890, he was in the Badlands of South Dakota, documenting the Plains Indian Wars. Traveling with the army, he experienced at first hand several brief skirmishes with the Sioux. The Wounded Knee Massacre, the last battle of the Indian Wars, took place a few miles from where he was situated.

When the Spanish-American War erupted, Remington, representing *Harper's Weekly* and William Randolph Hearst's New York *Journal*, went to Cuba. Arriving with the cavalry, he witnessed the assault of San Juan Hill. One of his paintings, *Charge of the Rough Riders of San Juan Hill* (1899), depicted Theodore Roosevelt, his friend of ten years, leading his men. Roosevelt's charge probably occurred more in Remington's imagination than in fact. Roosevelt, however, used the drawing to his advantage in creating his image as a soldier and hero that would later prove useful to his political future.

Remington illustrated not only articles but also books, the first being *Mexico Today* (1886) by Solomon Buckley Griffin. In 1890, nearly thirty, he illustrated Henry Wadsworth Longfellow's *The Song of Hiawatha* (1855), the popularity of which can be attributed partly to Remington's drawings. He illustrated books by Owen Wister, the noted writer of Western tales, and, in 1892, he did the drawings for Francis Parkman's *The Oregon Trail* (1892). In all, he illustrated more than 140 books.

Remington also wrote about the West he loved. His first signed articles, published in 1888, concerned the Sioux uprising. In 1895, he published the first of his eight books, *Pony Tracks*, a collection of his articles concerning army life. In 1902, he wrote a novel *John Ermine of the Yellowstone*, a romantic Western, which, in 1903, he adapted for the stage. The drawings for the novel posed a problem: How was he to illustrate a love story when he rarely sketched women? He solved his dilemma when he hired the well-known illustrator Charles Dana Gibson to draw the female figures.

In addition to being known as a pen-and-ink illustrator, Remington was also a popular oil painter. Beginning in 1887, his work was accepted in major exhibitions, often receiving prizes. He was an associate member of the prestigious National Academy of Design and a member of the National Institute of Arts and Letters. Remington's favorite subject for his paintings as well as for his illustrations was the Old West, a world full of cowboys, Indians, and horses. His paintings typically emphasize action; the scene might be of riders and horses wildly racing for safety, as in *A Dash for Timber* (1889), or of men besieged, as in *The Fight for the Water Hole* (probably painted 1895-1902). His paintings tell the story of the taming of the West. The fur traders, scouts, and soldiers populating his canvases conquer the West through their determination and strength while the Indians, noble but also cruel, are shown in their losing struggle.

In 1895, after watching the sculptor Frederic W. Ruckstull at work, Remington tried the new medium; the result was *The Bronco Buster*, a casting of which was later presented to Theodore Roosevelt by the Rough Riders on their return from the Spanish-American War. Over the next fourteen years, he produced twenty-five sculptures, all except one focusing on a Western theme. His bronzes have the same focus on action and the same attentiveness to details that distinguish his drawings.

Remington was a disciplined artist: He would rise at six and draw until the early afternoon; later in the evening, he would return to his studio to plan his work for the next day. He was also a highly successful artist. First known as an illustrator, he also made his mark as a writer, painter, and sculptor. On December 26, 1909, at the age of forty-eight, he died of complications from an appendectomy. His art can be found at the Remington Art Memorial, in

Ogdensburg, New York, and at the Amon Carter Museum of Western Art, in Fort Worth, Texas. The Thomas Gilcrease Institute of History and Art houses a large collection of Remington bronzes.

Summary

Through his illustrations, paintings, and bronzes, Remington created the image of the West held by most Americans. The lonely cowboy, the savage Indian, the limitless land, the noble horse, the brave soldiers who battle against overwhelming odds, and the pioneers who never question their right to settle the land are all in his paintings.

His illustrations and drawings have been valued as a documentary of the West. His rendering of the costumes of the Indian tribes, the different breeds of the horses, and the details of the soldier's dress have been praised for their authenticity. Some critics argue that Remington also romanticized the West, indicating the many buffalo skulls that litter his paintings, and others suggest that his work owes as much to his imagination as to fact, citing the historically inaccurate costumes of the Indians in *The Song of Hiawatha*. Both evaluations are correct. Remington was highly accurate in his early drawings, which were usually based on sketches done in the West, but the later paintings were often imagined reconstructions of fact and fantasy, portraying the spirit of the West rather than a particular moment. Yet whatever faults there might be found in his paintings, they do not obscure the fact that Remington had a tremendous impact on how Americans view the West. Many would agree with Owen Wister, "Remington is not merely an artist; he is a national treasure."

Bibliography

Ainsworth, Ed. *The Cowboy in Art*. New York: World Publishing Co., 1968. A history of the cowboy and the artists who painted him. Charles M. Russell and Remington are recognized as the greatest of the cowboy artists, but they are not discussed any more fully than a host of minor artists. A glorification of the cowboy. Filled with Western lore.

Baigell, Matthew. *The Western Art of Frederic* Remington. New York: Random House, 1976. Contains a short introduction to Remington's life and work followed by color plates of Remington's paintings from 1887 to 1909. Baigell is critical of Remington's portrayal of the West, suggesting that it is a romanticized version.

Ewers, John C. *Artists of the Old West*. Garden City, N.Y.: Doubleday and Co., 1973. Contains chapters devoted to the artists who popularized the West, including George Catlin, Albert Bierstadt, Frederic Remington, and Charles M. Russell. Discusses Remington's experiences during the Plains Indian War.

Jackson, Marta, ed. *The Illustrations of Frederic* Remington. New York:

Crown Publishers, 1970. A brief account of Remington's life, followed by drawings which are arranged by subject. Many of the drawings are not found in other books. Includes a brief commentary by Owen Wister on Remington's artistic contribution.

McCracken, Harold. *Frederic* Remington: *Artist of the Old West*. Philadelphia: J. B. Lippincott Co., 1947. A widely recognized biography. Contains colorful anecdotes gathered from Remington's friends and relatives. A glowing appraisal of Remington's artistic contribution. McCracken supplies a useful list of all of Remington's drawings, books, and bronzes. Included are forty-eight plates of paintings, pastels, and bronzes.

Richardson, E. P. *Painting in America: The Story of 450 Years*. New York: Thomas Y. Crowell, 1956. An authoritative study of American painting. Praises Remington as an illustrator who realistically recorded the West but criticizes the "crude and raw" color of his paintings.

Samuels, Peggy, and Harold Samuels. *Frederic* Remington. Garden City, N.Y.: Doubleday and Co., 1982. This massive but readable biography is the most thorough, most balanced study of Remington to date. While the authors hold their subject in high regard, they do not fail to acknowledge his flaws. Their account emphasizes the influence of Impressionism on his later work.

Vorpahl, Ben Merchant. *Frederic* Remington *and the West: With the Eye of the Mind*. Austin: University of Texas Press, 1978. Traces how Remington was influenced by the West and how he, in turn, shaped the public's image of the frontier. An academic study, ranging widely in literature and social history.

Wear, Bruce. *The Bronze World of Frederic* Remington. Tulsa, Okla.: Gaylord, 1966. Discusses the bronzes, how they were cast, Remington's involvement with the production, and the problem of forgeries. The text is followed by plates of the bronzes and pertinent information about each work.

Barbara Wiedemann

WALTER P. REUTHER

Born: September 1, 1907; Wheeling, West Virginia
Died: May 9, 1970; Pellston, Michigan
Areas of Achievement: Labor and social reform
Contribution: Committed to politically active unionism, Reuther helped organize the automobile workers in the 1930's and led that union in the support of a broad range of social and economic reform in post–World War II United States.

Early Life
Walter Philip Reuther was born September 1, 1907, in Wheeling, West Virginia, the son of a dissenting German Lutheran family. His father, Valentine Reuther, was active in local union activities and had become a convert to Debsian socialism, which advocated the gradual, democratic achievement of a humanitarian social order. The elder Reuther campaigned extensively for Eugene V. Debs for president, and he, himself, sought a state senate seat as a Socialist. He imbued his sons with the need for greater social and economic justice and the necessity of independent thinking, and he taught them the techniques of effective public speaking and debate. Valentine Reuther became convinced that the labor movement should be organized along industrial rather than craft lines and that workers should be encouraged to use the ballot box as well as the strike to advance their cause. Unions existed, he insisted, not only to promote the selfish interests of their members but also as instruments for the achievement of broad social equality and economic reform.

Young Reuther's own experiences tended to reinforce his father's teachings. At sixteen, he dropped out of school to work at Wheeling Steel Company. Excelling at die making, the production of exceptionally hard and precise steel forms for use as metal-shaping presses, Reuther was naturally attracted to Detroit, the center of the new automobile industry. Moving to Detroit in 1927, he worked briefly at Briggs Manufacturing Company before obtaining a job as a die maker at Ford Motor Company. During the five years he worked at Ford, Reuther earned relatively high wages, completed high school, and, along with his brother Victor, enrolled in classes at Detroit City College (later Wayne State University). At the same time, he noted the hectic, inhumane hours and work pace on the automobile assembly line and joined the small, ineffectual, left-wing Auto Workers Union. After 1930, while at Detroit City College, he and his brother organized a Social Problems Club, opposed the establishment of Reserve Officers' Training Corps on campus, and organized tours of the Depression-wracked city with its shantytowns and massive unemployment. They joined the Socialist Party and, in 1932, campaigned throughout southeastern Michigan on behalf of

Norman Thomas, the party's presidential candidate.

Laid off from his Ford job in 1932 (in part, he thought, because of his political and union activities), Reuther and his brother traveled extensively for almost three years. They bicycled through Europe, visited relatives, and established contact with the anti-Nazi underground just as Adolf Hitler was consolidating his power in Germany. In late 1933, they arrived in the Soviet Union and worked for almost two years at a massive automobile plant in Gorki. In letters to American friends as well as in interviews with Soviet newspapers, the stocky, redheaded, brash, idealistic, and self-confident Reuther spoke out on conditions inside the Soviet Union. Like many other Americans of left-wing sympathies, he praised the heroic purposefulness of the Soviet worker. Increasingly, however, he criticized the clumsy, inefficient, overly centralized state bureaucracy which slowed progress. In the fall of 1935, after further travels in the Soviet Union, China, and Japan, Walter and Victor Reuther returned to the United States.

Life's Work

Reuther threw himself into union activities upon arriving home. Despite New Deal legislation encouraging collective bargaining, labor organizing was a dangerous and uncertain undertaking in the mid-1930's. Industrialists in Detroit—a notoriously "open shop" city —opposed unions with all the resources at their command. When regular law enforcement personnel were not at their disposal, they sometimes employed violent gangs with underworld connections. They conducted extensive spying on union activities, fired organizers, and employed strikebreakers. Meanwhile, the work force was composed of a bewildering number of nationalities, speaking a variety of languages. Labor spokesmen, some influenced by Communist and Socialist ideologies, bitterly debated organizational strategies and engaged in internecine intrigue against one another. Reuther became an unpaid organizer for a small United Automobile Workers (UAW) local in early 1936. At the same time, he married May Wolf, a teachers union activist and member of the Marxist Proletarian Party. He addressed a labor rally the very evening of his marriage.

A shrewd strategist, Reuther understood the use of the dramatic in building UAW membership. Named president of a newly chartered west-side local in later 1936, he orchestrated a sit-down strike at Kelsey-Hayes, a major manufacturer of wheels and brakes for Ford Motor Company. Workers, in taking physical possession of the plant, prevented the introduction of strikebreakers and police by Kelsey-Hayes, whose owners naturally feared the destruction of company property in any possible scuffle. The successful Kelsey-Hayes confrontation was followed by the celebrated General Motors (GM) sit-down strike of 1937, in which Reuther's brothers, Victor and Roy, played principal roles. The controversial sit-down strategy, ruled illegal by the Supreme Court in 1941, proved enormously helpful in building UAW membership in GM and Chrysler factories. Reuther and other UAW officials attempted to recruit Ford workers in 1937 as well but were surrounded and physically beaten by company service detectives. Not until 1941 did Ford finally capitulate to organizing efforts. Although he had only a marginal role in the GM strike, Walter Reuther had demonstrated remarkable courage and ingenuity during the organizational successes of the late 1930's.

As a labor politician, Reuther engaged in acrimonious debate with critics, both on the Left and on the Right. In the mid-1930's, he was part of the UAW's Unity Caucus, composed of moderate nonideologues as well as Communists and Socialists. In 1937, he ran with Socialist Party backing for a seat on the Detroit Common Council but resigned from the party in 1939 and subsequently supported liberal, New Deal Democrats for public office. Although continually attacked by rivals as pro-Communist because of his stands in the mid-1930's, Reuther emerged, at the end of World War II, as the leading anti-Communist spokesman within the UAW. Gradually, he fashioned a middle position, opposing both Communism and Fascism and urging a program of government-encouraged production and abundance. During the war, he advocated a plan of rapid conversion of automobile manufacturing facilities to aircraft production but opposed a piecework incentive program proposed by union Communists. In an especially bitter strike at GM in 1945-1946, Reuther attempted to speak for inflation-conscious consumers as well as union members. He demanded a "look at the books" of GM, which he said would justify his request for an hourly pay hike without a corresponding price increase to automobile buyers.

Although the postwar GM strike failed, Reuther was able to capitalize on his imaginative leadership during the dispute. In 1946, charging that Communists as well as more orthodox labor leaders had sabotaged the strike, he won the presidency of the UAW. The subsequent year, he tightened his grip upon the union, appointed persons loyal to him to influential positions, and began to commit the UAW to a broad program of political activity. In 1947, he helped form the Americans for Democratic Action (ADA), the leading liberal anti-Communist organization of the postwar period. The ADA, heavily financed by the UAW, exercised considerable influence with the Democratic Party. It backed Harry S Truman's Fair Deal programs of government-encouraged economic growth, the creation of national health care and housing plans, an attack on racial segregation, and the repeal of the pro-business Taft-Hartley Act of 1947. Reuther and the ADA argued that the best guarantee against Communism, both domestically and internationally, was the expansion of material abundance and its more equitable distribution.

By winning major concessions for union members from the prosperous postwar automobile industry, Reuther was able to deflect internal criticism of his expansive reform activities. An exceptionally skillful negotiator, he won automatic cost-of-living adjustments in UAW contracts, improved medical and dental insurance coverage, and substantially advanced retirement and unemployment benefits. Multiyear contracts, moreover, brought a measure of stability to both the industry and the UAW work force. While his Left-liberal political positions and his strident, somewhat intolerant, style would hardly engender deep affection among most UAW members, Reuther clearly commanded their respect through his intelligence and stamina at the nego-tiating table. His personal courage, demonstrated during his recuperation from a serious wound suffered in a 1948 assassination attempt, added to his appeal among blue-collar automobile workers.

Beginning in 1952, Reuther played a major part in the merger of the Con-gress of Industrial Organizations (CIO) and the American Federation of La-bor (AFL). These two giant labor federations, the first based on industrial unionism and the second having its foundation in craft unionism, had been sometimes harsh rivals since the mid-1930's. With the deaths of the presi-dents of both organizations in 1952, serious talks about a merger became re-alistic. George Meany, a veteran labor politician, emerged as president of the AFL. Reuther overcame bitter opposition from the steelworkers union to become president of the CIO. (He also retained the presidency of the UAW.) Encouraged by progress in lessening interunion raiding, Meany and Reuther led their respective federations toward a merger in 1955. While Meany became president of the AFL-CIO, Reuther assumed the leadership of its Industrial Union Department and won Meany's promise to eliminate corrup-tion and racial discrimination in the new federation and to launch a major organizational drive.

From the beginning, the AFL-CIO proved to be a disappointment for Reuther. The much vaunted organizational blitz never took place; interunion rivalries precluded a genuine merger at the local level; and the percentage of the nonagricultural work force that was unionized began a slow decline. Reu-ther clashed openly with Meany's visceral anti-Communism, his foot-drag-ging on civil rights issues, and his reluctance to commit the AFL-CIO to a massive organizational drive. Meany, a gruff, cigar-smoking bureaucrat with a more traditional view of unionism, enjoyed the good life and the annual AFL-CIO conventions at posh resort areas. He had little in common with Reuther, an abstemious (he used neither tobacco nor alcohol) idealist who continually sought to commit the labor movement to a broad program of so-cial and economic reconstruction.

Frustrated with Meany and the AFL-CIO, Reuther enthusiastically em-braced the reform policies of the John F. Kennedy and Lyndon B. Johnson administrations. A longtime advocate of programs such as the Peace Corps, he was the most vocal and visible labor leader in support of the antipoverty and civil rights legislation of the 1960's. Because of his support for Johnson's domestic agenda, he only reluctantly expressed his reservations about American participation in the Vietnam War. By 1968, however, concerned about urban rioting, the assassinations of Robert Kennedy and Martin Luther King, and the disarray within Liberal circles, Reuther moved into open criticism of the war.

His painful break with the Administration coincided with his departure from the AFL-CIO. Disputes with Meany over the Vietnam War, civil rights, and other public issues underscored fundamental differences about unionism itself. The continued rejection by the AFL-CIO of his view that unions should transcend narrow bread-and-butter issues to become instruments of broad social reform proved increasingly intolerable to him. The unwillingness of the federation to support Cesar Chavez's United Farm Workers, in which Reuther took a deep personal interest, represented only the most recent example. In 1968, Reuther took the UAW out of the AFL-CIO and entered a loose partnership with the Teamsters called the Alliance for Labor Action (ALA). In the ALA, the Teamsters agreed to respect Chavez's organizational efforts and defer to Reuther on most issues of public policy. While still groping for ways to reinstill idealism and meaning into the labor movement, Reuther and his wife were killed in an airplane crash on May 9, 1970.

Summary

Reuther's death occurred at a time of deep division and disillusionment in the United States. Most labor leaders spurned his call to greater social activism. UAW members, mostly of post–Depression era age, cared far more about upward personal mobility than the heroic organizing struggles of the 1930's that had helped define Reuther. The American automobile industry, which had sustained high wages for the union, was plagued with antiquated productive facilities and faced increased foreign competition and a coming fuel shortage. Even Reuther's Liberal political allies, torn by war and domestic unrest, were entering a period of difficult redefinition.

While Reuther's active career spanned thirty-five years, his consciousness—thanks largely to his father—touched most of the twentieth century. He remained true to his father's Debsian Socialist vision even when circumstances and practicality mandated that he sever official ties with avowedly Socialist organizations. His goals of a purposeful, just, and humanitarian industrial order clearly date back to Valentine Reuther's teachings. His dramatic, confrontational style, molded in the contentious 1930's, remained his trademark even in the post–World War II period, when a lack of energy and idealism joined with rigid anti-Communism to produce the conservative "business unionism" of George Meany. More than any other union leader of his time, Reuther struggled to transcend narrow conceptions of legitimate union activity and to commit labor organizations to a broad, advanced program of social and economic justice.

Bibliography

Barnard, John. *Walter Reuther and the Rise of the Auto Workers*. Boston: Little, Brown and Co., 1983. An excellent introduction to Reuther by a respected academic historian. Especially good in defining Reuther's relationship with Debsian socialism. Barnard benefited from the extensive Archives of Labor History and Urban Affairs at Wayne State University.

Bernstein, Irving. *Turbulent Years: A History of the American Worker, 1933-1941*. Boston: Houghton Mifflin Co., 1969. The classic study of labor organizing efforts in the 1930's, including the passage of the Wagner Act, the rupture between the AFL and the CIO, and the growth of the UAW.

Cormier, Frank, and William J. Eaton. *Reuther*. Englewood Cliffs, N.J.: Prentice-Hall, 1970. A readable and sympathetic biography based heavily on interviews of Reuther and those close to him.

Dayton, Eldorous L. *Walter Reuther: The Autocrat of the Bargaining Table*. New York: Devin Adair Co., 1958. A hostile study by a right-wing writer, most useful as a summary of conservative anxieties about Reuther.

Goulden, Joseph C. *Meany: A Biography of the Unchallenged Strong Man of American Labor*. New York: Atheneum Publishers, 1972. Based heavily on interviews, this is the single best volume on Reuther's rival in the AFL-CIO. Goulden portrays Meany as a gifted labor leader, by background and temperament very different from the UAW leader.

Marquart, Frank. *An Auto Worker's Journal: The UAW from Crusade to One-Party Union*. University Park: Pennsylvania State University Press, 1975. A slashing indictment by an old-line UAW Socialist of Reuther's overweening control of the union. Marquart argues that Reuther rose to power within the union by Red-baiting his enemies.

Reuther, Victor G. *The Brothers Reuther and the Story of the UAW*. Boston: Houghton Mifflin Co., 1976. An indispensable defense. Victor Reuther emphasizes the impact of their father and the closeness with which the brothers operated. To the left of Walter on most issues, Victor Reuther was highly critical of Meany and cautioned against the merger in 1955.

Salvatore, Nick. *Eugene V. Debs: Citizen and Socialist*. Urbana: University of Illinois Press, 1982. A fascinating biography of Debs that provides excellent insights into early twentieth century American socialism.

Zieger, Robert H. *American Workers, American Unions, 1920-1985*. Baltimore: Johns Hopkins University Press, 1986. A first-rate historical overview of organized labor in the United States since World War I.

William Howard Moore

HENRY HOBSON RICHARDSON

Born: September 29, 1838; Priestley plantation, St. James Parish, Louisiana
Died: April 27, 1886; Brookline, Massachusetts
Area of Achievement: Architecture
Contribution: By absorbing early medieval stylistic ideas, suffusing them with his own vision, and adapting them to the needs of his own time, Richardson earned his reputation as one of America's greatest architects.

Early Life

Henry Hobson Richardson had a distinguished ancestor, one of the founders of modern chemistry, Joseph Priestley, whose granddaughter Caroline married Henry Dickenson Richardson, a partner in a Louisiana cotton business, and gave birth to the future architect in 1838. The boy attended school in New Orleans and was destined for West Point, but the academy rejected him for stuttering. Having shown early promise in drawing and in mathematics, young Richardson entered Harvard College, with the goal of becoming a civil engineer. His academic work was unspectacular; his friendships, however, were constructive ones. He numbered among his friends Henry Adams, the future historian, and several young men who later helped him obtain commissions.

Richardson's Class of 1859 photograph shows wide-set eyes in a rather long, thin face with dark, wavy hair. Although he looked serious, his classmates found him buoyant and personable. Another photograph taken in Paris, where he decided to study architecture at the École des Beaux Arts upon his graduation, confirms contemporary accounts of him as tall, slim, and clean-shaven.

Returning to the United States at around the end of the Civil War, Richardson chose New York over his native Louisiana as the best location for a beginning architect. His first commission, in 1866, for a new Unitarian church in Springfield, Massachusetts, most likely arose from his college friendship with the son of an influential supporter of the project. In January of 1867, his career well launched, he married Julia Gorham Hayden, to whom he had been engaged since before his Parisian sojourn. The couple would have six children. Several factors—among them, early commissions in New England and the fact that his wife was a native of Cambridge, Massachusetts—suggested a move to the Boston area, and by 1874 the Richardsons had settled in Brookline, where he would continue to live and work.

Life's Work

The Romanesque qualities for which Richardson would become famous began to appear in the third church he designed, the Brattle Square Church in Boston's Back Bay, for which he won a competition in 1870. Taking advantage of local materials, he chose Roxbury puddingstone for this building, whose most original feature is its 176-foot corner tower, which has arches forming a carriageway at the bottom and smaller belfry arches above a frieze of sacramental figures, with a pyramidal roof. The tower is somewhat detached from the church, in the manner of the Italian campanile.

One indication of Richardson's spreading fame was a commission for the Buffalo State Hospital buildings, also in 1870. Another was his selection, two years later, as designer of Trinity Church in Boston's Copley Square, while the Brattle Square Church was still under construction nearby. Because this part of Boston is built on fill and is watery below the surface, the weight of the planned church required four thousand wooden piles beneath its foundation, and construction took more than three years. This elaborate project included a sanctuary and a parish house which Richardson connected to the church by an open cloister. Built of granite with brownstone trim from local quarries and topped with a red tile upper roof, the church forms a Greek cross with a central tower based on one in Salamanca, Spain, as adapted by Stanford White, then Richardson's assistant and later a noted architect. John La Farge, one of the premier artists of his time, designed the windows and interior decoration. It is an elaborate and colorful church, both inside and out, with elements of Gothic and high, round Romanesque arches, all of which exemplify Richardson's genius for combining and modifying different styles to produce a unique, self-expressive result. Although additions, many of them unfortunate, have altered the church since Richardson's time, it remains one of his most famous and admired structures.

Richardson enjoyed the opportunity to work at a time when small towns and cities in New England were seeking larger and more gracious public library buildings. Beginning in 1877, Richardson designed libraries for Woburn, North Easton, Quincy, and Malden, Massachusetts, as well as one for the University of Vermont. Although his fondness for massive structures ran counter to the American Library Association's standards for flexibility in library design, all of his library buildings remained in use more than a century later. The Thomas Crane Public Library in Quincy, of Quincy granite, again with brownstone trim, is the simplest and is generally considered his finest. It is a rectangular structure of three main parts: stack wing with tiered alcoves, central hall, and reading room. Its asymmetrical front entrance is a low, broad Syrian arch surmounted by a gable. To the left of the arch is a circular stair tower with a low, conical roof. Asymmetrical end gables mark both ends of the building, for which Richardson also designed the original furniture.

Richardson also designed two additions to his alma mater: Sever Hall (1878) and Austin Hall (1881). The former uses red brick to harmonize with the older architecture of Harvard Yard, while the latter, for Harvard Law School, is sandstone with an elaborately carved entry arch and interior fireplace. More than a century after its construction, Austin Hall continued to be used mainly for its original purpose. Most architectural historians date Richardson's maturity from the period in which these two educational buildings were designed, as well as the Crane Memorial Library (1880).

Richardson worked as a collaborator on the sprawling Albany, New York, capitol over a period of many years beginning in 1875, but his most personal monument in Albany is its City Hall, with a beautiful 202-foot corner tower, another design of 1880. In that year, construction began on a more unusual project, the Ames Monument in Wyoming, which commemorated two brothers' contributions to the completion and administration of the Union Pacific Railroad. It is a granite pyramid, sixty feet square at its base and sixty feet high, erected near the railroad's highest point above sea level. Medallions bearing busts of Oakes and Oliver Ames decorate the east and west faces, respectively. Twenty years after it was built, the railroad relocated to the south, and the nearby town of Sherman lost its economic base and disappeared. For most of the twentieth century, the monument has stood isolated and reachable only by secondary roads.

Other Richardsonian structures have fared worse. A number of his Massachusetts railroad stations have been demolished, others violently altered or allowed to fall into ruin; few continued as stations in the 1980's. His most celebrated commercial building, the Marshall Field Wholesale Store in Chicago, designed in 1885, was made of rock-faced red Missouri granite and red sandstone. Groups of windows were topped by arches at the fourth floor level of this seven-story building; narrower arches capped single rows of fifth- and sixth-story windows. The simplicity and harmonious proportions of this store can be admired today only in photographs, for, in 1930, the owner demolished it in favor of a parking lot.

Among his many other structures, Richardson designed a stone and a metal bridge in Boston's Fenway in the early 1880's, the Allegheny County courthouse and jail in Pittsburgh (1883-1884), and a considerable number of private residences, both of wood stone, large and small, from the East Coast to St. Louis. Two of the latter, the William Watts Sherman House in Newport, Rhode Island (1874), and the J. J. Glessner House in Chicago (1885), have, along with Trinity Church, Sever Hall, the Allegheny County buildings, and the New York State capitol, been designated National Historic Landmarks.

Like all prominent architects, Richardson had to face the problems of popularity. As his work expanded, so did his work force, and he found it necessary to delegate more authority and exercise less personal supervision over his projects. In the 1880's, he took on too much work, but he chose his assistants and construction firms carefully and would not tolerate shoddy work. Charles McKim and Stanford White of his office went on to renown in a firm of their own.

Richardson was a convivial man who enjoyed good company, good food, and good wine. Photographs of him in his maturity show the formerly slender architect to be a massive man with a full mustache and a bushy beard. One anecdote has three of his assistants standing together able to wrap themselves in one of his coats. Although his creative energy continued to flow, Bright's disease took its toll in his final years, increasingly limiting the mobility of a man whose work was frequently in progress in several scattered locations. In 1886, only a year after an *American Architect and Building News* poll rated five of his buildings among the ten finest in the United States, with Trinity Church first, and while his fame was finally reaching Europe, where American building had never been taken very seriously, Henry Hobson Richardson died at the age of forty-seven.

Summary

When Richardson began his work in the 1860's, civic buildings in the United States were likely to follow classical or Renaissance styles, churches often followed the Victorian Gothic, while commercial structures were most often mere utilitarian boxes. Thus, Richardson's boast that he would design anything from a chicken coop to a cathedral reflects no mere indiscriminate appetite for building but a rejection of outworn conventions and an affirmation that a developed architectural sensibility might apply itself to any sort of building. The more one studies the range of Richardson's work—public, commercial, religious, and private buildings—the more clearly they can be seen as the expression of his artistic vision. A suburban or village railroad station was to be taken as seriously as a church and was as worthy of beauty.

At the same time, Richardson did not neglect the requirements of the task at hand. He preserved his independence and would not yield to clients' notions that were inconsistent with his own ideas, but neither was he indifferent to their requirements. His buildings became more functional and less ornate as his career proceeded. His placement of windows, for example, was dictated not by formal requirements of the exterior façade only but by interior needs. Richardson was the first American architect to combine creativity of the highest order with receptiveness to the needs of contemporaries. In a period of divorce between aesthetic and utilitarian concerns, Richardson united them in his mature work.

His influence, powerful for several decades after his death, was not always beneficial. Certain features of his design—the arches, towers, and rough stone exteriors—were easy to imitate, but the Richardsonian integrity that fused these and other less obvious elements into an artistic whole was not. In the years following his death, some of the most notable architectural talents occupied themselves with the requirements of the skyscraper, which implied not great masses of masonry but skeletons of steel and lower floor windows on a scale incompatible with typical Richardsonian materials and designs.

Although it is difficult to determine what contribution Richardson might have made had he lived longer, the work he left did not point toward the twentieth century. In large American cities, even Boston, which resisted it into the 1960's, the skyscraper became an economic inevitability. The glassy John Hancock Building now dwarfs nearby Trinity Church. Richardson's greatest commercial building, the Field Store, was wiped out as an anachronism as early as 1930 in downtown Chicago. Vast bland airports have supplanted Richardson's railroad stations as symbols of America on the move.

In recent decades, however, the value of Richardson buildings has been recognized more widely. The National Historic Landmark Program, which began in 1960, and the National Register of Historic Places Program, dating from 1966, offer substantial protection, the National Register including thirty-two of Richardson's works. The harmony and solid beauty of his best churches, libraries, and private homes continue to answer human needs left unsatisfied by the buildings which have come to dominate urban skylines.

Bibliography
Hitchcock, Henry-Russell. *The Architecture of H. H. Richardson and His Times*. Hamden, Conn.: Archon Books, 1961. The most thorough of the twentieth century studies of Richardson's work, this book contains some biographical facts and a learned, if often dogmatic, evaluation of his subject's significance.

—————————. *Richardson as a Victorian Architect*. Northampton, Mass: Smith College Pamphlets, 1966. A lecture based on a seminar given at Harvard University in 1965. Hitchcock adroitly relates Richardson's work to the diverse strands that make up the complicated conception that is "Victorian architecture."

Mumford, Lewis. *The Brown Decades: A Study of the Arts in America 1865-1895*. New York: Harcourt Brace and Co., 1931. Reprint. New York: Dover Publications, 1955. Mumford argues that Richardson, in using metal skeletons in two of his late commercial buildings, laid the basis for bridging the gap between stone construction and the ensuing steel-and-glass age. An eloquent appreciation of Richardson's contribution to his profession.

Ochsner, Jeffrey Karl. *H. H. Richardson: Complete Architectural Works*. Cambridge, Mass.: MIT Press, 1982. This handsome book includes not only photographs and plans of proposed and completed Richardson projects but also views of the author and his studios which provide valuable insights into his working habits. Biographical information is restricted chiefly to the details of his business life. Extensive bibliographies and appendices showing the locations of his buildings and indicating their preservation status mark this meticulously researched volume.

O'Gorman, James F. *H. H. Richardson and His Office: Selected Drawings*. Cambridge, Mass.: Department of Printing and Graphic Arts, Harvard

College Library, 1974. The thirty-page introductory essay by the most productive Richardsonian scholar since Hitchcock is particularly useful for its attention to the architect's working methods.

Roger, Laura Wood. *F. L. O.: A Biography of Frederick Law Olmsted*. Baltimore: Johns Hopkins University Press, 1974. Scattered references to Richardson and also a detailed account of the happy collaboration of Richardson with the greatest landscape architect of his time.

Russell, John. "Henry Hobson Richardson." *American Heritage* 32 (October, November, 1981): 48-59. A lively and beautifully illustrated essay by an art critic who sees Richardson as the transformer—even the creator—of the architectural profession in the United States.

Van Rensselaer, Marianna Griswold. *Henry Hobson Richardson and His Works*. Boston: Houghton Mifflin Co., 1888. Reprint. New York: Dover Publications, 1969. All students of Richardson are heavily indebted to Van Rensselaer, who wrote the only true biography of a man whom she knew personally and whose work she understood thoroughly. Commissioned as a tribute to Richardson shortly after his death, the book remains a readable and valuable account of his works. Virtually all of the limited personal information to be had about its subject is to be found here.

Robert P. Ellis

HYMAN G. RICKOVER

Born: August 24, 1898; Makow, Poland
Died: July 8, 1986; Arlington, Virginia
Area of Achievement: The military
Contribution: A specialist in electrical engineering, Rickover became a pioneer in nuclear propulsion after World War II. He headed the project that developed the *Nautilus*, the world's first nuclear-powered submarine, and remained a dominant personality in the navy and in public life for three decades.

Early Life

According to his public school records, Hyman George Rickover was born on August 24, 1898 (January 27, 1900, is the date of birth given by him), in the village of Makow, about fifty miles north of Warsaw, in what was then the Russian Empire. His parents were Abraham, a tailor, and Ruchal Rickover. In 1899, Abraham Rickover, like many other Jews, left the poverty and discrimination of Russia behind to try to achieve a better life in America. For several years the senior Rickover worked in New York City to save enough money to send for his wife and two children, Hyman and a daughter, Fanny. In 1904, or thereabouts (there are discrepancies surrounding many facets in Hyman Rickover's childhood), the family was reunited in New York. A second daughter, Hitel, usually known as Augusta, was born there. In 1908, the family moved to Chicago, where they settled in North Lawndale, a neighborhood of two-family homes that was a typical first step above the ghetto for families such as the Rickovers. Hyman attended public school in the neighborhood and worked at various jobs as he grew older. His high school record was by no means outstanding, but Rickover liked to think that his time-consuming work as a Western Union messenger kept him from achieving the grades of which he was capable. He did do well his final two years at John Marshall High School and was graduated early in February, 1918.

Rickover entered the United States Naval Academy later that year and graduated in 1922. Rickover's years at Annapolis were not happy ones, but as with so many other incidents in his life, inconsistencies exist between his version of events and the written record and/or the recollections of others. According to Rickover, anti-Semitism marred his years at the academy. Others recall that several Jews who were enrolled at the same time were very well liked and that Rickover was a loner because of his own desire to pass up social and athletic activities in order to study diligently. To use the slang of the time, it seems he was considered a "grind."

Of slender build and about five feet, six inches in height, Rickover never seemed to show an interest in sports or other recreational activities; he was, however, from his childhood years on, a determined worker. In Chicago, he had sometimes held two part-time jobs while attending school. At the academy, he became known for his zeal to get things done.

Life's Work

Commissioned an ensign in 1922, Rickover served the next two years on the destroyer *LaVallette*, holding the position of engineering officer during the second half of his tour. Rickover's next assignment was as electrical officer of the battleship *Nevada*. He then undertook advanced studies, first a year's course in electrical engineering at the Naval Academy's postgraduate school and then a year at Columbia University, where he received a master's degree in engineering. He was promoted to lieutenant while at Columbia. There, Rickover met Ruth Masters, a student in international law and subsequently a recognized scholar in the field. The two carried on a courtship, largely by correspondence, and in 1931 were married by an Episcopal minister. They had one son. (Two years after Ruth Rickover's death in 1972, Rickover married Eleonore Bednowicz, then a navy nurse; she retired after their marriage.)

In 1929, Rickover was accepted into submarine school. The training program lasted six months, after which Rickover was assigned to the submarine *S-48* as engineer and electrical officer. A year later, he was named executive officer and navigator, a position which he held until 1933. Although at this time in his career he was eligible to command an older submarine or an auxiliary such as a minesweeper, he was assigned to two years of shore duty in Philadelphia, where, with the Office of Naval Matériel, he was charged with inspecting supplies and equipment being produced for use by the navy. Next, Rickover was rotated to duty at sea as assistant engineering officer of the battleship *New Mexico*. Given much latitude by his immediate superior, Rickover was able to demonstrate his zeal for efficiency by instituting methods to save on fuel consumption. Not all of his innovations were popular, and Rickover could be hard on lax subordinates. He had the reputation for thoroughness, if not tact, and the *New Mexico* won the navy's prized E awards for efficiency in engineering each year of Rickover's tour of duty.

Ordered to the Asiatic Fleet in 1937, Rickover was promoted to lieutenant commander and given command of the old minesweeper *Finch*. This was his first and only command, and accounts differ regarding whether Rickover was merely striving to bring his customary efficiency to a ship where morale was already low or whether he bore down too hard on an otherwise decent crew. He was relieved of command after three months and assigned to the Cavite Navy Yard near Manila, in the Philippines, for duty as assistant planning officer. His responsibilities included planning the repair and overhaul of machinery for ships coming into the yard.

Rickover requested a transfer to the status of engineering duty officer, having recognized from the fact of his assignment to the *Finch* that his career as a line officer was headed toward a dead end. Since 1916 the navy had officially differentiated between line officers and EDO's. Line officers were trained, in effect, to command ships and eventually task forces and even fleets in the case of the most able. While outstanding line officers such as Chester Nimitz and Ernest King might in their younger days become expert in engineering matters, they would be rotated in the course of their careers to a variety of command and staff duties at sea and on shore so that they would be familiar with many aspects of the navy. In contrast, an engineering duty officer could design, operate, and maintain ships but could not command one.

After duty at Cavite, Rickover returned to the United States for assignment to the Bureau of Engineering, which later consolidated with another shore establishment into the Bureau of Ships in 1940. In an effort to prepare for World War II, the navy was undergoing rapid expansion. As head of the electrical section of the Bureau of Ships for much of the war, Rickover was responsible for organizing the design, construction, maintenance, and repair of the electrical apparatus in radios, radars, guns, lights, refrigerators, and propulsion. Promotion now came quickly; Rickover rose to commander in 1942 and some months later to the temporary wartime rank of captain.

Rickover's style of command was unconventional in that he ignored rank among the personnel detailed to his section, and he thought nothing of working late into the evenings or on Sundays. What mattered in wartime was that he got the job done, and he impressed his superior, Rear Admiral Earle Mills. Appealing to Mills for duty in a combat zone, Rickover, in 1945, received orders to develop and command a ship repair base on Okinawa. The war ended before the base became operational, and in a postwar navy due for retrenchment, Rickover, like many others, was an officer whose future career was uncertain.

Rickover, however, was destined to achieve fame as the father of the nuclear navy. Although the name of Rickover has become synonymous with the nuclear navy in popular accounts, the idea of a nuclear-powered submarine, a true submersible, had been batted around within the navy since 1939. Mills was certainly in favor of it, as were many experienced submariners, and so after the war, Rickover and a few other engineering officers were sent to Oak Ridge to learn about nuclear technology. Rickover assumed leadership of the group and so impressed Mills with his grasp of the subject that he became the admiral's assistant for nuclear matters until 1948, by which time the navy at last had made the decision to develop nuclear propulsion. Rickover received the two assignments that would place him at the center of what was to become the nuclear navy: head of the Nuclear Power Branch of the Bureau of Ships and, in early 1949, chief of the recently established Naval Reactors Branch of the Atomic Energy Commission.

For Rickover, there was a great advantage to the fact that he now held two positions, the former in the naval hierarchy, the latter in the civilian-run AEC: Depending on circumstances, he could initiate action either from his naval position or from the Naval Reactors Branch. Having already learned the ins and outs of military bureaucracy and how to deal with major defense contractors when he headed the electrical section of the Bureau of Ships, Rickover, still an obscure captain, became increasingly autonomous.

What became known as the Rickover style was again evident, and he gathered around him a group of bright and intensely loyal officers who worked diligently to overcome the myriad problems in harnessing a nuclear reactor for shipboard power. By the early 1950's Rickover began to receive the media attention that he worked hard to cultivate and had also made himself known to influential congressmen as an officer who got things done, perhaps the only one who could make the navy's nuclear propulsion program a success. Whether he was, he did have a demonstrated record of accomplishment and was both an engineer and an experienced submariner.

Rickover, nevertheless, had his problems, not only those involving the design of the submarine and the complex requirements for the prototype reactor to power the nuclear sub but also others involving naval politics. Twice he was passed over for promotion to rear admiral, meaning that he would have to retire; navy regulations so stipulated. His congressional supporters, however, rallied to him, and Secretary of the Navy Robert Anderson directed that a special board meet to select an engineering duty captain with experience in the nuclear field for promotion to rear admiral. As Anderson had known when he specified the criteria, Rickover was chosen. Just as this threat to Rickover's navy career was nearing resolution, the crucial Mark I nuclear reactor underwent a full-power test. Convinced that no excessive risk was involved, Rickover ignored advice to halt the test at the planned forty-eight-hour mark or less and ordered the test continued for ninety-six hours, enough time for a submarine to have crossed the Atlantic at full throttle. The successful completion of the test in June, 1953, generated much favorable publicity, soon to be surpassed by the achievements of the nuclear submarine itself.

In January, 1954, the *Nautilus*, the world's first nuclear submarine, was launched and a year later undertook her trial runs on nuclear power. The vessel was clearly a success, establishing all sorts of firsts and earning many laurels for the navy, for Rickover, and for the Eisenhower Administration, particularly with her August, 1958, submerged polar crossing. Rickover was now in a very real sense above the navy, for in a service whose personnel were routinely rotated to different assignments, he built an empire based in the Naval Reactors Branch of the AEC and in the Nuclear Power Branch of the Bureau of Ships and kept control for more than three decades. As the navy added more nuclear subs as well as surface vessels such as the cruiser *Long Beach* and the carrier *Enterprise*, Rickover was promoted to vice admiral (1958) and admiral (1973) and was continued on active duty by special presidential directive issued every two years, even after he reached the normal retirement age in 1962.

On the organization charts he was well down the chain of command. In fact, however, he was able to exert influence far beyond his official slot by insisting that safety considerations required him to approve personally the commanding officers of all nuclear-powered ships. As these officers spread throughout the navy in subsequent assignments, they carried the Rickover influence to many quarters.

By no means was Rickover's influence confined to the navy. Using reactor plans for a nuclear-powered carrier that had been cancelled, his organization, with some funding from private industry, developed for use by the Duquesne Light Company the nation's first nuclear-powered generating facility at Shippingport, Pennsylvania, in 1957. Although Rickover himself had little more to do with commercial nuclear power following the completion of the Shippingport facility, many men who learned their trade with NRB went on to become leaders in the growing nuclear power field in the 1960's.

For a time following the Soviet launching of their Sputnik satellite, Rickover also became widely known as an authority on American education. The lamentation about the spectacular Soviet first led to an uproar about the quality of education in the United States. Rickover was ready with an answer, criticizing what he considered its shortcomings and calling for standards of excellence such as those he had always imposed on himself.

Not until 1982 was Rickover retired from duty, and even then he remained a well-known figure, ironically making the news several times in 1984 when it was revealed that he had received expensive gifts from one of the major contractors with which he had dealt. He was reprimanded by the secretary of the navy. In July, 1986, he died at his Arlington, Virginia, home.

Summary

Hyman Rickover served on active duty longer than any previous naval officer in American history. His career was perhaps even more remarkable for its influence than for its longevity. In his tenacity and in his ability to use the media to advantage he displayed some of the characteristics of Douglas MacArthur and J. Edgar Hoover, two other public servants who far outserved most of their contemporaries.

Unlike MacArthur and Hoover, however, he labored in obscurity for a quarter of a century. Had he retired in 1945, his naval service would by no means have been without purpose, for Rickover was one of those scores of officers in such navy specialties as engineering, ordnance, logistics, and construction who, with little chance for popular recognition, provided the indispensable support for the fleets.

He became a public figure only around 1950, showing the same dedication and drive he had always demonstrated but doing it in the glamorous new area of nuclear power. Already experienced in the ways of bureaucracy, he developed a constituency among the media and in Congress and, with the support at crucial times of those who believed in him, guided the navy into the age of nuclear propulsion and made important contributions in the civilian power field as well.

Always he remained controversial. His detractors believe that by the 1960's he had become a conservative force in the navy, hindering innovation in submarine design and in the field of gas-turbine technology for surface ships. The charge has also been made that the overall strength of the navy was not what it might have been had not such emphasis been placed upon costly nuclear-powered ships at the expense of additional conventionally powered ships that could perform many missions just as well. Finally, it is charged that Rickover was vindictive to those who disagreed with him or to subordinates who failed to display the loyalty he demanded.

His admirers, however, are many. They applaud his part in the guiding of the navy into the nuclear age and his emphasis upon excellence at a time when standards throughout the armed forces and society as a whole appeared to be slipping. Whichever view more closely approximates the reality, much about the twentieth century navy cannot be understood without comprehending Hyman Rickover's role in it. A bureaucrat *par excellence*, he brought a uniquely personalized style of leadership—what has been termed a "rude genius"—to a service in the midst of technological revolution.

Bibliography

Anderson, William R., and Clay Blair, Jr. *Nautilus—90—North*. Cleveland: World Publishing Co., 1959. Written by Anderson, second skipper of the *Nautilus*, and journalist Blair, this book relates the *Nautilus'* crowning achievement—the voyage to the North Pole—perhaps Rickover's greatest triumph.

Beach, Edward L. *Around the World Submerged: The Voyage of the Triton*. New York: Holt, Rinehart and Winston, 1962. A fascinating account by the commander of the *Triton*, one of the first nuclear subs and the largest when built. Achieved invaluable publicity for Rickover with around-the-world voyage.

Blair, Clay, Jr. *The Atomic Submarine and Admiral Rickover*. New York: Henry Holt and Co., 1954. An authorized biography, with much information made available by Rickover, written when the controversy over Rickover's retention and promotion to rear admiral was under discussion. Lauds Rickover and downplays the contributions of others to the development of the *Nautilus*. What would become known as the Rickover mystique is seen throughout the pages of this book.

Hewlett, Richard G., and Francis Duncan. *Nuclear Navy: 1946-1962*. Chicago: University of Chicago Press, 1974. Factually reliable, concise, and clearly written narrative history of the building of the nuclear navy. Perhaps the best relatively brief study of the first fifteen years of Rickover's career in the nuclear navy.

Lewis, Eugene. *Public Entrepreneurship: Toward a Theory of Bureaucratic Political Power*. Bloomington: Indiana University Press, 1980. This valuable and interesting probe into the theory of bureaucracy uses Rickover (along with J. Edgar Hoover and Robert Moses) as one of three case studies in the gaining and wielding of bureaucratic power.

Polmar, Norman, and Thomas D. Allen. *Rickover: Controversy and Genius, A Biography*. New York: Simon and Schuster, 1982. Lengthy but readable study of Rickover. By no means friendly to the late admiral, it needs to be consulted by anyone interested in him or in the nuclear navy.

Rickover, Hyman G. *Education and Freedom*. New York: E. P. Dutton, 1959. A compilation of many of Rickover's speeches on education, this volume presents Rickover's views on a topic about which he felt strongly. Rickover authored several other volumes dealing with education.

Zumwalt, Elmo R., Jr. *On Watch*. New York: Quadrangle Books, 1976. Memoirs of a former chief of naval operations who once turned down a chance to serve as executive officer of the nuclear-powered *Long Beach*. No fan of Rickover, Zumwalt devotes many pages to a critique of the Rickover style and to an appeal for a balanced navy.

Lloyd J. Graybar

PAUL ROBESON

Born: April 9, 1898; Princeton, New Jersey
Died: January 23, 1976; Philadelphia, Pennsylvania
Areas of Achievement: Music, drama, and politics
Contribution: A Renaissance man, Robeson made unprecedented contributions to American and world history as an athlete, intellectual, performer, and internationally renowned peace advocate. In politics, he championed the cause of human rights for black Americans and other oppressed people throughout the world.

Early Life

Paul Bustill Robeson was born April 9, 1898, in Princeton, New Jersey, at a time when black Americans were politically disenfranchised, economically exploited, excluded from the mainstream of American life, and suffering the worst racial hostility since the abolition of slavery. Paul was the youngest of six children born to the Reverend Mr. William Drew Robeson and Maria Louisa Bustill Robeson. His mother, Maria Louisa, was a member of the prominent Bustill family of Philadelphia, some of whom were patriots in the American Revolutionary War. The Bustills helped to establish the Free African Society and produced a long line of teachers, artisans, and ministers to the Northern free black community. Paul's father, William Drew Robeson, was born a slave in Martin County, North Carolina. He fled to the North and, with the outbreak of the Civil War, joined the Union army. After the war, William Robeson attended Lincoln University and received a degree in divinity.

Paul was six years old when his mother died; the family moved to Sommerville, New Jersey, where Paul received most of his early education. The greatest influences on Paul for the remainder of his life were his family tradition, the environment of Jim Crow America, and the experience of being reared by his father. At an early age, Paul, who often worked with his father after school, sang in his father's church, listened to stories about slavery, and became imbued with several basic principles: to labor diligently in all endeavors, pursue worthwhile goals, maintain high standards, be of service to his people, and maintain his integrity.

At age seventeen, Robeson won a state scholarship to Rutgers University in New Brunswick, New Jersey. Those who knew him described him as a good-natured person who loved life. Striving for perfection in his work, this handsome six-foot, three-inch man maintained a sense of quiet, modest self-confidence. While attending Rutgers, he established an unprecedented academic record, achieving the highest grades in his class. He was also considered to be without equal in athletics.

Although football was his favorite sport, he participated in basketball, track and field, and baseball, winning an astonishing twelve major letters in four years. He was honored as the greatest athlete in Rutgers' history and elected to the All-American team twice (in 1917 and 1918) and has been called the greatest defensive back ever to tread the gridiron. Robeson brought the school national recognition by being the first player ever named All-American in any sport at Rutgers.

Robeson also loved public speaking and debate. A master in elocution contests, for four consecutive years he won first place honors in many speaking competitions, excelling in oratory, in extemporaneous speaking, and in forensics.

Robeson won admission to Rutgers' exclusive Cap and Skull honor association and the prestigious Phi Beta Kappa society. His senior thesis, "The Fourteenth Amendment: The Sleeping Giant of the American Constitution," by identifying several ways in which the law could be used to secure civil rights for black Americans, presaged by nearly forty years ideas adopted by the United States Supreme Court in the landmark decision, *Brown v. Board of Education* (1954). At commencement, he delivered the class oration, and afterward Rutgers honored him as the "perfect type of college man."

Life's Work

In 1920, Robeson began law school at Columbia University and played a few games of professional football to finance his education. While at Columbia, he met and married Eslanda Goode Cardozo. They had a son, Paul, Jr., in 1927. After his graduation, Robeson worked briefly for a New York law firm; after encountering considerable hostility in the legal profession, however, he took up acting as a career.

During his law school days, Robeson played Simon in a benefit play, *Simon the Cyrenian* (1921), staged at the Harlem Young Men's Christian Association by the Provincetown Players, a Greenwich Village theater group. His successful performance led to other parts, and he was offered the lead in two plays by Eugene O'Neill, *All God's Chillun Got Wings* (1924) and, in 1924, *The Emperor Jones* (1920). Robeson's acting was immediately acclaimed. He also made theater history, for that production of *All God's Chillun Got Wings* was the first in which a black man played the leading role opposite a white woman on the American stage. The young actor starred in numerous plays, including *Black Boy* (1925), by Jim Tully and Frank Dazey, *Porgy* (1927), by DuBose and Dorothy Heyward, and *Show Boat* (1927), by Jerome Kern and Oscar Hammerstein. He successfully toured Europe in the late 1920's and throughout the 1930's, drawing massive, enthusiastic crowds. Robeson played Othello in William Shakespeare's play at London's Savoy Theatre in 1930, where the opening performance received twenty curtain calls. He reached the pinnacle of his stage career in 1943-1944, with his New York performance in *Othello*, which holds the record for the longest run of any Shakespearean play produced on Broadway. His ovations were among "the most prolonged and wildest . . . in the history of the New York theatre."

In one scene from the 1924 production of Eugene O'Neill's *The Emperor Jones*, Robeson was asked to whistle; instead, he sang a black spiritual. To his listeners' delighted surprise, he had a marvelous voice. This event launched an illustrious musical career that brought additional celebrity. Robeson began augmenting his acting by singing spirituals. Robeson was the first person to give entire programs of exclusively Afro-American songs in concert to white audiences. This innovation made Robeson one of the most popular concert singers for more than a quarter of a century. Later, he broadened his repertoire to include the music of other nationalities. Accompanied on piano by Lawrence Brown, Robeson's magnificent baritone voice thrilled audiences around the world. Jerome Kern's "Ol' Man River" became his personal signature, concluding every concert.

Robeson made several films, the more significant being *The Emperor Jones* (1933), *Sanders of the River* (1935), *Show Boat* (1936), *The Song of Freedom* (1937), *King Solomon's Mines* (1937), *Jericho* (1937), and *Big Fella* (1938). He was particularly pleased with *Proud Valley* (1939), which depicted the harsh life of Welsh coal miners and gave a fair and accurate portrayal of black people, and his narration for *Native Land* (1942), a moving documentary on contemporary American life. Although British filmmakers, unlike their American counterparts, were willing to feature Robeson in major roles, with few exceptions these films depicted blacks in a demeaning manner. Disgusted at the results, Robeson picketed his own films, abandoned the cinema, and focused attention on the stage, where he could control and determine the images in every performance.

As Robeson became more successful in the theater and on the concert stage, he committed himself to improving the plight of blacks. He believed that with his singing and acting he could increase the white world's respect, knowledge, and understanding of his people. "They will," he said in 1932, "sense that we are moved by the same emotions, have the same beliefs, the same longings—that we are all humans together." Moreover, his prominence motivated him to reaffirm his black identity, and he started a campaign to educate black people about the virtues of their own cultural heritage, arguing that African history was as old and significant as that of the Chinese or Persians. Uncompromisingly, he maintained that "it should be the mission of Negro artists to earn respect as Negroes as a step toward making the white race eventually respect the black." He believed that blacks had a unique and valuable contribution to make in humanizing the world through their philosophy and art.

Robeson developed a sophisticated concept of cultural pluralism that had at its roots a deep respect for his own nationality. Living in Europe during the 1930's, he determined to use art to advance the cause of his own people and to use it on a grander scale to build a more humane world. Art would be the vehicle to unite all people against the common foes of poverty, exploitation, bigotry, political violence, and war. He began studying world cultures, history, politics, and economic and social systems, and he became fluent in more than two dozen languages, including Ashanti, Mande, Swahili, Yoruba, Hindustani, Arabic, Chinese, German, Russian, French, Spanish, and Finnish.

Robeson's cultural philosophy led him to more direct political activity. In 1934, at the invitation of Sergei Eisenstein, he made the first of several trips to the Soviet Union. He spoke out against the Fascist politico of the Nazis and was the only American entertainer to go to Spain and sing to Loyalist troops. At a rally sponsored to aid Spanish refugee children held in 1937 at London's Royal Albert Hall, he remarked, "The artist must take sides. He must elect to fight for freedom or slavery. I have made my choice." He raised money to fight the Italian invasion of Ethiopia and opposed all forms of colonialism. Robeson supported the Committee to Aid China, denounced Japanese imperialism, and made a special album of Chinese songs, *Chee Lai* (1940),which he recorded in the language to raise money for Chinese relief. The foremost spokesman against European colonialism, he led the campaign for African independence and became chairman of the Council on African Affairs, which he helped establish in 1937. With the outbreak of World War II, he supported the American effort by entertaining soldiers in camps and laborers in war industries. Many of his concerts were greeted by some of the largest military audiences and civilian workers ever assembled during wartime.

By 1946, Robeson became more determined than ever to work for an end to colonialism in Africa, Asia, and the Caribbean. For the second time in his life, black soldiers were returning from a war to preserve democracy only to be greeted with racism and bigotry. Robeson could no longer tolerate the status of second-class citizenship imposed on blacks. Jeopardizing his career and spending more than $100,000 a year, he devoted his time to campaigning for black civil rights. He spoke on behalf of trade unions who found their wartime, New Deal economic gains eroded, defended Native Americans, denounced sexism, backed Henry Wallace and the Progressive Party, and confronted President Harry S Truman, demanding that he put an end to lynchings in the South and segregation in the armed forces and that he enforce fair employment practices for minority laborers.

Disturbed by Robeson's militance, opponents labeled him a Communist to undermine his legitimate dissent and weaken his mass appeal. When Cold War tensions and McCarthyistic hysteria mounted, Robeson's detractors tried to discredit him, and on several occasions he was called to testify before government committees regarding his loyalty to the United States. Repeatedly he challenged the officials, reminding them of the unconstitutionality of these proceedings, and refused to be baited into identifying anyone of his associates or activities as being un-American.

As the fear of war between the United States and the Soviet Union escalated, Robeson, at the 1949 Paris Peace Conference, called for a cessation of hostilities and an end to the arms race. A cogent and powerful speaker, he articulated the similarities in attitude between many domestic and international policies, suggesting that the black people of the world, whether in the South or in colonies abroad, had no quarrel with Russia. Their grievance was more immediate; it was with those who oppressed them: "the senators who have just filibustered them out of their civil rights. . . . Milan in South Africa who, just like Hitler, is threatening to destroy eight million Africans and hundreds of thousands of Indians through hunger and terror."

In the 1950's, Robeson was viciously attacked for his statements. Riots occurred, disrupting his concerts in Peekskill, New York. His opposition to the United States' participation in the Korean War brought a barrage of criticism. Books and information about his achievements were removed from library circulation and stricken from histories, anthologies, and bibliographic references. Blacklisting and intimidation cost him his theatrical and concert bookings and a domestic audience. His passport was revoked, and he was barred from travel outside the United States. According to the State Department's brief, action was taken "solely because of his recognized status as a spokesman for large sections of Negro Americans . . . in view of his frank admission that he has been for years active politically in behalf of independence of the colonial people of Africa."

The government offered to return his passport if he signed a statement that he would not make any speeches while abroad; Robeson refused. He lost the lucrative income from concerts and an international forum. In the meantime, he continued to accept invitations to speak and sing before labor organizations, civic groups, and black churches. One amazing concert was mounted in 1953, when Canadians arranged to meet Robeson near the border at Blain, Washington, where he spoke and sang to nearly thirty thousand people who jammed the Peace Arch Park.

With the Supreme Court ruling in 1958, Robeson's passport was reinstated. He published his autobiography, *Here I Stand* (1958), and resumed a vigorous speaking and concert tour, traveling to Great Britain, the Soviet Union, Germany, New Zealand, and Australia. Dispelling any misconceptions about his actions, he stated, "The truth is, I am not and never have been involved in any international conspiracy or any other kind, and do not know anyone who is."

Whenever he spoke crowds gathered. Yet the physical strain of the previous decades had taken its toll. In 1961, illness caused him to retire from singing and acting, and in 1963 he returned to the United States, where he remained in seclusion until his death in 1976.

Summary

During his life, Paul Robeson received hundreds of awards and tributes for his superlative artistic achievements, phenomenal intellectual contributions, and unparalleled political sacrifices on behalf of world freedom and international peace. The British Parliament set aside a day to honor him. He won the Donaldson Award for Best Acting Performance, received the American Academy of Arts and Sciences' Gold Medal for Best Diction, and was awarded numerous honorary degrees from colleges. He was honored with the Badge of the Veterans of the Abraham Lincoln Brigade, for those who fought for Republican Spain against Francisco Franco, the Thirtieth Annual Spingarn Medal, and the National Federation for Constitutional Liberties' award. Further, he received the Lenin Peace Prize and the African Freedom Award, as well as other international honors. His prodigious career included eleven films, five documentaries, nearly two dozen plays, and hundreds of records. His meticulous and constant scholarship resulted in three dozen articles, one book, and hundreds of addresses and speeches.

Robeson believed that he could show the world through the media of entertainment that racism and exploitation of all people had to end. For him, art had a definite purpose. Aside from offering pleasure and joy, art was enhanced when it enlightened people; this was the true essence of art's potential to uplift the human spirit.

During the 1930's, Robeson integrated his artistic career with that of a political activist, a Socialist cultural philosopher, and a peace advocate. Seeing German Fascism at first hand compelled him to fight against it. He called for "immediate action" to save the Jews of Europe even though it might mean "heavy sacrifice and death." His interest in labor organization grew out of his pioneering effort as a founder of the Unity Theatre in England.

Robeson supported popular liberation movements in Asia, Africa, and the Caribbean in the 1930's and 1940's. He wrote on behalf of Philippine independence from the United States and was the most prominent voice against colonial rule in Africa. Robeson pioneered in the antiapartheid movement, counseling in the 1940's that "we cannot afford to tolerate the advocates of White Supremacy in South Africa, any more than we can agree to the activities of the Ku Klux Klan in Georgia or Mississippi."

Robeson was without peer in championing the cause of worldwide democracy; yet he became one of the greatest casualties of the Cold War. Actions which won approval and praise in the 1920's and 1930's brought derision and enmity in the late 1940's and 1950's. (Earl Schenck Miers, at the height of Robeson's vilification, wrote in *The Nation* that, "as a product of his times, Robeson today is perhaps more All-American than he was as a member of his college.") His constitutional rights were violated, and a torrent of hostility was directed against him.

A new generation of Americans, rediscovering Robeson in the 1970's, brought increasing recognition of his achievements. No doubt they would be reassured by his last public statement just before his death: "Though I have not been able to be active for several years, I want you to know that I am the same Paul, dedicated, as ever, to the worldwide cause of humanity, for freedom, peace and brotherhood." As William Shakespeare's Othello said in his last speech before they took him away: "Soft you; a word or two before you go. I have done the state some service, and they know't." With his genius and his humanism, Paul Robeson did indeed serve the state extraordinarily well.

Bibliography
Davis, Lenwood G. *A Paul Robeson Research Guide: A Selected Annotated Bibliography*. Westport, Conn.: Greenwood Press, 1982. All Robeson scholars must consult this very fine bibliography. Given the difficulty in identifying foreign and obscure domestic material on Robeson, this rather large compendium is a timely and essential reference.
Foner, Philip S., ed. *Paul Robeson Speaks: Writings, Speeches, Interviews, 1918-1974*. New York: Brunner/Mazel Publishers, 1978. This is an extremely valuable reader containing most of Robeson's major published material. Anyone interested in twentieth century history and politics must include this volume on his reading list.
Freedomways Associates. *Paul Robeson: The Great Forerunner*. New York: International Publishing Co., 1985. This anthology contains a number of short articles on various aspects of Robeson's life. Also included are a few documents and numerous tributes to the man from friends, associates, and admirers, who appreciated his contributions to humanity.
Gilliam, Dorothy Butler. *Paul Robeson: All-American*. Washington, D.C.: New Republic Book Co., 1976. This thoughtful biography of Paul Robeson is the best of the recent surveys of his life. The author, however, fails to explain adequately political events in the 1930's or Cold War issues that shaped his thinking.
Robeson, Paul. *Here I Stand*. New York: Othello Associates, 1958. Although short and succinct, this autobiography covers Robeson's life, beginning with his family and concluding with his sixtieth birthday. This fascinating personal account should be read by everyone.
Seton, Marie. *Paul Robeson*. London: D. Dobson Books, 1958. Seton, a longtime friend of Robeson since the early 1930's, has written the best biography of the man to date. Filled with many colorful insights, Seton endeavors to explain the origin of Robeson's radicalism in the 1930's. The work should be updated to cover the period from 1958 until his death in 1976.
Stuckey, Sterling. "'I Want to Be African': Paul Robeson and the Ends of Nationalist Theory and Practice, 1914-1945." *Massachusetts Review* 17 (Spring, 1976): 81-138. This stimulating article treats the development and

expression of Robeson's cultural nationalism in the 1930's. The author is correct in asserting that the actor had a profound understanding of African culture and its possibilities as a humanistic approach to life which, if accepted by the West, might benefit the entire world.

Wright, Charles H. *The Peace Advocacy of Paul Robeson*. Detroit, Mich.: Harlo Press, 1984. This short pamphlet provides valuable insight into a hitherto misunderstood aspect of Robeson's political activities: his role as one of the world's leading antiwar pioneers at the start of the nuclear age.

_____. *Robeson: Labor's Forgotten Champion*. Detroit, Mich.: Balamp Publishing, 1975. Although much has been written about Robeson, this book stands alone as the only treatment of his trade-union activities, a vital commitment to which the artist devoted much of his life. Another virtue of the book is its insight into labor's views and support for this champion of the working class.

Lamont H. Yeakey

JACKIE ROBINSON

Born: January 31, 1919; Cairo, Georgia
Died: October 24, 1972; Stamford, Connecticut
Areas of Achievement: Sports and civil rights
Contribution: Robinson was the first black to play in the major leagues and
as such is known for breaking the "color line" in baseball. A hero for his
brilliant career with the Brooklyn Dodgers, he was elected to the Baseball
Hall of Fame.

Early Life

John Roosevelt, or Jackie (as he was known throughout his adult life),
Robinson was the fifth child born to Mallie and Jerry Robinson, sharecroppers of Cairo, Georgia. Robinson's grandparents had been slaves. When
he was six months old, his father abandoned the family, and a year later his
mother took the family to Pasadena, California, where Robinson grew up.
Although poor, Robinson's mother saved money and ultimately purchased a
house in a previously all-white neighborhood. This was Robinson's first experience as a pioneer in integration. As a child, Robinson excelled in all sports.
In high school, junior college, and at the University of California at Los Angeles, Robinson starred in baseball, basketball, football, and track. In 1938,
at Pasadena Junior College, he broke the national junior college record for
the broad jump, previously set by his older brother, Mack Robinson, who
himself had won a silver medal at the 1936 Olympics. In 1939, he entered
UCLA, where he became the school's first letterman in four sports. Robinson's best sport was football; in 1941, he was named an All-American. That
year, he dropped out of college to earn money for his family.

In 1941, Robinson played professional football with the Honolulu Bears.
Drafted in 1942, Robinson applied for Officer's Candidate School at Fort
Riley, Kansas. Although admitted to the program, Robinson and the other
black candidates received no training until pressure from Washington forced
the local commander to admit blacks to the base's training school. Robinson's reputation as a sports hero helped to generate that pressure. As a second lieutenant, Robinson successfully challenged some of the Jim Crow policies at the base post exchange. He quit the base football team in protest
when the army agreed to keep him out of a game with the nearby University
of Missouri, because that school refused to play against black opponents.
Transferred to Fort Hood, Texas, Robinson protested segregation on an
army bus. His protests led to a court-martial, at which he was acquitted. In
November, 1944, he was honorably discharged. The army had little desire to
keep this black man who kept fighting against racism, and for his part,
Robinson was, as he later wrote in his autobiography, "pretty much fed up
with the service."

Life's Work

Out of the army, Robinson secured a tryout with the Kansas City Monarchs, a leading team in the segregated "Negro leagues." He was quickly offered four hundred dollars a month. In August, 1945, while playing for the Monarchs, Robinson was approached by a scout for the Brooklyn Dodgers. Dodger president Branch Rickey was publicly calling for a new black baseball league, with a team to be called the Brooklyn Brown Dodgers. Rickey wanted Robinson for the team and asked him to come to Brooklyn for a meeting.

Robinson traveled to Brooklyn to meet Rickey. The twenty-six-year-old Robinson was just under six feet tall and weighed 195 pounds. He was handsome, agile, and a natural athlete of almost limitless potential. He was also intelligent and articulate and one of the best-educated black baseball players in the United States. He had grown up in an integrated world and played on integrated teams in high school and college. He was the perfect candidate for Rickey's great experiment: the integration of the major leagues.

The meeting between Robinson and Rickey is a classic in American sports. Robinson expected to talk about a new black baseball team. Instead, Rickey asked him if he had a girlfriend, and on hearing about his college sweetheart, Rachel Isum, Rickey told him to marry her. Robinson was puzzled. Rickey continued the conversation, asking Robinson if he knew why he was there. Robinson mentioned the Brown Dodgers. No, Rickey told him, Robinson was brought there to play for the real Dodgers, to integrate baseball. Rickey then began to detail Robinson's life for him. Robinson had not been scouted simply for his baseball skills; he had been scouted for his character. Rickey wanted to know if he had the courage to be the first black athlete to play in the major leagues—if he could stand the insults, the racial slurs, the beanballs, without fighting back. Rickey swore at Robinson, called him the worst possible names, and tried in other ways to anger him. The meeting was "tough" according to Robinson, but necessary, because for Robinson, baseball would not simply be a matter of box scores. That day, he signed a contract for six hundred dollars a month with a thirty-five-hundred-dollar bonus. Rickey, who was a businessman as well as a man with a strong sense of social justice, knew that Robinson had only an oral contract with the Monarchs, which was renewed monthly. Thus, Rickey never offered to pay the Monarchs for the rights to Robinson's contract.

On October 23, 1945, the Brooklyn Dodgers shocked America by announcing that Jackie Robinson would be playing for their number-one farm team, the Montreal Royals. Southerners asserted that they would never play on the same team as Robinson; white sports reporters declared that he had few baseball skills and would never make it to the major leagues; owners of other baseball teams complained about Rickey's breaking the unwritten rule against hiring blacks. The manager of the Royals, a Mississippian, privately begged Rickey not to send Robinson to his team. In spring training in Florida, Robinson faced segregation as he had never seen it before. Buses, restaurants, hotels, and all other public facilities were rigidly segregated. On the way to Florida, Robinson and his new wife were twice asked to leave their airplane seats to make room for white passengers. Later, they were forced to move to the back of a bus. These were common experiences for Southern blacks but had been unknown to the California couple. During training, Robinson could not stay with the team at a local hotel but had to live with a local black family. Tensions were high throughout the spring.

Despite a poor spring training, Robinson started at second base for the Montreal Royals in the opening game. His performance was masterful. He had four hits, including a three-run home run, scored four times, and stole two bases. His baserunning so unnerved opposition pitchers that twice they balked with Robinson on third base, which allowed him to score. This was the beginning of a promising career.

That first year, Robinson faced hateful racist crowds and opponents in a number of cities. Often this only spurred Robinson on. For example, at Syracuse, the opposing players threw a black cat on the field, yelling, "Hey, Jackie, there's your cousin." Robinson then hit a double and shouted to the Syracuse bench, "I guess my cousin's pretty happy now." Robinson was totally unnerved by the crowd, however, when he played in Louisville in a post-season championship game. The Southern crowd mercilessly booed him with "a torrent of mass hatred," as he later described it. In Montreal, on the other hand, Robinson, nicknamed the "dark dasher" for his baserunning skills, was a star and a hero. When he made the game's winning hit in the last game of the "little world series," he was carried off the field by his teammates and had to run from an adoring crowd. One sportswriter noted that it was "probably the only day in history that a black man ran from a white mob with love instead of lynching on its mind."

In 1947, Robinson started for the Brooklyn Dodgers. Enormous pressures and racial insults hampered his playing. A few Dodgers, most notably Fred "Dixie" Walker, asked to be traded. The St. Louis Cardinals, playing in a segregated city, threatened to boycott Dodger games. The manager of the Philadelphia Phillies, Ben Chapman of Alabama, became so abusive that the commissioner of baseball, himself a Southerner, intervened. By the end of the season, most of Robinson's teammates were behind him, as were many opponents. Robinson smothered his temper, absorbed insults, and fought back only with his bat, glove, and baserunning. He led the league in stolen bases that year, batted .297, and electrified fans with his baserunning, including his ability to steal home. The *Sporting News*, which had initially predicted that he would never make it to the major leagues, voted him Rookie of the Year. More significant, a public opinion poll found him the second most popular man in America, behind the singer Bing Crosby.

Two years later, in 1949, Robinson led the National League in hitting with a .342 average and was named Most Valuable Player. By then, a few other blacks, including Roy Campanella, Don Newcombe, Larry Doby, and the legendary pitcher LeRoy "Satchel" Paige, had entered the major leagues. Most major league teams were beginning to scout black ballplayers. In 1950, Hollywood gave its stamp of approval to the experiment by hiring Robinson to star in a film about himself entitled *The Jackie Robinson Story*. Robinson was now making the rather princely sum of thirty-five thousand dollars a year from the Dodgers, as well as additional income from endorsements and promotions. The Dodgers were the dominant team in their league, and Ebbets Field was attracting large crowds. The experiment seemed to be paying off for all concerned. The owners of teams in the so-called Negro leagues, however, complained that their players were being stolen from them by the major league teams and that, with one or two exceptions, they were never compensated. The complaints were justified as Negro league stars such as Paige, Campanella, and Monte Irvin, and future great stars such Hank Aaron and Willie Mays, were indeed being hired by forward-thinking, previously all-white baseball teams. By the early 1950's, all but a few teams—most notably the New York Yankees and the Boston Red Sox—would have black players.

After the 1950 season, Rickey left the Dodgers and was replaced by Walter O'Malley. Robinson feuded with his new boss for the next six years. O'Malley seemed uninterested in challenging the status quo, while Robinson would no longer quietly accept racist insults. For example, O'Malley was unsympathetic to Robinson's demand that he be allowed to stay at the same hotels as his teammates. Robinson contemplated leaving baseball in 1954 and finally did so after the 1956 season. Robinson secretly sold the exclusive story of his retirement to *Look* magazine. Meanwhile, the Dodgers sold Robinson's contract to the New York Giants, their crosstown rival. Despite an offer of sixty thousand dollars a year, Robinson stuck to his plans and left baseball.

Robinson did not, however, fade from public life. He accepted a job with a New York restaurant chain and continued to work actively in civil rights causes. He became a major fund-raiser for the National Association for the Advancement of Colored People in the 1950's. In the 1960 presidential election primaries, he campaigned for Hubert Humphrey, but in a decision he later regretted, he supported Richard Nixon in the general election. Henry Cabot Lodge, Nixon's running mate, promised Robinson that Nixon would appoint a black to a cabinet position. In addition, Robinson was unimpressed with John F. Kennedy's record on civil rights. Robinson later wrote: "The Richard Nixon I met back in 1960 bore no resemblance to the Richard Nixon as President." After the 1960 election, Robinson became closely associated with Nelson Rockefeller, the New York liberal Republican governor. In 1964, he became one of Rockefeller's advisers on civil rights and a deputy director of his presidential campaign. After the nomination of Barry Goldwater, however, Robinson became national leader of the Republicans for Johnson. At about this time, Robinson also became involved in the formation of a black-owned bank in Harlem, the Freedom National Bank. Robinson correctly noted that white-owned banks offered few services to blacks, and he believed that the situation could be remedied only with black-controlled capital. In 1966, he accepted an appointment from Governor Rockefeller as a special assistant to the governor for community affairs.

While Robinson became involved in politics and business, he was never fully divorced from baseball. In 1962, he was elected to the Baseball Hall of Fame. In the early 1950's, he had publicly attacked those teams, such as the New York Yankees, which had not yet hired black players. In the late 1960's, he began to campaign for the hiring of a black manager. He accused the men of professional baseball of hypocrisy and of maintaining a double standard in allowing blacks to play but not to manage. In 1972, Robinson threw the first ball out at the World Series. Given a public forum, he declared, on national television, "I'd like to live to see a black manager; I'd like to live to see the day when there is a black man coaching at third base." When asked why he had to use the World Series to raise this issue, he responded, "What better place? What better time?" Nine days later, Robinson died at fifty-three of complications caused by diabetes.

Summary

The significance of Jackie Robinson was twofold. First, he was an outstanding athlete and one of the most exciting baseball players of his time. In the late 1970's, the New York Mets would use pictures of Robinson in their advertising, knowing that the memory of his playing could still thrill fans. In an age of power-hitters, Robinson brought back base-stealing, bunting for hits, and finesse. His ability to unnerve pitchers was uncanny. His daring in stealing home, even in a tight World Series game, brought spectators to their feet. He was a clutch player who came through with the big hit, or the big stolen base, at a crucial moment in the game. He was a star with charisma and class. He was truly one of the greatest sports heroes of his age.

Robinson was also a pioneer. While he had the backing of Rickey and the help of many players and fans when he integrated baseball, it was Robinson who had to bear the racial slurs, duck the beanballs, and dodge spikes aimed at his body. Robinson did this with grace and dignity, but he also did it with fire. Moreover, he was able to make the transition from turning the other cheek to fighting back verbally. He was the ultimate competitor, for after his baseball career was over, he continued to fight for racial justice and equality. To the end, Robinson spoke out against all forms of segregation.

Bibliography

Frommer, Harvey. *Rickey and Robinson: The Men Who Broke Baseball's Color Line*. New York: Macmillan, 1982. Excellent dual biography of Branch Rickey, the owner of the Dodgers who hired Robinson, and Robinson. Follows careers of both beyond their years in baseball, to their deaths.

Kahn, Roger. *The Boys of Summer*. New York: Harper and Row, Publishers, 1971. Written by a leading sportswriter, this is warm and readable history of the Brooklyn Dodgers in the age of Jackie Robinson.

Peterson, Robert. *Only the Ball Was White*. Englewood Cliffs, N.J.: Prentice-Hall, 1970. History of black baseball. Contains important information on early black players and the organization of the Negro leagues.

Robinson, John Roosevelt. *Baseball Has Done It*. Edited by Charles Dexter. Philadelphia: J. B. Lippincott Co., 1964. Part autobiography, part history of the integration of baseball, and part a history of the blacks who played in the Negro leagues, this book is also Robinson's first long statement about race relations and integration after he left baseball. Written during the early years of the civil rights revolution, this is an important book that links civil rights to baseball. The book also gives important details about the events leading up to Robinson's breaking of the color line.

_____. *I Never Had It Made*. New York: G. P. Putnam's Sons, 1972. Robinson's autobiography, published just before he died. A key source for Robinson's life, especially after he left baseball.

Rogosin, Donn. *Invisible Men: Life in Baseball's Negro Leagues*. New York: Atheneum Publishers, 1983. Study of black baseball before the integration of the major leagues. Based on extensive interviews with former players. Readable, yet scholarly.

Tygiel, Jules. *Baseball's Great Experiment: Jackie Robinson and His Legacy*. New York: Oxford University Press, 1983. Skillfully written, this is the best study of the integration of baseball. Written by a professional historian, based on archival work and interviews, this book is a joy to read and the place to start when reading about Robinson.

Paul Finkelman

JOHN D. ROCKEFELLER

Born: July 8, 1839; Richford, New York
Died: May 23, 1937; Ormond Beach, Florida
Areas of Achievement: Industry and philanthropy
Contribution: One of the major industrialists and philanthropists in the history of the United States, Rockefeller pioneered in bringing a new scale to business organization through his phenomenally successful Standard Oil Company; he also brought a new scale to philanthropic giving.

Early Life

John Davison Rockefeller was born on July 8, 1839, in Richford, New York, to Eliza Davison and William Avery Rockefeller. His father owned a farm and traded commodities, such as salt and lumber. The family, which included John's older sister, two younger sisters, and two younger brothers, moved frequently: first to Moravia, New York; then to Owego, New York; and finally, to Cleveland, Ohio. John's education was irregular, but he studied hard and did have two years at Cleveland High School. His father, who by that time had become a wandering vendor of patent medicine, encouraged him to go into business. John especially liked mathematics, and he took a three-month course in bookkeeping at Folsom's Commercial College.

In selecting a job, Rockefeller was not as much interested in the salary as he was in the possibilities a position offered for learning about the business world. He selected a large and diversified merchant firm and started as a bookkeeper at a salary of $3.50 per week. After three and a half years, he left to form his own wholesale grain and grocery business with Maurice B. Clark. Together, the two had only four thousand dollars; during their first year, however, they grossed $450,000 and netted a fourteen-hundred-dollar profit. The following year, the Civil War began. The war gave Rockefeller, along with a number of other leading postwar industrialists, the opportunity to make his initial pile of money. Business at Cleveland-based Clark and Rockefeller boomed with major orders coming in from the army, other cities, and Europe. Rather than miss these business opportunities fighting in the Civil War, Rockefeller avoided the draft by paying for a substitute to fight in his place.

During these early business years, Rockefeller displayed the character traits and personal life-style that would be with him throughout his life. A devout Baptist, Rockefeller remained active in that church, even after becoming fabulously successful in business. For years, he taught Sunday school and served on church boards with streetcar conductors and other working-class people He also took seriously the biblical injunction to give away one-tenth of what he earned, even when starting out at a very low salary. He lived simply, had few pleasures, and was devoted to his family. In

1864, he married Laura Celestia Spelman, whose father was a prosperous businessman. Eventually, they had four children who lived to adulthood: three daughters, Bessie, Alta, and Edith, and a son, John D. Rockefeller II, of whom his father was quite proud. The family lived in a large, comfortable, but not ostentatious house in Cleveland until moving to New York in the 1880's. Rockefeller instilled a sense of industry and public responsibility in his offspring that extended down to the third and fourth generations, producing one vice president (Nelson) and three state governors (Nelson of New York, Winthrop of Arkansas, and John D. IV of West Virginia). Of all the leading American industrial families, the Rockefeller dynasty became the most remarkable.

Life's Work

It was possible for John D. Rockefeller to gain a monopolistic fortune in the oil business because of certain conditions that existed at that time. Oil was first used for medicinal purposes. Yet oil strikes in Pennsylvania in the 1850's greatly increased the supply. To find other uses for the product, the Pennsylvania Rock Oil Company hired Yale chemist Benjamin Silliman, Jr. Silliman discovered that oil could be distilled into kerosene for burning in lamps, and he also noted its lubricating qualities. At the time, oil was obtained by skimming off what floated on the surface of water-filled ditches and springs. With other uses, however, drilling quickly became economically viable. Independent oil wells and small-scale refineries sprang up in great profusion in northwestern Pennsylvania, and refineries also proliferated in Cleveland. The oil business was chaotic, with numerous small operators, overproduction, cutthroat competition, and alternating periods of boom and bust. Rockefeller perceived that whoever could bring order to this industry could make a fabulous fortune.

In 1863, Rockefeller began his involvement with the oil business. He and his wholesale grocery partners, along with refining expert Samuel Andrews, built a refinery in Cleveland. His wholesale grocery partners proved too cautious for Rockefeller's taste. In 1865, he decided to buy out the three Clark brothers, get entirely out of the wholesale grocery business, and devote himself to oil. By the end of the year, the firm of Rockefeller and Andrews had an oil refinery that was producing at least twice as much as any other single refinery of Cleveland's nearly thirty refineries.

Rockefeller prospered more than his competitors because of his foresight, attention to detail, emphasis on efficiency, lack of toleration for waste, and growing reputation as a successful businessman. These qualities allowed him to borrow heavily from bankers and to attract partners who brought additional capital to his firm. Henry M. Flagler joined Rockefeller in 1867, bringing with him a substantial amount of money and the ability to negotiate ever lower railroad shipping rates. Railroad rates were unregulated then, with railroads commonly giving favored shippers rebates on their publicly stated rates. The larger the shipper, the more favorable the rate. Rockefeller was able to play two railroads off against each other and water transportation off against the railroads. In turn, his lower shipping rates allowed him to undersell his competitors, steadily driving them out of business.

Meanwhile, Rockefeller implemented a policy of vertical integration. To cut his firm's dependence on related businesses, he began making his own barrels and then bought his own timber tracts to supply his cooperage plant. He owned his warehouses, bought his own tank cars, and, to the extent possible, owned or produced the raw materials and transportation he needed to operate. Finally, he fought waste by using kerosene by-products to become the oil industry's leading producer of paraffin and machine lubricants.

In 1870, to accommodate additional growth, Rockefeller converted his partnership into a joint-stock corporation, the Standard Oil Company of Ohio. Meanwhile, Thomas A. Scott of the Pennsylvania Railroad began organizing certain railroads, oil refiners, and well owners into the infamous South Improvement Company. The purpose was to form a monopoly and get rebates on their competitors' shipments. The public reaction was hostile, and the South Improvement Company quickly lost its charter. Rockefeller had been part of this scheme, which badly tarnished his reputation. Yet, through the South Improvement Company, he acquired another wealthy partner, Cleveland refiner Oliver H. Payne.

Furthermore, Standard Oil decided to proceed on its own to create a monopoly in the oil business. Early in 1872, Rockefeller offered to buy out nearly all remaining Cleveland oil refineries. Owners could either accept a cash offer, take the offer in Standard Oil stock, or be driven out of business. With the South Improvement Company still a live entity and given the size of Standard Oil itself, most refiners sold out. Some claimed that they had been pressured into taking less than their businesses were worth, but those who acquired Standard stock did make small fortunes. Rockefeller accomplished this takeover of his Cleveland competitors in three months. From Cleveland, Standard then proceeded to acquire refineries in Pittsburgh, in Philadelphia, and on Long Island. By 1875, the firm was refining half of the oil products in the United States. Rockefeller's next step was to gain control of pipelines, oil terminals, kerosene distributors, and additional plants. He also attracted rival oilman John D. Archbold to his firm. By 1878, Rockefeller had secured his monopolistic position.

During the 1880's, Standard Oil continued to grow. The firm acquired new oil fields, built new refineries, and developed new refining methods. Under the direction of John's brother, William Rockefeller, the firm also expanded into the international market. Standard Oil products were a familiar sight in Asia, Africa, South America, and even Central Europe, where Standard encountered stiff competition from cheap Russian oil. Also, Standard Oil pioneered in corporate organization. Rockefeller employed the best legal talent to devise the concept of the trust. That meant that the stock of Standard's subsidiaries and related companies was combined with Standard's stock, new certificates were issued, and an executive committee with Rockefeller at the head assumed control. During 1883-1884, he transferred the corporate headquarters to New York City. Yet Standard Oil never took total control of the oil industry. While accounting for eighty to ninety percent of oil produced in the United States and making substantial profits, Standard did lower the price of its products. Rockefeller had stabilized a chaotic industry.

In the process, Rockefeller became very powerful and was feared and vilified. The lack of railroad rate regulation did much to make his monopoly possible. Unfair railroad rates upset many more people than Rockefeller's business competitors. The public began agitating for railroad rate regulation, first at the state level and then for the Interstate Commerce Act, passed in 1887. Since that law was largely ineffective, agitation continued until railroad rates were finally effectively regulated in the twentieth century. Throughout this agitation, the outstanding example of how unregulated railroad rates could lead to powerful monopolies was Standard Oil. The New York legislature investigated the company in 1879 and again in 1888. Henry Demarest Lloyd published an exposé in the *Atlantic Monthly* in March, 1881. Congress sought to dampen the public's concern with the Sherman Antitrust Act of 1890. When that law went initially unenforced, muckrakers again attacked. The best-known exposé was Ida M. Tarbell's *History of the Standard Oil Company* (1904). Rockefeller always refused to respond directly to these attacks. His attitude was that his products spoke for themselves. Not until 1905 did Standard Oil hire its first public relations expert. Nevertheless, the federal government proceeded to prosecute Standard Oil for violating the Sherman Antitrust Act. Under court order, the company broke into smaller, separate companies in 1911.

Rockefeller's wealth at one point approached $900,000,000. What to do with all this money posed a dilemma. He invested in the stock market and, in the 1890's, gained control of the Mesabi Range, the richest iron ore field in the United States. Within a few years, however, he sold his Range holdings to Andrew Carnegie. Increasingly, his interests were turning to philanthropy, where his impact was tremendous.

At first, Rockefeller's gifts to hospitals, colleges, and other institutions were haphazard, and his gifts were sometimes misused. Soon, however, he began to apply some of his principles for making money—of attention to detail and organization—to giving money away. He virtually made the University of Chicago with a founding gift in 1889 of $600,000 and later gifts (some from his son) totaling $80,000,000. He created the Rockefeller Institute for Medical Research in 1901 and the General Education Board in 1902.

The latter helped to revolutionize medical education, fought the spread of hookworm, and worked to improve Southern agriculture. His philanthropy was further systematized with the creation of the Rockefeller Foundation in 1913. He gave away more than a half billion dollars, and the influence of his philanthropic institutions has continued to grow after his death. Rockefeller had turned over active leadership of the Standard Oil Company in 1897 but lived until 1937, dying at the age of ninety-seven.

Summary

John D. Rockefeller succeeded as a businessman and a philanthropist in part because of his personal qualities and in part because of his times. He had an uncanny ability to identify and secure leading executive talent. The extreme care with which he made decisions was accompanied by a boldness of action and accuracy of vision unmatched in his field. Furthermore, he had the steadiness to compete in a rough, competitive, "survival of the fittest" environment where there were few laws and regulations. Indeed, he turned this freewheeling environment to his advantage. He was able to build Standard Oil because of such conditions as the general absence of effective railroad rate regulation and lack of an income tax. He went into the oil business at a time when it was taking off, and good luck was with him when the gasoline-powered automobile came along to increase demand. He regarded himself as a trustee of his wealth and became, perhaps, the outstanding philanthropist in the United States. Finally, he instilled an obligation for public service in his descendants. Of all the "robber barons" of his generation, his long-range impact may have been the greatest.

Bibliography

Abels, Jules. *The Rockefeller Billions: The Story of the World's Most Stupendous Fortune*. New York: Macmillan Publishing Co., 1965. Scholarly, readable, with a good selection of photographs of Rockefeller, his family, business associates, and houses. Generally, Abels is favorably disposed toward Rockefeller.

Carr, Albert A. *John D. Rockefeller's Secret Weapon*. New York: McGraw-Hill Book Co., 1962. Focuses on the role that the Union Tank Car Company, established by Rockefeller and the key to his transportation system, played in the success of Standard Oil. In 1891, the company became a separate corporation from Standard Oil in response to the Sherman Antitrust Act. Carr covers the history of Union Tank Car up to 1961.

Collier, Peter, and David Horowitz. *The Rockefellers: An American Dynasty*. New York: Holt, Rinehart and Winston, 1976. The bulk of this book is on John D. Rockefeller's descendants, down through his great-grandchildren, the impact his fortune has had on them, and their sense of public responsibility.

Hawke, David F. *John D.: The Founding Father of the Rockefellers*. New York: Harper and Row, Publishers, 1980. A chatty, popular account, this slim volume is not too extensively footnoted but is based on archival sources along with more detailed secondary sources, especially Nevins' 1940 biography.

Josephson, Matthew. *The Robber Barons: The Great American Capitalists, 1861-1901*. New York: Harcourt, Brace and Co., 1934. Reprint. Harcourt, Brace and World, 1962. In this critical account, Rockefeller is only one among many late-nineteenth century industrialists, but the book is excellent for setting him in the context of his time. Josephson is critical of the business practices and extensive power of Rockefeller and his associates.

Nevins, Allan. *John D. Rockefeller: The Heroic Age of American Enterprise*. New York: Charles Scribner's Sons, 1940. Nevins is the scholarly authority on Rockefeller. This two-volume work was the most comprehensive, carefully researched, and balanced source on Rockefeller until Nevins' 1953 book appeared.

_____. *Study in Power: John D. Rockefeller, Industrialist and Philanthropist*. New York: Charles Scribner's Sons, 1953. More of a second biography of his subject than a revision, this book incorporates material based on a large amount of documents not available to Nevins in his earlier biography; it also reflects a maturing of Nevins' analysis. Both Nevins biographies can be profitably consulted.

Judith Ann Trolander

RICHARD RODGERS

Born: June 28, 1902; New York, New York
Died: December 30, 1979; New York, New York
Area of Achievement: Musical theater
Contribution: In the course of his sixty-year career as a Broadway composer, Richard Rodgers helped to establish the prototype of the American musical.

Early Life

Richard Rodgers was born in New York City at the dawn of the twentieth century. Tensions created by live-in grandparents and a competitive older brother were dispelled when Dr. William and Mamie Rodgers gathered the family around the Steinway to sing and play songs from current Broadway shows. It was here that Richard Rodgers received his first taste of the Broadway musical.

Rodgers started to play the piano at age four. Although he was given formal lessons, he was much happier picking out show tunes by ear. The family marveled at the boy's achievements, and Rodgers quickly learned that music was a sure way of getting attention.

Rodgers had been stagestruck from his first visit to the theater. When he discovered the musicals of Jerome Kern, he quickly adopted Kern's ideals as his own. Rodgers aspired to create a new form of American musical theater free from European stuffiness and grounded in a conscious attempt to relate songs to story.

Rodgers' parents encouraged their son's ambition to be a Broadway composer. When Rodgers attempted his first amateur score at the age of fifteen, his father and brother Mortimer helped with the lyrics and, through his father's efforts, he got his first copyright on a song.

In order to pursue his career, he needed a lyric writer. When a mutual friend introduced him to Lorenz Hart, the professional attraction was immediate. They not only shared a disdain of the childish, old-fashioned quality of current musicals, but they also had a mutual hero in Kern. Hart's eccentric, disheveled appearance and mercurial personality, however, were the antithesis of his new partner's dependability and practicality. (Despite his boyish face and expressive eyes, Rodgers was known for his conservative habits and sober appearance.)

In 1919, Rodgers enrolled at Columbia University, primarily to be able to write the Varsity Show with his new partner. The team soon moved from amateur status to professional when Lew Fields, a respected Broadway producer, chose songs from two of the Varsity Shows for *A Lonely Romeo* (1919) and *Poor Little Ritz Girl* (1920).

Buoyed by the encouragement of his family and friends, Rodgers left

Columbia after two years to study music at Juilliard. By 1925, however, in debt to his father and frustrated by his inability to get professional recognition on Broadway, the young composer nearly took a job in the garment business. An offer to write *The Garrick Gaieties* (1925) for the Theatre Guild, one of New York's most prestigious producing organizations, became the unexpected opportunity that launched Rodgers and Hart's career on Broadway.

Life's Work

Rodgers and Hart rapidly became one of Broadway's most important songwriting teams. Between 1925 and 1930, they wrote fifteen full scores. Most were hits. Their greatest successes were shows in which they experimented with new subjects, ranging from the American Revolution to King Arthur's court.

Rodgers married Dorothy Feiner in 1930 and, in the same year, signed a film contract and moved to Hollywood. Although he and Hart were challenged by their early work, they missed New York. Both returned to Manhattan soon after learning in the press that they had been all but forgotten on Broadway.

The late 1930's were vintage years for Rodgers and Hart. *On Your Toes* (1936) was the first musical to incorporate a ballet into the story of a musical, *The Boys from Syracuse* (1938) was the first musical inspired by one of William Shakespeare's plays, and *Pal Joey* (1940) was one of the first musicals that did not sugarcoat the disagreeable qualities of its characters.

In the early 1940's, Hart became increasingly self-destructive and unpredictable. Despite the critics' doubts about Rodgers' ability to succeed without Hart, the composer had to find another collaborator. In 1943, Rodgers teamed up with Oscar Hammerstein II (an old friend from the Varsity Shows at Columbia), and together they wrote the landmark musical *Oklahoma!*

Hammerstein was a playwright as well as a lyricist. His work with Jerome Kern on *Show Boat* (1927) had been an attempt at the kind of cohesive musical play that Rodgers wanted to write. Their plan for *Oklahoma!* was to write a show in which the songs, story, dances, and stage design were so well integrated that no single element would overshadow any other. This not only represented a crystallization of the conceptual and structural ideals tested by Rodgers and Hart but also set a precedent for all subsequent Rodgers and Hammerstein collaborations. After Hart's death in 1943, Rodgers seized the chance for a second career with Hammerstein. Rodgers and Hammerstein also became business partners. They produced others' work in addition to their own—Irving Berlin's *Annie Get Your Gun* (1946) was their most successful venture—and established their own publishing house, Williamson Music, Inc.

In the 1940's, Rodgers and Hammerstein achieved unprecedented success.

Both *Oklahoma!* (which would hold the record for the longest-running musical in Broadway history for fifteen years) and *South Pacific* (1949) received Pulitzer Prizes; *Carousel* (1945) became their most ambitious attempt at the integration of song and story; and *The King and I* (1951), following the pattern of its predecessors, became the third Rodgers and Hammerstein musical to run for more than one thousand performances.

Rodgers was operated on for cancer of the jaw in 1955 and in 1957 was treated for depression. Returning to work proved to be excellent medicine: He teamed with Hammerstein to write *Flower Drum Song* in 1958 and *The Sound of Music* in 1959. Hammerstein died ten months after the opening of *The Sound of Music*, at the age of sixty-five.

Having outlived two of the most successful collaborations in the history of Broadway, Rodgers had to find a way of continuing to work after Hammerstein's death. After a failed attempt at forming a partnership with lyricist Alan Jay Lerner, he became his own lyric writer for *No Strings* (1962), which incorporated an onstage orchestra into the plot.

In the last years of his life, Rodgers continued to find new projects and collaborators to satisfy his indefatigable need to work. A heart attack and a second bout with cancer made it difficult for him to speak clearly and walk. Although he continued to write beautiful songs, neither the scripts nor the lyrics of his final projects could compare favorably with those of his successes with Hart and Hammerstein.

After sixty years in the professional theater, Richard Rodgers died on December 30, 1979, at the age of seventy-seven—seven months after the opening of his final musical, *I Remember Mama*.

Summary

Although the theater songs that were the result of Rodgers and Hart's twenty-five-year collaboration represent some of the best work of his career, the eighteen-year collaboration between Rodgers and Hammerstein proved to be the most influential partnership in the history of the American musical theater. As a result of the success of *Oklahoma!*, *Carousel*, *South Pacific*, and *The King and I*, the definition of the Broadway musical was irrevocably changed.

The most successful Rodgers and Hammerstein musicals were inspired by solid literary sources, were strictly American in character despite some exotic settings, and were painstakingly structured so that the songs would be believable expressions of the characters. Both men supervised every aspect of their productions and earned reputations for setting standards of excellence, fairness, and generosity in all of their dealings.

Ironically, the overwhelming popularity that came to Rodgers, combined with the disappointments of his last five musicals, generated a distorted perception of his career. Many came to view him as an outdated Establishment hero. A look at his contribution to the American musical theater from 1925 to 1962, however, reveals not only remarkable quality and quantity (he wrote fifty-nine musical scores and more than one thousand songs) but also a persistence in breaking with convention. His music has influenced generations of musical theater artists in America and has bolstered the reputation of the musical in the United States and throughout the world.

Bibliography

Engel, Lehman. *The American Musical Theatre*. New York: Macmillan, 1975. A history of the American musical theater and the best analysis of musical and dramatic structure based on the Rodgers and Hammerstein prototype.

Ewen, David. *Richard Rodgers*. New York: Henry Holt and Co., 1957. Draws upon reminiscences and firsthand information from Rodgers' family, friends, and colleagues. Includes photos, a copy of Rodgers' first copyrighted song, and many useful appendices.

Green, Stanley. *The Rodgers and Hammerstein Story*. New York: John Day Co., 1963. Focuses on the parallel careers of Rodgers and Hammerstein before and after their collaboration. Includes direct quotes from recorded conversations. A provocative concept but a generally uninspired text.

_____, ed. *Rodgers and Hammerstein Fact Book: A Record of Their Works and with Other Collaborators*. New York: Drama Book Specialists, 1980. The most comprehensive, meticulously researched reference book on Rodgers and Hammerstein. Includes biographical and production fact sheets and selected critical reviews from professional productions.

Rodgers, Richard. *Musical Stages: An Autobiography*. New York: Random House, 1975. Contains useful personal anecdotes, photos, descriptions of his working methods, and analyses of some of his most successful songs. Some insight into the forces that shaped his career. Written with characteristic modesty and dry humor.

Suskin, Steven. *Show Tunes: The Songs, Shows and Careers of Broadway's Major Composers*. New York: Dodd, Mead and Co., 1986. Annotated reference of all published songs. Valuable resource for musical theater scholars and enthusiasts. All entries are cross-referenced.

Wilder, Alec. "Richard Rodgers." In *American Popular Song: The Great Innovators, 1900-1950*. Edited by James T. Maher. New York: Oxford University Press, 1972. Analysis of Rodgers' most musically satisfying songs. Author admits preference for songs written with Hart. Analysis of songs based upon their inherent musical strength, rather than their dramatic contexts.

Marilyn Plotkins

JOHN AUGUSTUS ROEBLING

Born: June 12, 1806; Mühlhausen, Thüringen, Confederation of the Rhine
Died: July 22, 1869; Brooklyn Heights, New York
Area of Achievement: Civil engineering
Contribution: An academically trained civil engineer who worked in the middle decades of the nineteenth century when such talents were rare in the United States, Roebling fully exploited the potentialities of the suspension bridge, placing the United States in the forefront in construction of long-span, stable, heavy-load-bearing bridges for generations.

Early Life

John Augustus Roebling was born on June 12, 1806, in Mühlhausen, Thüringen, one of the German states of the Confederation of the Rhine, incorporated into Prussia in 1815. Prussia, the second largest of the German states, was in most respects the most advanced. Roebling's parents were respected citizens of the ancient walled town, which was rich in Gothic architecture that later became one of the motifs in Roebling's work. Mühlhausen similarly enjoyed a rich cultural heritage, Johann Sebastian Bach, among other noted figures, having worked there. Because rapidly growing Berlin was Prussia's political and cultural center, Roebling was sent to Berlin's Royal Polytechnic School in 1822. When he was graduated in 1826, he had studied civil engineering, architecture, mathematics, and philosophy (under Georg Wilhelm Frederich Hegel) and completed a senior thesis on suspension bridges.

Life's Work

Upon graduation, Roebling was employed for the next three years as a civil engineer on both public and military works for the Prussian government. Prussia, however, was an autocratic state in which the liberal, republican views that were to take root in the German state until 1848, views Roebling shared, withered. Because of such opinions, Roebling was officially listed as a subversive, and his career accordingly ended. Seeking a freer reign for his career and for his political convictions, he emigrated to Saxonburg in eastern Pennsylvania. For the next six years, he unsuccessfully attempted farming. With the craze for internal improvements, particularly for canals and railroads, in full swing and trained engineers rare, Roebling returned to engineering in 1837, initially as a surveyor for the Beaver River Canal, then shortly afterward for the Pennsylvania Railroad: a few years later, well on its way to becoming the world's largest corporation. The enormous anthracite deposits of northeastern Pennsylvania, the frenzy to find economical means of getting the coal to market as it increasingly became the nation's principal domestic and industrial fuel, ensured a demand for bridges. In 1844, at the age of thirty-eight, Roebling earned his first commission, partly on the strength of his invention, in 1840, of a method of manufacturing wire-rope cable, essential for stable, heavy-duty suspension work. His first project, built to carry the Pennsylvania State Canal across the Allegheny River at Pittsburgh, was a suspension aqueduct for canal boats. Its masonry towers foreshadowed an Egyptian motif later to reappear in the Brooklyn Bridge. Roebling's next four commissions, also aqueducts, were for the Delaware and Hudson Canal, a company then redesigning its anthracite-carrying canals from the coalfields of northeastern Pennsylvania to tidewater ports better able to compete with railroads. All were multispan suspension structures. Convenient for navigation, they were built without falsework—one of the advantages of suspension construction. Each consisted of troughlike flumes capable of carrying boats of sixty or more tons. The flumes were solidly embanked with fitted timbers and into transverse floor beams, all buttressed with sidewall trusses. As on the famed Delaware Aqueduct, which remained in use until the 1970's, the shore piers and masonry spans were company built. All the suspension work and its loads were designed and built by Roebling. Indeed, the Delaware Aqueduct was a handsome, thousand-foot span hung on eight-and-one-half-inch wrought-iron cables. Aware of the cable's coming importance, Roebling, in fact, founded his own wire-cable factory in Trenton, New Jersey, in 1849, just prior to completion of his Delaware and Hudson commissions.

In the meantime, a fire in Pittsburgh and the destruction of the Monongahela River's Smithfield Bridge in 1846 brought him a commission for his first vehicular suspension bridge. With two shore abutments and six river spans, it stretched fifteen hundred feet. The deck was carried by wrought-iron rods hung from wire cables, which Roebling spun onshore. Until traffic weights became too great, the bridge was in all regards a success, resulting, late in the 1850's, in construction of an identical bridge over the Allegheny River at Pittsburgh's Sixth Street. In this case, however, there were two differences: First, Roebling spun his wire cable on the bridge; second, his son, Washington, joined him, thus inaugurating his own career.

In 1851, John Roebling undertook his greatest challenge yet: construction of a railway suspension bridge across the Niagara River at Niagara Falls, New York. After a brilliant career, Charles Ellet, Roebling's predecessor, resigned his commission for the job, effectively ending his career. Moreover, leading engineers in both the United States and Europe considered the task impossible. Roebling designed a double-decked structure: the upper one carrying the mainline of the Grand Trunk Railway and the Great Western Railway of Canada; the lower one serving normal vehicular traffic. The Niagara gorge was deep; the river was deep and swift; the span to be covered on an absolute level was 821 feet from shore to shore. Roebling's design consisted of four ten-inch cables, each of 3,640 wires, hung from masonry towers. Characteristically, the load was carried by the cables and reticulations of radiating stays. Roebling completed this, the first of the world's railway suspension bridges, in 1855.

Meanwhile, Roebling rebuilt an Ellet bridge at Wheeling, West Virginia, and by 1856, he had embarked on ten years of frustrations—finances, ice, floods, and war—constructing a twelve-hundred-foot span across the Ohio River between Cincinnati and Covington, Kentucky. Since its opening in January, 1867, nevertheless, with its design unaltered, it continues in use, an even greater tribute to his engineering genius, tenacity, and industry than his remarkable Niagara Bridge.

Roebling's last and monumental work was begun in 1867, with his appointment as chief engineer for the New York Bridge Company, whose objective was bridging the East River between lower Manhattan and Brooklyn, then two separate cities. The growth of each dictated a need for the most efficient connections. River traffic was enormous; rail and shipping connections were awkward and inefficient; and, though a tidal river, the East River severed both cities and halted traffic by freezing over or being covered with ice floes periodically. Proposals for a bridge began at least by 1811, and, in 1857, Roebling made his own bid. The Civil War and objections from the United States Army Engineers shelved work until 1869. Roebling designed an unprecedented structure with a main span of 1,595 feet. Unfortunately, though built to Roebling's specifications, the great bridge, which came to symbolize not only New York's greatness but also the aesthetic and structural abilities of American engineering, was completed by Washington Roebling fourteen years after his father's death. On his initial survey in July, 1869, John Roebling's toes were crushed against pilings by a ferry, and he died of a tetanus infection July 22, 1869, in Brooklyn Heights, New York.

Summary

Though Roebling has been popularly identified with the design of the magnificent Brooklyn Bridge, an American symbol as well as an example of artistic engineering, one of his major contributions lies elsewhere: He, along with a handful of others, demonstrated the necessity for, and the superiority of, professionally trained engineers and the passing of those who, however ingeniously, even brilliantly, worked by "guess and by God." This was especially true of bridge builders, who were increasingly confronted by the broad, swift rivers of America and by the vastly heavier burdens that had to be borne by their structures during rapid industrialization. Roebling did not invent the suspension bridge: As a simple form it was thousands of years old. On a modest scale and in modest circumstances, suspensions were being improved even as his career began. The precision of his designs, his master of wire-cable manufacture and use, and his mathematical assessment of loads and stresses that lend special character to all of his constructions, whether his aqueducts, his Wheeling, Pittsburgh, Cincinnati, or Niagara structures, however, made him the acknowledged master of suspension forms. By his boldness in adapting his designs to the peculiar needs of the American environment, he revolutionized bridge construction throughout the world. This was a legacy passed on not only by his son's completion of the Brooklyn Bridge but also by professional engineers everywhere.

Bibliography
Condit, Carl W. *American Building: Materials and Techniques from the Beginning of Colonial Settlements to the Present*. Chicago: University of Chicago Press, 1982. A standard study; chapters 8 and 12 are on Roebling. Excellent technical discussion of bridge construction, including the suspension work of Roebling, among others. Also strong on historical contexts of these developments. Readable and widely available.

——————. *American Building Art: The Nineteenth Century*. New York: Oxford University Press, 1960. As excellent as all of Condit's studies. Concentration not only on building techniques but also on the aesthetics of structural architecture. Chapter 5 is particularly relevant to Roebling and suspension bridges.

Kirby, Richard S., and Philip G. Laurson. *The Early Years of Civil Engineering*. New Haven, Conn.: Yale University Press, 1932. Standard and excellent. Includes portraits and very brief biographical sketches of Roebling and many other major civil engineers of national and international note. Chapter 5 is especially relevant.

Latimer, Margaret, Brooks Hindle, and Melvin Kranzberg. *Bridge to the Future: A Centennial Celebration of the Brooklyn Bridge*. New York: New York Academy of Sciences, 1984. A literary as well as a technical survey. Sound and accurate.

Steinman, David B., and Sara Ruth Watson. *Bridges and Their Builders*. New York: G. P. Putnam's Sons, 1941. Expertly done by engineering scholars. A fine survey.

Vogel, Robert M. *Roebling's Delaware and Hudson Canal Aqueducts*. Washington, D.C.: Smithsonian Institution Press, 1971. Fine monograph on Roebling's early work. Technically detailed with reproductions of Roebling's designs. Useful for understanding Roebling's later works.

Clifton K. Yearley
Kerrie L. MacPherson

WILL ROGERS

Born: November 4, 1879; near Oologah, Indian Territory (modern
  Oklahoma)
Died: August 15, 1935; Walakpa Lagoon (near Point Barrow), Alaska
Areas of Achievement: Entertainment, journalism, and humanitarianism
Contribution: An internationally prominent humorist and satirist, Rogers
  functioned as a constructive social critic and humanitarian as well as an
  entertainer.

Early Life

William Penn Adair Rogers was born November 4, 1879, in the Indian
Territory of the United States of America near what eventually became
Oologah, Oklahoma. Both of his parents came from the Indian Territory and
contributed to his status as a quarter-blood Cherokee Indian. His father,
Clement Van (Clem) Rogers, was a rough and wealthy rancher, farmer,
banker, and businessman, in addition to being a prominent politician. His
mother, Mary Schrimsher Rogers, was a loving woman who came from a
financially successful and politically powerful family. Will was the youngest of
eight children, three of whom died at birth, and the only male to survive
childhood.

Rogers developed a lasting love for the life and basic skills of the cowboy,
horseback riding and roping, in his early years. At home, he adored his
affectionate mother but developed a complex and not completely positive
relationship with his father. Rogers clearly loved his father, who provided a
masculine establishment figure with whom to identify. At the same time, Will
possessed a strong personality which eventually clashed with that of the elder
Rogers. Then, at age ten, disaster entered the young Oklahoman's life when
his mother died and the closing of the open range heralded an end to the
cowboys' life. These conditions changed a relatively secure and happy child
into a sad wanderer who sought desperately to replace the love and sense of
purpose that had been taken from him.

Tension increased between Rogers and his father in the years following
Mary Rogers' death. The elder Rogers was particularly infuriated by his
son's uneven performance in school. Between the ages of eight and eighteen,
Rogers attended six different educational institutions and left each one under
questionable circumstances. His main interests during these years were playing the class clown and participating in theatrical activities. He also developed a growing fascination with trick roping. In 1898, after running away
from the last school he attended, the eighteen-year-old embarked on a seven-
year odyssey. He worked variously as a wandering cowboy, as the manager of
the family ranch, and as a trick-rope artist in Wild West shows, then turning
to vaudeville. His travels took him literally across the globe. Such behavior

merely increased the elder Rogers' dissatisfaction with his son. The son, on the other hand, manifested guilt at not having lived up to the father's expectations and example of success.

One final factor remains to be discussed in connection with Rogers' teenage and early adult years: his sensitivity to his Cherokee Indian heritage. This sensitivity was evident in his militant reaction to any criticism of Indians or those of Indian ancestry. Furthermore, because of his own Indian background, he was the victim of racial prejudice in trying to establish relationships with women.

The year 1905 proved to be a crucial one for Rogers. He went to New York and entered vaudeville as a trick-rope artist. At the same time, he began making serious proposals of marriage to Betty Blake of Roger, Arkansas, whom he had first met in 1899. When Rogers and Blake were married in 1908, the Oklahoman had taken the first step in what proved to be one of the most successful entertainment careers in American history. Perhaps more important, however, these events assisted Rogers in overcoming the sadness which had enshrouded him since youth: His marriage helped to replace the female love and sense of belonging he had lost when his mother died, while his success in show business enabled him to establish a more positive relationship with his father and compensated Rogers for the loss of the cowboy life.

Life's Work

Will Rogers' career can be divided into four periods. During the first, from 1905 to 1915, he became a successful vaudevillian. He began his stage career with a trick-roping act, in which he lassoed simultaneously a moving horse and its rider. Gradually, the young performer began making comical remarks as his lariats whirled about. By 1911, he was a bona fide monologuist, making humorous comments about other artists and the theater world. Traveling the famous Orpheum Circuit, he used the same material each evening. Rogers also toured England and Western Europe several times. The Rogers family numbered five by 1915: Will and Betty, William Vann Rogers, Jr. (born 1911), Mary Amelia Rogers (born 1913), and James Blake Rogers (born 1915).

The next stage in Rogers' rise to prominence started in 1915, when he began performing in Florenz Ziegfeld's Midnight Frolic. The Midnight Frolic was staged on the roof of the New Amsterdam Theater in New York City, the home of the Ziegfeld Follies. Rogers encountered a problem working in the Midnight Frolic. Since it attracted many repeat customers, he had to struggle to present new material each night. Eventually, the daily newspapers provided him with constantly changing material concerning contemporary society upon which he could base his humorous monologues.

Rogers' career received a giant boost in 1916, when he joined the Ziegfeld Follies. Within two years, Rogers had finished developing the basic characteristics of his humor. Fittingly, it was at this time that the budding comedian became known as the Cowboy Philosopher and began each performance with his famous line: "Well, all I know is what I read in the newspapers." Rogers' humor was based on the following precepts: Proven material was mixed with continually changing jokes about contemporary news; neutrality on controversial topics was maintained by poking fun at all sides; truth and realism, sometimes exaggerated, provided the best foundation for humor; the comical style involved the projection of Rogers' personality. With his humor resting on these tenets, Will quickly assumed the characteristics of a cracker-barrel philosopher and satirist who functioned as a constructive social critic. As such, he became increasingly serious about what he said.

An additional facet of Rogers' life emerged during World War I: his genuine humanitarianism. He pledged one tenth of what he made during the conflict to the Red Cross and the Salvation Army, and he was extremely active in raising funds for both organizations.

The third stage of the Rogers' career encompassed the years from 1918 to 1928. He became a national figure during this era, expanding into new fields of endeavor. Much of his success was a result of his physical appearance and bearing. Slender, athletic, six feet tall, with handsome facial features that reflected his Indian heritage, Rogers performed in cowboy regalia, chomping on an ever-present wad of chewing gum, and twirling ropes which he watched while making detached comments concerning contemporary events. His ungrammatical speech, Western accent, contagious smile, and unruly forelock merely added to the pretense of an illiterate, homespun yokel, perceptively satirizing society. This pose enabled Rogers to get away with saying things that other performers would never have considered saying.

In 1918, Samuel Goldwyn offered Rogers a starring role in the film *Laughing Bill Hyde*. The humorist hesitantly accepted, since the New Jersey shooting location of the film allowed him to continue working in the Ziegfeld Follies. *Laughing Bill Hyde* proved to be a reasonable success, and Goldwyn presented Rogers with a two-year contract to make motion pictures in California. He agreed to the arrangement and moved to Los Angeles. Rogers added another dimension to his work in 1919, with the publication of two books: *Rogers-isms: The Cowboy Philosopher on the Peace Conference* and *Rogers-isms: The Cowboy Philosopher on Prohibition* (1919).

The move to California was not without its troubles. The newest Rogers baby, Fred Stone Rogers, died of diphtheria when he was eighteen months old. The numerous two-reel motion pictures which Rogers made for Goldwyn did not turn the aspiring actor into a star, and when his contract with Goldwyn was not renewed in 1921, Rogers himself made three two-reel pictures in which he played the leading role. A complex set of circumstances resulted in his losing a large amount of money in the venture. Faced with bankruptcy, the determined performer left Betty and the children in California while he returned to New York and the Ziegfeld Follies. Between 1921 and 1923, Rogers launched a banquet-speaking career and began a syndicated weekly newspaper column, in addition to his work for Ziegfeld. Two years of laboring around the clock in this fashion enabled him to pay off his debts.

Rogers continued to pursue a career in motion pictures, despite his initial difficulties. Thus, in 1923, after he had taken care of his money problems, he returned to Los Angeles and signed a contract with the Hal E. Roach Studio to make a series of two-reel comedies. Thirteen films resulted from this agreement. They were more successful than the Goldwyn films but Rogers was still not a great motion-picture success. He eventually reached the conclusion that the problem resided with the unwillingness of studios and directors to allow him to project his own personality. Frustrated, the humorist once again returned to New York and the Ziegfeld Follies. A third book, *Illiterate Digest*, composed mainly of weekly newspaper articles, appeared in 1924.

Rogers added still another dimension to his work in the mid-1920's. He began his one-person lecture tour in 1925, repeating it in 1926 and in 1927, and periodically thereafter. Additionally, the energetic satirist published a number of magazine articles for the *Saturday Evening Post* and *Life* (at that time a humor magazine). In 1926, he began his short daily syndicated newspaper column, which frequently appeared under the caption "Will Rogers Says." Two more books followed quickly: *Letters of a Self-Made Diplomat to His President* (1926) and *There's Not a Bathing Suit in Russia and Other Bare Facts* (1927). These were collections of articles he had written for the *Saturday Evening Post*, as was his 1929 offering, *Ether and Me: Or, "Just Relax."*

In the 1920's, Rogers also expanded his humanitarian efforts. While in Europe during 1926, he traveled to Dublin, Ireland, and did a benefit for the survivors of a theater fire. The same year, he took similar action to assist survivors of Florida tornadoes and Mississippi River flood victims. His daily and weekly newspaper columns complemented these efforts, repeatedly appealing for public support.

The final phase in Rogers' professional evolution covered the years from 1929 to 1935. During this time, Rogers was catapulted into the elite arena of superstardom. His salary, popularity, influence, and the range of media he employed to communicate with his massive audiences all contributed to this achievement.

Rogers made his first sound motion picture, *They Had to See Paris*, in 1929 for Fox Film Corporation. It was successful, and Rogers became a star overnight. He soon signed a two-year contract with Fox to make five pictures. A leading figure in the development of sound films, in 1934 Rogers was voted the nation's most popular box-office attraction in a poll taken among independent theater owners. It is estimated that at the time of his death in 1935,

Rogers was making one million dollars a year performing in motion pictures, a sum then unsurpassed by any screen personality.

Rogers made infrequent radio appearances during the 1920's but did not feel comfortable with the medium. Nevertheless, he did seventy-five radio programs between 1927 and 1935. His radio appearances increased after 1930, when he did fourteen programs sponsored by E. R. Squibb and Sons. A longer but more sporadic series was sponsored by the Gulf Oil Corporation between 1933 and 1935. In time, Rogers became one of the most popular radio entertainers in the country; as early as 1930, he was receiving $350 per minute for his radio performances.

The onset of the Depression in 1929 elicited a predictable response from Rogers. He devoted more and more time to benefits for victims of all sorts of natural disasters and the disadvantaged. These activities took him all over the United States and as far afield as Nicaragua.

Haphazard vacation plans in August of 1935 resulted in Rogers joining the famous aviator Wiley Post on a flight in a newly constructed plane of Post's design. Plans called for the two to fly from Seattle, Washington, to Point Barrow, Alaska, with stops in between. The plane crashed on August 15, 1935, at Walakpa Lagoon, sixteen miles short of its destination. Both Rogers, age fifty-five, and Post were killed in what became one of the most famous air tragedies of the twentieth century.

Summary

Rogers' philosophy remained consistent throughout his career. He generally sided with the disadvantaged and weak against the powerful and wealthy on both domestic and international questions. This outlook in part reflected Rogers' early experiences. His Indian heritage, for example, exposed him to racial prejudice. Having experienced such prejudice, he became more understanding of society's disadvantaged people and more supportive of the weak and the poor.

Underlying Rogers' humor was a combination of realism and optimism. Regardless of how bad the truth seemed to be, there was almost always a positive message in what he said and wrote. This quality reflected the experience of his nation and region. In both, the task of carving a civilization out of a primitive environment made reality impossible to ignore and hope necessary for survival.

In the entertainment world, Rogers established several important precedents. His method of remaining neutral on controversial topics by criticizing all involved established an approach to satire which has been employed by succeeding generations of performers. His commitment to humanitarian activities set a standard which entertainers have followed. Finally, his reliance on contemporary news as the basis for his constantly changing material has been widely imitated.

Bibliography

Croy, Homer. *Our Will Rogers*. New York: Duell Sloan and Pearce, 1953. One of the numerous biographies available on Rogers, this volume is extremely valuable because of the interviews Croy conducted. Croy also knew Rogers personally during the latter's motion-picture career.

Day, Donald. *Will Rogers: A Biography*. New York: David McKay Co., 1962. This volume is unbalanced since it overemphasizes the importance of the early days in Rogers' relationship with his wife. Includes no footnotes or bibliography. Well written, but of questionable value for research.

Keith, Harold. *Boy's Life of Will Rogers*. New York: Thomas Y. Crowell, 1938. A valuable work for reminiscences by hundreds of Rogers' relatives and friends, supported by the author's study of books, magazines, and newspapers that contained information by or about Rogers.

Ketchum, Richard M. *Will Rogers: His Life and Times*. New York: American Heritage Publishing Co., 1973. This book is well written, accompanied by an excellent collection of photographs, and based on many materials not previously used. Unfortunately, it is not documented, fails to describe causative factors in Rogers' life, and does not analyze the humorist's philosophy.

Milsten, David Randolph. *An Appreciation of Will Rogers*. San Antonio, Tex.: The Naylor Co., 1935. Valuable for interviews with close friends and associates of Rogers.

Rogers, Betty. *Will Rogers: The Story of His Life Told by His Wife*. Garden City, N.Y.: Garden City Publishing Co., 1943. Betty's recollection of her life with Will is a key source. Contains no footnotes or bibliography. Rogers states that her direct quotes frequently come from her husband's newspaper articles.

Rogers, Will. *The Autobiography of Will Rogers*. Edited by Donald Day. Boston: Houghton Mifflin Co., 1949. Day mixes in various materials from numerous other sources and does not inform the reader. The work is not documented.

——————. *The Writings of Will Rogers*. 23 vols. Edited by Joseph A. Stout, Jr., Peter C. Rollins, Steven K. Gragert, and James M. Smallwood. Stillwater: Oklahoma State University Press, 1973-1984. A twenty-three-volume set of the edited, annotated writings of Rogers with some radio broadcasts included. Includes a subject index for the entire set; most of the individual volumes possess an index as well.

Rollins, Peter C.. *Will Rogers: A Bio-Bibliography*. Westport, Conn: Greenwood Press, 1984. The most significant resource for anyone doing research on Rogers. It contains a wealth of information ranging from a biographical overview to a complete listing of the available primary and secondary sources. This material is not only described, but much of it is also summarized and evaluated. A treasure trove without equal.

Trent, Spi M. *My Cousin Will Rogers: Intimate and Untold Tales*. New York: G. P. Putnam's Sons, 1938. Trent was a close companion of Rogers during the latter's youth and early adulthood. His work is a valuable source for those years. It must be used cautiously when dealing with the period after Rogers' marriage.

S. Fred Roach

ELEANOR ROOSEVELT

Born: October 11, 1884; New York, New York
Died: November 7, 1962; New York, New York
Area of Achievement: Reform
Contribution: While she never held a public position until she was appointed
United States Delegate to the United Nations in 1945, Eleanor Roosevelt
was the personification of liberal reform thought in the United States from
the 1930's to her death in 1962.

Early Life

Anna Eleanor Roosevelt was born October 11, 1884, into a patrician family in New York. The niece and godchild of Theodore Roosevelt, Eleanor was orphaned at age ten and brought up by her maternal grandmother. Her childhood was very unhappy, even while her mother and father lived; Eleanor was regarded as the "ugly duckling" of the family and was called Granny even as a young child. "I was," she said, "a solemn child without beauty. I seemed like a little old woman relatively lacking in the spontaneous joy and mirth of youth." Grandmother Hall, who cared only for her place in society, had Eleanor educated first by private tutors in the United States and finally in a private boarding school in England.

Perhaps one of her formative experiences came in that last stage of her formal education at Allenswood School outside London, England. There she studied, from age fifteen to age eighteen, under the direction of Marie Souvestre, a remarkable woman of strong personality and liberal mind. Eleanor's happiest childhood years seem to have been at Allenswood, where she experienced a theretofore unknown warm and loving acceptance. Headmistress Souvestre, not afraid to voice unpopular opinions, encouraged the young woman to think creatively and independently.

Returning to the United States at age eighteen, Eleanor exhibited an interest in and concern for the plight of the poor. Her experiences on her return to New York also established a lifetime pattern of involvement in two worlds: the patrician world of her family and the netherworld of the disadvantaged. On the one hand, she went through the ordeal of being a debutante. ("That first winter [back] when my sole object in life was society, nearly brought me to a state of nervous collapse.") At the same time, however, she joined the National Consumers' League—an organization concerned with problems faced by workers in clothing factories and sweatshops—and also engaged in some settlement-house work.

In 1905, when she was twenty-one, Eleanor married a distant cousin, the dashing and handsome Franklin D. Roosevelt, and her evolution into the American champion for the downtrodden was put on hold for nearly fifteen years. Between 1905 and 1920, Eleanor was, in her own words, a "conventional, quiet, young, society matron." During that time, she bore six children, five of whom lived, and tried to cope with her dictatorial mother-in-law. This period was important, however, in that FDR entered politics. He served in the New York state legislature and was appointed assistant secretary of the navy by President Woodrow Wilson. Late in this period of Eleanor's dormancy, in 1918, she discovered her husband's marital infidelity, a profoundly distressing situation and something which seemed to spark a new sense of independence in her.

Life's Work

In 1920, after FDR's campaign for the vice presidency ended in failure, Eleanor joined the League of Women Voters as well as the more liberal Women's Trade Union League. After FDR contracted polio in 1921, Eleanor (in conjunction with newsman Louis Howe) fought to keep alive her husband's dream of a political career. This struggle, against FDR's mother's demand that her son return to Hyde Park to live out his life as an invalid, was almost a metaphysical struggle for FDR's soul and Eleanor's independence. It was in the latter's phrase "the most trying winter" of her entire life.

By 1924, FDR was actively back in politics, despite being paralyzed, and nominated Democrat Al Smith for the presidency. Eleanor worked as a Democratic Party organizer and served as financial chairman of the women's division of the Democratic State Committee in New York. She campaigned in FDR's successful bid for the New York governor's office in 1928 and 1930 and toured the country in 1932 as FDR successfully campaigned for the presidency. Traveling the country that year, at the peak of the Great Depression, Eleanor's longtime concern for the poor and the oppressed intensified.

Between 1933 and 1945, what she called the White House years, Eleanor developed and broadened her image as an advocate for the forgotten and the powerless. During that time, she was indefatigable in her efforts on behalf of everyone from Southern tenant farmers to unemployed factory workers to West Virginia coal miners to oppressed black Americans. Although the president was irritated at first by her outspoken behavior and asked Eleanor to confine her attention "to the Girl Scouts," he changed his mind as he discovered the important role she was playing. She crisscrossed the United States (forty thousand miles in 1933 alone), assessing conditions and spreading goodwill on behalf of FDR wherever she went.

As her uncle, President Theodore Roosevelt, had once called the presidency a "bully pulpit," so Eleanor used her position as First Lady to dramatize social, economic, and racial injustice in the United States. She was a staunch advocate for black civil rights and more equitable living conditions for all people, and her life became a model for women who wanted to expand their horizons in socioeconomic and political terms. Eleanor, to be sure, was able to accomplish this goal at the personal and nonprofessional level and thus avoided being identified as a radical feminist.

In 1945, after FDR's death, she was appointed first American delegate to the fledgling United Nations. One of her finest hours came as chair of the United Nations Commission on Human Rights, which drafted the Declaration of Human Rights. Eleanor, who had much to do with the actual writing of that declaration, then steered it through hostile sessions to ratification. Her last formal role came during John F. Kennedy's presidency, when she chaired the Kennedy Commission on the Status of Women. That commission's report, which appeared almost simultaneously with Betty Friedan's powerful *The Feminine Mystique* (1963), did much to publicize the inequities women faced in the United States and to spur the modern femininst movement. Eleanor Roosevelt died November 7, 1962, of bone marrow tuberculosis.

Summary

There was something uncanny in the way that people outside the perimeters of power made their way to Eleanor's side—whether it was an Arkansas tenant farmer advocate such as H. L. Mitchell or a South American peasant. In 1952, American Ambassador Claude G. Bowers urged the United States State Department to have Eleanor represent the United States in Santiago at the inauguration of a new Chilean president. It turned out to be a diplomatic ten-strike. She was almost physically overwhelmed by the delighted throngs who followed her every movement. The diplomatic delegations of other countries were as nothing in comparison with Eleanor.

Eleanor Roosevelt is one of the great and towering human figures of the twentieth century, and she clearly deserved the designation by which she is often recalled, First Lady of the World. She was a hero whose values were correct. Perhaps her primary legacy to those people who came after her can be summed up in the words: "Choose you this day whom you will serve." She made a conscious choice to use her talents and gifts to advance the cause of mankind, and she provided a role model for all people. Instead of living out her life in comfort and ease, she chose to work at making society more humane by seeking to alleviate suffering and to establish a higher quality of life for the forgotten peoples of the world.

Bibliography

Boettiger, John R. *A Love in Shadow*. New York: W. W. Norton and Co., 1978. While many members of Eleanor's family have written about life as a Roosevelt, this volume is the most sensitive and offers a unique perspective. Boettiger, Eleanor's grandson, was Anna Roosevelt's son by her second marriage and tells his mother's story as he thinks she would have written it. There are many insightful passages about Eleanor.

Hareven, Tamara K. *Eleanor Roosevelt: An American Conscience*. Chicago:

Quadrangle Books, 1968. A perceptive and scholarly analysis of Eleanor's social thought, this volume was originally a dissertation at Ohio State University.

Hickok, Lorena A. *Reluctant First Lady*. New York: Dodd, Mead and Co., 1962. This book, written by a news reporter and one of Eleanor's most intimate friends, details the growth of her interests and abilities once she became First Lady.

Hoff-Wilson, Joan, and Marjorie Lightman, eds. *Without Precedent: The Life and Career of Eleanor Roosevelt*. Bloomington: Indiana University Press, 1984. This volume was the result of the celebration of Eleanor's centennial.

Kearney, James R. *Anna Eleanor Roosevelt: The Evolution of Reformer*. Boston: Houghton Mifflin Co., 1968. This book, too, was the outgrowth of a dissertation; it is well written and is invaluable to an understanding of Eleanor's transformation into a reformer

Lash, Joseph P. *Eleanor and Franklin: The Story of Their Relationship, Based on Eleanor Roosevelt's Private Papers*. New York: W. W. Norton and Co., 1971. This is the best and most detailed study of the Eleanor Roosevelt–Franklin Roosevelt relationship and is based in large part on Eleanor's private papers. Lash, a longtime friend of Eleanor, is an admiring biographer, and it is that admiration which makes this book more than a mere professional exercise.

_____. *Eleanor: The Years Alone*. New York: W. W. Norton and Co., 1972. A continuation of Eleanor's biography begun in *Eleanor and Franklin*, this volume maintains Lash's high-quality work. The two Lash volumes provided the basis for the highly acclaimed television productions of the mid-1970's.

Roosevelt, Anna Eleanor. *Autobiography*. New York: Harper and Row, Publishers, 1961. Reprint. Boston: G. K. Hall, 1984. This is an abbreviated (though augumented) version of several of Eleanor's earlier autobiographical works, including *This Is My Story* (1937), *This I Remember* (1949), and *On My Own* (1958). This volume will give the reader a flavor of Eleanor's "public face" as well as some insights into her view of herself as mother and wife.

Charles J. Bussey

FRANKLIN D. ROOSEVELT

Born: January 30, 1882; Hyde Park, New York
Died: April 12, 1945; Warm Springs, Georgia
Areas of Achievement: Politics and government
Contribution: Displaying extraordinary personal courage and perhaps the most astute political leadership America has ever witnessed, Roosevelt dominated American government for a longer period than has any other president of the United States.

Early Life

Born in Hyde Park, New York, on January 30, 1882, Franklin Delano Roosevelt was a member of an American aristocratic family of great wealth. James and Sara Roosevelt, of Dutch and English ancestry, educated their only child with private tutors and European tours. At Groton School in Massachusetts, Roosevelt came under the influence of Rector Endicott Peabody, who prided himself on grooming future politicians and instilling in his charges a lifelong commitment to public service.

By 1900, when Franklin enrolled at Harvard University, he was an impressive young man—six feet two inches tall, handsome, with a patrician nose and majestically deep-set eyes. In his junior year, he fell in love with his fifth cousin, Eleanor Roosevelt, a tall, slender woman whose pleasing face was punctuated by a prominent set of Rooseveltian teeth. Eleanor was the daughter of President Theodore Roosevelt's younger brother, Elliott, who died from alcoholism when she was ten. In 1905, Franklin married Eleanor, over the objections of his mother, who tried to postpone the wedding.

Following Harvard, Roosevelt dabbled briefly with the practice of law before turning to the real love of his life: politics. In 1910, he entered the political arena for the first time, running for the New York State Senate. Fellow Democrats skeptically observed his entrance into the race for several reasons: his aristocratic bearing, his tendency to look down his nose at people, his unfamiliarity with working-class voters in the Hyde Park–Poughkeepsie area, and the fact that he was a former Republican. The political climate, however, demanded a reformer and Roosevelt, following in the footsteps of his cousin Theodore, could fill the bill by pointing to the ugly specter of corruption within the opposition party. During the campaign, FDR (as he came to be known) showed he was different from the average "cheap-talking" politician, displaying a pragmatic unorthodoxy that later endeared him to the nation. He even campaigned for office in an automobile, an unusual political act for a time when most people eyed the horseless carriage with suspicion. Victory was his, however, and FDR became only the second Democrat elected from his district to the New York State Senate since the Civil War. He was on his way.

It was not an easy path to success. Experiences in the New York senate taught him the limits of progressive, reformistic power. When he challenged Charles F. Murphy's Tammany machine of New York City over the Democratic nomination for the United States Senate, he met defeat. He gradually learned, however, to moderate his reform tendencies. This later proved to be his first major lesson in the school of politics. Following his reelection in 1912, Roosevelt jumped at the opportunity to join Woodrow Wilson's administration in the capacity of assistant secretary of the Navy under Josephus Daniels. In doing so, young FDR may have imagined himself following the example of Theodore, who had achieved the governorship of New York, the vice presidency, and the presidency after serving in the same position. The Navy Department afforded Roosevelt a chance to hone his administrative skills and strengthen his political ties throughout the Democratic Party to the point that, by 1920, delegates to the national convention were willing to exploit his famous name by nominating him for the vice presidency as James M. Cox's running mate. Cox and Roosevelt suffered defeat in the Republican landslide that swept Warren G. Harding and Calvin Coolidge into office. FDR remained basically unchanged throughout these events, still a somewhat immature young man who maintained very few strong convictions.

All this changed in August, 1921, when Roosevelt contracted polio while vacationing at Campobello Island, his family's resort off the Maine seacoast. His health was shattered, but a new Roosevelt slowly began to emerge. Paralyzed from the waist down, and wealthy enough to retire at the age of thirty-nine, he fought to regain his vigor. First, he had to overcome the frustration that resulted from the wearing of heavy steel braces which prohibited him from walking unaided. Second, he had to ignore the pleas of his mother (whom he worshiped but who urged him to withdraw from politics) and listen to his wife and his personal secretary, Louis McHenry Howe, who plotted to restore him to some semblance of health. During this period of recovery, Eleanor became his "legs," going where he could not go, doing what he could not do physically, and generally learning the art of politics.

Life's Work

In 1924, FDR showed that Roosevelt the fighter had superseded Roosevelt the dedicated aristocrat when he appeared at the Democratic National Convention to give his "Happy Warrior Speech" nominating Alfred E. Smith for president. Smith lost the nomination but Roosevelt did not lose his political career to polio. Instead, it seemed to give him a strength of character he had rarely shown before the Campobello incident. In 1928, while Smith was losing his home state of New York by 100,000 votes to Herbert Hoover, FDR was winning the governorship by twenty-five thousand, thus becoming the front-runner for the 1932 Democratic presidential nomination. Reelected by an unprecedented 725,000 votes in 1930, Roosevelt, aided by his national campaign manager, James A. Farley, began his first run for the presidency. Capturing the nomination on the third ballot, Roosevelt pledged himself to create, if elected, a "new deal" for the American people.

The 1932 presidential campaign pitted FDR against the Republican incumbent, Herbert Hoover. With the country three years into the Great Depression, Roosevelt wisely ran a pragmatic campaign—fluctuating between alternative ideological positions, allowing Hoover's record to speak for itself and leaving the decision to the American electorate. On November 8, 1932, the people spoke—giving him a 472–59 electoral victory over Hoover. When Roosevelt took office on March 4, 1933, the nation was mired in the worst depression in American history. There were approximately thirteen million unemployed people—25.2 percent of the work force. As a mood of apprehension gripped the country, Roosevelt tried to calm the panic-stricken populace:

> So, first of all, let me assert my firm belief that the only thing we have to fear is fear itself—nameless, unreasoning, unjustified terror which paralyzes needed efforts to convert retreat into advance. In every dark hour of our national life a leadership of frankness and vigor has met with that understanding and support of the people themselves which is essential to victory. I am convinced that you will again give that support to leadership in these critical days.

During the crucial one hundred days that followed his inaugural speech, Roosevelt began the New Deal. He quickly satisfied the public's overwhelming desire for leadership and action by issuing executive orders and introducing legislation which a frightened Congress quickly rubber-stamped. FDR acted in four critical areas: finance, industry, agriculture, and relief (welfare). In combating the Depression, Roosevelt gave the nation no panacea but offered the means through which it might be able to survive the crisis. He did not end the Depression—but many of his programs and the laws he signed got the country through the Depression and remained an effective part of the federal government long after his death. In finance, the Emergency Banking Act (1933) and the Glass-Steagall Banking Act (1933) saved the banking structure and helped prevent a future crisis by creating the Federal Deposit Insurance Corporation. The Truth-in-Securities Act (1933) and the Securities Exchange Act (1934) brought Wall Street under tighter public regulation. In industry, the National Industrial Recovery Act (1933) offered both business and labor opportunities for greater self-government. Later, through the National Labor Relations Act (1935), he concentrated more on allowing labor unions the right to organize. In agriculture, Roosevelt tried to restore farmers' prosperity through the Agriculture Adjustment Act (1933) by subsidizing certain farm products they could not afford to sell at market prices. In relief, FDR straddled the line between welfare and public works. At first, the New Deal doled out money to unemployed people through the Federal Emergency Relief Administration (1933) and sent young men to work camps through the Civilian Conservation Corps (1933).

After the one hundred days had passed, FDR turned away from welfare and made government jobs a primary goal of his administration. Listening to his advisers, Harry Hopkins and Harold L. Ickes, Roosevelt made the federal government the employer of the last resort through the Civil Works Administration (1933), the Public Works Administration (1933), and the Works Progress Administration (1935). In particular, the WPA, which averaged 2,112,000 on its monthly payrolls from 1935 to 1941, was the largest, most visionary, and probably most effective federal relief program ever created. Perhaps the most long-lasting reform achieved by FDR was the Social Security Administration (1935) granting unemployment compensation and old-age pensions.

Roosevelt's New Deal programs generated billions of new dollars throughout the American economy increasing incomes and causing tax revenues to "trickle up" to the federal and state governments. The jobs also raised the hopes of millions of voters who came to believe that FDR had saved them from financial disaster. He was the man who put food on their tables, shoes on their feet, and a roof over their heads. In brief, the New Deal was political dynamite and Roosevelt was the New Deal. The president's charismatic leadership, his inspirational speeches and informal "fireside chats," made him an unbeatable campaigner, as his 1936 Republican opponent learned. Roosevelt crushed Kansas Governor Alfred M. Landon by the largest electoral margin in recent American history, 523 to 8.

In less than three years, Roosevelt created an imperial presidency and vastly enlarged the federal bureaucracy, thus prompting criticisms from conservatives and the Supreme Court. When the Court began invalidating some New Deal programs such as the National Industrial Recovery Act (*Schechter v. United States*, 1935) and the Agriculture Adjustment Act (*Butler v. United States*, 1936), he struck back. In 1937, FDR tried to pack the Court with New Dealers by introducing the Federal Judiciary Reorganization Bill. Although the bill failed to pass Congress, Roosevelt prevailed in this struggle, since the Court's later decisions proved more favorable to New Deal legislation. Still, the court-packing scheme suggested dictatorial ambitions and damaged FDR's reputation in some circles. His popularity further declined as the nation slid deeper into the Depression in 1938, and the president, determined to keep his working majority in Congress, attempted to purge conservative Democrats from his party. This tactic also failed. By 1939, the New Deal, for all practical purposes, was dead.

As the New Deal passed into history, new dangers loomed on the horizon. Totalitarian regimes in Germany, Japan, and Italy threatened America's position in the world. Roosevelt himself recognized that the leaders of these regimes, Adolf Hitler, Hideki Tojo, and Benito Mussolini, would necessitate some changes in American foreign policy when he said that "Dr. Win the War" would have to replace "Dr. New Deal." In this way, he reluctantly began to shift American diplomacy in the direction of confronting these aggressors. After Germany invaded Poland on September 1, 1939, precipitating a declaration of war by England and France, Americans debated whether their country should maintain its isolation or aid its British and French allies. While Roosevelt was preaching neutrality, he won an unprecedented third term, a 449–82 electoral victory over his 1940 Republican opponent, Wendell Willkie.

When the war came to America, it struck with a fury. Possibly no aspect of FDR's foreign policy has evoked more controversy than the role he played in leading the United States into World War II. On December 7, 1941, a little more than a year after he promised that "this country is not going to war," Japanese planes swept down on the American naval base at Pearl Harbor, Hawaii, nearly destroying the United States Pacific Fleet. The declaration of war that followed prompted his critics to complain that he had tricked his nation into war. While the Roosevelt Administration made numerous errors in judgment, FDR did not intentionally expose the military installation to attack in order to drag a reluctant and isolationistic American people into the war.

Shortly after the "day of infamy," Roosevelt met with British prime minister Winston Churchill in the first of several Washington conferences forming a "grand alliance" between the two world leaders and their nations. At the first meeting, Roosevelt agreed to the idea that the allies should place top priority on defeating Germany and Italy, while fighting a holding action against Japan in the Pacific theater. In fact, throughout the war, FDR actively planned and executed top military and diplomatic decisions that affected its outcome and the postwar world. Together with Churchill and Soviet premier Joseph Stalin, he agreed to the formulation of the United Nations. At the Yalta Conference (February, 1945), Roosevelt made another of his extremely controversial decisions that would affect public opinion long after he was gone. In return for Stalin's promise to enter the war against Japan and to allow free elections in the Soviet bloc nations, FDR acquiesced to Russia's hegemony in eastern Poland and other territories occupied by Soviet troops. Because these decisions were kept secret by the chief signatories, Roosevelt never felt the full fury of his critics before his death on April 12, 1945.

Summary

In electing Franklin D. Roosevelt to an unprecedented four terms of office, the American people lent credence to the belief that FDR was the greatest leader ever to hold the presidency. This view was further substantiated by the 1982 survey conducted by Professor Robert K. Murray of Pennsylvania State University among a thousand Ph.D. historians; only Abraham Lincoln ranked ahead of Roosevelt as the best president in American history. Nevertheless, Roosevelt certainly had his critics, and they made valid points: He seems to have had dictatorial ambitions when he circumvented the Constitution and tried to pack the Supreme Court. FDR may have gravely damaged the national economy by allowing the national debt to grow to astronomical proportions. Other presidents followed him down the path of "deficit spending," enlarging upon the problem that he had created in order to combat the Depression. Without a doubt, Roosevelt was one of the most controversial presidents in American history.

FDR created the imperial presidency, in the process setting a precedent for leadership by which all his successors have been evaluated. He took the executive branch, which had lost much of its power and glory, and expanded it beyond the limits achieved by any twentieth century American chief executive. Circumstances such as depression and war, and the force of his indomitable personal character shaped by the adversity of polio, allowed him to restructure the office into its present form—one that casually encroaches on the normal powers and functions of Congress and the Supreme Court. In 1939, for example, in an act that escaped virtually unnoticed by the nation's press, he issued Executive Order 8248, creating the Executive Office of the President and shifting the powerful Bureau of the Budget from the Treasury Department to the White House. Then, when the time came to run for an unprecedented third term in 1940, Roosevelt occupied a perfect position to manipulate the federal economy for reelection purposes, and manipulate it he did—setting another example that his successors have followed.

Although Roosevelt's primary claim to greatness lay in domestic achievements, he made major contributions in foreign policy as well. He was the president who led America to victory over the Axis powers and then achieved the first détente with the new superpower: Soviet Russia. It was in the arena of American politics and government, however, that FDR made his greatest imprint. Even his critics must concede that his impact on the nation was extraordinary.

Bibliography

Burns, James MacGregor. *Roosevelt: The Lion and the Fox*. New York: Harcourt Brace, 1956. The best political biography of Roosevelt. Burns stresses FDR's Machiavellian tendencies and his failure to implement an enduring reform coalition.

_____. *Roosevelt: The Soldier of Freedom*. New York: Harcourt Brace Jovanovich, 1970. One of the best books analyzing Roosevelt's role as commander in chief during World War II.

Dallek, Robert. *Franklin D. Roosevelt and American Foreign Policy, 1932-*

1945. New York: Oxford University Press, 1979. Dallek received the Bancroft Prize in history for this excellent analytical overview of FDR's foreign policy.

Divine, Robert A., ed. *Causes and Consequences of World War II*. Chicago: Quadrangle Books, 1969. Very good historiographical collection of essays and accompanying bibliography focusing on the prelude to and aftermath of World War II.

Freidel, Frank. *The Apprenticeship*. Boston: Little, Brown and Co., 1952. The first of a projected six-volume biography. *The Apprenticeship* covers the period from Roosevelt's birth through his tenure as assistant secretary of the Navy. Some reviewers thought this volume suffered from an overemphasis on FDR's early life.

_____. *The Ordeal*. Boston: Little, Brown and Co., 1952. The second volume covers the era from 1919 to 1928, including FDR's contracting polio in 1921, his comeback (firmly established by the "Happy Warrior Speech" in 1924), and his election as governor of New York in 1928.

_____. *The Triumph*. Boston: Little, Brown and Co., 1956. The third volume addresses the subject of Roosevelt's two terms as governor of New York culminating with his election as President of the United States in 1932. This is a very dispassionate analysis of Roosevelt's emergence as the master politician who crushed Herbert Hoover's hopes in the 1932 presidential election.

_____. *Launching the New Deal*. Boston: Little, Brown and Co., 1973. Focuses on the winter of 1932-1933 through the completion of the "One Hundred Days" Congress of June, 1933. This is a very detailed, well-documented study of the early New Deal, although it omits Harry L. Hopkins' Federal Emergency Relief Administration. (Freidel's four-volume series on Roosevelt provides an unusually well-balanced account. The first three volumes constitute the definitive analysis of FDR's early years.)

Leuchtenburg, William E. *Franklin D. Roosevelt and the New Deal*. New York: Harper and Row, Publishers, 1963. This overview of Roosevelt's foreign and domestic policy up to 1940, the best one-volume treatment of its subject, is scholarly yet highly readable.

Schlesinger, Arthur M., Jr. *The Age of Roosevelt: The Crisis of the Old Order, 1919-1933*. Boston: Houghton Mifflin Co., 1957. This is the first of four projected volumes focusing on the changes experienced by the United States during Franklin Roosevelt's career. Essentially the first volume analyzes the political, economic, and social currents of the 1920's, culminating with FDR's first presidential election in 1932. Somewhat flawed by the author's tendency to allow his liberalism to prejudice his historical analysis of the period.

_____. *The Age of Roosevelt: The Coming of the New Deal*. Boston: Houghton Mifflin Co., 1959. The second volume of Schlesinger's series analyzes the first two years of Roosevelt's presidency and the New Deal from 1933-1935. The problem of Schlesinger's pro-Roosevelt bias is less serious in this work than in his first volume.

_____. *The Age of Roosevelt: The Politics of Upheaval.* Boston: Houghton Mifflin Co., 1960. The third volume (to date) of Schlesinger's multivolume study of Roosevelt carries the analysis of FDR through his reelection in 1936. As with the first and second volumes, this work is characterized by Schlesinger's highly subjective analysis of political, economic, and social history, but it solidifies Schlesinger's major contribution to the literature on Roosevelt.

J. Christopher Schnell

THEODORE ROOSEVELT

Born: October 27, 1858; New York, New York
Died: January 6, 1919; Oyster Bay, New York
Areas of Achievement: Politics, writing, and war
Contribution: As twenty-sixth president of the United States, Roosevelt energetically led America into the twentieth century. Popular and effective, he promoted major domestic reforms and a larger role for the United States in world affairs. In so doing, he added power to the presidential office.

Early Life

Theodore Roosevelt, twenty-sixth president of the United States, was born October 27, 1858, to a moderately wealthy mercantile family in New York City. His father, Theodore, Sr., was of mostly Dutch ancestry; his mother, Martha Bulloch of Georgia, came from a slaveholding family of Scots and Huguenot French. (During his political career, Roosevelt would claim an ethnic relationship with practically every white voter he met; among his nicknames—besides TR and Teddy—was Old Fifty-seven Varieties.) He was educated at home by tutors and traveled with his parents to the Middle East and Europe.

As a child, Roosevelt was puny, asthmatic, and unable to see much of the world until he was fitted with thick eyeglasses at the age of thirteen. He grew determined to "make" a powerful body, and by strenuous exercise and force of will, young Roosevelt gradually overcame most of his physical shortcomings. Shyness and fear were other weaknesses he conquered. "There were all kinds of things of which I was afraid at first," he later admitted in his *Theodore Roosevelt: An Autobiography* (1913). "But by acting as if I was not afraid I gradually ceased to be afraid." Insecurity, however, was one demon which he never exorcised.

While becoming athletic and assertive, young Roosevelt retained his wide-ranging intellectual curiosity. At Harvard, from which he was graduated in 1880, his absorption with both sports and books made him something of an oddity. Yet career plans remained uncertain. Dull science classes at Harvard dimmed his earlier interest in becoming a naturalist. A year at Columbia University Law School (1880-1881) did not stimulate him toward a legal career. While attending Columbia, he married Alice Lee, completed his first book, *The Naval War of 1812* (1882), and entered politics in the autumn of 1881 by election to the New York legislature as a Republican representative from Manhattan. For the remainder of his life, except for brief military glory in the Spanish-American War, writing and politics would absorb most of his overflowing energy.

Life's Work

At the age of twenty-three, Roosevelt, the youngest member of New York's legislature, attracted attention because of his anticorruption stance and his flair for the dramatic. He instinctively knew how to make his doings interesting to the press and the public. Personality flaws were obvious from the beginning of his political career (egotism, impulsiveness, a tendency to see everything in black or white, and occasional ruthlessness), yet Roosevelt's virtues were equally apparent and won for him far more admirers than enemies: extraordinary vitality and intelligence, courage, sincerity, conviviality, and, usually, a willingness to make reasonable compromises.

Family tragedy, the death of his young wife, prompted Roosevelt to retire from politics temporarily in 1884. During the next two years, he operated cattle ranches he owned in the badlands of the Dakota Territory, where he found time to write *Hunting Trips of a Ranchman* (1885), the first of a trilogy of books on his Western activities and observations. Ranching proved financially unprofitable, but outdoor life made Roosevelt physically more robust and helped ease the pain of Alice's death. In 1886, he returned to New York and married Edith Kermit Carow, who would bear him four sons and a daughter and rear the daughter, Alice, born to his first wife. That same year, Roosevelt was the unsuccessful Republican nominee for mayor of New York City; he also commenced work on a six-volume history of America's Western expansion, *The Winning of the West* (1889-1896).

Roosevelt did not seek another elective office until he won the governorship of New York in 1898, but in the meantime, he served in three appointive positions: member of the United States Civil Service Commission (1889-1895), president of New York City's Board of Police Commissioners (1895-1897), and assistant secretary of the navy (1897-1898). He resigned the latter post when war with Spain broke out in 1898. Eager for combat, he organized a volunteer cavalry regiment known as the Rough Riders. Most of the land fighting between the United States and Spain occurred in Cuba; the image of Colonel Roosevelt leading a charge up San Juan Hill (in actuality, Kettle Hill) became a public symbol of this brief, victorious war. "Teddy" was a national hero. In November of 1898, he was elected governor of New York and quickly published a new book, *The Rough Riders* (1899), which a humorous critic said should have been titled "Alone in Cuba."

As governor of New York (1899-1900), Roosevelt pursued a vigorous program of political reform. The Republican state machine, wanting him out of New York, promoted his nomination for vice president on the national ticket in 1900. With reluctance, thinking that office might be a dead end, Roosevelt was finally persuaded to accept the nomination, thus becoming President William McKinley's running mate in 1900.

Within a year, McKinley died by an assassin's bullet, and Theodore Roosevelt, at age forty-two, was sworn in as the youngest chief executive in the nation's history. Physically, the new president had an aura of strength despite his average height, spectacles, small hands and feet, and high-pitched voice. His wide, square face, prominent, firm teeth, and massive chest overrode any hint of weakness.

The presidency, Roosevelt once observed, was a "bully pulpit," and he wasted no time in exhorting America toward new horizons in both domestic and foreign policy. Yet Roosevelt was painfully aware that he had become president by mishap. Not until his overwhelming election to a full term in 1904 did he believe that the office was truly his.

Within the nation, President Roosevelt called for a Square Deal for both capital and labor. He saw himself as chief arbiter of conflicts between economic groups; government, he believed, should represent everyone equitably. Believing in capitalism yet convinced that big corporations were too powerful and arrogant, he began a policy of "trust busting." Roosevelt's administration was the first to use successfully the Sherman Anti-Trust Act (passed in 1890) to break up business monopolies. Actually, Roosevelt believed more in regulation than in "busting," but he hoped to frighten big business into accepting regulation. Privately, he was convinced that, for modern America, industrial and financial combinations were inevitable; he desired to subordinate both big business and labor unions to a stronger central government, which he viewed as the proper instrument for protecting the general interest.

The Hepburn Act, which for the first time gave the Interstate Commerce Commission regulatory power over railroads, was a signal accomplishment of Roosevelt's presidency, as was the Pure Food and Drug Act and the Meat Inspection Act, all passed in 1906. Conservation of natural resources was another Roosevelt goal. Over both Democratic and Republican opposition, he cajoled Congress into limiting private exploitation of the nation's wilderness, mineral, and water resources. His administration doubled the number of national parks and tripled the acreage of national forests. Fifty-one wildlife refuges were established. Conservation was probably Roosevelt's most passionate cause and one of his most enduring legacies.

In foreign policy, Roosevelt is remembered by the proverb he once used: "Speak softly and carry a big stick." In practice, however, he bifurcated that approach; he spoke softly toward nations whose power he respected, while saving the big stick for small or weak countries. High-handedly, he "took Panama"—to use his own words—away from the nation of Colombia in 1903, so as to build an isthmian canal; the next year, he proclaimed a protectorate over all of Latin America—the Roosevelt Corollary to the Monroe Doctrine. As for the Far East, Roosevelt worried over but respected the rising power of Japan. He wanted the Japanese to thwart Russian expansionism but not to dominate Asia. He assumed that Great Britain and the United States would draw closer in worldwide interests; he viewed Germany, Japan, and Russia as probable enemies of a future Anglo-American alliance.

Roosevelt did not run for reelection. He had pledged after his 1904 triumph that he would not seek or accept another nomination. It was a promise he later regretted. The Republican Party in 1908 chose Roosevelt's close personal friend William Howard Taft who, with Roosevelt's blessing, easily won the presidency. Yet Taft's troubled term (1909-1913) split the Republicans into Progressive and Old Guard wings, and by 1910, Roosevelt angrily decided that Taft had capitulated to the Old Guard. Consequently, Roosevelt attempted to regain the White House in 1912. After losing a bitter contest to Taft for the Republican nomination, Roosevelt burst into the general election as a third party (Progressive, or Bull Moose Party) candidate, thus virtually guaranteeing victory for Democratic nominee Woodrow Wilson. Roosevelt's personal popularity allowed him to finish second in the 1912 presidential election, but without a viable national organization, he lost heavily to Wilson in the electoral count. Taft ran third.

Roosevelt spent most of the remainder of his life writing books, exploring Brazil's backcountry, and criticizing President Wilson, whom he hated. He wanted to fight in World War I but was refused a commission. His health weakened by infections contracted in Brazil, Theodore Roosevelt died in his sleep on January 6, 1919, at the age of sixty.

Summary

"The Republican Roosevelt," as one historian termed him, is usually ranked among the best American presidents. An inspirational leader and superb administrator, he revitalized the presidency. His career seemed to defy the adage that power corrupts. In mental prowess, he had few equals in American political history; indeed, Roosevelt ranks among the rarest of human types: an intellectual who was also a man of action.

Ideologically, Roosevelt defies simple definition. Whether he was an "enlightened conservative" or a "Progressive liberal" remains in dispute. Roosevelt himself refused to accept pat labels. He viewed himself as a moral leader who combined practicality and idealism for the purpose of unifying the nation's opposing economic and social interests into a mutually beneficial synthesis.

Coming to the presidency at the dawn of the twentieth century, Roosevelt understood that America was fast becoming a complex urban, industrial nation and that a new balance was needed between individualism and the collective good. In foreign policy, Roosevelt acted upon his conviction that the old isolationism was no longer possible and that the United States, because of its growing strength, was destined to be a world power.

Bibliography
Beale, Howard K. *Theodore Roosevelt and the Rise of America to World Power*. Baltimore: Johns Hopkins University Press, 1956. Best study of

Roosevelt's foreign policy. Beale demonstrates that Roosevelt had prophetic insights yet was blind toward the nationalistic aspirations of "backward" colonial peoples.

Blum, John M. *The Republican Roosevelt*. Cambridge: Harvard University Press, 1954. "Brilliant" is the usual word for characterizing this book. Blum explains Roosevelt as an astute conservative who welcomed change as the only means of preserving what was vital from the past.

Chessman, G. Wallace. *Theodore Roosevelt and the Politics of Power*. Boston: Little, Brown and Co., 1969. Most recommended brief biography of Roosevelt. Sympathetic to Roosevelt, it is a skillful blend of narrative and analysis.

Harbaugh, William Henry. *Power and Responsibility: The Life and Times of Theodore Roosevelt*. Rev. ed. New York: Oxford University Press, 1975. The most thorough full-length biography of Roosevelt. Judiciously balances his virtues and limitations.

Morris, Edmund. *The Rise of Theodore Roosevelt*. New York: Coward, McCann and Geoghegan, 1979. Splendidly written, insightful treatment of Roosevelt's life from birth to the beginning of his presidency in 1901. Especially good for Roosevelt's ranching days in the Dakota Territory and his exploits during the Spanish-American War.

Mowry, George E. *The Era of Theodore Roosevelt: 1900-1912*. New York: Harper and Row, Publishers, 1958. The standard study of the first dozen years of twentieth century America, when Roosevelt was the central political figure. Invaluable for understanding Roosevelt's actions within the context of his time of ascendancy.

Pringle, Henry F. *Theodore Roosevelt: A Biography*. New York: Harcourt, Brace and Co., 1931. This readable Pulitzer Prize biography of Roosevelt was long considered the definitive work, but later historians tended to fault Pringle for overemphasizing Roosevelt's immaturity and bellicosity.

Roosevelt, Theodore. *The Writings of Theodore Roosevelt*. Edited by William H. Harbaugh. Indianapolis: Bobbs-Merrill Co., 1967. An excellent one-volume anthology of Roosevelt's own words, including excerpts from his autobiography.

William I. Hair

ELIHU ROOT

Born: February 15, 1845; Clinton, New York
Died: February 7, 1937; New York, New York
Areas of Achievement: Government and diplomacy
Contribution: As secretary of war under William McKinley and Theodore
  Roosevelt, Root administered territories gained at the end of the Spanish-
  American War and initiated reforms in army administration. He pursued a
  conservative line as secretary of state under Roosevelt and later as United
  States senator from New York, and argued for the value of international
  law as a political instrument.

Early Life

Born in Clinton, New York, on February 15, 1845, Elihu Root was the
third of four sons of Oren and Nancy Buttrick Root. His father was professor of mathematics at Hamilton College in Clinton, and Elihu was valedictorian of the Hamiton class of 1864. He was graduated from New York University Law School in 1867. Root's legal career was successful from the start; in
time he became one of the leading members of the American bar. Specializing in cases involving large corporations, he was labeled a Wall Street lawyer.
Among his corporate clients were the Havemeyer Sugar Refining Company
and the traction syndicate controlled by William C. Whitney and Thomas F.
Ryan. Root's success as a lawyer and later as a member of McKinley's and
Roosevelt's cabinets came from his capacity to master detail, the concise and
logical qualities of his written arguments, and his ready wit. Reserved and a
bit stiff with those he did not know well, Root formed strong friendships with
men such as Theodore Roosevelt, William Howard Taft, and Henry Cabot
Lodge.

Prior to his appointment as secretary of war in 1899, Root was involved in
Republican Party politics on the local and state levels. He served from 1883
to 1885 as United States attorney for the district of Southern New York; he
was a manager of the New York State constitutional convention of 1894. His
association with Roosevelt began around 1882, when Root provided legal
advice about an obstacle to Roosevelt's running for the state legislature.
Root ran Roosevelt's unsuccessful campaign for mayor of New York City in
1886, he provided advice when Roosevelt served as city police commissioner,
and in 1898 he resolved a question about Roosevelt's legal residence that enabled him to run for and be elected governor.

A thin, wiry man of average height, Root had closely clipped hair and a
full mustache, both of which turned white in his old age. In 1878, he married
Clara Frances Wales. An attentive husband and father to his daughter,
Edith, and sons, Elihu and Edward Wales, Root often made decisions about
his public career based upon his wife's distaste for life in Washington, D.C.

Life's Work

While Root declined President McKinley's offer to serve on the commission concluding a peace treaty with Spain, he accepted appointment as secretary of war in 1899. McKinley said that he wanted a lawyer in the job because of the need to administer the territories acquired during the war. The legal problems posed by the American occupation of Puerto Rico, Cuba, and the Philippines were complex, and the transition from military to civilian governments required a different solution in each case. In all three territories, however, Root favored improvements in education, health care, and transportation.

The absence of a strong movement for independence in Puerto Rico led Root to conclude that the best solution would be an indefinite period of American control. He proposed a highly centralized governmental structure centered on a governor and legislative council appointed by the president. Root persuaded McKinley that Puerto Rico's economic well-being depended upon an exemption from the Dingley Tariff rates, but the Administration accepted a temporary lower rate in the Foraker Act of 1900. Congress also provided for a popularly elected lower house in a bicameral Puerto Rican legislature, and Root accepted the change.

The terms of the peace treaty with Spain called for Cuban independence, and by 1902 Root had established a native government for Cuba and had withdrawn American military forces. He first replaced General John R. Brooke with General Leonard Wood as the military governor, and he instructed Wood to mount a program to repair war damage and to modernize schools, roads, and systems of sanitation. A constitutional convention met in 1901; the delegates were elected by Cubans, but Root had restricted the vote to property owners, former soldiers, and those who were literate. The constitution produced by the convention contained guarantees of American interests originally outlined in the Platt Amendment to the Army Appropriation Act of March 2, 1901. The government of the United States was granted the right to buy or lease bases on Cuban soil, and it was given the right to intervene with troops if Cuban independence or the stability of the Cuban government were threatened.

Root faced a more difficult task in dealing with the situation in the Philippines. Forces led by Emilio Aguinaldo were in revolt against the American military government, and Root, as secretary of war, had both to bring home the twenty-one thousand troops in the islands whose enlistments were running out and to replace them with an effectively trained force which eventually numbered seventy-four thousand. It took two years to end the guerrilla war, and in the interval the report of a commission headed by President Jacob Schurman of Cornell led Root to conclude that the Philippines were not ready for independence or for a great degree of self-government. In 1900, McKinley and Root sent Judge William Howard Taft to Manila at the head of a second commission charged with replacing the military government. Taft became governor general, and a bicameral legislature was created. Root's instructions to the Taft commission, adopted by Congress in the Organic Act of 1902, became the formula for government of the Philippines pursued by the Roosevelt Administration.

Partly as a result of his activities as a colonial administrator, Root saw the need for reforming the army bureaucracy. He instituted a general staff system headed by a chief of staff directly responsible to the secretary of war, and he ended the practice of making permanent army staff appointments in Washington. There was a regular rotation of officers from the staff to the line. Root called for legislation which established the Army War College and which made the national guard the country's militia. He took steps to see that the guard received the same training and equipment as the regular army.

Root resigned as secretary of war on February 1, 1904, despite the objections of President Roosevelt, but he returned to the cabinet as secretary of state on July 7, 1905. He played no part in Roosevelt's arbitration of an ending to the Russo-Japanese War by means of the Treaty of Portsmouth; nor did he have anything to do with securing for the United States the right to build a canal through the Isthmus of Panama. Root's chief actions as secretary of state were designed to bolster the fabric of international agreements ensuring world peace. He placed emphasis on friendly relationships with the nations of South America, and in 1906 he undertook a lengthy personal tour of that continent which led to Latin American participation in the Second Hague Peace Conference in 1907.

In the area of Canadian-American relations, Root resolved the North Atlantic coastal fisheries dispute. With the help of Lord Bryce, the British ambassador in Washington, he found a solution to the Alaska boundary issue. Root negotiated a voluntary immigration restriction agreement with Japan after the unrest in California over Japanese labor precipitated exclusion laws. By means of the Root-Takahira agreement and an arbitration treaty concluded in 1908, he established mechanisms for consultation between the governments of the United States and Japan. Root was committed to voluntary arbitration of international disputes, and during his tenure as secretary of state, he negotiated bilateral arbitration agreements with twenty-four foreign governments. In 1912, he was awarded the Nobel Peace Prize for these efforts to move international disagreements within a judicial framework.

In the instructions that were given to the American delegates to the 1907 Hague Peace Conference, Root outlined plans for a permanent court of arbitral justice and committed the American government to its establishment. The nations represented at the conference, however, could not agree on a procedure for selecting judges. The idea was put aside until 1920, when Root, invited by the League of Nations, served on the committee that drafted the statute establishing the World Court. Root worked with President Warren G. Harding and Secretary of State Charles Evans Hughes to gain approval for American membership in the court, but congressional opposition led by Senator Henry Cabot Lodge frustrated the effort. In 1929, Root returned to Geneva to serve on the committee revising the 1920 statute, and he devised a compromise on advisory opinions, usually termed the "Root formula," meeting United States objections to certain classes of cases coming before the World Court. Delays in submitting these changes to Congress and the changing political situation led to the treaty's eventual defeat in 1935.

By that time, Root was ninety years old, and his public career was behind him. He had resigned as secretary of state on March 5, 1909, before assuming the office of United States senator, to which he had been elected by the New York State legislature. Root's career as a senator was less significant than his previous career as a member of the McKinley and Roosevelt cabinets. Root lacked sympathy with the Progressive legislation supported by William Howard Taft, Roosevelt's successor, and he grew disenchanted with Woodrow Wilson's policy of neutrality toward the conflict in Europe that developed into World War I.

Root supported Wilson's efforts to mobilize once the United States entered World War I, and in 1917 he went to Russia as head of a mission to the Provisional Revolutionary Government. Wilson did not appoint Root as an American representative to the peace conference at Versailles, but the former secretary of state gave public support to Wilson's plan to join the League of Nations. He had reservations about Article X of the League Covenant and wanted modifications in the terms of the treaty, but he encouraged Senator Lodge to support American membership. Lodge, however, came out in opposition to both the Treaty of Versailles and membership in the League of Nations.

Elihu Root died in New York City on February 7, 1937. He was buried in the cemetery on the Hamilton College campus in Clinton, New York, his birthplace and family home.

Summary

The achievements of Elihu Root's long period of public service fall into two categories. The first is a set of pragmatic solutions to specific problems. His differing approaches to the governing of Puerto Rico, Cuba, and the Philippines, like the reforms he initiated in the structure and training of the army, testify to his skills as a lawyer. Root's work as secretary of war demonstrates the ability of the United States at the beginning of the twentieth century to take on the responsibilities of a global power. The second category of achievement is Root's consistent efforts to forge a judicial system to interpret a growing body of international law. His work as secretary of state on a series of bilateral arbitration treaties, his support of Wilson's call for a League of

Nations, and his efforts to establish the World Court testify to his commitment. Root declined an appointment to the World Court itself. Given the fact that the United States was not a party to the treaty establishing the court, he believed that it was inappropriate for him to sit as a judge.

Root's skills were best suited to administration and negotiation. In addition to his work on behalf of the League of Nations and the World Court, he was one of four American delegates to the Conference on the Limitation of Armaments held in Washington, D.C., between November 12, 1921, and February 6, 1922. He served as president or chairman of a number of the organizations founded by Andrew Carnegie, including the Carnegie Endowment for International Peace, and he advised every administration through that of Franklin D. Roosevelt in the area of foreign affairs.

Bibliography
Coletta, Paolo E. *The Presidency of William Howard Taft*. Lawrence: University Press of Kansas, 1973. A clear account of the Roosevelt-Taft split, this study notes Root's ties to both men and examines the 1912 election campaign.
Gould, Lewis L. *The Presidency of William McKinley*. Lawrence: University Press of Kansas, 1981. Gould argues that McKinley shaped military and foreign policy more aggressively than previous scholars have believed.
Jessup, Philip C. *Elihu Root*. 2 vols. New York: Dodd, Mead and Co., 1938. The most complete account of Root's public career and his political views, this book was begun during Root's lifetime and benefited from the use of his papers.
Leopold, Richard W. *Elihu Root and the Conservative Tradition*. Boston: Little, Brown and Co., 1954. Leopold traces Root's political conservatism but also shows his pragmatic interest in international law.
Millett, Allan Reed. *The Politics of Intervention: The Military Occupation of Cuba, 1906-1909*. Columbus: Ohio State University Press, 1968. This study stresses the role of the United States Army in the policy-making process which determined the nature of the American occupation of Cuba.
Mowry, George E. *The Era of Theodore Roosevelt: 1900-1912*. New York: Harper and Row, Publishers, 1958. Granting Root's service to Roosevelt, Mowry notes that the president's growing progressivism was matched by Root's increasing conservatism.
Pratt, Julius W. *America's Colonial Experiment: How the United States Gained, Governed, and in Part Gave Away a Colonial Empire*. Englewood Cliffs, N.J.: Prentice-Hall, 1951. Pratt's study pulls together the story of America's involvement in Cuba, the Philippines, Puerto Rico, Hawaii, and Central America.

Robert C. Petersen

JOHN ROSS
Coowescoowe

Born: October 3, 1790; Turkey Town, Alabama
Died: August 1, 1866; Washington, D.C.
Area of Achievement: Statesmanship
Contribution: As a leader of the Cherokee nation during its ordeal of forced removal and civil war, Ross is the supreme example of nineteenth century Native American statesmanship.

Early Life

John Ross was born October 3, 1790, at Turkey Town, a Cherokee settlement near modern Center, Alabama. He was by blood only one-eighth Cherokee. His mother, Mollie McDonald, was the granddaughter of a Cherokee woman, but his father, the trader Daniel Ross, and all of his mother's other ancestors were Scottish. His father, while securing a tutor for his children and sending Ross to an academy near Kingston, Tennessee, did not want to stamp out his children's Cherokee identity, and his mother gave him a deep sense of loyalty to the tribe, to their ancient lands and traditions, and to the ideal of Cherokee unity. As a son of three generations of Scottish traders, Ross early showed an interest in business. In 1813, he formed a partnership with Timothy Meigs at Rossville, near modern Chattanooga, and two years later another with his brother Lewis Ross; during the Creek War of 1813-1814, when Cherokee warriors fought in Andrew Jackson's army, he did a lucrative business filling government contracts. During the Creek War, he served as adjutant in a company of Cherokee cavalry.

By the mid-1820's, his increasing involvement in the political affairs of the Cherokee nation caused him to abandon business. In 1827, he settled at Coosa, Georgia, thirty miles from the new Cherokee capital at New Echota, and established himself as a planter, with a substantial house, orchards and herds, quarters for his twenty slaves, and a lucrative ferry.

Ross served as a member of four Cherokee delegations to Washington between 1816 and 1825 and was president of the tribe's National Committee in 1818, when it resisted the attempt of Tennessee to persuade the tribe to surrender their lands in that state. In 1822, he was a cosigner of a resolution of the National Committee that the Cherokee would not recognize any treaty which surrendered Cherokee land. In 1823, Ross earned for himself the undying loyalty of the majority of the tribe when he rejected a bribe offered by federal commissioners and publicly denounced them in a meeting of the National Committee.

Life's Work

Ross was president of the convention which in 1827 produced the Cherokee constitution. This document, in its assignment of powers to three branches of government, its bicameral legislature, and its four-year term for the principal chief, was modeled on the Constitution of the United States. In 1828, he was elected principal chief, an office which he held until his death, and in 1829 he went to Washington on the first of many embassies which he undertook in that capacity.

The Cherokee established their republic within the context of an ongoing struggle to maintain their traditional claims against state governments, particularly that of Georgia. In 1802, Georgia had ceded to the United States its western territory (what later became Alabama and Mississippi) in exchange for a promise that all Native Americans would be removed from Georgia. A substantial number of Cherokee, accepting removal, surrendered their land rights and moved west. (One of them was the great Cherokee genius Sequoya, who gave his people a syllabary for their language.) With the inauguration of Andrew Jackson, who was determined to send the Cherokee west, and the discovery of gold on Cherokee land, it was clear that removal was inevitable. Ross was determined to exhaust every legal and political recourse, however, before submitting to the superior physical might of the United States government. Though Jackson was willing to assert the power of the federal government—even if it meant war—to put down any movement in South Carolina for "nullification" of the Constitution, he declared that in the Cherokee case he would not interfere with state sovereignty. As a result, his Indian Removal Bill of 1830 included the provision that any Native American who chose not to remove was subject to state law. Georgia therefore refused to recognize the legitimacy of the Cherokee republic and made no effort to prevent white squatters from moving into the Cherokee country. These official attitudes and the chaos caused by the gold rush produced a state of anarchy in which, on one occasion, Ross himself barely escaped assassination.

By 1833, pressure by the government of Georgia and by the Jackson Administration was producing dissension among the Cherokee themselves. John Ridge, son of an influential Cherokee family, and Elias Boudinot, editor of the *Cherokee Phoenix*, were both working for acceptance of removal and were thus undermining the efforts of Ross, who wanted the tribe to resist removal, and if it were inevitable, to accept it only on the best possible terms.

In 1835, returning from a trip to Washington, Ross found his land and house occupied by a white man, who was able to present a legal title granted by Georgia. In the same year, the Ridge faction signed the Treaty of New Echota, accepting removal. In spite of the fact that it was signed by only a handful of Cherokee, in spite of opposition by the Cherokee who had already settled in the West, in spite of a protest signed by fourteen thousand Cherokee, and in spite of Henry Clay's opposition in the Senate, it was approved by the Senate in May, 1836, and signed by Jackson.

Under the conditions of the treaty, the Cherokee were given two years to prepare for removal, and Ross spent that time in further hopeless efforts to persuade the government to give the entire Cherokee people opportunity to accept or reject the treaty. The removal itself was flawed by looting, arson, and even grave-robbing by white squatters; disease was inevitable in the stockades which served as holding pens; of the thirteen thousand who were removed, probably four thousand, including Ross's wife, died on the "Trail of Tears."

In his first years in Oklahoma, Ross devoted all of his energies to his efforts to unite three Cherokee factions: his own Nationalist followers, the Ridge-Boudinot faction which had accepted removal, and the Old Settlers, who had formed their own government and did not want to merge with the Easterners. In July, 1839, a convention wrote a new constitution, virtually the same as that of 1827, and passed the Act of Union, which was ratified by all parties. In spite of Ross's efforts for Cherokee unity, however, extremists in his own party exacted the traditional Cherokee penalty for selling tribal lands when they murdered Ridge and Boudinot. Ross was not involved in these crimes and did not condone them, but they were a source of disharmony in the tribe as long as he lived, and they were the primary reason that he had difficulty negotiating a new treaty with the government in an attempt to guarantee Cherokee claims to their Oklahoma lands. Ross had opposed removal because he knew that if the government were allowed to confiscate the Georgia lands they could confiscate lands in Oklahoma later. The government refused to agree to guarantees, however, because the followers of Ridge and Boudinot claimed that Ross was responsible for the murders; finally, in 1846, the Polk Administration signed a treaty acceptable to all parties.

On September 2, 1844, Ross married Mary Bryan Stapler, daughter of a Delaware merchant, who bore him two children. The period from the 1846 treaty until the Civil War was a relatively happy time for Ross and for his people. He prospered as a merchant, raised livestock, and contributed much of his wealth to charities on behalf of poor Cherokee; under his guidance, seminaries and a Cherokee newspaper were established.

Though, by 1860, Ross owned fifty slaves, he opposed slavery on principle, and this issue in the 1850's was another source of tribal dissension, his full-blood followers opposing it and the mixed-bloods favoring it. When the war began and agents were working among the Oklahoma tribes on behalf of the Confederacy, Ross favored neutrality and adherence to the 1846 treaty. Only when the neighboring tribes accepted a Confederate alliance and the Cherokee nation was virtually surrounded was Ross willing to accept an alliance. Yet in June, 1862, when Union forces finally arrived from Kansas, he welcomed them, though he and his family were forced to leave the Cherokee country as refugees when the Union forces withdrew. His four sons by his first wife served in the Union Army, and one of them died in a Confederate prison.

For the next three years, Ross was in the East working to persuade the Lincoln Administration to send federal troops to the Cherokee country and to feed the six thousand pro-Union Cherokee who had taken refuge in Kansas. The last year of the war was a particularly unhappy time for him because of the illness of his wife, who died in July, 1865.

When Ross died on August 1, 1866, he was in Washington negotiating a peace treaty with the United States government and fighting the efforts of the Cherokee faction which had been pro-South in the war to get federal approval of a permanently divided tribe. The treaty which was proclaimed ten days after his death was his last contribution to the cause of Cherokee unity.

Summary

John Ross was passionately devoted to the ancestral homeland of the Cherokee and to their cultural traditions, but when he recognized that removal was inevitable he submitted to it in order to reestablish a unified Cherokee nation on the frontier; his people's achievement of a remarkable blend of tribal traditions and white man's political and economic methods was his greatest monument. Though he was "by blood" only one-eighth Cherokee, he grew up as a Cherokee, identified with the Cherokee people, and devoted his life to the great cause of tribal unity. The Cherokee tragedy, which remains permanently fixed as one of the most disgraceful acts of the American people, stands in contrast to the life of the man who was probably the most distinguished Native American political leader of the nineteenth century and who resembles Lincoln both in his political skills and in his vision of union as the only basis for peace and justice.

Bibliography

Eaton, Rachel Caroline. *John Ross and the Cherokee Indians*. Chicago: University of Chicago Press, 1921. A doctoral dissertation which concentrates on the political ordeal of the Cherokee during Ross's lifetime. Essentially accurate, though apparently written without access to all the early documents.

Meserve, John Bartlett. "Chief John Ross." *Chronicles of Oklahoma* 13 (December, 1935): 421-437. A brief but balanced account of Ross's life, though flawed by several errors in detail.

Moulton, Gary. *John Ross: Cherokee Chief*. Athens: University of Georgia Press, 1978. The best and most nearly definitive account of Ross's life and political struggles. Most useful because of its copious notes, which provide all the apparatus necessary for further study.

Starkey, Marion L. *The Cherokee Nation*. New York: Alfred A. Knopf, 1946.

A semipopular account of Cherokee history from the beginnings to removal, with a final chapter devoted to later events. Written from the point of view of the missionaries to the Cherokee and perhaps overly sympathetic to the Treaty Party.

Wardell, Morris L. *A Political History of the Cherokee Nation, 1838-1907.* Norman: University of Oklahoma Press, 1938. A scholarly account of the Cherokee from removal to Oklahoma statehood. Refers to Ross in passing.

Woodward, Grace Steele. *The Cherokees.* Norman: University of Oklahoma Press, 1963. The best general account of the full range of Cherokee history, from first white contact to the late twentieth century. A fuller and much more balanced history than Starkey's book.

Robert L. Berner

JOSIAH ROYCE

Born: November 20, 1855; Grass Valley, California
Died: September 14, 1916; Cambridge, Massachusetts
Area of Achievement: Philosophy
Contribution: Royce was the last major philosopher of the twentieth century
   to integrate theological or religious topics with idealistic philosophy and to
   present his system to the general reader in terms of community and loyalty.
   He advanced philosophic idealism and played a significant role in Harvard
   University's intellectual development.

Early Life

Josiah Royce was born November 20, 1855, in Grass Valley, California.
His parents, Josiah Royce, Sr. (1812-1888), and Sarah Bayliss Royce (1819-
1891), had come to California during the gold rush of 1849. They were pious,
evangelical Christians. Since Royce's father was never successful in any of his
various business activities and, as a salesman, was often absent from the
home, his mother played a major role in shaping young Josiah's world. He
was a sickly boy, short, freckled, with wild red hair; his mother did not allow
him to play with the other children in the community. According to later
autobiographical remarks, Royce was fascinated by the problem of time: He
considered his hometown old, yet people referred to Grass Valley as a "new
community." Meanwhile, in 1866 Royce entered Lincoln Grammar School in
San Francisco, the family having moved there for better economic opportunities and educational possibilities for "Jossie." After a year at San Francisco
Boy's High School, which in 1869 had a distinct militaristic manner that
Royce hated, he entered the preparatory class at the University of California
in Oakland. Within five years, Royce received his bachelor of arts degree in
classics. As a result of his achievement, local patrons of the university sponsored him for a year's study in Germany.

Accordingly, from 1875 to 1876, Royce studied at Heidelberg, Leipzig, and
Göttingen. His area of study was philosophy. His early concerns about time,
the individual, and the community now found expression in his study overseas and at The Johns Hopkins University, the pioneer in graduate study and
research. Enrolling in 1876, Royce completed his Ph.D. degree at Johns
Hopkins within two years. Jobs teaching philosophy were scarce, and—very
unwillingly—Royce returned to the University of California, where he
taught English rhetoric and literature for the next four years. He did not,
however, give up his study of philosophy.

In 1880, Royce married Katharine Head; the couple produced three sons.
Royce kept his public role and private life separate, although the latter often
indirectly revealed itself in his letters. Having met William James while at
Johns Hopkins, Royce corresponded with him, and in 1883 Royce joined the

Harvard faculty as a temporary replacement for James, who was on academic leave. Royce could now be a full-time philosopher.

Life's Work

Having published fifteen articles by the time of his temporary appointment, Royce worked very hard, teaching and writing, to gain a permanent place on the Harvard faculty. Within six years he would achieve tenure and have a nervous breakdown. *The Religious Aspect of Philosophy* (1885) was based on lectures which he published as a book. This was a method he used for nearly all of his books. Exceptions were *California from the Conquest in 1846 to the Second Vigilance Committee in San Francisco, 1856: A Study of American Character* (1886), a state history, and *The Feud of Oakfield Creek* (1887), a novel; both books were early reflections of Royce's lifelong interest in community and individual behavior.

After spending most of the year 1888 traveling to Australia as a cure for his nervous condition, Royce returned to Harvard with a fuller grasp of his ideas as well as the energy to express them. After publishing *The Spirit of Modern Philosophy* (1892), he was appointed professor of the history of philosophy at Harvard. He continued to write on an extraordinary range of topics, but his basic focus was on religious values and philosophy; *The Conception of God* (1897) and *Studies of Good and Evil* (1898) were typical expressions of that focus. During the years 1894 through 1898, Royce was chairman of the Department of Philosophy, and he significantly shaped the courses and the faculty at Harvard.

Royce published his Gifford Lectures as *The World and the Individual* (1899-1901). In the last sixteen years of his life, his scholarship was truly remarkable. His writing continued to be both broad and technical; *Outlines of Psychology: An Elementary Treatise, with Some Practical Application* (1903), *The Philosophy of Loyalty* (1908), and *Race Questions, Provincialism, and Other American Problems* (1908) were the results of his efforts to have philosophy inform both the scholar and the general public.

While his scholarly achievements were many, in his personal life Royce suffered many setbacks. His marriage was a strain. His wife was often caustic and hypercritical, and his children disappointed him in various ways. Christopher, his oldest son, who suffered from mental illness most of his adult life, was committed to Danvers State Hospital in 1908. Christopher died two years later. A month before, William James had died; he was Royce's closest and dearest friend.

Despite these tragic events, Royce continued to work, publishing *William James and Other Essays on the Philosophy of Life* (1911). Within a year he had completed *The Sources of Religious Insight* (1912). Despite a major stroke, Royce struggled back to health and continued his philosophic work with a significant book, *The Problem of Christianity* (1913).

World War I was a philosophical crisis for Royce. After much thought, he became a strong advocate for American intervention. Worn out by personal worries and poor health, Royce died on September 14, 1916, in Cambridge, Massachusetts.

Summary

Royce left no school of thought or prominent disciples. His philosophy of metaphysical idealism fell out of fashion as pragmatism, logical positivism, and existentialism gained currency in the academic and the larger society. His use of the German idealism of Immanuel Kant and Georg Wilhelm Friedrich Hegel also limited Royce's appeal. It would, however, be premature to downgrade Royce's lasting contributions.

In his varied writings, Royce stressed the primacy of the individual while holding fast to his emphasis on community. Royce recognized the damage done to individuals and to society by the alienation in American life. Also significant in his thought was the distinction between the world of appreciation or value and the world of factual description. The world of appreciation gives meaning, shape, and value to the human condition.

Finally, Royce was not a naïve thinker. He recognized evil in the world in various manifestations. His philosophy of the Absolute recognized three kinds of evil: metaphysical evil—anything short of the Absolute is not perfect; natural evil—anything that offends man's ethical sense or which man cannot accept because of his limited human intelligence (the problem of Job); and human evil—sin or voluntary inattention. Royce was a philosopher whose ideas have application to the modern world. Along with Charles Sanders Peirce and William James, Josiah Royce during his lifetime and in his writing contributed to the golden age of American philosophy.

Bibliography

Buranelli, Vincent. *Josiah Royce*. New York: Twayne Publishers, 1963. In this brief biography the focus is on Royce's philosophy, particularly its origins in German idealism. According to Buranelli, Hegel was the major philosophic influence on Royce's intellectual development.

Clendenning, John. *The Life and Thought of Josiah Royce*. Madison: University of Wisconsin Press, 1985. Based essentially on Royce's letters, this biography follows a chronological scheme in which the philosopher's writings are related to the personal developments in his life. Royce's personality is clearly presented. He had a strong sense of humor and an attraction toward the ironic. The thesis is that a close relationship exists between the particulars of Royce's life and the universality of his system of thought.

Kuklick, Bruce. *Josiah Royce: An Intellectual Biography*. Indianapolis: Bobbs-Merrill Co., 1972. A solid history of Royce's ideas, this book relates him to the issues of his time. In the process, Royce's place in the history of American philosophy is clearly developed.

_____. *The Rise of American Philosophy: Cambridge, Massachusetts, 1860-1930*. New Haven, Conn.: Yale University Press, 1977. An outstanding history of the Department of History at Harvard University, this book clearly places Royce in the changing context of American philosophy as it moved from a gentlemanly pursuit of the truth to being part of academic professionalism. Well written; includes extensive bibliography.

Oppenheim, Frank M. *Royce's Voyage Down Under: A Journey of the Mind*. Lexington: University Press of Kentucky, 1980. With a modest use of psychohistory, Oppenheim's book explores the philosophical consequences of Royce's trip to Australia as a cure for his nervous condition. In fact, Royce's greatest philosophical achievements were ahead when he returned to Harvard.

Powell, Thomas F. *Josiah Royce*. New York: Washington Square Press, 1967. A solid but brief treatment of Royce's life and thought. The later scholarship of Clendenning, Kuklick, and McDermott has undermined the importance of Powell's book.

Royce, Josiah. *The Basic Writings of Josiah Royce*. Edited by John J. McDermott. 2 vols. Chicago: University of Chicago Press, 1969. A handy introduction to Royce's writings, since some of the original editions are out of print. Organized by topic. The introduction is informative. The annotated bibliography of Royce's publication makes this book an invaluable source.

_____. *The Letters of Josiah Royce*. Edited by John Clendenning. Chicago: University of Chicago Press, 1970. The introduction places the letters in their proper historical and philosophical contexts. The letters reveal a man who moved from the mundane to the sublime often in the same letter. Taken together, the letters constitute an interesting autobiography.

Royce, Sarah B. *A Frontier Lady: Recollections of the Gold Rush and Early California*. New Haven, Conn.: Yale University Press, 1932. A personal narrative of the Royce family overland trip to California as written by Josiah's mother. A basic document in understanding her influence on Royce's later philosophy on community and history.

Santayana, George. *Character and Opinion in the United States*. New York: Charles Scribner's Sons, 1920. An often caustic and ironic account of the academic world that Royce shared with Santayana, his former student and fellow faculty member.

Starr, Kevin. *Americans and the California Dream, 1850-1915*. New York: Oxford University Press, 1973. A solid presentation via cultural history and analysis and biographies of the California of Royce's youth. Starr explains how the state rapidly changed as a result of many types of influences (not the least of which was to gain wealth) and how Royce's philosophic concern for community grew out the state's colorful past.

Donald K. Pickens

BENJAMIN RUSH

Born: January 4, 1746; Byberry, Pennsylvania
Died: April 19, 1813; Philadelphia, Pennsylvania
Areas of Achievement: Medicine, psychiatry, and chemistry
Contribution: In his day, Rush was widely regarded as the most important American physician and professor of medicine; today he is more likely to be remembered as a signer of the Declaration of Independence and an enthusiastic supporter of the Constitution.

Early Life

Benjamin Rush was born January 4, 1746, in Byberry, Pennsylvania, the fourth child of seven in the family. His father, John, a farmer and a gunsmith, died when Benjamin was five years old. As a result, his mother, Susanna (Hall) Harvey Rush, had to open a grocery store in order to support her family.

When Benjamin was eight, he entered a school operated by his uncle, the Reverend Mr. Samuel Finley, and it was there that the boy came into contact with the tenets of the Great Awakening, a movement that was stirring the inert religious energies of the Colonies.

Rush, who remained a devoutly religious man throughout his life, went to the College of New Jersey (founded the same year he was born, later to become Princeton University) fully expecting to emerge a minister like his uncle. Acting on the advice of others, he began to consider other career possibilities, however, and finally chose medicine.

After receiving his degree in 1760, Rush studied medicine as an apprentice under Dr. John Redman in Philadelphia, where he also attended medical lectures at the College of Philadelphia. In 1766, he enrolled in the University of Edinburgh, in Scotland, where many other Americans had studied medicine. He received his M.D. in 1768, having concentrated on the study of chemistry; his dissertation, on the human digestive system, was the product of much experimentation on his own digestive system.

Following graduation, Rush spent some time visiting England and then returned to Philadelphia, where he began his own practice in 1769. In that same year he was appointed professor of chemistry at the College of Philadelphia, which today is the Medical College of the University of Pennsylvania. He was the first professor of chemistry in North America.

Life's Work

Although the impact of the Great Awakening was always a part of his thinking, Rush was also a man of the Enlightenment. Along with his friend Benjamin Franklin and other enlightened Americans, he was humanistic and optimistic, believing that "natural philosophy" was the key to expanding man's knowledge.

Unlike Franklin, Jefferson, Adams, and others, however, there is little that seems brilliant or original about Rush's thinking. He authored the first chemistry text by an American-born individual (*Syllabus of a Course of Lectures on Chemistry*) in the second year of his teaching career, yet it contained no genuinely original work. He taught the importance of hypotheses in medical and scientific inquiry, but, strangely for a man of the Enlightenment (and very unlike Franklin or Jefferson), Rush eschewed experimentation that would test hypotheses. Finally, Rush became more and more convinced that all fevers were the result of arterial tension, and thus the only way to cure a fever was to relieve that tension through bloodletting. In his enthusiasm for the method Rush was led to insist that in cases of severe fever, as much as four-fifths of a patient's blood should be drained away. He was certainly not the only one to subscribe to this erroneous view—indeed, for a long period bloodletting was a universally accepted practice. Unhappily, as the most famous physician in the United States, Rush was in a position to influence, rightly or (in this instance) wrongly, countless other physicians of his own generation and of generations to come.

The year 1776 was an important year for Rush. In that year he married Julia Stockton, with whom he would have thirteen children (including James, who would follow in his father's footsteps as a physician and medical educator); joined the Continental Congress; and signed the Declaration of Independence. During the Revolution, he served briefly as surgeon general to the Armies of the Middle Department, and he also served on a governmental committee which encouraged the local production of gunpowder. In this latter endeavor, his knowledge of chemistry came in handy, and his instructions for the manufacturing of saltpeter were widely circulated. Rush was also an early and enthusiastic supporter of the Constitution, a member of the convention that framed it, and a member of the Pennsylvania Convention which ratified it.

After the war, Rush resumed his teaching and his medical practice—a practice that originally had been mostly among the poor but now grew to encompass many of the most prominent of Philadelphia's citizenry.

In 1787, Rush took charge of the branch of the Pennsylvania Hospital that housed and treated the insane, and in this new position he showed a deep understanding of the problems of the mind—an understanding that resulted in his study *Medical Inquiries and Observations upon the Diseases of the Mind* (1812), the first book on psychiatry written by an American.

In 1789, Rush surrendered his teaching post in chemistry in order to accept the position of professor of theory and practice of medicine at the College of Philadelphia. There, Rush began to refine his theories on bloodletting, which he put into vigorous practice during Philadelphia's great yellow-fever epidemic of 1793. His example would, unfortunately, be followed by many physicians during yellow-fever epidemics for almost a century.

In 1791, Rush was appointed professor of institutes of medicine and clinical practice, and in 1796 he became professor of the theory and practice of medicine. He was at the height of his career, the most famous physician in the United States, and the inspiration of a whole generation of medical students, whom he served as both teacher and friend. In addition to his teaching and his medical practice, Rush was also very active in social and humanitarian work, opposing slavery and capital punishment while supporting improvements in education (especially for women), temperance, and prison reform.

In 1797, Rush accepted the position of treasurer at the United States Mint—an office he still held at the time of his death on April 19, 1813. He was sixty-seven years of age.

Summary

As an enlightened American, Rush was a man of wide-ranging interests throughout his life. He was an ardent patriot, a signer of the Declaration of Independence, and a strong supporter of the Constitution. In addition, he took part in a movement to give his home state of Pennsylvania a new constitution in 1788.

His support of numerous social causes was always strong, and many of his views on the insane, slavery, and education were in advance of their time. As a teacher, Rush inspired and nurtured many hundreds of students throughout his long teaching career. As a physician, the most famous of his time, Rush unfortunately fell under the sway of theories that were often prejudicial to the health of his patients—theories which have been thoroughly discredited as medical knowledge has increased.

Bibliography

Binger, Carl. *Revolutionary Doctor: Benjamin Rush, 1746-1813*. New York: W. W. Norton and Co., 1966. An imperfect examination of the life of Rush which attempts to interpret that life within the psychological context of the early death of his father and his excessive attachment to his mother.

D'Elia, Donald J. "Dr. Benjamin Rush and the American Revolution." *Proceedings of the American Philosophical Society* 110 (1966): 227-234. Concentrates on the life of Rush between the years 1769 and 1813. Argues that Rush's ardent republicanism shaped his views on medicine and healing and that his American medical system was a scientific counterpart to the political and social aspects of the American Revolution.

Goodman, Nathan G. *Benjamin Rush: Physician and Citizen*. Philadelphia: University of Pennsylvania Press, 1934. The first biography of Rush. It portrays him in his many and varied roles as professor, practitioner, politician, and crusader for reform. Perhaps its most important contribution, however, was to reveal Rush as a pioneer practioner in the field of psychiatry.

Hawke, David. *Benjamin Rush: Revolutionary Gadfly*. Indianapolis: Bobbs-Merrill Co., 1971. The best biography of Rush, this study takes the story of his life up to 1790, at which time the author claims that Rush became politically inactive. Prior to that date, however, Rush was almost compulsively active in politics as well as social causes, medicine, and a score of other pursuits. The work reveals Rush in all of his frenetic activities and shows the numerous and baffling contradictions and paradoxes in his behavior. The amount of detail supplied is enormous, as Rush's opinions on myriad subjects are carefully presented.

Powell, John H. *Bring Out Your Dead: The Great Plague of Yellow Fever in Philadelphia of 1793*. Philadelphia: University of Pennsylvania Press, 1949. A popular but well-researched account of the 1793 yellow-fever epidemic in Philadelphia which shows Rush to have been a courageous and tireless worker among the sick, but one who probably killed more of them with his purging and bleeding than he saved. The book is useful, too, for its account of the debate Rush conducted with other physicians of the city over the question of the contagiousness of yellow fever.

Rush, Benjamin. *The Autobiography of Benjamin Rush*. Edited by George W. Corner. Princeton, N.J.: Princeton University Press, 1948. A collection of notebooks kept by Rush throughout his lifetime. The collection clearly reveals the personality and character of the man, as well as his views on the times in which he lived. Thus such varied subjects are treated as the war between England and the American Colonies, the medical practices of Indians, the character of the French, and Philadelphia's great yellow-fever epidemic of 1793.

_____. *Letters of Benjamin Rush*. Edited by Lyman H. Butterfield. 2 vols. Princeton, N.J.: Princeton University Press, 1951. These volumes contain an enormous wealth of information on Rush as a teacher and practitioner of medicine, as an essayist, as a political activist, and as a tireless worker for the abolition of slavery, the modernization of education, temperance, and prison reform.

Shryock, Richard Harrison. "The Medical Reputation of Benjamin Rush: Contrasted over Two Centuries." *Bulletin of the History of Medicine* 45 (1971): 507-552. Considers the changing reputation of Rush as a physician. When he died he was eulogized. Over time, however, physicians and historians came to realize the consequences of the "heroic" methods of bloodletting and purging which Rush urged.

Weisberger, Bernard A. "The Paradoxical Doctor Benjamin Rush." *American Heritage* 27 (1975): 40-47, 98-99. Presents Rush as a man of enormous contradictions in both medicine and politics, who was often quarrelsome in the latter instance and usually wrongheaded in the former.

Kenneth F. Kiple

BILL RUSSELL

Born: February 12, 1934; Monroe, Louisiana

Area of Achievement: Basketball
Contribution: Revolutionizing the strategy of basketball, Russell introduced to the sport a style of play never before used or advocated.

Early Life

William Felton Russell was born February 12, 1934, in Monroe, Louisiana. His mother, Katie, who died when Bill was twelve, exerted a strong, lasting influence. She named Bill for William Felton, president of Southeastern Louisiana College, and made it clear that her children would be college graduates. Bill's father, Charles Russell, was a hardworking wage earner who held several jobs: factory laborer, truck driver, construction worker, hauling business owner, and ironworker in a foundry. He was also a semiprofessional baseball player, as had been his brother, Robert. Robert Russell, just short of making the Negro Major Leagues, blamed his failure on his being right-handed. Robert insisted that his nephew do everything with his left hand.

When Bill was nine, the family left Louisiana for better economic opportunities in Detroit, Michigan, but soon afterward moved to West Oakland, California. Bill's brother, Chuck, proved to be an outstanding athlete in baseball, football, basketball, and track. Two years older than Bill, Chuck cast a shadow over Bill through high school. Unlike Chuck, Bill was not gifted with coordination and muscle until late in his senior year. His gawkiness and awkwardness gave him a self-admitted inferiority complex which, through later athletic stardom, was replaced by an outgoing, although enigmatic, personality.

Russell, six-foot, ten-inches and 215 pounds in his prime, is noted for his fierce integrity, frequent cackling laugh, incisive wit, competitive intensity, and far-ranging, intellectual mind. His interests run from music appreciation and reading to assembling electric trains and investing in a Liberian rubber plantation. His ego was described by Boston Celtic teammate Tom Heinsohn as the largest on the team, while another Celtic teammate, Tom Sanders, emphasized Russell's capacity to needle people and keep them slightly off balance. Twice married, Russell has three children, William Felton, Jr. (called Buddha), Jacob Harold, and Karen Kenyatta.

Life's Work

Russell's older brother, Chuck, was named to Bay Area all-star teams in basketball, football, and track, playing for Oakland Tech. When Bill enrolled at McClymonds High School, he intended to escape Chuck's shadow. Instead, coaching personnel and students expected him to lead McClymonds in similar fashion. Russell proved instead to be skinny and awkward. One sport in which Russell became proficient, however, was table tennis, which improved his reflexes and coordination. As his height and weight increased, Russell's efforts in basketball and track improved.

In his senior year, Russell was a starter as McClymonds won the Bay Area basketball championship. A winter graduation enabled him to be chosen for a California high school all-star group which toured northward into Canada, playing against top high school and even small college competition. The trip was a turning point for Russell, his play dramatically improving and his mind constantly analyzing the game. He also gained his first insight into his jumping ability.

Despite Russell's starting role on a championship team and noticeably improved play with the touring group, only the University of San Francisco offered a basketball scholarship. Russell had never heard of the school. While waiting for University of San Francisco (USF) head coach Phil Woolpert to contact him, Russell took a job as an apprentice sheet-metal worker. Playing in a McClymonds alumni game, Russell experienced a first, enjoyable and terrifying at the same time: He jumped high enough to look down into the basket. A new dimension entered Russell's expanding range of skills.

Russell's freshman coach at USF, Ross Giudice, introduced him to the hook shot and spent innumerable postpractice and weekend hours helping Russell sharpen his game. During that season, Russell averaged twenty points per game and started to develop the most remarkable defensive skills basketball would ever witness. Giudice was so impressed that he told Woolpert that the potential was there for Russell to become the greatest player in history.

Another great help to Russell was K. C. Jones, his dormitory roommate and teammate. Jones and Russell decided that basketball was a geometric game, and repeated analyses led them to develop and redevelop concepts and strategies from that time throughout their careers. Their approach eventually revolutionized theories of rebounding and defense, but it did not result in instant success. The varsity fell well short of championship-level play. A ruptured appendix removed Jones as soon as the season started, and other illnesses and injuries depleted the roster. Russell looked back with no excuses, however, and ascribed the squad's mediocrity to lack of teamwork.

In Russell's junior year, everything changed. Jones was back, Russell was the acknowledged leader, and tough team defense keyed San Francisco to an amazing year. After losing to the University of California at Los Angeles (UCLA) in their third game of the season, the USF Dons swept their next twenty-six to win the National Collegiate Athletic Association (NCAA) championship. By then, Russell had been tabbed by Howard Dallmar, coach of Stanford and a former standout player in the National Basketball Association (NBA), as one who could stop George Mikan, then professional basketball's best. The Eastern press was not convinced, though, calling Tom Gola, senior leader of defending champion La Salle, college basketball's best player. The issue was settled in the NCAA title game. Russell scored twenty-three points, had twenty-two rebounds, and constantly harassed La Salle shooters, while teammate Jones kept Gola scoreless from the field for twenty-one minutes, in an 89-77 win. Russell tallied 118 points in five play-off games, breaking Gola's NCAA record of 114, and was named the tournament's Most Valuable Player.

Russell's defensive play had created controversy, tied to what appeared at times to be both offensive and defensive goaltending. The NCAA rules committee widened the free-throw lane from six to twelve feet, a move quickly referred to as the "Bill Russell rule." After his junior year, Russell was invited by President Dwight D. Eisenhower to the White House to discuss a national fitness program. Russell was designated the college basketball representative on a physical-fitness council, joining the likes of Willie Mays and Bob Cousy.

Russell, by then, had tried varsity track and became a friend and intense rival of another USF high jumper, Johnny Mathis, who was destined to be a popular singer. At the Modesto Relays, Russell outjumped Mathis, six feet seven inches to six feet six inches. Russell's interest in track lasted past his graduation when, intent on being a 1956 United States Olympian, he entered both the basketball and high-jump trials. The high jump narrowed to four contestants for three spots, and Russell tied Charlie Dumas—who would later be the first man to leap seven feet—for first place. Since Russell had already been selected as one of only three collegians on the twelve-man United States Olympic basketball team, he withdrew his name from the high-jump ranks.

Prior to that, Russell had led San Francisco to an undefeated season and a second consecutive NCAA title. In the process, the Dons had won fifty-five games in a row, then an NCAA record. When the NBA draft came around, Russell discovered that the Boston Celtics had dealt veteran scorer Ed Macauley and rugged Kentucky all-American Cliff Hagan to the St. Louis Hawks for their draft rights. The Rochester Royals selected first, taking Sihugo Green, a top-rated guard, bypassing Russell because they believed that Maurice Stokes, the NBA Rookie-of-the-Year, supplied them with the same kind of rebounding strength. Additionally, Russell's presence on the Olympic team would remove him from much of the regular season. It was rumored, too, that the Harlem Globetrotters would outbid any NBA team to get Russell.

Arnold "Red" Auerbach, coach of the Celtics, picked Russell anyway. His Celtics had always been a high-scoring team but needed a strong big man. Russell led an undefeated Olympic team to a gold medal and then rejected a Globetrotter offer which was well above Boston's offer. By the end of his first

NBA season, Russell proved to be the Celtics' long-needed ingredient. They celebrated their first NBA championship, and Russell had turned pivot play around forever. Thus, in one year, Russell had been the dominant force on three championship teams, in the NCAA, in the Olympics, and in the NBA.

In his second year, Russell was severely injured during the third game of the championship finals. Boston, without its shot-blocking, rebounding genius, lost to the Hawks in six games. During that season, Russell set a single game rebounding record of forty-nine, which he later increased to fifty-one, set a play-off single game rebounding record, a single season's rebounding record, and was the runaway choice as the league's Most Valuable Player. Curiously, he was bypassed on the All-League team.

In the following season, Russell broke his own season's rebounding record, enjoyed a .598 shooting percentage from the field (the best of his career), and led Boston to a sweep of the Minneapolis Lakers for the league crown. He was named All-League center. Over the next seven seasons, Russell led the Celtics to eight league championships in a row and nine out of ten. During that period, Russell was constantly compared to Wilt Chamberlain, the seven-foot, two-inch record-breaking scorer whose style of play contrasted sharply with Russell's. Opinion was divided as to which powerful center was better, but Russell wore the championship rings.

In 1966-1967, Russell succeeded Auerbach as head coach and, though leading the Celtics to a 60-21 slate, finished behind the Chamberlain-powered Philadelphia 76ers, whose 68-13 mark set an NBA record. The 76ers throttled Boston four games to one in the play-offs, and many believed that Russell and the Celtics were an item of the past. Instead, Boston came back in 1967-1968, to beat Philadelphia in three straight play-off games, after being down, three games to one, and then whipped the Los Angeles Lakers in six games, for their tenth title in twelve years. When Russell took them to another title in 1968-1969, the Celtics claimed the best championship streak in sports history, eleven titles in thirteen tries, and Russell had been the central figure in each. After the season, Russell retired.

Russell took up golf, ventured into films, did several radio shows for the American Broadcasting Company, basketball broadcasts for ABC-TV, and later held television contracts with the Columbia Broadcasting System and the Turner Broadcasting System. He also did lecture tours, Bell Telephone commercials, and even served as a substitute host for Dick Cavett.

Sam Schulman, principal owner of the then hapless Seattle SuperSonics, lured Russell back into NBA coaching in 1973. In Russell's initial season, the SuperSonics won ten more than their previous year, and in 1974-1975, Seattle made the play-offs for their first time. They repeated that achievement in 1975-1976, but Russell had already started to lose faith in too many of his players. He started a fourth and final season with little determination and regretted that he had not resigned earlier.

Summary

   Russell's fame was a result of his consistently superb efforts as an unselfish team player who intimidated enemy shooters, whose blocked shots almost always triggered fast breaks for his team, whose belief in and use of psychology constantly worked to his team's advantage, and whose leadership was undenied. Auerbach, knowing the importance of winning in professional sports, guaranteed Russell that he would never talk statistics at contract time. This was exactly what Russell, the ultimate team player, wanted to hear. In his own view, he never graded himself higher than sixty-five against a perfect game standard of one hundred.

   More important, Russell recognized that there was far more to life than basketball. From his pedestal of fame, he stood taller, making himself heard in matters that counted. Teammate Cousy referred to Russell as a crusader. Certainly, Russell was among the first blacks in sports to speak out on issues. He remembered his being regularly stopped on Oakland's streets as a teenager, the police routinely harassing him with racial epithets. He remembered the mayor of Marion, Indiana, presenting each Celtic with a key to the city. Then, with K. C. Jones, Russell was refused service in a restaurant. He remembered honors being given him in Reading, Massachusetts, where he lived, the citizens of a wealthy section of town then circulating a petition to keep him out, when they learned that he planned to move there. Similar hurts were experienced in his hometown of Monroe, in Lexington, Kentucky, and elsewhere. Teammate Heinsohn remarked that Russell led the league in regrets. Russell also remembered, however, his grandfather's crying when, in the Celtic locker room, he had seen white John Havlicek showering alongside black Sam Jones.

   Russell spoke out against the NBA's unwritten, but patently obvious, "quota" rule, and was fined. He was among those who defended Muhammed Ali, while condemning newspapers and magazines for their yellow journalism. When he was the first black selected to the Basketball Hall of Fame, already in its fifteenth year of operation, he refused to be inducted, criticizing the hall's standards and terming their leadership racist. He took up the cudgels when he could, on one hand speaking about blacks nationally, on the other being active in Boston school issues. This is the Russell who has affected America, a sports hero who insists on being judged as a total person.

Bibliography

Auerbach, Arnold "Red," and Joe Fitzgerald. *Red Auerbach: An Autobiography.* New York: G. P. Putnam's Sons, 1977. A breezy study which contains the drive to win not only of Auerbach, but also of his Celtics.

Cousy, Bob, with Ed Linn. *The Last Loud Roar.* Englewood Cliffs, N.J.: Prentice-Hall, 1964. A very revealing book. Cousy tells his story as frankly as any athlete ever has. Much insight into league and team methods is contained here.

Harris, Merv. *The Lonely Heroes*. New York: Viking Press, 1975. A valuable work on professional basketball's big men, dependable in its facts, written with an effort to achieve balance.

Havlicek, John, with Bob Ryan. *Hondo: Celtic Man in Motion*. Englewood Cliffs, N.J.: Prentice-Hall, 1977. Candid descriptions of Boston plus very interesting insights into Russell's youth make this a worthwhile book. As with all books by Celtic personnel, Russell's personality, as well as his value to the club, is assessed.

Heinsohn, Tommy, with Leonard Lewin. *Heinsohn, Don't You Ever Smile?* Garden City, N.Y.: Doubleday and Co., 1976. Easily the most humorous of all Celtic literature. In his discussion of Russell, Heinsohn may get closer to the truth of how Russell and his teammates related than any other work yet written.

Hirshberg, Al. *Bill Russell of the Boston Celtics*. New York: Julian Messner, 1963. A slick, useful study, discussing Russell's youth very well. Its value is diminished only because it was published before Russell's career had closed.

Linn, Ed. "I Owe the Public Nothing." *Saturday Evening Post* 237 (January, 1964): 60-63. An article which, because Russell spoke out so candidly, created controversy. Permits a quick study of Russell's pride and philosophy.

Russell, Bill, and Taylor Branch. *Second Wind: The Memoirs of an Opinionated Man*. New York: Random House, 1979. The second of two Russell autobiographies, this concentrates considerably more on his private life and behavior and rearticulates his philosophy. This is the better of the pair.

Russell, Bill, as told to William McSweeny. *Go Up for Glory*. New York: Coward-McCann, 1966. Though surpassed by Russell's second autobiography, this stands as an outstanding work. Contains valuable statements about sports and goals achievable within competition.

Russell, Bill, with Tex Maule. "I Am Not Worried About Ali." *Sports Illustrated* 26 (June, 1967): 18-21. Concentrating on Muhammed Ali's problems, the article reveals the passion and attitudes of Russell in several matters.

John E. DiMeglio

BABE RUTH

Born: February 6, 1895; Baltimore, Maryland
Died: August 16, 1948; New York, New York
Area of Achievement: Baseball
Contribution: A remarkably talented athlete with a great flair for showmanship, Babe Ruth has come to symbolize baseball, the American national pastime.

Early Life

George Herman Ruth was born in Baltimore, Maryland. His father was George H. Ruth, Sr. (1871-1918), and his mother was Kate Schamberger (1875-1912). Some confusion exists about the younger Ruth's actual date of birth. For many years, George Ruth believed that he had been born on February 7, 1894, but his birth certificate gives February 6, 1895, as his date of birth. George Ruth was the eldest of the eight children born to the Ruths, although only he and a sister (later Mrs. Wilbur Moberly) survived to adulthood. George Ruth's mother (whose maiden name is sometimes spelled Schanberg) lived until her eldest son was thirteen. His father survived until young George's second year in the major leagues.

The Ruths attempted to support their family through the operation of a barroom. Of his childhood, the dying Ruth told Bob Considine in 1947, "I was a bad kid. I say that without pride but with a feeling that it is better to say it." Having discovered that their eldest child, George, was a fractious youth, George and Kate enrolled him in St. Mary's Industrial School in Baltimore, Maryland, in 1902. Under the direction of the Xaverian Catholic Brothers, St. Mary's served as a vocational school as well as an orphanage, boarding school, and reform school. It was at St. Mary's that young Ruth studied to become a tailor and also learned to play baseball. Brother Matthias of St. Mary's would hit fungoes to Ruth, who quickly seized upon the game as a release from the studies and chores at St. Mary's as well as a chance to demonstrate what Brother Matthias recognized as a remarkable skill in the popular game. To Ruth, Brother Matthias was not only a fielding, hitting, and pitching coach, he was also "the father I needed." Years later, at the height of his fame and popularity, Babe Ruth never forgot St. Mary's or the Xaverian Brothers who had taught him so well.

In Baltimore, in 1914, there was a professional baseball team named the Orioles. At the time, the Orioles were a minor league team, owned and managed by Jack Dunn, who, after learning about Ruth's great baseball promise, signed the young athlete to a contract. Ruth discovered that he did not have to become a tailor; he could make a living doing what he enjoyed most: playing baseball. On February 27, 1914, George Ruth left St. Mary's to join the Baltimore team. During his first few days of spring training, Jack Dunn's new "babe" was the subject of some good-natured baseball pranks. Eventually, the new arrival on the team became Babe Ruth, arguably the greatest and most colorful player in the history of the sport he loved so well.

Life's Work

Young Babe Ruth was a left-handed pitcher, and the high prices being offered for Ruth's pitching ability soon proved too tempting for the financially distressed Orioles to resist: Ruth was sold to the Boston Red Sox in July, 1914. On July 11, 1914, Babe Ruth pitched and was victorious in the first major league baseball game he had ever played. With his tremendous speed and sharp breaking ball, Ruth impressed Red Sox manager Bill Carrigan. Still, it was clear by August that the Red Sox would not win the American League pennant from Connie Mack's Philadelphia Athletics. Ruth was therefore sent down to the Red Sox minor league team in Providence, Rhode Island, to help them win the International League pennant. Providence manager "Wild Bill" Donovan was credited by Ruth for his effective pitching coaching, later of value to Ruth in his Red Sox career.

Throughout his long and colorful career, Ruth was criticized for financial, gastronomic, and sexual excesses. As with other legendary personalities, however, his sins as well as his successes may have been exaggerated. In his major league career, spanning 1914 to 1935, the Babe (as he was called) was an exciting, intelligent, and astonishingly well-rounded ball player, suggesting that the tales about his endless hedonism were largely, if not entirely, fictitious. On October 17, 1914, Babe Ruth married Helen Woodford, a waitress whom he had met in 1914, while with the Red Sox. In 1922, the Ruths adopted a baby girl named Dorothy. In 1926, the Ruths separated; in January, 1929, Helen Ruth was killed in a tragic fire. Three months later, Ruth married a beautiful widow named Claire Merritt Hodgson and adopted her daughter Julia. Ruth remained with his second wife until his death in August, 1948.

In 1915, the Boston Red Sox won the American League pennant, winning 101 games, of which Ruth had won eighteen, and losing only fifty. In the 1915 World Series, the Red Sox defeated the Philadelphia Phillies, four games to one. In 1916, Ruth won twenty-three games—a figure he matched in 1917. Overall, Babe Ruth won ninety-two games as a pitcher, and lost only forty-four; his earned run average was a remarkable 2.24. Ruth pitched for Boston in three World Series: 1915, 1916, and 1918. He won three World Series games, lost none, and sported an earned run average of 0.87. Had he continued as a pitcher, Ruth's pitching record could have been as remarkable as his hitting record.

The Red Sox now faced a problem with Ruth. In 1918, Ruth was recognized as one of the finest pitchers in baseball. He also hit eleven home runs, knocked in sixty-four runs, and batted .300. Ruth was too good a hitter to pitch every four days, resting between starts. He was too good a pitcher, however, to play the outfield or first base every day. It is some indication of Ruth's phenomenal baseball ability that from 1914 to 1919, while he was principally a pitcher, Ruth had 342 hits in 1,110 at-bats, with forty-nine home runs and 230 runs batted in. He simply had become too powerful as a hitter to keep as a pitcher. He also had become too expensive. Babe Ruth's 1917 salary was five thousand dollars, in 1918 it was seven thousand, and by 1919, it had grown to ten thousand. In January, 1920, Babe Ruth was sold again—this time by the Red Sox to the New York Yankees. The price tag was $100,000 and a loan of $350,000.

The season of 1920 was a turning point in the history of baseball. In that season, Ruth smashed an incredible fifty-four home runs, driving in 137. A new national hero was born, and the game of baseball began to change from a short game (meaning a game of bunts, sacrifices, and steals) to a long game (meaning home runs and big-scoring innings). There had been great concern for the future of the national pastime when it was revealed that some Chicago White Sox players had been bribed in the 1919 World Series, which they lost to Cincinnati. Ruth's amazing feats, however, drove the 1919 scandal from fans' minds. As *The New York Times* reported: "Inside of a fortnight the fandom of the nation had forgotten all about the Black Sox, as they had come to be called, as its attention became centered in an even greater demonstration of superlative batting skill by the amazing Babe Ruth." In 1921, Ruth hit an astounding fifty-nine home runs and drove in 170, while batting .378. Ruth's Yankees won ninety-eight games in that season and beat their cross-town rivals, the New York Giants, five games to three, in the World Series. It was no wonder, *The New York Times* reported, that "the baseball world lay at his feet."

The Yankees won the pennant again in 1922, 1923, 1926, 1927, 1928, and 1932; they won the World Series in 1922, 1923, 1927, 1928, and 1932. In the World Series games in which he played as a Yankee, Ruth hit fifteen home runs, drove in twenty-nine runs, and hit .347. Obscured by his extraordinary totals as a hitter (and pitcher) is Ruth's fielding, throwing, and baserunning ability. Numerous baseball fans and analysts testify to Ruth's superb skills as an outfielder and daring, aggressive baserunner. Ruth's attempted steal of second base in the final game of the 1926 World Series, which the St. Louis Cardinals won, is part of baseball folklore. With two outs in the ninth inning of the deciding Series game, Ruth walked. Trailing 3-2 in the ninth inning, the Yankees had two outs, but powerful Bob Meusel was at bat. With one strike on Meusel, Ruth attempted a delayed steal of second but was thrown out. The game was over, and the Cardinals were world champions. Baseball fans still argue the wisdom of Ruth's attempted steal. There is another Ruth legend associated with the 1926 World Series, the validity of which is still debated by baseball mythologists. A young boy, John Sylvester, was seriously ill during the 1926 Series. When he asked his father for a ball autographed by Ruth, the older Sylvester wired that request to the Babe. Players of both teams autographed balls which were sent to the Sylvester home. Johnny Sylvester did recover, but reports that Ruth promised to hit a home run for Johnny which, when executed, led to the boy's recovery, are in error.

In 1927, the New York Yankees, led by Ruth's herculean hitting (sixty home runs, 164 runs batted in, batting average of .356), won the World Series in a four-game sweep of the Pittsburgh Pirates. The 1927 Yankees are properly regarded by baseball historians as the greatest of all baseball teams. Ruth had by that time accumulated 416 home runs, batted in 1,274, and was batting .349. He was regarded as the great turnstile whirler, and it seemed as though people everywhere knew of Babe Ruth. In 1927, the Yankees paid Ruth an unbelievable seventy thousand dollars—a figure they matched in 1928 and 1929. In 1930 and 1931, he received eighty thousand dollars per season. Ruth's earnings over twenty-two seasons in the majors were estimated to be $896,000, in addition to World Series shares of $41,445 and approximately one million dollars from endorsements and barnstorming tours. Despite the high cost, Ruth was an asset to the Yankees: He attracted so many fans to Yankee Stadium, which opened in 1923, that it was nicknamed "the House that Ruth Built."

Although 1927 will always be associated in sports history with Babe Ruth, the years 1928-1933 are equally, perhaps even more, impressive. In those years alone, Ruth batted .341, hit 270 home runs, and drove in 852 runs. It was spectacular. It was the golden age of sports, and Babe Ruth came to symbolize it all. Americans needed a diversion: The Depression had hit, and prohibition was not repealed until December, 1933. The public followed Ruth's successes and his failures, his heroics and his occasional misconduct, with enthusiasm.

In 1934, Babe Ruth spent his last full year in the major leagues. His average sank to .288; he hit twenty-two home runs and batted in eighty-four. It would have been an excellent season for most players, but it signaled the end for Babe Ruth. In 1934, the Yankees failed again (as in 1933) to win the pennant. Ruth left the Yankees and signed on for the 1935 season with the Boston Braves of the National League. He played in only twenty-eight games for the Braves, hitting six homers, driving in twelve runs, and batting .181. Ruth never attained his goal of becoming a major league manager, although he did coach in 1938 for the Brooklyn Dodgers. Statistics do not always reliably convey the value of a ballplayer, but, in Ruth's case, the evidence is clear: In his major league career, he played in 2,503 games; he batted 8,396 times and had 2,873 hits, of which 714 were homers. His lifetime batting average was .342. At the time of his death in 1948, Babe Ruth held fifty-four major league records. Although some of those records have now been captured by more recent players, Babe Ruth, the famous Number Three of the Yankees, is still the standard against which ballplayers are measured.

In June, 1948, Ruth, a dying man, stood in Yankee Stadium to say good-bye to thousands of fans. About two months later, he died of cancer at a New York City hospital. On the evening of August 17, 1948, Ruth's body lay inside the main entrance to Yankee Stadium. It is estimated that more than 100,000 fans passed by to pay their respects. The Babe was dead, but, as Marshall Smelser put it, "one with ears tuned and eyes alert will hear or read his name almost monthly. Even without any imposing monument his memory will last in this country till memory be dead."

Summary

In March, 1944, during the bitter fighting on Pacific Islands, Japanese soldiers attacked United States Marine positions, screaming in English: "To hell with Babe Ruth." Babe Ruth had come to symbolize not only American baseball but also America. As Robert Creamer, the baseball historian, reported, Ruth once said of himself: "I swing big, with everything I've got. I hit big or I miss big. I like to live as big as I can." Here was an indigent boy who rose from the obscurity of a Maryland boys' home to become one of the most famous Americans, whose death was reported in the headlines of *The New York Times*. Although he only lived to be fifty-three, Ruth's life seemed curiously long and complete. Ruth had a remarkable flair for the spectacular and the flamboyant. He lived his life with a zest which his countrymen seemed able to share. As he was dying, he told his biographer, Bob Considine, that "I want to be a part of and help the development of the greatest game God ever saw fit to let man invent—Baseball." Even in death, Ruth will always be associated with baseball, and with America. Marshall Smelser summarized the importance of Babe Ruth in American life thus: "[H]e is our Hercules, our Samson, Beowulf, Siegfried. No other person outside of public life so stirred our imaginations or so captured our affections."

Bibliography
Creamer, Robert W. *Babe: The Legend Comes to Life*. New York: Penguin Books, 1974. A very well-written and well-researched biography. A balanced account of Ruth's life, neither iconoclastic nor hagiographic. Probably the best general account of Ruth's life, although there is little documentation for the close reader.
Ruth, Babe. *Babe Ruth's Own Book of Baseball*. New York: G. P. Putnam's Sons, 1928. No credit is given in this volume to any assistant writer, although there very probably was at least one. This is an interesting book because it contains details about Ruth's life—as well as about his baseball beliefs—which are rarely referred to elsewhere. Anecdotal. It provides an interesting view of baseball strategy in the 1920's.
Ruth, Babe, as told to Bob Considine. *The Babe Ruth Story*. New York:

E. P. Dutton, 1948. A surprisingly well-done and frank account of Babe's life, written in the last months of that life. Although bowdlerized, the book contains the Babe's views of many important episodes in his life and is enjoyable reading for the Ruth fan.

Smelser, Marshall. *The Life That Ruth Built.* New York: Quadrangle/The New York Times Book Co., 1975. By far the best study of Ruth yet to emerge. Balanced account, if rather forgiving of Ruth in certain areas. Superbly researched and documented. Thoughtful and analytical. Thorough. Attempts to place Ruth into his historical context. Indispensable for those wishing a deeper study of the Ruth legend.

Wagenheim, Kal. *Babe Ruth: His Life and Legend.* New York: Praeger Publishers, 1974. A very good popular account, overshadowed by Creamer's when both appeared at about the same time. Although this volume is not as thorough as Creamer's—and certainly not as thorough as Smelser's—it is a useful and readable account.

Weldon, Martin. *Babe Ruth.* New York: Thomas Y. Crowell Co., 1948. A book appearing about the same time as *The Babe Ruth Story*, this book was never given close attention, but it is a short, readable account without documentation. Tends to be rather flattering of the Babe. This book, like Claire Ruth's memoir *The Babe and I* (with Bill Slocum), published by Prentice-Hall in 1959, becomes a philippic against organized baseball for not embracing Babe as a manager after his playing career was done. Useful if read with other accounts.

James H. Toner

SACAGAWEA

Born: c. 1788; along the Continental Divide, western Montana, eastern Idaho, perhaps near modern Tendoy, Idaho
Died: December 20, 1812; Fort Manuel, Dakota Territory (modern South Dakota)
Area of Achievement: Exploration
Contribution: In addition to providing important geographical information to the Lewis and Clark Expedition (1804-1806), Sacagawea has come to symbolize the diverse lives and struggles of women in the American West.

Early Life

The Shoshone Indian woman Sacagawea was born about 1788 in a native hunting camp somewhere along the Continental Divide between Montana and Idaho. Her people, the Shoshones, often frequented the area around present-day Tendoy, Idaho. The Shoshones were a hunting, fishing, and gathering people. The young girl who became known as Sacagawea must have spent her first years like other women in her band, learning skills ranging from cooking and child care to making clothes and digging the wild roots that were a staple in the Shoshone diet.

Each fall the Lemhi Shoshones joined their Flathead Indian neighbors for a grand buffalo hunt in what is now western Montana. On that hunt in 1800, Sacagawea's life was forever changed. While camped with her relatives near Three Forks, Montana, she and several other Shoshones were kidnaped by Hidatsa Indian raiders. The raiders took Sacagawea and the others back to the Hidatsa village of Metaharta on the Knife River in modern North Dakota. There Sacagawea and one other Shoshone woman were sold as wives to a French-Canadian fur trader named Toussaint Charbonneau.

Life's Work

Had it not been for the arrival of the Lewis and Clark Expedition near the Hidatsa villages in the fall of 1804, Sacagawea would have lived out her life as an adopted Hidatsa woman, hoeing corn, cleaning the traditional earth lodge, and caring for a growing family. The presence of the American explorers at Fort Mandan, just south of her village, changed the course of Sacagawea's life. Already planning for the final leg of their great journey to the Pacific, Meriwether Lewis and William Clark knew that they would need extra help from those native peoples who might know the ways West. Even more important, the expedition would require experienced interpreters. Although Charbonneau had not traveled beyond the Yellowstone River, he was engaged by the expedition as an interpreter. Because Lewis and Clark planned to use horses from the Shoshones to cross the Great Divide, employing Charbonneau's wife also made good sense.

When the expedition left Fort Mandan for the Pacific in April, 1805,

Sacagawea was very much a part of the adventure. She now traveled with her infant son Jean-Baptiste, born only two months earlier. Her role in the journey to the Pacific has long sparked controversy among Western historians. Some have forcefully argued that Sacagawea "guided" Lewis and Clark through hidden passes and down treacherous rivers. Other historians, more interested in fact than fiction, have sought a more balanced evaluation of her place in Western exploration. Sacagawea was not hired to guide Lewis and Clark. At no point during the expedition's journey did she play an active part in selecting one route over another. In June, 1805, when Lewis and Clark had to make a crucial decision about the true course of the Missouri River, Sacagawea's advice was not requested. Only twice did the Indian woman provide what might be called "guide services." In the late summer of 1805, when the expedition was making its way through western Montana, she recognized important landmarks on the way to the Shoshone camps. It so happened that the band headman of these Shoshones was Sacagawea's brother Cameahwait. The chance meeting between Sacagawea and her brother did not materially affect expedition-Indian relations, since Cameahwait had already decided to help the explorers. In fact, the chief virtually ignored his sister, and she showed no interest in remaining with her own people. On the eastward return journey in 1806, Sacagawea accompanied Clark's party on a reconnaissance of the Yellowstone country. She provided Clark with valuable information about what was later called Bozeman Pass. Clark recognized Sacagawea's contribution to this part of the expedition, describing her as of "great service to me as a pilot."

If Sacagawea was not the expedition's faithful Indian guide, she did make important contributions in other areas. Clark summed up her most valuable duties by describing her as "interpretress with the Snake Indians," Snake being a common frontier synonym for Shoshone. Much of the success, and even the very survival of the expedition depended on reliable communication and translation between the explorers and the native people. Sign language, while a useful means for basic conversation, could not cope with the complex exchanges required by the expedition. Here Sacagawea had a vital part to play. Both east and west of the Great Divide she served the expedition well, patiently helping to move each Indian word along a cumbersome translation chain that often stretched from Shoshone to French and on at last to English.

The expedition also benefited from the physical presence of Sacagawea and her infant son. Western Indians who might have viewed the expedition as a threatening war party were reassured by the presence of the Shoshone woman and her child. As Clark put it, "The Wife of Shabono [Charbonneau] our interpreter we find reconsiles all the Indians, as to our friendly intentions a woman with a party of men is a token of peace."

Two other controversies continue to surround Sacagawea. Her name—its meaning and spelling—still rouses debate. Sakakawea, Sacajawea, and

Sacagawea all have their passionate advocates. The concern about spelling is not simply a debate about handwriting. If the woman's name was Sacajawea, the word might be Shoshone, meaning "boat launcher." Yet if the spelling was more properly Sacagawea, the name would be Hidatsa and translate as "bird woman." The evidence from the journals of the Lewis and Clark Expedition appears to support a Hidatsa name. On May 25, 1805, Lewis wrote: "Sah ca gah we ah or bird woman's River" to name what is now Crooked Creek in north-central Montana. The Sacagawea spelling is now accepted by most historians as well as by the National Park Service.

If Sacagawea's life, accomplishments, and name remain open to some question, there has also been much argument about the time and place of her death. When Grace R. Hebard published her *Sacajawea* in 1933, she claimed that the Indian woman had lived the remainder of her life at Wind River, Wyoming, under the name Porivo. Hebard insisted that Sacagawea died in 1884. It is now plain that Hebard misinterpreted some evidence and ignored much more. The state of Wyoming continues to mark the supposed grave site and indicate its location on tourist maps. Reliable historical evidence from Clark and fur trader John C. Luttig make it plain that Sacagawea died on December 20, 1812, at Fort Manuel in present-day South Dakota. Luttig was the trader at Fort Manuel and wrote in his record book the following brief but touching obituary. "This Evening the wife of Charbonneau, a Snake Squaw, died of a putrid fever she was a good and the best woman in the fort, aged abt 25 years."

Summary

When the traveler Henry Marie Brackenridge saw Sacagawea in St. Louis the year before her death, he described her as "a good creature, of a mild and gentle disposition, greatly attached to the whites, whose manners and dress she tries to imitate." To the citizens of St. Louis, Sacagawea was no ordinary Indian. She was instantly recognized as a member of the great Lewis and Clark Corps of Western Discovery. William Clark, who did much to care for young Jean-Baptiste after his mother's death, honored her courage on the trek to the Pacific. Writing soon after the expedition returned from the West, he recalled her presence on "that long dangerous and fatigueing rout to the Pacific Ocean." Clark was only sorry that the Indian woman could not have been given a greater reward for "her attention and services."

The Shoshone woman Sacagawea earned an important place in the history of the American West. That place does not depend on some false and inflated role as expedition guide. Like other members of the great exploring venture, it was enough that she persevered and stayed the course. When the expedition reached the Pacific in December, 1805, Sacagawea was not included in the first parties to see the great ocean. Plucky as ever, she bitterly complained that she "had traveled a long way with us to see the great waters." Sacagawea had indeed earned the right to gaze upon the Western sea. The Indian woman remains a complex symbol in the story of Western expansion. She stands for courage and determination on the trail. As a Native American, she is a reminder of the violence that lay behind American expansion into Indian homelands. In all, Sacagawea exemplifies a Western destiny filled with bright days and gathering shadows.

Bibliography
Anderson, Irving. "A Charbonneau Family Portrait." *American West* 17 (Spring, 1980): 4-13, 58-64. A popular but reliable account of the Charbonneaus—Toussaint, Sacagawea, and their son Jean-Baptiste.
_____. "Probing the Riddle of the Bird Woman." *Montana: The Magazine of Western History* 23 (October, 1973): 2-17. A thoroughly documented study of the circumstances surrounding Sacagawea's death.
Clark, Ella E., and Margot Edmonds. *Sacagawea of the Lewis and Clark Expedition*. Berkeley: University of California Press, 1980. A reasonably accurate biography that is weakened by uncritical acceptance of the Porivo legend.
Howard, Harold F. *Sacajawea*. Norman: University of Oklahoma Press, 1971. Despite some confusion about Sacagawea's name, this is the best book-length biography of the Indian woman.
Jackson, Donald. *Thomas Jefferson and the Stony Mountains: Exploring the West from Monticello*. Urbana: University of Illinois Press, 1980. The best general introduction to Western exploration in the period.
_____, ed. *The Letters of the Lewis and Clark Expedition with Related Documents, 1783-1854*. 2d ed. 2 vols. Urbana: University of Illinois Press, 1978. A comprehensive collection of materials about the expedition, including correspondence touching on the life of Sacagawea.
Lewis, Meriwether. *The Original Journals of the Lewis and Clark Expedition*. Edited by Reuben Gold Thwaites. 8 vols. New York: Dodd, Mead and Co., 1904-1905. The standard collection of expedition diaries. A fuller, more completely annotated edition is in progress, edited by Gary E. Moulton, to be published by the University of Nebraska Press.
Madsen, Brigham D. *The Lemhi: Sacajawea's People*. Caldwell, Idaho: Caxton Printers, 1979. A generally sound study of the tribal group to which Sacagawea belonged.
Ronda, James P. *Lewis and Clark Among the Indians*. Lincoln: University of Nebraska Press, 1984. The only full-scale study of relations between native peoples and the expedition. Contains an appendix that summarizes and evaluates books and articles dealing with Sacagawea.

James P. Ronda

AUGUSTUS SAINT-GAUDENS

Born: March 1, 1848; Dublin, Ireland
Died: August 3, 1907; Cornish, New Hampshire
Area of Achievement: Art
Contribution: Saint-Gaudens' memorial statues of America's greatest men and women are generally regarded as among the most beautiful and inspired examples of late nineteenth century artistic realism.

Early Life

Augustus Saint-Gaudens was born March 1, 1848, in Dublin, Ireland. His father was Bernard Paul Ernest Saint-Gaudens, formerly of the village of Aspet in southern France, a shoemaker who emigrated to London and then Dublin. It was in the latter city that he met and married Mary McGuiness, a handcrafter of slippers formerly from Bally Mahon, County Longford. Their first children, George and Louis, died in childhood; then Augustus was born in Dublin; finally, Andrew and another Louis were born in the United States.

Emigration from Ireland to the United States took place in 1848, during Augustus' infancy and the ruinous Potato Famine. The small family arrived at Boston but soon moved to New York City. Here the children were brought up in the Catholic faith and attended public schools.

A patron of the arts, Dr. Cornelius Rea Agnew, saw some pen-and-ink drawings by the child Augustus in his father's shop and recommended that he be apprenticed to an artist. Accordingly, in 1861, when he was thirteen, the boy began his apprenticeship under a stern taskmaster named Avet, a stone-cameo cutter.

The Civil War years and the personalities of that era impressed themselves upon the sensitive mind of the budding artist. Later, he would portray several of them in examples of his greatest works. He came to detest Avet, however, and almost turned his back on portraiture until he found employment with the shell-cameo artist Jules LeBrethon and was accepted as a student at the distinguished drawing school of the Cooper Institute. Before the war drew to a close in 1865, he was admitted to the still more prestigious National Academy of Design. His skills greatly heightened and his family's finances much improved by his earnings, Saint-Gaudens sailed for Europe at the age of nineteen.

Life's Work

In Paris, Saint-Gaudens obtained employment with an Italian cameo cutter and enrolled in a small art school and then in the world famous school of fine arts, L'École des Beaux-Arts. Here, Saint-Gaudens learned much of low relief and the special art of sculpture. In 1868, the American produced his first such work, a bronze bust of his father.

Several lifelong friendships were formed in the five years before Saint-Gaudens returned to the United States in 1872, one with Alfred Garnier, one with Paul Bion and another with the Portuguese Soares dos Reis. These accomplished young artists reinforced one another's desire to persevere in the face of brutal criticism and dwindling funds. Saint-Gaudens, with some of his friends from L'École des Beaux-Arts, lived for a while in Rome; there he completed several classic busts and his statues *Hiawatha* and *Silence*, later placed in Saratoga and New York City, respectively.

His brief return home, to New York, led to several commissioned works. During this time, his patrons included Senator William Evarts of New York, Edward Stoughton, Edward Pierrepont, Elihu Root, and L. H. Willard. Now a productive artist, he chose to live in Rome for the next three years, returning to the United States to stay in 1875. Before his return, he met and became engaged to an American girl in Rome, Augusta F. Homer.

The wedding took place at Roxbury, Massachusetts, on June 4, 1877. Both Augustus and Augusta were dark, average in height, and slim. She was considered by far the better-looking of the two, his chin and nose being long and angular. He also maintained a mustache and, generally, a beard of some kind. Their one child, Homer, was born in 1880. Back in New York, artist John La Farge helped Saint-Gaudens obtain such important assignments as the statue of Admiral David Farragut for placement in Madison Square, New York City, the St. Thomas (Episcopal) Church reliefs, also in New York, and those of the Edward King tomb in Newport, Rhode Island.

Early in the 1880's, Saint-Gaudens began a friendship which was to have a great impact on both his life and his work. A Swedish-born model, Alberta Hulgren or Hultgren, became his mistress; rechristened Davida (she later used the name Davida Johnson Clarke), she became his muse as well. The details of this relationship, long suppressed, remain sketchy. For many years, Saint-Gaudens maintained a separate household for Davida, by whom he had a son; her likeness is evident in a number of Saint-Gaudens' idealized female figures.

It was during this decade, too, that Saint-Gaudens fully established himself as an artist. By 1880, he had already completed the Morgan Tomb's *Angels*, the statue of Robert Richard Randall for Sailors' Snug Harbor, Staten Island, and several medallion and plaque low reliefs such as those of fellow artist Bastien-Lepage and friend Dr. Henry Shiff. A friend of whom he did caricatures was Charles Follen McKim. Another friend and patron, Stanford White, made valuable contacts on his behalf. In the years that followed, Saint-Gaudens added to his fame with statues or reliefs of Robert Louis Stevenson, William Dean Howells, the children of Jacob H. Schiff, Kenyon Cox, Peter Cooper, Princeton president James McCosh, Mrs. Grover Cleveland, General John A. Logan, General William T. Sherman, and Abraham Lincoln. The Lincoln statue was very highly regarded, and it came to rest, appropriately enough, in Lincoln Park in Chicago.

Other works included *The Puritan*, in Springfield, Massachusetts, a winged *Victory* on the Sherman Monument, *Silence*, *Amor Caritas*, caryatids, other glorified women, eagles for gold coins, horses, and angels. He taught courses at the Art Students' League in New York, accepted pupils readily at his studio on Thirty-sixth Street (most notably Frederick W. MacMonnies) and helped found the Society of American Artists and other groups to promote and advance the fine arts. His advice to aspiring artists was to "conceive an idea and then stick to it." Those who "hang on" will be "the only ones who amount to anything."

In 1891, Saint-Gaudens' most celebrated creation was unveiled: The slim nudity of his *Diana*, high on the tower of Stanford White's Madison Square Garden, provoked comment throughout the city of New York. (A second *Diana*, slightly altered and improved, later took the place of the first.) Many artists today, however, regard Saint-Gaudens' 1891 monument to Mrs. Henry Adams in Rock Creek Cemetery, Washington, D.C., and especially the relief he did there, commonly entitled *Grief*, as his greatest work.

Late in life, Saint-Gaudens suffered two great shocks: He lost his studio in a fire, and then he lost his fast friend and patron White to a pistol bullet. The fire, in October, 1904, destroyed many small pieces of his life's work. The murder of White, a noted architect with a flamboyant life-style, was carried out by crazed playboy Harry K. Thaw in June, 1906, and was a scandalous affair. Saint-Gaudens died August 3, 1907, following a bout of poor health, in his beloved vacation site of Cornish, New Hampshire.

Summary

Realistic sculpture reached its zenith of popularity during the lifetime of Augustus Saint-Gaudens, and his own contributions helped to keep it popular. While many of his works, busts, reliefs, and complete statues are simply of wealthy patrons and their friends, his most memorable creations are largely associated with the great men and women of his lifetime, including Lincoln, Farragut, and Sherman.

His work is both inspired and inspirational, ideal for the dramatic memorial and the noble sentiment. It expresses feelings of passion, confidence, and courage; it is timely yet timeless.

Bibliography

Cortissoz, Royal. *Augustus Saint-Gaudens*. Boston: Houghton Mifflin Co., 1907. The author, a specialist in the field of American art and artists in the nineteenth century, has produced in this book an effective though somewhat rambling biography.

Cox, Kenyon. *Old Masters and New*. New York: Fox, Duffield and Co., 1905. Cox was a close friend of Saint-Gaudens, and his insight into the subject's work is especially valuable. While dealing with such different artists as Michelangelo and James Whistler, he does set aside a chapter entitled "The Early Work of Saint-Gaudens," wherein the sculptor's Sherman is given particularly close inspection.

Greenthal, Kathryn. *Augustus Saint-Gaudens: Master Sculptor*. New York: Metropolitan Museum of Art, 1985. An excellent, thoroughly researched study. Among the 181 illustrations are twelve superb color plates. Includes an extensive bibliography.

Hind, Charles Lewis. *Augustus Saint-Gaudens*. New York: International Studio, John Lane Co., 1908. The author, a prolific biographer at the turn of the century, produced in this volume a very well illustrated if rather shallow biography.

Saint-Gaudens, August. *The Reminiscences of Augustus Saint-Gaudens*. 2 vols. Edited by Homer Saint-Gaudens. New York: Century Co., 1913. The son of the subject and himself a knowledgeable artist, Homer Saint-Gaudens speaks with authority. Inasmuch as he quotes his father extensively, Homer Saint-Gaudens is regarded as the editor, but he is generous with his own observations.

Taft, Lorado. *History of American Sculpture*. New York: Macmillan, 1903. This book is the best illustrated work available on the masterpieces of Saint-Gaudens and his contemporaries. Taft's lucid commentaries and beautiful full-page photogravures were so well received that this book went through several revisions and reprints.

Wilkinson, Burke. *Uncommon Clay: The Life and Work of Augustus Saint Gaudens*. San Diego, Calif.: Harcourt Brace Jovanovich, 1985. The work of a novelist and popular biographer, this spirited account portrays Saint-Gaudens as part passionate romantic, part "Renaissance soldier of fortune." Provides information unavailable elsewhere, particularly concerning Davida Clarke, whose role in Saint-Gaudens' life is perhaps exaggerated by Wilkinson. Well documented; includes a useful section of illustrations.

Joseph E. Suppiger

J. D. SALINGER

Born: January 1, 1919; New York, New York

Area of Achievement: Literature
Contribution: Although Salinger wrote only one novel and thirty-five stories, he attained a degree of international recognition and popularity that is unequaled by most twentieth century American authors.

Early Life

Born in Manhattan, the setting (or focal point) for most of his best fiction, Jerome David Salinger was the second child and only son of Sol and Marie Jillich Salinger. His paternal grandfather, Simon, born in Lithuania, was at one time the rabbi for the Adath Jeshurun congregation in Louisville, Kentucky. His mother, reared a Christian, converted to Judaism upon marrying Sol and changed her name to Miriam. Salinger's father, an importer of meat (hams from Poland in particular), was a highly successful businessman. The family lived on Riverside Drive during Salinger's early years. The Salingers were not conventionally religious; the children were exposed primarily to the ideas of Ethical Culture. In 1930, young Salinger, or "Sonny" as he was called by his family, spent the summer at Camp Wigwam in Harrison, Maine (the probable source for the setting of his last published story).

Salinger attended Manhattan public schools until, at age thirteen, he was enrolled in the McBurney School, also in Manhattan, where he earned below-average grades but became manager of the fencing team and was elected sophomore class president in his second year there. In the fall of 1934, hoping for better academic performance from his son, Salinger's father sent him to Valley Forge Military Academy in Wayne, Pennsylvania, where he participated in all the usual activities, was literary editor of the yearbook, and maintained about a B average.

After Salinger was graduated from Valley Forge in 1936, he attended the Washington Square campus of New York University. He took the following year off to travel with his father in Austria and Poland; while in Europe, Salinger learned German and familiarized himself with the family business. This experience led him back to academe, to Ursinus College in Collegeville, Pennsylvania, in the fall of 1938. The columns that Salinger wrote for the Ursinus College newspaper reveal a very literary man most unhappy with college life. Salinger abruptly left Ursinus in December; his train voyage home to New York was perhaps the inspiration for a similar scene in *The Catcher in the Rye* (1951).

In the spring of 1938, Salinger enrolled in the Extension Division of Columbia University and attended Whit Burnett's writing class. Within a year, his first story, "The Young Folks," was published in Burnett's *Story* magazine; another appeared in the *University of Kansas City Review*. In 1941, he cracked the slick magazines, with one story each in *Collier's* and *Esquire*. Thereafter, for ten years or more, regardless of his life circumstances, Salinger regularly published stories in these and such other magazines as *The Saturday Evening Post*, *Good Housekeeping*, *Cosmopolitan*, *Harper's*, and *The New Yorker*. Several of Salinger's stories, even some of those written as early as 1941, concern a young man named Holden Caulfield, who would become the hero of Salinger's first and only novel, *The Catcher in the Rye*.

Meanwhile, in the spring of 1942, Salinger was drafted into the United States Army, serving first in the Signal Corps and then later in the Counter-Intelligence Corps, where he was assigned to the Twelfth Infantry Regiment of the Fourth Division. He sailed with the latter for England in January of 1944. On D-Day, Salinger, by then a staff sergeant, landed on Utah Beach with his regiment, five hours after the first assault. The fighting that Salinger witnessed provided the background for the story "For Esmé—with Love and Squalor" (1950). In August of 1944, Salinger had a friendly meeting with Ernest Hemingway, in France. Until his discharge in the spring of 1946, Salinger's duty was to interrogate captured German soldiers and French civilians. In 1945, he married a French psychiatrist, from whom he was divorced soon after.

For the next several years Salinger moved quite often; he lived first with his parents on Park Avenue, then in Westport, Connecticut, and finally in an apartment on East Fifty-seventh Street in Manhattan—all the while writing stories, cruising around Greenwich Village in his sports car, and working on the final drafts of *The Catcher in the Rye*. This remarkable novel about the odyssey of a teenage boy spiritually lost in nighttime Manhattan was an immediate popular success. Salinger obligingly sat for interviewers and photographers. One particular picture of him—the one that appeared on the dust jacket of the first printing of *The Catcher in the Rye* (and frequently elsewhere)—became so well-known to the public that it became a kind of icon. It shows a handsome young man in three-quarters profile, with dark eyes in a slender and sensitive face and a mouth anticipating a possibly sad smile. The owner of this iconic face was six feet, two inches tall—and soon to be disillusioned about the rewards of popularity.

Life's Work

The novel *The Catcher in the Rye* illustrates well the basic features of Salinger's art. In his novel, as in most of his short stories, Salinger identifies with the concerns of young people who suffer from the hypocrisy of the adult world, and he effectively re-creates their speech. The book also contains numerous examples of Salinger's distinctive humor—often considered vulgar—for which the book was banned from many libraries and school reading lists. Finally, in a plot development typical of Salinger's fiction, the protagonist is transformed through spiritual insight, allowing him to accept, at least temporarily, the world as it is. The quest of many of Salinger's protagonists is religious in character, usually containing elements of both Buddhism (recognition of the pain of life) and of Christianity (Holden, in his desire to protect the children in the field of rye, acting as a savior or Christ figure). Some critics found Salinger mannered, sentimental, and insufficiently interested in social questions, but readers around the world—not merely in the United States—identified strongly with Salinger's adolescent protagonist. Many readers, together with numerous magazine reporters, sought out the young writer.

To escape from his fans, Salinger ordered his portrait removed from all later printings of *The Catcher in the Rye*, refused all requests for interviews, and finally, in January of 1953, retired from the world altogether by moving to a rustic cottage near Cornish Flat, New Hampshire—located on a dirt road in the woods, about a mile from St. Gaudens Memorial Park. In the same year Salinger's collection *Nine Stories* was published, notable for its chronicles of the Glass family, its use of Zen Buddhist motifs, and for its remarkable "For Esmé—with Love and Squalor," a story which presents the agony of war, the Dostoevskian premise that hell is the suffering of being unable to love, and an offer of hope through love from a young girl in England to a battle-weary American sergeant.

Also in 1953, Salinger met nineteen-year-old Claire Alison Douglas at a party in Manchester, Vermont. An English debutante, she had studied at the best private schools and was then a top student at Radcliffe College. She was much influenced by Salinger's religious preoccupations and became in part the model for Franny Glass, the protagonist of "Franny" (1955). Franny is memorable for her antipathy toward ambitious, egotistical English instructors and for her desperate effort to escape the pain of the world by endlessly repeating the Jesus Prayer of Russian Orthodoxy. Despite her attraction to Salinger, Claire Douglas married (in August of 1953) her fiancé, Colman Mockler, a student at the Harvard Business School. Within a short time, however, this marriage was annulled. On February 17, 1955, Salinger and Claire Douglas were married. On December 10 of that year their first child, Margaret Ann, was born, and on February 13, 1960, their second and last child, Matthew Robert, was born.

During the late 1950's and early 1960's, Salinger completed his cycle of Glass family stories, publishing two stories each in the books *Franny and Zooey* (1961) and *Raise High the Roofbeam, Carpenters and Seymour: An Introduction* (1963). In 1965, he published "Hapworth 16, 1924" in *The New Yorker*, consisting chiefly of a long letter home written from camp by Seymour Glass at the age of seven. This strange and precocious document would be the last work of fiction published by Salinger, at least through the late 1980's.

In 1967, Salinger and Claire Douglas divorced. The cottage was sold. When the children were grown, Claire moved to San Francisco and established herself as a Jungian psychologist. Salinger continued to live in his hilltop chalet, writing daily and trying to avoid intrusive fans and reporters, who, once a year or so, invaded his retreat, hoping to engage him in conversation for a few minutes or at least catch a glimpse of him. To some, Salinger's withdrawal into almost total privacy seemed psychotic; he has not, however, completely isolated himself from society. For example, romantic interests have been reported in the press—with the nineteen-year-old novelist Joyce Maynard in 1973 and with actress Elaine Joyce in 1982. In 1978, he attended a testimonial dinner in Queens, New York, for an old army buddy. As to what Salinger has written since 1965, Truman Capote reported shortly before he died: "I'm told, on very good authority, that . . . he's written at least five or six short novels and that all of them have been turned down by *The New Yorker*. And that all of them are very strange and about Zen Buddhism."

Summary

Salinger's major work, *The Catcher in the Rye*, had, by the late 1980's, been translated into thirty-five languages and sold more than twelve million copies in English-language editions alone. Indeed, it is the income from such unprecedented sales that has allowed Salinger to live his monkish life and to write for himself alone, refusing to conform to the expectations of publishers. Foreign readers have found it easy to identify or sympathize with the sensitive Holden Caulfield. Russians in particular have fallen in love with the young protagonist. Many editions of *The Catcher in the Rye* (to say nothing of the stories) have been published in the Soviet Union not only in Russian but also in other Soviet languages. (A Russian edition of Salinger's collected works in one volume was published in fifty thousand copies as late as 1983.) In this way, Salinger has made an important contribution to international understanding and therefore to world peace. Indeed, *The Catcher in the Rye* has probably done more than any other American novel—in part precisely because of the attacks on it by book censors—to introduce young people to great literature.

Bibliography

Alsen, Eberhard. *Salinger's Glass Stories as a Composite Novel*. Troy, N.Y.: Whitston Publishing Co., 1983. A fascinating summary and analysis of the Glass family stories. Includes a helpful chronology of events in the lives of both Buddy and Seymour, as well as of the other siblings. Although little is said about Salinger's own life, autobiographical elements in the Glass stories become apparent under Alsen's treatment. Especially useful is a list of all the books that form the basis of Seymour's (that is Salinger's) eclectic religious philosophy. All are mentioned in the Glass stories, and they are essential to Alsen's analysis of Salinger's religious views.

French, Warren. *J. D. Salinger*. Rev. ed. Boston: Twayne Publishers, 1976. Both critical and biographical. Has a useful chronology of life and work, updated from the 1963 edition, and a selected bibliography, also updated.

Grunwald, Henry Anatole, ed. *Salinger: A Critical and Personal Portrait*. New York: Harper and Row, Publishers, 1962. A good early collection of critical articles, most of them favorable to Salinger. A detailed "biographical collage" forms the first chapter.

Laser, Marvin, and Norman Fruman, eds. *Studies in J. D. Salinger: Reviews, Essays and Critiques of "The Catcher in the Rye" and Other Fiction*. New York: Odyssey Press, 1963. Balanced collection of critical articles which include incidental biographical information. A checklist of Salinger's work is appended.

Lundquist, James. *J. D. Salinger*. New York: Frederick Ungar Publishing Co., 1979. Excellent critical analysis of the fiction, with a chronology of life and work and an extensive bibliography.

Sublette, Jack R. *J. D. Salinger: An Annotated Bibliography, 1938-1981*. New York: Garland Publishing, 1984. Well-organized bibliography of 1,462 items, with author and title indexes and a detailed chronology of life and work. Annotations are extensive, especially in the section on biography, which contains 175 entries. Sublette's bibliography essentially incorporates all previous bibliographies and is indispensable to any serious study of Salinger.

Donald M. Fiene

JONAS EDWARD SALK

Born: October 28, 1914; New York, New York

Areas of Achievement: Medicine and immunology
Contribution: Salk developed the first effective vaccine for polio, and he marshaled the nation's resources to help eradicate the disease.

Early Life

Jonas Salk was the firstborn child of Daniel B. Salk and Dora Press. His father was a garment maker, and both of his parents encouraged their children to do well in school. Salk attended Townsend Harris High School for the gifted and received his B.A. from College of the City of New York in 1934. He received his M.D. from New York University in 1939 and interned at Mount Sinai Hospital, where he studied immunology. Salk was recognized as an able scientist by his teachers, and during World War II he was a participant in the army's effort to develop an effective vaccine for influenza. He continued this interest in his first academic appointment at the University of Michigan, developing such a vaccine with his more senior colleague and former mentor, Thomas Francis, Jr. This established Salk's reputation professionally as an ambitious, bright, and innovative scholar who could organize a laboratory and work well under pressure.

Salk was restless and wanted independence from the projects of his senior colleagues so that he could try out some of his own unconventional ideas. He astounded his peers by accepting a position at the University of Pittsburgh Medical School, which, at that time, had no record of basic research in medicine. Salk got the space he needed and rapidly put together a team of laboratory workers to help him study infectious diseases. Not intimidated by authority, Salk used his managerial skills and cultural breadth to convince philanthropists and university administrators to equip his laboratory. His driving energy resulted in the publication of many important papers that caught the attention of the National Foundation (March of Dimes) and its director, Daniel Basil O'Connor. The National Foundation had for many years supported treatment and rehabilitative programs for paralytic polio victims. Salk was one of many younger investigators whom O'Connor hoped to recruit for the research that would lead to a vaccine for that dreaded disease.

Life's Work

Salk's greatest contribution to immunology was his insight that the killing of a virus by chemical treatment need not profoundly alter the antigenic properties of the virus. Any foreign material in a body can serve as an antigen and provoke the body's immune system to form antibodies to attack it. This is one of the body's major defenses against the invasion of bacteria and viruses. A virus may have complex proteins that coat its deadly infectious nucleic acid. Chemical treatment by formaldehyde may damage some of the genes of the virus so that they cannot multiply in the body, but they may not appreciably change the shape of the surface proteins of the virus. It is the surface proteins, and not the inner core of genes contained in the viral nucleic acid, that provoke antibody formation.

Salk's success in developing a vaccine for polio depended on the discoveries of many other researchers in immunology and virology. Originally polio could only be grown in live monkeys. Attempts in the 1930's to use a vaccine prepared from the killed extracts of infected monkey brains resulted in deaths of several children from meningitis and other reactions. It was also erroneously thought that polio grew only in nerve tissues, but infected humans produced large amounts of viruses in their feces, suggesting that it also grew in the intestines. John F. Enders and his colleagues succeeded in growing polio virus in tissue culture using embryonic cells, a major breakthrough that led to their being awarded a Nobel Prize in 1954. Polio also turned out not to be one virus but at least three different types of viruses, each type having many different strains, some highly infectious and others only weakly so. It was this need to type the polio viruses that brought O'Connor to Pittsburgh. Salk developed new methods to type the viruses rapidly and new methods to grow the viruses in large quantities. He realized that this work could not be done with a few animals and he organized a large laboratory, heavily funded, to maintain and use thousands of monkeys for his experiments. Salk made good use of the facilities and support; he soon proved his hunch that the antigenic properties of killed polio virus were not impaired by the formaldehyde treatment of the viruses.

Two additional findings were important for Salk's future work in developing a polio vaccine. Isabel Morgan Mountain succeeded in immunizing monkeys against polio by using formaldehyde-killed virus. Hilary Koprowski used live viruses whose properties had been attenuated or weakened by passage through rats; he fed twenty-two human subjects with the altered virus, and none showed symptoms, although all had developed antibodies against the fully infectious strain of polio virus.

Salk rejected two prevailing views at the time. Many immunologists believed that purified antibody, gamma globulin, would be effective in preventing polio. Gamma globulin, however, was expensive, and it afforded protection for only a short time. Many other immunologists were convinced that a killed virus would not work or that it could not be purified without contamination of the proteins from the cells on which it grew. Salk proved that these two views were mistaken; with the backing of the National Foundation, he prepared the purified killed polio virus vaccines against all three types of polio. Although the virus was rendered inactive after three days, Salk kept the virus in formaldehyde for thirteen days to guarantee that no live virus was present. By 1954, all the difficulties were resolved, and Salk began the crucial human experimentation to confirm the results obtained on monkeys. He and his laboratory workers immunized themselves and their families and then began field-testing the vaccine. The virus proved better than ninety percent effective. The first seven million doses of the vaccine were administered in 1955. A contaminated source from a California pharmaceutical firm was noticed, and the trials were held up until the purification procedures were standardized. Salk then initiated a nationwide program from 1956 through 1958. Almost immediately after this massive program of immunization, the United States was polio-free.

Salk's killed virus vaccine required four injections, one for each type plus a booster. Additional boosters were necessary as the antibody levels gradually fell. The National Foundation, aware of this possibility, had also backed Albert Sabin to develop a live polio vaccine. The live vaccine, which then required fewer visits to a physician for booster doses, replaced the Salk vaccine, The killed virus vaccine does not cause polio in its recipients or in individuals who have never been vaccinated; the live vaccine, however, occasionally does cause polio in family members or neighbors who have never been vaccinated. For this reason, Salk urged the use of killed vaccine in areas where compliance with vaccination requirements was inadequate. Although live vaccine was more frequently used in the years following Salk's campaign, polio had already been defeated and in the public's mind Salk had become a national hero. Among the many honors showered on him was the Lasker Award in 1956 and the Presidential Medal of Freedom in 1977.

Salk's popularity with the National Foundation and with philanthropists led him to a second major venture. He proposed an institute for biological research which would permit the most talented scientists in the world to carry out research that would lead to new advances in knowledge beneficial to health and human happiness. The Salk Institute for Biological Studies was founded in 1960, and a building for it opened in 1963. The building, chiefly funded by the National Foundation, was constructed at La Jolla, a suburb of San Diego noted for its beautiful scenery and beachfront. The Salk Institute attracted many Nobel laureates; the freedom to do full-time research and thinking was a major feature of its design. Salk thought of the institute as an experiment in the sociology of science, with a primary mission to study and initiate modern trends in biology tempered with a conscience for humanity. Among the seven original resident fellows of the Institute was Jacob Bronowski, a mathematician turned philosopher, whose television series *Ascent of Man* reflected the optimism of the Salk Institute—the conviction that knowledge of the universe enriches both human understanding and human welfare. Salk maintained a laboratory to study multiple sclerosis, and he also devoted much of his energy to writing books about the philosophy and social role of science.

Summary

Salk's national immunization campaign in 1956-1958 administered more than two hundred million doses of killed vaccine without a single individual becoming infected with the disease. This remarkable achievement reflected Salk's talent for establishing quality control as he shifted from a single laboratory to the national level in carrying out his project. The disease was particularly frightening to parents, who witnessed the devastating paralysis it produced in schoolchildren and the helplessness of its most severely affected survivors, who had to live in "iron lungs," expensive and bulky machines that kept them breathing. The disease had also taken on national importance as Americans admired the courage of President Franklin D. Roosevelt, who had survived polio and went on to guide the nation through the Great Depression and World War II while confined to a wheelchair.

Salk represented a new generation of scientists who required funded research to accomplish their goals. Directing a large laboratory with many technical assistants and advanced students involves management skills, inspired leadership, the ability to write convincing grant applications and progress reports, and a personality that thrives on hard work and the occasional successes that careful scientific research yields. Jonas Salk was a model of this new breed, but he was also unique in extending his efforts to involve an entire nation in his enterprise.

Bibliography

Carter, Richard. *Breakthrough: The Sage of Jonas Salk*. New York: Trident Press, 1965. This popular biography covers Salk's life through 1965. Salk's energy and personality are well depicted, although specific experiments are only mentioned and not analyzed.

Salk, Jonas. *Anatomy of Reality: Merging of Intuition and Reason*. New York: Columbia University Press, 1983. Salk relates metabiological ideas to biological and cultural evolution. He proposes more efforts to view life and the universe from both rational and intuitive, especially value-laden, perspectives.

_____. *Man Unfolding*. Edited by Ruth N. Anshen. New York: Harper and Row, Publishers, 1972. Salk introduces the idea of biological dualisms as attributes of the human condition, whose unresolved conflicts lead to social unrest and conflict. He uses biological processes as guides or analogies for constructing psychological and social models that attempt to resolve the conflicts.

_____. *The Survival of the Wisest*. New York: Harper and Row, Publishers, 1973. Salk greatly extends his concept of dualisms and introduces the idea of metabiology, a philosophic extension of the life sciences. From this perspective, Salk argues that resolution of conflicts arising from dualisms is not only possible but also necessary.

Salk, Jonas, and Jonathan Salk. *World Population and Human Values: New Reality*. New York: Harper and Row, Publishers, 1981. The ideas of Salk's metabiology are applied to the population problem. Each concept is provided a separate diagram to reinforce the verbal reasoning. A perspective on the world is attempted by use of United Nations vital statistics and population trends in different continents and cultures.

Elof Axel Carlson

MARGARET SANGER

Born: September 14, 1879; Corning, New York
Died: September 6, 1966; Tucson, Arizona
Areas of Achievement: Public health and social policy
Contribution: Through the establishment of low-cost birth control clinics, Sanger made birth control information and contraceptive devices available to American women of all social classes.

Early Life

Born in Corning, New York, to poor Irish parents, Margaret Higgins was the sixth of eleven children. Her mother died at the age of forty, and Margaret always believed that her mother's premature death was a consequence of excessive childbearing. During her mother's illness, Margaret acted as a nurse and also helped care for her younger siblings. Margaret enjoyed a close relationship with her father, who worked as a headstone carver. Higgins advised his resourceful children to use their minds to make a contribution to the world and to try to leave it better than they found it.

As a young girl, Margaret formed the conclusion that poverty, illness, and strife were the fate of large families, whereas small families enjoyed wealth, leisure, and positive parental relationships. Being from a large family, Margaret always felt inferior, and she longed to be rich and comfortable.

After the death of her mother, Margaret decided to become a nurse. During her final training at a Manhattan hospital, she met an architect named William Sanger, who fell in love with her at first sight. Margaret married Bill Sanger in 1902 after a six-month courtship. Over the next few years, Bill continued his work as an architect and Margaret stayed home with their three children. Sanger's restlessness and boredom in her role as a housewife led to her return to obstetrical nursing in 1912. She felt a need to regain her personal independence, and her mother-in-law agreed to move in and take care of the children. At the same time, Margaret and Bill Sanger began attending Socialist meetings in Greenwich Village. Margaret observed forceful speakers, such as Emma Goldman, who were rethinking the position of women and the future of worldwide political and economic systems. Sanger was considered a shy, delicate woman who rarely voiced her opinion at meetings.

Sanger's speaking debut was as a substitute before a group of working women. Her topic was family health. The working women liked Sanger's demeanor and believed what she said. Throughout her life, much of Sanger's impact was attributable to her personal appearance: She was petite, feminine, and demure. Sanger invariably gained support after the publication of her picture in the newspaper. Although her appearance was described as Madonna-like, Sanger was single-minded, stubborn, and intolerant; she was also charming, personable, and energetic. Sanger's personality was such that people either worshiped her or despised her.

Life's Work

During her years as an obstetrical nurse, Sanger frequently made house calls to the Lower East Side of New York City to attend poor women who were giving birth or experiencing complications from self-induced abortions. These women were worried about the health and survival of the children they already had and were desperate to find a way to stop having more children. They would beg Sanger to tell them "the secret" of the rich women and would promise that they would not tell anyone else. Sanger would suggest coitus interruptus or the use of condoms, but she quickly realized that the women rejected initiating these methods, placing contraceptive responsibility on men. Sanger herself never believed in male-oriented contraceptives because she saw men as opponents, rather than partners, in the struggle for conception control.

A turning point in Sanger's life occurred when she met a young mother of three named Sadie Sachs. Sanger was called to nurse Sadie during the sweltering summer of 1912. Sadie had attempted an abortion and was near death when Sanger was called to the apartment. Two weeks later, Sadie was finally out of danger. Sadie believed that another pregnancy would kill her and she pleaded with the attending physician to help prevent another pregnancy. The doctor callously told Sadie that she could not expect to have her cake and eat it too. His only suggestion, jokingly added, was that she have her husband, Jake, sleep on the roof. After the doctor left, Sadie turned to Sanger, who was more sympathetic than the doctor but who had no better suggestion for contraception. Sanger promised the anguished woman that she would return at a later date and try to provide helpful information. Sanger did not return, and three months later she was again summoned to the Sachs apartment. Sadie was in critical condition from another abortion attempt, and this time she died minutes after Sanger arrived. Sanger was burdened with guilt over the death of Sachs and resolved that she would find out how to prevent conception so that other women would be spared the pain, suffering, and heartache of unwanted pregnancies.

After two years of research, including a trip to France, Sanger decided to publish a journal aimed at working women which would encourage them to rebel and to insist on reproductive freedom. It was at this time that Sanger coined the term "birth control." In 1914, the first issue of *The Woman Rebel* was published. Although Sanger advocated that women limit births, she was prohibited by Anthony Comstock from explaining to women the precise methodologies for limiting births. Comstock was the head of the New York Society for the Suppression of Vice, and Sanger had experienced problems with him several years earlier when she wrote articles for *The Call*, a labor publication. Sanger's health-oriented column on venereal disease was aimed at adolescent girls, but Comstock refused to allow the column to be published. He had been instrumental in seeing that no obscene materials were distributed through the United States mail, and Comstock made it clear to publishers of *The Call* that he considered Sanger's article obscene and that its publication would result in immediate revocation of their mailing permit. Both Sanger and Comstock wanted to protect America's young people. Comstock sought to protect the young by distancing them from information on venereal disease, while Sanger thought that the protection of the young could best be achieved by exposing them to and educating them about the realities, dangers, and treatment of venereal disease.

Thousands of women responded to Sanger's articles in *The Woman Rebel*, once again pleading for information about the prevention of pregnancy. Sanger wrote a pamphlet called *Family Limitation* which provided practical, straightforward information in language that women of all social classes could understand. Sanger included descriptions and drawings of suppositories, douches, sponges, and the cervical pessary. Sanger also advocated sexual fulfillment for women, which was a radical idea in the early 1900's. After twenty refusals, Sanger found a printer for *Family Limitation*. With the help of friends, Sanger began distributing the pamphlet and was arrested immediately. The possibility of prison was overwhelming to Sanger at this time, so she sailed for Europe before she came to trial, leaving her husband and children behind. She settled in London and was accepted into the intellectual circle of people on the vanguard of sexual and contraceptive thought. Sanger discovered that the Netherlands, because of an emphasis on child spacing, had the lowest maternal death rate and infant mortality rate in the world. In addition, contraceptive clinics had been in operation for thirty years. When Sanger visited the Netherlands, she received trained instruction on the fitting and insertion of the diaphragm, which came in fourteen sizes. Sanger became convinced that she not only would have to overcome the restraint on free speech in the United States but also would have to provide women with access to trained people, preferably physicians, who could fit them with contraceptives.

Sanger returned to the United States to stand trial, but the charges against her were dismissed. Anthony Comstock had died while she was away, and the mood of the people was now supportive of Sanger.

In October of 1916, Margaret Sanger opened the nation's first birth control clinic. The clinic provided birth control and venereal disease information and birth control instruction. Most important, the clinic kept detailed medical records and case histories of patients. Although Sanger and her sister Ethel Byrne were imprisoned for their role in the new birth control clinic, public sentiment was in their favor. In the next few years, Sanger began publishing the *Birth Control Review*, a scientific, authoritative journal intended for health care professionals. In 1921, Sanger organized the first national birth control conference, which attracted physicians from all over the country.

Margaret and Bill Sanger were divorced in 1920, and in 1922 Margaret married a wealthy businessman named Noah Slee. Slee contributed many thousands of dollars to his wife's cause but always stayed in the background of her life. Sanger was a national figure by this time and a frequent speaker who enthralled her audience. She traveled internationally and made a great impact on the birth control movements in both Japan and India. In her efforts to establish international unity, Sanger established a World Population Conference, and years later, in 1952, the International Planned Parenthood Federation.

Throughout her career, Sanger lamented the absence of a safe, easy, effective contraceptive. She believed that some sort of contraceptive pill would best meet the needs of women, and she called such a pill her "holy grail." When she discovered that scientists John Rock and Gregory Pincus were experimenting with hormonal methods of contraception, Sanger convinced Mrs. Stanley McCormick, a wealthy widow, to provide funding for Rock and Pincus to continue their research for a contraceptive pill.

Sanger continued to be an active force in the birth control movement until very late in her life. As a nursing home patient in Tucson, Arizona, she was irascible and stubborn and insisted that since she was rich and smart she would do exactly as she pleased. She did just that until she died in 1966 of arteriosclerosis, one week before her eighty-seventh birthday.

Summary

In her lifetime, Margaret Sanger was jailed eight times, yet she never relented in her efforts to promote, and democratize access to, birth control. The medical records of patients visiting Sanger's birth control clinic provided the basis for the initial studies on the effects of child spacing on maternal health and marital satisfaction. These records also yielded information on the efficacy of various birth control methods for different groups of women.

Sanger's early efforts to disseminate contraceptive information were condemned by the church, the press, and the medical profession. Her belief that sex is a normal part of human life which requires a rational response led her to search for easy and safe contraceptives that would allow women to choose maternity while attaining freedom through control of their bodies. Sanger believed that in some way every unwanted child would be a social liability, and that a society should try to maximize its social assets by having children that are wanted by their parents. Sanger insisted that the best measure of the success of her work was in the reduction of human suffering.

Availability of contraceptive information and birth control devices has had widespread implications for Americans, both individually and collectively. Maternal death rates and infant mortality rates have declined, child spacing spans have increased, and total family size has decreased. Control of conception is a subject taught in classes throughout the country, and American women and men take for granted the fact that contraceptives are sold in drugstores and are easily obtained from physicians. As a result of the achievements of Margaret Sanger, control of conception has become a reality for many women throughout the world.

Bibliography
Chandrasekhar, Sripati. *"A Dirty Filthy Book": The Writings of Charles Knowlton and Annie Besant on Birth Control and Reproductive Physiology*. Berkeley: University of California Press, 1981. Includes essays by Sanger's American and British predecessors who laid the foundation for her work. Provides an account of the Bradlaugh-Besant trial in 1877 and its impact on the British birth rate.
Dash, Joan. *A Life of One's Own*. New York: Harper and Row, Publishers, 1973. A somewhat psychoanalytic portrait of Sanger and the men in her life. Provides a chronological account as well as descriptions of Sanger's public and private activities.
Douglas, Emily Taft. *Pioneer of the Future*. New York: Holt, Rinehart and Winston, 1970. A thorough work documenting the milestones of Sanger's life. Good in-depth account of research, events, and individuals who gave Sanger the basic knowledge, ideas, and encouragement from which to proceed.
Gray, Madeline. *Margaret Sanger: A Biography of the Champion of Birth Control*. New York: Richard Marek Publishers, 1979. Excellent, well-researched biography with one of the few in-depth examinations of Sanger's later years, including her addiction to Demerol.
Kennedy, David M. *Birth Control in America: The Career of Margaret Sanger*. New Haven, Conn.: Yale University Press, 1970. Focuses on Sanger's public career in the United States and illuminates American society in the years prior to 1945. Describes the social context in which Sanger worked and the attitudinal, behavioral, and institutional responses she evoked.
Sanger, Margaret. *Margaret Sanger: An Autobiography*. New York: Dover Publications, 1971. A factual description of the life of the author without much insight and introspection. Describes people who influenced Sanger, including the C. V. Drysdales and Havelock Ellis in England, and Dr. Aletta Jacobs, birth control pioneer in Amsterdam.
_____. *Motherhood in Bondage*. New York: Brentano's, 1928. Reprint. New York: Pergamon Press, 1956. Composed of letters written to Sanger by women desperate to discover a method of preventing conception. Tragic, heart-wrenching accounts.
_____. *Woman and the New Race*. New York: Brentano's, 1920.

Attempts to convince working-class women that control of reproduction is the key to a healthier, more satisfying life and a better world. Advocates rebellion in order to gain access to contraceptive information.

Lesley Hoyt Croft

GEORGE SANTAYANA

Born: December 16, 1863; Madrid, Spain
Died: September 26, 1952; Rome, Italy
Areas of Achievement: Philosophy and letters
Contribution: Combining a deep sense of the enduring and ideal nature of classic Greek culture with a learned sense for the immediate and natural, Santayana produced a series of philosophical and literary works as well as personal commentaries on the life and cultures of his times. He has been deemed the "Mona Lisa" of philosophy.

Early Life

George Santayana was born December 16, 1863, in Madrid, Spain. His mother, Spanish by birth, was first married to a member of the Sturgis family of Boston, an American merchant in the Philippines, where, until her husband's death in 1857, she lived and reared three children. Santayana's father was a friend of the Sturgis family, having served as a civil servant in the Philippines and authored a book on the natives of the Island of Mindanao. In 1862, the couple returned to Spain and were married in Madrid. Shortly thereafter, Santayana's mother returned to Boston with her older children while Santayana remained with his father in Spain. In 1872, he was brought by his father to Boston.

When Santayana arrived in Boston, he knew no English, and only Spanish was spoken in his home, but he soon picked up English outside the home and from his reading and was able to speak it without a marked accent. He attended Brimmer School, Boston Latin School and Harvard College, where he was graduated summa cum laude in 1886. In 1883, after his freshman year at Harvard, he returned to Spain to see his father. There, he considered a career in either the Spanish army or as a diplomat but decided instead to return to the United States and pursue a career as a writer. His attachment to Europe, however, remained strong.

At Harvard, Santayana had studied with both Josiah Royce and William James. Having already published since 1880 in *The Boston Latin School Register*, he became a regular contributor of cartoons and literary pieces to the *Harvard Lampoon*. He helped found *The Harvard Monthly* and provided it with a continuous flow of poetry and articles.

In physical appearance, Santayana was a gentle looking man of medium size. He had lively eyes, was bald, and for a while wore a handsome beard; later, he wore a mustache. He was fastidious about his clothes, often wearing black.

Life's Work

Santayana's first major philosophical work, *The Sense of Beauty: Being the*

Outline of Aesthetic Theory, was published in 1896 when he was thirty-three. A book of sonnets and a series of pieces of literary criticism were also published that year. This was also the year that Santayana went to study with Dr. Henry Jackson at Trinity College, Cambridge. He undertook careful examination of the works of classical Greece, particularly those of Plato and Aristotle. This experience led to the production of one of Santayana's major philosophical works, the five-volume *The Life of Reason: Or, the Phases of Human Progress* (1905-1906). In it, Santayana attempted to present a summary history of the human imagination, a panorama of the whole life of reason and of human ideas as they are generated out of and controlled by man's animal life and nature. This was Santayana's first major effort at combining a skeptical naturalism-humanism with a Platonic idealism. A variety of pieces of literary philosophical criticism followed, and in 1914 his famous piece "The Genteel Tradition in American Philosophy" appeared.

In that year, Santayana received news of a legacy. He promptly retired from Harvard at the age of fifty and in January, 1912, he left the United States for Europe, never to return. Santayana had been an extremely gifted teacher, and his sudden departure for Europe astonished his colleagues. Yet, although he was interested in his students, he disliked academic life and wished to devote himself to his writing. Also, his dual Spanish-American heritage, although contributing extraordinary range and perspective to his thinking, awoke in him conflicts from which he was thankful to escape. He went to France, Spain, and England, and finally to Rome, Italy, where he lived for eleven years in the monastery of the Blue Sisters. From there, Santayana produced a number of penetrating pieces on the life and culture of his times, including *Winds of Doctrine: Studies in Contemporary Opinion* (1913) and *Egotism in German Philosophy* (1916), a book much read by the Germans during the war, although it strongly demonstrated his loyalty to the Allied cause. In 1920, he wrote *Character and Opinion in the United States*. A major philosophical work appeared in 1923, *Scepticism and Animal Faith*, followed by his magnum opus, the four-volume *Realms of Being* (1927-1940). In 1936, he produced a novel reflective of his American experience entitled *The Last Puritan: A Memoir in the Form of a Novel*.

Santayana's *Persons and Places* (1944-1953), a kind of autobiographical travelogue, captures much of the spirit of all of Santayana's writing. It presents him as a traveler who, however appreciative or critical of the places and people encountered, is always a stranger, catching glimpses of people and places and recomposing these images as an artist would a painting. Santayana, in his work, too, conveys a constant sense of detachment, reflecting his reclusive spirit. Yet his works of speculative philosophy, with precision, depth, and coherence, elucidate complex ideas with what has been described as "luminous succinctness."

Santayana's life ended with characteristic ambiguity. Although he considered himself Catholic and lived among the nuns for eleven years, he did not officially return to the Roman Catholic Church and he did not receive the Sacraments on his deathbed. He died in September, 1952, a few months before his eighty-ninth birthday. He was buried in Rome, on ground reserved for Spanish nationals.

Summary

To many Americans, George Santayana was a great man of letters, a civilized hermit, an isolated sage. His works were eloquent and penetrating but always a bit of a mystery. Santayana spent forty years in the United States and wrote eleven books as well as numerous other works. Yet he left the United States in 1912 never to return. As Santayana himself noted, however, his intentional detachment from America must be balanced by the fact that he was detached from every other place as well. He never did have a sense of home, yet he clearly believed that "it was as an American writer he was to be counted."

Like Ralph Waldo Emerson, Santayana was essentially concerned with the conditions of life, with the bearing of events on men, and with the emergence of values and the possibilities for happiness. His account of the many sides of human experience, ethical, social, artistic, and religious, shows an interweaving of themes normally kept separate in modern philosophy and is expressed in prose that is polished to great beauty. Although his philosophy was much influenced by classical culture, it also contains much of the dynamic, fresh, naturalistic aspects of American culture. Santayana's profound belief in the life and power of the human mind and imagination and in the creativity and freedom of the human spirit produced a series of truly noteworthy works which expressed the American spirit at its best.

Bibliography

Cory, Daniel. *Santayana: The Later Years*. New York: George Braziller, 1963. This book presents a collection of recollections by Santayana's close friend. Contains also various letters from Santayana and gives an excellent personal picture of the man and his thoughts.

Howgate, George W. *George Santayana*. Philadelphia: University of Pennsylvania Press, 1938. This book deals with the various aspects of Santayana as a person and professional, namely, the poet, the critic, the moral philosopher, the writer, the metaphysician. Using abundant quotes from Santayana's writings, Howgate traces the influences that have shaped his thought and tries to show the interrelationships and underlying unity of various aspects of Santayana's personality and thought. The author also frequently takes issue with some of Santayana's opinions.

Munson, Thomas N. *The Essential Wisdom of George Santayana*. New York: Columbia University Press, 1962. This is an exposition of Santayana's philosophical positions, primarily from the viewpoint of neo-Thomist philosophy. The book is interesting in this respect and also because its appendices contain several letters from Santayana to the author raising critical questions about Munson's interpretations.

Schilpp, Paul Arthur, ed. *The Philosophy of George Santayana*. Vol. 2. Evanston: Northwestern University Press, 1940. In this volume, the writings of Santayana are scrutinized and evaluated by eighteen of his philosophical contemporaries. Almost every aspect of Santayana's work is covered. Further, Santayana has written an *Apologia Pro Mente Sua*, in which he replies to his critics. The volume also contains Santayana's autobiography and a complete bibliography of Santayana's writings from 1880 to October, 1940.

Singer, Beth J. *The Rational Society*. Cleveland: The Press of Case Western Reserve University, 1970. This book focuses on Santayana's social thought and depicts him as a metaphysician of human experience and culture. Professor Singer gives primary attention to two of Santayana's works, *Reason in Society*, a volume of *The Life of Reason*, and *Dominations and Powers* (1951). A critical and analytical study directed primarily to professional philosophers.

Singer, Irving. *Santayana's Aesthetics*. Cambridge, Mass.: Harvard University Press, 1957. This book presents Santayana's aesthetics and philosophy of art as seen in the light of his later writings on ontology and metaphysics. It also uses Santayana's work to suggest some new approaches to traditional problems in the fields of aesthetics and the philosophy of art.

Sprigge, Timothy L. S. *Santayana: An Examination of His Philosophy*. Boston: Routledge and Kegan Paul, 1974. A detailed examination of Santayana's philosophy, treating such topics as skepticism, animal faith, the doctrine of essence, spirit and psyche, and the material world. It also gives an outline of Santayana's philosophical development.

Jacquelyn Kegley

JOHN SINGER SARGENT

Born: January 12, 1856; Florence, Italy
Died: April 15, 1925; London, England
Area of Achievement: Art
Contribution: Sargent was renowned for his magnificent portraiture, which earned for him a reputation as a modern Van Dyck.

Early Life

Mary Newbold Singer Sargent, the artist's mother, was an incurable romantic. In 1854, she induced her husband, Dr. FitzWilliam Sargent, to abandon his medical practice and their comfortable, predictable bourgeois existence and move to Europe. Mary had recently come into a decent inheritance from her father, a wealthy fur merchant, and now saw no reason to live out her life among the dull, middle-class surroundings of Philadelphia. The transplanted Sargents usually spent their summers in northern France, Germany, or England, and headed to southern France or Italy during the winter, living in rented apartments. Florence, Italy, could be characterized as the family's "home base." There, the Sargents' eldest child, John, was born and attended school.

John Singer Sargent displayed a high degree of intellectual maturity, but his formal education was frequently interrupted by the family's travels. In addition to English, he spoke Italian, German, and French fluently; he became an accomplished pianist; he knew European literature, history, and art. His mother constantly hauled him around to museums and cathedrals; she was an enthusiastic watercolorist and encouraged him to make art his career, much to the dismay of her husband, who wanted his son to become a sailor. It was Mary Sargent who had her way, and John was allowed to attend the Academy of Fine Arts in Florence. The young student enthusiastically filled sketchbooks with drawings of classical monuments, copies of old master paintings, and still lifes; he drew people and scenes that he observed on his various travels. His parents showed his work to professional artists, and, when these experts confirmed John's talent, it was decided that he should be sent to Paris to further his studies.

Sargent arrived in the French capital in late spring of 1874 and was accepted by Charles Jurand Carolus-Duran, a famous academic portraitist, to join his atelier for advanced students; Sargent also passed the examinations for admission to the École des Beaux-Arts. He thus received one of the best formal art educations of his day. The Beaux Arts gave him a solid grounding in academism; Carolus-Duran taught him to paint in half-tones and trained him to eliminate all that was not essential from his composition. Sargent was also influenced by such artists as Édouard Manet and Eugène Boudin and some of the Impressionists; like them, he spent his summers in the French provinces painting outdoors. His progress was rapid. One of his paintings, *En route pour la pêche* (also known as *The Oyster Gatherers of Cancale*), which resulted from a summer in Brittany, won a second-class medal at the Salon of 1878, a great personal achievement for a young unknown artist. Carolus-Duran thought so highly of his pupil that he invited him to help paint the *Triumph of Marie de' Medici*, a large mural commissioned for the ceiling of the Luxembourg Palace. Sargent helped color the design but was also allowed to paint the two allegorical figures on either side of the principal portrait of Marie de' Medici; he also painted a bystander with the features of Carolus-Duran, who was so pleased that he allowed his pupil to paint a more formal portrait of him. The work, a remarkably perceptive representation done in half-tones and selective highlights, was artistically the culmination of the lessons Sargent had been taught. The portrait, both chronologically and artistically, marked the beginning of his professional career.

Life's Work

Sargent established his own studio (first on the rue Notre-Dame des Champs, later on the rue Berthier) and began to enjoy life as a rising young society artist. It was extremely difficult for a foreigner to break into the French market, however, and most of his commissions at that time came from wealthy foreigners living or visiting abroad. He did do an uncommissioned full-length portrait, *Madame Gautreau* (1884), which he hoped would open some doors, but the work was badly received at the Salon of 1884. Nevertheless, Sargent hardly suffered from lack of praise. According to Henry James, he was so talented that even on the threshold of his career he had nothing more to learn.

During this period, Sargent also did some subject paintings, such as the exotic *El Jaleo* (1882), a picture of a Gypsy dancer he saw while on a visit to Spain. For the most part, however, he did not stray very far from his main source of income, although he became increasingly disenchanted with working in the French capital. His commissions had begun to decline, and he had not received the proper respect he thought he deserved. From time to time, his work had taken him to England as the wealthy British had less hesitation about having their portraits painted by foreigners than did the French.

Sargent passed the summer of 1885 at Broadway in the Cotswolds, where he did a number of landscapes. At that time, he apparently decided to make his residence in the British Isles more permanent; the following year, he closed down his Paris studio and moved to London, renting a studio previously occupied by James McNeill Whistler. The British capital would be his home for the rest of his life.

Commissions for portraits came slowly at first—some potential patrons, accustomed to the formalism of the Royal Academy, found his technique a bit too avant-garde—but gradually, he was commissioned for more and more work, until he had almost more than he could handle. Although the English art scene was not as exciting as the one he had left in Paris, Sargent's personal associations in the British capital were more congenial and fulfilling. Many of his clients were wealthy Americans, and one of these, Henry Marquand, invited him, in 1887, to come to the United States (to Newport, Rhode Island) to paint a portrait of his wife with the prospect of other commissions from Marquand's well-heeled friends.

Sargent's trip to the United States lasted eight months. He completed twelve formal portraits and had a one-man show in Boston in January, 1888, which received rave reviews. Everywhere he went, he was treated as a great artist and was appreciated in a way it seemed he had never been in Europe. Still, he returned to England; during the summer of 1888, he painted a series of pictures in the Impressionist style of Claude Monet, for whom he had an intense admiration. After this interlude, he returned to full-time portraiture. One of his most famous, *Ellen Terry as Lady Macbeth* (1889), he solicited himself. He returned to the United States in December, 1889, for another series of portraits, but he was also commissioned to decorate the upper landing of the Boston Public Library, a project that would occupy him intermittently for the next quarter of a century. As his theme, Sargent chose the development of religious thought from its pagan origin, through Old Testament times, to Christianity. The actual painting was done in England on canvas and transported to Boston. Although Sargent considered the work to be one of his major contributions to contemporary art, the murals did not display his talent at its best.

Throughout the last years of the Victorian period and the following Edwardian period, Sargent was widely regarded as the greatest portrait painter in England, his status confirmed by the number of commissions he was now receiving from the British aristocracy and by his election to full membership in the Royal Academy in 1897. Yet the more famous he became and the greater the requests for his services, the more his interest in portraiture declined. He undoubtedly recognized that his work was suffering from repetition and a tendency toward formalism and artificiality. Consequently, from 1910 onward, he devoted the major part of his time to landscapes, journeying to Spain, the Holy Land, Egypt, Majorca, Corfu, and, especially, the Alpine region and Italy, for subject matter. He chose the subjects that pleased him, beginning his work early in the day, having plopped his easel down wherever the spirit moved him. Sargent continued to work in oils, but most of his production was now in watercolors.

Sargent was in the Austrian Tirol when World War I broke out. The local military authorities refused him permission to leave the country, and he remained in the village of Colfushg and continued to paint. He apparently took little interest in the course of hostilities, which he regarded as collective madness; he naïvely believed that fighting was suspended on Sundays.

Finally, he managed to leave Austria and make it to Italy, through France, and back to England, where he resumed work on the mural for the Boston library.

He came again to the United States in 1916, and, on this trip, accepted another commission for a mural: for the rotunda of the Boston Museum of Fine Arts. When he returned to England in April, 1918, he was asked by the Ministry of Information's War Artists Committee to do a painting emphasizing wartime Anglo-American cooperation. He went to France to do research, staying there six months until October, one month before the armistice. The result was *Gassed*, painted in his London studio, which shows a line of Allied soldiers, eyes bandaged, being led one after the other toward a dressing station. The picture was displayed at the Royal Academy in 1919 and became an instant sensation, being judged one of the best paintings to come out that year.

Sargent now came more frequently to the United States, his work on his wall decorations monopolizing much of his time and energy. He was there from 1919 to 1920; he returned again in 1921 and in 1923, and he was planning to make a return trip to oversee the installation of his museum paintings. Just before he was scheduled to leave, on April 15, 1925, Sargent died of a heart attack, following a farewell party given by his sister. He was found with an open copy of Voltaire's *Philosophical Dictionary* (1764) beside him. His death drew national attention, marked by a memorial service in London's St. Paul's cathedral.

Summary

Like a great actor who devotes too much of his talent to soap operas instead of to the classics, Sargent for most of his productive life painted works lacking in spiritual depth and imaginative force, works that he was later to regret having done. "I *hate* to paint portraits! I hope I never paint another portrait in my life. . . . I want now to experiment in more imaginary fields," he said. Yet portraits were what he did best; when he was good, he was excellent; when he was bad, he was still extraordinary. For example, his portrait *Woodrow Wilson* (1917), not generally considered to be one of his best, is remarkable in the way it captures the humorless, messianic Wilsonian stare. Sargent's misfortune was to live at a time when painting the famous and haut-monde was increasingly looked on with derision.

Although he refused to accept any commissions in which he did not have complete artistic freedom, he remained acutely sensitive to the social and professional stature of his subjects, whom he frequently placed in his paintings in theatrical or symbolic surroundings. Sargent was a businessman who gave his sitters what they paid for. He posed them on Louis XV settees, in front of marble pillars, standing beside huge cloisonné vases, some wearing top hats and highly polished riding boots, as in *Lord Ribblesdale* (1902), or plumed bonnets, as in *Lady Sassoon* (1907), or adorned, as in *The Wyndham Sisters* (1899), in dresses worth small fortunes. Sargent was clearly an artist of *fin de siècle* conspicuous consumers, and he served them well.

The Americans claimed him as one of their own, but in training and performance he was completely European. Sargent based his style on Europe's traditional artistic values as expressed by the artists he admired. He never tired of going to museums to learn from the great artists of the past, such as Diego Velázquez, Titian, Tintoretto, Peter Paul Rubens, and, above all, Frans Hals, whose loose brushwork became Sargent's own trademark. Sargent's painterly style was enlivened with splashes of clear color that attested the lessons he had learned from the Impressionists. He was never able to adapt his palette completely to theirs, however, and sometimes he became too garish or somber. "One day the American painter Sargent came here to paint with me," Monet recalled. "I gave him my colors and he wanted black, and I told him: 'But I haven't any.' 'Then I can't paint,' he cried and added, 'How do you do it!'" Sargent came the closest to Impressionism in his watercolors, especially those he did in Venice, which also reveal him at his spontaneous and individualistic best. Yet, if Sargent had failings as a painter, they were failings of theme, not of expertise, for his was overpowering and could rival that of the finest painters of any age.

Bibliography

Charteris, Evan Edward. *John Sargent*. New York: Charles Scribner's Sons, 1927. This official biography is built largely from quotations, letters, and anecdotes. The author, who was a personal friend of Sargent, was too close to his subject to be truly objective, and the painter's personality remains elusive. Sargent is revealed as tremendously dedicated, hard-working, and self-critical, but such traits alone are hardly the stuff of drama.

Lubin, David M. *Act of Portrayal: Eakins, Sargent, James*. New Haven, Conn.: Yale University Press, 1985. Contains extensive sexual-sociological analysis of Sargent's famous portrait of the Boit children, *The Daughters of Edward Boit* (1882). Essentially an exercise in speculation and provocation, showing that what is not known about a painting need not stand in the way of intellectualizing about its meaning.

McSpadden, J. Walker. *Famous Painters of America*. New York: Dodd, Mead and Co., 1916. A brief description of Sargent's life and work, written during his lifetime in obvious recognition and appreciation of his genius. Argues that, despite Sargent's thoroughly European training and formation, "Americans may rightfully claim Sargent."

Memorial Exhibition of the Works of the Late John Singer Sargent. Boston: Museum of Fine Arts, 1925. A catalog of some of Sargent's most famous works, shown to commemorate the unveiling of his mural decorations in the Boston Public Library. The works on display came almost exclusively from American collections and thereby help to reinforce the artist's image as a native son.

Mount, Charles Merril. *John Singer Sargent*. New York: W. W. Norton and Co., 1955. A complete, well-researched, and lavishly documented account in which even the most insignificant aspects of Sargent's life seem worthy of inclusion. Mount, who is also a portraitist, offers intelligent and perceptive commentary about his subject's style and techniques.

Olson, Stanley. *John Singer Sargent: His Portrait*. New York: St. Martin's Press, 1986. A literate, sympathetic, but objective biography, particularly strong in its portrayal of the varied figures who played a part in Sargent's life. Includes a small selection of illustrations.

Ormond, Richard. *John Singer Sargent: Paintings, Drawings, Watercolors*. New York: Harper and Row, Publishers, 1970. An oversized book with many plates of Sargent's principal works, too many, unfortunately, reproduced in black and white. The commentary on each is informative and incisive, however, as is the biography, highlighting the major periods of the artist's life.

Wm. Laird Kleine-Ahlbrandt

CARL SCHURZ

Born: March 2, 1829; Liblar, Prussia
Died: May 14, 1906; New York, New York
Areas of Achievement: Politics and journalism
Contribution: Recognized as a leader of the German-American community in the United States, this partisan of liberty fled from Germany after the revolutions of 1848 and made a career as a journalist and politician, serving as a Union general in the Civil War, a senator from Missouri, and a secretary of the interior.

Early Life

Carl Schurz was born to Christian and Marianne (Jüssen) Schurz on March 2, 1829, in one of the outbuildings of a moated castle in the Prussian Rhineland (modern West Germany), where his grandfather worked for Baron Wolf von Metternich. His family was of humble origin but was respected in the local context of village life; his grandfather was the count's estate manager, one uncle was the mayor of a neighboring village, and his father was the Liblar schoolmaster. Schurz was reared a Roman Catholic, but with a strong dose of Enlightenment skepticism; as an adult, he considered himself a "freethinker." As a boy, he enjoyed the run of Metternich's estate, its formal gardens, its forests, and its farmlands. His parents noted his unusual intelligence and his musical skill and resolved to make sacrifices to give him a higher education. Thus he left his father's school in the village, going to preparatory school at neighboring Brühl and then at Cologne, several miles away. When he was seventeen, the family moved to the nearest university town, Bonn, so that the boy could study there, even though his parents had suffered financial reverses which temporarily put his father in debtors' prison.

At Bonn, Schurz began to make a name for himself both in the politically liberal fraternal organizations and as a budding scholar, under the tutelage of the young Romantic, Gottfried Kinkel. Then came the revolutionary fervor of 1848. Immediately, Schurz interrupted his formal education and turned to a life of political activity. Like many young men of his generation, he saw 1848 as the opportunity to achieve a unified German state with a liberal-democratic constitution. Too young to stand for election himself, he turned to journalism and popular agitation to support his goals. His zeal for freedom and justice, his skills as a writer and speaker, and his tireless and combative commitment to his cause were characteristics that would distinguish him as a prominent American statesman years later. He joined the revolutionary army which fought against the old monarchies and barely escaped with his life when it was forced to surrender. In 1850, he returned to Prussia from exile in France and Switzerland in disguise and rescued Professor Kinkel from the prison to which the Prussians had condemned him. After spending a brief time in Paris and London, where he wooed and married Margarethe Meyer, daughter of a well-to-do Hamburg mercantile family, he decided to leave the Old World for America. If he could not be a citizen of a free Germany, he concluded, he would become a free citizen of the United States.

The tall, slim young man with thick glasses affected the flowing hair and mustache of a Romantic liberal in 1848; as he matured, he was recognizable for his bushy beard and sharp features, so often caricatured by Thomas Nast.

Life's Work

Schurz and his young wife arrived in the United States in 1852, staying first in Philadelphia and eventually settling in Watertown, Wisconsin, in 1855. As an immigrant, he was neither tired nor poor. His wife's dowry was enough to set him up in business. His fame as a daring fighter for freedom in Germany, his solid education, his gifts as a writer and speaker, and his political ambition combined to make him a well-known figure almost immediately. Although he rarely stood for election himself, his persuasiveness with German-American voters made him a force to be reckoned with in the ethnic politics of that age.

He led the Wisconsin delegation to the Republican National Convention in 1860. Though originally pledged to William H. Seward, he became an avid supporter of Abraham Lincoln once he had received the nomination. Schurz traveled more than twenty-one thousand miles campaigning for Lincoln, speaking in both English and German, and was credited with swinging much of the German-American vote away from its traditional inclination for the Democratic Party and into Lincoln's camp. In gratitude, Lincoln appointed him minister to Spain and, after the onset of the Civil War, brigadier and then major general in the Union army. Schurz's military career did little to enhance his reputation. He was only in his early thirties, and his high rank was clearly a result of political influence rather than demonstrated military skills. Schurz did his best, however, to contribute to the Union cause, seeing action at the Second Battle of Bull Run, Gettysburg, and Chancellorsville. Lincoln invited Schurz to report directly to him on the wartime situation, which Schurz did with great energy, pressing the president to emancipate the slaves.

After the war, Schurz settled in St. Louis as part owner and editor of the German language *Westliche Post*. His wife never liked the American Midwest, however, and so she spent much of her time in Europe. While visiting his family in Germany in 1868, Schurz made a widely reported visit to Berlin, where the onetime revolutionary was warmly received by Otto von Bismarck, now prime minister of Prussia and chancellor of the emerging German Empire.

Schurz was critical of President Andrew Johnson but enthusiastically supported Ulysses S. Grant in the 1868 elections. German-American forces were influential in Missouri politics, and the state legislature sent him to Washington, D.C., as a senator. Once there, he became disillusioned with the apparent corruption in the spoils system, and he turned his polemical skills to the issue of civil service reform. This challenge to the status quo alienated many of his party allies, and he was not returned to office in 1874. The Senate provided a platform for Schurz's oratorical skills, and he gained a national reputation as a spokesman for reform and for the German-American community. Because of his criticisms of United States politicians, some alleged that he was not a patriotic American. He responded with a turn of phrase which has become famous: "My country right or wrong: if right, to be kept right; and if wrong, to be set right."

No partisan loyalist, Schurz was active in founding the Liberal Republican Party which supported Horace Greeley for president over Grant in 1872. With the election of 1876, however, he returned to the Republican Party, supporting Rutherford B. Hayes, and after Hayes's victory, Schurz was made secretary of the interior. He attempted to initiate environmental controls, particularly over forest lands, and to follow a humanitarian policy with respect to the Indians. Inevitably, his liberal idealism was unable to overcome deep-seated interests which opposed his policies. He left government office in 1881, never to serve again, and pursued his career as a journalist, author, and lecturer. He made New York his home, where he became editor in chief of the *Evening Post* and eventually *Harper's Weekly*.

As an independent, he found himself among the "Mugwumps," who were more committed to his liberal ideals, especially civil service reform, than to any political party. Looking at his record, one sees a man who supported James A. Garfield (Republican) in 1880, Grover Cleveland (Democrat) in 1884, 1888, and 1892, William McKinley (Republican) in 1896, William Jennings Bryan (Democrat) in 1900, and Alton B. Parker (Democrat) in 1904. In an age when corruption was often an accepted part of the political process, Schurz remained free of its taint. His nineteenth century liberalism has been criticized as being narrow and doctrinaire, a *laissez-faire* philosophy which had little room for labor unions and social programs. Yet his concepts of personal liberty, due process of law, and clean government surely put him in the mainstream of American political thought and action. He favored suffrage for blacks (but not for women) and spoke out strongly against anti-Semitism. In the 1890's, he looked with dismay upon American diplomatic and military expansion and, polemically as ever, crusaded as an anti-imperialist. The onetime general loathed war and its accompanying atrocities; moreover, he seemed to fear that an active policy overseas by the United States might at some time lead to a conflict with the land of his birth, Germany. As a man in his sixties and seventies, he traveled and spoke as avidly against an

American empire as he had once fought for Lincoln's election and freedom for the slaves. Though he no longer was alleged to be able to swing the German-American vote in major elections, he was widely praised as that community's leader and was showered with honors. He died peacefully at his home in New York City at the age of seventy-seven.

Summary

Schurz saw himself as "the main intermediary between German and American culture." He continued to be equally fluent in German and English, writing his widely read memoirs in both languages. He traveled back and forth many times between the United States and the old country, filled with pride for both. When accused of mixed loyalties, he responded that he loved equally his "old mother" and his "new bride." Stalwart and eloquent, he vigorously defended the cause of freedom, as he saw it, in Germany and in the United States. His stubborn dedication to his principles and his combative temperament sometimes earned for him the enmity of political opponents. Surely not even all German-Americans supported him on every issue. As a group, however, they were proud of his accomplishments, the most impressive of any German immigrant at that time, and they agreed with him that fondness for their country of origin did not diminish their patriotism as Americans. Schurz would have been deeply saddened by the political and diplomatic events of the first half of the twentieth century which brought the United States and Germany into conflict, but much heartened by the development of a firm alliance between America and a liberal-democratic Germany after 1945.

Bibliography

Easum, Chester V. *The Americanization of Carl Schurz*. Chicago: University of Chicago Press, 1929. A brief, older work, upon which further scholarship on Schurz has depended.

Fuess, Claude M. *Carl Schurz, Reformer: 1829-1906*. Edited by Allan Nevins. New York: Dodd, Mead and Co., 1932. A gentlemanly biography by a scholar of German-American parentage.

Schurz, Carl. *Intimate Letters of Carl Schurz: 1841-1869*. Edited and translated by Joseph Schafer. Madison: State Historical Society of Wisconsin, 1928. Hitherto unpublished letters, mostly to members of his family, which shed light on Schurz's career and personal life beyond that shown in the six-volume set cited below.

_____. *The Reminiscences of Carl Schurz*. 3 vols. Garden City, N.Y.: Doubleday and Co., 1907-1908. An entertaining and enlightening view of Schurz as he saw himself, with insightful sketches of the great men he knew, especially Lincoln, Bismarck, and a long list of American political figures. A modern abridgement by Wayne Andrews (New York: Scribners, 1961) is available, with an introduction by Allan Nevins.

_____. *Speeches, Correspondence and Political Papers of Carl Schurz*. Edited by Frederic Bancroft. 6 vols. New York: G. P. Putnam's Sons, 1913. The vast array of Schurz's political output is set forth in this old, but well-edited, collection of his works.

Trefousse, Hans L. *Carl Schurz: A Biography*. Knoxville: University of Tennessee Press, 1982. A scholarly study of Schurz, based on exhaustive study of the printed and manuscript sources, in the United States and in Europe, including some private letters to his companion in later life, Fanny Chapman. Excellent notes and bibliography.

Gordon R. Mork

WINFIELD SCOTT

Born: June 13, 1786; Petersburg, Virginia
Died: May 29, 1866; West Point, New York
Area of Achievement: The military
Contribution: Scott, whose military career spanned more than fifty years, left his mark by showing the power of volunteer troops fighting in a republican army.

Early Life

Winfield Mason Scott was born June 13, 1786, near the tobacco market town of Petersburg, Virginia. His father William, a captain on the patriot side in the American Revolution, died in 1791, leaving only a modest inheritance and little in the way of a memory for the young boy. His mother, Ann Mason, was descended from an important Virginia family, and she spent her widowhood teaching her son the ways of the Virginia gentry until her death in 1803.

Young Scott was educated by private tutors in Petersburg and at the new capital at Richmond. At age nineteen, he enrolled at the College of William and Mary. He showed little aptitude for college work and left the Williamsburg school after a year without earning a degree. The young man decided on a career in the law, and in accordance with the custom of the day, studied law with an established attorney. When a war scare after 1807, however, caused Congress to vote funds to enlarge the United States Army in anticipation of war with Great Britain, Scott abandoned a legal career for the sword. In May, 1808, Scott became a captain in the regular army.

Scott was exceedingly tall by the standards of his day—six feet, five inches—and in his younger years, muscular but not fat. Photographs of the elderly Scott showing his three-hundred-pound bulk do not give an accurate picture of the young captain. Along with a striking figure, Winfield Scott bore a somewhat haughty manner. This was characteristic of many Virginia gentlemen of the time, but Scott was both especially quick to take offense at perceived snubs and insults and not shy about voicing his own opinions. Indeed, his lack of tact got him court-martialed during his first tour of duty at Natchez in the Mississippi Territory in 1810. Captain Scott openly proclaimed the former commanding officer General James Wilkinson a traitor in league with former vice president Aaron Burr. For this affront, Wilkinson had the young man disciplined for disrespect to a superior officer. Scott postponed marriage until the age of thirty; when he did wed, he chose Maria Mayo, the daughter of an important Richmond editor, for his bride.

Life's Work

The War of 1812 brought a host of young officers forward into national prominence. At the start of the war, the United States Army was commanded by men who had learned their military skills back in the Revolutionary War. Most of the commanders of the first year of the war were simply incompetent to fight a war on the offensive as called for by the leaders in Washington, and not until they were replaced by younger men did the war go more favorably for the Americans. The two great young generals who emerged in 1813 and 1814 were Andrew Jackson and Winfield Scott, a pair of men who later became bitter rivals.

The great task for an American commander in the War of 1812 (as in the Revolution) was to solve the problem of making raw American troops stand up in the field to trained British regulars. Much of the American force consisted of state militiamen serving limited terms with little training. Too often in battle, the militia ran or refused to fight. Scott, more than any other commander on the Canadian front, managed to shape an army of militiamen and regulars into an effective fighting force. A measure of the success of his efforts may be seen by looking at the first and last battles on the Niagara Frontier, the stretch of land connecting Lake Erie to Lake Ontario and separating the United States from British North America. In October, 1812, shortly after gaining the rank of lieutenant colonel in the United States Army, Scott participated in the Battle of Queenstown on the west bank of the Niagara River. The attack was a disaster for the Americans, as a large body of American militia refused to cross the river, claiming that their mission included only defense of New York and not the invasion of Canada. Scott's party, outnumbered and badly outfought, was captured by the British, and the young Virginian had to spend an enforced stretch in British captivity until he could be exchanged.

During the summer campaign of 1813 on the lakes, Scott distinguished himself by leading a successful assault on the British Fort George on the Niagara River and, later, by aiding in the burning of York (modern Toronto). The next spring—May, 1814—Scott was promoted to brigadier general and was given responsibility for training the men under the command of General Henry Dearborn for a campaign to clear the Niagara Frontier of British forces. In July, Scott led American troops, both regulars and state militiamen, in the fierce battles of Chippewa (opposite Buffalo) and Lundy's Lane (near Niagara Falls). The latter battle was perhaps the bloodiest of the war, with four hundred killed on both sides. The effect of the July fighting was to establish American control of the Niagara region and to show that Americans could stand up to British veterans who had fought successfully against Napoleon. At Lundy's Lane, Scott himself showed extraordinary personal courage: He had several horses shot from under him and was hit twice by bullets, in the ribs and shoulder. He spent a month recovering in Buffalo before journeying to Philadelphia for further treatment, and at war's end Major General Scott was still recovering from his wounds.

In 1816, Scott journeyed to Europe not so much to sightsee as to interview veterans of the Napoleonic Wars. He came back filled with new ideas about how to train and lead a new American army and over the next thirty years put his ideas into practice. In 1817, he was called to New York City to head the Eastern Military District, a command he held until 1831. During these years, the general devoted himself to improving the training of troops, an effort that first saw print in his 1821 publication *General Regulations for the Army: Or, Military Institutes*. This writing consisted of rules for camp life and drill and reflected Scott's experiences in the War of 1812 and his European interviews. He later amplified his ideas on the use of the foot soldier in his *Infantry Tactics* (1835), a manual used by the army until the Civil War.

The 1830's were an extraordinarily busy time for the middle-aged Scott. He did more hard riding during this decade than any other. In the summer of 1832, President Jackson ordered him to take a regiment west to help in the suppression of the Sac rebellion led by Black Hawk. This was only one of a series of wars between Native Americans and white Americans prompted by Jackson's "Removal" policy. The Sac were defeated by Illinois and Wisconsin militiamen before Scott reached the Upper Mississippi country; unfortunately, the regiment was badly decimated by a cholera epidemic. Scott remained long enough to negotiate Black Hawk's surrender and the removal of the Indians west of the Mississippi. Next, the general traveled to Charleston, South Carolina, on a confidential mission for the president to survey the state of federal installations in the city and harbor in light of the threats made by the "nullifiers" in the Palmetto State. Scott made sure the hotheads in South Carolina knew that the federal government stood prepared to defend its property and the right to collect tariff duties.

After the successful defusing of the Tariff showdown, Scott's next field assignment came in early 1836, when President Jackson sent him to Florida to put down the Seminole rebellion (again in response to Jackson's removal policy) led by Osceola. After six months with little success against the Indians, Scott was recalled to Washington and there faced a "court of inquiry" about his conduct in prosecuting the Florida war. Scott was enraged at this insult from the President but still managed to convince the court that his strategy of fortifying outposts in the swamps to launch small raids against the Indians was preferable to marching columns of hundreds of men back and forth in search of the Indians. The court cleared Scott of any malfeasance, and in the end, his strategy of counterguerrilla warfare against the Seminoles proved successful.

Almost as soon as the Washington charges were settled, Scott had to deal with a series of frontier crises. First, in January, 1838, he traveled to Buffalo to prevent the smuggling of American arms to Canada after the famous Caroline Affair. His apt diplomacy, surprising to some in a military man, helped ease a potential *causus belli* between the United States and Great

Britain. Then, in May, Scott traveled to Tennessee to organize the army's handling of the removal of fifteen thousand Cherokee westward to the trans-Mississippi Indian Territory. Again, the army was needed to enforce a Jackson removal treaty, but the results were especially horrible as thousands of Indians suffered on what became known as the Trail of Tears. By the time the march was actually under way, however, Scott was otherwise engaged in more frontier diplomacy, this time at Detroit where he sought to prevent a new border skirmish between the Americans and the British across the river. That task accomplished, the general ventured in winter across the northern United States to the Maine–New Brunswick border to prevent yet another border flare-up from exploding into war, this time in March, 1839, the so-called Aroostook War over the proper boundary along the St. John's River. While Scott was engaged in his journeys for peace, leaders of the Whig Party mentioned his name as a candidate to run for the presidency in 1840. Though he never became president, Winfield Scott hoped for the next twenty years to achieve that goal, and in 1852 he did get the Whig nomination but failed to convince the electorate.

In 1841, Scott finally became the senior officer in the United States Army and alternated his attention between military affairs and his political ambitions. His job was made harder in 1845 when a Democratic administration, hostile to Scott, came into office determined to engage in a war with Mexico. Scott was thought too old to command in the field the American detachment sent to acquire the Rio Grande territory in 1845 and 1846, and when this force did provoke a war, Scott's subordinate Zachary Taylor earned the glory at Monterrey and Buena Vista. President Polk found winning a peace harder than winning battles, however, and in the late fall of 1846 had to turn to Scott to lead a campaign to bring the Mexicans to surrender.

From March through September of 1847, Scott led one of the most brilliant campaigns in the history of the United States Army. Against a larger enemy fighting to defend its own capital, Scott captured Mexico City despite disease, despite the forces of Mexican General Antonio López de Santa Anna, and despite the sniping of various Democratic politicians (one of whom was on his staff by presidential order). The campaign began at Vera Cruz with an amphibious landing, the first such coordination between the army and navy in United States history. Scott laid siege to Vera Cruz for a week, bombarding the city daily and earning a reputation among the Mexicans as a barbarian because of the hundreds of women and children killed in the shelling. Scott then began his march to Mexico City, first defeating the Mexican Army at the mountain heights of Cerro Gordo where the enemy had hoped to bottle up the Americans. From April 19, 1847, through mid-May of the same year, Scott and his army advanced along the National Road toward Mexico City. When he got within fighting distance, the Mexicans asked to begin peace negotiations. Scott's army had decreased to five thousand men because of disease, and he used the summer months of negotiation to rebuild his army to fourteen thousand well-drilled men. In August, when negotiations collapsed, Scott made his famous daring march south along Lake Chalco and flanked the Mexican forces, attacking Mexico City by the back door along the road from Acapulco. On August 20, Scott's men captured the mountain pass at Cherabusco, just four miles south of the capital. Again, the Mexicans asked to negotiate, and again the talks led nowhere. From September 8 through September 13, Scott carried out a series of feints against the Mexican forces and, at the climactic battle of Chapultepec, stormed into the city. His smaller army defeated the Mexican army of thirty thousand men.

The peace that followed was anticlimactic, and Scott became embroiled in charges and countercharges with Democratic officers in the army and politicians back in Washington. While he was the acknowledged conqueror of Mexico, he was not universally seen as a hero, and he had to watch the junior Zachary Taylor receive the Whig nomination for the presidency in 1848. The difference in popular estimation between the two generals may be seen in their nicknames: Taylor was "Old Rough and Ready," Scott "Old Fuss and Feathers." When Scott did finally run for the White House in 1852, his opponent (and former subordinate in Mexico) Franklin Pierce trounced him, mainly because Scott's Whig Party had self-destructed over a number of issues. Scott was honored for his services in 1853 and became lieutenant general of the army, a post he held until his retirement in October, 1861. He distinguished himself when the Civil War broke out, first by not succumbing to rebel blandishments to join the Confederacy and second by devising a plan that ultimately was carried out in defeating the rebels, the so-called Anaconda Plan. The plan bore that name because Scott envisioned a slow, squeezing attack against the South, first down the Mississippi, then a gradual frontal attack in Virgina, combined with a naval blockade to cut off the South's commerce. The strategy worked, though at a terrible cost that Scott could not foresee: 600,000 died. The old man spent much of the war working on his memoirs and, when he felt the end near, asked to be carried to West Point so that he could die at the Military Academy. Scott's death came on May 29, 1866.

Summary

Winfield Scott came into the army when it was a tiny force and the nation was still a small, self-conscious republic; when he left the United States Army, it was on the verge of becoming the army of the "Coming of the Lord," the Union Army of two million soldiers that destroyed slavery and the rebel republic. The problem with which he wrestled as a military man was the same on the Niagara Frontier as in Mexico and would be, too, for the Union Army at the Battle of Bull Run: how to take an army of raw volunteers and make them an army capable of fighting European regulars. In other words, how could one ask amateurs to kill and be killed? This was a task at which George Washington had failed until the last year of the Revolution, and it is to Scott's credit that he succeeded in 1814 and in 1847. Indeed, most European observers had expected the Mexicans to win the war in 1846 precisely because Mexico had an army trained by Europeans and the Americans were still the same amalgamation of volunteers and militia that had performed so poorly in the War of 1812. Scott's solution to the problem of how to make obedient but innovative soldiers out of the manpower of a democratic society was to emphasize drill as well as humane treatment. During his commands after 1817, he sought to make the life of the common soldier more comfortable and less harsh, on the theory that men fought better when not brutalized by their own officers. The outcome at Lundy's Lane and Chapultepec shows that Scott indeed did adjust the hierarchical organization of military life to the democracy of the new republic.

Bibliography
Bauer, Jack K. *The Mexican War: 1846-1848*. New York: Macmillan Publishing Co., 1974. This volume in the "Wars of the United States" series is useful for those interested in Scott as a strategist. It contains a very good account of the Vera Cruz to Mexico City campaign, along with fine maps.
Johannsen, Robert. *To the Halls of Montezuma: The Mexican War in the American Imagination*. New York: Oxford University Press, 1985. This work discusses how contemporaries saw the Mexican War and is especially perceptive about why Zachary Taylor became a hero and Scott did not.
Mahon, John K. *The War of 1812*. Gainesville: University of Florida Press, 1972. This book gives Scott his due as part of the new generation of commanders who emerged in 1813. Helpful maps show the battles along the Niagara Frontier.
Potter, David M. *The Impending Crisis: 1848-1861*. New York: Harper and Row, Publishers, 1976. This political history of the coming of the Civil War treats Scott's election campaign of 1852 in the context of the breakup of the Whig Party. The author finds Scott a better general than a politician.
Scott, Winfield M. *Memoirs of Lieut.-General Scott*. 2 vols. New York: Sheldon and Co., 1864. This is the essential starting point for Scott students. It is long-winded and touchy about points of honor, but Scott does get the final say against his critics. Scott's *Memoirs* are thin with regard to the subject's political career, emphasizing instead his military exploits.
Victor, Orville James. *Life and Military and Civic Services of Lieutenant General Winfield Scott*. New York: Beadle and Co., 1861. All the 1852 "campaign biographies" are inaccessible except in a few research libraries; the Victor book appears in a popular microfilm series and gives a straightforward account of the details of Scott's military career.

Weigley, Russell F. *History of the United States Army*. New York: Macmillan Publishing Co., 1967. The author evaluates Scott both as a strategist in war and as a molder of the army. He sees Scott as an excessively vainglorious man, but still the builder of the professional officer corps.

James W. Oberly

GLENN THEODORE SEABORG

Born: April 19, 1912; Ishpeming, Michigan

Areas of Achievement: Nuclear science and education
Contribution: Codiscoverer of ten transuranium elements and numerous radioisotopes with wide applications in research, medicine, and industry, Seaborg served under five United States presidents in establishing policy regarding the role of science and uses of atomic energy.

Early Life

Glenn Theodore Seaborg was born in Ishpeming, Michigan, a small iron-mining town on the Upper Peninsula, in April, 1912. His mother, Selma O. Erickson, came through Ellis Island from Sweden in 1904 to join family members in a predominantly Swedish immigrant section of Ishpeming. There she met and married his father, Herman Theodore Seaborg, whose father and mother had moved from Sweden to Michigan in 1867 and 1869. Young Glenn's first language was Swedish, and his early years were strongly influenced by Swedish cultural traditions.

When he was ten years old and starting the fifth grade, his parents decided to leave Michigan and move to Southern California to take advantage of a better climate and broader opportunities for their children. They settled in Home Gardens (now South Gate), which, as a brand-new subdivision, did not have any schools during their first year there. Seaborg and his younger sister, Jeanette, attended part of a year of grammar school and, later, four years of high school in the Watts district of Los Angeles. His schoolmates in Watts came from many different ethnic backgrounds: European, Chinese, Mexican, Japanese, black, Filipino. This early exposure to different cultures may have contributed to Seaborg's later facility in getting along well and communicating effectively with a wide range of people.

Seaborg was urged by his parents to undertake a commercial course in high school, which they believed was the most secure route to a respectable, white-collar job, their fondest dream for the son of a long line of machinists. Seaborg, however, elected to take college preparatory courses and, in his final two years of high school, thanks to the inspiration of a fine science teacher, discovered the excitement of science, in which he would make his career.

When Seaborg started college in 1929 at the University of California, Los Angeles (UCLA), there were only four permanent buildings and much mud at the newly established Westwood campus. There were, however, gifted teachers who encouraged his scientific curiosity and told him about the thrilling new discoveries being made in the field of nuclear science in Europe and at the Berkeley campus. He became determined to work in this new frontier.

After earning his undergraduate degree in chemistry from UCLA in 1934, the tall (six-foot, three-inch), lanky young man moved north to Berkeley to undertake graduate work. Berkeley was a mecca for scientists; its chemistry and physics faculties were among the finest in the world, with such notable pioneers as the chemist Gilbert N. Lewis and the physicist Ernest O. Lawrence. Intense and hardworking, Seaborg could hardly believe his good fortune. At weekly seminars, he was enthralled by reports of the results being obtained by Lawrence at the twenty-seven-inch cyclotron and delighted to have the chance of working the graveyard shift to complete experiments for his thesis on the inelastic scattering of neutrons, for which he earned his Ph.D. in chemistry from University of California, Berkeley, in 1937. During the years immediately following, he developed two associations which would have great influence on his life: He served as personal research assistant to Lewis, and he met and courted Lawrence's secretary, an attractive woman named Helen Griggs.

His career as a published nuclear scientist actually began in 1936 when physicist Jack Livingood asked him to perform the chemical separations on a target just bombarded at the cyclotron in order to identify the radioisotopes it had produced. During the ensuing five years of collaboration with Livingood, they discovered or identified a number of radioisotopes (iodine-131, iron-59, cobalt-60) which are still widely used in medicine for diagnosis and therapy. In 1938, with Emilio Segre, Seaborg discovered technetium-99m, which is the most widely used diagnostic radioisotope in nuclear medicine.

Seaborg has often described the exhilaration he and his colleagues felt when they learned in 1939 about the experiments Otto Hahn and Fritz Strassman were performing in Germany, which gave the first evidence of a nuclear fission reaction. The next year, Edwin M. McMillan and Philip Abelson discovered the first transuranium element, element 93, which they named neptunium. McMillan then began the search for element 94, but was called away in 1940 to work on important war research on the East Coast. As a young assistant professor, Seaborg took over this work and enlisted the help of his graduate student Arthur C. Wahl and a fellow chemistry instructor, Joseph W. Kennedy. In February, 1941, through bombarding uranium with deuterons in the sixty-inch cyclotron, they discovered element 94, plutonium, in the form of plutonium-238. With the added collaboration of Segre, they discovered plutonium-239, which proved to be a fissionable isotope that might serve as the explosive ingredient in a nuclear weapon and as a nuclear fuel. In 1942, John W. Gofman, Raymond W. Stoughton, and Seaborg created and identified a second major source of nuclear energy, the isotope uranium-233, which is the key to the use of the abundant element thorium as a nuclear fuel.

On his thirtieth birthday, April 19, 1942, Seaborg arrived at the University of Chicago Metallurgical Laboratory to join the Manhattan Project as leader of the group working on the chemical extraction of plutonium. This began his long career as a scientific leader, employing his gift for communication and talent for administration as well as his instinct for science.

Life's Work

Seaborg has often described the years in Chicago working on the Manhattan Project as the most exciting and most challenging of his life. The team of dedicated scientists worked around the clock in what they believed was a race against the Nazis to produce the first atomic bomb and, later, an attempt to save thousands of lives in the Pacific theatre. In June, 1945, when their part of the project was successfully completed, Seaborg joined six colleagues in signing the Franck report, which recommended that the bomb be demonstrated, rather than used against a civilian Japanese population. Nevertheless, President Harry S Truman made the decision to go ahead and drop the bomb. The second atomic bomb, dropped on Nagasaki, Japan, on August 9, 1945, was fueled with plutonium. The "Atomic Age" had begun, and Seaborg shared the conviction of others that control of nuclear weapons was now the most critical question of our times. He joined in the debate about implications for the future of our planet and served on the first General Advisory Committee to the Atomic Energy Commission, participating in difficult decisions about the development of more advanced nuclear weapons (for example, the hydrogen bomb) and in explorations of the peaceful uses of atomic energy.

During the years in Chicago, Seaborg and his coworkers also discovered two new transuranium elements, americium (element 95) and curium (element 96). He holds patents on these elements, making him the only man ever to hold a patent on a chemical element. In 1944, he formulated the actinide concept of heavy element electronic structure, which accurately predicted that the heaviest naturally occurring elements together with synthetic transuranium elements would form a transition series of actinide elements in a manner analogous to the rare earth series of lanthanide elements. This concept, the most significant change in the periodic table since Dmitri Mendeleev's nineteenth century design, shows how the transuranium elements fit into the periodic table and thus demonstrates their relationships to other elements.

When Seaborg returned to Berkeley in 1946 with his wife, Helen, whom he had married on a brief return visit to Berkeley in June, 1942, he dedicated himself to two efforts: establishing the world's premier research group working on transuranium elements and starting a family. Now a full professor of chemistry at the University of California and soon to become associate director of the Radiation Laboratory, he brought back from Chicago with him a number of the brightest young scientists in the nation, and together, this team discovered six more transuranium elements, elements 97 through 102.

He and Helen were also successful in attaining their goal of a large family— they had six children. A highlight of the first years back in Berkeley was the receipt of the Nobel Prize for Chemistry with McMillan in 1951 for their work on the chemistry of the transuranium elements. The visit to Stockholm to receive the prize from the King of Sweden was a dream come true for this son of a Swedish immigrant.

In 1958, Seaborg's talents as an administrator were presented with a new challenge. He became the second chancellor of the University of California, Berkeley, and served during a period (1958-1961) of tremendous growth and development at the university. The Master Plan for Higher Education in California (1959) set an ambitious agenda for the state university and college systems. A long-range physical plan was developed for the Berkeley campus, which was undergoing an unprecedented period of building; the College of Environmental Design and the Space Sciences Laboratory were both established at that time. Students were beginning to shake off postwar apathy and became actively involved with such issues as free speech, the draft, and racial discrimination in housing.

Caricatures of Seaborg at this time began to make use of his dramatic bushy eyebrows, yet these depictions were generally in good humor. Seaborg somehow had a talent for keeping people on opposite sides of fences talking to one another and seeking compromise solutions to problems. Some of these negotiating techniques were no doubt the result of experience leading groups of scientists with diverse interests and opinions; his interpersonal skills had been further honed by serving as faculty athletic representative for the Berkeley campus during an era of corruption and controversy in the Pacific Coast Intercollegiate Athletic Conference, which ended with the establishment in 1959 of a new conference: the Athletic Association of Western Universities (now known as the Pac Ten), of which Seaborg was chief architect.

The Soviet launch of Sputnik in 1957 provoked a wave of concern in the United States about the need for improved science education for schoolchildren. Chancellor Seaborg, who had always had a particular interest in this area, served as a leader in the movement to improve science education. He served as chairman of the Steering Committee for CHEM Study (an innovative new chemistry curriculum still widely used throughout the world), as chairman of the Panel on Basic Research and Graduate Education of President Eisenhower's Science Advisory Committee, as a member of a national committee on the application of the National Defense Education Act of 1958, as a member of the Board of Directors of the National Educational Television and Radio Center, and as initiator and chairman of a committee to establish a memorial for Ernest Lawrence (who died in August, 1958) on the Berkeley campus.

In 1961, Seaborg was appointed Chairman of the Atomic Energy Commission (AEC), a position in which he served for ten years. The AEC engaged in a wide range of activities: the development and testing of nuclear weapons; the sponsorship of nuclear energy as a source of electricity; the production of nuclear material; the conduct of reactor research and development for the armed services (including the nuclear navy); the sponsorship of research in high-energy and low-energy nuclear physics, in chemistry, and in biology; the support of educational activities in schools; the production and sale of radioisotopes for use in medicine, agriculture, industry, and research; the licensing of the use of nuclear materials for power plants and other peaceful purposes; and international cooperation in science. Seaborg was responsible for overseeing all these varied activities, supported by a budget of two and a half billion dollars.

As a chief adviser to the president, Seaborg also played an important role in establishing policy regarding arms control agreements. He went to Moscow as a part of the American delegation for the signing of the Limited Nuclear Test Ban Treaty of 1963, which prohibited the testing of nuclear weapons in the atmosphere, in outer space, and underwater. He also participated in laying the groundwork for the Non-Proliferation Treaty of 1970 by helping to establish safeguards that would assure that nuclear materials intended for peaceful uses were subject to appropriate inspections and controls by the International Atomic Energy Agency and to ensure that they were not diverted for military purposes. During his ten years as Chairman of the AEC, Seaborg traveled to more than sixty countries, promoting international cooperation in science.

After he returned to his professorship at the University of California in 1971, University Professor of Chemistry Seaborg continued to pursue the goals of international cooperation in science and the attainment of arms control agreements. He helped to establish the International Organization for Chemical Sciences in Development (IOCD), which facilitates collaboration between chemists in developed countries and chemists in developing countries in the search for solutions to Third World problems, and became its president in 1981. He has written and lectured extensively about the need for a comprehensive test ban treaty, which would extend the prohibition of testing of nuclear weapons to underground testing. Among the many books he has authored are two on the subject of arms control history: *Kennedy, Khrushchev and the Test Ban* (1981, describing the negotiations during the Kennedy Administration for the Limited Test Ban Treaty) and *Stemming the Tide: Arms Control in the Johnson Years* (1987, featuring a description of the negotiations that led to the Non-Proliferation Treaty).

In 1974, Seaborg's research group at the Lawrence Berkeley Laboratory discovered element 106. It is there that Seaborg continues to work as an active research scientist, helping to direct a research group in the search for new isotopes and new elements at the upper end of the periodic table, including a search for the "superheavy" elements. The group is also investigating the mechanism of the reactions of heavy ions with heavy element target nuclei. Another aspect of the research program is concerned with the determination of the chemical properties of the very heaviest synthetic chemical elements.

Deeply involved in the effort to improve mathematics and science education, Seaborg has served as President of Science Service from 1966 and as head of the Lawrence Hall of Science since 1982. He also served on the National Commission on Excellence in Education, which published the much-publicized report, "A Nation at Risk," in 1983.

He began keeping a diary at the age of fourteen and has maintained a detailed record of his daily activities since that time. This personal historical record (which also contains less significant childhood entries such as "took a bath") is a valuable resource for his work on the history of science, recording much about critical decisions in the nuclear age. An avid hiker, he also served as vice president of the American Hiking Society, helped to establish the "Golden State Trail," the California segment of a cross-country hiking route, and is an eloquent supporter of conservation of natural resources and protection of wilderness areas.

Summary

Seaborg's discovery of several radioisotopes has revolutionized medical science. Seventy percent of all diagnosis and treatment in the United States employs nuclear techniques. By 1970, ninety percent of the eight million administrations per year of radioisotopes in the United States utilized cobalt-60, iodine-131, or technetium-99m. Technetium-99m is the workhorse of nuclear medicine; in 1985, it accounted for more than seven million diagnostic procedures per year in bone, liver, lung, thyroid, cardiovascular, and brain scanning and imaging. Millions of people have already benefited (including Seaborg's own mother) and will continue to benefit directly from his research and from his support of research and development during his chairmanship of the AEC through advanced diagnostic and therapeutic applications.

It is impossible to overstate the impact of the discovery of the element plutonium on our times. It has been argued that the existence of weapons of mass destruction has acted as a deterrent and prevented the outbreak of a major conflict between the superpowers for a longer period than at any other time in history. Certainly, knowledge of the potential for destruction of our planet has cast a pall over the lives of all human beings. The other side of the coin is the potential which plutonium has to serve as a virtually inexhaustible source of electrical energy, on which the world depends more each day. Considering the horrifying threat of nuclear war, Seaborg's efforts to prevent the development of still more potent weapons (the Limited Test Ban Treaty of 1963) and to limit the spread of ownership of these weapons to more countries (the Non-Proliferation Treaty of 1970) are of critical importance to the world's future. In Seaborg's view, the need to control nuclear weapons is urgent. The epilogue of his book, *Kennedy, Khrushchev and the Test Ban*, ends thus:

> . . . we are negotiating at a higher and more dangerous level. If we allow the present opportunity to slip away, however, the next one, if there is a next one, will be at a level still higher and more dangerous. The hour is late. Let us hope not too late.

Bibliography

Seaborg, Glenn T. *Nuclear Milestones: A Collection of Speeches*. San Francisco: W. H. Freeman and Co., 1972. A unique compilation of historical insights with many unpublished photographs of the scientists and laboratories responsible for the nuclear age. In this book, through a selection of speeches he gave while chairman of the Atomic Energy Commission, Seaborg tries to present some of the reminiscences and reflections of the scientific accomplishments to advance mankind.

_____. *The Transuranium Elements*. New Haven, Conn.: Yale University Press, 1958. Seaborg tells for the first time the full and dramatic story of plutonium, with emphasis on the men who did the work.

Seaborg, Glenn T., with Benjamin S. Loeb. *Kennedy, Khrushchev and the Test Ban*. Berkeley: University of California Press, 1981. Seaborg tells the story that made the signing of the Limited Test Ban Treaty on August 5, 1963, possible.

_____. *Stemming the Tide: Arms Control in the Johnson Years*. Lexington, Mass.: Lexington Books, 1987. A description of the efforts in arms control during the Johnson administration, including the attainment of the Non-Proliferation Treaty of 1970.

Sherrill Whyte

SAINT ELIZABETH ANN BAYLEY SETON

Born: August 28, 1774; New York, New York
Died: January 4, 1821; Emmitsburg, Maryland
Areas of Achievement: Religion and education
Contribution: Through her resourceful, independent, and pioneering spirit, Elizabeth Seton had a profound influence on nineteenth century American education, laying the foundations of the Catholic parochial school system.

Early Life

Elizabeth Bayley Seton was born August 28, 1774, in New York City. Her father, Dr. Richard Bayley, was an eminent surgeon and professor of anatomy at King's College (later Columbia University). Her mother, Catherine Charlton Bayley, was the daughter of the rector of an Episcopalian church in New York. Little else is known of her, and she died when Elizabeth was three. Bayley remarried, but Elizabeth never formed a close bond with her stepmother. As a child, Elizabeth was a lively, exuberant girl. She was educated at a private school, excelling in French and enjoying dancing and music. She also had a strong introspective tendency and a profoundly religious temperament. Her early upbringing was unsettled; her father was dedicated to his work and gave her little close attention (although there is no doubt of his love for her), and she and her seven half brothers and half sisters were frequently sent to stay with relatives in New Rochelle.

As a young woman, Elizabeth was under medium height, but she was well proportioned and graceful; her features had a pleasing symmetry, and her dark, lively eyes attracted attention. She radiated intelligence and charm. In 1794, at the age of nineteen, she married William Magee Seton, the son of a prominent New York businessman. It was by all accounts a successful and happy marriage, and between 1795 and 1802, Elizabeth Seton gave birth to two sons and three daughters.

She was not, however, to have a conventionally serene and prosperous life. Forced by circumstances to mature early, responsibility for the welfare of others became a constant feature of her life. The death of her father-in-law in 1798 left her in charge of six more young children, and the death of her own father in 1801 was another severe blow. In the meantime, William Seton's business affairs had foundered, and the family was faced with a financial crisis, which was complicated by a steady deterioration in her husband's health. Doctors recommended a sea voyage, and in 1803 William, Elizabeth, and their eldest daughter, Anna, sailed for Italy. William survived the voyage but died in Pisa, Italy, just after the family had been released from quarantine at Leghorn.

It was while in Italy, where Seton stayed for three months following her husband's death, that she first came into contact with Roman Catholicism.

This contact was through her friendship with the Filicchi family, particularly the two brothers, Philip and Antonio. Her interest in religion, which had never been far from the surface, had earlier been stimulated by Henry Hobart, the gifted Episcopalian minister who preached at Trinity Church in New York. Now she felt the attraction of Catholicism, and her stay in Italy initiated a period of intense inner turbulence, the issue of which was to have momentous consequences.

Life's Work

On her return to New York in 1804, she was torn between the Catholic faith which she now wished to embrace and the innumerable ties which held her to the Protestant religion into which she had been born. For a year, she struggled to make a decision, corresponding with the Filicchis, John Carroll, Bishop of Baltimore, and Bishop John Cheverus of Boston, while also receiving the opposite counsel of Henry Hobart. Finally, on March 14, 1805, she publicly professed her allegiance to the Roman Catholic faith and began to attend St. Peter's Church, the only Catholic church in New York City. Thus began a period of three years in which her new faith was tested to its utmost. She had exchanged social position and respectability, the security of being in the majority, for a minority faith composed mainly of poor immigrants. Her family and friends reacted with coolness to her decision, turning to dismay when Seton's sister-in-law, Cecilia Seton, became a convert to Catholicism in 1806.

Seton's most pressing need at this time was to establish a secure home for her young family. She took part in a scheme to establish a small school at which she would be an assistant teacher, but the enterprise failed. Following this failure, with financial support from her friend John Wilkes, Seton established a boardinghouse for boys. This, however, was also a short-lived venture.

By 1808, at the instigation of Father William Dubourg, the president of St. Mary's College at Baltimore, she had left New York for Baltimore to take charge of a boarding school for girls located in Paca Street, next to St. Mary's Chapel. The school got off to a slow start, with only two pupils, rising to ten by the end of the year. During this period of one year, Elizabeth's vocation was becoming clear to her; she wanted to form a religious community. By March of the following year, in consultation with her friends and advisers, she had agreed to move to the village of Emmitsburg, about fifty miles from Baltimore. The new settlement was to be financed by Samuel Cooper, a Catholic convert. Seton took vows of poverty, chastity, and obedience, was adopted as the head of the community, and became known as Mother Seton.

On June 21, 1809, accompanied by her eldest daughter and three other women, she traveled to Emmitsburg. The Sisters of Charity of St. Joseph had been formed. Father Dubourg became the first superior, and the new community adopted a slightly modified version of the constitution and rules of the French community, the Daughters of Charity of St. Vincent de Paul. By December, sixteen women were living in a simple cottage known as the Stone House, which was the community's first home. There were only five rooms, one of which was set aside as a temporary chapel, and it was with some relief that the sisters moved into their more spacious permanent home, known as the White House, in February, 1810.

From this point onward, growth was rapid. By the summer, there were forty pupils at the school, many from well-to-do families, and by 1813, the number of sisters had increased to eighteen. The curriculum consisted mainly of reading, writing, spelling, grammar, geography, and arithmetic. Music, language, and needlework were also taught. Mother Seton played some part in teaching, but as the school became established, she spent more time in administration and supervision. The success of the school was a result of the effective inculcation of piety and strict morality, reinforced by firm but compassionate discipline. It is through her work at Emmitsburg that Mother Seton is rightly known as the founder of the Catholic parochial school system in the United States. She worked indefatigably—encouraging, consoling, admonishing, mothering, and organizing. She translated religious texts from the French, prepared meditations, gave spiritual instruction, kept a journal, and still had time to carry on a lively correspondence.

Mother Seton continued to be surrounded by the illnesses and deaths of those she loved. Her half sister Harriet died in 1809, and Cecilia Seton followed four months later. The death of her eldest daughter, Anna Maria, in 1812, affected her more deeply than any other. Yet her strength of character, serenity, and resilience were never more apparent than in adversity. Her ability to rise above sorrows and maintain her devotion to her calling ensured the survival and growth of the community in the difficult early years.

Within a short period, the community was expanding. By 1814, the St. Joseph orphanage in Philadelphia had applied to the Sisters of Charity for the services of a matron and two sisters, and in the following year, four other sisters were sent to Mount Saint Mary's College in Emmitsburg. In 1817, the first establishment of the Sisters of Charity was founded in New York City, originally as an orphanage, but like the earlier community in Philadelphia, quickly expanding into a school. Plans were made for schools in Baltimore, and the first of these was established in 1821. Mother Seton, however, did not live to see it. After several years of declining health, she died on January 4, 1821, at the age of forty-six.

Summary

Born two years before the declaration of the Republic, Elizabeth Seton grew up in a land which was alive with a newfound sense of freedom, of its own vast potential. She, too, was an American pioneer, although her expertise was not in the claiming and cultivation of land but in the edification and training of the young and in the schooling of souls. In addition to her profound contribution to nineteenth century education, she offered comfort, support, and hope to an untold number of people who came under her care. She combined the American virtues of innovation, self-sufficiency, and independence with the spiritual values of humility and service. Neither mystic nor theologian, she was a practical woman who emphasized simplicity and efficiency in daily affairs, both spiritual and material.

It had always been clear to those who came into contact with her that she was a woman of exceptional spiritual stature. Some recognized, with prophetic accuracy, that she would make her mark on history. As early as 1809, before Seton had even moved to Baltimore, Bishop John Cheverus envisaged "numerous choirs" of her order spreading throughout the United States, and she herself expected "to be the mother of many daughters." At her death, her confessor, Father Simon Bruté, instructed the Sisters of Charity to preserve every scrap of her writing for posterity. After her death, her communities quickly spread across the land: to Cincinnati, Ohio, in 1829; to Halifax, Nova Scotia, in 1849. By 1859, a community had been formed in Newark, New Jersey, and by 1870, Greensburg, Pennsylvania, had been added to the list.

It was not until 1907, however, that the cause for her canonization was introduced. In 1959, her life was declared heroic, and she received the title of Venerable. Two miraculous cures, which had taken place in 1935 and 1952, were attributed to her intercession, and Beatification followed in 1963. In 1975, Pope Paul VI proclaimed her a saint. The poor widow who had endured many trials, the convert who had founded a holy order, had become, 154 years after her death, the first American-born saint of the Catholic Church.

Bibliography
Dirvin, Joseph I. *Mrs. Seton: Foundress of the American Sisters of Charity*. Rev. ed. New York: Farrar, Straus and Giroux, 1975. One of the three biographies which were reissued to mark the occasion of Mother Seton's canonization. Strongly Catholic in tone yet also scholarly and well documented, it presents a warm, sympathetic portrait which captures the essential, simple goodness of the woman as she went about her daily affairs.
Feeney, Leonard. *Mother Seton: Saint Elizabeth of New York*. Rev. ed. Cambridge, Mass.: Ravengate Press, 1975. Concise biography which will appeal to Catholic readers. Others may find themselves alienated by the author's stylistic eccentricities and his conservative religious point of view, which tends to intrude upon his subject.
Heidish, Marcy. *Miracles: A Novel About Mother Seton, the First American*

Saint. New York: New American Library, 1984. Notable for the ingenious device of using as narrator a fictionalized version of a priest who sat on the tribunal investigating one of the miraculous cures attributed to Mother Seton. His job is to be devil's advocate. The flaw in the novel is that the down-to-earth, skeptical priest, full of doubt and wry humor, becomes far more interesting than the heroine.

Hoare, Sister Mary Regis. *Virgin Soil.* Boston: Christopher Publishing House, 1942. Detailed examination of the American Catholic parochial school system, and convincing argument for Elizabeth Seton as its founder.

Kelly, Ellin M., ed. *Numerous Choirs: A Chronicle of Elizabeth Bayley Seton and Her Spiritual Daughters.* Vol. 1, *The Seton Years, 1774-1821.* Evansville, Ind.: Mater Dei Provincialate, 1981. Useful primarily for the long extracts from Seton's letters and journals, which form the core of the narrative and give vivid insight into her mind. Arranged in strict chronological order, with as little editorial comment as clarity permits.

McCann, Sister Mary Agnes. *The History of Mother Seton's Daughters: The Sisters of Charity of Cincinnati, Ohio, 1809-1917.* 3 vols. New York: Longmans, Green and Co., 1917. The story of the first ninety years of the Cincinnati community. The chief interest centers on the stormy episode in 1850, when the Cincinnati Sisters refused to join the other communities in affiliating themselves to the French Sisters of Charity of St. Vincent de Paul (see volume 2).

Melville, Annabelle M. *Elizabeth Bayley Seton: 1774-1821.* New York: Charles Scribner's Sons, 1976. Definitive biography, scholarly and objective, free of the hagiographic tone of many other biographies.

Bryan Aubrey

WILLIAM H. SEWARD

Born: May 16, 1801; Florida, New York
Died: October 10, 1872; Auburn, New York
Areas of Achievement: Politics and foreign policy
Contribution: As an antislavery leader who helped to found the Republican
Party during the 1850's, Seward, who contested Lincoln for the presiden-
tial nomination in 1860, went on to become one of the United States'
greatest secretaries of state.

Early Life

The ancestors of William Henry Seward came to America from England
during the early eighteenth century. His parents, Samuel and Mary Seward,
reared five children. Young Seward was influenced mainly by his father, who
valued discipline and wealth. At age fifteen, Seward left home for Union
College in Schenectady, New York. A financial dispute with his father led
him to leave Union College for Georgia, where he taught school (and observed slavery at first hand) for a short time. Returning to New York State,
he completed his studies at Union College. He then worked for two law firms
before being admitted to the bar in 1822. The following year, Seward moved
to Auburn, near Syracuse, where he joined the law firm of Judge Elijah
Miller. Judge Miller provided him not only a job but also a bride, for Seward
married the judge's daughter, Frances, in 1824.

For men such as Seward, Auburn proved to be a great source of political
opportunity. By the mid-1820's, Seward had already become very active in
the National Republican Party, which supported John Quincy Adams, and he
then became active in the Antimasonic Party, which not only challenged the
"secret government" of the Masons but also advocated protective tariffs and
government support for the construction of roads, canals, and railroads. It
was as an Antimason that Seward launched his public career. He won a seat
in the state senate, and he increasingly became a favorite of the leading
political organizer of his party, Thurlow Weed (also of Auburn). The two
men became close friends and established a lifelong political relationship
which soon brought Seward to national prominence. Weed first carried Seward into the new Whig Party as it emerged during the winter of 1833-1834,
then engineered Seward's nomination for governor. Although Seward lost
when he first ran for the office in 1834, he triumphed four years later.

By the time he became governor, Seward had proven himself to be highly
ambitious, often unprincipled, and tough. He stood for the Whig economic
program of tariffs, internal improvements, and the national bank, and took a
daring position in support of temperance, prison reform, and the abolition of
jail sentences for debtors. On race issues, however, he was inconsistent.
Although he detested slavery, he opposed, with equal vehemence, granting

the right to vote to blacks. Yet he recognized that the controversy over slavery might offer him political opportunities, and he grabbed them during the next twenty-five years.

Life's Work

Portraits of Seward show a handsome man about five feet, six inches tall, with a graceful, thin face marked by an aquiline nose, a ruddy complexion, and wavy, red hair. Early photographs of Seward are not as flattering: The lines in his face are less graceful, his look less direct. This discrepancy can be observed also in his political career, for Seward often offered less than met the eye. As governor, he became well-known for his opposition to slavery and his support for the education of Catholic immigrant children in the face of nativist Protestant objections, and he continued to advocate high tariffs and internal improvements. Yet he took none of these positions without first having carefully assessed their potential impact on his career. When the Whigs in New York suffered reverses during the mid- and late- 1840's, they turned to Seward as their best chance to regain a seat in the United States Senate. Their plan succeeded. In 1849, the Auburn lawyer moved to Washington.

The next twenty years witnessed the zenith of Seward's political career. Opposing the Compromise of 1850 because it did not end the expansion of slavery, Seward delivered his most famous speech. He argued before the Senate that there existed "a higher law than the Constitution" that prohibited the movement of slavery into free territory. This speech, which was reprinted thousands of times during the following decade, turned Seward into one of the leading symbols of the antislavery movement, a hero to Northerners, a demagogue to Southerners. Moreover, Seward's "higher law" speech guaranteed that when the Whig Party disintegrated during the period between 1852 and 1854, Seward would be called upon to lead the Republican Party, which replaced it. Seward in New York, Abraham Lincoln in Illinois, and Salmon Chase in Ohio all came to lead the new party that was both sectional (not national) and fundamentally opposed to the expansion of slavery into the territory acquired by the United States following the Mexican War.

Yet both Seward's friends and his foes exaggerated his opposition to slavery, for he was first and foremost a nationalist—and, as such, hardly a radical within the abolitionist cause. Slavery, he believed, would impede national development, but he was against so rapid and wrenching a transition away from slavery as might lead to war and destroy the Union. Seward favored gradual, not immediate, abolition. He advocated compensation for slaveholders who freed their slaves. A conservative and traditionalist, unlike many abolitionists, he continued to praise the Constitution. That Seward was a nationalist also explains his support of federal funding of internal improvements, tariffs, and development of the West. He remained suspicious of executive power, although not when it was used to assert the national interest against foreign competitors. Seward believed that, eventually, the United States would extend its boundaries from coast to coast and would encompass Canada and Mexico and Alaska (which he helped to purchase from Russia in 1867). As a nationalist, he believed, as did his hero John Quincy Adams, that Providence intended for the United States to dominate the Western Hemisphere. He believed that the political and moral contradictions of slavery would discredit this mission.

Seward viewed the systems of the nation's free and slave states and territories incompatible. This incompatibility would, he claimed in an 1858 speech, lead to "an irrepressible conflict," meaning that the United States would eventually have to extend either the free or the slave system to all of its borders. Lincoln shared this conviction, and the likelihood that either Lincoln or Seward would become the Republican Party nominee for president in 1860 led many influential Southerners to advocate secession.

Seward desperately wanted to become president, but, for a number of reasons, he failed to receive his party's nomination. The "irrepressible conflict" speech had become so notorious that many Republicans feared that its author could not win the election. Furthermore, Seward's long-standing support for Catholic education, stemming back to the New York education quarrels of the 1840's, left nativists in his party dissatisfied. (As for Thurlow Weed, another likely candidate that year of 1860, he was simply outmaneuvered by the opposition—a rare but important occurrence in his political career.) Thus, the Republican Party named Abraham Lincoln its candidate for the presidency. Seward's defeat was a bitter blow, yet—although he genuinely believed Lincoln to be less qualified than himself—Seward loyally supported Lincoln in the general election. Lincoln rewarded this loyalty, offering Seward the post of secretary of state following his electoral victory.

During the next eight years, Seward proved himself to be among the nation's most outstanding State Department chiefs, though it was not immediately apparent. He began his work in a provocative manner. He proposed that Lincoln, in effect, serve as a figurehead president while Seward assume the real powers of the presidency. He threatened war against England and France in order to motivate the South to return to the Union in a burst of nationalistic fervor. He insulted the British at a moment when the Union needed foreign support against the challenge of the Confederacy.

If his early diplomacy appeared belligerent, however, he quickly mended his ways. From the beginning of the Civil War in 1861, Seward's major task was to minimize foreign support for the Confederacy. The South not only sought diplomatic recognition from the Europeans; it also sought military aid in the form of loans and equipment, especially naval craft that could challenge the Union blockade of Southern ports.

Preoccupied with military and political matters, Lincoln gave Seward a free hand in the diplomatic arena. Seward played it well. When a Union naval captain plucked two Confederate officials off the *Trent*, a British frigate, officials in London threatened war. Seward avoided conflict in a very adroit maneuver in which the British, for the first time since the American Revolution, accepted the American view of neutral rights on the high seas. In like manner, Seward, through a combination of bluff, public appeal, and skillful negotiation, discouraged both the British and the French from aiding the Confederacy either diplomatically or materially.

Seward's skill was evident in more than simply wartime diplomacy. He shrewdly unveiled the Monroe Doctrine when the French installed a puppet regime in Mexico, and he effectively laid the foundation for American financial claims against London stemming from damage inflicted on Union shipping by a Confederate cruiser, the *Alabama*, constructed in Great Britain. More important, his vision of an American continental empire culminated in his imaginative purchase of Alaska in 1867. "Seward's Folly," his critics called the acquisition, but even an unfriendly Congress recognized its potential value.

The plot to kill Lincoln also targeted Seward, who was severely wounded. He recovered to serve President Andrew Johnson as secretary of state, generally endorsing Johnson's Reconstruction policy. The fact is that Seward remained willing to subordinate black rights to what he believed to be the main task, that of the reconciliation of the North and the South.

Nevertheless, it was foreign policy, not Reconstruction politics, for which he would be remembered. Retiring from public life in 1869 and returning to Auburn, he died three years later, October 10, 1872.

Summary

William Seward's career touched upon virtually all the major issues of the pre–Civil War era. He became one of the country's leading Whig (and later Republican) leaders in part because he thoroughly supported the main Whig principles: nationalism, a limit on executive power, strict support for the Constitution, a high tariff to fund internal improvements, and low land prices in order to stimulate westward expansion. Yet it was antislavery that, above all, shaped his career. Seward became a leading opponent of the expansion of slavery, and he nearly rode this issue into the presidency.

What Seward lacked, however, was conviction. Seward never conveyed Lincoln's sense that slavery was a genuine American tragedy. To an extent, Seward was victimized by his evident ambition. He was not fully trusted, in large measure because he was not fully trustworthy. Too often he subordinated political principle to personal interest, a weakness which limited his effectiveness with allies and foes alike.

Nevertheless, his skepticism about principle allowed him to compromise where compromise was necessary and made him a particularly effective diplomat. Next to John Quincy Adams, he had the broadest vision of any secretary of state in American history. He was a practical man, a man of action rather than an intellectual. Whatever the flaws in his character, his record speaks for itself.

Bibliography

Adams, Ephraim D. *Great Britain and the American Civil War*. 2 vols. New York: Longmans, Green and Co., 1925. Adams, while very sympathetic toward the British, nevertheless provides a fair and detailed account of Seward's first four years as secretary of state.

Case, Lynn M., and Warren F. Spencer. *The United States and France: Civil War Diplomacy*. Philadelphia: University of Pennsylvania Press, 1970. An excellent survey of Seward's foreign policy from a Continental perspective. Seward is viewed with grudging respect.

Ferriss, Norman B. *Desperate Diplomacy: William H. Seward's Foreign Policy, 1861*. Knoxville: University of Tennessee Press, 1976. A sympathetic account of Seward's diplomacy, with a focus on the *Trent* affair.

_____. *The Trent Affair: A Diplomatic Crisis*. Knoxville: University of Tennessee Press, 1977. A thorough but dull account of the crisis that nearly brought Great Britain and the United States to war in 1861.

Paolino, Ernest N. *The Foundations of American Empire: William Henry Seward and U.S. Foreign Policy*. Ithaca, N.Y.: Cornell University Press, 1973. The author views Seward as defining a commercial imperial mission for the United States. Curiously, the book ignores the Civil War.

Seward, William H. *William H. Seward: An Autobiography from 1801-1834, With a Memoir of His Life, and Selections from His Letters*. 3 vols. Edited by Frederick Seward. New York: Derby and Miller, 1877. The editor was Seward's son. This volume provides a look at Seward's entire life from his own perspective.

Van Deusen, Glyndon G. *William Henry Seward*. New York: Oxford University Press, 1967. The best one-volume biography. Van Deusen is sympathetic to but rarely uncritical of Seward, whom he views as a man both unprincipled and practical.

Warren, Gordon H. *Foundation of Discontent: The Trent Affair and Freedom of the Seas*. Boston: Northeastern University Press, 1981. This work is less kind to Seward than the work of Ferriss. It is very helpful in clarifying the complex legal issues of the affair.

Gary B. Ostrower

ROGER SHERMAN

Born: April 19, 1721; Newton, Massachusetts
Died: July 23, 1793; New Haven, Connecticut
Areas of Achievement: Politics and law
Contribution: Sherman's political wisdom and facility for compromise helped create the United States Constitution. He also served ably as a Colonial leader in Connecticut during the American Revolution.

Early Life

Roger Sherman was born on April 19, 1721, in Newton, Massachusetts, outside of Boston. He was the second son born to William Sherman and Mehetabel Wellington Sherman; their family later grew to include seven children. The infant Roger was named for Roger Wellington, his maternal great-grandfather. The Sherman family had first arrived in America in 1636 when their ancestor, Captain John Sherman, migrated from Essex, England, to Watertown, Massachusetts.

In 1723, William Sherman moved his young family to a section of Dorchester, Massachusetts, that was incorporated as Stoughton in 1726. It was there that Roger Sherman was reared. He was taught by his father to be a cobbler, or shoemaker, and they also farmed the family land together. The latter work required Roger's full attention in the spring and summer months. When winter approached, he attended a one-room school located a mile and a quarter from his home. The education the boy received there was rudimentary, but he improved on it himself. When he traveled from house to house with his cobbler's tools, he also took along books to read while he made or repaired shoes. One of his earliest interests was mathematics; he also read widely in law, astronomy, history, philosophy, and theology. The last of these subjects probably became of interest to young Sherman from his association with the Reverend Samuel Dunbar, an influential Congregationalist preacher in Stoughton. Despite his curiosity about theological matters, Roger Sherman did not officially join Dunbar's congregation until he was twenty-one, on March 14, 1742. This delayed declaration of faith was rather unusual in Colonial America, where a person's religious affiliation was highly important in the community.

Sherman met his first wife, Elizabeth Hartwell, the daughter of a local church deacon, while he still resided in Stoughton, though Sherman did not marry her until a few years had passed. The death of his father intervened in 1741; Roger Sherman found himself suddenly responsible for the support and education of the younger children in his family. In order to facilitate family matters, Roger moved to New Milford, Connecticut, in 1742; he accomplished this by walking more than one hundred miles from his Massachusetts' home. Once in New Milford, he helped his older brother William manage the general store he had already established in that farming community. On November 17, 1749, Roger Sherman married Elizabeth Hartwell. Their marriage would produce seven children, but only four survived infancy. Elizabeth herself died at age thirty-five in October of 1760.

Roger Sherman had varied interests in his first years in Connecticut. He produced an almanac (modeled after that of Benjamin Franklin) which predicted weather, gave advice to farmers, and quoted proverbs and poetry. Sherman continued this enterprise until 1761.

Roger Sherman found his most lucrative employment in 1745, when he was appointed as land surveyor for New Haven County; he received this position for his superb mathematical ability. At this time, surveyors were at a premium in the Colonies, and so, when Litchfield County was formed in northwestern Connecticut in 1752, Sherman became its surveyor as well. Because of these jobs, he was able to speculate in real estate dealings, much to his success. Also, his work in court to defend the land boundaries of plaintiffs drew Sherman more into an interest in law. He read more intensely in the law during these years, and in February of 1754, he was admitted to the bar. Because of his growing popularity and reputation for fairness, New Milford's citizens began electing Sherman to a series of political offices. He served on their grand jury, as selectman, as justice of the peace, and finally, as their delegate to the Connecticut General Assembly.

Life's Work

Sherman's life in New Milford, however, despite his popularity, became increasingly difficult after the death of his wife in 1760. The following year, he decided to move to New Haven, where he established a general store next to the Yale College campus. Because of his proximity to the college and local churches, Sherman sold many books; some of his best customers were students and ministers. Sherman's devotion to reading increased at this time; he also began to take more of an interest in Colonial politics. Sherman was still serving as a delegate to the Connecticut General Assembly, a position he first held in 1755 and (except for the years of 1756-1757) would continue to hold until 1761. In 1759, he had also been named a justice of the County Court of Litchfield. In 1766, he was appointed a judge in the State Superior Court of Connecticut. Connecticut's original charter from England had granted the colony the most carefully structured and autonomous government enjoyed by any colony. This is a fact that Sherman cherished and which he put to work in his later dealings in the congresses of the emerging nation.

Although Roger Sherman's record as an office holder in Connecticut's distinct government seems impressive in itself, his most valuable contributions to American society were yet to be made. With Sherman's selection to the First Continental Congress in August of 1774, his work as one of the Founding Fathers of the United States truly began. He served diligently in this congress, despite the fact that he was one of the oldest delegates. Sherman was also sent to represent Connecticut in the Second Continental Congress, which convened in May of 1775. It was becoming evident by the time of this second congress that a war for independence from England was inevitable for the thirteen colonies. Shots had been fired in Massachusetts between British redcoats and Colonial patriots in April of 1775. In this second congress, Sherman served on a committee of five men who drafted the Declaration of Independence, although most of the actual writing of the document was done by Thomas Jefferson. Once war had been declared, Sherman labored long hours on vital committees managing the Revolution. He headed efforts to raise ten million dollars to fund the war, and he organized the purchase of the Colonial army's supplies.

In his home state of Connecticut, Sherman also served on the Council of Safety during these years, and he stockpiled munitions at his New Haven store for the army. While at home in New Haven, he founded the New Haven Foot Guards, a unit of militiamen drawn together to defend the city and its residents. Despite these efforts, Sherman's house, as well as his son's, was raided by the British in an attack on New Haven in 1779.

Yet Sherman was not too weighed down by the burdens of his war work. He also enjoyed a happy family life during this period. On May 12, 1763, he had married a beautiful young woman, Rebecca Prescott of Danvers, Massachusetts. Together they had eight children who kept Sherman's home life joyful and lively. One pretty young daughter's quick wit was commented on by a guest at their home: General George Washington.

Sherman, in the area of law and political compromise (an art he perfected), was to play an important role in the founding of the nation that Washington's army had fought to achieve. At the war's end, the thirteen colonies were rather loosely bound together by the Articles of Confederation, which Sherman had also worked to establish in the Grand Committee of the Continental Congress of 1776. It became evident, especially after Shays' Rebellion in Massachusetts, that a stronger central government was needed; powers the government had to have, such as taxation and treaty-making, were lacking. Sherman had served as a delegate to the Congress of the Confederation beginning in 1781. Then, he was also elected to represent Connecticut in the Constitutional Convention held in Philadelphia in the summer of 1787. It was there that Sherman made vital political compromises that helped establish the United States Constitution. Sherman, representing a middle-sized state, effected a successful compromise over an issue that had deadlocked this convention. He sought to establish a manner of legislative voting that would guarantee large states (such as New York and Virginia) and small states (such as Delaware and Rhode Island) an equal and fair voice in making laws. Sherman suggested the establishment of the two houses of the United States Congress as they now exist. The Senate has equal representation for each state, and the House of Representatives has representation proportionate to a state's population. Sherman's compromise was accepted on June 11, 1787; it is known by his name, as the Great Compromise, or as the Connecticut Compromise.

Sherman made other contributions to the founding of the American government. He favored the election of the president by the state legislatures, but he did not win this point. When the popular election of the president is held, however, the decisive recorded vote still comes in the electoral college, which Sherman was instrumental in establishing. He was also responsible for the concept of the congressional override on legislative bills vetoed by the president. Sherman also proposed that the trial for a president's impeachment be held in the House and the Senate (instead of in the Supreme Court, as other delegates had suggested).

From records of his service in the various Colonial congresses, particularly the Constitutional Convention, one may draw a physical picture and character study of Sherman. His fellow delegates wrote in high praise of his conscientious work but also detailed his awkward physical and vocal mannerisms. From these Colonial leaders, one learns that Sherman was a tall man with broad shoulders; he was rugged-looking with a jutting jaw, wide mouth, and deep-socketed, piercing blue eyes, all set in a large head. He wore his brown hair cut close to his head in a conservative style and did not wear a powdered wig as did the men of the Colonial aristocracy. Sherman was one of the poorest delegates to the Constitutional Convention; he barely had enough money to feed his children during the difficult inflationary period caused by the war. Sherman's poverty and lack of a formal education were always evident in his speech, which contained slang terms and was delivered in a rustic accent. Nevertheless, no one writing of Sherman for posterity denied his effectiveness as a statesman. He knew how to make his points in debates, and while he spoke very frequently, he was always concise. In committee work and in informal discussions among delegates, Sherman often saw the issues more clearly than anyone else. He had foresight as to what the United States Constitution had to include and what it had to avoid; here, he was a great advocate of states' rights. For all of his levelheadedness, earnestness in debate, dedication in his service, and honesty in his dealings, Sherman won the sincere praise of his peers.

Connecticut's citizens returned Sherman to serve as a United States congressman in the fall of 1789. He was also appointed to a seat in the Senate in 1791, an office which he held until his death. Sherman died from typhoid fever on the evening of July 23, 1793, in New Haven, Connecticut.

Summary

Sherman's distinguished career as a Colonial political leader and statesman afforded him the title the Great Signer. Because of his almost continual service in the various American congresses, Sherman was the only man to sign all the following major documents: the Articles of Association of 1774, the Declaration of Independence, the Articles of Confederation, the Federal Constitution, the Declaration of Rights, and the Treaty of Paris (with Great Britain).

Sherman also enjoyed a prestigious career as a founding father of New Haven, Connecticut. He was the treasurer of Yale College from 1765 to 1776; in its early years, he often paid the school's bills with his own money to prevent its closing. He was elected the first mayor of New Haven, and while in office (from 1784 until his death), he built new schools and renamed the city streets for American patriots rather than British monarchs. He also built up the city's business and shipping enterprises by offering special loans to new merchants moving into New Haven.

The people of Connecticut expressed their gratitude to Roger Sherman for leading their state out of the struggles of a war for independence into the security of a new nation with a sound and wisely planned government—they named a city after him in 1802, Sherman, Connecticut.

Bibliography

Beals, Carelton. *Our Yankee Heritage: New England's Contribution to America's Civilization*. New York: David McKay Co., 1955. Beals entitles his chapter on Sherman "Shoemaker Statesman." In it, he emphasizes the patriot's early life as well as his political career. This chapter contains many details of Sherman's personal life not found in other sources. Beals also provides a thoughtful analysis of Sherman's character traits.

Boardman, Roger S. *Roger Sherman: Signer and Statesman*. Philadelphia: University of Pennsylvania Press, 1938. A readable, carefully researched study of Sherman's life and career, with much documentation—such as a full listing of the committees on which he served. A bibliography lists other important references. Focuses on Sherman's public career rather than on his personal life.

Bowen, Catherine D. *Miracle at Philadelphia: The Story of the Constitutional Convention, May to September, 1787*. Boston: Little, Brown and Co., 1966. Bowen describes the daily workings of the Constitutional Convention in great detail. A helpful item for the reader is the inclusion of a full text of the United States Constitution, as well as a bibliography. The text is readable and enlightening. The Founding Fathers come through as human beings with distinct personalities and interests.

Collier, Christopher. *Roger Sherman's Connecticut: Yankee Politics and the American Revolution*. Middletown, Conn.: Wesleyan University Press, 1971. The book's title accurately reflects its dual subjects—Roger Sherman and the Connecticut of his era. Collier notes the lack of personal materials available on Sherman; only his public life is recorded in any detail. Thus,

Collier's well-documented study covers the broader range of the statesman in his native state. A substantial bibliography is provided.

Rommel, John G. *Connecticut's Yankee Patriot: Roger Sherman*. Hartford, Conn.: American Bicentennial Commission of Connecticut, 1979. This is a slender but useful volume; it was prepared as one in a series of historical works on Connecticut topics for the two hundredth anniversary of the Declaration of Independence. It re-creates Sherman's political career accurately and concisely, concentrating on his work during and after the Revolutionary War. A small reading list is included.

Rossiter, Clinton. *1787: The Grand Convention*. New York: Macmillan Publishing Co., 1966. This book covers fully the 1787 convention, focusing on the men present and the work achieved there; Rossiter details also the later lives of the convention delegates. A careful factual accounting of a fateful political convention and the government it established. The Founding Founders are somewhat idealized here.

Van Doren, Carl. *The Great Rehearsal: The Story of the Making and Ratifying of the Constitution of the United States*. New York: Viking Press, 1948. A classic book on how the United States government was founded. Since no formal record was kept for much of the 1787 convention, the author works from the delegates' diaries and notes. Accuracy is a primary feature here, but the narrative remains lively and interesting. The author shows the delegates' personalities as well as their contributions to the final document. An informative appendix is included.

Patricia E. Sweeney

WILLIAM TECUMSEH SHERMAN

Born: February 8, 1820; Lancaster, Ohio
Died: February 14, 1891; New York, New York
Area of Achievement: The military
Contribution: One of the architects of the Union victory in the Civil War and a father of modern warfare, Sherman was also a leader in the nation's late nineteenth century Indian wars in the West.

Early Life

Tecumseh Sherman was born February 8, 1820, in Lancaster, Ohio. His father, Charles R. Sherman, was a lawyer and Ohio Supreme Court justice. His mother, Mary Hoyt, was a graduate of an Eastern school for women. They migrated from Connecticut to Ohio in 1811 and produced there a family of eleven children, including later senator and cabinet member, John Sherman. Tecumseh (Cump) was their sixth child.

When Tecumseh was nine years old, his father died suddenly, and his family was broken up. He was taken up the street to live with the family of Thomas Ewing, later United States senator and cabinet member. There he was baptized in the Catholic Church and received the Christian name, William, to go with his Indian one. From then onward, he was William Tecumseh Sherman. Ewing never adopted him, but he always treated him like a son.

Sherman had a happy childhood, enjoying his friends and relatives and often participating in innocent pranks. He received the best education Lancaster had to offer and, at the age of sixteen, Ewing arranged a West Point appointment for him. Sherman endured the military academy boredom and was graduated sixth in his 1840 class.

During these early years, Sherman came to admire his foster father and adopt many of his Whig Party attitudes. At the same time, he always felt a need to prove himself capable of survival without Ewing's help. At West Point, he accepted the aristocratic concept of the superiority of the professional soldier over the volunteer. Sherman came to view his military friends as his family and throughout his life always felt most comfortable around them.

Upon graduation, Sherman received a commission in the artillery and assignment to Florida, where he participated in the Second Seminole War. Though combat was rare, he came to see the Indians at first hand and developed the mixture of admiration and repugnance toward them that he was to hold all of his life. In March, 1842, he was sent to Fort Morgan, in Mobile Bay, where he first experienced the pleasures of polite society. His June 1, 1842, transfer to Fort Moultrie, near Charleston, allowed him to continue his socializing, of which he soon tired. For four years, he lived a boring existence, brightened only by his passion for painting, a furlough back to Ohio highlighted by his first trip down the Mississippi River, and investigative duty in the area of his later march on Atlanta. He also became engaged to Ellen Ewing, his foster sister, with whom he had corresponded since his 1836 departure for West Point. Sherman never painted much after he left Fort Moultrie in South Carolina, but all these other experiences were to have a profound effect on his later life.

When the Mexican War erupted, Sherman hoped to participate in the fighting. He was instead sent to Pittsburgh on recruiting duty. He chafed under his bad luck and jumped at the chance to travel around the Horn to California. By the time he arrived, however, the war there was over, and he found himself adjutant to Colonel Richard B. Mason, spending long hours battling correspondence, not Mexicans. He became very depressed. The 1849 discovery of gold provided him with new excitement, and he absorbed all he could of the gold fever, though the inflation almost ruined him. In 1850, he was sent East with messages for General Winfield Scott, and on May 1 he married Ellen Ewing. Their wedding was an important Washington social event, as Thomas Ewing was then a member of President Zachary Taylor's cabinet.

During the decade of the 1850's, Sherman fathered six children and tried unsuccessfully to support them. From 1850 to 1853, he served in the Army Commissary Service in St. Louis and New Orleans, at which time he resigned his commission to open a branch bank in San Francisco for some St. Louis friends. The pressures of banking in the boom and bust California economy, his chronic asthma, and a homesick wife who wanted to return to her father's house caused Sherman to spend the years from 1853 to 1857 in recurring depression. When the bank closed in 1857, he took on as personal debts the unsuccessful investments he had made for army friends. He carried that financial burden to New York, where he opened another branch bank only to see it fail during the Panic of 1857. He was crushed; no matter what he tried, he met failure. Instead of establishing independence from his foster father, he repeatedly had to look to him for support. Thomas Ewing continued to hope that Sherman would agree to manage his salt interests in Ohio, but Sherman refused. Instead, he went to Kansas as part of a law and real estate business, along with two Ewing sons.

The business failed, and Sherman desperately tried to return to the army for his economic (and psychological) salvation. There were no openings, but an officer friend told him about a new Louisiana military seminary looking for a superintendent. Sherman applied and became founding father of what became modern Louisiana State University. When secession came, duty convinced him he had to leave the job and the people he had come to love. He believed that he had to sacrifice his economic well-being for the sake of the Union.

Life's Work

After leaving Louisiana in February, 1861, Sherman became angry over alleged Northern nonchalance toward Southern secession. He found a position with a St. Louis street railway company, determined to remain aloof from the national crisis until he could see a change. Thomas Ewing and John Sherman urged him to reenter the Union army, and, through their efforts, he was named a colonel of the Thirteenth Infantry Regiment in May, 1861. He stood over six feet tall, with long legs and arms, piercing blue eyes, sandy red hair that seemed always to be mussed, a grizzly reddish beard, and a generally unkempt appearance. He spoke rapidly and often, his mind able to reach conclusions before his charmed listeners understood his premises.

Before he could serve with the Thirteenth Infantry, he was appointed to a staff position under Winfield Scott and, in July, 1861, commanded a brigade at Bull Run. He saw that fiasco as further proof that the North was not taking the war seriously enough.

He was happy to leave chaotic Washington for Kentucky to help Fort Sumter hero Robert Anderson organize the Union war effort there. Upon arrival, he quickly convinced himself that the Confederate forces were much larger than his were and that it was only a matter of time before they would overrun him. He sank into depression and lashed out at newspaper reporters for allegedly publicizing his weaknesses. At his own request, he was transferred to Missouri in November, 1861, where his outspoken negativity convinced many that he was unbalanced. He took a twenty-day leave in December, 1861, and was mortified to see his sanity unfairly questioned in the press. When he returned to duty and was given command over a training facility in Missouri, his depression deepened and he even contemplated suicide. The Union war effort and his own career seemed hopeless.

His transfer to Paducah, Kentucky, in February, 1862, and his association with the successful Ulysses S. Grant slowly lifted his spirits. He distinguished himself as a division commander in the bloody battle of Shiloh in April, 1862, and he then defended Grant and other generals against press and political criticism of their roles in the battle. When he was promoted to major general of volunteers and took part in Henry W. Halleck's capture of Corinth in May, 1862, he began to believe that the Union effort had hope and he could play an important role in any success.

In July, 1862, Grant appointed Sherman to the post of military governor of recently captured Memphis. Sherman was able to use both his banking and military experience to govern that hotbed of secession sentiment. It was there that the activities of Confederate guerrillas caused him to see at first hand that the war was not simply a contest between professional soldiers. The general populace had to be controlled if the Union effort was to be successful. When guerrillas fired on a boat in the Mississippi River, Sherman leveled a nearby town. He had long recognized the determination of the Southern populace, and he now began to see that only a destruction of this stubborn intensity would resolve the conflict in the Union's favor. He would utilize this insight at the appropriate time.

In December, 1862, Sherman led an unsuccessful assault on the heights above Vicksburg. When the press resuscitated the insanity charge against him, he court-martialed a reporter, the only such event in American history. The trial, though it might have been an excellent exposition of the inevitable conflict between the military and the press in wartime, proved to be little more than a conflict of personality. It settled little.

Sherman was part of Grant's enormous army which captured Vicksburg in July, 1863, and he was made brigadier general in the regular army as a reward. He became commander of the Army of Tennessee when Grant became supreme commander in the West; he participated in the successful November lifting of the Confederate siege at Chattanooga. In January, 1864, he commanded the Meridian, Mississippi, expedition, which showed him yet again the effectiveness of the destructive activity he was later to use during his March to the Sea.

In the spring of 1864, Grant moved East to become general-in-chief of all Union armies, and Sherman took command over Western forces. On May 5, 1864, Grant attacked Lee in Virginia, and Sherman took on Joseph E. Johnston in Georgia. After first organizing railroads to supply his troops, Sherman battled Johnston throughout the spring and summer of 1864, slowly but inexorably pushing the Confederates from the Chattanooga region toward Atlanta. Jefferson Davis became nervous at Johnston's constant retreat and replaced him with offensive-minded John Bell Hood. The new Confederate commander attacked Sherman and was defeated. Atlanta fell in September, in time to influence the reelection of Abraham Lincoln that November.

Sherman then showed the Confederates that war had indeed become total. He ordered the civilian evacuation of Atlanta. When his order was met with shocked protests, he responded: "War is cruelty, and you cannot refine it." He did not: In November, he began his March to the Sea, revolutionizing warfare by cutting himself off from his base of supplies, living off the countryside, and destroying goods and property. His aim was to convince the Confederates that their war effort was doomed. He became the father of psychological warfare. On December 21, 1864, his army reached Savannah and made contact with the Atlantic fleet. His presentation of the Georgia city to Lincoln as a Christmas present electrified the North.

On February 1, 1865, Sherman began his march through the Carolinas. On April 17, Johnston and his Confederate forces surrendered at Durham Station, North Carolina. Sherman, who had retained his affection for Southerners throughout the war and had only conducted his total warfare as the most efficient way to end the hostilities quickly, demonstrated his feelings in the peace agreement he made with Johnston. He negotiated political matters, neglected to insist that slavery was over, and, in general, wrote an agreement very favorable to the South. In Washington, the Administration, just then reeling from the assassination of Lincoln, was shocked. Secretary of War Edwin Stanton and General Henry W. Halleck led the opposition to the agreement, and Sherman was forced to change it, suffering sharp criticism from both the public and the press.

With the war over, Sherman became commander of troops in the West. He fought the Indians and helped construct the transcontinental railroad. When Grant became president in 1869, Sherman became commanding general, a position he held until his retirement in 1883. His tenure was filled with controversy as he battled secretaries of war and Congress over his authority, his salary, and sufficient appropriation for the troops. When he published his memoirs in 1875, the blunt directness of those two volumes created a controversy, including a bitter exchange with Jefferson Davis.

From his retirement in 1883 until his death in 1891, Sherman kept busy attending veterans' reunions and the theater, while also becoming a popular after-dinner speaker. In 1884, he categorically refused to run for the presidency, establishing a standard which allegedly reluctant office seekers have been measured against ever since. In 1886, he and his family moved from St. Louis to New York. On February 14, 1891, he died from pneumonia.

Summary

William Tecumseh Sherman was one of the leaders of the successful Union war effort that prevented the disruption of the United States. He helped introduce the nation and the world to the concept of total war, his Civil War activities serving as a harbinger of the kind of conflict to be fought in the twentieth century. He devised his mode of warfare as a way to end the hostilities quickly, but it helped prolong Southern animosity toward the North into the twentieth century. Still, when Sherman toured the South in 1879, he received a friendly greeting.

Sherman's life, apart from his Civil War years, is important in itself. Before the war, he attended West Point with many of the other military leaders of the Mexican and Civil wars. He served in the army in Florida during the Second Seminole War. In California, he composed a report to President James K. Polk which announced the discovery of gold and helped set off the famous Gold Rush of 1849. During the 1850's, as a banker, he was one of San Francisco's leading businessmen during its formative years. In 1860, he helped found what is modern Louisiana State University. After the war, Sherman's tenure as general-in-chief of the United States Army from 1869 to 1883 allowed him to influence the direction of such events as the Indian Wars, Reconstruction, and the disputed election of 1876. Thus, Sherman influenced the development of American society throughout his life. He was one of the major figures of the nineteenth century.

Bibliography

Athearn, Robert G. *William Tecumseh Sherman and the Settlement of the West*. Norman: University of Oklahoma Press, 1956. A thorough study of Sherman's participation in the postwar Indian troubles and his role in the construction of the transcontinental railroad. Sherman was neither as harsh toward the Indians as the West desired nor as lenient as the East wished. He believed that the completion of the railroad would force the hostile Indians onto reservations.

Barrett, John G. *Sherman's March Through the Carolinas*. Chapel Hill: University of North Carolina Press, 1956. A detailed military history of Sherman's final campaign through North and South Carolina. Sherman reluctantly put his concept of total war into practice during this march from Savannah, Georgia, to Raleigh, North Carolina. His army inflicted special punishment on South Carolina because the soldiers blamed the Palmetto State for starting the war.

Glatthaar, Joseph T. *The March to the Sea and Beyond: Sherman's Troops in the Savannah and Carolinas Campaigns*. New York: New York University Press, 1985. An excellent analysis of the makeup and attitudes of the common soldier in Sherman's army during his marches. The author analyzes the soldiers' views about their cause, black Southerners, white Southerners, camp life, and pillaging.

Lewis, Lloyd. *Sherman: Fighting Prophet*. New York: Harcourt, Brace and Co., 1932. Though dated and written without the benefit of all the now available Sherman documentation, this is still a valuable and very readable biography. It puts special emphasis on Thomas Ewing's influence on his foster son. The vast bulk of the book details the Civil War years, and coverage of the postwar years is unfortunately brief.

Liddell Hart, Basil H. *Sherman: Soldier, Realist, American*. New York: Harcourt, Brace and Co., 1958. A fine study of Sherman's Civil War military activities by a leading military historian. The author states that Sherman was far ahead of his time and that later generations of military men might have profited from his example had they paid attention.

Marszalek, John F. "Celebrity in Dixie: Sherman Tours the South, 1879." *The Georgia Historical Quarterly* 46 (Fall, 1982): 368-383. An account of Sherman's postwar tour through most of the sites of his Civil War battles. The author finds that Sherman received a warm response in Atlanta, New Orleans, and everywhere else he went in the South.

_____. *Sherman's Other War: The General and the Civil War Press*. Memphis, Tenn.: Memphis State University Press, 1981. A thorough account of Sherman's battles with reporters during the war, this study also contains an extended analysis of his personality during this period. Argues that Sherman fought the press in a constitutional battle formed more by personality than by First Amendment principles.

Merrill, James M. *William Tecumseh Sherman*. Skokie, Ill.: Rand McNally, 1971. A detailed popular biography which has the benefit of the major Sherman manuscript collections. It discusses all aspects of Sherman's life but is especially valuable for its coverage of his postwar years.

Sherman, William T. *Memoirs of General William T. Sherman*, 2 vols. New York: D. Appleton and Co., 1875. Reprint. Introduction by William S. McFeely. New York: Da Capo Press, 1984. Sherman's controversial and absorbing account of his life from 1846 to the end of the Civil War, originally published in 1875. This is an essential source for gaining an understanding of Sherman's perception of the battles in which he participated and the leaders with and against whom he fought.

John F. Marszalek